Neil Moonie
Beryl Stretch
Mark Walsh
David Herne
Elaine Millar
David Webb

Heinemann Educational Publishers
Halley Court, Jordan Hill, Oxford OX2 8EJ
Part of Harcourt Education

Heinemann is the registered trademark of Harcourt Education Limited

© Neil Moonie; Beryl Stretch; Mark Walsh; David Herne; Elaine Millar; David Webb

First published 2003

08 07 06 05 04
10 9 8 7 6 5 4 3

British Library Cataloguing in Publication Data is available
from the British Library on request.

ISBN 0 435 45465 X

Typeset by Techtype, Abingdon, Oxon
Printed and bound in Great Britain by The Bath Press Ltd.

Tel: 01865 888058 www.heinemann.co.uk

Contents

Acknowledgements

The authors and publishers would like to thank the following individuals and organisations for permission to reproduce material and photographs:

Alamy page 325
Camera Press pages 326 and 364
Camera Press/ILN page 318
Corbis pages 337 and 482
Gareth Boden page 339
Getty pages 118, 341 and 373
Getty News pages 10 and 421
Hulton Getty pages 119, 321, 322 and 352
PA photos page 10
Photodisc pages 210, 463 and 366
Sally & Richard Greenhill page 120
Tony Larkin/Rex Features page 10

The DDC, Dewey and Dewey Decimal Classification, summary on pages 301–2 is a registered trademark of the OCLC Online Computer Library Centre, Inc. Permission to reproduce it has been granted by OCLC, to whom the copyrights in the material belong.

Crown copyright material on pages 12, 107, 108, 109, 110, 131, 134, 138, 139, 140, 148, 152, 153, 154 and 333 reproduced under Class Licence Number C01W0000141 with the permission of the Controller of HMSO and the Queen's Printer for Scotland.

Every effort has been made to contact copyright holders of material reproduced in this book. Any omissions will be rectified in subsequent printings if notice is given to the publishers.

Websites

Please note that the examples of websites suggested in this book were up to date at the time of writing. It is essential for tutors to preview each site before using it to ensure that the URL is still accurate and the content is appropriate. We suggest that tutors bookmark useful sites and consider enabling students to access them through the school or college intranet.

Introduction

About this book

This book is designed to support students wishing to achieve the Level Three BTEC National qualification in Care for Edexcel. This book can also be used as a useful resource for many other basic care qualifications.

Course structure

The BTEC National Diploma in Care is a specialist vocational programme available for full-time study and is equivalent to three A levels. A Certificate programme is available for part-time students who may already be in employment.

The Diploma programme consists of eight core units (with a unit value of nine) and nine specialist option units. The Certificate programme comprises seven core units (unit value 8) and four specialist option units. Both the Diploma and Certificate awards are designed to assist entry into most higher education professional care training programmes.

The BTEC National programmes encourage and stimulate student achievement through innovative learning and assessment styles and by focusing on the applied knowledge and understanding of the care sector. Valued by both the sector and higher education, they allow vocational theory to be applied in practice through a minimum of 400 hours compulsory vocational work placements, in a variety of care settings. You will demonstrate how you have reflected on and improved your basic practitioner skills and how you have linked knowledge and understanding to your practice. Emphasising the importance of this, the Vocational Practice unit extends throughout the length of the programme and has a value of two units.

This book covers the eight core units and four of the specialist option units.

The core units comprise:

- Equality, Diversity and Rights*
- Communication and Supportive Skills*
- Research and Project
- Introduction to Sociology
- Vocational Practice
- Protecting Self and Others
- Applying Psychology
- Personal and Professional Development

The specialist option units comprise:

- Care Services
- Health Promotion
- Practical Caring Skills
- Lifespan Development

*These units are externally assessed.

Assessment

With the exception of the first two core units, you will produce a portfolio of evidence to match the assessment criteria detailed within each unit specification. Your tutors will set assignments to meet these criteria and indicate a date for completion and submission. The assignments will be marked and graded by your tutors. A random sample will then be selected and reviewed by Edexcel to ensure fair marking for all students. The grades you receive for these assignments each have a point value. Your final grade is worked out based on the number of points you have achieved throughout the programme.

The Integrated Vocational Assignment (IVA) will form the complete assessment for the first two units and is taken towards the end of the learning programme. The IVA requires students to apply their newly acquired knowledge and skills to practical work-related situations. Students must show maturity of learning and understanding in their approach to this time-constrained assessment. You cannot be awarded your qualification until this assessment has been satisfactorily completed. The completed IVA assessment will be marked by your tutors using a marking scheme supplied by Edexcel. It will then be re-marked by an external assessor to ensure that marking across all national centres is fair and accurate.

Features of this book

Throughout this text there are a number of features that are designed to encourage reflection and discussion and relate theory to practice in a care context. These features are:

- What you need to learn   A list of the knowledge points that you will have learned by the end of the unit
- Think it over   Thought-provoking questions and dilemmas that can be used for individual reflection or group discussion
- Theory into practice   Practical activities that require you to apply your theoretical knowledge to the workplace
- Key issues   Contemporary issues in care that you need to be aware of
- Case studies   Examples of "real" situations to help you link theory to practice
- Assessment activities   Activities that assist you in meeting the assessment requirements of the unit.
- End of unit test   Questions to help consolidate the knowledge that you have acquired in the unit.

Each unit also contains a glossary to explain the technical terms used in the book and a comprehensive list of texts for further reading.

A wide range of experienced professionals have contributed to this text in order to support you in your studies and to provide you with a firm knowledge foundation to extend and build upon for your future in a care profession. We all hope that you enjoy your BTEC National programme and wish you every success in achieving your award now and in your future careers.

Beryl Stretch

Equality, diversity and rights

This chapter introduces you to the rights of individuals, and how some groups in society are denied those rights as a result of individual and structural discrimination in society. It encourages you to think about the negative effects that discrimination has on all members of society, and the corresponding benefits of diversity.

It shows how equality, diversity and rights are central to the delivery of care services, and describes the systems, structures and policies that attempt to prevent discrimination and promote the rights of service users. It explains the statutory background to some service users' rights, and the circumstances in which the law allows those rights to be overridden.

It explains the role of the individual worker in promoting equality, diversity and rights, and how it is necessary for them to understand the origins of discriminatory behaviour and examine their own prejudices in order to do so.

What you need to learn

- The importance of equality, diversity and rights to care services
- How care services recognise and promote equality, diversity and rights
- How the individual care worker can promote equality, diversity and rights in their own practice

The importance of equality, diversity and rights to care services

Principle of equity

The principle of equity is that all people should have equal opportunities. This does not mean that everyone should have equal wealth, status and power. This is impossible to achieve in a free society. It does mean that everyone should have the same rights under the law, and the right to services provided by the state on the basis of their need. Individuals should be free from discrimination. Discrimination means treating someone differently because of something about them – their race, age or sex, for instance – which is not relevant to the situation. It results in people being unfairly denied opportunities.

Concept of tolerance

Tolerance is essential if everyone is to have equal opportunities. It means that people recognise and respect the rights of others who are different. Prejudice prevents some people from doing this. A prejudice is judgement made without evidence, and sometimes in the face of evidence to the contrary. Prejudice results in discrimination. The law supports the rights of some groups that suffer from prejudice and discrimination. The Race Relations Acts, the Sex Discrimination and Equal Pay Acts and the Disability Discrimination Act make some forms of discrimination illegal.

Cycle of disadvantage

The cycle of disadvantage describes how inequalities combine and relate to each other in a way that makes it very difficult for people to escape from them.

A section of society suffers discrimination in many different aspects of their lives. The groups most likely to be overrepresented in this excluded section of society are older people, people with disabilities, people from some ethnic minority groups, and single parents (the great majority of whom are women). A common feature of nearly all of these people is dependence on benefits.

Low income results in unequal access to education and health services, and an inability to afford good-quality diet and housing. Low educational achievement results in fewer job opportunities and a greater likelihood of unemployment, which limits income. Poor diet and housing result in ill health, which further damages employment prospects.

The effect is cumulative, and results in marginalisation. Some commentators speak about the formation of an underclass. Others dislike this term, and say it blames the individual when the real cause is structural discrimination in society. They prefer the term socially excluded.

The Black Report (1980) identified a strong link between membership of the lower social classes and poor health.

Figure 1.1 Factors that contribute to social exclusion

Think It Over

Look at these factors which contribute to social exclusion. Write a brief life story of an individual from birth to death. Your account should show how these factors work together to create a cycle of disadvantage over the individual's lifetime.

Care values

The basic care values are that services should be available to everyone on the basis of need and that they should be delivered in a way that promotes users' rights.

Many people requiring services are members of vulnerable groups and suffer disadvantage. Care services must not exclude or discriminate against any group in society. The way care services are delivered should empower service users and promote their dignity.

This is done by applying the Care Value Base in every aspect of care work. The Care Value Base is embodied in health and social care qualifications and in the service standards of care agencies. There are three areas in which care workers have particular responsibility to respect service users' rights, as shown in the diagram below:

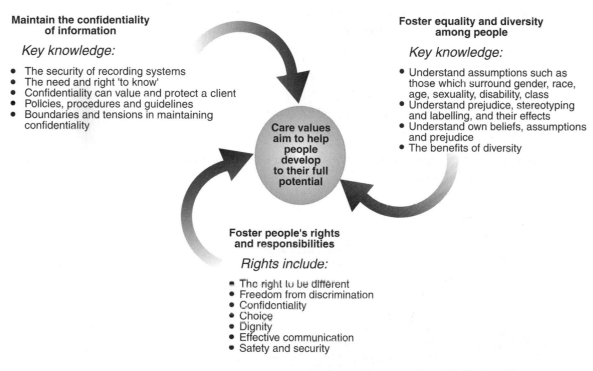

Maintain the confidentiality of information

Key knowledge:

- The security of recording systems
- The need and right 'to know'
- Confidentiality can value and protect a client
- Policies, procedures and guidelines
- Boundaries and tensions in maintaining confidentiality

Foster equality and diversity among people

Key knowledge:

- Understand assumptions such as those which surround gender, race, age, sexuality, disability, class
- Understand prejudice, stereotyping and labelling, and their effects
- Understand own beliefs, assumptions and prejudice
- The benefits of diversity

Care values aim to help people develop to their full potential

Foster people's rights and responsibilities

Rights include:

- The right to be different
- Freedom from discrimination
- Confidentiality
- Choice
- Dignity
- Effective communication
- Safety and security

Figure 1.2 The Care Value Base

Care work should empower service users in order to promote people's rights and responsibilities. This means that workers must recognise the right of people to make decisions about their own lives. Service users should have choices wherever possible. Nothing should be done without their agreement unless the law permits it (see page 19). Wherever necessary, service users should be provided with the necessary information to complain about infringement of their rights.

Workers should respect service user's individual and social characteristics and their views and beliefs to encourage diversity in people and further equality. They should challenge discrimination and oppression whenever it occurs. The worker should know how to get support for service users being oppressed and discriminated against.

Workers need to understand service users' moral and legal rights to confidentiality, but also the limits to confidentiality. They should respect confidentiality, but be open with people about the limits resulting from agency policy and the law (see pages 21 and 29).

Moral rights of individuals

The principle of equity is based on the idea that individuals have the moral right to equal opportunities. There are a number of other moral rights that support this. There have been many attempts to define these rights. These include the United Nations Universal Declaration of Human Rights, the United Nations Convention on the Rights of the Child and the European Convention on Human Rights.

Some attempts have been criticised because some of the rights are thought too ambitious, and very difficult to achieve. The rights of one person are obligations on others. They are meaningless unless others accept these obligations, and the means exist to enforce them.

One attempt to define human rights which does appear to be realistic and is enforceable is the European Convention on Human Rights. The Convention was incorporated into UK legislation in October 2000 as the Human Rights Act. For the first time there is a statement of what constitutes human rights in UK legislation (see pages 17–19). This means that people can go to court if necessary, to enforce their rights.

Key issues

In small groups, spend ten minutes making a list of the moral rights which every individual should have. When you have finished, compare with the list to the Articles of the European Convention on Human Rights (see page 17).

How does your list differ?

Have you things on your list that do not fit into the Convention?

Are they true rights?

If there are rights in the Convention, which are not on your list, say why they are important.

How people who use care services may be subject to inequality generally within society

Many service users will be subject to inequality in a number of ways. In the course of their everyday lives they may experience:

- individual discrimination because of the prejudices of others. This includes unfair treatment, exclusion, insults, harassment and violence.
- institutional discrimination as a result of organisations failing to provide appropriate services because of prejudiced or ethnocentric attitudes of service providers (see pages 8–9).
- structural discrimination or a general disadvantage because prejudiced attitudes are common throughout society and its institutions. An example of this is the way some ethnic minority groups experience discrimination in education, health, social care, housing employment and the law.

Effects of inequity on people

Despite anti-discriminatory legislation, people's life chances are still affected by prejudice and discrimination. National statistics on health, wealth, employment and

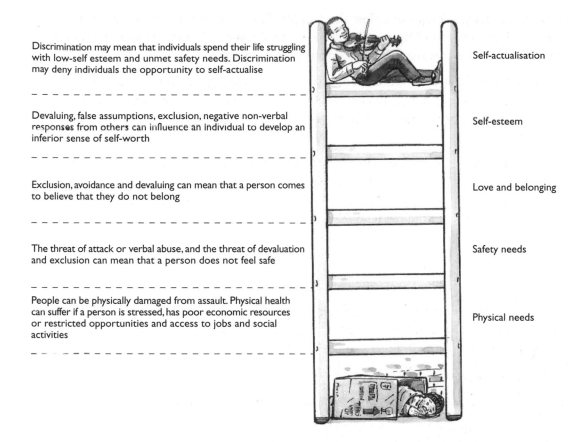

Discrimination may mean that individuals spend their life struggling with low-self esteem and unmet safety needs. Discrimination may deny individuals the opportunity to self-actualise

Self-actualisation

Devaluing, false assumptions, exclusion, negative non-verbal responses from others can influence an individual to develop an inferior sense of self-worth

Self-esteem

Exclusion, avoidance and devaluing can mean that a person comes to believe that they do not belong

Love and belonging

The threat of attack or verbal abuse, and the threat of devaluation and exclusion can mean that a person does not feel safe

Safety needs

People can be physically damaged from assault. Physical health can suffer if a person is stressed, has poor economic resources or restricted opportunities and access to jobs and social activities

Physical needs

Figure 1.3 Discrimination can block human needs (as described by Maslow) and change people

education show it on a structural level. Regular press reports of Employment Tribunal findings and court judgments show it on a personal level. Individuals' prospects are directly affected because they are denied opportunities by overt or covert discrimination. Overt discrimination is open, though not always deliberate. Covert discrimination is more subtle (or hidden), such as failing to invite someone rather than deliberately excluding them.

There are further effects resulting from discrimination operating against the whole range of human needs as identified by Maslow.

Exposure to discrimination may affect the individual's self-image. If people have a poor self-image, they will have low self-esteem, which will further limit their opportunities. They may believe that opportunities are not open to them, so there is no point in trying for them. If their self-esteem is poor, they may not present themselves to the best advantage. They may feel that others have low expectations of them, perhaps in education or work, and end up fulfilling those expectations.

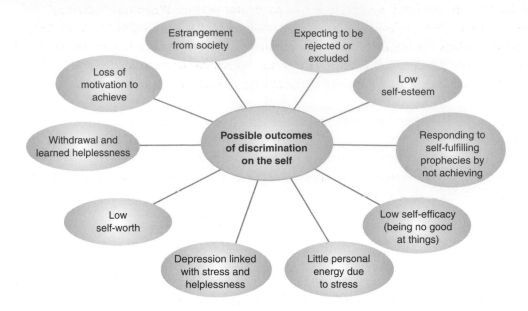

Figure 1.4 Some of the effects of discrimination

This is an example of how low self-esteem may affect opportunities:

Case Study

Sean and Daniel are both interviewed for a job, but neither gets it. Sean has high self-esteem. He is disappointed, but thinks that he was unlucky, or that he didn't have the skills the employer was looking for. He asks the employer for some feedback on his performance in the interview and looks at ways in which he can acquire the skills he needs, and present the skills he has in future applications. He is more confident the next time he applies for a job, and is successful in his application.

Daniel has low self-esteem. He gets very depressed by being rejected and thinks it must be his fault. He goes along to his next interview feeling very low and expecting to be rejected again. He doesn't present himself very well, and doesn't get the job. He is even less confident when the next opportunity arises.

Suggest some ways to help Daniel raise his own self-esteem.

An individual with a good self-image and high self-esteem will see rejection as a short-term set back. If self-image has been eroded by constant exposure to prejudice, discrimination and abuse, then they may find it much more difficult to handle setbacks.

Stereotyping and labelling

Stereotyping is based on prejudice, and means holding beliefs that all members of a group are the same. Stereotypes are often based on inaccurate, negative and damaging beliefs about a group. They are damaging even when they appear positive because they make people unreceptive to the differences between individuals. The subject of the stereotype may be forced into a mould unsuitable to their interests and talents. Even qualities that are generally true of groups will not be true of all individuals in that group.

Labelling means applying a stereotype to a particular person. When one individual labels another, they are less likely to accept evidence which contradicts the label. This means that labels are often self-fulfilling prophecies. Prejudice, stereotypes and labelling result in individual discrimination, which is one individual treating another differently, usually worse, because of a physical characteristic or membership of a group.

Think It Over

Consider one example when you have stereotyped an individual and, therefore, labelled that person. What prompted you to do this? If the individual had known of your action, how do you think they would have felt?

Have you ever been knowingly labelled by someone else?

How did you feel about it?

The effects of marginalisation and disempowerment

The victims of prejudice and discrimination are often marginalised, which means forced to the edge of society. As a result they are cut off from economic, cultural, political and social activities, and do not enjoy the full rights or benefits of citizenship. They do not have the economic power to purchase services for themselves. Services provided by the state are not distributed fairly. The Aicheson Report (1998) identified that it was often the communities with the greatest need which got the poorest services, and better-off communities which got the better services. Marginalisation is one of the mechanisms of the cycle of disadvantage, working to prevent people from improving their disadvantaged position.

Disempowerment results when people are denied choice. It usually happens when service users are expected to fit in with services, rather than services being designed to meet users' needs. Sometimes users are not given the information needed to make decisions about their lives. Many users do not have the money to purchase what they need for themselves. If the professionals they rely on to arrange their care do not consult them or offer them choice, individuals lose control over important parts of their lives. These may include things such as where and how they live, how they spend their day, who they associate with, what they eat and drink and what time they get up and go to bed. If people are disempowered they are likely to have a poor self-image and low self-esteem.

Think It Over

Consider your own self-image and self-esteem for a few moments.

What questions would you ask yourself in order to assess these?

Identification of vulnerable groups

Discrimination takes place on the basis of sex, race, age, disability, sexuality, religion, health status and class. This does not mean that everybody in these groups experiences disadvantage. For example:

- although women are underrepresented in higher paid jobs, many women do have successful careers.
- there is widespread racial discrimination in society, but not all groups suffer the same levels of disadvantage. Pakistanis and Bangladeshis experience the worst levels of economic disadvantage. People of Caribbean and Indian origin are not as seriously disadvantaged. African, Asian and Chinese people appear to suffer little economic disadvantage.
- whilst many older people are poor, increasing numbers have occupational pensions and enjoy high standards of living.

If we think about these characteristics as playing cards, the more supposed positive cards a person holds (for instance a young, white heterosexual man in good health and without a disability), the greater their chances of success.

Groups open to structural inequality are those dependent on state benefits – the long-term unemployed, single parent families and older people relying on the state pension. The more supposed negative cards a person holds, the more likely they are to be a member of these vulnerable groups.

- Young Caribbean men may be over-represented amongst the long-term unemployed if they underachieve in education because of institutional racism in the education system. They may start in a less competitive position even in the absence of racial discrimination by employers.
- Older men who lose their jobs may join the long-term unemployed because of ageist attitudes of employers. Someone with a disability or from an ethnic minority group in this position would find themselves doubly disadvantaged.
- Women are very overrepresented amongst single parent families as it is usually the mother who has the child care responsibility. Women from the lower social classes will find it harder to obtain work that pays well enough to pay for child care.
- People from the lower social classes, those with disabilities and members of economically disadvantaged ethnic minority groups are less likely to have a good employment record in a well paid job. They are less likely to have an occupational pension, and are more likely to be dependent upon state benefits in old age.

Equal access to services

Some groups are denied access to services because of institutional discrimination by organisations in society. Institutional racism was defined by Sir William McPherson in the Stephen Lawrence Enquiry Report as 'The collective failure of an organisation to provide an appropriate and professional service to people because of their colour, culture or ethnic origin. It can be seen or detected in processes, attitudes and behaviour which amount to discrimination through unwitting prejudice, ignorance, thoughtlessness and racist stereotyping which disadvantage minority ethnic people.' This does not mean that all the workers in an organisation are prejudiced against a particular group. They may have **ethnocentric** attitudes. This means they do not question ways of working which are based on incorrect assumptions that disadvantage some groups.

Many of the report's findings apply to education, health and social care services. The report raised awareness of the extent to which institutional discrimination exists in health and social care services.

There is evidence of institutional racism within the National Health Service. A number of studies have suggested that non-white patients are treated differently from white patients within mental health services. This has been confirmed by a recent Mental Health Act Commission report which found that non-white patients, and particularly people of Afro-Caribbean ethnicity, were far more likely to be compulsorily detained (sectioned) under the Mental Health Act 1983.

Social services departments have also been accused of institutional racism. It is suggested that in some cases they have made incorrect assumptions about ethnic minority populations. One assumption is that ethnic minority populations are made up of stable, multigenerational families who care for their own older people through community organisations or the extended family. This has led to failures to make appropriate provision for elders from ethnic minorities. Children of Afro-Caribbean and mixed parentage are overrepresented in the care system, and there is frequent failure to recruit sufficient foster parents and prospective adopters from appropriate ethnic backgrounds.

Other groups are widely discriminated against by public services. In March 2001, the Health Secretary launched a national framework for older people, to prevent older people being denied the services they needed. Whilst there are good reasons why an older person should receive different health treatment from a younger one, there was evidence that this was often happening because of the prejudices of doctors and nurses. In October 2000 health workers were told they should stop deciding not to resuscitate older patients if they fell into a coma, without prior consultation with the patients or their families. People with learning disabilities have also experienced discrimination in the health service, and in particular children with Down's syndrome have been refused heart surgery.

Ensuring equal access to services requires structural changes in the way those services are provided. Many organisations that discriminate against groups in society have equal opportunities policies, but they are not working.

Key issue

Think about what care organisations should do to make services more accessible to:

* members of ethnic minority groups
* individuals with physical, sensory or learning disabilities
* older people.

Advantages of diversity in British society

There are two reasons to respect the diversity of others. The first reason is that it is unfair, and often illegal, to treat members of minority groups in a discriminatory way. The second, equally important, reason is that there are positive benefits to diversity for all members of society.

The dimensions and advantages of diversity in British society

Ethnocentricity is the unthinking assumption that the individual's viewpoint from their own cultural perspective is normal or superior, without considering that there could be

The Notting Hill Carnival

other points of view. It is a narrow and limiting attitude, the opposite of valuing diversity that enriches a person's life. Valuing diversity opens people to new experiences, and to new ways of looking at things. Being open to others' cultures enriches everyone and means that our everyday lives are more interesting, even at such basic levels as the types of food we eat. Fashion often borrows from other cultures, and popular music has benefited from diverse cultural influences.

Many people find that experience of other philosophies, and the use of techniques such as yoga, alters their view of the world and makes them more creative. Others benefit from forms of complementary medicine, such as acupuncture, massage and aromatherapy, which have their roots in other cultures.

Not only do we benefit culturally from being open to diversity, but we also benefit from the contribution of people as individuals who would otherwise be excluded. If people are excluded, they cannot make a full contribution to society, and everyone loses. For example:

- If people from some ethnic minority groups underachieve in the education system, society suffers as it is deprived of their potential contribution to the workforce.
- If women are discriminated against in employment and are excluded from certain jobs, or do not achieve the highest positions, their contribution at this level is lost.
- If people with disabilities do not have equal opportunities, they will have unrecognised talents which remain unused.
- If older people are devalued, their skills and experience are lost to society.

David Blunkett and Stephen Hawking have made important contributions to society despite their disabilities

Assessment activity 1.1

Choose an aspect of culture that interests you – food, music, film, literature, fashion, medicine. Write a report on how it has been influenced as a result of being open to other cultures.

How care services recognise and promote equality, diversity and rights

Formal policies on equality and rights

Formal polices on equality and rights include legislation, such as the following:

- Mental Health Act
- Children Act
- Race Relations
- Sex Discrimination Act
- Disability Discrimination Act
- Human Rights Act
- Data Protection Act.

The government issues Codes of Practice and Guidance alongside the legislation to tell care organisations and individual professionals how laws should be implemented. All care organisations should have formal policies on equality of access and service user rights which is incorporated into all their procedures.

All care workers are bound by the law and the Care Value Base, but workers in particular services will also be bound by Codes of Practice and Charters. Health Service workers must comply with the Patient's Charter which promotes equal rights by stating patients' rights and the standards that they can expect from services. The Community Care Charter fulfils a similar role for social services workers.

Some workers will be bound by codes of conduct issued by their professional organisations. The Nursing and Midwifery Council Code of Professional Conduct contains a number of provisions protecting patients' rights to equal treatment.

Summary

As a registered nurse, midwife or health visitor, you must:

- respect the patient or client as an individual
- obtain consent before you give any treatment or care
- co-operate with others in the team
- protect confidential information
- maintain your professional knowledge and competence
- be trustworthy
- act to identify and minimise the risk to patients and clients

Figure 1.5 Summary of the NMC's Code of Professional Conduct
Source: Nursing and Midwifery Council

Patient's Charter

Everyone has the right under the charter to:

- receive health care on the basis of clinical need
- be registered with a GP and change your GP easily and quickly if you want to
- get emergency medical treatment at any time
- be offered a health check when you join a GP's list
- ask your GP for a health check if you are aged 16 – 74 years and have not seen your GP for the past three years
- be offered a health check once a year in your GP surgery, or at your own home if you prefer, if you are 75 years or over
- receive information about the services your GP provides
- decide which pharmacy to use for your prescription and have the appropriate drugs and medicines prescribed
- get your medicines free if you are a pensioner, a child under 16, or under 19 in full-time education, pregnant or a nursing mother, suffering from one of a number of specified conditions, or on income support or family credit
- be referred to a consultant, acceptable to you, when your GP thinks it is necessary, and to be referred for a second opinion if you and your GP agree this is desirable
- have any proposed treatment, including any risks and any alternatives, clearly explained to you before you decide whether you agree to it
- receive dental advice in an emergency (if you are registered with a dentist) and treatment if your dentist thinks it is necessary
- receive a signed written prescription immediately after your eye test
- see your own health records, subject to any limitations in law, and know that everyone working in the NHS is under a legal duty to keep your records confidential
- choose whether or not you wish to take part in medical research or medical student training
- information about the standards of services you can expect, waiting times and local GP services
- have a complaint about NHS services investigated thoroughly and receive a full and prompt reply from the Chief Executive or General Manager
- be told before you go into hospital, except in an emergency, whether it is planned to care for you in a ward for men and women.

Figure 1.6 The Patient's Charter
© Crown copyright

Soon, all care workers will be covered by similar standards when the Care Standards Act 2000 sets up the General Social Care Council.

Documents such as the Wagner Report (1988), Home Life (1984) and A Better Home Life (1996) set standards for care in residential homes and nursing homes. Community Life (1990) sets standards for people being cared for in their own homes.

Assessment activity 1.2

Divide into four groups, each group finding the key points relevant to equality, diversity and rights in the four documents mentioned in the previous paragraph. At a plenary discussion, find similar themes and discuss their importance to service users.

Positive promotion of individual rights

The positive promotion of individuals' rights is possible only if they know what their rights are. Care organisations should have policies on equal opportunities, confidentiality and access to records, and complaints. They must also have guidance for people whose rights are being infringed, for instance under the Mental Health and Children Acts. Organisations' policies must be widely available to service users. This means they must be accessible, readable and comprehensible. This may involve providing leaflets and translating them into ethnic minority languages and Braille to ensure equal access. Where service users are unable to represent themselves, it may be necessary for the organisation to arrange advocacy services for them.

Advocacy

To have choice, individuals must be able to understand what is available and express an opinion. Some individuals cannot do either of these things. Advocacy is the process by which they can be helped to do so. Sometimes an advocate may make decisions in their interests and on their behalf. The dictionary defines an advocate as someone who pleads, intercedes or speaks for another.

Service users may be unable to exercise choice for many reasons, for instance:

- Children may lack the maturity to understand the reasons for, or the implications of, things that are happening to them.
- People with learning disabilities may be unable to fully understand their circumstances.
- Some older people may be confused or have a memory problem which calls into question the validity of choices they make.
- Some people with disabilities, for instance those who have had strokes, may be unable to communicate their wishes.
- People from a different cultural background may not understand systems and processes for securing their rights.
- For a number of reasons service users may lack knowledge or confidence to deal with officials.

Many of these people will have friends or family to advocate on their behalf. If they do not, then they risk becoming disempowered and marginalised unless they have an independent person to support them.

Personal advocacy may take two forms:

- Professional advocacy, such as a lawyer or other professional representing a person in court, or any other formal hearing, such as a tribunal or complaints procedure.
- Citizen advocacy, when an independent volunteer acts on behalf of a service user with a service provider.

Think It Over

Have you ever spoken for someone else? Why did you do that? Was the result satisfactory or did the individual wish they had spoken out for themselves?

Public advocacy is a different type, where a voluntary organisation represents a whole group. The purpose is to get a message across better than the members of the group could do as individuals. An example of this is the work of the Terence Higgins Trust in relation to people with HIV/AIDS.

Care workers may act as advocates for service users, but may have problems when there are conflicts between the role of advocate and the role of employee of a service provider. This is especially true when the service user is complaining about that provider.

Think It Over

Think about examples from your own care experience when a service user would have benefited from advocacy. Were there any arrangements in place for them to be represented? What were the arrangements? If there were no arrangements, what were the effects on the service user?

Work practices

The role of work practices in promoting service users' rights is particularly important. Services should be provided in a way that respects the privacy and dignity of service users.

- They should be able to protect their private space, to lock the door to their room, and expect staff to ask permission before entering.
- They should have choice over what to eat and wear, what activities they participate in, and how they are addressed by staff.
- Service users' needs should be more important than the routine of the organisation, and they should be able to choose when to get up, have meals and bathe.
- Dignity and privacy must be a particular consideration when helping service users with intimate care tasks.
- Care should be offered in a way that maximises independence and service users should be encouraged to do things for themselves, rather than the worker taking over to save time.
- Service users must be kept safe but not overprotected. They have the same right to take risks as others. They should be discouraged from activities only after a clear decision that a risk outweighs the service user's right to independence.

Theory into practice

Think about ways in which service users' rights may conflict with the needs of an organisation. Design a leaflet to be given to service users on admission to a care setting. Explain to the service user how the day-to-day working practices in the establishment support their rights.

Organisational policies

Employing organisations may include standards for staff behaviour in their contracts of employment. They will issue general guidelines which regulate workers day-to-day relations with their service users. These will cover areas such as confidentiality, and when it is permissible to accept a gift from a service user. There will be procedures for staff dealing with people who are particularly vulnerable, such as child abuse and elder abuse procedures. Organisations will also have mission statements and service standards which inform workers and service users about expected standards. All of these polices should include the organisation's policy on equal opportunities.

Complaints procedures

If service users do not have the right to complain, they have no way of standing up for their rights. An accessible and easily understood complaints system is a basic part of any organisation's policy on equal opportunities. In the case of a Social Services department, for instance, a common form or complaint procedure would be:

- In the first instance, to speak with the member of staff concerned or their manager to see if the issue can be resolved informally.
- If that does not resolve the issue, to make a complaint to a senior manager of the department.
- If the matter is still not resolved, to request the matter to be referred to a review panel, which will have lay members as well as a representative of the Social Services department.
- If the complainant is not satisfied, they have the right to refer the matter to the Local Government Ombudsman.

A similar system operates for the Health Service. The first stage is local resolution, if the complaint can be dealt with informally by the provider of the service. If not, the complaint moves to an independent review, when the complaint may be reviewed by a panel. Patients who are not satisfied with the outcome of their complaint may approach the Health Service Commissioner (Ombudsman). It is one of the roles of Community Health Councils to advise and assist patients who want to make a complaint about health services.

Theory into practice

Investigate how to make a complaint against a large service provider such as a social services department or an NHS Trust. How can you establish what your rights are? How can you get a copy of the complaints procedure? How easy is it for individuals to complain? How can individuals contact sources of support?

Affirmative action

Affirmative action is positive discrimination. It means identifying individuals or groups which are disadvantaged or marginalised and taking compensating action to promote the equality of their opportunities. This is often completely uncontentious, for instance in the case of services for older people and people with physical disabilities. Sometimes it may be more controversial. There have been cases where the provision of services to disadvantaged groups has been resented, usually by other marginalised groups who feel they also deserve special treatment.

Sometimes affirmative action is very controversial. For instance, some political parties have attempted to redress the underrepresentation of women in parliament by proposing all-women shortlists. Some men have complained about this on the grounds that it may exclude better-qualified men. Some women have also felt uneasy because of concerns that people will think that they have not succeeded on their own merits.

The argument against this is that discrimination and disadvantage are so deep rooted in society that, without affirmative action, these inequalities will never be removed.

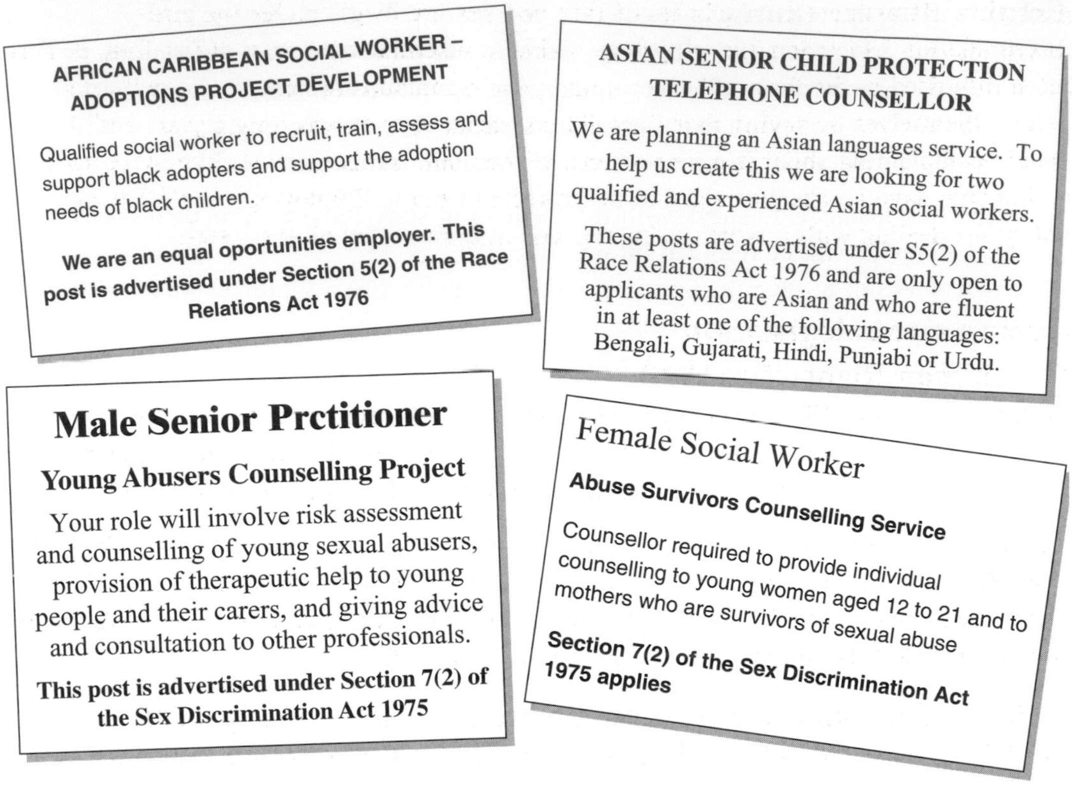

> **AFRICAN CARIBBEAN SOCIAL WORKER –
> ADOPTIONS PROJECT DEVELOPMENT**
>
> Qualified social worker to recruit, train, assess and support black adopters and support the adoption needs of black children.
>
> **We are an equal opportunities employer. This post is advertised under Section 5(2) of the Race Relations Act 1976**

> **ASIAN SENIOR CHILD PROTECTION TELEPHONE COUNSELLOR**
>
> We are planning an Asian languages service. To help us create this we are looking for two qualified and experienced Asian social workers.
>
> These posts are advertised under S5(2) of the Race Relations Act 1976 and are only open to applicants who are Asian and who are fluent in at least one of the following languages: Bengali, Gujarati, Hindi, Punjabi or Urdu.

> **Male Senior Prctitioner**
>
> **Young Abusers Counselling Project**
>
> Your role will involve risk assessment and counselling of young sexual abusers, provision of therapeutic help to young people and their carers, and giving advice and consultation to other professionals.
>
> **This post is advertised under Section 7(2) of the Sex Discrimination Act 1975**

> **Female Social Worker**
>
> **Abuse Survivors Counselling Service**
>
> Counsellor required to provide individual counselling to young women aged 12 to 21 and to mothers who are survivors of sexual abuse
>
> **Section 7(2) of the Sex Discrimination Act 1975 applies**

Figure 1.7 Job adverts should not discriminate against groups in society

The Race Relations Act allows affirmative action in the provision of services to ensure the welfare of particular groups, or to promote the participation of underrepresented groups. Both the Sex Discrimination Act and Race Relations Act allow discrimination in employment where there is a genuine occupational qualification.

Key issue

Look in the social work press for job advertisements claiming exemption under s5(2)d Race Relations Act and s7(2) Sex Discrimination Act. Why are the advertised posts exempt from the anti-discriminatory legislation? What are the arguments for and against this type of affirmative action?

Think It Over

Have you ever met affirmative action in your own life or heard a friend or relative complain about someone else receiving affirmative action? How would you support affirmative action if it disadvantaged someone you care for? It can be very difficult under such circumstances.

Freedom from harassment

Harassment is an expression of prejudice, in an intrusive form, which is harmful to the victim. It involves verbal or physical abuse, unwanted attention, bullying, jokes and exclusion. Harassment on the bases of race and sex are illegal under the anti-discrimination legislation, but all groups liable to discrimination may suffer from it. It is often disguised in the form of humour, and people committing harassment will often defend themselves by saying that they did not mean it, or it was only a joke, and that people complaining about it have no sense of humour. Harassment is never acceptable and people have an absolute right to be protected from it. Employers should have a policy for dealing with it which is known and understood by all their staff.

Human rights legislation

The Human Rights Act 1998

Until October 2000, UK law covered only three areas of discrimination: race, sex and disability. This changed in October 2000, when the European Convention on Human Rights (see page 4) was incorporated into UK law as the Human Rights Act 1998.

It is too early yet to predict how the implementation of the Human Rights Act 1998 will affect the way that care organisations and individual care workers work with service users. It will enable people to enforce their rights under the Convention in British courts, and all other legislation must be compatible with the Act.

Main sections and implications for health, care or early years

The following are some of the effects which the Human Rights Act may have on care practice:

Article 2 – Protection of life
The right to life provision of the convention will be very important in health settings. It will have to be considered in matters such as abortion and in end of life decisions, such as whether to switch off life support systems. It will question the legality of postcode rationing of services on resource grounds, particularly of life saving operations and medications. Children on the child protection register not allocated a social worker may be covered, as well as the closure of nursing homes or care homes which often results in residents being moved, perhaps reducing their life expectancy.

Article 3 – Prohibition of torture and inhuman and degrading treatment
Neglectful treatment of service users in residential homes, the failure to provide proper health care or social care and failure to protect children from abuse may be covered by this Article. It has been suggested that refusal of contact between parents and children in care may be contested on this ground. Life prolonging treatment which causes pain and suffering may also be covered.

Article 5 – Right to liberty and the security of the person
The arrangements for compulsory admission to hospital under the Mental Health Act will have to meet the requirements of this Article. Delays in making practical arrangements for the discharge of people no longer suffering from mental disorder may infringe it. It may have repercussions for locking the door of an elderly resident's room, even if they are at risk of wandering.

Article 6 – Right to a fair and public hearing
Lack of openness or failure to involve service users in any proceedings, such as child protection conferences, adoption panels and mental health review tribunals may infringe this Article. Disciplinary committees of professional bodies such as BMA and UKCC will have to consider this Article when the outcome would affect a person's right to work.

Article 8 – Right to respect for private and family life, home and correspondence
This article will be important in any procedure that involves removing children from their parents, and any refusal of contact. Closure of care and nursing homes will be covered. It may provide a positive duty on social services to help older people to stay in their own homes. It might be a breach of their rights if they have to go into hospital or residential care because care was not provided in the community. Older people kept in hospital when their needs could be better met by a care package at home may also argue that their rights under this Article have been breached.

Article 9 – Freedom of thought, conscience and religion
This Article will promote the ability of service users to practise their religion. Matching children with foster homes and adoptive homes of the same faith may become a more important consideration. The right of residents in care homes to follow religious practices will also be protected.

Article 12 – Right to marry and found a family
Organisations turning down people as prospective adoptive and foster parents may have to justify their decisions under this article. It may also cover people with physical or learning disabilities who are discouraged from becoming parents, or have children removed from them.

Article 14 – Prohibition of discrimination on the grounds of: sex, race, colour, language, religion, political or other opinion, national or social origin, association with a national minority, property, birth or other status
This article cannot be applied on its own, but applies to all the other rights in the Convention. The term 'other status' may have a wide interpretation, and make discrimination illegal in a range of situations not otherwise mentioned in the Act.

Key issue

Watch the press for stories linked with the Human Rights Act, or use the Internet to search a newspaper archive. Write a report on how the Act is changing the way care services are delivered.

The rights of an individual may need to be overridden

Although the Human Rights Act guarantees the rights of individuals, not all of these rights are guaranteed in all circumstances. The right to life and the freedom from degrading and inhuman treatment are absolute. However, many other rights are called qualified rights. This means that they can be set aside in some circumstances. The right to liberty may be lost if detention is based in law, such as the Mental Health Act (see page 20), or if a crime is committed. The right to privacy may be limited by the need to prevent crime, to safeguard the individual or to protect others.

This recognises that not everybody's rights can be enforced as there may be tensions and contradictions between two rights of one individual, or between competing rights of different individuals. There is more about this on page 22.

The use of power and force

Carers have power over service users, because they have control over some aspects of their lives. This power is not legitimate. It should be limited by giving service users choice whenever possible. Power that is not legitimate is oppression.

Force means using physical means to make someone do something, or to prevent them from doing something. It should only be used as an absolutely last resort, and when there is legal authority to do so (see below). It should be extremely rare for a care worker to use force of any kind with an adult. If things are serious enough to justify the use of force, the police will usually be called. There may be occasional situations in working with children when restraint is justified.

Everybody takes risks in their everyday lives – driving and crossing the road are not risk free activities. It is sometimes difficult for care staff to accept that service users should be allowed to take risks, because they feel responsible for them. In some ways this is true, and it is important that care organisations have a policy on what is acceptable risk, so that workers understand what the limits are.

A form of discrimination often applied to older people is to suggest that things should be done to them against their will, if it is for their own good. This is discriminatory, patronising and illegal. Service user choice should always be respected, unless there are very good reasons for doing otherwise

---

Think It Over

An older person is living alone and at risk because she cannot look after herself and sometimes falls. She refuses to consider residential care. Should she be made to go into care? What is the difference between this older person and the younger person who wants to go rock climbing, which also involves risks?

Statutory powers

The law assumes that all adults are able to make decisions about their lives unless it is shown otherwise. This concept is known as competence. It does not automatically apply to children. The law demands that children show competence, or understanding, before they are allowed to make important decisions for themselves, such as consenting to medical treatment. Children of any age can consent to medical treatment, providing that they fully understand what is proposed. This principle was established by the Gillick case (*Gillick v West Norfolk and Wisbech Health Authority*). A child can refuse consent to treatment on the same basis, but the refusal can be overridden by anybody with parental responsibility giving consent.

The Children Act

The Children Act 1989 introduced the concept of parental responsibility to replace parental rights. Although parental responsibility is not clearly defined, this is an important change because (see page 4) a responsibility is something which safeguards the rights of another. Here it is the rights of the child which are the more important. This reinforces the central principle of the Children Act 1989 which is the paramountcy of the welfare of the child. The Act has two main aims:

- to safeguard and promote the welfare of children
- to promote the upbringing of children by their families.

Parents and children have rights under the Human Rights Act (see page 17). The Children Act recognises that it is not always possible to reconcile everybody's rights, for example when a child is abused. Then the parents' rights take second place to the welfare of the child. If attempts to help a child within the family fail, then there are powers to remove them. To do this, the social services have to satisfy the court that:

- the child is suffering, or at risk of suffering, significant harm and
- this is the result of the care being given to the child, or because the child is beyond parental control.

The magistrates can make a care order only if they are satisfied that these conditions are met, and that it is in the best interests of the child to do so. The police can also take a child into protection for up to 72 hours if they have reason to believe that the child would otherwise suffer significant harm.

The Mental Health Act

Because all adults are assumed to have competence, the law requires that certain conditions have to be satisfied before their right to choice is removed.

The Mental Health Act 1983 allows someone to be taken to hospital and kept there against their will for assessment or treatment if:

- they are suffering from a mental disorder and
- being kept in hospital against their will is the only way to protect their health, to prevent them from harming themselves or otherwise coming to harm, or to protect others from harm.

Two doctors and a social worker (or the patient's nearest relative) must agree compulsory detention is necessary. In an emergency, one doctor and a social worker may do so. The police also have powers to detain someone in a public place if they have reason to suspect that they are suffering from a mental disorder.

Case Study

Mrs Greene has become very agitated. She has not slept for three nights and is not eating or drinking. She is talking continuously and constantly active with pointless tasks such as moving the furniture around. Her husband calls the GP. She is in danger of becoming exhausted and dehydrated, but refuses to take medication or go to hospital, as she does not believe she is ill. The GP calls the social worker and the psychiatrist.

- What should the doctors and social worker be considering before deciding whether it is justified to make Mrs Greene go to hospital? It may help you to think about this if you read through the section below first.

Common law

Some situations where service users' right may be overridden are not covered by legislation (statute law), but by the common law. Common law is law that has built up over the years from custom and the decisions of judges. This does not mean that it is less important than statute law. There is no statute law against murder for instance, which is a common law offence.

Common law allows things to be done to people without their consent if they lack competence. They must be done in that person's best interests and only if they are unable to make the decision for themselves. This may be because they are prevented by a mental disability, or if they are unable to communicate a decision because they are unconscious or for any other reason. The safeguards are that in deciding someone's best interests, consideration should be given to:

- their past and present wishes
- the need to maximise their participation in the decision
- the views of others (eg relatives) about the person's wishes and feelings
- the need to do what is least restrictive to their freedom.

It is an important role of advocacy (see page 13) to make sure that these conditions are met.

Think It Over

You are working as an assistant in a care home. A resident demands to leave. What factors would you take into account before deciding you were justified in stopping them?

Staff actively promote equality and individual rights
Treating people equally

Treating people equally does not mean treating everybody the same. It means to treat people in such a way as to give them equal access to services. It also means providing services in such a way that all service users get equal benefit from them. The following are some examples of how it might be necessary to treat people differently in order to treat them equally:

- A person who does not have English as their first language may require a translator in order to understand the services available and to express a choice about them.
- For cultural reasons, a Moslem service user may require the services of a carer of the same sex to perform intimate tasks.
- A child with a disability may be allocated a classroom assistant to enable them to take full advantage of mainstream education.

Theory into practice

Plan the development of a nursery to meet the needs of a diverse service user group. Consider the staffing, building, equipment and activities required to provide an equal opportunities environment. Make notes of your reasons for each suggestion.

Confidentiality

There can be no such thing as complete confidentiality. Information about service users has to be shared between workers in health and care organisations to ensure continuity and good quality care. It has to be shared with managers to ensure worker accountability. Sometimes it will have to be passed to another agency to ensure that service users get the care they need. Service users should understand what information is held about them, with whom it will be shared, and under what circumstances. Their permission should be sought before sensitive information is passed to others. Whenever possible they should be able to control disclosure about themselves. Care staff should only seek information about service users on a need to know basis.

21

There are circumstances where even very sensitive information may have to be passed on, even if the service user objects. This happens when there is a likelihood of harm if the information is not disclosed. This consideration will override the confidentiality of professional relationships. Examples are:

- A GP has a patient suffering from a serious mental disorder, in need of hospital treatment but refusing it. The GP would have to provide information about the patient's condition to a social worker to enable the social worker to decide whether to make an application for compulsory admission to hospital.
- A social worker suspects that a service user is physically abusing their children and a Child Protection Case Conference is convened. The professionals concerned must share information in order to protect the child.

Tensions and contradictions

For every right, there is a corresponding duty and responsibility on another person. The examples above show that there is no guarantee that rights and duties will never conflict. Because of this, care workers in all situations encounter tensions and contradictions in their roles. These differ from straightforward choices between right and wrong, because there is an element of right on both sides. These tensions arise for a number of reasons:

1 The rights of one person may clash with the rights of others.

Case Study

An older person is confused and wanders at night, repeatedly waking the neighbours with claims that they have been burgled. The neighbours demand something is done but when a social worker offers the older person residential care, they refuse it.

The right of the person to choose conflicts with the right of the neighbours to lead an undisturbed life. Whose rights should take precedence?

2 Two different rights a person has may conflict.

Case Study

An elderly person in a residential home is confused and thinks that her parents are still alive. She insists on leaving the home at night to look for them. The weather is bad, and the home is on a busy road. The resident would not be safe outside.

The resident's right to choose is conflicting with the right to be protected from harm. Which right is more important?

3 Two obligations of a care worker may conflict.

Case Study

A home care assistant has a good relationship with a service user who is severely disabled with a degenerative disease. They call one day and discover that the service user has taken a large overdose of medication, and left a note saying that they wish to be left to die. The care assistant knows that the service user has thought this through. They have responsibilities as an employee of a social services department.

What is the first responsibility of the worker?

4 Cultural values may conflict.

Case Study

A young child requires an operation. The parents, who are Jehovah's Witnesses, refuse permission for the child to have a blood transfusion. The doctors can either operate without a transfusion, which increases the risk to the child, or overrule the parents.

Is the parents' right to bring up the child as they wish more important than the duty of the doctors to carry out the operation in the safest way possible?

5 Resource allocation often has a moral dimension.

Case Study

The NHS Trust has a limited budget, and cannot meet all the health needs of its population. A patient in a Persistent Vegetative State has a limited chance of recovery, and is taking up a scarce bed in an Intensive Care Unit. The patient has the right to life, but the bed could be used for other critically ill patients with a better chance of recovery. How should this choice be made?

Think It Over

Choose one of the case studies and discuss the arguments on both sides in a group.

Staff development and training

One of the responsibilities of a manager is the professional development of their staff. This may be done formally through supervision sessions, or more informally in the course of day-to-day working. The manager should supervise the work of their staff, offer advice and guidance in difficult situations and help the workers identify training opportunities to improve their practice.

Education and training will help a worker recognise tensions in their work roles, how to begin to deal with them, and when to seek management advice. These tensions may go unrecognised without a sound knowledge of service user rights and the Care Value Base. Workers who go on to further professional training will be equipped by their training to make more complex decisions that respect service users' rights in difficult situations.

Professions have codes of conduct to guide their members in how to carry out their work, and there may be a controlling body with disciplinary procedures to deal with workers who do not meet acceptable standards (see page 11).

Practice implications of confidentiality

Every organisation should have a confidentiality policy to protect their service users and meet the requirements of the Care Value Base, but also of the Data Protection Act 1998.

The Data Protection Act 1998 has eight key principles which apply to both paper and computer records. These principles govern the way health and care services deal with information they hold about users.

1 **Personal data must be obtained and processed fairly and lawfully**
   Service users must be told that records are kept about them, and how and why these records are kept. They must be told who the information may be shared with, and why, and should be asked to give their consent. Service users must also be told of their rights of access to information held about them.

2 **Personal data shall be held only for one or more specified and lawful purposes**
   Organisations must have a lawful reason to hold data on individuals, for instance to enable them to provide, monitor and review services, and to provide statistical information to central government

3 **Personal data must be relevant, adequate and not excessive**
   Organisations should only keep information they need to provide a service, nothing more and nothing less.

4 **Personal data shall be accurate and kept up to date**
   Facts should be checked before being recorded and the records of service users should be reviewed regularly to make sure that information held about them is correct. If service users' details change, the record must be amended as soon as possible.

5 **Personal data must not be kept for longer than is necessary**
   Organisations should have a disposal date for records, and they should be destroyed when the date arrives. Some records, such as those concerning people who have received services, may be destroyed within a few years of the service ending. Others, such as adoption records and the records of people who have committed offences which may make them a danger to children, may be kept for as long as 100 years.

6 **Personal data must be processed in accordance with the rights of data subjects**
   Individuals have rights of access to their records and rights about when information is passed to others. There are exemptions, which cover situations where people would be at risk, but generally users should be able to see information held about them, and control who that information is given to.

7 **Personal data must be kept secure from unauthorised access, alteration, disclosure, loss or destruction**
   Paper records should be stored safely. There should be a system for removing and returning files. Electronic records should be protected by passwords and backed up regularly.

8 Personal data shall not be transferred to a country outside the European Economic Area unless that country ensures an adequate level of protection
Principle 8 is unlikely to affect health and care organisations, and is intended to ensure that data is only transferred to countries where there are appropriate safeguards about how it will be dealt with.

Every organisation should have a nominated member of staff to act as data controller. If an individual believes that their rights under the Data Protection Act have been infringed, they should complain to the data controller within the organisation. If they are not satisfied with how the complaint is dealt with, they can complain to the Data Protection Commissioner.

Think It Over

Think about an organisation you have experienced. How well did the policies and procedures of the organisation protect individuals' confidentiality?

How the individual care worker can promote equality, diversity and rights in their own practice

The bases of discrimination and how these may be reflected in the behaviour of care workers

Every care worker should have an understanding of the bases of discrimination within society. Because bases of discrimination are cultural features, they will all have widely held stereotypes associated with them. Everyone will have been exposed to these at some level, and some of them will have been absorbed. If they are not questioned, then they will be reflected in our behaviour. It is important to identify your own beliefs and prejudices because much discrimination is unintentional, the result of learned attitudes and lack of knowledge.

Identifying one's own beliefs and prejudices

There is a natural tendency for human beings to classify things into groups. This had evolutionary advantages. When all humans were hunter-gatherers, it would have been extremely important to make quick decisions about what was a predator and what was prey, on the basis of very limited information. People unable to do this would either not eat, or be eaten. This is a skill which is still important today, for instance when crossing the road there is not time to consciously process a lot of information about size, shape and colour before deciding that the object approaching is a car.

The pictures, although very different, are all chairs. In recognising them, we are demonstrating that we have a stereotype of a chair, and by calling them all chairs, we are labelling them.

Figure 1.8 Labelling

This ability to classify objects and make judgements on limited information is very useful. However, it is damaging if applied to people. It may lead to discrimination through prejudice, stereotyping and labelling. We must accept that we all have this tendency.

Changing one's own beliefs and prejudices

There are two steps to changing one's beliefs and prejudices. The first is for the individual to think about their attitudes, and accept that some may be based on prejudice. The second step is to seek out accurate information about the area, since prejudice can only flourish with ignorance. It will probably be necessary to do this in co-operation with others, perhaps in the context of support groups or awareness training. You may have the opportunity to check your beliefs and attitudes about a group with a member of that group. This would have to be done with great tact.

Key issues

In a group, spend a few minutes thinking about what your life might be like when you are 80 years old. Write down some notes about your thoughts. Share these notes with the other group members. What do they tell you about your attitudes towards older people? Are the thoughts of the entire group similar? What does this tell you? Do any of the group have very different ideas? How have these arisen?

Challenging oppressive and discriminatory behaviour

Good care practice is anti-discriminatory, not just non-discriminatory. It is important to challenge oppressive and discriminatory behaviour whenever it happens. Ignoring it or doing nothing about it is not a neutral option. If oppression is ignored and not opposed, this is the same as accepting it, and it will be reinforced in the minds of both the oppressor and the oppressed.

To challenge oppression, a worker must be aware of their beliefs and prejudices, and have examined them. They have to be confident in their knowledge of the rights of service users, and of the values, laws, codes of practice and procedures which support them. To support service users, it may be necessary to know the means of redress open to them, such as complaints procedures, and the roles of support groups and statutory bodies such as:

- the Equal Opportunities Commission
- the Commission for Racial Equality
- the Disability Rights Commission
- the Data Protection Commissioner.

It is also necessary to have an assertive approach, as challenging people over discriminatory behaviour may lead to defensiveness, and possibly even aggression. It is important for the worker challenging discriminatory behaviour to know how they can get support from colleagues and within the management structure of their organisations.

Think It Over

In a group, consider the following situation. You are an assistant in a nursery class. One of the children makes racist remarks about another child. Discuss how you would deal with this situation.

Bases of discrimination in society and the links between discrimination and behaviour

All bases of discrimination have linked prejudicial attitudes which directly affect the behaviour of those who hold them. Here are some examples:

Older people may be thought of as a burden, or a drain on resources, resulting in their being begrudged appropriate services, and preference given to younger people when resources are limited. Older people are often treated like children and patronised and not consulted when decisions are made about them, resulting in disempowerment. Sometimes illnesses are seen as an inevitable result of old age, and not investigated or treated appropriately.

People with disabilities may experience similar attitudes to older people. They are often patronised by others pitying them, regarding them as objects of charity or remarking on their bravery. This is a stereotype which, although apparently positive, is damaging (see page 7). They may be treated as though their disability were general rather than specific, and ignored by others – the 'does he take sugar' syndrome – and excluded from social contacts and decisions about themselves. People with learning difficulties are particularly vulnerable to being treated as children.

Figure 1.9 It is wrong to assume that people in wheelchairs cannot speak for themselves

People with mental disorders may similarly be regarded as dangerous to others. Some may be, but so are many people without a mental disorder. Of those people with mental disorders who harm someone, far more harm themselves than harm other people. Fear may result in people being treated in a more restrictive way than is necessary for their or others' safety.

People with HIV/AIDS will be open to to discrimination if people do not understand how the virus is transmitted. If they wrongly believe it can be caught from touch, or sharing crockery and cutlery, they may exclude them from normal social contact. If care workers are not well informed, it will result in service users getting a poorer service.

Think It Over

Choose another basis of discrimination. What stereotypes are attached to people who have this characteristic? How are these stereotypes likely to affect the way they are treated?

Appropriate use of language

No competent care worker uses overtly discriminatory language, but it is also necessary to be aware of more subtle ways in which language can devalue service users. Some words have fallen into disuse because they have acquired negative connotations. No one would use words such as cripple, imbecile or lunatic, though at one time all were in common use. Workers should be aware that this is a continuing process. A handicap now is regarded as a socially constructed disadvantage that results from a disability, because of the attitudes of others or the lack of appropriate resources and facilities. The two terms should not be confused. Similarly, learning difficulty is a more appropriate term to use than mental handicap.

Workers should also be aware of the danger of stereotyping and labelling service users by grouping them together in relation to a single characteristic – an illness, for instance. To call individuals schizophrenics, rather than people with schizophrenia, makes their illness the most important thing about them, and devalues them by ignoring their other qualities. Individuals should not be described as suffering from an illness, because this turns them into passive victims. Referring to them as having an illness is more empowering and conducive to an open-minded approach to them as individuals. Terms such as 'confined to a wheelchair' are similarly unacceptable and patronising. People with disabilities regard themselves as 'wheelchair users', and the wheelchair as something which enables, not confines them.

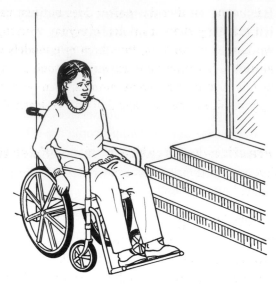

Figure 1.10 'Disability or handicap?'

Figure 1.11 'Confined to a wheelchair'

Think It Over

Think about the language you use in relation to a group within society, for instance older people or people with disabilities. Discuss this in a group. Is any of the language you use unconsciously discriminatory?

Role modelling

Care workers are important role models because discriminatory attitudes are learned. We have already seen on page 26 that failing to challenge discriminatory behaviour will reinforce it, and the reverse is true. If discriminatory behaviour is challenged, then the person discriminating may rethink their attitudes, especially if their behaviour was unconscious or unthinking. The person discriminated against will at least know that not everybody shares the same discriminatory attitudes.

It is important that the worker does not just pay lip service to anti-discriminatory practice, but that they show it in their everyday working lives. This is particularly true when working with children, for whom role models will be more influential in forming their attitudes. If services are delivered in such a way that they conform to sexual stereotypes, or fail to respect different cultures, then whatever statements are made about equal opportunities, the message that will be learned is that it is all right to discriminate.

Practice implications of confidentiality

Every worker has a statutory and professional duty to protect information about service users.

Interviewing

Interviews with service users when sensitive information is being discussed should always be somewhere they cannot be overheard. Workers should always be aware that service users have the right to keep back information, and should not pressurise service users or be oppressive in their questioning if this happens.

Recording

Workers should take care to distinguish between facts and opinions when recording information about service users. They should only record information necessary for the organisation to carry out its responsibilities.

Storage of information

Electronic data should be protected with passwords. Workers must never use somebody else's password, and should not let anyone else use theirs. When using a computer, workers should make sure that screens are positioned so that unauthorised people cannot see them.

Files and other paper records should be kept securely where unauthorised people cannot get access to them, and never left lying around. Workers should only remove files from their secure location when there is a good reason for doing so.

Sharing of information

Workers should ask the service user's permission before passing on sensitive information to others. They should check that any enquirer has the right to the information and the need to know. If in doubt, they should consult a manager. They should check the identity of people requesting information, to ensure that they are who they claim to be. Sometimes information may have to be given over the telephone, in which case it is good practice to ring back to confirm the person's identity.

Workers should take care, when passing information to authorised people, that sensitive information is not overheard by people who do not have the right or need to know. They should never gossip about the private affairs of service users, either between themselves or outside work with friends and family.

Theory into practice

Design a leaflet to be given to people on admission to a residential home. Explain their rights to confidentiality and access to information to the resident. Explain the procedures of the establishment which support these rights.

End-of-unit test

1 Why doesn't equality of opportunity lead to equality of outcome?
2 What are the problems in defining the moral rights of individuals?
3 Identify two reports which provide evidence for a cycle of disadvantage. State the main findings of each.
4 What is the contribution of the McPherson Report to our understanding of unequal access to services?
5 What is the difference between a prejudice and a stereotype?
6 What is the difference between statute and common law?
7 Identify three pieces of anti-discriminatory legislation.
8 How might the Human Rights Act cause a tension between the rights of children and their parents in cases of suspected child abuse?
9 How do the main aims of the Children Act meet the requirements of the Human Rights Act?
10 A very confused resident of a care home wants to leave in the early hours of the morning. The resident is very frail, the weather is bad, and the resident has nowhere to go. Do the staff have any right to stop the resident?
11 Why might it be necessary to treat people differently in order to treat them equally?
12 What are the arguments for and against affirmative action?
13 What are the limits to confidentiality in the service user/carer relationship?
14 Which organisation assists patients who wish to complain about health services?
15 Describe a situation in statute law which allows someone to be compulsorily detained, other than if they are suspected of a criminal offence.

References and further reading

Bagilhole, B. (1998) *Equal Opportunities and Social Policy,* Harlow: Longman

Brading, J. and Curtis, J. (1996) *Disability Discrimination, A Practical Guide to the New Law,* London: Kogan Page

British Medical Association and the Law Society (1995) *Assessment of Mental Capacity – Guidance for Doctors and Lawyers,* London: BMA

Centre for Policy on Ageing (1984) *Home Life – a code of practice for residential care,* London: CPA

Centre for Policy on Ageing (1986) *A Better Home Life – a code of practice for residential and nursing home care,* London: CPA

Clarke, L. (1995) *Discrimination* (2nd ed) Wimbledon: Institute of Personnel Development

Donnellan, C. (ed) (1999) *Issues for the Nineties: Vol. 6 Racial discrimination, Vol. 13 What are Children's Rights? Vol. 17 Disabilities and Equality, Vol. 18 Gender and Prejudice,* Cambridge: Independence Educational Publishers

Family Welfare Association Guide to the Social Services 2001/2002

Fenwick, H. (1998) *Liberties* (2nd ed), Harlow: Longman

Linden, J. (1998) *Equal Opportunities in Practice,* London: Hodder

Moonie N. (ed) (2000) *Health and Social Care,* Oxford: Heinemann

Thompson, N. (2000) *Anti-discriminatory Practice,* Basingstoke: Macmillan

Webb R. and Tossell D. (1993) *Social Issues for Carers,* London: Edward Arnold

Communication and supportive skills

This unit explores the skills of effective interpersonal interaction and communication. It examines the factors that enhance and inhibit communication and provides guidance on how to communicate effectively with service users; including how to provide support to distressed individuals.

Providing assessment evidence for Unit 2

In order to achieve this unit you must produce reports of interactions that you have undertaken which meet the grading criteria requirements. It may be easier to report a small range of different interactions that demonstrate different aspects of the criteria for passing this unit, than to attempt to meet all the criteria with just one report.

The criteria for this unit require students to demonstrate a number of practical skills. Students must show that they have understood the major factors which influence communication and that they understand the role of advocates and interpreters. Students must also show that they have reviewed their own personal communication methods, demonstrated the use of supportive skills, used communication skills effectively and appropriately, demonstrated ways of overcoming or minimising barriers to communication and used examples from placement to explain how communication skills can support vulnerable or distressed individuals. In order to gather evidence of these criteria, it may be useful to maintain a logbook that records details of conversations and other interactions which have occurred in placement settings. These records can then be used to create detailed transcripts of interactions which can be evaluated in order to meet the grading criteria.

What you need to learn

- Interpersonal interaction and communication
- Supportive skills
- Communication skills
- Supportive skills with distressed individuals

Interpersonal interaction and communication

Many animals and insects communicate information between individuals, but no other species can communicate in the complex range of ways that human beings can. There are many different ways in which people communicate with each other. These can include: language, body language, signs and symbols, written communication, art and music. Recorded information also enables communication to take place.

Types of interpersonal communication

Language

Spoken, signed, or written communication can communicate complex and subtle messages between individuals or groups of people. Language not only enables people to communicate information, but it also provides a basis for people to develop concepts. Concepts influence the way individuals think. Concepts enable us to group experiences together to help us understand events that we have experienced. Concepts also enable us to predict the future. Human civilisation has developed because of our ability to classify experience using language.

Language does not have to be based on sounds which are heard. Signing systems such as British Sign Language provide a full language system for people who do not use spoken language.

Body language

Facial expressions, body posture and muscle tone all provide messages as to how we feel and perhaps what we are thinking. Mime and drama use body language to communicate complex ideas and emotions.

Signs and symbols

Gestures made with hands or arms, written symbols or diagrams such as traffic signs all communicate messages to people.

Humans can communicate across distance and time by using the following:

Written communication

Books, e-mail, text messages and so on, allow people to communicate around the planet and even across centuries of time. Written communication does not have to be visual. Braille (a system of raised marks that can be felt with your fingers) provides a system of written communication for people who do not use visual systems of communication.

Artwork and other objects which are designed or built

Paintings, photographs, sculptures, architecture, ornaments and other household objects can communicate messages and emotions to people. People often take photographs or buy souvenirs to remind them of happy experiences. Many individuals earn their living by designing and developing artwork.

Music

Music can provide an effective communication system for expressing emotion. Music is sometimes called the language of emotion.

Recorded information

Books, magazines, newspapers, films, videos, tapes, CDs and other electronic media enable us to re-experience events or messages from the past.

Communicating simple messages

Some forms of communication involve simply sending a message within a fixed unambiguous system of meaning. An example might be an airline pilot trying to park an aircraft. The pilot might be guided by a member of ground staff using arm signals.

The arm signal clearly indicates the direction that the aircraft must turn towards. Each arm signal will have a simple meaning, which is exactly the same for pilots, and for the ground crew; the message cannot be misinterpreted.

Communicating complex messages

Most communication between people is not simple and unambiguous. Artwork, for example, rarely communicates straightforward information. It is normal for people to experience completely different messages from the same piece of artwork. Paintings, sculptures and poems are not designed to give people information but to stimulate thoughts and emotions in people. Beauty is said to be in the eye of the beholder –

Figure 2.1 Communication through signals

this phrase means that what we experience depends on the way we think, as well as what it is that we hear or are looking at.

Within care settings a great deal of communication with members of the public will be complex. It is vitally important to understand that each person will have their own ways of interpreting things that are said to, or done to them. Communication with members of the public should not be a simple matter of trying to pass on information. Effective communication will depend on engaging in a 'communication cycle', which takes into account the way information is being received by the other person. Different people will interpret messages in different ways. Effective communication requires much more than giving clear information.

The communication cycle

When we communicate with other people we become involved in a process of expressing our own thoughts and interpreting the other person's understanding of what we are communicating. This process should usually involve the steps set out below:

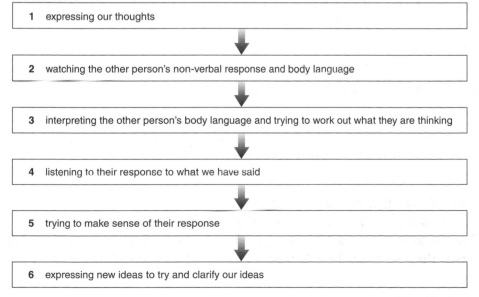

1. expressing our thoughts

2. watching the other person's non-verbal response and body language

3. interpreting the other person's body language and trying to work out what they are thinking

4. listening to their response to what we have said

5. trying to make sense of their response

6. expressing new ideas to try and clarify our ideas

Figure 2.2 Communication

Communication needs to be a two-way process where each person is trying to understand the viewpoint of the other person. The communication cycle requires professionals (at least) to have advanced listening skills and the ability to check their understanding of others' responses.

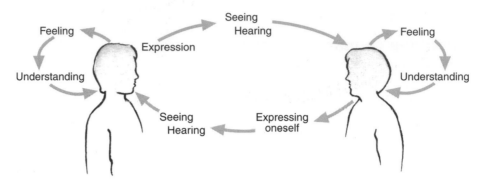

Figure 2.3 The communication cycle

Listening is not the same as hearing the sounds people make when they talk. Listening involves hearing another person's words – then thinking about what they mean – then thinking what to say back to the other person. Some people call this process 'active listening'. As well as thinking carefully and remembering what someone says, good listeners will also make sure their non-verbal communication demonstrates interest in the other person.

Skilled listening involves:

1 looking interested and ready to listen
2 hearing what is said
3 remembering what is said
4 checking understanding with the other person.

It is usually easier to understand people who are similar to ourselves. We can learn about different people by checking our understanding of what we have heard.

Checking our understanding involves hearing what the other person says and asking the other person questions. Another way to check our understanding is to put what a person has just said into our own words and to say this back to them, to see if we did understand what they said.

When we listen to complicated details of other people's lives, we often begin to form mental pictures based on what they are telling us. Listening skills involve checking these mental pictures to make sure that we understand correctly. It can be very difficult to remember accurately what people tell us if we don't check how our ideas are developing.

Good listening involves thinking about what we hear while we are listening and checking our understanding as the conversation goes along. Sometimes this idea of checking our understanding is called 'reflection' because we reflect on the other person's ideas.

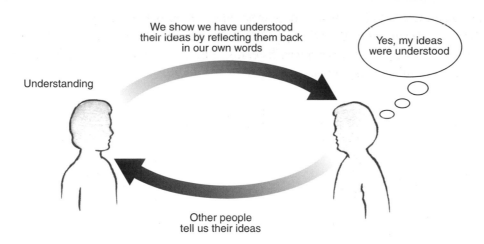

Figure 2.4 Reflection

Good listening is hard work. Instead of just being around when people speak, we must build up an understanding of the people around us. Although listening is difficult, people who are attracted to work in care roles may often enjoy learning about other people and their lives.

Assessment activity 2.1

You need to correctly identify different types of interpersonal interaction and communication. To do this, you could identify two contrasting examples of interpersonal interaction that you have had. One could be spoken, for example a conversation with someone you know well. The other example could be written; perhaps letters or e-mails you have exchanged.

For each example, describe the interaction and evaluate how effective it was. If your interaction was effective and meanings were understood, can you identify how the communication cycle worked? If there were problems then how far were these problems caused by an ineffective communication cycle? Your work may contribute towards a merit grade if you can explain the ways in which verbal and non-verbal communication can affect the communication cycle.

Barriers to effective interpersonal interaction

Communication can become blocked if individual difficulties and differences are not understood. There are three main ways that communication becomes blocked:

1 A person can't see, hear or receive the message.
2 A person can't make sense of the message.
3 A person misunderstands the message.

Examples of the first kind of block, where people don't receive the communication, include visual disabilities, hearing disabilities, environmental problems such as poor lighting, noisy environments, and speaking from too far away.

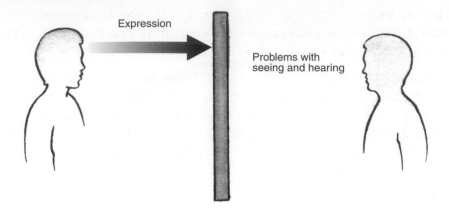

Figure 2.5 Environmental problems like noise and poor light can create communication barriers

Examples where people may not be able to make sense of the message include:

- the use of different languages, including signed languages
- the use of different terms in language, such as jargon (technical language), slang (different people using different terms), or dialect (different people making different sounds)
- physical and intellectual disabilities, such as dysphasia (difficulties with language expression or understanding), aphasia (an absence of language ability), being ill, or suffering memory loss, or learning difficulty.

Reasons for misunderstanding a message include:

- cultural influences – different cultures interpret non-verbal and verbal messages, and humour, in different ways
- assumptions about people – about race, gender, disability and other groupings
- labelling or stereotyping of others
- social context – statements and behaviour that are understood by friends and family may not be understood by strangers
- emotional barriers – a worker's own emotional needs may stop them from wanting to know about others
- time pressures can mean that staff withdraw from wanting to know about others
- emotional differences – emotional differences can sometimes be interpreted as personality clashes, or personality differences. Very angry, or very happy, or very shy people may misinterpret communication from others.

Effective communication requires that care workers evaluate possible barriers to communication and find ways of overcoming these barriers.

Communication and culture

Non-verbal communication is a language. There are many languages in the world and they do not all have the same concepts and sounds. Non-verbal communication is not the same everywhere. For example, in Britain the hand gesture with palm up and facing forward, means 'Stop, don't do that'. In Greece it can mean, 'You are dirt' and is a very rude gesture.

Why do the same physical movements have different meanings? The answer lies in culture. One explanation for the hand signs is that the British version of the palm-and-fingers gesture means, 'I arrest you, you must not do it', whereas the Greek interpretation goes back to medieval times when criminals had dirt rubbed in their faces to show how much people despised them.

Without looking at history and culture, it is confusing to consider why gestures mean what they do. No one knows all the history and all the cultural possibilities of body language and non-verbal communication. But it is vitally important that carers should always remember that people have different cultural backgrounds. The carer's system of non-verbal communication may not carry the same meanings to everyone. We can easily misinterpret another person's non-verbal messages.

Personal space and culture

Sometimes cultural differences are very marked. White British people are often seen as 'unusual' or odd when they go outside Europe, because they keep a large personal space around them. Other people are not allowed to come too near when they speak, or to touch them. In many other cultures, standing close is normal and good manners – touching an arm or shoulder is just usual behaviour. Some British people feel threatened by such non-verbal behaviour because it is not what they have grown up with. For some British people, strangers who come too close or who touch are trying to dominate or have power over them. They become afraid or defensive. However, things work out fine when this need for space and distance is understood and allowed for by people from other cultures.

Using care values means that care workers must have respect for other people's culture. People learn different ways of communicating, and good carers will try to understand the different ways in which people use non-verbal messages. For instance, past research in the USA suggests that white and black Americans may have used different non-verbal signals when they listened. It suggests that some black Americans may tend not to look much at the speaker. This can be interpreted as a mark of respect – by looking away it demonstrates that you are really thinking hard about the message. Unfortunately, not all white people understood this cultural difference in non-verbal communication. Some individuals misunderstood and assumed that this non-verbal behaviour meant exactly what it would mean if they had done it. That is, it would mean they were not listening.

Learning the cultural differences

Words do not have precise unchanging meanings. Understanding another person involves making sense of the things that they say.

Think It Over

What does the phrase: 'we can fish' mean?

If you were talking to someone whilst walking along a riverbank – holding a fishing rod – there would be an obvious interpretation. But if you were walking around a factory and you had just asked 'What do you do in this factory?' the phrase above could be the answer!

Making sense of spoken language requires knowledge of the context and intentions of the speaker. Understanding non-verbal communication involves exactly the same need to understand 'where the person is coming from', or to put it more formally, what are the circumstances and cultural context of the other person.

There is an almost infinite variety of meanings that can be given to any type of eye contact, facial expression, posture or gesture. Every culture develops its own special system of meanings. Carers have to understand and show respect and value for all these different systems of sending messages. But how can you ever learn them all?

No one can learn every possible system of non-verbal message – but it is possible to learn about the ones people you are with are using! It is possible to do this by first noticing and remembering what others do – what non-verbal messages they are sending. The next step is to make an intelligent guess as to what messages the person is trying to give you. Finally, check your understanding (your guesses) with the person: ask polite questions as well as watching the kind of reactions you get. So, at the heart of skilled interpersonal interaction is the ability to watch other people, remember what they do, and guess what actions might mean and then check out your guesses with the person.

- Never rely on your own guesses, because often these turn into assumptions.
- If you don't check assumptions with people, you may end up misunderstanding them.
- Misunderstandings can lead to discrimination.

Think It Over

Imagine you are working with an older person. Whenever you start to speak to her she always looks at the floor and never makes eye contact. Why is this?

Your first thought is that she might be sad or that you make her sad. Having made such an assumption, you might not want to work with this person – she is too depressing and you do not seem to get on. You might even decide that you do not like her. But you could ask: 'How do you feel today; would you like me to get you anything?' By checking what she feels, you could test your own understanding. She might say she feels well and is quite happy, and then suggests something you could do for her. This means that she cannot be depressed.

Why else would someone look at the floor rather than at you?

- It could be a cultural value. She may feel it is not proper to look at you.
- She may not be able to see you clearly, so she prefers not to try to look at you.
- She may just choose not to conform to your expectations. Looking at the floor may be important to some other emotional feeling that she has.

So it would be unfair to assume that she was difficult or depressed just because she did not look at you when you talked to her.

Good caring is the art of getting to understand people – not acting on unchecked assumptions. So non-verbal messages should never be relied on; they should always be checked. Non-verbal messages can mean different things depending on the circumstances of the people send them. But all messages are like this. Words can be looked up in a dictionary, and yet words do not always carry exactly the same meaning.

As well as looking at the whole picture of people's words, their non-verbal messages and where they are, it is also necessary to understand their culture, their individuality and how they see their social situation. This is why caring is such a skilled area of work. People can improve their skills constantly through experience, and through linking new ideas to their experience. The main thing is always to check assumptions. It is important to remember that it is easy to misunderstand others. By checking ideas it is possible to reduce the risks of being uncaring or discriminatory.

Culture, age and gender

A person's understanding of him or herself will be strongly influenced by past personal history and current social context. Socialisation into the rules of a culture has a major part to play in the way individuals form their self-concept.

Perceptions of age-appropriate behaviour and gender-appropriate behaviour are strongly influenced by culture. Culture is the term used to describe the norms and values which belong to an identifiable social group. People are socialised into the norms and values of a culture; they learn the socially accepted rules of their group. Group norms and values – the 'rules' for behaviour – vary between different religious, ethnic, class, gender and age groups.

Norms and values which influence interpersonal interaction vary a great deal between different class groups and different regions of Britain. Not only do norms of interaction vary, but they also constantly evolve and change. It might be possible to invent a dictionary of rules for understanding the meanings of verbal and non-verbal behaviours; but such a dictionary would need constant revision for it to be accurate.

People of different age groups have usually been socialised into different norms with respect to interpersonal behaviour.

Case Study

Florence Tucknell was born in 1922. When she was young there was a cultural norm that only close friends and family would call her by her first name. She was Miss Tucknell to everyone else. For a stranger to call her 'Florence' would be a sign of disrespect, a sign that they thought they were socially superior or more powerful than she was. When Florence went into a respite care home for a week she was upset that everyone used first names. She knows that this is what goes on nowadays, but this was not how she was brought up to behave.

Miss Tucknell was very pleased to be greeted by her key worker who introduced herself as, 'I'm Anthea Shakespeare, may I ask your name?'

Miss Tucknell replied, 'I'm Miss Tucknell, please.'

'Shall I call you Miss Tucknell then?'

'Yes please.'

Miss Tucknell was annoyed with one of the other staff who said 'Hello Flo, I've come to take you into lunch'. Miss Tucknell avoids this care worker whenever she can.

1 How do you think Miss Tucknell felt when she was addressed as 'Flo'?
2 What effect is this likely to have on her relations with this member of staff?
3 What actions could the member of staff have taken to avoid this problem?
4 Why is it important to use appropriate language with service users?

Case Study

Martin Howarth was born in the north of England in 1956. He recently moved to the south-east of England and took a job as a care worker. Martin was surprised to find that many of his younger female colleagues were complaining about his behaviour. Martin has been socialised into the norm of calling women 'Flower' or even 'Petal.' When Martin used these terms he was expecting to communicate approval, comradeship and warmth. Martin believed that these were universal terms of endearment, i.e. 'You are likeable, we're all working together, we get on – don't we?'

His new colleagues in the south had never been referred to as 'Flower' before and saw it as sexist: 'You are saying that I am weak, short-lived and that all that matters about my existence is my degree of sexual attractiveness!' Martin soon learned that age, gender and region affect how words are understood. Words change their value with time.

Assessment activity 2.2

Mr A came from Bangladesh to the UK to live with his son and daughter-in-law ten years ago. Recently he has become forgetful and has also had some difficulty in hearing speech when there is any background noise. Mr A and his son approach the enquiries desk of a local authority social services department in order to ask them what help may be available. A young white woman staffs the desk.

What barriers to communication might arise in this interpersonal situation? Describe the barriers you can identify, giving reasons why these barriers could prevent effective communication. Your work on this issue might contribute to the examples of overcoming barriers to communication that are needed for this unit.

Supportive skills

Care workers often work with people who have experienced abuse, are afraid, or who do not understand what might happen next. Members of the public are often vulnerable people – people who feel threatened by what they are experiencing. Care staff must have advanced interpersonal skills if they are to be effective in meeting the needs of the people they work with.

Human needs are complex. In the past it was sometimes assumed that physical needs should always take priority over other social and cultural needs. Nowadays physical needs are often seen as the foundation for working with people, but not always the most important issue to address. One way of understanding human needs is through the work of Abraham Maslow (1908–70). Maslow's theory was that the purpose of human life was personal growth; that is, the quality of a human life can be understood in terms of an individual's development of their own ability and potential. Before a person can fully develop his or her potential, there are levels of need called deficiency needs which first have to be met. Maslow's levels of need are often set out as a pyramid (as shown in Figure 2.6) on the left-hand side of the diagram. The role of communication in meeting human need is described on the right-hand side of the diagram.

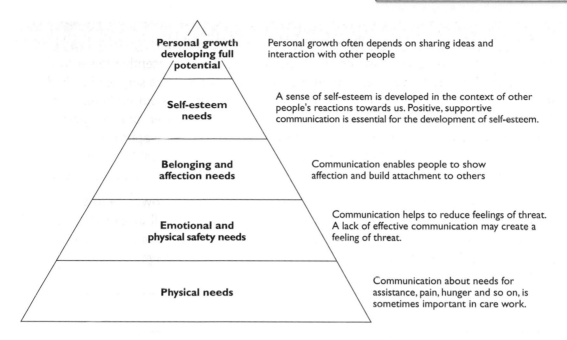

Figure 2.6 Communication within Maslow's levels of need

Effective communication needs to operate at every level of the triangle above. It is important to give and receive clear information about physical needs in order to respond to those needs. A lack of clear communication may result in a person's physical needs being unmet.

Listening skills are vital in order to create the basis for psychological safety and to reduce the threat that members of the public may feel. If a person does not feel that they have been listened to they may feel that they are not being respected. A lack of respect may create a feeling of low self-esteem and emotional vulnerability. As well as this, the individual may feel that they are physically at risk because their needs have not been understood. Effective body language is vital to establish professional relationships and create a sense of safety and belonging with people who we work with.

Supportive skills are essential if workers are to meet the self-esteem needs of others. If workers can build an understanding of other's needs, then patients may feel that they have been respected and valued. Listening and supportive skills convey a sense of value to others.

An overview of supportive skills

Effective supportive behaviour will depend on a range of verbal and non-verbal skills together with the ability to reflect on our own personal behaviour and to work in a context which enables effective communication.

Supportive body language

Muscle tone, facial expression, eye contact and posture can send messages of being friendly. When meeting a person it is usually appropriate to smile, to express interest through eye contact and to maintain a relaxed posture – free of muscle tension, which indicates a readiness to talk and listen. It is difficult to define a simple set of rules for supportive body language because each individual will have their own expectations

41

about what is appropriate and normal. Settings where conversation takes place can influence how people should behave. The most important thing about supportive body language is to learn to monitor the effects that our behaviour is having on another person. Being supportive involves being aware of your own non-verbal behaviour and monitoring how your non-verbal behaviour is affecting others. The section on communication skills in this chapter explores the detail of components of non-verbal communication in more depth.

Think It Over

Imagine that you feel sad about something and that you explain your problems to a friend. How would you feel if your friend did not look at you and instead seemed interested in what was happening outside the window? How would you feel if your friend just 'parroted' things you said back to you? How would you react if he or she just said things like ' I know', or 'Yes' all the time – without sounding sincere or interested?

Being a good friend involves supportive behaviour – how good are you at showing others that you understand their feelings?

Personal space

There are different social and cultural expectations about how close another person should be when they talk to you. For many British people face-to-face contact where the two people are less than an arm's length apart suggests either intimacy (love and affection) or aggression. These interpretations are naturally suspended when a worker is performing a socially understood role such as personal care. Even so, some members of the public may feel threatened because their personal space has been entered. It may be important to establish a sense of trust through smiling and talking to the individual before coming close to them.

Listening skills

Listening is an essential skill for supportive communication. As explained in the previous section, listening is an active process which involves thinking carefully about the content of the other person's speech and checking this understanding as the conversation progresses. It can also be important to plan even brief conversations so that there is an emotional structure to conversation.

Usually we start with a greeting or ask how someone is. Conversations have a beginning, middle and an end. This means that we have to create the right kind of atmosphere for a conversation at the beginning. We might need to help someone relax – we might need to show that we are friendly and relaxed. We then have the conversation. When we end the conversation we usually say something like 'See you soon.' When we end a conversation we have to leave the other person with the right feelings about what we have said.

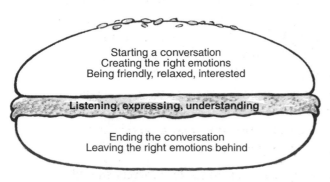

Figure 2.7 The conversation sandwich

Specialist skills for supportive communication

The skills for creating a sense of emotional safety were first identified by Carl Rogers (1902–87). Originally these skills were seen as a basis for counselling relationships, but they have since become adopted as a basis for any befriending or supportive relationship. There are three conditions for a supportive conversation and these are that the carer must show (or convey) a sense of warmth, understanding and sincerity to the other person. These conditions sometimes have other names:

- warmth (sometimes called acceptance)
- understanding (originally called empathy)
- sincerity (originally called genuineness).

Conveying warmth

Conveying warmth means being seen as a warm, accepting person. In order to influence another person to view you this way you will need to demonstrate that you do not stereotype and label others. You will need to demonstrate that you do not judge other people as good or bad, right or wrong. This is sometimes referred to as a non-judgemental attitude. Warmth means not comparing people to see who is best!

Conveying warmth means being willing to listen to others. It means being able to prove that you are listening to a person because you can remember what they have said to you. Warmth involves using reflective listening. That is, you give your attention to the person when they talk, and remember what they say. You can then reflect the words back again.

Service user	'I hate it here, you don't know what it's like, there's no one to talk to, they're all too busy, no one cares about me.'
Worker	'I suppose they are busy and you feel that no one cares.'
Service user	'That's right, they don't – you aren't so bad, but you won't be here tomorrow.'
Worker	'Well that's right, I can't come in tomorrow but we could talk for a while now if you would like that.'

The worker is able to show the service user that they are listening by repeating some of the things that the service user has said. The repetition is not 'parrot fashion'; the worker has used his or her own way of speaking. The worker has also avoided being judgmental. When the service user said that no one cared, the worker did not argue with him or her. The worker might have felt like saying, 'How can you say that – don't you know how hard we work for you? You want to think yourself lucky, there's plenty of people who would be pleased to be here, other people don't complain'. This advice to think yourself lucky and make comparison with other people is judgemental, it does not value the other person, and it is not warm. If the worker had said these things it would have blocked the conversation. Warmth makes it safe for the service user to express their feelings. Warmth means that the worker could disagree with what a service user has said, but the service user needs to feel safe that they will not be put down.

In developing the skill of showing warmth, it is important not to judge. Workers should accept that people have the right to be the way they are, and to make their own choices.

While you may disapprove of a person's behaviour, you must show that you do not dislike them as an individual. This is particularly important when working with people with difficult behaviour. It is essential that individuals know it is the behaviour which is disliked, not them as a person.

Conveying understanding

Understanding means learning about the individual identity and beliefs that a person has. Carl Rogers saw the idea of understanding or empathy as 'the ability to experience another person's world as if it was your own world' – the key part being the 'as if'. We always keep an idea of our own world and we know that other people have different experiences from our own. It is important to try to really understand the thoughts and feelings of others.

Reflective listening provides a useful tool to help staff to gradually learn about people. By keeping a conversation going, a person may feel that they are understood; the worker is warm and non-judgemental, so it becomes safe for a person to tell the worker something about their life. If the worker checks that they understand the person, they may feel valued. As the person feels that they are valued, so they may talk more. The more the person talks, the more the worker has a chance to learn about their views.

Service user	'So anyway, I said to the doctor look these pills are only making me worse, I don't want them.'
Worker	'So you told him to stop them.'
Service user	'That's right, I don't believe in pills – you end up rattling round with all that lot inside you – if you're meant to get better you will, that's what I say.'
Worker	'Have you always believed that pills don't help?'
Service user	'Yes, well ever since I was young, I put my faith in God.'

By listening and conveying warmth the worker is being given the privilege of learning about the person's religious views and perhaps even needs. Understanding can grow from a conversation which conveys value for the other person. If you can get to understand people a sense of trust may develop. If a person is understood and not judged they may consider it safe to share thoughts and worries with staff.

Conveying sincerity

Being sincere means being open about what you say and the way that you speak. It means not acting, not using set phrases or professional styles which are not really you. In some ways being sincere means being yourself, being honest and real! Being real has to involve being non-judgemental though, trying to understand people rather than trying to give people advice. If being honest means giving other people your advice – don't do it! However, when you listen and learn about other people, do use your own normal language. Think about ways you might describe yourself and occasionally share details of your own life with people you are helping. Sometimes it is necessary to share your thoughts to keep a conversation going. Sharing information from your own life might help to convey sincerity or genuineness in some situations.

| Service user | 'But what's the point in talking to you, I mean you don't really care, it's just your job.' |
| Worker | 'It is my job, but I do care about you, and I would be pleased to talk with you. I chose this work because I care and so I can make the time to listen if you want to talk about it.' |

Understanding, warmth and sincerity have to be combined in order to provide a safe, supportive setting.

Learning to create a supportive relationship with people will involve practice and a great deal of self-monitoring and reflection. It will be necessary to get feedback from colleagues, supervisors and most importantly members of the public, when you practise conveying warmth, understanding and sincerity.

You may be able to tell if your communication is effective because the other person may reflect your behaviour. That is, if you are warm and understanding the other person may come to trust you; then you may find that this person is warm and friendly toward you. If you are honest and sincere, people may be honest and sincere with you. The quality of a supportive relationship can become a two-way process. You may find working with others more enjoyable because you become skilled at warmth, understanding and sincerity.

Theory into practice

The following are ideas for developing supportive skills.

1 Work with a friend. Take turns in imagining that you are upset or sad whilst the other person uses reflective listening skills. Tape-record the conversation. Play the tape back and evaluate your performance in terms of warmth, understanding and sincerity.
2 Watch videos of conversational skills or counselling situations where warmth, understanding and sincerity are demonstrated – discuss how this is effective and how you might develop your own conversational skills.
3 Think about your own conversations with service users – keep a logbook to reflect on your own skills development.
4 Practise being warm, understanding and sincere with your supervisor or tutor – ask them for feedback.
5 Work on supportive behaviour as part of a group project. Practise being supportive whilst undertaking some problem-solving work.

Assertive skills

Some people may seem shy and worried; they say little and avoid contact with people they don't know. Other people may want people to be afraid of them, they may try to dominate and control others. Fear and aggression are two of the basic emotions that we experience. It is easy to give into our basic emotions and either become submissive or aggressive when we feel stressed. Assertion is an advanced skill which involves controlling the basic emotions involved in running away or fighting. Assertion involves a mental attitude of trying to negotiate, trying to solve problems rather than giving in to emotional impulses.

Winning and losing

A simple way of understanding assertion is to look at people's behaviour when they have an argument. An aggressive person will demand that they are right and other people are wrong. They will want to win while others lose. The opposite of aggression is to be weak or submissive. A submissive person accepts that they will lose, get told off or put down. Assertive behaviour is different from both these responses. In an argument an assertive person will try to reach an answer where no one has to lose or be 'put down'. Assertion is a skill where 'win-win' situations can happen – no-one has to be the loser. For example, suppose a service user is angry because their carer is late:

Person	'You're late again – I'm not putting up with it – I'm going to make a formal complaint about your behaviour.'
Aggressive response	'Don't you talk to me like that – you're lucky I'm here at all – don't you know how hard we work, there are other people to look after as well as you, you know!'
Submissive response	'I'm terribly sorry, I promise I won't be late again.'
Assertive response	'I'm sorry that you're angry, but I really couldn't help it, please let me explain why I had to be late today.'

The assertive response aims to meet the emotional needs of both people without anyone being the loser. The aggressive response tries to meet the needs of the worker and not the member of the public – it aims to give the worker power and keep the other person vulnerable. The submissive response may allow the service user to control and dominate the worker. Assertive skills can help enable carers to cope with difficult and challenging situations.

Aggressive behaviour	Assertive behaviour	Submissive behaviour
Main emotion: anger Wanting your own way Making demands Not listening to others 'Putting people down' Trying to win Shouting or talking very loudly	*Main emotion:* staying in control of emotions Negotiating with others Trying to solve problems Aiming that no has to lose Showing respect for others Keeping a clear, calm voice	*Main emotion:* fear Letting others win Agreeing with others Not putting your views across Looking afraid Speaking quietly or not speaking at all
Threatening non-verbal behaviour including: fixed eye contact, tense muscles, waving or folding hands and arms, looking angry	**Normal non-verbal behaviour** including: varied eye contact, relaxed face muscles, looking 'in control', keeping hands and arms at your side	**Submissive non-verbal behaviour** including: looking down, not looking at others, tense muscles, looking frightened

To be assertive a person usually has to:

- understand the situation that they are in – including facts, details and other people's perceptions
- be able to control personal emotions and stay calm
- be able to act assertively using the right non-verbal behaviour
- be able to act assertively using the right words and statements.

Learning to stay calm and use the right verbal and non-verbal behaviour is a skill which can be developed by watching other experienced professionals and copying their performance. Role-play and reflection on practice can also help to develop assertive skills. Some verbal and non-verbal behaviours involved in assertion are summarised in the table on page 46.

Assessment activity 2.3

Use an example of a conversation you have had whilst on placement in order to provide examples of how you have used supportive skills effectively and appropriately in practice. You should produce a written report which explains how supportive skills were involved in your conversation and describe how you have used listening skills to build an understanding of the other person's point of view. To contribute towards a merit grade you should continue your report with an analysis of ways in which listening and positive communication skills can contribute to self-esteem.

You may wish to make reference to the communication cycle and to the three conditions identified by Carl Rogers. You should evaluate your own communication skills in order to work towards a distinction grade. You might also consider evaluating how far supportive skills are used within your various placement settings in order to contribute towards the criteria for a distinction.

Advocacy

Sometimes, when people have a very serious learning disability or an illness (such as dementia), it is not possible to communicate with them. In such situations care services will often employ an advocate. An advocate is someone who speaks for someone else. A lawyer speaking for a service user in a courtroom is working as an advocate for that person and will argue the service user's case. In care work, a volunteer might try to get to know someone who has dementia or a learning disability. The volunteer tries to communicate the service user's needs and wants – as the volunteer understands them. Advocates should be independent of the staff team and so can argue for the service user's rights without being constrained by what the staff think is easiest or cheapest to do.

Advocacy often provides a way to make sure of that people's needs are not overlooked. Advocacy is not straightforward however; volunteers may not always understand the feelings and needs of the people that they are advocating for. Some people argue it would be better if service users could be trained and supported to argue their own case. Helping people to argue their own case is called self-advocacy. Self-advocacy may work very well for some people, but others may need very considerable help before they can argue or explain their needs.

Another kind of advocacy is called group-advocacy. This is where people with similar needs come together and receive support to argue for their needs as a group. Group-advocacy may provide an answer for some people who need extensive support to be able to self-advocate. Different people may need different kinds of advocacy support.

Interpreters and translators

Interpreters are people who communicate meaning from one language to another. This includes interpreting between spoken and signed languages such as English and British Sign Language. Translators are people who change recorded material from one language to another.

Translating and interpreting involve the communication of meaning between different languages. Translating and interpreting is not just a technical act of changing the words from one system to another. Many languages do not have simple equivalence between words or signs. Interpreters and translators have to grasp the meaning of a message and find a way of expressing this meaning in a different language system. This is rarely a simple task even for professional translators.

Think It Over

There are many funny stories of misunderstandings that arise when translators fail to translate the meaning of a message and simply change words from one language to another. One story is of a drinks company who used the slogan 'turn it loose' in English. When this slogan was translated literally into Spanish it conveyed the meaning of 'this drink will give you diarrhoea'.

Interpreters can be professional people who are employed by social services or health authorities in order to communicate with people who use different spoken or signed languages. Interpreters may also be friends or family members who have sufficient language ability to be able to explain messages in different circumstances. A mother might learn sign language in order to communicate information to a deaf child. A child might have learned to speak a language such as English more effectively than their parents. It is possible for family members to interpret for each other.

Interpretation and translation are vital in any setting where communication is blocked because individuals rely on different languages or communication systems. Many people live in communities where English may not be the first language. When these people need to access health care or social services, or when members of these communities need legal support, the services of translators and interpreters are likely to be needed. People who are deaf from birth often develop a signed language such as British Sign Language. British Sign Language is not a version of the English language; it is an independent language system, which is as different from English as Spanish is. Many people from the deaf community rely on their own language system (BSL) and may be unable to access written or spoken communication in English.

Interpreting and communicating using interpreters raises a number of important issues. See page 56 for further details.

Assessment activity 2.4

Write a report which describes the role of advocates, interpreters and translators in care work. Find out from your placement how and when these services might be used. For each of these three roles, give an example of their use with a service user. If possible, base these examples on practical work that takes place during your placement.

To meet the criteria for a merit grade your report should provide a discussion of the various issues and problems that need to be taken into account when using advocates, interpreters and translators in care settings. At distinction level you will need to provide an example of a specific interaction and provide an evaluation of the advantages and disadvantages of using an advocate, translator or interpreter in this situation.

Communication skills

Verbal and non-verbal behaviour

Non-verbal communication

When we meet and talk with people, we will usually be using two language systems.

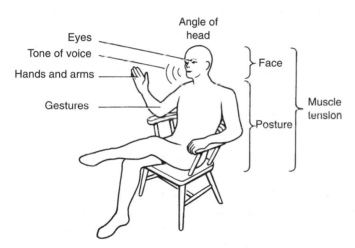

Figure 2.8 Non-verbal behaviour sends messages

We will use a verbal or spoken language and non-verbal or body language. Effective communication in care work requires care workers to be able to analyse their own and other people's non-verbal behaviour. Our body sends messages to other people – often without us deliberately meaning to send these messages. Some of the most important body areas that send messages can be seen in Figure 2.8.

The eyes

We can guess the feelings and thoughts that another person has by looking at their eyes. One poet called the eye 'the window of the soul'. We can sometimes understand the thoughts and feelings of another person by eye-to-eye contact. Our eyes get wider when we are excited, attracted to, or interested in someone else. A fixed stare may send the message that someone is angry. Looking away is often interpreted as being bored or not interested within European culture.

angry
aggressive

interested
happy

bored

Figure 2.9 The face and communication

The face

Our face can send very complex messages and we can read them easily – even in diagram form.

Our face often indicates our emotional state. When a person is sad they may signal this emotion with eyes that look down – there may be tension in their face, their mouth will be closed. The muscles in the person's shoulders are likely to be relaxed but their face and neck may show tension. A happy person will have 'wide eyes' that make contact with you – their face will smile. When people are excited they will move their arms and hands to signal their excitement.

Voice tone

It's not just what we say, but also the way that we say it. If we talk quickly in a loud voice with a fixed voice tone, people may see us as angry. A calm, slow voice with varying tone may send a message of being friendly.

Body movement

The way we walk, move our head, sit, cross our legs and so on, send messages about whether we are tired, happy, sad or bored.

Posture

The way we sit or stand can send messages. Sitting with crossed arms can mean 'I'm not taking any notice'. Leaning can send the message that you are relaxed or bored. Leaning forward can show interest. The body postures (right) send messages.

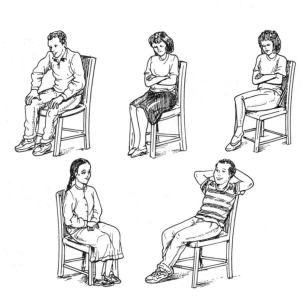

Figure 2.10 Body postures that send messages

Muscle tension

The tension in our feet, hands and fingers can tell others how relaxed or how tense we are. If someone is very tense their shoulders might stiffen, their face muscles might tighten and they might sit or stand rigidly. A tense face might have a firmly closed mouth with lips and jaws clenched tight. A tense person might breathe quickly and become hot.

Gestures

Gestures are hand and arm movements that can help us to understand what a person is saying. Some gestures carry a meaning of their own. Some common gestures are shown in Figure 2.11.

Touch

Touching another person can send messages of care, affection or power over them, or sexual interest. The social setting and other body language usually help people to understand what touch

'I don't know'

'stop, don't do that'

'success – everything's going well'

'perfection' or 'perfect'

Figure 2.11 Some gestures common in Britain

might mean. Carers should not make assumptions about touch. Even holding someone's hand might be seen as trying to dominate them!

Proximity

The space between people can sometimes show how friendly or 'intimate' the conversation is. Different cultures have different behaviours with respect to space between people who are talking.

In Britain there are expectations or 'norms' as to how close you should be when you talk to others. When talking to strangers we may keep an arm's-length apart. The ritual of shaking hands indicates that you have been introduced – you may come closer. When you are friendly with someone you may accept them being closer to you. Relatives and partners may not be restricted in how close they can come.

Proximity is a very important issue in care work. Many service users have a sense of personal space. A care worker who assumes it is all right to enter a service user's personal space without asking, or explaining, may be seen as being dominating or aggressive.

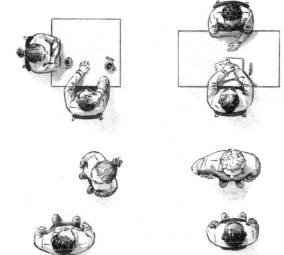

Face-to-face positions (orientation)

Standing or sitting eye to eye can send a message of being formal or being angry. A slight angle can create a more relaxed and friendly feeling.

Verbal skills

Keeping a conversation going

Keeping a conversation going is like the old-fashioned game of keeping a plate spinning on the end of a stick – you have to keep turning the stick to keep the plate spinning – otherwise it will

Figure 2.12 Face-to-face interaction

fall off! In the same way you need to keep working on conversation otherwise it will stop. It can be hard to get to know people unless you can keep a conversation going.

Starting a conversation is often easy. We ask someone how they are today, we introduce ourselves or we ask a question. If we remember, we can mention things that have been talked about before such as, 'How did you get on at the dentist yesterday?'

Once a conversation has started, the trick is to keep it going long enough. Skills which help with this are turn taking, using non-verbal communication to show interest, being good at asking questions using prompts and using silence at the right times. Conversations involve taking turns to listen and talk. If you are trying to get to know a service user you will probably do less talking and more listening. People need to take turns for a conversation to work. People normally show when they want you to talk by slowing down the rate at which they speak their last few words, changing the tone of the voice slightly and looking away from you. The person will then stop speaking and look directly at you. If you are sensitive to these messages you will be ready to ask a question or say something which keeps the conversation going.

Another important skill is looking interested in what a service user is saying. Looking interested is one way we can show respect – carers should be interested in what people say because learning about others is part of the professional skill of a carer. So carers should show interest even if the member of the public is talking about things which would be boring in private life.

Showing interest involves giving the other person your full attention. Non-verbal messages which usually do this include:

- eye contact – looking at the other person's eyes
- smiling – looking friendly rather than 'cold' or frozen in expression
- hand movements and gestures that show interest
- slight head nods while talking non-verbally say 'I see,' or 'I understand,' or 'I agree.'

Showing interest can be a good way of keeping another person talking.

Asking questions

Some questions don't really encourage people to talk. Questions which do not encourage people to talk are called closed questions. Closed questions are not very useful when trying to get to know people. Questions like 'How old are you?' are 'closed'. They are closed because there is only one, right, simple answer the person can give: 'I'm 84', and so on. Closed questions don't lead on to discussion. 'Do you like butter?' is a closed question – the person can say only yes or no. 'Are you feeling well today?' is a closed question – the person may say only yes or no.

Open questions are 'open' for discussion. Instead of giving a yes or no answer, the person is encouraged to think and discuss their thoughts. A question like 'How do you feel about the food here?' means that the other person has to think about the food and then discuss it.

Open questions keep the conversation going. Sometimes closed questions can block a conversation and cause it to stop.

The more we know about someone the more we can be sensitive about the type of questions that we ask. Some people don't mind questions about their feelings or opinions, but do dislike questions which ask for personal information. Getting to know people often takes time and usually involves a number of short conversations – rather than one long conversation.

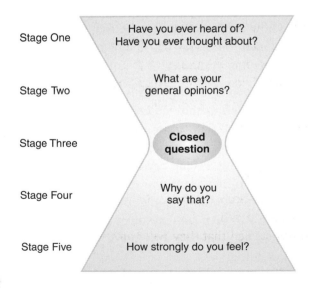

Stage One — Have you ever heard of? Have you ever thought about?

Stage Two — What are your general opinions?

Stage Three — Closed question

Stage Four — Why do you say that?

Stage Five — How strongly do you feel?

In some formal conversations it can be important to ask direct closed questions; but the best way to ask closed questions is to ask open questions beforehand. There is an old saying that if you really want to find out what someone else thinks then 'Every closed question should start life as an open one'.

There is a technique called **funnelling**, which uses this principle in formal interviewing. First the interviewer asks general open questions, then narrower questions, then a closed question. The answer to the closed question can be followed up using probes and prompts.

For example, a care worker might be trying to find out about the life history of an older

Figure 2.13 The funnelling technique

service user. Perhaps the worker wants to ask, 'Were you interested in music?' It can be 'cold' and even aggressive to just fire questions like this at people. Instead, the question could be funnelled.

Worker	What was it like in the evenings before television came along? [open question]
Other person	Well, we used to get together and make our own entertainment.
Worker	So what sort of activities did you do? [open question]
Other person	Oh, gossip, talking to neighbours, sing-songs.
Worker	Were you interested in music? [closed question]
Other person	Well a bit – I used to have piano lessons – but we couldn't afford a piano at home.

Funnelling is a skill which enables carers to lead into questions 'gently', it is a great alternative to asking too many closed questions.

Silence

One definition of friends is 'people who can sit together and feel comfortable in silence'. Sometimes a pause in conversation can make people feel embarrassed – it looks as if you weren't listening or interested. Sometimes a silent pause can mean 'let's think' or 'I need time to think'. Silent pauses can be all right as long as non-verbal messages which show respect and interest are given. Silence doesn't always stop the conversation. Some carers use pauses in a conversation to show that they are listening and thinking about what the service user has said.

Probes and prompts

A probe is a very short question such as 'Can you tell me more?' This kind of short question usually follows on from an answer that the other person has given. Probes are used to 'dig deeper' into the person's answer, they probe or investigate what the other person just said.

Prompts are short questions or words which you offer to the other person in order to prompt them to answer. Questions such as, 'So was it enjoyable or not?' or, 'Would you do it again?' might prompt a person to keep talking. Sometimes a prompt might just be a suggested answer – 'More than 50?' might be a prompt if you had just asked how many service users a carer worked with in a year and they seemed uncertain.

Probes and prompts are both useful techniques to improve questioning skill, when you are trying to keep a conversation going.

To sum up, if you need to keep a conversation going you can:

- use non-verbal behaviour like smiling and nodding your head to express interest
- use short periods of silence to prompt the other person to talk
- paraphrase or reflect back what the other person has said so that they will confirm that you have understood them
- ask direct questions
- use probes and prompts to follow up your questions.

Listening skills

Listening means hearing another person's words, thinking about what they mean and planning what to say back to the other person. Hearing means picking up the sounds that another person is making. Listening and hearing are quite different activities. Listening involves hearing and then remembering what has been said; if we are going to remember what someone else has said we have to understand it first. Some psychologists believe that people usually remember only about one out of every 2000 pieces of information that are heard in a day. Most of the sounds that come to our ears are not important enough to bother about remembering.

Think It Over

Last night you may have watched TV or talked to family and friends – just how much can you recall of what you heard last night? If you cannot remember much, perhaps it does not matter; a lot of conversation may just be for creating a social atmosphere.

Listening is a central skill in care work. Listening enables workers to develop an understanding of the people that they work with. Listening provides a way of showing respect and value for others. Listening enables the worker to learn about the lifestyle beliefs and personal needs of others.

Sometimes, getting ready to listen involves switching into a store of knowledge and understanding. For some people this is a conscious 'switching on' process. We switch on by remembering another person's name or face; perhaps we can recall when we last talked to them and what they said. Listening skills depend on being able to remember important details about other people. Listening can be hard mental work. Instead of just living in our own private worlds we have to think about other people. So, if someone is saying that he or she is sad about something we first have to hear their words and then imagine how the other person feels. We have to make sense of what is said, perhaps imagining how we would feel if it happened to us. Having thought through what we have been told, we have to think again before we speak. Effective listening takes time and effort; too often people do not bother to listen.

Communication differences and overcoming barriers to effective communication

Ways of overcoming difficulties in communication

It is always important to learn as much as possible about other people. People may have 'preferred forms of interaction'. This may include a reliance on non-verbal messages, sign language, lip-reading, use of description, slang phrases, choice of room or location for a conversation and so on. Everyone has communication needs of some kind.

The next page shows some ideas for overcoming barriers to communication.

Visual disability

- use language to describe things
- assist people to touch things (e.g. touch your face to recognise you)
- explain details that sighted people might take for granted
- check what people can see (many registered blind people can see shapes, or tell light from dark)
- check glasses, other aids and equipment.

Environmental constraints

- check and improve lighting
- reduce noise
- move to a quieter or better-lit room
- move to smaller groups to see and hear more easily
- check seating arrangements.

Preventing misunderstandings

- try to increase your knowledge of different cultures
- watch out for different cultural interpretations
- avoid making assumptions about, or discriminating against people who are different
- use reflective listening techniques to check that your understanding is correct
- stay calm and try to calm people who are angry or excited
- be sensitive to different social settings and the form of communication that would be most appropriate in different contexts
- check your work with advocates who will represent the best interests of the people that you are working with.

Hearing disability

- don't shout, keep to normal clear speech and make sure your face is visible for people who can lip-read
- show pictures, or write messages
- learn to sign (for people who use signed languages)
- ask for help from, or employ a communicator or interpreter for signed languages
- check that hearing aids and equipment are working.

Language differences

- communicate using pictures, diagrams and non-verbal signs
- use translators or interpreters
- be careful not to make assumptions or stereotype
- increase your knowledge of jargon, slang and dialects
- re-word your messages – find different ways of saying things
- speak in short, clear sentences.

Physical and intellectual disabilities

- increase your knowledge of disabilities
- use pictures and signs as well as clear, simple speech
- be calm and patient
- set up group meetings where people can share interests, experiences or reminiscences
- check that people do not become isolated
- use advocates – independent people who can spend time building an understanding of the needs of specific individuals to assist with communication work.

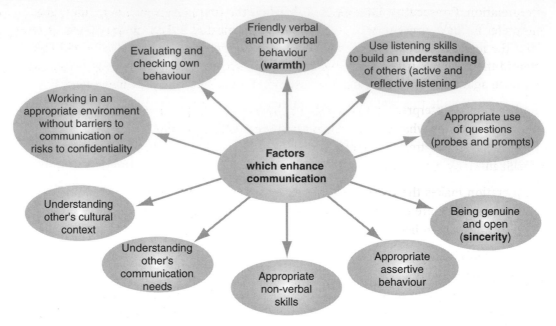

Figure 2.14 Ways to enhance communication

Emotional barriers which can inhibit communication

Sometimes it is very difficult to listen to and communicate with others. Service users often have very major emotional needs, they are afraid or depressed because of the stresses they are experiencing.

Listening involves learning about frightening and depressing situations. Carers sometimes avoid listening to avoid unpleasant emotional feelings.

Communication can be inhibited because care workers:

- are tired – listening takes mental energy
- do not have sufficient time to communicate properly
- are emotionally stressed by the needs of service users
- do not understand the culture or context of others
- make assumptions about others or label or stereotype others.

Labelling and stereotyping

People who have difficulty hearing or seeing are sometimes assumed to be awkward or mentally limited. Older people are sometimes seen as demented or confused if they do not answer questions appropriately.

People can also be labelled or stereotyped when they use different language systems. Some people will shout at those who don't speak the same language, as if increasing the volume would help. People who sign to communicate are sometimes thought to be odd or to have learning difficulties, because they don't respond to written or spoken English.

Some issues associated with using interpreters

Translation and interpretation involves conveying what a person means from one language to another. This is not as simple as just changing words or signs from one system to another. When an interpreter works with people, they will become part of the communication cycle. It will often be important that the interpreter can confirm that they have understood things correctly before they attempt to pass that understanding on to another person. Much interpretation in care and social work settings is consecutive interpretation. Consecutive interpretation is when the first person pauses to allow the interpreter to make sense of what they have communicated. When the interpreter is clear about the message they communicate it to the second person. The interpreter will then listen to the response from the second person. The second person will need to pause so that once again the interpreter can make sense of what they wish to communicate.

Another kind of interpretation is called simultaneous interpretation; this is when an interpreter explains what another person is saying while they talk. Because of the need to clarify subject matter and emotions this kind of interpretation is likely to be more difficult in many care settings.

Interpretation makes the communication cycle more complicated. There is a range of other issues which are critically important when considering working with an interpreter, as shown below.

Knowledge of the subject matter
An interpreter is likely to be more effective when they understand the issues involved. A professional interpreter may be able to explain details of legislation or procedures for claiming benefit because they understand the issues. If a relative or friend is acting as an interpreter they will have to make sense of the technical details before they can communicate clearly. Knowledge of languages alone is not always sufficient to enable clear and effective communication.

Trust
It is important that people have confidence in somebody who is acting as an interpreter. People from specific communities may find it hard to trust a member from a different community. Many women may not feel safe and confident discussing personal issues using a male interpreter. The issue may not be about the interpreter's language competence, but about the interpreter's ability to empathise with, or understand and incorrectly convey what a person wants to say.

Social and cultural values
Many people may wish to use a professional interpreter, or a specified member of their community or gender group, because of social norms. Many people may feel that it is inappropriate to discuss personal details using an interpreter of the opposite sex. Some deaf people do not feel confident using interpreters who have not experienced deafness themselves. Choice of an interpreter must support the self-esteem needs of people who need to access interpretation services.

Confidentiality
Confidentiality is a right enshrined in the 1998 Data Protection Act as well as an ethical duty on professional staff. Professional interpreters are likely to offer guarantees of confidentiality. Using a relative or volunteer may not necessarily provide people with the same guarantee of confidentiality. Confidentiality may be an issue which needs to be checked, before interpretation begins.

Non-judgemental support
A professional interpreter who has trained in social work is likely to offer advanced interpersonal skills which include the ability to remain non-judgemental when undertaking interpretation work. Volunteers, relatives and friends may have language competence, but they may not necessarily be able to interpret meaning without biasing their interpretation.

Assessment activity 2.5

You will need to produce a report which demonstrates with examples ways of overcoming or minimising barriers to communication. To do this you might choose an example of an interaction you have witnessed or been involved in whilst on placement. Use the Barriers to Communications grid set out below in order to identify factors which can create barriers to effective communication.

The Barriers to Communication grid

Rating Scale: 1 Good – there is no barrier.
    2 Quite good – few barriers.
    3 Not possible to decide or not applicable.
    4 Poor – barriers identified.
    5 Very poor – major barriers to communication.

In the environment

Lighting	1	2	3	4	5
Noise levels	1	2	3	4	5
Opportunity to communicate	1	2	3	4	5

Language differences

Carers' skills with different languages	1	2	3	4	5
Carers' skills with non-verbal communication	1	2	3	4	5
Availability of translators or interpreters	1	2	3	4	5
Assumptions and/or stereotypes	1	2	3	4	5

Emotional barriers

Stress levels and tiredness	1	2	3	4	5
Carers stressed by the emotional needs of service users	1	2	3	4	5

Cultural barriers

Inappropriate assumptions made about others	1	2	3	4	5
Labelling or stereotyping present	1	2	3	4	5

Interpersonal skills

Degree of supportive non-verbal behaviour	1	2	3	4	5
Degree of supportive verbal behaviour	1	2	3	4	5
Appropriate use of listening skills	1	2	3	4	5
Appropriate use of assertive skills	1	2	3	4	5
Appropriate maintenance of confidentiality	1	2	3	4	5

Once you have identified factors which can create barriers to communication you need to write about ways in which you could have overcome or minimised these barriers to communication. You should discuss how your own conversation created or reduced communication barriers. Your work for this task might provide the evidence needed at merit level, that you can analyse the potential effects of your communication style on communication barriers. Your work might also enable you to use a placement example in order to minimise barriers for a specific interaction.

To contribute towards a distinction grade your report might include an evaluation of how effective communication is within the placement settings you have worked in. This work might meet the criteria for evaluating the ways in which care settings use communication skills.

Self-esteem and the development of self-concept

In Western culture it is necessary to develop an individual sense of self, in order to have the confidence to work independently of others and to make appropriate interpersonal relationships. A sense of individual self develops slowly as children grow up. Our self-concept or identity is never complete; it keeps evolving and developing as we grow older.

A child's sense of self will be influenced by the beliefs, values and norms of their initial family or care-giving group. Later, children will be influenced by the beliefs, values and norms of the friends with whom they mix and play. Children adopt others' values and norms in order to be accepted into social groups. They will need to understand the rules of games or sports that they wish to join in. To be liked and to be popular, they have to show that they fit in with others. Mead (1934) believed that children come to learn general social rules and values at this stage. They might be able to imagine 'generalised others' or general social demands which they need to live up to.

Mead believed children might learn to display emotion as expected within the social roles and cultural context that they live in. They do not simply do what others teach them to do, however. Instead they internalise values that are built into a sense of self. This sense of self determines what they actually do. These roles may become part of the child's self concept and social identity.

This sense of self will guide the individual to exaggerate, suppress or even substitute emotional feelings. In some social classes and geographical areas, boys may learn to exaggerate feelings of anger and aggression in order to achieve social status. In another social class group, boys may learn to express anger in terms of clever verbal behaviour with little hint of emotion. Some girls may learn to suppress feelings of distress in order to look 'in control'.

It is tempting just to say that society does this to people – that people develop the emotions for which society trains them. Mead's theory provides an explanation of how social influences work on an individual. It is the idea of a self, a 'me' that explains how social values influence individual behaviour.

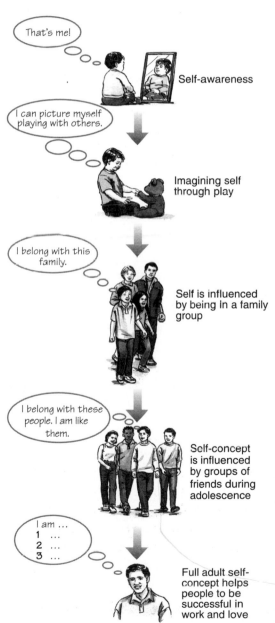

Figure 2.15 The development of self-concept begins with self-awareness

That's me! — Self-awareness

I can picture myself playing with others. — Imagining self through play

I belong with this family. — Self is influenced by being in a family group

I belong with these people. I am like them. — Self-concept is influenced by groups of friends during adolescence

I am ...
1 ...
2 ...
3 ... — Full adult self-concept helps people to be successful in work and love

During adolescence this sense of self becomes of central importance. Erik Erikson (1963) believed that biological pressures to become independent would force adolescents into a crisis, which could only be successfully resolved if the individual developed a conscious sense of self or purpose. He wrote, 'In the social jungle of human existence, there is no feeling of being alive without a sense of ego identity'. Other theorists have regarded the development of self-concept or identity as more gradual, and less centred on biological maturation. A clear sense of self may lead a person to feel worthwhile and to have a sense of purpose. A sense of self might provide a person with the confidence to cope with changes in life.

The development of a secure sense of self may be needed in order to:

1 make effective social and sexual relationships with others
2 cope with work roles where we have to make independent decisions
3 cope with complex interpersonal situations where 'emotional intelligence' (Goleman, 1996) is needed in order to use appropriate skills such as assertion
4 cope with our own internal or interpersonal feelings in order to enable us to motivate ourselves
5 develop self-confidence in social or work settings.

General factors which will influence the development of self-concept include:

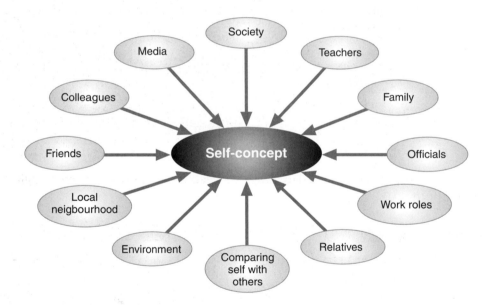

Figure 2.16 Influences on self-concept

Think It Over

Examine the list of influences above. How have each of these issues influenced your own sense of who you are – what are the most important influences on your life?

An overview of the developmental stages of self-concept might be summarised as in the table below:

Age	Stage of development
1½–2 years	Self-awareness develops – children may start to recognise themselves in a mirror.
2½ years	Children can say whether they are a girl or a boy.
3–5 years	When asked what they are like, children can describe themselves in terms of categories, such as big or small, tall or short, light or heavy.
5–8 years	If you ask children who they are, they can often describe themselves in detail. Children will tell you their hair colour, eye colour, about their families and to which schools they belong.
8–10 years	Children start to show a general sense of 'self-worth', such as describing how happy they are in general, how good life is for them, what is good about their family life, school and friends.
10–12 years	Children start to analyse how they compare with others. When asked about their life, children may explain without prompting, how they compare with others. For example: 'I'm not as good as Zoe at running but I'm better than Ali'.
12–16 years	Adolescents may develop a sense of self in terms of beliefs and belong to groups – being a vegetarian, believing in God, believing certain things are right or wrong.
16–25 years	People may develop an adult sense of self-concept that helps them to feel confident in a work role and in social and sexual situations.
25 onwards	People's sense of self will be influenced by the things that happen in their lives. Some people may change their self-concept a great deal as they grow older.
65 onwards	In later life it is important to be able to keep a clear sense of self. People may become withdrawn and depressed, without a clear self-concept.

The differences in expression of self-concept between the various age groups might be summarised in the table below:

Age group	Expression of self-concept
Young children	Self-concept is limited to a few descriptions, e.g. boy or girl, size, some skills.
Older children	Self-concept can be described in a range of 'factual categories', such as hair colour, name, details or address, etc.
Adolescents	Self-concept starts to be explained in terms of chosen beliefs, likes, dislikes, relationships with others.
Adults	Many adults may be able to explain the quality of their lives and their personality in greater depth and detail than when they were adolescents.
Older adults	Some older adults may have more self-knowledge than during early adult life. Some people may show 'wisdom' in the way they explain their self-concept.

According to Maslow (1908–70) the goal of living is self-actualisation; this means to fulfil potential and to become everything that a person is capable of becoming. Deficit needs such as physical illness, not feeling safe, not having a sense of belonging, or having low self-esteem prevent people from developing fulfilled and happy lives.

The way other people communicate with us will be one factor which can influence our feelings of safety, secure self-concept and the ability to value what we think we are.

Think It Over

Imagine you went into a shop and tried to pay for some goods. Imagine that the shop assistants were unfriendly and ignored you. Imagine that they told you to shut up and wait your turn when you tried to attract their attention. How would you react to this and what impact would this have on your self-esteem?

Most people would be very angry in this situation but their self-esteem would not suffer greatly because they would think to themselves: 'I'm not using this shop again, I'll take my business elsewhere.'

Now imagine that every day you get the same treatment. Imagine that you live with people who are unfriendly and ignore you. When you talk more senior people tell you to shut up. How will this affect you and how will this affect your self-esteem?

Most people would be angry but they might also become emotionally damaged. If other important people treat you as if you don't matter, it is hard for you to value yourself.

The key difference between being mistreated in a shop and mistreated in a care setting is one of power. Where you believe that you hold the power, your self-esteem will not be vulnerable. If you think that other people have all the power, your self-esteem is likely to be at risk.

A loss of general self-esteem is associated with depression and withdrawal (see the next section on learned helplessness).

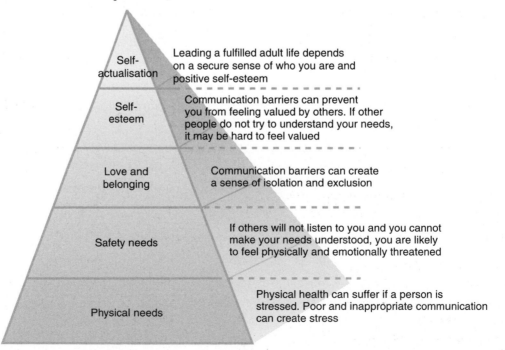

Figure 2.17 Communication barriers can damage a person's quality of life

Assessment activity 2.6

To achieve this unit you need to produce evidence that you have reviewed your own personal communication methods. You need to demonstrate how communication skills have been used effectively and appropriately, and describe the major factors which have positive and negative effects on communication. One idea for addressing these tasks is to prepare a role-play or simulated discussion where one person interviews or leads a conversation with another person. Audio or videotape this conversation and use the rating scale set out below in order to analyse ways in which verbal and non-verbal communication affect the communication cycle. To achieve a merit grade you will need to provide an analysis of the factors which affected this interaction. At distinction level you will need to evaluate your own skills with respect to different types of interaction and provide a discussion which judges the significance of different factors in influencing the interaction.

The rating scale: how good were different aspects of non-verbal communication?

Eye contact	1	2	3	4	5
Facial expression	1	2	3	4	5
Angle of head	1	2	3	4	5
Tone of voice	1	2	3	4	5
Position of hands and arms	1	2	3	4	5
Gestures	1	2	3	4	5
Posture	1	2	3	4	5
Muscle tension	1	2	3	4	5
Touch	1	2	3	4	5
Proximity	1	2	3	4	5

How to rate behaviour:

Place a circle around the number 1 when you have seen very effective and appropriate use of a skill.

Place a circle around the number 2 when you have seen some appropriate use of the skill.

Place a circle around the number 3 when you have not seen the skill demonstrated or if it does not seem appropriate to comment on the area.

Place a circle around the number 4 when you have seen some slightly ineffective or inappropriate behaviour in relation to the area.

Place a circle around the number 5 when you have seen very inappropriate or ineffective behaviour in relation to the area.

How good were verbal communication and listening skills?

Encouraging others to talk	1	2	3	4	5
Reflecting back what others have said	1	2	3	4	5
Using appropriate questions	1	2	3	4	5
Use of prompts	1	2	3	4	5
Using silence as a listening skill	1	2	3	4	5

Clarity of conversation	1	2	3	4	5
Pace of conversation	1	2	3	4	5
Turn taking	1	2	3	4	5

(Use the same rating instructions as for non-verbal communication above.)

When you have completed your ratings you should discuss ways in which you might improve specific aspects of your communication skills in relation to the role-play or conversation that you undertook. If you can make detailed plans for developing your skills this may help to meet the grading criteria for a distinction grade.

Supportive skills with distressed individuals

Care work and social work often involves working with people who are experiencing strong emotions. People may be angry because they feel that others have power over them. People may feel anxious or vulnerable about what might happen to them or their family. Many older people who are assessed in terms of their community care needs may feel threatened or depressed. People who have experienced long-term ill-health may also become depressed to the point where they withdraw from human interaction.

Reasons for distressed behaviour

Some reasons for distressed, angry or withdrawn behaviour include the following:

1 **Pain** – People in pain often find it difficult to control emotion. Pain can cause people to become aggressive or to give up and withdraw.
2 **Fear** – Some people may not know what to expect in a care setting or from a social work assessment. Fear of the unknown can cause people to feel out of control and become angry or upset.
3 **Grief** – A major loss of a person or of a lifestyle may result in a feeling of being out of control. Emotions of anger, guilt, depression and withdrawal may result from a loss.
4 **Frustration** – Some people will become frustrated because they cannot do things as easily as they could before experiencing an illness. Other people will experience frustration because their needs are not being fully met. Services often have limited resources which limit the help that can be offered. Frustration often leads to anger.
5 **Communication differences** – Where people use a different first language, or use a signed language, or where there are sensory disabilities there is always a risk of inappropriate assumptions, stereotyping, or labelling. People may feel vulnerable or that their rights have been infringed.
6 **Feeling vulnerable and threats to self-esteem** – Some people may be afraid of losing their dignity, others may feel that they had been discriminated against, or simply just that their needs have not been addressed. Pain, fear and grief can all create a feeling of vulnerability. Unwanted change can threaten self-esteem.
7 **Past learning** – Some adults and children may have learned that being aggressive is one way to get things that they need. Some people may be used to starting arguments or fighting as part of their way of life.

Anger and withdrawal

Case Study

Mr Mansel is 84 and moved into a rest home after having a stroke. Mr Mansel grew up in Jamaica but moved to Britain 50 years ago. Unfortunately he has been placed in a nursing home some distance from his friends and receives few visits. None of the staff understand Mr Mansel's history or cultural background. The home has a number of staff vacancies and is currently short staffed. Staff have little time to talk to Mr Mansel. The stroke has affected Mr Mansel's speech and staff find communication difficult and time consuming. Other residents in the home have communication differences including hearing disabilities and disorientation and memory loss.

Some residents avoid Mr Mansel and appear to label him as different from themselves. Mr Mansel feels isolated and distressed.

Ineffective communication, such as Mr Mansel is experiencing can result in:

1 a loss of self-esteem – you can't be worth much if people don't communicate
2 a loss of purpose in life – you might feel excluded, or alienated from others if you cannot communicate
3 a loss of support – you may find life difficult to cope with if your social and emotional needs are not met
4 a feeling of being threatened – if people do not communicate, you may not be able to predict what is likely to happen.

These problems may result in a belief that we can no longer control our life circumstances.

Martin Seligman (1975) published a theory of 'learned helplessness' which explains how a loss of control over our life circumstances can result in a process of learning to become withdrawn, depressed and helpless (see Figure 2.18).

Helplessness starts when a person learns that no matter what they do they cannot control what is going to happen. People can develop a general helpless attitude to daily living when major needs like communication are 'out of control'.

According to Seligman the first stages in the process of becoming helpless are to react with frustration and anger. In the case study above, Mr Mansel may become aggressive, perhaps shouting at others or damaging property. In the past, such problems were often regarded as being due to 'confusion', 'age', or dementia. Seligman explains that aggression can be a last attempt to control – when nothing else works you can lose your temper. In a 'stressed' care environment Mr Mansel's anger is unlikely to get him the attention he needs. Instead he may be labelled as disturbed or difficult and isolated further.

The next step in the process is learning to 'give up'. Giving up saves energy. Withdrawal from trying to communicate may be the best coping strategy. Being 'withdrawn' can protect a person. Mr Mansel cannot get his social and self-esteem needs met but there may be a sense of safety in not attempting to communicate. Ineffective communication may not matter so much if you come to expect no communication at all.

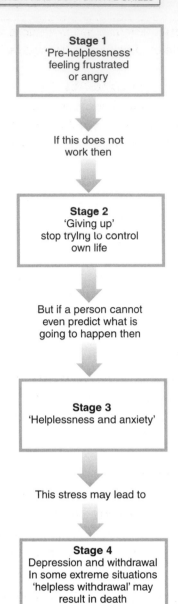

Figure 2.18 The process of learned helplessness

The process of learning to become helpless does not stop with withdrawal. If a person cannot predict what is likely to happen to them then they are likely to become anxious. The stress of anxiety can cause a deeper level of withdrawal, a withdrawal into depression. Seligman argued that helplessness and anxiety could result in clinical depression due to changes in brain chemistry.

A lack of communication could be enough to cause anxiety. Mr Mansel may not know what is happening around him or what to expect from staff. If he feels unable to respond to discrimination and exclusion he may experience anxiety and withdrawal. Serious mental ill-health may result.

Finally, Seligman believed that severe depression resulting from learned helplessness could be fatal. This may be particularly true when an individual is in poor health.

Effective communication is not just a right which service users may expect – not just a quality issue. Effective communication is necessary to protect the mental well-being of vulnerable people. Poor communication can be understood as a form of abuse. If Seligman's theory is correct then it is possible to argue that this abuse may be enough to cause death.

Think It Over

Many distressed individuals feel that they cannot control their situation. Consider the emotions of the people below:

1 Sheena had a stroke at the age of 65, but at first she tried hard to follow exercises designed to help her improve her speech and mobility. She tried to regain the ability to do housework that she had lost because of the stroke. After a few weeks, Sheena became frustrated with daily living activities. She was assessed as needing home care support. A few weeks later, she stopped her exercises and announced that she would never recover. She has since become withdrawn and refuses to acknowledge the need for housework – she seems disinterested and leaves everything to her home care worker.

2 Michael is a 30 year-old man with learning difficulty. He attends a centre which offers classes in cooking. At first Michael used to join in with the other students,

although he found it very difficult to follow the activities. Michael has now taken to sitting in the corridor when the classes begin. He becomes angry and even aggressive if centre staff try to encourage him to join in.

3   Zehra is two years old. She is playing in the garden and is fascinated by the colourful flowers she sees. Zehra touches and tries to taste the flowers, but her parents keep stopping her and saying 'No don't do that.' Zehra cannot make sense of what it is that she must not do. She freezes and after a few moments she begins to cry.

Can you see how a process of learning to give up could start in each of these people's situations? Learned helplessness may starts with frustration and aggression. Sheena may have become angry with herself, the home care worker may not have experienced her frustration. Michael's anger is obvious to the instructors in the centre but the process of helplessness may not be so obvious. Zehra does not know how to respond so a helpless response sets in quite quickly, although some frustration may have been visible on her face. When aggression fails it is possible that these people's distress will turn into depression and withdrawal. Sheena and Michael have withdrawn from situations that they cannot control. Zehra has withdrawn into crying.

A lot of angry and aggressive behaviour experienced by staff in care settings may be a result of members of the public feeling that they have lost control of the situation they are in. The theory of learned helplessness provides a useful way of understanding some causes of anger and withdrawal.

What happens when people become aggressive?

Anger is a powerful emotion and it often looks as if people suddenly lose their temper. A person will suddenly start shouting; a service user will suddenly start making abusive comments. In many situations a person will already feel stressed long before an outburst of anger. Frustration and tension can grow as an individual fails to control their own emotions and their circumstances.

As tension mounts it may take only a single remark or some little thing that has gone wrong, to push the person into an angry outburst. People who feel stressed may need only a trigger incident to set off an explosion of anger that has built up inside them.

After an explosion of anger, stressed people can still feel tense. Very often they may feel that is someone else's fault that they have been made to feel so angry. Anger can flare up again if the person is not given respect and encouraged to become calm. As time passes, tension may reduce as stress and levels of high emotional arousal decrease.

Not all angry outbursts follow this pattern. Some people learn to use aggression to get their way and some people can switch aggressive emotions on and off as they wish. Being angry can sometimes be a reaction that a person has chosen. But it is wrong to assume that all aggression and anger are deliberate. A great deal of aggression experienced by healthcare workers will be an emotional response to not being able to control circumstances.

When people are aggressive or abusive they may make care workers feel threatened. The simple in-built emotional response to threat is to want to run or fight. An unskilled response to aggression is to be aggressive back. This will escalate into a conflict situation which is unlikely to have a positive outcome.

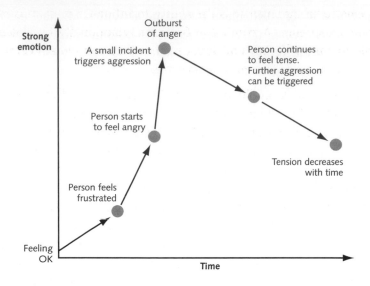

Figure 2.19 Stages in the development of aggression

For example, suppose an immobile resident in a care home has asked for a commode but has been left waiting, they may react aggressively with accusations such as: 'You don't care about me, you're too lazy to do your job properly' and so on. An unskilled response to this abuse might be to shout back at the resident returning the abuse with statements such as, 'You're not the only person here you know, I've only got one pair of hands' and so on. The problem with responding to aggression by being aggressive is that one or both people have to lose. The purpose of care is to provide a good quality of life as well as to provide for basic needs such as food, shelter and warmth. If a care worker it is successful in putting down a service user they are likely to increase that person's sense of being out of control and create increased helplessness in the individual. Depressed or withdrawn people may seem easier to manage than aggressive ones, but turning aggression into depression can hardly rate as a satisfactory care outcome.

Even in mildly aggressive encounters one or both people are likely to feel resentment towards each other. It cannot be a good outcome for members of the public to feel that social work or care staff are rude and abusive. Equally, most workers are unlikely to have job satisfaction if they develop resentment towards a significant number of the people that they work with.

There is, of course, no guarantee that the care worker will be the winner in every conflict situation. Some members of the public can become physically violent and cause physical as well as emotional injury to staff. Other members of the public may make successful formal complaints if they have received abuse. A professional skilled response is to stay calm, be assertive rather than aggressive, calm the other person, and resolve the situation without creating resentment. This is easier to say than it is to do.

Skills for working with individuals
Emotional intelligence and staying in control
Daniel Goleman (1996) published a theory of emotional intelligence. Whilst people vary in their degree of intellectual ability, Goleman's theory is that people also vary in their ability to manage and use their own emotions. Education and training can improve intellectual performance and it can also improve emotional performance.

One aspect of emotional intelligence is the ability to influence or even control the emotions that we experience. According to Goleman, emotionally intelligent people are likely to be able to control feelings of threat so that they can remain calm in situations involving people who are distressed or aggressive.

Humans have two systems to guide behaviour. We can think and reason using the outer part of the brain called the cortex and we can react to experiences with emotion - a system which is built in to our mid-brain. Emotion is designed to enable us to respond rapidly if we are threatened. If you switched on the lights as you entered a room in your house and you saw a large bear coming towards you – your emotional systems would make you respond with fear – you would attempt to run away. If you suddenly realised that this was a friend wearing a fancy dress costume, your fear response would switch off. You would probably laugh because your emotions had made you react inappropriately. Thought takes time and is much slower than your emotional responses. But thought can influence our perception of threat. Emotional intelligence involves the ability to use thought to moderate and control our emotional responses.

If someone is aggressive towards us, the immediate emotional response is to feel threatened and to fight back or run. We do not have to be fixed by this first emotional reaction. It is possible to rethink what we are experiencing and re-interpret the threat. A professional person may see a distressed person who is in danger of becoming helpless – as person who they can help. An unskilled person may simply experience the emotions of threat and danger. The professional person can switch off the emotions associated with being attacked, and may think 'This person is distressed but I'm sure I can work with them, they will not harm me.' Learning to reinterpret threats means that professional people can choose the emotions that they need to be able to work effectively with people. Untrained and unskilled people may be controlled by their emotions. People who have developed good levels of emotional intelligence can often make their emotions work for them – they may literally be able to choose their emotional state.

Figure 2.20 It is not reality that creates emotions in us; the way we perceive and think controls what we experience

Care workers are unlikely to be able to switch off feelings of being threatened simply by wishing them away. Usually workers will switch off the threat using positive thoughts about their own past experiences, their skills in being able to calm people, or just by using their own professional role to protect themselves from feeling 'got at'. If a care worker can think 'this person is distressed because of their situation', rather than 'this person is out to get me' they may be able to switch off the emotions that create a sense of being threatened.

Staying calm

Being calm depends on the thoughts that we have, but it is also a practical skill which can be acted out and rehearsed. If a worker can appear to be calm their own behaviour may have a calming effect on others. Non-verbal signs of being calm are summarised in Figure 2.21.

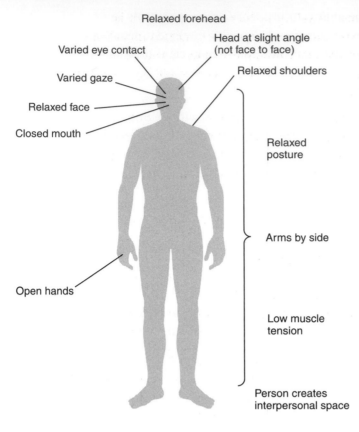

Relaxed forehead

Head at slight angle
(not face to face)

Varied eye contact

Relaxed shoulders

Varied gaze

Relaxed face

Closed mouth

Relaxed
posture

Arms by side

Open hands

Low muscle
tension

Person creates
interpersonal space

Figure 2.21 Non-verbal signs of being calm

It is important to remember to breathe gently and slowly; slow, careful breathing can help to create relaxation and calmness as well as looking calm to others. Sometimes it is appropriate that body posture should be at a slight angle towards an angry person. A face-to-face posture is sometimes interpreted as an attempt to dominate or be threatening. The volume of speech should not be raised, it is important to talk in a normal tone and volume and to display that you do not feel threatened or angry.

Communicating respect and value

It is important to acknowledge the feelings and complaints that distressed people may be experiencing. If the other person feels that they are being taken seriously and are being listened to, this may have a calming effect. Reflective listening skills and the ability to keep the conversation going will be very important. A professional conversation should be warm and sincere whilst also seeking to build an understanding of the situation. Thanking a person for clarifying issues may be one way in which a worker can reduce the frustration that another person may feel. If a worker can communicate that they understand the other person's point of view this may go a long way toward calming a situation and preventing further outbreaks of anger.

Assertion

Staying calm and in control of your own emotions, displaying respect and value for others, reflective listening and building an understanding of another person's viewpoint are central assertive skills. Assertion is the skill of being able to understand another person's viewpoint whilst being able to help them to understand your own viewpoint. Assertive skills create a situation where negotiation is possible. Assertive skills will therefore be very important when working with distressed individuals. More details comparing assertion with aggression and submissive behaviour can be found on page 45. More detail on listening skills can be found on page 54.

Creating trust and negotiating with distressed individuals

If you can successfully calm an angry or distressed person, the next step will be to try and establish a sense of common ground or liking between each other. It is at this stage that a skilled worker will attempt to build an understanding of the other person's viewpoint. Creating trust involves meeting the other person's self-esteem needs. In some situations it may be necessary to make the other person feel important. Sometimes it may be appropriate to say just a little about your own feelings, background and so on if this helps to build bridges and create a sense of safety with the other person. It is usually appropriate to come across as open-minded and supportive but it is important that you do not agree with everything that the other person demands. It will be important to keep the conversation going and to keep the other person talking – perhaps using questioning and reflective listening skills.

Once you have built a level of understanding with a distressed person, it may then be possible to try and sort things out and to negotiate what kind of help or support you can offer. At this stage in the interaction it may be possible to take a problem-solving approach. Problem solving may start off by clarifying the issues that are involved and exploring alternative solutions.

Sometimes it may be necessary to structure expectations. This means gently introducing ideas of what is possible and not possible. It is important not to argue with a distressed person as this may only force them back to being aggressive or withdrawn. If you have to say 'no' to a demand, it may often be better to slowly lead up to the expectation that you will say no, rather than directly confronting a person with a 'stone wall' rejection of their views. For instance, 'I understand what you're saying and I'll see what I can do, but it would be wrong to promise anything', or 'We can try but I am not hopeful'.

Negotiation often depends on factual information and it may be important to bring factual information into the conversation at this stage. It will be important not to appear patronising when offering information. It will also be important to clearly explain technical information that the other person may not clearly understand.

Sometimes it will not be possible to reach agreement with a distressed person and in these circumstances it will be important to conclude the conversation leaving a positive emotional outcome, even if agreement has not been reached. It may be possible to agree to resume a conversation tomorrow, or to thank the person for their time and offer to talk again. It will always be important to leave the person with an increased sense of self-esteem even if they did not agree with your viewpoint.

Stages in managing a conversation with an angry person

1 stay calm
2 try to calm the other person using appropriate non-verbal behaviour
3 listen to the other person
4 build trust and meet the other person's self esteem needs
5 negotiate and try and solve problems.

Real conversations do not always follow simple stages but is important not to attempt to negotiate and solve problems before listening and building trust.

Managing a difficult conversation

The brief example below is designed to illustrate some of the principles explained in this section. Real conversations may often be longer and more complex than this example. One way of developing skills in conversation management might be to analyse real conversations using the principles set out above. The conversation below takes place in a care home for older people.

Relative	What have you done to my mother! She's so much worse than before – you aren't looking after her properly. She can't eat because of the rubbish food you give out.
Worker	Your mother does look worse today, perhaps you would like to sit down and we can talk.
Relative	Well you tell me what is going on then and why the food is such rubbish!
Worker	I'll explain what we're doing if you like and I'm sorry that your mother doesn't like the food. Could tell me what sort of things does she really like to eat?
Relative	Not the rubbish here.
Worker	Sometimes it's possible to increase a person's appetite by just offering a very small tasty piece of something they really like, perhaps fruit or a tiny piece of bread and jam?
Relative	What, and you are going to sort that out, are you!
Worker	I've found that it works for a lot of people – but can you give me some ideas of what your mother would like?
Relative	Well she likes pears and cherry jam, but good stuff – not like here.
Worker	Ok. Could you possibly bring some of her favourite things in and we could try and see if that would help.
Relative	Why should I?
Worker	Well it might help, everyone is different and you are the person who would really know what your mother is likely to enjoy.
Relative	Can't you do something about the food here?
Worker	I'm afraid that the choice of food is limited, but we might be able to work together to improve your mother's appetite as a first step to making things better.
Relative	I suppose it's not up to you to change the food. I'll bring the jam in but I still think it's not right.
Worker	I'm sorry that you're not happy about the food but perhaps we can talk again tomorrow.
Relative	Well, thank you for your time – at least I could talk to you.

Discussion

This conversation starts with the relative making aggressive accusations. The worker responds by remaining assertive and not arguing, or going straight into discussing the complaints that the relative has raised. Instead the worker attempts to calm the situation and invites the relative to sit down. By inviting the relative to sit down the worker is taking control of the conversation and creating a situation where she can use her listening skills.

At several points the angry relative is still challenging the worker with complaints and aggressive statements. The worker is careful not to respond to these challenges and risk triggering more aggression. The worker is able to stay calm and to build a sense of trust by keeping the conversation going. The worker is able to ask the relative questions about his mother's needs. The worker is also able to meet the relative's self-esteem needs by pointing out that he is the person who would really know what his mother likes.

In this conversation the worker negotiates that the relative will bring some food in. The worker structures the relative's expectations by mentioning the limited choice of food. Because the relative has been listened to he is willing to stop complaining – he compliments the worker with the statement that at least she listened.

The conversation ends on a positive emotional note, even though the problems of catering in this care setting have not been resolved. The point of this conversation was to meet the emotional needs of the distressed relative and not to find technical solutions to catering problems!

Sources of support for carers

Working with distressed people is stressful. Even highly skilled and experienced professional staff sometimes fail to manage conversations appropriately, or to manage their own emotions. It is important that staff receive practical advice and emotional support if they are to develop or even maintain their skills.

It is difficult to provide emotional support for others if you do not receive emotional support yourself. An organisation that blames and criticises staff rather than supporting them is unlikely to employ staff that can provide effective support to its service users or customers.

Sources of practical and emotional support for staff include:

1 Formal supervision

Formal supervision is where a worker discusses their work with a senior member of staff. The supervisor may provide feedback on the quality of the worker's practice. Formal supervision may also be used to discuss training needs, or to review specific incidents which have occurred in practice. Formal supervision might be an appropriate setting to discuss the development of communication skills.

2 Peer support

Peer support involves the help and guidance that can be gained from colleagues. Sometimes this support can be formal, for instance where workers have a mentor or advisor, who may be a more experienced colleague. Very often peer support is informal – workers may talk through incidents that have happened during a coffee break. Workers may ask one another for ideas and advice or simply just share experiences.

3 Counselling

There is an old saying that a problem shared is a problem halved. Counselling services provide a service where individuals can discuss their thoughts and feelings in a totally confidential setting. Counselling can help people to make sense of practical and emotional problems that they are experiencing. Many people experience emotional stress when working with people who are distressed. Counselling provides a vital support service to help cope with stress.

4 Training

Recent legislation is likely to result in most care workers achieving appropriate qualifications. Training enables people to reflect on their practice, to explore new ideas and to develop their own personal and professional skills. The development of new ideas and skills can help to increase confidence in working with people.

5 Support within own social network

Many people rely on the emotional support that partners, family and friends supply. When things go wrong, friends and family can provide an emotional 'buffer' which takes the stress out of some aspects of life. Many people develop a positive sense of belonging and self-esteem through their relationships with friends and family. Friends and family can provide a useful source of emotional support which can promote self-confidence when working with other people.

Assessment activity 2.7

You need to produce evidence, using examples from a placement or case study, to explain how communication skills can support a distressed individual or manage challenging behaviour.

For this piece of work you might write a theoretical account of how you might have worked. You might choose to base your account on a real situation which you have observed. You are not required to have demonstrated advanced emotional and conversation management skills for this exercise, but you are required to discuss the theory involved in communicating with distressed individuals.

To contribute towards a merit grade you might write about the importance of conversation management within care settings in order to meet the criteria of 'considering the implications of good communication skills for care settings'. To contribute towards a distinction grade a discussion of conversation management might include an evaluation of the extent to which these skills are, or could be, used within the care settings you have experienced.

End-of-unit test

Read the short conversation set out below between a care assistant and a resident in a rest home setting and then answer the questions that follow.

Carer	Come on Bill, it's time for lunch. What's the matter, don't you want any?
Resident	What's the time?
Carer	12 o'clock, come on now, look lively.
Resident	But I'm not hungry.
Carer	Aren't you indeed, well I bet you will be later. You just come with me and everything will be all right.
Resident	What's for dinner?
Carer	Can't you remember – you had a menu this morning!
Resident	I never did. I don't remember any menu.
Carer	Yes you did, but I can't waste time arguing with you. You will just have to get what you're given!

Resident	I'm not having pork, or any of that sweetcorn rubbish – animal food that is what we get here.
Carer	Well don't start on me, just leave anything you don't like. Look here we are – just sit here!
Resident	But this isn't where I usually sit.
Carer	Well it will have to do today, I haven't got time to mess about. There are other people to look after as well you know!
Resident	*(No answer but responds with non-verbal messages which suggest anger and frustration.)*

1 Identify some of the inhibiting factors which may prevent this conversation from meeting the resident's needs.

2 List three types or levels of need that the resident may have had in a care setting.

3 Why are closed questions often inappropriate in caring conversations?

4 Identify the barriers to effective communication in the conversation above.

5 Explain the consequences that may follow for the resident if he is constantly treated the same way as in this conversation during his stay in care.

6 Explain the difference between listening and just hearing.

7 List three important qualities that a supportive conversation should include.

8 What risks might patients face if they felt that they were being ignored and could not control what was happening to them? Explain the process of learned helplessness.

9 What is an advocate? Why might a person need the services of an advocate within a care context?

10 List three types of support that staff might receive while working with people with challenging behaviours.

References and further reading

Goleman, D. (1996) *Emotional Intelligence,* London: Bloomsbury

Hargie, 0., Saunders, C. and Dickson, D. (1987) *Social Skills in Interpersonal Communication,* London: Routledge

Maslow, A. H. (1970) (2nd edn) *Motivation and Personality,* New York: Harper & Row

Pease, A. (1997) *Body Language,* London: Sheldon Press

Rogers, C. R. (1951) *Client Centred Therapy,* Boston: Houghton Mifflin

Sanders, P. (1994) *First Steps in Counselling,* Manchester: PCCS Books

Seligman, M. (1975) *Helplessness,* San Francisco: W. H. Freeman and Co.

Thompson, N. (1996) *People Skills,* Basingstoke: Macmillan Press

Research and project

This unit introduces you to the theory and practice of research in care settings. Research investigation is now a key feature of many areas of care work and provides important knowledge that care practitioners use in their work with service users. The skills needed to carry out research investigations and to understand research reports are learnt by students on a variety of pre-qualifying care training courses and have also become an important part of professional training for qualified care workers. Developing basic research skills is now seen as a means by which care workers can improve standards of evidence-based practice.

What you need to learn

- The purpose and role of research
- Research methods
- The research process
- Obtaining research data
- Ethical issues and their implications
- Planning and presenting your own research
- Producing a bibliography

The purpose and role of research

What is research?

Research is a widely used term. For example, market researchers who approach shoppers with their clipboard in shopping centres and high streets throughout the UK typically ask people to spare 10 minutes to take part in 'research'. You may also have seen and completed a questionnaire in a magazine or newspaper that is 'researching' readers' views and attitudes.

Research is now a vital area of work in the care field. In fact, scientific and social research into care-related issues is such a huge and rapidly expanding enterprise that it is impossible for practitioners to keep up with all of the new research findings that are published. However, care workers do need to know about, understand and make use of the relevant research findings – that is, those that can be used to develop practice and improve treatment in their area of care work.

Ideas about research

Before we consider the possible reasons for carrying out research into care-related issues, it's important to clarify how we're going to use the term 'research' in this chapter.

People tend to use the term research to indicate that they're seeking information about something. In a nutshell, this is what research is – a search for information. However, as you'd probably expect, carrying out a research investigation in a care setting involves a lot more than simply looking for information on a topic. The types of care-related research that we'll learn about in this chapter involve searching for particular forms of information (data) in particular ways and for clearly identifiable reasons.

Figure 3.1 Research takes many forms

Think It Over

Can you think of any situations where you have completed a research questionnaire or have taken part in any other kind of research project? Describe your experience of being a research participant to a class colleague.

What is involved in doing research?

Professional and academic researchers argue that in a true research investigation the researcher(s) will :

- ask questions or put forward ideas (hypotheses) that can be tested against evidence
- collect information in a systematic way
- analyse the information that they find
- reach conclusions about the questions or ideas on the basis of their research evidence
- work in an ethical and unbiased way.

A researcher needs to carry out their investigation in a practical, effective and efficient way whilst also ensuring that it incorporates these criteria. To achieve this, researchers construct and follow a **research process**. In effect, they break up their investigation into a number of stages and then work through each of them in a careful, considered sequence. This means that a research investigation will involve planned, thoughtful and systematic information seeking.

Researchers tend to include and work through the same general types of activity when following a research process. The activities that need to be covered include:

- choosing a research topic
- identifying specific questions to explore, or hypotheses to test
- identifying potential sources of data
- selecting methods for collecting the data
- carrying out data collection
- analysing data
- writing up and presenting the findings.

In practice, individual researchers tend to work through these activities in the same logical order as they're listed. However, researchers don't all do exactly the same things in exactly the same way. As individuals, researchers tend to modify the way they carry out each activity to meet the particular needs of their own investigation.

Why carry out research?

Generally, researchers aim to produce knowledge that is useful and which extends human understanding. Most of the care-related research that is carried out is practical or applied research and is useful to both care practitioners and to care service users. For example, care practitioners benefit from research that extends understanding of the effectiveness of treatment methods. In addition, care-related research is undertaken to:

- extend care practitioners' knowledge about the way that the human body normally works, how disease occurs and how illness affects people
- develop and assess the effectiveness of care and treatment methods
- identify the care needs of different service user groups, such as premature babies, older people and disabled people
- assess the impact of care policies
- identify situations where there are gaps in service provision
- evaluate and understand the effectiveness of different care practices
- analyse the impact of changes that may have been made in the way services are provided.

Research knowledge is valued highly by care practitioners because it is based on evidence rather than on unquestioned, 'taken for granted' assumptions.

Research methods

There are a number of ways of identifying and describing the methods that people use to carry out **empirical** research investigations. Researchers need to be aware of the range of possible research methods that are available to them so that they can select those that are most appropriate for their proposed investigation.

Types of research method

At some point in every research investigation a researcher will be asked 'What type of research are you doing?' This is a question about the overall strategy or approach to the research investigation. Researchers can answer the question in a number of ways. However, people often describe their research in terms of whether it is a **quantitative** or a **qualitative** research study and whether they are carrying out **primary** or **secondary** research.

Quantitative research methods

Researchers often distinguish between quantitative and qualitative research methods, even though they frequently use both in the same study. The main characteristic of quantitative research is that the researcher will use some sort of measurement tool and will be seeking numerical data. For example, a quantitative study might involve a researcher asking questions that include the words 'how many...', 'how often...' or 'what percentage or proportion of...'. The focus of all of these questions is measurement and the answers are likely to consist of numerical or at least quantifiable data.

When a researcher decides to do a quantitative study some consequences will inevitably follow on from this. For example, if you're going to measure things ('how much...' or 'how often...') you'll collect a lot of numerical data which you'll have to make sense of. The process of making sense of data is called **analysis**. The analysis of quantitative data involves doing some mathematics to produce **statistics** that summarise and describe the numerical patterns and relationships that exist in the data.

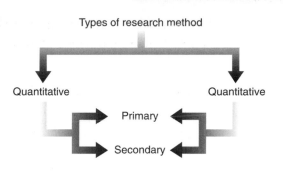

Figure 3.2 The different types of research

Qualitative research methods

Qualitative research methods are often presented as the alternative to quantitative research methods. The obvious way in which qualitative research methods differ from quantitative methods is that they don't usually involve measuring things. This means that the researcher(s) collect non-numerical forms of data. For example, asking people how they *feel* about something, to describe their *experience* of something or what something or somebody *means* to them will produce responses expressed in words rather than numbers. Feelings, experiences and meaning are not easily reduced to numbers. Furthermore, researchers don't always want to collect measurements of things.

Choosing to use qualitative research methods results in consequences for researchers in a similar way as described in the section on quantitative research. For example, researchers who decide to use qualitative research methods generally use a **naturalistic approach** to investigate people's feelings, beliefs and ways of life. This means they'll collect a lot of word-based data (spoken and written) through the **interviews** and **observations** that they carry out. As a result, qualitative analysis involves a process of identifying themes and patterns of meaning in the word-based data rather than doing any kind of mathematics or producing statistics.

Combining quantitative and qualitative research methods

In practice, researchers tend to favour either quantitative or qualitative research methods but use both in their research investigations. For example, a researcher investigating the effectiveness of a busy health centre could use quantitative research to measure things like waiting times, how long service users spend with their doctor and how often they make appointments. The data would be mainly numerical and statistics could be produced to show the findings. But statistics can't be used to summarise people's feelings about and experiences of the health centre. The researcher would have to ask some questions and record what the service users say about this. In this way, they would be supplementing the numerical data with qualitative data. In essence the study would mainly use quantitative methods but this wouldn't exclude the use of some qualitative methods.

Primary and secondary research

A second way of identifying the type of research investigation is to describe the researcher's role in generating data. Researchers can do one of two things – they can either collect new data for their investigation or they can re-use data that was originally collected for a different research study.

Primary research involves the researcher collecting 'first-hand' or new data specifically for the research investigation that they're working on. For example, if you were asked to

79

carry out primary research into the effectiveness of a specific health centre, you'd have to go and obtain research data yourself. The data that you'd obtain is known as primary data – new, original research information directly obtained by the researcher.

It is rare to find a topic so new and unusual that no other research data exists on it. Most research investigations are conducted into topics that have links to previous research. Researchers find out about previous research that is similar to their own by carrying out a **literature review**. The researcher will search through specialist research journals and books related to their research topic to find data produced by other people that could be of use to them. This is known as *secondary data*. It is 'second-hand' data, generated by somebody else for a separate research investigation.

Professional and academic researchers use secondary data in a number of different ways. For example, a researcher will use secondary data to explain what's already known about their research topic and to show how their research study will contribute to knowledge and understanding of the general subject area. Secondary data is also commonly used in the final, writing up stages of primary research. Typically a researcher will analyse his or her primary data and will then compare and contrast the findings they've obtained with those obtained by other researchers who've conducted similar studies. This comparison strategy helps to put the researcher's primary data into context.

A researcher who wants to make greater use of existing findings may also, for example, analyse secondary data to check the original researchers' conclusions or to test out new methods of data analysis that have been developed after the original study was completed.

Think It Over

What do you think is the best source of primary data on teenagers' attitudes to healthy eating? Where might you look to obtain secondary data on this topic?

Approaches to research investigation

We have said that it is possible to think of research as qualitative and/or quantitative, and as primary and/or secondary. **Deductive** and **inductive** approaches to research provide a third way of thinking about types of research.

The deductive approach

Researchers who adopt a deductive approach in their research investigation begin with a specific theoretical idea or **hypothesis** in mind and then set out to test it against empirical evidence. This is the commonest way of thinking about research investigation.

The researcher generates ideas about the area they wish to investigate, states a clear hypothesis and then carefully plans and develops their research methods to collect evidence of the phenomena that

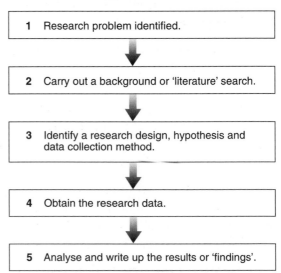

1	Research problem identified.
2	Carry out a background or 'literature' search.
3	Identify a research design, hypothesis and data collection method.
4	Obtain the research data.
5	Analyse and write up the results or 'findings'.

Figure 3.3 The deductive approach

specifically interest them. The hypothesis, and the theory that it is based on, drives the data collection part of the research process. This might seem very logical, especially if you believe that the role of research is to discover scientific 'facts' or truths.

Deductive research is commonly used in the natural sciences (physics, chemistry and biology). It is also widely used by psychology and medical researchers. Deductive research investigations typically involve an attempt to control and test relationships between '**variables**' so that 'cause and effect' relationships can be identified. The laboratory experiment (see page 92) is the classic 'controlled' research method. Medical researchers frequently use laboratory experiments to test the effects of new medicines. Careful control of conditions inside the laboratory will enable the medical researcher to claim that their findings can be '**generalised**'. That is, they will be able to argue that their findings are 'true facts' that can be repeated under the same conditions and can be applied from the laboratory research setting to the world in general.

Researchers who adopt a deductive, scientific approach claim that it is important to maintain a separation between themselves as researcher and what happens in the research situation. Deductive researchers do this to avoid influencing the people or the conditions they are studying. Researchers who adopt an inductive approach to research use a contrasting method.

The inductive approach

Inductive research is approached from the opposite direction to deductive research. That is, an inductive researcher does not begin with a theory or hypothesis that they want to test against data. Instead they collect lots of data from research on a particular topic and then find ways of making sense of it. Researchers who adopt an inductive approach often begin their investigations with a general research question or an interest in researching a particular setting (such as accident and emergency departments) rather than with a specific hypothesis.

Inductive research is not usually aiming to find or test 'cause and effect' relationships. Typically, researchers using this approach look in detail at a specific group of people or at a particular situation.

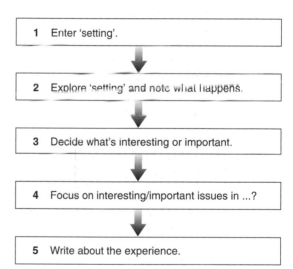

Figure 3.4 An inductive research approach

As a result, a researcher using an inductive approach tries to gain an awareness and appreciation of how particular individuals or groups of people view and experience the world in their 'natural settings'.

The inductive approach to research is strongly associated with the disciplines of anthropology and sociology. In care-related research it is likely to be used by members of non-medical disciplines like social workers, nurses and occupational therapists who want to understand the experiences of the individuals and groups whom they study.

Most researchers who adopt an inductive approach to their investigations accept that they inevitably play a part in the research situation. Researchers acknowledge this to different degrees when they write up their research investigations.

Theory into practice

Second thoughts on folic acid

Swedish researchers have found that women who take folic acid before and during pregnancy are more likely to have twins. Of 2569 women who used folic acid supplements 2.8 per cent gave birth to twins. This compares to a twin birth rate in the general Swedish population of 1.5 per cent. Researchers have calculated that if 30 per cent of 100,000 women in Sweden took folic acid there would be 225 extra pairs of twins. These twins would have a lower birth weight and an increased risk of cerebral palsy. This should be weighed against the benefit of avoiding four or five spina bifida cases. Not all researchers are convinced that the link between twins and folic acid is real though and further research is urged. (*New Scientist*, 28 July 2001, p.19)

1 Using the key terms outlined in the previous section of the chapter, describe the type of research investigation that has been carried out in Sweden.
2 What do you think the main goal or purpose of this research was?
3 Describe ways that care practitioners could make use of the findings of this research investigation.

The research process

The secret of success when planning and conducting a research study is to follow what is called a **research process**. This is simply an organised, logical and systematic strategy or approach to research investigation. There are a number of different ways of organising a research process. For example, deductive researchers tend to follow a linear research process. Figure 3.5 shows how this involves a series of sequential steps that are not repeated. However, inductive researchers tend to follow more of a cyclical approach. Figure 3.6 shows how this also involves the

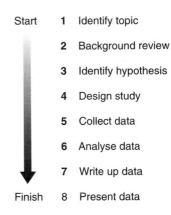

Start	1	Identify topic
	2	Background review
	3	Identify hypothesis
	4	Design study
	5	Collect data
	6	Analyse data
	7	Write up data
Finish	8	Present data

Figure 3.5 A linear research process

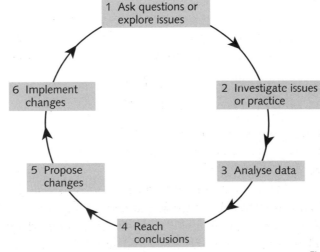

1 Ask questions or explore issues
2 Investigate issues or practice
3 Analyse data
4 Reach conclusions
5 Propose changes
6 Implement changes

Figure 3.6 A cyclical research process

researcher following a series of steps that are repeated during the data collection and analysis phases.

Identifying a topic to research

The first task for any researcher is to identify a research topic. Researchers are often directed to research particular topic areas or even specific questions. For example, they may be given a topic to research as part of their work role or because somebody has commissioned them to carry out a specific piece of research.

Where the researcher has to identify their own topic, they will usually begin by identifying general topic areas that are researchable. Essentially, you can research a topic only if it is possible to obtain **evidence** about it.

Identifying care-related topics

A common way of identifying a research topic is to do a lot thinking about different possibilities and then to gradually focus down on an area of special interest. It is important to keep practical considerations in mind when thinking about the topics that you could research as a student. Peter Langley (1993) suggests that you should ask the following questions about the ideas that you come up with:

- 'Is the proposed research possible?' You need to be sure that you can obtain primary and secondary data on the subject you're interested in. Specialist and sensitive topics may seem glamorous and exciting but won't be researchable if you can't obtain data on them.
- 'Is the idea relevant to your course?' The reason for your student research project is to develop and demonstrate your understanding of care-related research skills.
- 'Is the project interesting enough to you?' Research projects usually take quite a long time to complete. The topic that you choose will need to be interesting enough to motivate you all the way through.
- 'Is the proposed research ethically justifiable?' That is, can you be sure that your research will not cause harm or offence or get you into difficulties yourself? A project that involves any risk to yourself or others cannot be justified (see page 96 for further detail on research ethics).

You should try to avoid topics that are personally upsetting or sensitive or which provoke you to express very strong opinions. Topics like abortion, child abuse and euthanasia fall into this category for some people. If you cannot be objective and open-minded in your research study you will not produce good research.

Identifying a topic will give you a sense of direction for your investigation. A good way of getting started is to think about the subjects or issues that positively motivate you in your course. Whatever your initial idea, you will need to work on it to develop it into a researchable topic.

What factors influence choice of research topic?

- An individual researcher's obsession with a topic!
- Researchers are sometimes commissioned to research specific topics by government departments or business organisations.
- A researcher's values and beliefs can influence their choice of research topic. For example, they may want to expose injustice or promote change.
- A researcher may identify a gap in knowledge and understanding about a topic in their academic discipline or area of professional practice.

- Research topics are often chosen because they address social, psychological or health problems.
- The amount of time and money available to the researcher is an important influence on choice of topic.

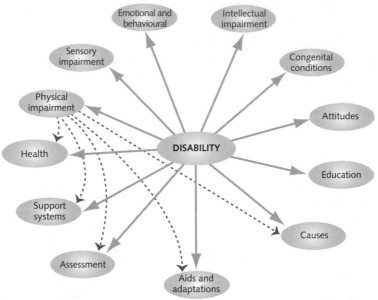

Figure 3.7 Focusing on disability

Think It Over

Draw your own version of this spider diagram. What other sub-topics would you add to your spider diagram to focus more clearly on an interesting and researchable idea?

Obtaining and reviewing background information

The literature review, or 'review of the field', occurs in the early planning stages of a research investigation. The researcher carries out a literature search in which they find and review all the relevant information and previous work done by others on their chosen research topic.

Professional and academic researchers put a lot of their time and energy into literature reviews. They use specialist academic libraries that hold research journals and an extensive range of books on their chosen topic. Once they've obtained copies of the relevant books and articles they carry out a review of them and summarise the important parts.

Why obtain background information?

1 *To clarify the research problem* – The process of searching through and reviewing information sources helps to focus a research idea more clearly.
2 *To develop the research methodology* – Accounts of previous investigations on a topic help a researcher to think about the methods that they could use themselves.

Sometimes it is appropriate to try something different from previous researchers but there may also be very good reasons for replicating the methods used in other studies.

3 *To improve understanding of the research topic* – Reviewing the background literature, theories and studies that already exist gives a deeper understanding of the topic area and helps the researcher understand where their investigation fits in.

Sources of background information

A number of information sources provide useful, relevant background information for a research investigation. These include textbooks, topic books, journals, magazines, newspapers and CD-ROMS obtained from, or used in, public, school and college libraries as well as the Internet, the mass media and organisations that are willing to provide information.

Textbooks

Textbooks tend to provide summaries of theories and research findings on specific topics. You may also find useful statistics and quotes that relate to your topic. However, textbooks can provide only a limited amount of **secondary data**. This might be useful in the early stages of a literature search but will need to be supplemented with other information sources later on. The index and references section of a textbook are always worth looking at as they can point you to other specialist topic books that may or may not be primary sources, but which are likely to have more detail than a textbook can give.

Topic books

A subject or key word search on a computerised library database is a quick way of producing a list of book titles on your topic. Specialist topic books are a good source of detail and add depth to your background information. You will have to work at identifying and summarising the interesting and relevant bits of information that you need. Again, try using the index and reference sections to spot the parts of the book that will be most useful to you.

Journals

Professional and academic researchers try to have their research reports published in specialist research journals. These specialist journals are difficult to obtain unless you happen to have access to a higher education library. A small but growing number are freely available on the Internet.

Newspapers and magazines

Newspapers and magazines often publish articles containing research studies and findings. These can provide useful and accessible background information. However, it is important to think carefully about the reliability of any information found in newspapers and magazines if the main aim of the publication is to entertain readers. For example, specialist care magazines aimed at professional practitioners and care students are likely to be more reliable sources of background information for a care-related research investigation than Sunday supplements or 'glossy' monthly magazines. Similarly, broadsheets (big papers) tend to be more reliable and impartial than tabloid newspapers.

CD-ROMs

CD-ROMs provide quick and easy access to a lot of information. CD-ROM encyclopaedias tend to have good summaries of social science, psychology and health-related topics. However, bear in mind that the information is always limited and is likely to be at least a little out of date because it's not possible to update a CD-ROM. You will always need additional information and are unlikely to find up-to-date statistics or accounts of research studies on CD-ROMs.

The Internet

Students and professional researchers increasingly use Internet websites as a source of background information. However, information available on the Internet has not usually been through the same impartial editing and checking process as would information in most print-based sources. You should therefore be careful about verifying the accuracy of the information you obtain from online sources.

Key issues

Guidelines for using the Internet as an information source

1 Make use of *both* library and online resources.
2 Cross-check any information obtained from the Internet with authoritative library resources.
3 Evaluate the Internet sites that you use. Ask the following questions:
   a Can you identify the author(s) of the web pages or sites?
   b Are the author(s) well known in the area you are researching?
   c Do the authors give their credentials and reasons for publishing the information?
   d Is the site linked to other authoritative and reputable sites?
   e Where did the author(s) gather the information?
   f Is the information based on original research or secondary sources?
   g When was the information published? (Many sites are never updated or maintained.)
   h Is the information academic (produced by researchers), popular (produced for the general public), governmental or commercial (produced by a business for commercial reasons)?
   i Does the information express an opinion or claim to be factual?
   j How does the information compare with what you already know? Does it add anything to your understanding of the topic?
4 Keep a detailed record of the sites that you use and the sources of the information you use. It's best to bookmark the good sites that you use and organise them in a directory so that you'll be able to find them again.
5 Reference the sites that you use in your final report.

Organisations

A large number of business, voluntary sector and government organisations produce research reports. Some will provide copies of their reports and publications on request. You should bear in mind that organisations don't usually publish research unless it suits their commercial or other purposes. The impartiality and objectivity of the research can therefore be doubtful.

To assess the objectivity of the background information that you find, it's best to search and review a variety of sources and to cross-check between them. This helps you to make judgements about the reliability of each source and the validity of the background information you've collected.

Writing a literature review

When sufficient background information has been obtained the researcher has to summarise it. This typically involves writing an overview of the main issues, theories and research findings in the topic area. The review should be written with your proposed research topic in mind. That is, only information that appears to be relevant to your topic area should be selected and summarised. A lot of other information will have to be left out. Your literature review should focus on key points and should conclude by identifying where your own research topic fits into the overall topic area.

Identifying a research question or hypothesis

Once a research topic has been identified, the next step is to look at the topic in a very focused way to identify a research question or hypothesis. Initially this involves focusing on a specific aspect of the general research topic and then identifying possible research questions or hypotheses that emerge or can be brainstormed out of it.

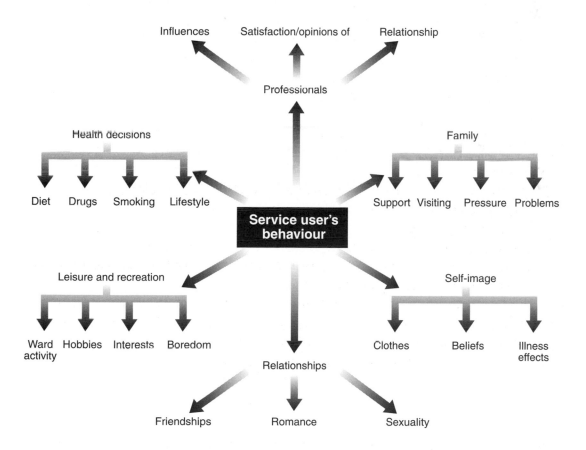

Figure 3.8 Brainstorming

A clearly stated hypothesis or research question should provide a sharp focus to a research investigation. The decision about whether to use a research question or a hypothesis depends on the type of research being undertaken and the theoretical approach that the researcher takes.

Hypotheses

A hypothesis is simply a statement that makes a prediction (expressing your belief) about what you will find or what will happen. Some researchers decide to investigate a

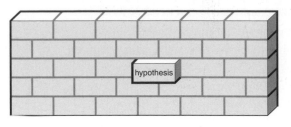

particular topic because they have a 'hunch' or belief about something or because they want to test an existing theory. In these kinds of situations it is usually appropriate to develop a hypothesis. A hypothesis is like a brick in a bigger 'theory wall'.

The researcher's task is to test the hypothesis (the prediction) by assessing whether the empirical evidence supports or contradicts it. Researchers who develop hypotheses are using what we

Figure 3.9 The 'theory wall'

referred to earlier as a deductive approach to their research investigation. They are trying to deduce, or work out, whether there is evidence to support the hypothesis or 'hunch' that they're putting forward. If the empirical evidence doesn't support the hypothesis the researcher is likely to question and doubt the bigger theory. However, if the empirical evidence does support the hypothesis, it is likely to strengthen the researcher's belief in the bigger theory.

Researchers usually develop two hypotheses for an experimental research study. An **experimental hypothesis** is a prediction about the type of changes or relationships that the researcher expects to occur because of the effect of independent variable(s). For example, 'the tomatoes will increase in size when given more water and sunlight'. The **null hypothesis** states that any change or lack of change that occurs in the experimental situation is due to chance or some factor other than the independent variable(s). For example, 'the tomatoes will increase in size due to chance factors'. Hypotheses are **directional** if a prediction is made about the way in which a change will occur (such as an increase or decrease in size) and **non-directional** if the researcher simply predicts that a change will occur.

Think It Over

Can you think of a directional, experimental hypothesis that you could use to investigate the possible connection between eating salt and high blood pressure?

Research questions

Research questions are clearly focused questions that can be investigated. That is, the researcher can obtain evidence to answer (or at least respond to) the question. Researchers don't always have a hypothesis to test in their investigations. Researchers who use an inductive approach, for example, don't start with any kind of theory or hypothesis in mind. Usually they want to collect data before working out any theoretical explanation for their findings. Nevertheless, researchers still need something to focus their investigation. Instead of a hypothesis, inductive researchers will develop and use a research question. Examples include:

- How does the work experience of school children affect their future career choices?
- What attitudes do teenage girls have towards careers in the engineering sector?
- What impact do anti-drink-drive campaigns have on the behaviour of middle-aged men?

- Does the role of house-husband affect a man's self-esteem?
- What does it mean to be a social worker?

A research question doesn't involve a prediction and is likely to be more open-ended than a hypothesis. Research questions need to be written in clear, precise, unambiguous language. They should focus the researcher on a specific topic in a clear way.

Operationalising concepts

Creating a clear, unambiguous research question or hypothesis involves creative thinking. However, the question must also be precise. All the terms used in it must be clearly defined. This is known as operationalising the concepts and variables.

Case Study

Look at the following analysis of a research question and response:

'How good are early education organisations at providing child-care services?'

The terms 'early education organisations' and 'child-care services' need to be operationalised to make the research question clear and unambiguous. The researcher must say what counts as an early education organisation and what, precisely, they mean by a child-care service. They may only want to include businesses such as private nurseries and play groups. Or they might also include individual childminders and primary schools in a broader definition of 'early education organisation'. Whatever they choose to include, the researcher must come up with a definition of the term 'early education organisation' that all readers of the report understand in the same way. The same point applies to the term 'child-care service'.

As well as the two terms that we've discussed, the researcher also needs to say what they mean by the phrase 'how good'. This term could be understood and measured in a variety of ways. Does 'how good' refer to parents' sense of 'satisfaction' with the services provided or does it refer to the 'effectiveness' of the service in achieving specific goals such as teaching children to write, play together or make friends? It could mean any of these things. The term 'good' is, in fact, the critical element of the research question. It is the concept that the researcher is actually trying to measure. As a result, the researcher has to identify at least one clear indicator of what counts as 'good'.

When your research question or hypothesis has been operationalised, you will have a much better idea of the possible data sources that are most appropriate for your investigation. For example, if an 'early years organisation' is defined as meaning a business or voluntary group providing child care, you won't need to contact any childminders who work on their own. If 'good' is indicated by a parent or primary carer's self-defined level of satisfaction with the organisation, you'd need to decide how best to collect this type of 'opinion' data. It would seem that you'd be better off asking parents or primary carers questions, using a questionnaire or interviews, rather than observing their behaviour when they collect their children from the nursery or play-group.

Think It Over

Why do you think that having clearly operationalised concepts is vital to the success of a research project?

Obtaining research data

When you have developed a research question or hypothesis you will then have to choose the best way of obtaining data to address the question or test the hypothesis. To choose the most effective methods for your investigation, you'll need to understand the strengths and weaknesses of the various options available.

Using questionnaires

A research questionnaire usually contains a series of questions, rating scales and 'forced choice' data collection items. Questions can be open or closed depending on the type and depth of data being sought.

- **Closed questions** are used where a specific, clear response is required. For example, 'do you eat meat?' is a closed question with a 'yes' or 'no' answer.
- **Open questions** allow the respondent to give a broader, more in-depth answer. For example, 'what are your views on eating meat?' is an open question that allows the respondent to express their personal views on this subject.

Rating scales are a special type of closed question. The respondent has to choose one option from a limited range of possible responses. Usually the researcher will ask the respondent to indicate a degree of preference for or against something. A questionnaire on food choices could, for example, include the following rating scale:

Indicate the extent to which you agree with the statement: 'Eating meat is necessary for a balanced, healthy diet'.	
Strongly agree	☐
Agree	☐
Neither agree or disagree	☐
Disagree	☐
Strongly disagree	☐

Forced choice items also set out a limited range of possible answers for the respondent to choose from. However, they are different from rating scales as they do not usually involve any kind of preference to be expressed. They simply ask the respondent to choose a 'best fit' answer. You should be able to answer the following forced choice item by choosing the category that best fits your own current age.

> Which of the following age groups do you currently belong to?
>
> 14–16 ☐
>
> 17–19 ☐
>
> 20–22 ☐
>
> 23 and over ☐

Questionnaires are used by researchers when they want to obtain relatively large amounts of quantitative data. They are frequently used to conduct large-scale surveys on specific topics. However, researchers who survey the population on a subject can't include all possible respondents because there are usually too many people involved and contacting them would take too much time and cost too much money. The solution to this problem is to use a **representative sample** of the population.

Advantages and disadvantages of questionnaires

Advantages
- cheap and efficient
- produce a large volume of data quickly
- very reliable
- allow the researcher to compare different respondents' answers and produce statistics.

Disadvantages
- response rates often low
- often limit the range of responses that can be given
- researcher cannot be certain that respondents have understood the questions, cannot use follow-up questions to explore unusual answers and may not know who actually filled in the questionnaire
- people who complete questionnaires may have unrepresentative views on the subject.

Interviews

Interviews are also based on a series of questions. The interviewee has to be able to understand and respond honestly to the questions for a research interview to be successful. The different styles of research interview include:

- **Structured interviews** – based on a pre-written and organised list of questions. All interviewees are asked the same questions in the same order.
- **Unstructured interviews** – much looser and focus more generally on topic areas rather than very specific pre-written questions. The researcher uses the topic areas to develop a 'guided conversation' with the interviewee.
- **Semi-structured interviews** – somewhere in between the previous styles. The researcher will use a mixture of structured questions and general topic ideas to develop questions during the interview itself.

The main advantage of using an interview to gather research data is that the researcher is present during data production. The researcher can use the interview situation to encourage people to provide full answers to the questions and can use their judgement to make adjustments to the interview questions or ask follow-up answers where they think this is required. A disadvantage of the researcher's presence is that some respondents say what they think the interviewer wants them to say rather than what they really think or feel.

Advantages of semi-structured interviews
- They avoid limiting possible responses because questions are not usually pre-determined.
- They allow the researcher to explore what the respondent says because they do not have to follow the same restricted list of questions with everyone. More in-depth data can be obtained as a result.
- Response rates are higher because the researcher is present during data collection.
- The researcher can give help and guidance, explaining questions and providing additional information where required.

Disadvantages of semi-structured interviews
- A researcher can't be totally confident that each interviewee has told the truth or that they have all remembered events correctly.
- Recording what people say can be difficult. For example, note-writing affects the flow of conversation. Tape recording can put interviewees off even where they've given full consent for it to be used.
- Interviews usually produce too much data. Most of it will not be useful and will be too detailed.
- Interviews take a lot of time to conduct. Time also needs to be put aside for transcribing notes and tapes into a complete record of what each interviewee said.
- Interviews can produce very different kinds of response from different interviewees. This makes the comparison of data very difficult.

Scientific experiments

Experiments are widely used to obtain data in biological, psychological and natural science research investigations. Social researchers do use experimental methods but their use is quite rare in the social research field.

Types of experiment

Laboratory experiments are carried out in a highly controlled and closed research setting. Researchers who use these experiments are generally investigating possible 'cause and effect' relationships. Whilst many scientific experiments investigate chemicals or other substances, people can also take part in experimental research. For example specialist 'hearing' or 'sleep' laboratories exist specifically to research cause and effect relationships in these two areas of human experience.

Social researchers tend to use **field experiments** when they conduct experimental research. The conditions under which field experiments are conducted are much less controlled than laboratory experiments. In fact, field experiments usually take place in everyday settings.

Clinical trials are a type of experiment somewhere between laboratory and field experiments. They are widely used to investigate the effectiveness of medicines and other treatments for physical or psychiatric problems. Clinical trials are not carried out in closed laboratory environments. However, they do involve a carefully chosen population of people whose reactions to experimental medication or treatments are carefully monitored so that researchers can understand cause and effect relationships.

Characteristics of experiments

The key feature of an experiment is the attempt by the researcher to identify the relationship between two or more '**variables**'. Basically, the researcher manipulates, or changes, what they call the **independent variable** to see what effect it has on the other **dependent variable(s)**.

An independent variable is a 'factor' such as social class, a 'behaviour' such as smoking cigarettes, or a 'substance' such as aspirin, which the researcher thinks might cause a change in something else – this something else being the dependent variable. For example, in an experiment to investigate the effects of alcohol on physical co-ordination, alcohol would be the independent variable and physical co-ordination would be the dependent variable. In short, loss of physical co-ordination can be shown to be dependent on level of alcohol consumption. The more a person drinks the less control they have over their ability to co-ordinate their movements.

In an experiment, the dependent variable is the thing that the researcher wants to explain. Usually, the researcher is trying to identify what affects the dependent variable. To do so, they'll generally 'control' or manipulate one or more independent variables to assess their effects on the dependent variable.

Experiments generate quantitative data. They are also part of a deductive approach to research investigation. Researchers who use experiments observe and measure what happens in the experimental situation very carefully in order to identify cause and effect relationships. In such situations, care must be taken to isolate the crucial dependent and independent variables so that their interaction isn't influenced by **extraneous variables**. These are factors that can also affect the relationship between the dependent and independent variables.

Experimental researchers use a number of methods, including control groups, placebos, and 'blind' and 'double-blind' protocols, to minimise the possible impact of extraneous variables. This is called 'controlling for' extraneous variables and is done to protect the validity of the research.

- A **control group** is a part of the research population that is deliberately not experimented on. For example, the control group could be a group of people who have been specially selected because they match the qualities and characteristics of the experimental (tested) group. The researcher will carry out their experiment, testing a dependent variable in the experimental group. The findings that are obtained from the work with the experimental group are then compared to those obtained from the control group to identify any differences.
- A **placebo** is an inert substance (usually a 'sugar pill' containing Vitamin C) that has no known effect on the dependent variable being tested. In clinical drug trials, where placebos are often used, the researcher may give one 'tested' half of the participants an experimental drug, whilst the other (control group) half are given the placebo. People in the tested group will experience significantly greater change in the dependent variable (such as pain reduction) than people who have received the placebo if the experimental drug is effective. Members of the control group who

think that they are receiving the experimental drug but who are actually receiving the placebo may experience what is known as the 'placebo effect'. That is, they will experience changes or improvements in the dependent variable (such as reduced pain) that can't be attributed to the experimental drug!

- Medical research into new medications typically uses the clinical trial type of experiment. Here the researchers are likely to also use **blind** or **double-blind protocols**. In blind protocol research, the participants don't know whether they are receiving the experimental drug or the placebo. In a double-blind study the participants are placed in the 'experimental' and the 'placebo' groups by an independent person who has no part in the data collection process. The researchers who collect and analyse the data also don't know which participants are in the experimental group and which are receiving the placebo. When the data have been collected and fully analysed the independent person will reveal which participants belonged to which group. The researchers will then check whether the two sets of people experienced different effects from the medications they took.

Control groups, placebos, blind and double-blind protocols are all used in experimental research to minimise potential bias and clarify the 'cause and effect' relationship between dependent and independent variables

Advantages of experiments
- produce very reliable data – the reliability of experimental data can be checked simply by repeating the experiment under the same conditions
- produce quantitative data that can be analysed statistically – this means that the researcher can compare whether differences occur in the data when different independent variables are manipulated
- 'scientific' status of experiments gives them a lot of status and credibility.

Disadvantages of experiments
- produce data on only a very specific, narrow topic (the relationship between two variables) – they are not flexible beyond this
- validity of experimental data can be doubted unless the researcher is certain that the effects of all extraneous variables have been excluded
- data validity is sometimes questioned on the grounds that what happens in the laboratory under controlled conditions may not happen in the less controlled real world outside
- experimenting on human beings in care situations raises difficult ethical issues – in particular, people have feelings and human rights that chemicals and placebos do not have!

Observational methods

Observational methods of data collection involve watching people's behaviour or looking at some other phenomenon. Observational research can be formal and highly structured where the researcher uses a checklist or some other device to record specific observations, or it can be more informal with the researcher noting interesting things that they have seen but had not really planned to look for.

Structured

Observational research is useful for finding out how people actually behave. Often people say they think or believe something but, in reality, they behave differently. Observational research can be used in studies that adopt either a deductive or an inductive approach. For example, in a deductive study, a researcher may identify a hypothesis about students' behaviour in classrooms (perhaps 'The people at the back will pay less attention') and produce a structured checklist or form to record her observations of this. In this kind of situation, the researcher would probably conduct observations overtly. That is, the students in the class would know that the researcher was collecting data, even if they didn't know what this was about. An alternative is to conduct observations covertly. This involves the researcher observing and recording their observations without people knowing that they're doing this. There are a number of ethical problems with covert observation (see pages 96–9) but there are circumstances where it is the only method of finding out how people truly behave.

Less structured

Researchers who use an inductive approach tend to use a form of participant observation to obtain their data. This is less structured than a checklist approach but still involves making and writing about a lot of observations. Participant observers generally join a group of people or a community or somehow enter the setting that they want to research. They do this to get to know the group or situation from 'the inside'. The aim is to understand the real *motives* and *meanings* of the people, community or culture being studied in a natural setting. The researcher believes that their experience of the group will give them access to data, via observation, that can't be obtained using other methods like questionnaires, interviews or experiments.

Advantages of observational methods
- Observational methods can provide access to highly valid 'real life' data.
- Observational data can be 'rich' in meaning and can enable researchers to obtain sensitive data that would otherwise be 'hidden'.
- Participant observation allows researchers to obtain very detailed data over a long period of time.
- The researcher doesn't have to decide what they are looking for in advance of beginning their study. They can make decisions about which observations are or are not significant as events occur naturally.

Disadvantages of observational methods
- Participant observers can find it hard to remain objective because they become too involved in the research setting.
- Participant observers sometimes influence behaviour or events in the research setting if they become too involved.
- Researchers may never really understand the group or setting they're studying if they are unable to appreciate the deep meaning and significance of behaviour from the standpoint of a detached outsider.
- Observational studies tend to be small-scale and the group being studied may not be representative of any other social group (therefore findings can't be generalised).
- Covert observation has serious ethical problems associated with it. For example, informed consent cannot be obtained before covert observation is carried out.
- The reliability of observational data is generally low. Observations are often personal and can't be replicated by the researcher or others.

Ethical issues and their implications

The popular image of research is that it is a positive way of extending knowledge and improving our general quality of life. However, many people are wary of researchers because they worry about the potential harm that might result from being involved in a research investigation. The potential physical or psychological risks involved in any research investigation should never be treated lightly. As a consequence, care organisations, practitioners and potential research participants expect researchers to be aware of all the ethical issues involved in their research investigations.

Ethics are moral principles or codes of behaviour. Research ethics cover the principles and codes of behaviour that we expect researchers to abide by when planning and conducting their research investigations. People who wish to conduct research investigations in real care settings usually have to demonstrate that their proposed investigation conforms to the ethical **codes of practice** of several different organisations who will regulate or have an interest in the research study.

Ethical codes of practice

Registered care professionals, including nurses, occupational therapists and medical practitioners, are subject to the rules and regulations of their respective professional regulatory bodies such as the General Nursing Council, the College of Occupational Therapy and the General Medical Council. Each of these bodies produces a code of research ethics that registered members must follow when conducting research. Academic researchers may also belong to other professional associations and academic societies, such as the British Sociological Association, or the British Psychological Society, and will have a contract with the business, university or government that employs them or supervises their research studies. All of these different associations, societies and organisations are likely to produce, and require members and employees to follow, a code of research ethics.

Researchers usually have to do a lot of planning and preparatory work before they can say that their research proposal meets the requirements of all of the ethical codes that apply to them. Despite this, research cannot take place in a care setting until the research proposal has been formally approved by the care organisation's **ethics committee**. This consists of a group of professional experts, care organisation staff, lay people and representatives of service users. The ethics committee will scrutinise every research proposal for ethical issues and will discuss their implications and ways of dealing with them in great detail. A care organisation is likely to produce its own specific ethical code of practice and will not give permission for research to be carried out unless its requirements are completely met.

General ethical issues in research

People who read and review research studies tend to do so with a number of general questions about ethical issues in mind. These include:

Who has commissioned and funded the research?
It is important to ask this question because there is an expectation in the academic and professional care fields that researchers are able to work independently and their reports will be truthful and unbiased. The unspoken concern is that a government, business or

other politically motivated organisation may commission research to deliberately produce 'evidence' that supports their particular aims. This would not be unbiased, independent research and would therefore be unethical.

Are the human rights of the participants observed and protected?

As a general principle, every research subject should participate voluntarily, should have full knowledge of the nature of the research, should be allowed to withdraw at any point in the research process and should not be harmed by their participation in the research. Care practitioners and researchers, as well as members of the general public, would condemn as unethical research investigations that directly or indirectly abused the human rights of vulnerable care service users. Researchers who work in care settings are expected to go to great lengths to ensure that the interests of vulnerable service users are fully protected if they participate in a research study.

Are the intended benefits or consequences of the research investigation positive and constructive?

Research should aim to improve or increase knowledge for a positive purpose. It should not be carried out for frivolous reasons, for the sake of it or simply to benefit the reputation of the researcher. If a researcher begins their investigation with a positive and constructive aim, and honestly believes their study could have a beneficial outcome, it would ethically justifiable. It would be unethical if the research involved illegal behaviour or unjustifiable suffering, or was never intended to benefit anybody.

Specific ethical principles

Codes of research ethics usually contain specific guidelines on the ethical ways of treating and managing relationships with research participants. In particular, the principles of informed consent, confidentiality and honesty are fundamental to the research relationship.

Informed consent

Every research participant has a basic right to full information about aims, processes and procedures involved in the investigation. Research participants should never be tricked or pressured into taking part in a study.

Ethics committees always assess how a researcher intends to gain informed consent from their intended research participants. It is vital that participants have a full understanding of any potential risks that they may face if they participate. This is especially important for care service users. Side effects or possible hazards of experimental treatments must always be fully explained to anyone who is persuaded to take part in medical research, for example. Where a person has a mental health problem, a learning disability or is very old or too young to understand an explanation of possible risks, their 'informed' consent cannot be obtained. People who cannot consent fully and freely should not be recruited to participate in research investigations. Where they are, an ethics committee is likely to refuse permission for an investigation to proceed in order to protect the interests of such vulnerable people.

A common strategy for obtaining informed consent is to write a brief statement explaining what the research study involves. This is then shown or read to each potential participant. Other methods include holding briefing meetings for people interested in taking part, asking people to read a description of the research study and to then complete a form demonstrating their understanding of, and willingness to participate in, the study and interviewing potential participants. Whichever method is used, participants must be allowed to withdraw from the study at any time during the research. It is unethical to prevent or refuse this.

Confidentiality

People who participate in research have the right to remain anonymous and to have the confidentiality of their data protected. Typically, research participants expect the researcher not to name them in the final research report. This is because disclosure of personal details could have a negative impact on the person's life or on others who know them. For example, the views and feelings that they expressed towards a sensitive research topic could affect a person's family, friends, neighbours or work colleagues directly or indirectly. Confidentiality is one way of protecting other people from this kind of negative outcome of research. Confidentiality also allows participants to express their real views and describe their true experiences because the principle protects them from receiving direct personal criticism for doing so. For this reason protecting confidentiality reassures most people enough for them to tell the truth and give what is sometimes very personal information.

Researchers protect the confidentiality of participants in various ways. For example, they often avoid using the real names of the people, places or organisations from where they obtained data. Some researchers make up fictitious names for places ('West Town') and are vague about the part of the country where the research was conducted ('a hospital in the North East of England'). Referring to a specific setting, town or organisation can sometimes allow readers to identify people who may have participated in the research even when their real names are not used.

Honesty and integrity

There is a general expectation that researchers will act with honesty and integrity when carrying out their investigations. In particular they are expected to report their findings truthfully. It is unethical to distort or falsify findings or to fail to point out errors or problems that affected the investigation. Unfortunately, researchers have failed to meet these basic ethical requirements in the past. A lack of honesty and integrity by care researchers is both unethical and potentially dangerous. It is the responsibility of individual researchers, the wider research community and organisations that support and sponsor research to ensure that honesty and integrity are features of every researcher's approach to research investigation.

Theory into practice

'Talented' children

In the late 1960s, a group of researchers conducted an investigation in which they randomly selected children within school and then told each child's teacher that they were 'talented'. The researchers didn't actually assess or measure the abilities or skills of any of the children. They simply wanted to know what effect giving teachers such information would have on a child's educational experience and future development. It was found that the selected children achieved better results than their peers even though they were not necessarily more able initially.

Metabolism study

From 1946 to 1956 nineteen mentally retarded boys living at the State Residential School, Fernald, Massachusetts were fed radioactive iron and calcium in their breakfast cereal. The researchers sought to obtain data on the links between nutrition and metabolism. Parents consented to the study on behalf of their children but were not told about the addition of the radioactive substances.

1 Identify the main ethical issues that result from each of these research investigations.
2 Why do you think the subjects in the research studies didn't give informed consent to the researchers?
3 If you were the parent of a child in either study, which ethical principle(s) would you use to prevent your child from participating?
4 Do you think that either of the studies could be modified to make them ethically acceptable? Outline and explain your views.

Judging validity and reliability

When care practitioners read research reports they tend to ask a couple of fundamental questions about the research methods. In particular, they want to know whether the data collection methods produce valid data and whether these methods are reliable. A data collection method that obtains the kind of data that the researcher sets out to obtain with it has a high **validity**. Researchers must choose the right kind of method to obtain valid data. For example, using observational methods to assess nurses' attitudes to patients is unlikely to produce valid data. The researcher would have to reach a conclusion on the basis of assumptions about what their observations mean. An interview or structured questionnaire is likely to produce more valid data. A method that can be repeated to produce the same data in very similar circumstances is a highly reliable method. **Reliability** is concerned with the method being reproducible.

Think It Over

Why do you think that an experiment is likely to be a more reliable data collection method than an unstructured interview or an observational method?

Planning and presenting your own research

So far we have covered the topics and issues that should have given you a good understanding of research methods and the research process. You now need to put this knowledge and understanding into practice by developing your own research project. Essentially, you now need to produce a detailed plan, or **research proposal**, outlining your intended investigation. This will set out what you want to investigate, how you intend to go about it and what you hope to gain or achieve through the research investigation.

Writing a research proposal should help you to think through, refine and express your research intentions. It is best to include a schedule of work that identifies key dates and the different stages of your investigation in your plan. When you try to schedule the work required you may realise that you need to rethink or develop certain parts of your intended project. The proposal should alert you and other interested parties to any potential workload, practical or ethical problems at an early enough stage for you to still do something about them.

Assessment activity 3.1

Developing a research idea

This activity provides you with an opportunity to develop a research proposal for a care-related research investigation. You should propose a project that you would like to carry out yourself once the proposal has been approved.

1 Brainstorm possible research ideas.

2 From the ideas that you've generated, identify a research topic and develop a hypothesis and a research question that are relevant to the care field.

3 Explain and justify your choice of research topic and hypothesis.

4 Develop an alternative to your preferred hypothesis that would require similar sources and provide a different perspective on the data and findings.

5 Describe the type of research investigation that you intend to carry out. You should comment on the overall approach and data collection methods that you intend to use and should make clear the types of data that you will be seeking.

6 Carry out a background literature review to identify and summarise relevant previous studies or theories on your chosen topic. You should try to use information technology when searching for and summarising the existing literature.

7 Describe the main ethical issues that result from your proposed research investigation. You should also explain how you intend to address each issue to ensure that your research is ethically acceptable.

Identifying and selecting data sources

When you've decided on the data collection methods that you'll use, you will need to have a clear, practical idea of your main data sources. If you decide to use questionnaires, you're likely to be doing a survey. In this case, you'll need to identify who your research population is and work out how you are going to sample them.

Sampling

Sampling involves selecting a representative group of respondents from a larger **research population**. If your sample is representative of the research population, you will be able to generalise your findings from the sample to the population as a whole. To avoid choosing a biased sample, the process should normally involve the selection of a **random sample** of respondents. In essence, every member of the research population should have an equal chance of being selected for the research sample.

Sampling methods

There are a number of ways of sampling the research population, including:

Sampling method	What does this involve?
Random sampling	Subjects are randomly chosen from a 'sampling frame' (a population listing) that has been constructed by someone else. Basically, the researcher numbers everyone in the list and then selects entries by extracting those that match the numbers that they choose from the random number table.
Systematic sampling	All items are listed and numbered in a sampling frame. The researcher selects every 'nth' item. For example, every fifth item starting from the beginning of the list. This goes on until a full sample has been chosen.
Stratified or quota sampling	This involves dividing the population into discrete groups or strata, such as people aged 16–24, 25–30 and 30+. A random or systematic sample of each strata is then taken until the desired quotas have been chosen for each strata.
Opportunity sampling	This involves simply selecting cases or respondents on the basis of personal knowledge or contact. An opportunity sample is not chosen randomly in the same way that the previous sampling methods are.
Snowball sampling	This is similar to the above but introduces a random element. Initially people volunteer or are specifically chosen to be part of the sample on an 'opportunity' basis. They then introduce or identify others who also fit the population criteria to the researcher.

Theory into practice

To use the Random Number table, let us suppose you need a random sample of 10 under-20-years-olds from a group of 50. Allocate each person in the group a number, then starting at the top left-hand corner of the table and moving down the column, select the first ten numbers that are 50 or less. You should get the numbers 20, 22, 45, 44, 16, 4, 32, 3, 1 and 27. These are the people that you will choose.

Collecting primary data

When you have written your research proposal, obtained ethical approval to begin your study and selected your data sources, you can start to collect data. It is best to begin your data collection by running a pilot study. This is a small-scale trial run of your investigation. It gives you a chance to check out whether the procedures and methods that you intend to use will actually work. The pilot study should help you to avoid later problems as well as helping you to gain some confidence and develop the basic practical skills that you will need for the real study.

If you do want to carry out a pilot study, you should ensure that you allow enough time for it. You also need to avoid using up too much of your main data source(s) doing it.

Random Number Table

20	17	42	28	23	17	59	66	38	61	02	10	86	10	51	55	92	52	44	25
74	49	04	19	03	04	10	33	53	70	11	54	48	63	94	60	94	49	57	38
94	70	49	31	38	67	23	42	29	65	40	88	78	71	37	18	48	64	06	57
22	15	78	15	69	84	32	52	32	54	15	12	54	02	01	37	38	37	12	93
93	29	12	18	27	30	30	55	91	87	50	57	58	51	49	36	12	53	96	40
45	04	77	97	36	14	99	45	52	95	69	85	03	83	51	87	85	56	22	37
44	91	99	49	89	39	94	60	48	49	06	77	64	72	59	26	08	51	25	57
16	23	91	02	19	96	47	59	89	65	27	84	30	92	63	37	26	24	23	66
04	50	65	04	65	65	82	42	70	51	55	04	61	47	88	83	99	34	82	37
32	70	17	72	03	61	66	26	24	71	22	77	88	33	17	78	08	92	73	49
03	64	59	07	42	95	81	39	06	41	20	81	92	34	51	90	39	08	21	42
62	49	00	90	67	86	93	48	31	83	19	07	67	68	49	03	27	47	52	03
61	00	95	86	98	36	14	03	48	88	51	07	33	40	06	86	33	76	68	57
89	03	90	49	28	74	21	04	09	96	60	45	22	03	52	80	01	79	33	81
01	72	33	85	52	40	60	07	06	71	89	27	14	29	55	24	85	79	31	96
27	56	49	79	34	34	32	22	60	53	91	17	33	26	44	70	93	14	99	70
49	05	74	48	10	55	35	25	24	28	20	22	35	66	66	34	26	35	91	23
49	74	37	25	97	26	33	94	42	23	01	28	59	58	92	69	03	66	73	82
20	26	22	43	88	08	19	85	08	12	47	65	65	63	56	07	97	85	56	79
48	87	77	96	43	39	76	93	08	79	22	18	54	55	93	75	97	26	90	77
08	72	87	46	75	73	00	11	27	07	05	20	30	85	22	21	04	67	19	13
95	97	98	62	17	27	31	42	64	71	46	22	32	75	19	32	20	99	94	85
37	99	57	31	70	40	46	55	46	12	24	32	36	74	69	20	72	10	95	93
05	79	58	37	85	33	75	18	88	71	23	44	54	28	00	48	96	23	66	45
55	85	63	42	00	79	91	22	29	01	41	39	51	40	36	65	26	11	78	32

Researchers usually discard the pilot data that they obtain before they begin the real, larger investigation. They don't save it to use in any final data analysis because they often have to adjust their data collection methods as a result of the things that they learn from the pilot study. This also means that the people who participate in the pilot cannot be asked to do so again in the full research project.

Practical tips for data collection

- Plan your data collection activity in a careful, practical way.
- Make sure that your questions are clear and easy to understand – test them out in a pilot study or have them vetted by your tutor.
- Prepare a clear but brief explanation of your research and how you'll protect respondents' confidentiality.
- Choose a suitable location and time when you can approach people with your questionnaire or observe them.
- Be polite if people decline to take part and do not take this as a personal rejection. A lot of people will decline to participate because they're busy, not interested or have other reasons for not helping. Accept this graciously and move on.
- Make sure that you have more than enough questionnaires or observation sheets with you – some always get spoiled or lost.
- If you're doing a group project, ensure that everyone is clear about their role and that they're all following the same procedures.

Assessment activity 3.2

Identifying possible data sources

1 Describe the likely sources of your research data. You should identify who or what the research population consists of, the key characteristics of the people or situations from whom you will obtain your data and the usefulness and appropriateness of the sources that you've selected.

2 Explain how you plan to actually obtain your research data. You should outline and justify the procedures and methods that you intend to use to obtain research data. Refer to sampling methods if you intend to use them.

3 Explain how you will try to ensure that your data are both reliable and valid.

4 Use at least one primary and one secondary source to obtain research data that will test your research hypothesis and/or research question.

Analysing your research data

Once you have obtained your research data, you will be well on the way to completing your research investigation. However, there is still quite a lot of work to be done. The first stage of this is to analyse, or make sense of, the data that you have obtained. This will take more time, and involve more effort, than you'll probably anticipate. Even so, it is essential that you prepare and analyse your data carefully.

It is likely that your research investigation will have produced both quantitative and qualitative data. Because of their differing characteristics, these forms of data need to be prepared and analysed in slightly different ways.

Quantitative data analysis

Quantitative data are numerical items of information. Quantitative data analysis usually involves collating and counting data response items and producing some simple statistics to make sense of the data set.

Two of the main types of statistics used by researchers who carry out small-scale investigations are descriptive and inferential statistics.

Descriptive statistics provide simple methods of describing aspects of the data set. For example, the **mean, median** and **mode** are all ways of describing **average** features of the data. **Inferential statistics,** by contrast, are methods of identifying relationships between aspects of the data. For example, that women who smoke are less likely to do regular exercise than women who don't.

Understanding the data

The type of statistics that can be generated from a data set depends on the type of quantitative data that have been obtained. This needs to be taken into account before data collection begins. The different kinds of data and their analysis possibilities are outlined below.

- **Nominal data** (category data) have no natural numerical properties. Instead they are given a number or 'code' to identify them. For example, biographical data about sex, ethnicity and place of birth can all be given numerical codes. These coded items can be categorised and counted to reveal their frequency in the data set.
- **Ordinal data** (ranking scales) are given numbers by the researcher to indicate an order or rank between them. For example, strongly agree=5, agree=4, no opinion=3, disagree=2, strongly disagree=1 are numerically ranked ordinal data items. Again, it is possible to produce frequencies and simple descriptive statistics from this kind of data.
- **Interval data** do have their own numerical qualities but there is no true zero in this kind of data. Whilst the starting and ending points of the numerical scale are arbitrary, the intervals between the points on the scale are measurable. For example, in a temperature scale it is possible to say that the distance between 10, 11 and 12 degrees is numerically the same. Interval data can be used to produce some basic descriptive statistics.
- **Ratio data** are natural measurements that do have a true zero. Age is an example of this kind of data item. For example, a person who is 20 years old is numerically twice as old as a child who is 10 years old. It is possible to produce a variety of statistics from this type of data.

The type of quantitative data generated in a research investigation will determine the extent to which statistics can be obtained from a data analysis. If the researcher asks questions that produce only nominal data all they can do is count up the responses and *report* them. The researcher would need to also produce some ordinal and, ideally, interval and ratio, data to generate more interesting statistics.

It is best to identify the kinds of data that will be produced by your data collection methods before using them.

Preparing quantitative data

Analysis of quantitative data usually involves some basic arithmetic. The preparation of quantitative data begins before any data has been collected. This is because all possible quantitative responses need to be numerically 'coded' in the data collection tool to allow for analysis later.

The main methods of collecting quantitative data in student research are through the use of questionnaires. Most student questionnaires have a mixture of 'open' and 'closed' questions. Possible responses to the closed questions need to be pre-coded. This is quite an easy thing to do. For example, imagine that you are conducting a questionnaire survey on teenager's attitudes to career choice. The first two questions request basic demographic information whereas the third and fourth questions seek data on factors affecting career choice:

Question		Code	Type of data
1 What sex are you?			
	Male	(1)	Nominal data
	Female	(2)	
2 How old are you? (Years only)			Ratio data
	15	(1)	
	16	(2)	
	17	(3)	
	18	(4)	
	19	(5)	
3 Choose *one* response that most clearly matches your view of the statement below:			
'A job that allows me to earn a high salary is more important to me than the kind of work the job involves.'			
I strongly agree		(1)	Ordinal data
I agree		(2)	
I neither agree or disagree		(3)	
I disagree		(4)	
I strongly disagree		(5)	
4 What factors will influence your choice of career?			

You will note that the first three questions are 'coded'. The possible answers have been given a code number in advance. When the researcher has collected all of the data, they will produce a table of coded responses. The following is an example of answers given by five respondents to the three questions above:

Question	1	2	3
Respondent 1	1	1	2
Respondent 2	2	4	1
Respondent 3	2	4	1
Respondent 4	1	3	3
Respondent 5	2	2	1

If you code all closed question and fixed response items in your questionnaire before you collect any data, you can just circle the response code that matches a respondent's answer as you go through the questions. When all of your data has been obtained you will need to enter the response codes into a coding sheet such as the one above. If you can do this on a computer spreadsheet (or transfer your data to one) such as Microsoft Excel, the programme will calculate a variety of simple statistics for you.

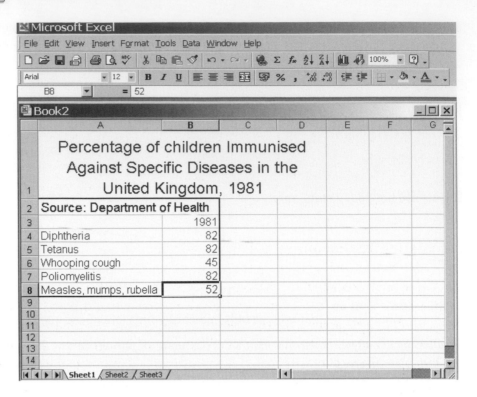

Figure 3.10 An Excel spreadsheet Screenshot reproduced with the permission of the Microsoft Corporation

Analysis methods

Data analysis begins with a preparation stage when the numerical data items that you've obtained are counted and collated. Typically this involves producing some frequency tables. From these it is possible to calculate descriptive measures such as the mean, median or mode. These statistics provide a summary of the pattern of information that can be found in a sample. The statistics do not say anything about whether the patterns in your data are likely to apply in, or can be generalised to, the population as a whole.

Producing a frequency distribution

A frequency distribution is a tally or count of how often (or frequently) certain data items occur within a data set. Frequency distributions give basic descriptive information about your data. To produce a frequency distribution, total up the number of times each type of response is given to a particular question or the number of times each type of observation has been made. The tallies can be used to produce a frequency table (see Figure 3.11), a bar chart or a pie chart.

Calculating a percentage is another way of working out the frequency with which a type of answer or response occurs. In the table below, percentages were calculated by dividing the total number of items (34) into each frequency. The result is expressed as a percentage. For example, 12 responses divided by the total of 34 is the equivalent of 35 per cent.

'Students should be paid generous grants'			
	Code	Frequency	%
Strongly agree	1	12	35
Agree	2	8	23.5
Neutral	3	5	15
Disagree	4	8	23.5
Strongly disagree	5	1	3
Total		34	100

Figure 3.11 A frequency table

Calculating the mean, median and mode

The mean, median and mode are all measures of 'central tendency'. The mean is the numerical value around which the data is centred. A researcher will calculate the mean of their data to get an idea of the average value. Researchers often collect data items that are not numerical but still want to know what the most common or midpoint items are. The mode, which is the most frequently occurring data item, can be used for this. Alternatively, the median will tell the researcher where the midpoint in the data set is. Figure 3.12 gives an example of these three descriptive statistics.

5, 6, 7, 7, 8, 8, 8, 9, 9, 25

Mean = 9.2
Median = 8
Mode = 8

Figure 3.12 Cups of coffee reportedly drunk by a group of 10 students over a two-day period

Presenting quantitative data graphically

The best way to present quantitative data in a research report is in the form of statistical graphs or charts. These present an easy to read visual summary of the main features of the data. The types of statistical graph that are most frequently used to present quantitative data are pie charts, bar charts, histograms and graphs.

Pie charts

These are used when the researcher has a number of related categories within their data, each with a single value. For example, data on the percentage of young people who use different types of drugs could be presented in the form of a pie chart.

Type of drug	Numbers (thousands)
Cannabis	28
Amphetamine	9
Ecstasy	4
Poppers	4
Magic mushrooms	4
Cocaine	1
LSD	2
Total	52

© *Source*: British Crime Survey

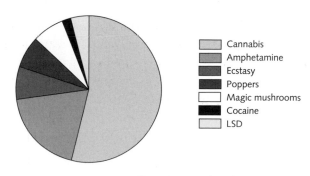

Cannabis
Amphetamine
Ecstasy
Poppers
Magic mushrooms
Cocaine
LSD

Figure 3.13 Pie chart showing numbers (thousands) of 16–19 year olds using selected drugs in 1998
© Crown copyright *Source*: Office of National Statistics

It is best to avoid using pie charts to present data summaries where there are too few (less than three) or too many (more than eight or nine) different categories within the data.

Bar charts

These are easy to calculate and provide an alternative to pie charts. They are especially useful when you have a lot of categories to display. The data can be presented in either percentage or 'raw' number form. Essentially, a bar chart is a kind of graph. You will need to construct and label the vertical axes carefully to ensure that the graphic makes sense to readers. The table below outlines the number of children who received support from Children and Family Services Teams in England during one week in February 2000. The bar chart indicates the different reasons why these children received social services support.

Category of need	Numbers receiving support
Abuse or neglect	79 740
Disability	30 310
Parental illness / disability	13 800
Family in acute distress	26 685
Family dysfunction	31 155
Socially unacceptable behaviour	14 045
Low income	14 195
Absent parenting	7 340
Cases other than CIN	12 065
Total	229 335

Source: Department of Health
© Crown copyright

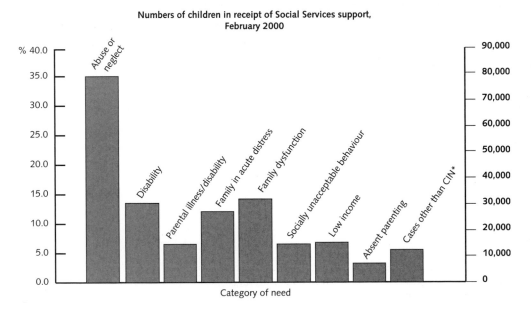

Figure 3.14 Bar chart showing the number of children receiving support from social services in one week in February 2000 by category of need
Source: Department of Health
© Crown copyright

Bar charts can also be used to show trends and make comparisons between different types of data category (see Figure 3.15 below), though you should be careful of including too many different categories in a chart as this will make it difficult to read.

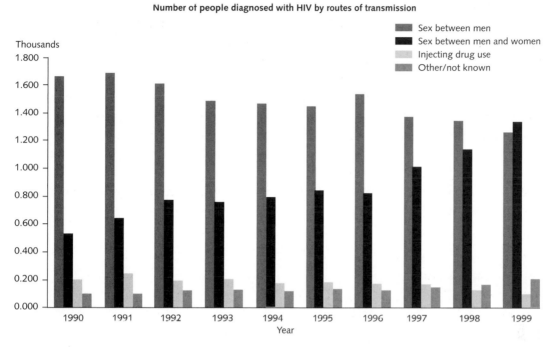

Figure 3.15 Bar chart showing numbers (thousands) of adults diagnosed with HIV in the UK by probable routes of transmission between 1990 and 1999
Source: Contents of graph from Public Health Laboratory Service

Histograms

A histogram is a graph that shows the frequency of values in a similar way to a bar chart. The difference is that the values are plotted (as on a graph) and a histogram can only be used with continuous data. The data need to be grouped into 'class intervals' (see Figure 3.16 below) where the number of items falling into each 'class' is identified. This means that a tally chart or frequency count needs to be produced before the histogram can be constructed.

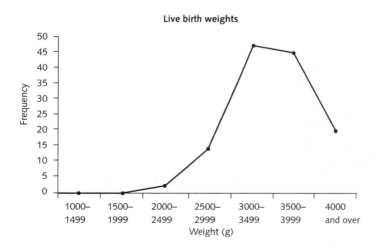

Source: Office for National Statistics
Figure 3.16 A frequency distribution to show live birth weights of babies
© Crown copyright

Weights (g)	Tally	Frequency
1000–1499		0
1500–1999		0
2000–2499	‖	2
2500–2999	‖‖ ‖‖ ‖‖‖	14
3000–3499	‖‖ ‖‖ ‖‖ ‖‖ ‖‖ ‖‖ ‖‖ ‖‖ ‖‖ ‖‖ ‖	47
3500–3999	‖‖ ‖‖ ‖‖ ‖‖ ‖‖ ‖‖ ‖‖ ‖‖ ‖‖	45
4000+	‖‖ ‖‖ ‖‖ ‖‖	20

Figure 3.17 Tally chart of live birth weights of babies born to a random sample of 128 women
Source: Office for National Statistics
© Crown copyright

Line graphs

Line graphs are the most common type of statistical graphic used to present research data. They are useful when the researcher has a lot of data that can be displayed in a chronological way. Figure 3.18 plots the trend in live births in the United Kingdom between 1961 and 1999.

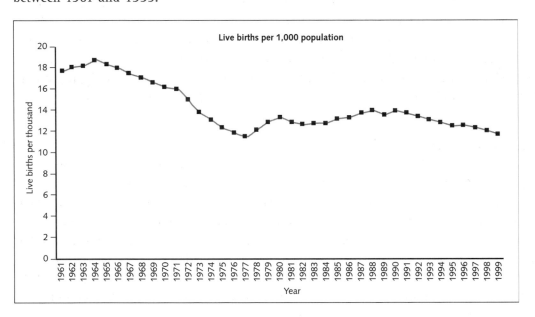

Figure 3.18 Line graph showing live births per 1,000 population from 1961 to 1999
Source: Office for National Statistics
© Crown copyright

It is possible to display several different lines of data on the same graph. For example, if we had the data to do it, it would be possible to display the trend in live births according to the ethnic origin of the baby or the baby's mother. This would allow the reader to visually compare data for several different ethnic groups. However, it is important to avoid having too many different lines on the one graph as this will make it messy to look at and hard to read.

Use and misuse of statistics

If you read that 72.3 per cent of statistics used in textbooks are based on lies and deception, you'd be right to feel suspicious. In fact, many feel suspicious about the kinds of 'truth' that statistics are often used to reveal. The attraction of statistics to researchers is that they're a very useful way of summarising and communicating complex data patterns. However, whilst a lot of researchers would insist that they use statistics only for this positive purpose, it is also the case that statistics can be created and presented for other, less positive purposes. For example, researchers and organisations have been known to present their data in a selective way – the way that suits their purpose or case – and in doing so ignore other evidence that doesn't help or support them.

Not everyone who misuses statistics does so deliberately. Some people make mistakes in their research investigations or use statistics inappropriately because they lack a clear understanding of what they're doing. For example, if you inadvertently selected an unrepresentative sample of people for a survey and then claimed that the statistical findings could be generalised to the population, you would be using the statistics in a misleading way. Inaccurately recording data would lead to a similar problem. Deliberately misinterpreting data to obtain a preferred outcome (one that supported a hypothesis, for example) or analysing or revealing only the part of the data that suits your purpose are more sinister and unethical ways of misusing statistics.

In order to use statistics appropriately, you need to be careful, thorough and honest when constructing quantitative data collection tools and when you are analysing the findings you get from using them. To avoid being misled by somebody else's use of statistics you should always ask questions about the basis on which the statistics have been compiled (who/what do they refer to? over what period of time? how big was the sample? how did they select participants? are there any obvious problems?) and remain sceptical about claims that are not clearly supported by the figures that you can see.

Qualitative data analysis

Qualitative data collection methods give the researcher less control over the type and range of data that will be collected than quantitative methods such as questionnaires. For example, researchers using in-depth interviews or observational methods can never be sure what respondents will say, how they will behave or what they might see. Qualitative data also generally consists of word or image-based information items rather than numbers. These factors can make qualitative data analysis more problematic than quantitative analysis. However, the key to this kind of data analysis is to apply the same principles as in quantitative analysis – prepare the data carefully, collate it and then apply your chosen analysis methods consistently.

Preparing qualitative data for analysis

Analysis of qualitative data is often a time-consuming process. Preparation of the data into a manageable form can take a long time. You may have different types of data to analyse. For example, you might have questionnaires with written answers to open questions. You might also have tape-recorded interviews to transcribe. This all needs to be reorganised.

The first step in qualitative data analysis is preparation. Where possible, the two tasks of coding and collating data should be followed. A difficulty when working with qualitative data is that the useful items of information are usually hidden in a much larger body of less useful (and sometime useless!) information.

Preparing written data responses

The first step in analysing qualitative data that consists of written responses is to make a copy of the original data. Keep your original data for reference. Use the new copy to do your analysis on. With written data it is best to collate the responses to each question. You might want to cut the relevant sections out of the copied questionnaires. After reading the responses several times, think about and identify the similarities between them. These similarities should allow you to group the responses into distinct categories. It's best to repeat this several times, looking for themes and patterns each time. When you have identified themes and patterns you will need to describe them, using direct quotes as examples wherever possible, in a discussion of your findings.

Preparing taped data

One of the strategies that researchers use to 'capture' data during interviews is to tape record a conversation. The researcher will get a word for word record of the interview but has to then write it all up. This is called **transcribing** and can be very time consuming. Researchers sometimes say that they learn a lot about their data by doing this. Others avoid transcribing whole conversations by re-playing their tapes and using the 'pause' button to allow them to transcribe the most interesting and useful sections. This is one way of beginning the process of coding data.

If you have conducted interviews on a specific topic with several people, or if you have observed a number of similar situations, there will probably be some similar patterns and themes in the data. These are the things that qualitative researchers look for during analysis. Generally they identify themes, name them and then allocate similar data items to their theme categories. This means that the researcher has to read through all of their data to assess the 'meaning' of each answer before deciding to allocate it to a category.

Presenting qualitative data

Quantitative data is quite easy to present in a graphical format because it is numerical. Qualitative data on the other hand needs a word-based style of presentation. Researchers usually present qualitative data in a written discussion. They use short verbatim quotes of what respondents said or wrote to provide evidence of typical or important responses and statements. These quotes are often used to clarify and illustrate the key themes and patterns in the data. Some researchers, depending on the nature of their study, include short case studies or brief descriptions of events and significant observations. In addition, qualitative researchers tend to also comment on the similarities and differences between respondents and on what was lacking from the data.

Qualitative research reports generally depend on a written discussions of findings but it is also possible to make use of other presentation methods, such as images, tape recordings, diagrams and flow charts, for example, if the data allows this. Whatever method is used the validity of the data should always be preserved.

Assessment activity 3.3

1 Prepare and collate your research data so that you can analyse the findings.
2 Use statistical skills (and other qualitative methods where appropriate) to interpret and describe the research data.
3 Produce appropriate statistical tables, charts and graphs to present your quantitative findings. Use an appropriate format to present your qualitative findings. You should also write a brief account of the reasons why you chose to use these particular data presentation methods.
4 Write a discussion of your research findings to show how they relate to the original hypothesis and/or research question.

Presenting research findings

The final stage of the research process is the presentation of findings. This typically involves producing a report of the research investigation and also, though not always, making a presentation of the study to other interested parties.

There are various ways of writing research reports. Professional and academic researchers tend to write up their research for publication in a specialist journal. As a result, they have to follow the writing and format guidelines set down by the journal. These can be quite specific, detailing the sections and word counts that the researcher must include. Similarly, researchers who are conducting investigations as part of a course of study (such as a BTEC or degree programme) will probably be given some guidance on the expected format and features of the final research report by their awarding body or academic institution.

Writing a research report

A research report should be written in a way that communicates clearly the *process* (what you did) and the *findings* (what you discovered) of the investigation. Research reports are usually divided into a number of sections. This is sometimes called the IMRD approach. These letters stand for Introduction, Methods, Results, and Discussion. These main stages of the research report allow the researcher to tell the 'story' of their investigation in an objective and informative way.

Whilst IMRD describes the key sections of a research report, most reports also contain a few other standard sections too. A standard research report structure is described below with some guidance on the content of each section.

Research report section	What does it contain?
Title	An informative and descriptive title of the investigation.
Abstract	A short summary (100–150 words) of the aims, methods and findings of the research investigation.
Introduction	A brief outline of the rationale for the investigation, a summary of the background literature and an explanation of the research questions or hypotheses. The aim is to put the research project into some kind of context.
Methods	A description of the data sources (population), data collection and analysis methods and procedures, and a discussion of the ethical issues associated with the research investigation.
Results	A description, using words, graphical images and statistics (where appropriate) of the findings. No analysis or comment should be made here.
Discussion and conclusions	A detailed analysis and discussion of the main patterns, features and possible ways of explaining the data results. All points made in the discussion should be supported by the data. Researchers typically provide a critical evaluation of the validity of their findings and the

	extent to which they provide answers to the research questions or support/refute the initial hypotheses. It's also a good idea to compare and contrast the findings with those of other similar studies and with existing theories.
Recommendations	Some researchers follow their discussion by recommending ways the research could be extended or modified to further improve knowledge and understanding of the research area.
References	This is a listing of the information sources (books, journals, websites) that were used in planning or conducting the investigation or which are referred to in the final report. The listing should be alphabetical and follow a standard referencing system so that the source can be traced (see below).
Appendices	Occasionally researchers will include additional materials, such as a copy of the questionnaire or interview questions, in an appendix at the end of the report. 'Raw' data is not usually included.

The final research report should be written in a clear style that assumes no specialist knowledge of your topic on the part of readers. The convention is to write the report in the third person and to avoid using first person 'I' statements ('I did this because...').The focus of the report should be on the topic and the data not on the researcher. It may be tempting to try and extend the report by padding out what you've got to say with further information, extensive background and pictures. You should avoid doing this, as 'padding' can be easily spotted and will detract from the quality of your report.

Don't worry if your hypothesis is not supported by your findings. In practice, this often happens. It's not a sign of 'bad' research. Resist all urges to falsify your results or to become less objective in your analysis if your hypothesis isn't supported by the data. The important thing is to conduct the research and analysis correctly so that you can identify whether your hypothesis is not supported by the data! You won't lose any marks for it if this situation occurs. You will lose marks if you falsify the data and therefore cheat!

Producing a bibliography

Checking that you have correctly referenced all of the books, articles and other data sources that you refer to in your report is an important part of the writing up process. If you kept a record of the sources that you used during your background information search, referencing should be straightforward. If you didn't, you will need to find the details of all of the sources you've used before you can complete the report.

Referencing your research

Academic and professional researchers use a number of referencing systems. Often the organisation publishing, commissioning or supervising the research will specify the referencing system that they want the researcher to use. Where a system isn't specified, the researcher has to simply choose one and then use it correctly and consistently. The **Harvard** and the **Vancouver systems** are referencing systems that are commonly used in research publications.

Under the Harvard system

- references are cited in the main text of the report by including the author's surname followed by the year of publication in brackets. For example, Foley (2002)
- where there are two authors included in the text as, surname and surname (year). For example, Millar and Millar (2000)
- where there are more than two authors include as, first author surname *et al.* For example, Seymour *et al* (2000)
- direct quotations must be in quotation marks followed by author surname and year and page number of reference (in brackets). For example, 'representativeness refers to the question of whether the group or situation being studied are typical of others.' (Griffiths, 1997)
- references are listed in alphabetical order at the end of the text in the same way as on page 117.

A journal example using the Harvard system is: Parker, T (1999) Psychiatric patients in hospital: do they receive enough money from benefits? *Nursing Times* 99 (16) 38–39. A book example using the Harvard system is: Parker, T & Webber, R (1983) *Recovery from Mania* Oxford: Basic Books.

Under the Vancouver system

- references are numbered (number in brackets) consecutively through the text
- each reference is then listed in numerical order at the end of the text
- journals are assigned standard abbreviations from 'Index Medicus', the American National Library of Medicine's catalogue of terms and abbreviations.

A journal example of a Vancouver reference is: Parker T. Psychiatric patients in hospital: do they receive enough money from benefits? *Nursing Times* 1999 Apr 17–23; 102 (16): 38–39.

A book reference example using the Vancouver system is: Parker T, Webber R. *Recovery from Mania.* Oxford: Basic Books, 1993

Assessment activity 3.4

1 Collect together and read through all of the work that you have produced for your research investigation.

2 Reorganise the material that you've produced so that it fits into an appropriate research report structure. You may have to rewrite some parts of your work whilst other parts may slot directly into the report structure.

3 Complete your report by ensuring that it is referenced using a standard referencing system.

Assessment activity 3.5

1 Evaluate your experience of conducting a research investigation. You should comment on your experience of trying to follow a research process, any problems or difficulties that you encountered and say how you overcame or adapted to them.

2 How valid are your research findings? Explain what they tell you and identify their limitations.

3 With the benefit of hindsight, draw some conclusions about the effectiveness of your research and suggest how the investigation could be changed in order to improve it.

End-of-unit test

1   Describe the key characteristics of a research investigation.
2   Explain why researchers should follow a research process during their research investigations.
3   Outline three ways in which research can contribute to the work of care practitioners.
4   Explain the differences between:
    a Quantitative and qualitative research
    b Primary and secondary data
    c Inductive and deductive approaches.
5   Why do researchers carry out literature reviews?
6   Describe what researchers do when they 'operationalise' their concepts and variables.
7   Identify four different data collection methods commonly used in care research.
8   Outline the main reasons why medical and scientific researchers commonly use experiments in their research investigations.
9   Explain why researchers should follow standard ethical codes of practice when carrying out their research studies.
10   Explain the meaning of the terms:
    a Validity
    b Reliability
    c Sampling.
11   Explain why researchers often try to obtain research samples that are representative of their general population.
12   What do the mean, median and mode statistics reveal about a set of data?
13   Explain the purpose of the abstract section of a written research report.
14   Name two different referencing systems that are commonly used by researchers when writing their research reports.

References and further reading

Gillham, W. (2000) *Developing a Questionnaire*, London: Continuum

Langley, P. (1993) *Doing Social Research*, Ormskirk: Causeway

Walsh, M. (2000) *Research Made Real*, Cheltenham: Nelson Thornes

Applying sociology

The chapter will increase your understanding of social, economic and political arrangements in British society. We will consider the role of the individual and the family within society, the inequalities that exist in modern day British society and the demographic structure and patterns of social change that are apparent. When working with individuals, it is important that carers develop an awareness of, and respect for, the variety of human experiences in society. The chapter will help you to explore the range of factors that can affect quality of life and the extent to which individuals can access care service provision.

What you need to learn

- Theoretical approaches used in sociology
- Sociology and the role and significance of the family
- Social stratification in British society
- Demographic trends and social change

Theoretical approaches used in sociology

What is sociology?

Auguste Compte first used the term 'sociology' in 1838 to describe what he called 'the science of the associated life of humanity'. In twenty-first century language, he might have said that sociology is a subject that involves the study of social arrangements and their effects on people's lives. Sociologists refer to these social arrangements as **social institutions**. All societies are based around social institutions such as the family, education services and law and order systems. Sociologists study the ways that social institutions like the family work. They carry out research to investigate the main factors that cause social institutions to change and develop, and also explore and describe the impact that current social institutions have on different social groups in the population.

Sociology, like social care, is really about people. Studying sociology involves exploring and trying to understand:

- different types of social 'world' that people live in
- different ways in which people make sense of and give meaning to their social experiences
- problems that result from the way society is currently organised
- possible ways of improving social arrangements to overcome these problems.

Britain is a multicultural place

Sociology and social care

Sociology is a subject that is now a part of all social care and welfare training courses. A significant feature of social care work is that it involves helping and supporting people who are experiencing some difficulty in living their lives independently. Social care professionals need a good understanding of the ways in which society is organised, how social institutions work and where their service users fit into all this so that they can offer them appropriate help and support. Whilst sociology, as a subject, is based on a lot of theories and research investigations, the task of a social care professional is to find ways of using and applying sociology to best understand and help the people they work with.

One of the distinctive features of sociology as a subject is that it includes a number of different kinds of sociological perspectives. These are simply ways of seeing society. Sociology is also distinctive in the way that it is based on a range of fundamental concepts or 'building-blocks'. An understanding of basic concepts such as **culture**, **socialisation** and **social class**, for example, is necessary before you can begin applying sociology to the lives and problems of social care service users. We will consider a range of the building-block concepts used in sociology throughout the chapter, showing how they can be used to make sense of society and the situations that people experience.

Sociological perspectives

There is a wide range of different ways of looking at society. Sociologists refer to these ways of viewing a society's institutions, practices and general social arrangements as **sociological perspectives**. Before we consider the major sociological perspectives, it is important to explain two other features of sociology which make it a distinctive subject and which will also help you to understand why these different, competing perspectives exist.

'Debunking' common-sense and nature

One of the enjoyable features of sociology is that using sociological perspectives, and developing what is more broadly called a **sociological imagination,** allows you to think critically and question ideas, explanations and commonly held assumptions about the social world we live in. This can be very irritating to people who have a vested interest in maintaining the status quo (the way things are) in society but is potentially helpful and liberating for those people who would like their lives to improve and things to be different.

Sociological perspectives tend to question both the idea of 'common sense' and also the types of common sense that are used to explain social relationships, social institutions and the structure of society as being somehow inevitable and natural.

Sociological perspectives question the 'truth' behind everyday, uncritical ways of understanding the social world. Often, they seem to expose taken for granted assumptions as false. Common-sense explanations tend to be based on an individual's limited personal experience and learnt cultural beliefs that are often myths. Typically, people don't question, or think critically about, their daily life or the nature of the social institutions that are part of their lives. 'Common sense' suggests, for example, that manual labourers tend to have poorer health, and on average live shorter lives, than qualified medical practitioners, primarily because they live less healthy lives and don't look after themselves as well. Sociologists would use both research evidence and more critical sociological perspectives to contest and 'debunk' this as a common-sense myth. In fact, sociological evidence suggests that a person's social class rather than their lifestyle has a greater influence on health experience and life chances.

Similarly, sociologists who study and try to explain features of social behaviour use research and critical perspectives to debunk the idea that certain kinds of social behaviour and social relationships occur because they are biologically 'natural'. One of the main obstacles that women had to overcome in their campaign for equality of opportunity in education and work, was the myth that a woman's 'natural' role is that of housewife and mother. For many decades this cultural myth acted as a barrier to equality of opportunity. Sociologists, particularly those using **feminist perspectives,** have contested the idea that men and women have 'natural' roles in life that are the result of their different biological characteristics. Sociological concepts, such as socialisation, **gender** and **power,** can now be used to explain how individuals learn to behave and relate to others in 'gendered' ways. The significance of inborn biological differences between men and women has been so widely contested since the 1960s, when feminism became a powerful sociological perspective, that most people now accept that male and female members of society should enjoy equality of opportunity.

A 1950s stereotypical image of a mother and housewife

Think It Over

Complete the table below with examples of common-sense or natural and sociological explanations for each of the social facts.

Social fact	Common-sense or natural explanation	Sociological explanation
A woman is more likely than her male partner to do the housework and the cooking at home, even if they both have full-time jobs.	Biologically, this is more of a natural role for a woman than for a man.	
Black people are more likely than white people to experience unfair discrimination in work and education situations.		British society tolerates a degree of racism at a personal, institutional and societal level.
People over the age of 75 are more likely to commit suicide than any other age group in the population.	Old people have nothing to live for and can't cope with worsening health problems.	

Which sociological perspective is best?

A sociological perspective is simply a way of looking at and understanding society. There are a variety of different ways of looking at and thinking about the structure and processes of society. However, sociologists tend to suggest (usually implicitly but sometimes explicitly) that the perspective they use provides the *best* way of gaining a clear and truthful understanding of society. The result of this is that sociologists and others who use sociological perspectives tend to 'contest', or argue about, the validity of each other's way of understanding social phenomena. Arguments about how society *really* works and how it *ought* to be changed are a constant, common feature of sociological debate. Nevertheless, it's probably best to accept that different perspectives can be used to analyse and understand the same social phenomena in equally valid ways.

Who is Mr or Mrs Normal?

It is likely that after studying and using different sociological perspectives for a while, you'll develop an affinity or liking for one or more of them at the expense of others. However, you should be careful of becoming blindly committed to one perspective on the grounds that it *really* does offer an answer to every sociological issue or problem. This is never the case. Instead you should try to retain a sceptical and critical view by considering what each of the available perspectives has to offer when they're used to analyse particular issues or social phenomena. It appears that different perspectives tend to focus on, and offer useful insights into, different features of society.

The various sociological perspectives that exist adopt one of two different approaches to social phenomena. That is, perspectives focus on either the structural aspects of society or on the social actions of groups or individuals in society.

Structural approaches

Structural approaches try to identify the ways that society is structured. They focus on the social institutions (such as the family and care services) that are part of this structure and which are seen to influence individuals' social experiences.

Functionalism

This perspective is also sometimes called **structural functionalism**. Its main argument is that society is organised around several vital social institutions that have an important function for society. Taken together these social institutions provide a structure that we think of as 'society'. A commonly used functionalist analogy is that society is organised, and functions, like a human body. The social institutions are the 'organs' of society and all must work well together if society is going to be 'healthy' and avoid being dysfunctional.

Functionalists argue that society, like the human body, has certain needs, which they call 'prerequisites', which have to be met for it to survive. For example, people have to be socialised into the culture of society, they must develop knowledge and skills for work and they must remain healthy to be economically productive. This is why we have social institutions like the family, schools and care services. Their function is to ensure that society's **functional prerequisites** are met. Sociologists who use a functionalist perspective argue that when social institutions are working well, there will be **social cohesion** or stability and productivity in society.

Marxism

This political and sociological perspective was developed from the work of Karl Marx. The Marxist perspective questions the functionalist idea that modern capitalist society is based on consensus (agreement) between the various social groups in society and harmony between social institutions. Instead, Marxists argue that society is really based on the distribution of economic power and wealth. Marxists believe that there are basically two social classes in capitalist societies, such as that of Britain. These consist of the **bourgeoisie** (wealthy people) who own the 'means of production', and the **proletariat** (working class) who sell their labour to the owners of the means of production for wages. Marxists believe that the capitalist bourgeois class exploit the proletariat and wield both economic and cultural power over them. This leads to a society that is characterised by antagonism and 'class conflict'.

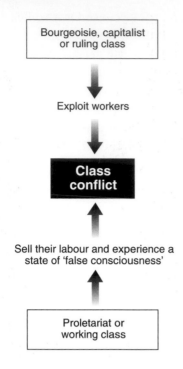

Figure 4.1 Marxist view of a capitalist society

Sociologists who use a Marxist perspective argue that the interests of the bourgeoisie are pursued at the expense of the proletariat, and vice versa. Marx himself argued that the bourgeoisie partly controlled society by developing and enforcing what he called a **ruling ideology**. This is a 'package of ideas' that protects and approves the interests of the bourgeoisie. For example, the belief that everyone could achieve success by working hard, that wealth is the best measure of success and that business owners and 'bosses' are morally entitled to keep profits for themselves are all, arguably, part of the ruling ideology in capitalist societies.

Marxist sociologists argue that by accepting a 'ruling ideology' the proletariat don't act in their own best interests and are oppressed by a **'false consciousness'**. According to Marxism, a revolutionary reaction and a communist system of state-controlled services would produce a better society that worked in the interests of everybody rather than for a privileged, powerful bourgeois minority. For Marxists, society functions to keep the bourgeoisie in power and the proletariat in a subservient position. Society is organised to ensure that this relationship continues and that class conflict is minimised.

Both the functionalist and the Marxist perspectives focus on the structure of society and the ways in which it influences, or determines, the identity and social experiences of the individual. As a result, both of these perspectives view the individual as relatively powerless to influence their destiny and life chances. An alternative to this type of structural approach is the social action or interpretative approach to understanding society.

Social action or interpretative perspectives

The social action approach focuses on the experiences, social behaviour and everyday lives of individuals and groups in society rather than on the way that society is structured. For example, sociologists who use social action perspectives believe that it's better to look at the micro-level behaviours of people and the social processes that occur in care settings (the 'sick role', doctor-patient relationships, **labelling** processes) rather than at the macro-level structures and social trends that occur at a more abstract societal level.

The social action approach is based on the idea that people are relatively free to influence their social experiences and life chances and play an important part in constructing the social institutions that are a feature of everyday life. This means that macro-level social forces (like social class) are seen as less powerful and deterministic than in the structural approach. According to social action theorists, people have more power and influence to shape their own lives and destiny than structural perspectives suggest.

Interactionist approaches argue that people create or construct their social experiences through the cultural meanings that they develop and apply in different social situations. Therefore, individual behaviours and the way of life of different groups in society need to be explored and understood in terms of the specific cultural meanings that group members attribute to them. This sociological point is important for social care workers who are required to work with a culturally diverse range of people. In a culturally diverse society, a service user's problems or difficulties can only be understood by appreciating their cultural perspective and way of life. A social care worker who is not culturally sensitive and assumes that everyone views and experiences life in the same way will fail to identify why a person has problems and what can be done (appropriately) to help them overcome their difficulties.

Figure 4.2 Are people controlled by social forces? Or do we pull the strings in our own lives?

Social interactionism

The most prominent sociological perspective that adopts a social action approach to the social world is symbolic interactionism. This perspective focuses on understanding the meaning and processes that occur in face-to-face social interactions. One of the main areas in which this perspective has contributed to social understanding is labelling of behaviour. The interactionist approach has enabled sociologists to study and theorise about the ways that people come to be classified (and then behave) in particular ways in care and criminal justice settings.

Contemporary standpoint perspectives

Feminism, anti-racism, New Right politics and environmentalism are more recent 'ways of seeing' society and understanding social processes. These new approaches are known as standpoint perspectives. They are the viewpoints of specific social, political or sub-cultural groups who feel that their experiences are not recognised or represented by sociologists who use the more traditional structural or action perspectives. A key argument of the standpoint perspectives is that the more established sociological perspectives haven't recognised the significance of social and cultural diversity and change in British society, and falsely assume that their general sociological analyses and claims can be applied to all social groups.

Feminist perspectives

A variety of different feminist perspectives have been developed to analyse and account for women's experiences of society. **Marxist feminists** use the basic conflict model of Marxism to explain how women are exploited both in terms of social class and as women in a male-dominated society. This feminist perspective offers a structural, conflict viewpoint of society (see page 121). **Radical feminists** view society primarily in terms of the conflict of interests and fundamental differences in power between men and women in society. The main argument of this approach is that society is **patriarchal** and works to ensure that male dominance is perpetuated at the expense of women. Finally, **liberal feminists** are concerned with achieving equality of opportunity in the society that we have rather than in overturning the current social system. They identify sexual discrimination as a major barrier to women's equality and try to change social processes and relationships to counteract this.

Anti-racist perspectives

These perspectives understand and explain society from the perspective of minority ethnic groups. The key argument is that society is racially structured and works to protect the interests of the dominant white majority at the cost of minority ethnic groups. As such, anti-racist perspectives see racial discrimination at individual, institutional and societal levels as playing a powerful role in determining the life chances and experiences of non-white individuals and social groups. The policy goal of anti-racist sociologists is to challenge and change social processes and relationships that are based on racial discrimination.

The New Right perspective

This way of viewing society is more of a political philosophy than a sociological perspective. In this sense it is associated with branches of Conservative political thinking (especially Thatcherism) and the Republican Party in the USA. The New Right perspective has been most influential when used by politicians to suggest how society ought to be run rather than as a way of explaining social processes or of understanding social structure.

Users of the New Right perspective argue that governments should avoid regulating individuals' lives and should promote, or at least allow, individual freedom and liberty. New Right thinkers argue that the 'free market' will produce better solutions to social problems than government intervention. Individual responsibility and personal choice are seen as preferable to a state-controlled welfare system that is seen to be ineffective and the cause of 'welfare dependency'.

The New Right perspective implicitly makes judgements about the 'types' of people there are in society. For example, it makes a distinction between those who 'deserve' welfare because they are in poverty or experiencing problems through no fault of their own and 'undeserving' people who 'waste' their abilities and settle for a life on welfare rather than make a personal effort to better themselves. This way of viewing society assumes that everybody can succeed if they want to, that society is 'naturally' structured to allow the 'best', the 'winners', to rise to the top and the 'worst', the less able and the 'losers' in life to sink to the bottom of the social hierarchy. This conception of society is widely disputed and rejected by most sociologists. The main criticism of such an account is that it uncritically accepts and legitimates the way things are in an unequal society. Many sociologists would argue that the New Right approach fails to consider how cultural, political and economic barriers restrict the lives of marginalised, less powerful groups other than to say that people in these groups are somehow inferior and life's 'natural' losers.

Environmentalist perspectives

Environmentalism is an approach to understanding society that has grown in significance since it first emerged in the 1970s. In the same way as feminism, anti-racism and New Right approaches, environmentalism falls outside of the traditional scope of sociological perspectives. However, so-called 'Green' thinking and politics that argue for a better, sustainable balance between people and the natural environment frequently have a 'social responsibility' element to them.

Environmentalism has had only an indirect effect on the way that we understand society. Essentially, politicians and social policy-makers now consider environmental needs, and the environmental impact of their policies on local areas and communities, alongside more traditional social, cultural and economic factors. Environmental perspectives do not claim to describe the structure of society or social processes in new enlightening ways; rather, they are more significant in alerting sociologists to the impact of industrial and population development on the broader physical environment in which 'society' is located.

Sociological concepts

We said earlier that sociologists use various concepts and perspectives to 'debunk' both common-sense and natural explanations of social phenomena. Sociologists use concepts such as socialisation, culture and **social control**, for example, to answer basic sociological questions such as:

- How do people become members of society?
- What factors enable people to live together and create a distinct, recognisable society?
- Why do people generally co-operate and support each other in modern society?

Socialisation

The first question concerns the relationship between the individual (the 'self') and broader society. When a baby is born it is relatively helpless and is more of a biological entity than a 'person' in the sense of having a developed personality, relationships with others or the interpersonal skills needed to live in modern society. An important question that sociologists have addressed is how does this baby become a socially and culturally sophisticated adult? The sociological answer is that we are all the products of a lifelong socialisation process.

Essentially, socialisation involves learning the culture and values of the society in which you live. Sociologists argue that every society has a socialisation process to achieve this purpose. In Britain, and all modern Western societies, the family carries out **primary socialisation**. This involves ensuring that children learn and internalise the culture, values and the expected standards of behaviour of the society in which they live. Primary socialisation processes shape each person's personality and behaviour and quickly turn every 'biological baby' into a socially competent member of society.

Sit up straight Amina

Figure 4.3 Babies learn from their carers

Secondary socialisation involves the individual learning how social rules and ways of behaving apply outside of their immediate family. Secondary socialisation is carried out through school and workplace experiences and via the mass media. It is a continuous, ongoing process in which a person learns more about general social values and also develops an understanding of the differing social rules and ways of relating to others that apply in specific settings such as the school classroom, the office or a care setting.

Figure 4.4 Secondary socialisation might start at school

Culture

Sociologists generally use the term culture to refer to the beliefs and behaviour guidelines that exist in any society. Culture is learnt, or transmitted, from one generation to another, through the process of socialisation. The concept of culture is often used very broadly by sociologists to include the language, **values** and **norms**, the customs, forms of dress, type of diet, the **social roles** and the knowledge and skills that are part of the way of life of a given society. Most people will view their own culture as natural and 'normal' and will often not be aware that their beliefs and behaviours are culturally determined. People become more aware of the ways in which they implicitly use culture to make sense of everyday life when they encounter another culture (on holiday, for example) or when they observe people who are unfamiliar with the subtle social norms and rules that apply in mainstream British society.

Figure 4.5 What is the social norm?

It is important to note that cultures change over time and that there is a range of cultural difference within diverse, multicultural countries like the United Kingdom. Cultural variations tend to occur when a society is ethnically and religiously diverse. Members of different ethnic groups tend to develop and apply social values and norms of behaviour that are partly inherited from their cultural forefathers and partly from the mainstream society in which they live. In this way culture helps people to make sense of, or give meaning to, their everyday surroundings, social situation and heritage.

Social control

This concept refers to the various methods that are used to persuade or force people to conform to the dominant social norms and values of a society. Methods of social control prevent high levels of **deviance** (and therefore encourage conformity) in a society and can be used to punish those who challenge established norms and values.

Social control can be applied formally or informally. **Formal social control** takes the form of laws, official rules and other legally sanctioned punishments. **Informal social control**, on the other hand, takes the more subtle forms of peer pressure, public opinion and the withdrawing of love or approval by people we respect and care for. Social control is achieved by rewarding people with positive sanctions (for example praise, sweets or money) for appropriate or socially desired behaviour, and by punishing them with negative sanctions (such as disapproval, 'being grounded' or a ban) for behaviour that is socially unacceptable.

Sociologists use the concept of social control to identify and explain how social rules are used to encourage people to conform to the social expectations of the society in which they live. Social control can't be achieved without effective socialisation. People must first learn the appropriate ways of behaving in society (how to conform) before formal and informal social control methods can be used to maintain their conformity.

A wide variety of social institutions apply methods of social control in society. The family, schools, peer groups, the mass media and our workplace relationships all have an impact on how we behave and the extent to which people conform or break social expectations and 'boundaries'.

Theory into practice

Social control can be achieved through the use of various sanctions that reward or discourage a person's behaviour. Reorganise the following list of negative sanctions into two separate columns that distinguish between 'formal' and 'informal' negative sanctions that people use in school and work situations.

Ridicule	Fines
Arguments	Jokes
Gossip	Corporal punishment
Dismissal from work	Written warnings
Being ostracised ('sent to Coventry')	Disciplinary hearings

Methods of research and social investigation

The concepts that sociologists use to understand society play an important part in the research investigations that they undertake. Researchers use sociological perspectives and concepts to try and gain an evidence-based or **empirical** understanding of the social world. This involves testing out theoretical ideas and concepts in real social settings.

Sociologists study a huge range of different social phenomena. Despite this, sociologists typically carry out their investigations to either describe a social phenomenon or to explain how or why society works in a particular way.

Descriptive research

Descriptive research investigations aim to discover the 'facts' about society. Sociologists who carry out descriptive studies tend to ask 'what' or 'how many' questions. For example, 'What function does the family perform?', 'What types of family exist in modern Britain?' and 'How many women are employed in managerial posts in social services departments?' are all questions that could guide a piece of descriptive research. This type of sociological research provides 'snapshots' of the ways that society works or is structured. However, it doesn't explain why things are the way they are.

Explanatory research

Explanatory research, on the other hand, aims to find the causes of particular forms of behaviour or the reasons for particular social phenomena (such as high death rates in certain social groups). Explanatory researchers tend to ask 'why' and 'how' questions because they are looking for causes. A sociologist conducting this type of research will generally begin with a theory that they wish to test. The theory that the researcher starts with is usually a tentative answer (an example hypothesis – 'if X happens, then I think Y will follow') that is tested out in a research situation. This is known as a deductive or 'scientific' approach to research investigation.

However, deductive methods are not the only way of approaching sociological research. A second strategy involves using an **inductive** approach. This is often used to conduct a descriptive study and doesn't involve using a theory (the hypothesis or tentative answer) as a starting point. For example, sociologists who carry out **ethnographic research** tend to begin by immersing themselves in a research setting or by joining a social group whom they wish to study (see page 80 for further details). The inductive researcher then becomes surrounded by 'data' and gradually tries to make sense out of it. Their findings tend to be descriptive rather than explanatory.

Types of research data

The 'data' that sociological researchers collect can be **quantitative** or **qualitative**. Quantitative data are based on numerical items of information whilst qualitative data are non-numerical and can be much more diverse. Different data collection methods tend to be used to produce these different types of data.

Primary data collection method	Quantitative data	Qualitative data
Participant observation		✓
Direct observation	✓	✓
Experiments	✓	
Interviews		✓
Questionnaires	✓	✓
Case study		✓
Content analysis	✓	✓

Think It Over

Why do you think that sociologists tend to avoid using experiments to carry out research into social problems or the lives of care service users? Discuss possible reasons with a class colleague.

Primary data are items of information that have been collected directly by the researcher. **Secondary data** are items of information that have originally been collected, and (usually) processed by, other researchers but which the researcher reuses or revisits in their own investigation.

Sociological research investigations are carried out by professional and academic sociologists and by a range of professionals who wish to understand and develop their knowledge of the ways that society works or has an impact on their lives. There is now a huge body of sociological research on which to draw, and more is always being carried out to try and keep up with the changing nature of society. The main methods of carrying out a social research investigation are described in more detail between page 98 and page 113 in Unit 3.

Assessment activity 4.1

Research into the structure and functioning of society or the impact of social problems can be useful to social care practitioners who often need this kind of background research to help them in their work with individuals and families. In this activity you're asked to outline a possible research project that is concerned with investigating a social care issue.

1 Identify a topic area linked to social care that you believe would be interesting and useful to investigate.
2 Clearly describe how the topic could be approached using three different sociological perspectives or theories. You should explain how the topic could be understood using each perspective, and should critically evaluate what each perspective or theory offers, before arriving at a conclusion about which perspective or theory you would choose to adopt in your investigation.
3 Identify appropriate research methods and explain how you would use them to investigate your chosen topic.

Sociology and the role and significance of the family

The family is an important focus of sociological investigation. Many sociologists identify the family as the 'building block' of society and claim that it exists, in some form, in all known societies. Sociologists have tended to ask a range of questions about the family, including:

- What is 'a family'?
- Why do families exist?
- What differing forms of 'family' exist in modern society?
- What kinds of roles and relationships are there within modern families?
- Have roles and relationships within families changed in recent times?
- Is the family becoming a less stable social institution?

Traditional extended family

Traditional nuclear family

Step-parent family

Reconstituted family

Lone-parent family

Cohabiting family

Same-sex family

Figure 4.6 The word 'family' can cover a vast spectrum of meanings

Some of these questions appear relatively straightforward and easy to answer. For example, you might think that a description of the way that your own family is organised, and the types of relationship that exist within it, would provide an answer to the question 'what is a family?' However, as we've mentioned earlier, sociologists who use research methods to investigate relatively large sections of the population would say that this is an inadequate answer. They would argue that an answer based only on personal experience fails to acknowledge or describe the diversity of family structures that currently exist within modern British society. A sociological answer to the question 'what is a family?' must go beyond our own everyday, personal experience and respond to the question in a broader, objective and evidence-based way.

The range and cultural diversity of family structures

A key point about the characteristics of the modern family is that there are now many forms of 'family' in Britain. The stereotypical notion of a married mum and dad and 2.4 children is a myth. Very few people live in this so-called 'typical family' (see Figure 4.7) Despite this, most people do live within some form of family structure.

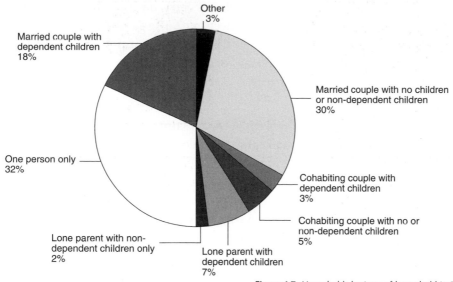

Figure 4.7 Households by type of household in Britain (2000)
© Crown copyright

Think It Over

What do these statistics reveal about the current forms of family structure and the patterns of change that have occurred?

One of the main reasons for the existence of a range of family types is that Britain is now a multicultural society. However, this is not the only reason for family diversity. Social change is another important factor. British society is continually changing and evolving. Social change has had a significant impact on personal relationships, family structures and roles within the family over the last fifty years. For example, some of the consequences of changes in women's roles and in attitudes to marriage and divorce can be seen in the growth of **lone-parent** and **reconstructed families**. We will consider these changes and the new forms of family that result from them later in the chapter.

Why do families exist?

We have said that the family is a very important social group in most cultures and societies. A strategy used by some sociologists, when trying to understand how a society works, is to ask what function the different parts (institutions) of the society perform. Sociologists argue that the modern family performs a number of functions.

Economic function

Firstly, the family has an important **economic function**. Most present-day families are units of consumption rather than units of production. However, before nineteenth century industrialisation many **extended families** worked together as agricultural producers. At the beginning of the twenty-first century this is rarely the case. Some farmers and small-business owners, such as shopkeepers, still rely on family members working together for their income. However, the economic function of the majority of contemporary families is that of consumers of goods and services.

Protection and child rearing

Protection and child rearing is a second important function of the modern family. Most people are born into and grow up in some form of 'family'. Families are expected to provide protection for and to socialise children whilst they are still dependent on their parents for help and care. If the family didn't carry out this function for the individual, how would society ensure that it occurred? The family is seen as, and is now expected to be, the best environment in which children can develop socially and emotionally and learn the culture or 'rules of behaviour' expected of independent adults in wider society.

Social control

A third feature of the family's role involves its **social control function**. Family relationships always involve formal and informal 'rules of behaviour'. These are the limits on behaviour that every family imposes on its members. Primary socialisation establishes this moral framework, building up each individual's conscience, thereby ensuring that people generally behave in socially acceptable ways. The responsibility of the family for ensuring that members behave appropriately is also formally reinforced through a number of laws that make parents legally responsible for their children's behaviour. Laws such as the Children Act 1989 and the Education Act 1944 allow the courts to impose sanctions on parents where they fail to supervise or control their children's behaviour.

Political function

Historically, the family has also performed an important **political function**, acting as a channel of social power and prestige. This was particularly important in **feudal** and patriarchal societies where a person's position was largely determined by the status of the family into which they were born. Whilst this situation is now possibly limited to the British Royal family and a very small number of landowning and financially powerful families, a person's family background still plays some part in determining their access to social influence and wealth.

Care and companionship function

In contrast to the ways that the economic production role of families has declined since the beginning of the twentieth century, the care and companionship function of the family has grown. Families now provide a close, relatively private emotional and social sphere where adults and children spend most of their time. Both adults and children are now likely to spend the majority of their non-working leisure time with other family members, whether this is in the context of family trips and holidays or just time spent being at home with each other.

Using these functionalist arguments, it could be said that the family exists because it performs important functions for the individual in society and for society as a whole. The family, as a social institution, has been adapted to meet the changing economic, social control, political, child-rearing and companionship needs of modern industrialised, capitalist society. It's important to note that it follows from this argument that the functions of, and relationships within, 'the family' will inevitably develop and change in the future as society continues to evolve.

What is 'a family'?

Sociologists have made the point that definitions of 'the family' are not usually broad enough to cover all types of modern family. Social and cultural diversity means that any notion of *the* family is a stereotypical myth.

Whilst most people do have a sense of what 'a family' involves in their particular society, it is important to note that these ideas are historically and culturally specific.

For example, at this point in history and in multicultural Britain, children appear to play a core part in our ideas about 'family'. If a person or a couple, whether they are married or not, are childless they are not commonly thought of, or referred to, as 'a family'. The number of parents doesn't seem to affect the definition. 'A family' exists, officially and informally, if there are children who live with a lone parent. The children don't have to be the biological offspring of either parent to be thought of as being part of 'a family'. Adopted children may live with two adults who are their non-biological parents. It is also becoming more common for children to live in so-called **reconstructed families** where one of their biological parents has remarried or cohabits with a new partner who is not the child's biological parent.

Though sociologists do have some difficulty in arriving at a precise and clear definition of what 'a family' involves, they use a number of terms to describe differing types of family structure.

Nuclear and extended families

The family structure that involves a man and woman and one or more dependent children, living as a distinct household unit, is referred to as a **nuclear family**. This form of family organisation is usually contrasted with the extended family. An **extended family** is basically a nuclear family with additional relatives living in the same household. The nuclear family is now a more prevalent form of family structure than the extended family.

A number of socio-economic and cultural factors influenced the emergence of the nuclear family, and the relative decline of the extended family, in the twentieth century. These included:

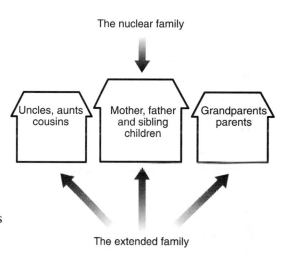

Figure 4.8 The nuclear and extended family

- Improved educational opportunities for men and women throughout the twentieth century. This allowed young people to leave the areas in which they grew up to pursue work and better jobs elsewhere. Inevitably, this led to the creation of new nuclear families whose connection to a wider extended family of relatives was weaker.
- The changing nature of work, particularly in areas where traditional industries such as mining, pottery or fishing declined, led to the loosening of attachments to local communities based around the extended family as people moved away in search of work.
- House building and slum clearance schemes, particularly in the first half of the twentieth century, broke up close-knit local communities and led to the dispersal of many extended families to newly constructed towns and residential areas throughout Britain. Raising housing and general living standards in this way had the effect of reducing the need for and prevalence of extended families sharing accommodation.
- The growth of state welfare services, including national health services, has taken an important 'caring' function away from the extended family. People can now make use of their entitlements to professional care and avoid asking, or relying on,

133

relatives to care for their children or elderly parents. As a result, part of the practical purpose of the extended family has been removed.

- Technological developments during the twentieth century, including a growth in private car ownership, home ownership and access to communication tools (such as the telephone and more recently to e-mail) have enabled people to move to different parts of the country and keep in touch with relatives if they wish. Many people now find it easier to organise their life around a nuclear family and see life in an extended family as a less attractive option.

Functionalist sociologists argue that the nuclear family became more prevalent in the twentieth century because it is best suited to the social and economic conditions in modern society. However, this doesn't mean that the extended family is an undesirable or unsuitable way to organise family life. It certainly has not died out and remains a significant element in the diverse range of family structures in multicultural Britain. Continuing social change is, in fact, leading to new forms of family organisation, challenging the prevalence of the nuclear family at the beginning of the twenty-first century.

New forms of family organisation

The two new forms of family organisation that have become more prevalent at the beginning of the twenty-first century are the lone-parent family and the reconstructed family.

Lone-parent families

Lone-parent families are the fastest growing type of family structure. During the 1990s the number of families headed by a lone parent increased by 30 per cent in the United Kingdom. A woman nearly always heads a lone-parent family. Another significant feature of this family type is the relative lack of children in the family. About one-third of lone-parent families consist of a woman and a single child. An increasing proportion of women who head lone-parent families have never been married or lived with a partner. However, most lone-parents have either cohabited previously or have been married and become lone parents when their relationship breaks down.

The marital background of lone parents	
Status	%
Divorced	35
Widowed	4
Separated	22
Unmarried	39
	100

Figure 4.9 Marital background of lone parents
Source: Labour Force Survey 2000, Office for National Statistics
© Crown copyright

The reconstructed family

Many lone-parent families subsequently evolve into reconstructed families when the adult head of the family forms a new relationship, and marries or begins to cohabit with a new partner. About 12 per cent of lone parents find a new partner and create this form of family organisation each year.

Typically, a reconstructed family is created through a 'merger' of two sets of people who previously lived in separate nuclear families. This means that the new partners often bring dependent children from their previous relationships with them. A reconstructed family takes on a further dimension when the new partners produce children themselves. Approximately six million people now live in reconstructed families in Britain. The ten per cent of all children who live with step-parents are part of these families. Reconstructed families provide a safe and happy environment for many people. However, research also shows that step-families are likely to be poorer than average, and that parents in these families are more unhappy about relationships than parents in first families. Families where both new partners acquire step-children, and also go on to produce their own children, report the highest levels of unhappiness.

Theory into practice

A variety of social and cultural factors have influenced the development of new types of family structure in the late twentieth century. Identify as many sociological reasons as you can for the emergence of:

1 lone-parent families;
2 reconstructed families.

You should try to explain why these types of families have emerged at this point in history by referring to the social, cultural and/or political factors, pressures or opportunities that you believe have allowed or have triggered this to happen.

Criteria	Descriptive term	Key features
Marital arrangement	Monogamous	Families can be based on a monogamous relationship between adult partners.
	Polygamous	Families can be based on polygynous (1 man, several wives) or polyandrous (1 woman, several men) relationships.
Type of household	Nuclear	Small families based on close relationships
	Extended	Families with looser kinship relationships
	Reconstructed	Families involve the 'merger' of previously separate nuclear families.
Power	Patriarchal	Families where the sources of power, prestige and wealth come from and are controlled by the male line.
	Matriarchal	Families where the sources of power, prestige and wealth come from and are controlled by the female line.
	Egalitarian	Families where authority is shared equally between the sexes.

Descent	Patrilineal	Families where descent and inheritance occur through the father.
	Matrilineal	Families where descent and inheritance occur through the mother.
	Bilineal	Families where descent and inheritance can occur through either the father or the mother.
Location	Patrilocal	Families who settle in or near to the husband's parents' home.
	Matrilocal	Families who settle in or near to the wife's parents' home.
	Neolocal	Families who settle away from both the husband and wife's parents' homes.
Marital/partnership choice	Endogamous	Families who develop out of marriages or partnerships between people who live within or share a common circle of relatives or a close community.
	Exogamous	Families who develop out of marriages or partnerships between people who do not live within or share a common circle of relatives or community.

Figure 4.10 Differing patterns of family organisation

Think It Over

1 Which of these terms would you use to describe your own family? Try to attach a descriptive term to your family for each of the criteria.
2 If you were to generalise, which terms best describe the commonest types of family arrangement in Britain today?

Roles and relationships within families

We noted earlier that the structure and function of the family has changed since the beginning of the twentieth century, largely in response to social and economic changes in British society. The next issue that we need to address is the impact that these changes have had on roles and relationships within modern families in Britain.

Changing relationships in the family

We mentioned earlier that the nature of the modern family has been affected by a decline in the prevalence of the extended family and an increase in the diversity of family types. A very important area of social change that has contributed to this, and which has affected roles and relationships within the family, has been the changing expectation about the respective roles of men and women, both in the family and in wider society.

The traditional, stereotypical view of male and female roles in the family is that a woman's primary status, and 'duty', is that of housewife and mother. The traditional expectation, widely common until the powerful feminist challenges of the 1960s, was that married women should stay at home to concentrate on 'maternal' tasks such as cooking, cleaning and childbearing. Men, on the other hand, were expected to take on a more limited paternal role within the family and to spend most of their time working to provide for the family's needs. As such, men gained most of their status from work roles and the authority position ('head of the household') they held within the home. Until these differing maternal and paternal roles were challenged from the 1960s onwards, they seemed inevitable and 'natural'.

Changing maternal and paternal roles

Gradually the 'traditional' pattern of family roles has changed. Increasingly, fathers take on more practical responsibility within the home and generally make a much greater contribution to childcare provision than in the pre-1960s era, for example. Women have made a lot of progress in terms of gaining greater access to, and equality in, the workplace. However, recent reports of the emergence of a 'New Man' who takes on his share of responsibilities within the family is disputed (see below).

The changing role of women

Women's roles in the family gradually changed during the twentieth century as a result of a decline in male authority and dominance. Women are no longer expected to play a subservient, supporting role to their male partners and now enjoy greater equality with men in the family and in wider society. Sociological reasons for this include the following:

Figure 4.11 The New Man?

- **Changes in childbirth patterns.** Women now have fewer children than in the past and are more likely to have them at a later age. This means that women spend less time in child-rearing and have more opportunity to establish and develop their careers.

- **An increase in the proportion of women in employment.** This is obviously related to the changing patterns of childbirth but is also due to the increased availability of childcare, nursery education and maternity pay.

- **A change in social attitudes** has made work more accessible for women. They are now able to demand equal pay and equal treatment with men at work, as well as more family-friendly, flexible work hours. Changing values in society as a whole during the 1960s and 1970s led to a reappraisal of women's roles and their right to equality generally. By the 1970s sociologists were suggesting that a more **'symmetrical family'** had developed in which the relationship between adult partners was more equal and co-operative.

New Man?

The recent claims that relationships within the family are now equal because so-called 'New Men' do their share of the practical tasks is disputed and difficult to find hard evidence for. Maternal and paternal roles have converged a great deal since the 1950s. However, women still seem to actually carry out most of the practical household tasks, even though their male partners argue that they 'help'. The primary responsibility for what was seen as the 'maternal' role still appears to lie with women, even though it is accepted that this is no longer a biologically 'natural' role for women as was previously claimed.

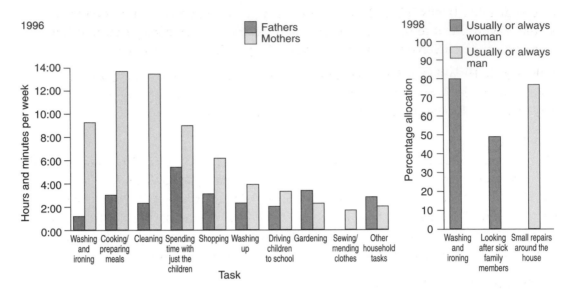

Figure 4.12 Division of labour within families in Britain
Source: Based on data from British Social Attitude Surveys (1992, 1994), *Social Trends* (1997) and British and European Social Attitudes Report (1998)
© Crown copyright

Privatisation and the family

Two sociologists, Peter Wilmott and Michael Young, developed the concept of a privatised, nuclear family to describe the main form of contemporary family structure. These sociologists argued that the structure of the family has gradually evolved through three different phases:

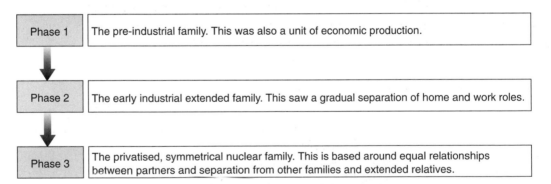

Figure 4.13 Three phases of family structure

Recent developments, such as the growth in prevalence of reconstructed and lone-parent families, and the apparent fact that many nuclear families maintain close links with relatives who live in other parts of Britain and abroad, can be used to contest the argument that the nuclear family is isolated. Many sociologists argue that whilst privatisation of the family has occurred throughout the twentieth century, the structure that has developed is really a modified form of extended family – that is, several linked nuclear families maintaining close and regular contact with each other.

Stability and the family

The changing nature of family structures, particularly the growth of lone-parent families and reconstructed families, has led people to question the stability and future of the family as a social institution. Common themes in media and political debates include:

- the idea that family life in Britain is less happy and supportive than it used to be
- the alleged threat to the future of the family posed by social changes such as the growth in the divorce rate and a decline in the popularity of marriage.

If the family is, in fact, a fundamental social institution, its stability is important. Conflict and significant changes in the structure and function of the family will, according to this view, have a major impact on wider society.

Conflict

Changes in traditional maternal and paternal roles within modern families may have led to a more equal set of relationships but have not necessarily reduced the levels of conflict that exist within families. In fact, the changing expectations of men's and women's roles is now a considerable source of potential conflict in the family. In effect, both adult members of a family are now less certain of what is expected of them and may have increasingly conflicting expectations of each other's roles.

Marriage and cohabitation

Fewer women and men are getting marred than 20 years ago (see Figure 4.14). Despite this, most British adults will get married at some point in their life. In 2000 there were 267,961 marriages. However, of this number only 81,848 of the men and 80,244 of the women were getting married for the first time. The remainder were remarriages. There are now fewer first marriages because the average age of first marriage has increased (28 for men, 26 for women) and more people now cohabit, or live together without marrying. Approximately 10 per cent of adults in Britain are cohabiting at present – this includes 30 per cent of adults under 35 years of age. This doesn't mean that marriage is less popular than it used to be. On the contrary, many people who divorce remarry and many couples who cohabit go on to get married. Cohabitation and divorce are nevertheless seen as social trends that potentially threaten the stability of the family where people view marriage as the most stable form of adult relationship.

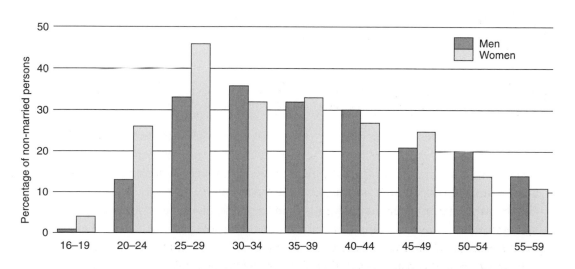

Figure 4.14 Marriage and cohabitation figures
Source: Living in Britain, based on General Household Survey, 2000. Office for National Statistics
© Crown copyright

Divorce

The growth in divorce in Britain began after the **Divorce Reform Act 1969** was passed. This Act allowed partners to divorce after a minimum of two years separation if both parties agreed. If only one partner wished to get divorced, they had to wait five years. This divorce legislation both reflected and created new attitudes towards marriage. Whilst this, and subsequent, changes in the law have resulted in an increase in the divorce rate, other sociological factors have also contributed to rising divorce figures. For example:

- The growth in prevalence of a privatised nuclear family has put greater pressure on marital relationships – more partners divorce because of the increased intensity of modern marriages.
- The breakdown of traditional roles within the family has led to increased uncertainty and tension within marital relationships.
- Greater equality of opportunity at work has increased the likelihood of people having extra-marital relationships with work colleagues – affairs are often a cause of divorce.
- Greater longevity leads to an increased likelihood that people will divorce – 20 per cent of divorcees have been married to their partners for more than 20 years.
- The social stigma relating to divorce has decreased since the late 1960s and the introduction of legislation that allows 'no fault' divorce.
- Welfare benefits and equality laws reduce the economic impact of 'penalties' associated with divorce.

Decrees absolute granted UK	
Year	*Numbers*
1990	167 555
1992	175 144
1994	173 611
1996	171 729
1998	160 057
2000	154 628

Figure 4.15 Divorce statistics
Source: Annual Abstract of Statistics, 2000. Office for National Statistics
© Crown copyright

Divorce now happens in one in every three marriages. The social care and welfare consequences of this are higher state welfare spending, an increased demand for social housing and higher rates of psychological distress and mental health problems. It has been estimated that divorce increases welfare spending by about £1.4 billion per year. This money is spent on items such as housing benefit, legal aid costs, income support and state child-care costs. Additionally, the psychological costs of divorce can be considerable for both adults and children involved. The Joseph Rowntree Foundation (1998) reviewed 200 studies on the social and psychological effects of divorce. They concluded that children affected by divorce are twice as likely as children from nondivorced families to experience social problems such as poor school achievement, are more likely to misuse alcohol and drugs and also have a greater incidence of psychiatric disorders later in life.

Social policy and the family

The family is very important as both a concept and a social institution for government policy-makers. Social and welfare policy-makers tend to assume that families will be the basic social unit in society and will play an important role in providing welfare for its members. Politicians frequently argue about how the family ought to be organised and function. The main theme of these political debates centres on the extent to which the 'traditional' (that is, nuclear) family is the best model of the family organisation compared with newer forms such as lone-parent and reconstructed families.

State intervention and the family

Social policy-makers generally expect men and women to perform different roles within the family. For example, the Beveridge Report of 1942 (see page 321) included an assumption that the family would be based around a married couple. It also assumed that women were going to have a life-long domestic, caring role within the family. Husbands would spend most of their time out at work and would earn money to provide for their wives and children. These assumptions clearly had implications for women's opportunities and affected their ability to claim benefit and develop careers. For a long time, welfare benefits (and pensions) were based upon assumptions made about women being part of a married couple. This effectively excluded women from receiving many welfare benefits as a right until the law was changed at the end of the twentieth century.

Reactions to changes in the family

By the 1980s, social changes affecting the family, such as a rise in lone-parent families, an increase in the rate of teenage pregnancies, and an increase in divorce rates, led to a political reaction against changes in the family. Conservative government policy at the time sought to target welfare benefits and policy initiatives on 'normal' families and to reject and tackle families who were felt to be abusing the welfare system. New forms of family organisation, particularly lone-parent families, came to be seen as the *cause* of social problems rather than as the victims or consequence of them. As a result social policy and welfare benefits were used to reinforce the 'traditional' caring role of the family. At the same time, the Conservative government sought to reduce the intervention of local and national government in providing welfare and social care services for 'problem' families.

The family and care in the community

The recent policy shift to providing care in the community has had significant consequences for families containing one or more people who require health or social care services. The **NHS and Community Care Act 1990** set out the principles on which community provision would be based. An essential ingredient of this piece of legislation is the idea that the family has the primary responsibility for caring for its members. The legislation resulted in the closure of a large number of institutional, residential services but funding was not made available to support people at home instead. Instead their families (that is, women in the family) were expected to the care for them when the state withdrew.

Tackling absent fathers

The increasing incidence of lone-parent families and teenage pregnancy in the 1980s and 1990s led to concern about the role, and absence, of men in the family. One of the main policy initiatives set up in 1993 to tackle this was the Child Support Agency. The goal of the agency was to reduce state support for lone-parent families and hold absent fathers financially responsible for their children. The policy clearly drew on the idea that men have a financial responsibility to support their children and also expressed the view that lone-parent families were a social problem.

New Labour, the family and social policy

Since being elected to government in 1997, New Labour appears to have accepted that there are diverse family structures and has not explicitly sought to return to 'traditional' family values or structures. New Labour has introduced policies that are more supportive and less stigmatising of lone-parent families, particularly focusing on combining welfare entitlement with taking up work and training opportunities. For example, lone parents can now get financial support for child-minding but only if they take up work or training opportunities. New Labour policy towards the family still sees it as an ideal form of social institution. Recent policy initiatives have sought to improve standards of parenting, have considered the issue of paternity leave for fathers and have reinforced the view that parents should be held accountable for the behaviour of their children.

The legal framework and the family

Every government develops social policy initiatives that relate to and have an effect on the family during the government's period of office. However, fewer governments pass legislation that has an ongoing impact on the structure and role of the family. Despite this, there is a considerable body of family law in Britain. A number of the main provisions, or milestones, are outlined in the table below. Many of the statutes referred to were passed to improve the legal rights and social position of women in society.

Legislation	Main provisions
Married Women's Property Act 1882	This gave married women the right to keep their own earnings, take out life assurance and own property worth up to £20. The Act also enabled women to sue and be sued in Court. Before this, women were, in effect, the property of their husbands.
Suffrage Acts 1918	Gave women the right to vote.
Matrimonial Causes Act 1923	This Act awarded women equal rights to obtain a divorce.
Matrimonial Proceedings and Property Act 1970	This Act entitled women to a share in their home.
Equal Pay Act 1970 and 1975	These statutes gave women the right to receive the same pay as men for doing similar work.
The Family Law Act 1996	This Act makes substantial changes to the law on marital and relationship breakdown. It covers divorce, mediation, financial provision and pension rights.

Changes in the law throughout the twentieth century have established a situation where married women now have legal equality with their husbands.

Children's rights

The legal rights of children have also gradually improved over the last century. Children now have a right to primary and secondary education, adoption rights, protection from exploitation in employment and protection from neglect and abuse through child protection laws. **The Children Act 1989** brought together much of the care and welfare-related law affecting children. In essence, it established that a child's welfare and development were to be the 'paramount' considerations in any legal case that had an impact on their life.

Assessment activity 4.2

Sociologists claim that the family plays a vital role in the development of children. In this activity you are asked to describe how the family contributes to a child's social and emotional development and to evaluate the implications of this for society as a whole.

1 Describe how families socialise babies and children into the social norms, values and culture of the society in which they live. You should explain what the socialisation process involves and give some examples to illustrate how children learn and internalise cultural values.

2 Explain what secondary socialisation involves, illustrating your explanation with examples of how people learn and internalise cultural values through their experiences of school, work and the mass media.

3 Critically evaluate the importance of the socialisation process (primary and secondary) for society. You should assess the significance of socialisation for the cohesion and functioning of society, consider the possible implications of a breakdown in socialisation processes and also consider any reasons to criticise the view that socialisation is a vital social process.

Social stratification in British society

The term 'stratification' is used by sociologists to refer to the different ways in which society is structured (stratified) and in which people are classified. According to sociologists, social stratification doesn't simply result from the 'natural' ordering of people into different social groups. In fact, the concept of social stratification is often used by sociologists to draw attention to, and to challenge, the artificial, discriminatory and culturally produced divisions that exist in society. Sociologists, together with many social care and welfare workers, argue against the view that people have different 'natural' positions in society. They maintain that this kind of viewpoint undermines the idea of equality of opportunity, fails to question why some people are seen and treated as more important than others and accepts that social inequality and discrimination are somehow inevitable.

In the next section of the chapter we will consider the different forms of social stratification that make British society unequal and will also consider the effect that this can have on individual's life chances.

Theoretical perspectives on social stratification

Sociologists have identified a range of ways in which British society is stratified according to social characteristics. For example, age, gender, ethnicity and social class are all seen as social characteristics that affect a person's position in society. The main consequence of social stratification is that a hierarchy develops in which people are ranked according to their social characteristics. For example, a white, middle-class male's social characteristics will give them a better position in the social hierarchy than a black, working-class woman. The important impact of this is that people who are higher up the social hierarchy have better access to scarce resources (money, work opportunities, power) than people at the bottom. For many sociologists the existence of a social class hierarchy in British society has the most profound effect on people's life chances and is the main way in which society is socially stratified.

Social class

Social class is a term used to identify a group of people who are similar in terms of their wealth, income and occupation. Sociologists argue that the current social class system emerged as a result of the development of capitalism and the decline of the feudal ordering of British society from the early nineteenth century onwards.

Britain's feudal society was rigidly stratified according to an individual's ownership or non-ownership of land. The monarch (king or queen) who was at the very top of the social hierarchy owned all land. They had the right to distribute land to members of the aristocracy who lay beneath them in the feudal hierarchy. Land was then leased or rented to people further down the hierarchy. However, there was always a significantly large group of ordinary people, the peasants or serfs, who had little economic power because they owned no land in what was an agricultural economy. Ordinary people owed their loyalty and allegiance to their land-owning 'superiors' and had little or no opportunity to acquire land or improve their social position. As a result very little **social mobility** occurred in British society until the emergence of a **capitalist economic system**.

The capitalist economic system that emerged during Britain's industrial revolution in the late eighteenth and nineteenth centuries, ended feudalism in Britain. Industrial employers were able to develop new employment relationships with workers that didn't involve any kind of 'feudal' duty to a powerful landowner. In the capitalist system a new 'social class' hierarchy emerged. This was based on a person's occupation and the social status that this had in society. People who had highly sought after and prestigious occupations belonged to higher social classes, and vice versa. A further consequence of the new economic basis of social classification, was that upward social mobility became possible because people were able to work their way up (or slip down!) the social class structure. Social position was no longer determined by birth.

Whilst this is a simplified account of the way that social classes emerged, it is still the case that a person's occupation is seen as the key characteristic when dividing people into social class, or **socio-economic**, groupings.

The three-class pyramid

The classic way of thinking about social class in Britain is to identify the working class, the middle class and the upper class as the three distinct social classes. In this model, the working class forms the largest social group at the base of the social class hierarchy or pyramid (see Figure 4.16.) The main characteristic of people in this social class is that they, or the male head of their household, have a manual occupation. By contrast the smaller proportion of people who make up the middle class are identified as people who belong to a household where the male head has a non-manual occupation. The upper class is a relatively small proportion of people who are wealthy, powerful and have a lot of social status.

This three-tier social class pyramid provides a relatively crude way of looking at the way in which social stratification occurs on economic grounds. Whilst each social class has 'in-class' economic gradations that differentiate it further, other methods of classifying people into social classes offer more wide-ranging and subtle criteria.

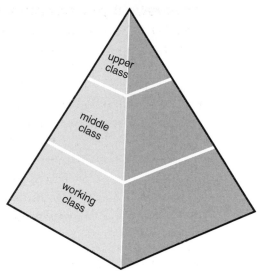

Figure 4.16 The social pyramid

The Registrar-General's scale

The social classification system used to identify and record an individual's social class until 2001 was known as the Registrar-General's scale. Statistics based on this scale were developed from census records that held details of the occupation of the male head of each household in Britain. The scale consisted of six social classes (see Figure 4.17) that were organised into a hierarchy linking occupations to social status.

Social Class	Types of occupation	
Class 1	Professional occupations	Lawyers, doctors
Class 2	Intermediate occupations	Executives, shopkeepers
Class 3N	Skilled, non-manual occupations	Clerks, policemen
Class 3M	Skilled, manual occupations	Electricians, coal miners
Class 4	Partly skilled occupations	Farm workers, bus drivers
Class 5	Unskilled	Labourers, cleaners

Figure 4.17 Registrar-General's social class scale

At the beginning of the twenty-first century, the Registrar-General's scale was felt to be out of date and an inadequate method of classifying the class structure of modern Britain. A new scale was developed for use in the 2001 Census.

The National Statistics Socio-Economic Classification

This social classification system has been developed to incorporate the changes that have occurred in Britain's class structure over the last few decades of the twentieth century. The main change involved expanding the classification system to reflect the growth of middle-class occupations and the changing nature of the kinds of work that people do as well as the levels of social esteem that these jobs attract. There are now eight major social classes in the NSS-EC scale (see Figure 4.18).

Social class	Types of jobs included
Higher managerial and professional occupations	Doctors, lawyers, dentists, professors, professional engineers
Lower managerial and professional occupations	School teachers, nurses, journalists, actors, police sergeants
Intermediate occupations	Airline cabin crew, secretaries, photographers, firemen, auxiliary nurses
Small employers and own account workers	Self-employed builders, hairdressers, fishermen, car dealers and shop-owners
Lower supervisory and technical occupations	Train drivers, employed craftsmen, foremen, supervisors
Semi-routine occupations	Shop assistants, postmen, security guards
Routine occupations	Bus drivers, waitresses, cleaners, car park attendants, refuse collectors
Never worked or long-term unemployed	Students, people not classifiable, occupations not stated

Figure 4.18 The National Statistics Socio-Economic Classification

How useful are these scales? Sociologists recognise that social class is not as important in the way that people define themselves as it used to be. The fact that society appears to be becoming more differentiated suggests that there are fewer major distinctions within the population (e.g. between working and middle class) than was previously the case. However, despite the suggestions of some politicians, Britain is far from a 'classless' society. Sociological evidence, from the census and other research investigations, shows that there is a socio-economic hierarchy in Britain.

Social mobility

The concept of social mobility is used by sociologists to describe and monitor the extent to which individuals and specific social groups are able to move up or down the social hierarchy from one social class to another.

The amount of social mobility that exists tells us whether Britain is an open, meritocratic society or not. In a meritocratic society people who have the most talent and those who work the hardest can be successful and move up the social hierarchy on merit. In a true **meritocracy**, there would be no artificial social, cultural, economic or political barriers to prevent people from achieving their true potential. This would mean that a person's ability and effort would determine their social status rather than the fact that they were born into a high-status or wealthy family background.

Figure 4.19 Social mobility

Sociologists measure social mobility by comparing an individual's occupation with that of their father (inter-generational mobility) or by comparing a person's first occupation with their present career or job role. Generally, sociologists have found that there is only 'short-range' social mobility in Britain. Studies show that people rarely move more than two occupational groups up or down, whichever measure of social mobility is used. Additionally, the statistics show that 50 per cent of those children who are born into the highest social class move into occupations that ensure they remain at the top of the social hierarchy. Women with children appear to be less socially mobile than women who've never had children. Nevertheless, sociologists have also found that women who are more socially mobile tend to be able to move up the social hierarchy in only a relatively narrow range of occupations (related to caring, teaching and public service) when compared to more socially mobile men.

Key issue

To what extent is modern Britain a meritocracy? You could research this issue by evaluating recent statistics on social mobility and social class in Britain, and by surveying people on the extent to which they believe that personal success and achievement in society are 'open to all' or are based on some kind of 'old boy network'.

Does social class matter?

Many sociologists believe that social class is the key form of social stratification in modern society. Sociological research has repeatedly shown that social class has a greater effect on a person's life chances than other important social factors such as their gender, ethnicity, age and experience of disability. For example, people in the new top social class are generally seven times more affluent than people in the bottom class, despite within-class differences in other social characteristics. This doesn't mean that these other features of social stratification are not important in modern British society. However, their impact should always be considered alongside an individual's social class position.

In addition to having access to similar financial resources, people in the same social class also appear to enjoy similar life chances. The broader impact of social class on life chances is outlined in more detail on page 150.

Income and wealth distribution

Income and wealth are economic resources that have an important effect on a person's life chances. **Income** refers to sources of money that people receive. Most people receive their income from the wages or salary that they receive from an employer. **Wealth**, on the other hand, refers to the financial or economic assets that people possess. Both income and wealth are unevenly distributed in British society.

The distribution of income in Britain

Source of income	Percentages					
	1971	1976	1981	1986	1991	1995
Wages and salaries[1]	68	67	63	58	58	56
Self-employment income[2]	9	9	8	10	10	10
Rent, dividends, interest	6	6	7	8	9	7
Private pensions, annuities and so on	5	5	6	8	10	11
Social security benefits	10	11	13	13	11	13
Other current transfers[3]	2	2	2	3	2	3
Total household income (= 100%)						
(£ billion at 1995 prices[4])	314	365	398	472	573	599

[1]Includes forces' pay and income in kind.
[2]After deducting interest payments, depreciation and stock appreciation.
[3]Mostly other government grants, but including transfers from abroad and non-profit-making bodies.
[4]Adjusted to 1995 prices using the consumers' expenditure deflator.

Figure 4.20 Household income in the UK
Source: adapted from *Social Trends 27* (1997:90), using figures from the Office for National Statistics
© Crown copyright

The present unequal distribution of income occurs for a number of reasons. For example, people who work in professional and managerial occupations tend to receive significantly higher pay than unskilled workers. The proportion of people who now live on less than half of the average income has risen from 8 per cent in 1982 to 19 per cent in 1993. The living standards of people at the bottom of the incomes league table haven't improved significantly since the late 1970s. On the other hand, people who are at the top of the income league table have enjoyed a significant increase in their income. This means that the gap between those at the bottom and those at the top of the income league table has increased during this period. The social groups who are now most likely to have low incomes include lone-parent families, older people, and disabled people. Families headed by members of ethnic minority groups are also more likely to be living on very low incomes.

The distribution of wealth in Britain

The distribution of wealth in Britain is massively unequal – the top 10 per cent of the population own half of all wealth. This includes:

- **marketable wealth** or assets that can be sold or cashed in (for example, property and shares)
- **non-marketable wealth** or assets that can't be sold or cashed in (for example, pension rights).

Most people hold the largest part of their wealth in the properties that they own. About 1 per cent of the population with wealth above £500,000 hold most of their wealth in shares or other non-property assets.

	Percentages				
	1976	1981	1986	1991	1993
Percentage of wealth owned by:					
Most wealthy 1%	13	11	10	10	10
Most wealthy 5%	26	24	24	23	23
Most wealthy 10%	36	34	35	33	33
Most wealthy 25%	57	56	58	57	56
Most wealthy 50%	80	79	82	83	82
Total marketable wealth (£ billion)	472	1036	1784	3014	3383

This applies to the adult population aged 18 and over. The estimates for 1976, 1981, 1986 and 1991 are based on the estates of persons dying in those years. The estimates for 1993 are based on estates notified for probate in 1993–94. The estimates are not strictly comparable between 1993 and earlier years.

Figure 4.21 The distribution of marketable wealth plus pension rights in the UK
Source: adapted from *Social Trends 26* (1996:111), using figures from the Inland Revenue

The *Sunday Times Rich List* indicates that there are about 1000 very wealthy people in Britain. Between them, these people own almost £115 billion.

Hardship in Britain

Social inequality and poverty has increased sharply in Britain since the late 1970s. The Institute for Fiscal Studies produced a number of reports on the growth of hardship in Britain during this period. The findings indicated that:

- the richest 10 per cent of the population now receive as much income as the bottom (poorer) half of households
- families with children have suffered a greater reduction in income than households without children
- the number of children living in poverty has increased threefold since the 1970s.

As a consequence of the increase in social inequality in Britain, a large proportion of the population are now said to live in **relative poverty**. This term is used to refer to a situation where some people can't afford goods or services that are part of the normal, expected standard of living in a society. For example, having a telephone, heating and a fridge at home are things that the majority of people now enjoy and which are an expected part of the ordinary standard of living in Britain. Some sociologists argue that people who live on less than half of the average income experience relative poverty. This means that 50 per cent of the British population will have average or below average income. Another method that sociologists use to assess relative poverty is to conduct a survey to find out what people expect is an acceptable minimum lifestyle. People who don't have the resources to afford this minimum level are said to experience relative poverty.

Think It Over
Who is poor? What are the 'basic necessities' of life in modern Britain? Make a list of the goods, services and conditions that you believe provide a minimum standard of living today. Compare and discuss your list with class colleagues.

The effects of social class on life chances
Sociologists have conducted a large number of research studies on the effect that social class has on life chances. A persistent finding is that a person's social class is the most important predictor of health experience and other life chances.

Social class and health
There is a clear link between the risk of illness and premature death and a person's social class. Infant mortality rates, for example, are twice as high for the children of unskilled manual workers than they are for the children of professionals. Sociological research in Britain consistently shows that this class-related pattern is linked to health chances and life expectancy for all age groups.

Richard Wilkinson, a sociological researcher, wrote a letter to a social science journal called *New Society* in 1976 about this apparent connection. He asked the Labour government of the time to set up an urgent inquiry into the causes of the link between social class, health experience and death rates. The **Black Report** was the result of the inquiry. This produced hard, empirical evidence of considerable social class differences in health experiences. The report showed that unskilled workers had a two and a half times greater chance of dying before retirement than professional people. The Black Report showed that the difference in death rates between those at the top and those at the bottom of the social class hierarchy had increased during the twentieth century despite the emergence of the National Health Service. For example, in 1930 unskilled workers were 23 per cent more likely to die prematurely than professional workers. By 1970, the likelihood had increased to 61 per cent.

Education
All children in Britain have a right to receive state education between the ages of 5 and 16. The vast majority of children in Britain do attend state schools and an increasing proportion go on to further and higher education. However, research studies show that the best schools, colleges and universities tend to recruit students from families higher up the social class scale, whereas students from families in the lower social classes tend to enjoy opportunities in institutions that are less well funded and which produce poorer results.

In a comprehensive report on health inequalities, Sir Donald Acheson noted that people living in the most disadvantaged circumstances were least likely to gain access to the types of high-quality education services that they would most benefit from. Educational attainment statistics have repeatedly shown that the children of higher social class families generally achieve more than their lower social class counterparts. Local education authorities that provide a high percentage of free school meals (a general indicator of lower social class) also have a lower percentage of pupils achieving five or more GCSEs levels 'A star' to 'C'.

Assessment activity 4.3

A person's life chances are closely linked to their social class. In this activity, you are asked to research and present evidence that illustrates the link between personal health experience, mortality and social class.

1 Carry out research to identify evidence of the link between social class and a person's life chances. Summarise the sociological research evidence that you obtain in a short report entitled 'Social class and health experience'.

2 As a second part of your report, discuss the possible effects on life chances that social mobility (upward and downward) is likely to have on a person's life chances.

3 Evaluate the validity and relevance of two systems of social classification that have been used to study the links between social class and life chances.

Demographic trends and social change

The changing population structure in Britain

Demography is the study of population characteristics and trends. Sociologists have studied the changing features of Britain's population since census figures were identified as a useful source of sociological data. Whilst demographic data is expressed in terms of statistics, it's important to note that many of the measures and figures are, in fact, based on estimates and projections. This means that the figures are rarely exact but they're still useful as a way of understanding the general population situation and the likely pattern of change that will occur in the future. For example, health and social policy, makers rely on demographic statistics like those below to plan care services.

Demographic indicator	What information does this provide?
Birth rate	The number of live births, usually per 1000 of the population, per year.
Death rate	The number of deaths, usually per 1000 of the population, per year.
Life expectancy	The average number of years that a member of a specified group can expect to live from an identified moment in time (usually birth).
Infant mortality rate	The number of deaths of live-born infants, usually per 1000 of the population, per year.
Age structure	The proportion, percentage or actual number of people within specified age groups in the population at a particular point in time.
Ethnic structure	The proportion, percentage or actual number of people within specified ethnic groups in the population at a particular point in time.
Migration patterns	The actual number, or percentage, of people entering (immigration rate) or leaving (emigration rate) the United Kingdom as their main country of domicile.

You will need to understand definitions like these when you read tables of demography statistics. However, you should always check the basis on which demography statistics are compiled as they may use different definitions from those above.

Examination of demographic trends

The population of the United Kingdom has grown from about 1 million people in the eleventh century to about 60 million people today. The population of the United Kingdom grew rapidly during the nineteenth century. This was partly due to a decline in death rates, improved medical knowledge and better public health conditions, amongst other factors.

UK population in millions			
	All	*Males*	*Females*
1851	22 259	10 855	11 404
1931	46 038	22 060	23 978
1971	55 928	27 167	28 761
1991	57 814	28 428	29 566
2001*	59 987	29 605	30 382

*This is a projection based on 2000 data

Figure 4.22 Population statistics
Source: Abstract of National Statistics, 2000. Office for National Statistics
© Crown copyright

An ageing population

The population structure of the United Kingdom has changed over the twentieth century as birth rates slowed at the same time as life expectancy grew. The effect of this is now being felt as the proportion of older people expands in relation to the proportion of younger people.

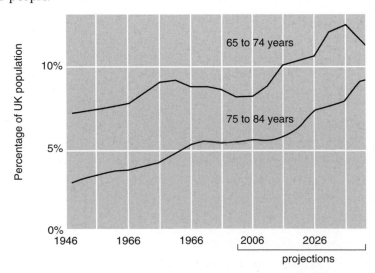

Figure 4.23 Age structure of population statistics
Source: Annual Abstract of National Statistics, 2000. Office for National Statistics
© Crown copyright

The changing age structure of the population concerns government policy-makers who foresee problems in funding pensions and care services for this growing number of older people. Amongst the potential solutions being considered are policies of discouraging early retirement, making personal pensions compulsory, raising the retirement age and making younger people pay higher taxes to fund provision.

> ## Key issue
> We are facing a demographic crisis. What do you think the government should do now to deal with the problem of funding care services for the large numbers of older people who will require them over the next 40 years?

Population movement

Historically, in the UK the movement of population has been from rural, countryside areas to urban, city areas. This happened on a large scale during industrialisation as people sought work in the new factories but has been a general trend throughout the twentieth century. Over one-third of the population of the United Kingdom now live in major conurbation areas.

Geographic location of the population in England (2000)	
Area	*000's*
North	3068
Yorkshire and Humberside	5058
East Midlands	4208
East Anglia	2214
South East	18 735
South West	4975
West Midlands	5335
North West	6403
	49 997

Figure 4.24 Geographic location statistics
Source: Annual Abstract of National Statistics, 2000. Office for National Statistics
© Crown copyright

The consequences of a high population density in urban areas include environmental and social problems. Crime rates, pollution and traffic congestion are much higher in urban areas. Inner city areas often have the poorest social and housing conditions. Whilst the more affluent people are able to move away or choose the better parts of a city to live in, older and poorer people tend to suffer the health, psychological and social exclusion effects of inner city deprivation.

Unemployment patterns

The occupational system of British society is continually changing in small ways as organisations and industries adjust to technological, scientific and social developments. At certain points in history, major changes in industry and the economy have produced large-scale occupational changes and high unemployment levels. For example, during the 1970s and 1980s an economic recession combined with the loss of traditional industries (such as coal mining and steel making) together with an increase in the number of women and young people seeking work, produced high unemployment figures.

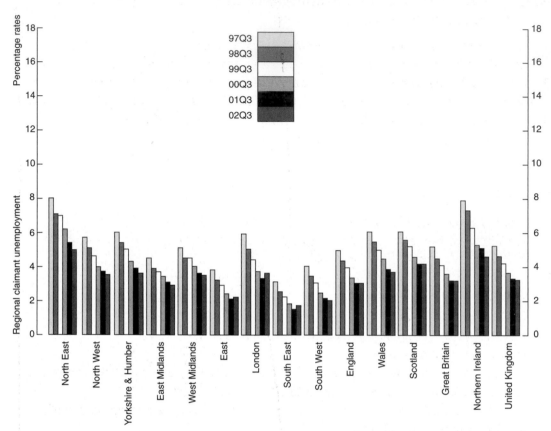

Figure 4.25 Statistics on regional unemployment
Source: Economic Statistics, 2002. Office for National Statistics
© Crown copyright

The development of new types of work, particularly based around the computer and telecommunications industries, and an improvement in the economy have gradually reduced unemployment levels to those we see at the beginning of the twenty-first century. However, significant changes in ways of working have also helped to reduce unemployment levels. Job-sharing, reduced overtime working, early retirement, more part-time working and self-employment have all changed the occupational structure of the United Kingdom since the recessions of the 1980s.

Unemployment has significant negative effects on individuals, families and society in general. Individuals tend to become socially isolated and experience psychological problems (including loss of confidence and a sense of shame) when they experience unemployment for long periods. Because unemployment tends to affect local areas and regions in a general way, communities affected by unemployment tend to suffer problems of drug abuse, higher crime and loss of social cohesion. For some communities, long-term unemployment has become a way of life and has led to the social exclusion of sections of the population.

Demographic changes in relation to family structure and family breakdown are outlined and discussed in more detail on pages 130–6.

Assessment activity 4.4

Changes in the size, location and structure of the population of Britain has implications for those who plan health, social care and welfare provision. In this activity, you are asked to explain the nature of recent demographic trends and to suggest how they have influenced care provision.

1 Using statistical sources, describe significant demographic changes that have occurred in Britain since the beginning of the twentieth century.
2 Using sociological knowledge and understanding, explain the implications of these significant demographic changes that you've identified for care provision.
3 Using two examples, describe how demographic changes can influence the development of specific forms of care provision.

End-of-unit test

1 Identify three social institutions that a sociologist might study.
2 Explain what the term 'sociological perspective' means, referring to an example that you've learnt about in this chapter.
3 Describe how a structural approach to sociology differs from a social action approach.
4 Explain how Marxist sociologists view society and its main problems.
5 In what ways are feminist perspectives distinctly different from other forms of sociological perspective?
6 Describe how an understanding of the concept of socialisation could be helpful to care professionals who work with children and their families.
7 Identify two other sociological concepts and explain how they could be usefully applied in social care situations.
8 Sociologists argue that the notion of a 'typical' British family is a myth. Explain why.
9 How has social change during the twentieth century affected the role of women in the modern family?
10 Identify three ways in which British society is seen by sociologists to be stratified.
11 Outline the main findings and implications of the Black Report into health inequalities.
12 Describe the general relationship between social class and health experience in Britain.
13 Explain what demographic trends describe.
14 Identify a current demographic trend or feature of social change and explain how it may affect the need for social care and welfare services in the future.

References and further reading

Clarke, A. (2001) *The Sociology of Health Care*, New Jersey: Prentice Hall

Moore, S. (2001) *Sociology Alive!*, Cheltenham: Nelson Thornes

Rodgers, B and Pryor, J. (1998) *Divorce and Separation: the Outcomes for Children*, York: Joseph Rowntree Foundation

Willmott, P. and Young, M. (1975) *The Symmetrical Family*, Harmondsworth: Penguin

Vocational practice

An essential part of your programme of learning about social care will be your structured vocational placement, which will occupy a minimum of 400 hours of your time. Unit 5 is closely linked to the vocational placement programme and as such stands alongside it to draw on knowledge, skills and understanding from all the other core and specialist optional units that you will study. For these reasons, this unit runs through the whole of your programme. To demonstrate the importance of the unit it has a value of *two* units.

This unit allows you to demonstrate to others that you can apply your learning in the workplace and gain personal competence. As you move through the programme, you will be helped to acquire the basic hands-on caring skills such as helping at mealtimes, assisting with personal hygiene and communicating with service users with different disabilities. Later, you will be critically analysing your own performance in the workplace, setting targets for both your personal and career development and comparing and contrasting different aspects of care-work, staff training and development and implementation of policies.

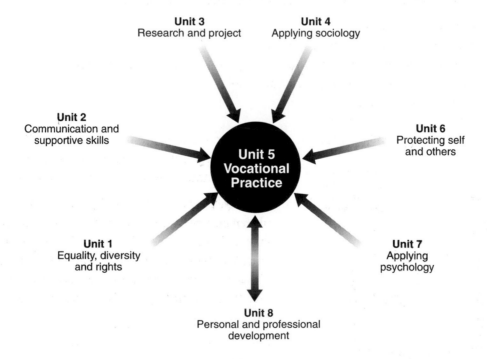

Figure 5.1 Diagram to show the pivotal role of Unit 5 in the programme

What you need to learn

- Common and particular features of each vocational placement
- Base knowledge and skills of an effective practitioner
- Principles of team work, work relationships, roles and responsibilities
- Equal opportunities
- Care programmes
- Personal career goals

Common and particular features of each vocational placement

Your tutors will have expended many hours of their time planning a programme of vocational placements that will provide you with suitable tasks to develop your basic skill base and to stimulate your enquiring mind. In some educational establishments, placement is organised around one particular day in the week. In others, specified placement weeks interrupt the more traditional lesson structure and in yet other schools and colleges these two arrangements are combined. You are likely to experience between four and six different types of placement and will need to be able to identify certain common and particular features, as well as comparing and contrasting other aspects. To accomplish all of this in a successful way you will need to:

- plan ahead carefully
- collect or photocopy required documents
- prepare your own worksheets for completion at the appropriate time
- ask to the right people the right questions
- make notes as appropriate
- demonstrate basic care skills
- reflect on your skill acquisition and improve weak areas
- have a pro-active approach to the unit
- show enthusiasm in the work placement.

The paperwork that you will generate from your placements must be kept carefully in a special file that will become your Vocational Practice Log or VPL. You will also be able to present your VPL file at job and career interviews because it is directly relevant to your future in care work.

You will find more information to help you with the VPL on page 187 of the Assessment guidelines.

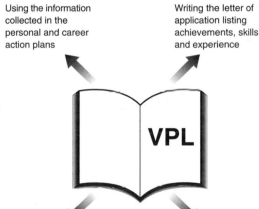

Using the information collected in the personal and career action plans

Writing the letter of application listing achievements, skills and experience

Compiling the evidence to support the application from the development of knowledge, skills and understanding from work in diverse care settings and demonstrating the use of reflective practice

Offering the VPL for perusal at interview, (time will permit only a short look or glance, but you have shown organisation and enthusiasm)

Figure 5.2 Using your VPL in applications

Placement structure

Some educational establishments may be fortunate enough to allow each student to select their own placement; others will have little or no choice because of the difficulty in obtaining a sufficient number of placements. You should remember from the outset that your tutors have worked extremely hard to get the vocational placements for you, so be reliable, punctual, polite and enthusiastic in your approach.

Wherever possible, you should attempt to cover a wide variety of placement care settings and not be blinkered from the start. Occasionally, students will declare that they wish to work only in centres related to children, drug rehabilitation or probation for example, and be resentful and uninterested if they have to work with elderly service users. This is a poor start to caring, as all carers must be able to value the equality and diversity of all service users and be able to respond to their needs. Such students would be well advised to consider different courses of study if these are available, as they are unlikely to become flexible, adaptable and useful carers. An open, enquiring mind and a willingness to learn in all areas is required from the beginning of your programme of studies.

Many students are anxious to gain vocational placements in hospitals, drug rehabilitation centres or children's homes, probably because this is where they see their future career or it seems exciting and dramatic, apparently at the cutting edge of care. Establishments are now very aware of the expensive litigation they can face if service users are disadvantaged by the results of their programme of care; they are also short of staff and under pressure to cut waiting lists, meet government targets and balance budgets. As a result, many organisations are increasingly reluctant to offer vocational placements, so do not be disappointed if you do not get your first choice of social care placement. It is worth remembering that more people are cared for in other settings than inside establishments, with service users' homes representing the largest percentage of all. There are so many varieties of care settings in which you can develop your caring skills and knowledge that this should not concern you at all and will be to your advantage when you eventually begin your professional training.

Assessment activity 5.1

Allow two or three days to carry out the research for this activity and, if possible, work in groups of three or four, eventually comparing group results in a plenary session.

- Research all the different types of care settings in your neighbourhood using local information, telephone directories, family and friends, libraries and any other appropriate sources of information. Think very broadly; it does not matter if the setting is large or small, public or private, residential or day-care, or managed by a charity. When your group feels that their list is complete, write the names on strips of card and mix them up. Exchange cards with another group and distribute them among group members. Each individual tells the group the name on the card, and a few sentences about the type of care given in the care setting and the service users who may be involved. Ask the rest of the group if they wish to make any contributions. Join two groups together and clear up any gaps in knowledge, seeking assistance from the tutor if required.
- Finally, join all the groups together and discuss your results before making a large wall chart display of the cards with accompanying notes. Title the display 'Types of care settings in our locality'. A display such as this will assist in the planning of your programme of vocational placements.

Mission statements

From the activity you will have learned that there is a wide variety of care settings and each will have a set of policies, procedures and a statement of aims, sometimes called a mission statement or a statement of principles, such as the one in the box below.

Statement of principles for a primary school

Children are happy when they are learning how to do things. We want our children to learn how to read and write, how to play together, how to discover, how to make things and, last but not least, how to behave towards each other, teachers, parents and society in general.

Aims are broad general statements of the purpose of the organisation and are usually fairly short.

A policy is a formal written statement explaining what to do within an organisation or work setting; workers must abide by the policies of the organisation. Policies usually arise from European or government requirements and can exist at international, national or local levels.

Policies will cover many areas such as health and safety, manual handling and lifting, confidentiality, equal opportunities, bullying and harassment and dealing with aggression and violence. You will find these policies operating in all care sectors, so it is a good place to start. If there are several students working at your vocational placement try to organise that a copy of each policy is available in a locality with access by students, this may be in the workplace or in the educational establishment. It is costly and time-consuming for workplace staff to provide multiple copies at different times for different students.

Large establishments will have a very large number of policies and procedures (probably over two thousand) and you will not be able to manage more than a few of these; smaller units such as residential homes will have only a few so be aware of this type of incompatibility.

Procedures detail the steps an employee should take in a particular situation such as a fire, when faced with violence, etc. A procedure should be followed as laid down in the written document, and if not followed will undoubtedly lead to a post-incident investigation. They exist to help employees in difficult situations and have been agreed by management and employees as the best way forward. Policies and procedures exist to protect service users and staff from harm in the workplace.

Assessment activity 5.2

This activity should take place after students have been on their first vocational placement, with a short pre-placement tutor discussion regarding the methods to be employed. The activity can provide new students with guidelines for their VPL work.

- In your tutor group suggest titles of policies that should/could exist in a wide range of care establishments. Provide ideas in the form of thumbnail sketches about the purpose and rough content of each policy.

- Working as a group, decide on one important care policy to research in your first placement. This could be confidentiality, equal opportunities, or health and safety. Each group member should obtain a copy of this policy and four others of their choice during the placement.
- Make key notes on your chosen policy during your placement days. Bring these notes to your next lesson.
- In your group, say which policies were collected and then provide one key point on the chosen policy until all issues have been raised.
- With guidance from your tutor, compare similarities and differences on the raised key points. Highlight major points on a chalkboard or flip chart.
- Being conscious of confidentiality, you should be able to say whether you were aware of any incidents, actions or behaviours observed during your placement that did not conform to the policy in general and the possible reasons for this. You should also be able to reflect on your own performance and critically analyse yourself in relation to the policy. For example:
  - Confidentiality – did any student discuss a service user's problem with friends or at home? Why?
  - Equal opportunities – did students have some favourite service users and avoid others? Why?
  - Health and safety – did unknown visitors walk by the student without enquiry? Why?

This activity will stimulate awareness and provoke thought and reflection about policies in general, and implementation in the workplace. You will be able to transfer ideas gained from this activity to analysing aims, policies and procedures from other placements for your VPL and to reflect and analyse your own and other's performance in the workplace.

Roles and responsibilities of the staff structure

The size of the establishment or organisation will influence the staff structure, the proportion of management to other staff and the mix of skills found in the care setting. A nursing or residential home might have only a few qualified care staff on the payroll and a majority of 'hands-on' care assistants with or without NVQs. A charitable organisation will have a much larger number of part-time volunteers and few or no staff with care qualifications. A specialised setting, such as a Social Services department supervising care in the community, will have an even greater proportion of qualified social workers, care assistants, qualified nursery nurses, occupational therapists, community psychiatric nurses and all manner of other staff. A privately run playgroup might have only three paid staff, so whether the care setting is run by the state (i.e. statutory), privately owned or run by voluntary agencies (such as charities) will also make a difference to the management structure and proportion of staff.

Nearly all care settings will produce an annual report or information leaflet and these will usually provide the staffing information. A website providing statistics such as the proportion of nurses and doctors in hospitals to 100 patients can be found at www. goodhospitalguide.co.uk

You can also compare one care setting or hospital with another with this website. You will have to ask someone for this information at a smaller care setting.

You may also be able to obtain one or two copies of job and person descriptions for vacancies in the establishment. A job description clearly sets out the roles and responsibilities for the person holding that position. A person description sets out the knowledge, skills and abilities required for the job, for example, a person dealing with the general public might be required to have excellent communication skills, be patient and even-tempered and dress appropriately. Paid employees should be able to help you with short descriptions of their job roles and to whom they make reports or receive their vocational tasks from.

A role will carry certain rights and obligations, including who to report to and who reports to the person in that role. There may be in-built authority with certain roles, for instance head teachers and principals in schools and colleges. Most organisations have a hierarchy that is a 'higherarchy' – from a majority of lower-grade employees at the bottom to one or a few higher-grade personnel at the top. This is often known as a pyramidal hierarchy.

Think It Over

When an incident or crisis occurs in a care establishment and the media wish to interview people to gain more information, it is always someone at the top of the hierarchy in an establishment who faces the cameras and the journalists. Why?

Why is there usually a delay in providing the interview?

Assessment activity 5.3

Before you go into your first vocational placement, write a short job description of the tasks you expect to do and include the person(s) to whom you expect to report. Reporting in your placement may include simply starting and finishing your placement day and passing on any information that you think is important. Word-process your job role. Save to disk and print one hard copy (dated) for your VPL. After your placement experience, modify the job description to match your actual experience, date and place an up-dated hard copy in your VPL. Repeat this activity before and after each placement.

Service users – how their needs are met in each setting

You will need to find out about the people who use the services of your placements. You need to consider:

- single or mixed genders and approximate numbers of each
- age ranges
- general or particular environments that the service users come from, such as a local community or a broad regional basis
- social classification – mixed or specific. For example, a private hospital is more likely to take service users from the middle and upper social classes whereas a local authority nursery for single working mothers is more likely to have service users from the lower social classes.

You must be careful not to stereotype service users, and are required to give a broad picture only. You will also need to consider the reasons why service users need the services and how their needs are met by the service.

Figure 5.3 The needs of service users

Assessment activity 5.4

1 Using Figure 5.3 as a guide, provide four brief, imaginary case studies for each broad heading to explore the diverse reasons for service users requiring care services. You can carry out this task on your own or in small groups and compare the findings.

2 For each individual in your imaginary case study, give two ways in which their needs might be met.

Services and resources provided by associated organisations

Links to other organisations

Many care settings have links with other organisations that carry out different tasks associated with the service. In a residential home for the elderly, for example, might be visiting hairdressers, physiotherapists and occupational therapists, chiropodists, social workers and, certainly, visiting doctors. Social services might be involved with financial assistance for many service users.

Charities for elderly people might help with clothing and small gifts; local communities often assist with fund-raising and social events. If you are in placement approaching Christmas, you will probably have plenty of links to report on as local schools sing carols and make gifts. Schools have close links with the police and fire services who often give talks on road safety, particularly for pedestrians and cyclists, and to emphasise fire safety. You will only find out about such links by being alert and asking for information from

Figure 5.4 A sleepy link with an organisation

the care workers. Think broadly and do not be afraid of making suggestions as busy people might forget the special occasions.

Loaning resources

Many organisations, as well as providing a service, also loan resources. These can be as diverse as toilet frames for otherwise healthy people who have fractured limbs, information leaflets about specific conditions such as meningitis or immunisations and materials to relieve pressure sores for people who have certain mobility problems.

Assessment activity 5.5

Explore the links that your educational organisation has with other establishments and make a group or class pattern diagram of your findings. Write short descriptions of the purpose of these links. You can construct similar diagrams for your placement links and make comparisons.

Do you think that links will be stronger in statutory, private or voluntary organisations?

Role and performance in each placement

You may be given a written sheet of general guidance by your tutors before you attend your placement or provided with verbal instructions. You should use this information to help in writing a job description for yourself in the placement. This should include:

- your aims for the placement
- your objectives in the placement
- the tasks you will be expected to perform.

The aims are broad general statements of your expectations from the placement while objectives are measurable goals, which you can expect to achieve during your period in the setting. You will find the headings for this chapter useful in defining your goals.

Assessment activity 5.6

Imagine that next week you will be going to a local residential home for elderly people for your first two-week block vocational placement. Write a job description for this placement before you go, stating your aims, objectives and expected tasks. You may need to look through the headings of this chapter first.

Evaluating your performance

With any learning it is essential to evaluate performance after the experience.

Your aims and objectives might have been totally unrealistic for the skills, knowledge and abilities that you possess initially and by evaluating your work and performance after each placement you will soon become an expert at job descriptions! You should also find that your skills, knowledge and abilities become increasingly sophisticated as you progress through your placements over the two years of your programme. Do not be afraid of self-criticism; many students feel that they must always say good things about themselves. One tends to think that if someone is reading your work and you mention a task or event that you did not handle well, then the reader will think poorly of you. Being able to criticise one's own performance is a higher-level skill and consolidates learning. Some examples of evaluation of personal performance are provided below:

- I was pleased with the way I comforted Mrs K because I empathised rather than sympathised with her loss.
- I felt that my irritation with Mr B showed in my body language and I was ashamed of myself later on. I need to learn to be more tolerant of demanding service users.
- When chatting to a care assistant about something personal a service user told me, I forgot about confidentiality. I need to be more alert about confidentiality; it is easy to forget.
- I avoid talking to a severely deaf service user because I am embarrassed when I speak loudly and feel everyone around is listening. I am discriminating against this service user because of his disability due to my personal feelings.

You can see how these statements are producing good self-evaluations and should lead to an improved performance. With no analysis, there will be no change in behaviour. After judging your effectiveness, you can then plan to improve this skill next time, thus providing aims and/or objectives for your next period of experience. You will be able to see how your performance can improve with increasing skills, knowledge and ability. Do not be too hard on yourself, however; you are allowed a 'pat on the back' as well – if you are pleased with the way you handled something, then say so.

Base knowledge and skills of an effective practitioner

Having a job means being paid for the time and effort that you give to the workplace, but having a vocation means a sense of being called to the occupation. When you feel called upon to be a carer you will wish to make a difference to your service users. In other words, you will desire to be an effective practitioner having a specialist knowledge and appropriate caring skills.

Below you will find lists of basic tasks that you will be expected to perform in most placements.

Links between theory and practice in the health and care field

It is important to realise that however many lectures you attend, books that you read or accounts that you write, you will not be effective in your placement, and subsequent career, if you don't use your knowledge practically. You will need to show that you can transfer the knowledge that you gain into your practice. There are numerous ways of doing this, for example:

- Demonstrating how you put equal opportunities theory into your workplace by anti-discriminatory practice or challenging (politely) a discriminatory view or opinion of someone else that is not acceptable to you.
- Respecting confidentiality in your placement.

- Using your knowledge of psychology to help someone through a difficulty.
- Using your communication skills in appropriate ways such as checking understanding, asking open questions and not being judgemental.
- Helping a service user with meal planning and using your knowledge of the components that constitute a healthy diet.
- Promoting a healthy lifestyle with different service users by providing information and guidance so that service users can make informed choices.
- Being aware of potentially harmful environmental problems and seeking ways to overcome them.
- Using knowledge of growth and development or human physiology to appreciate and be alert to potential problems.
- Planning research to aid practice.

These are necessary general statements and you will be able to find many other links over your two-year programme. By actively considering such links, you will not only increase your personal development, but also improve your practice and increase the service that you are able to give to service users.

Developing skills

It is essential that you take the opportunity to work with different service user groups because you will develop different skills with each group. Although there will be many common themes with each placement, you will manage each situation differently. Intellectual stimulation for instance will be quite different with elderly people, adults, people with learning disabilities and children.

Assessment activity 5.7

Developing skills with different service user groups (1)
Using the four service user groups mentioned above devise suitable activities that will provide for both social and intellectual needs and explain why you have chosen these activities and the possible benefits to the service users.

Your practical care skills will also be quite different with different groups.

Developing skills with different service user groups (2)
Using 'assisting with personal hygiene' as an example of a practical skill, brainstorm all the important points you should be aware of and then say how these might be different between helping a three-year-old child in a nursery and an elderly lady with limited mobility and moderate arthritis. When you are doing this exercise remember that all service users should be encouraged to be as independent as possible.

Communication

A whole chapter in this book and an essential unit in this qualification is devoted to communication in the caring professions. You may think that you are a good talker already, but that is not enough. Talking is very personal and you may have to think again about the way you speak with service users. General chat mainly revolves around expressing one's own views, asking closed questions and using language that might be all right with one's peers, family and friends but not with vulnerable service users.

It takes a lot of practice to get it right and can be frustrating at first; you will not be used to trying to edit and review what you want to say in your head before you say it. Students often say that they cannot do it; you will develop the skill but you have to keep trying. Not only do you have to re-think what you say but also the way you say things and who you are saying them to. There would be no point in using Cockney rhyming slang to a Scotsman, and similarly there is no point in using modern slang to an eighty-five-year-old lady – neither party would understand a word! You would need to use simple, short sentences without complex words when speaking with a service user with learning disabilities or a young child.

Negatives can also have a confusing effect on certain service user groups who 'home' in on certain words, ignoring the negative. 'We are not going swimming today' can send some service users dashing off to fetch their bathers and towel, much to the frustration of the carer!

Performance analysis

You will find that your communication skills develop rapidly through contact with different service user groups and you will be able to analyse your performance better after a course year (and some varied placements). You will also gradually improve your knowledge and skills enough to judge when you need to refer something you have seen, done or heard to a supervisor. At first, you will probably refer most events or none at all depending on your personality, but later you will develop a better sense of proportion. It is probably wise to refer more rather than less! As you gain more experience of your service users and the settings, you will understand their physical, social, emotional, spiritual and intellectual needs and be able to help meet these needs. Some service users will yearn for peace and quiet and need to be left alone whereas others may need social intercourse and intellectual stimulation. If you are unsure, ask the service user and then you will know. Do not try to guess their needs, you may guess completely wrongly and give the appearance of not caring for them as people. Remember that people have a right to choose the care they receive and the way in which they receive it.

Communication skills

The real importance of non-verbal and verbal communication cannot be emphasised enough. In this section, you will be considering how to overcome communication barriers. When you fail to get through to someone, you have to think about possible barriers in the interaction. When you have identified the problem you will see how to overcome the barrier.

Barriers

Firstly, is it you who is preventing communication? Here are some of the points you may be failing to address:

- Are you not listening actively?
- Have you checked the service user has understood at frequent intervals?
- Are you distracted by something else?
- Are you interrogating the service user by asking repeated closed questions?
- Did you introduce yourself and your purpose?
- Have you adopted a poor position and/or posture?
- Is your body language implying that you are disinterested in the service user?
- Is your voice too quiet/loud/fast/shrill/low/anxious?

- Are you giving poor responses such as dismissing the service user's feelings?
- Did you make the conversation too complex?
- Did you summarise and close the dialogue appropriately?
- Did you let the service user down the last time you spoke?
- Have you respected the service user as a person with feelings and rights?

This appears at first to be a daunting list and you can probably think of other items to add to it but you will be able to check through this very quickly. Once you have identified the error you will know how to overcome it. Assuming that you feel that you have done your best with these points, you now have to consider other barriers. These barriers are probably still your error as you should have checked on these points at the start of your conversation or better still, before beginning the conversation at all! The pattern diagram in Figure 5.5 will provide you with food for thought. You will be able to overcome these when you have identified the difficulty.

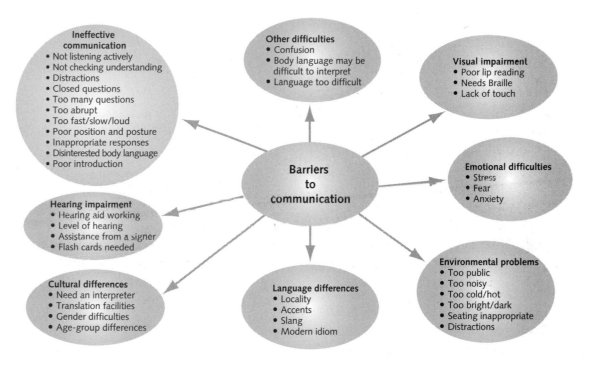

Figure 5.5 Barriers to communication

Non-verbal language

When someone speaks a different language and an interpreter is not available, try to learn a few appropriate words yourself and introduce picture flash cards with the English words on. Remember that non-verbal language is the major part of communication, so touch, smile, open posture and friendly demeanour are as important as words.

Solutions

People who have impaired hearing may need to be referred to an audiologist for a hearing aid or repair to an aid. Sometimes a new battery or cleaning is all that is required. Similarly, service users who are visually impaired may need suitable glasses to watch facial expressions and pick up on non-verbal communication. It is not unusual to hear an individual say 'Wait until I get my glasses on so that I can hear you'. Do not shout at service users; rather repeat your message a few times clearly in a moderate voice. Some severely deaf service users may have a text-messager attached to a mobile phone (using a type-talk service) on which they can communicate.

People who are confused or have learning difficulties respond to short, simple repeated messages at the right level. It is important to leave enough time to get the information across and not to become impatient with the service user. Picture boards and flash cards can again prove useful, but should not entirely take the place of verbal and non-verbal communication.

You should respect confidentiality with all service users at all times unless you have fears for someone's safety; if you do feel the need to pass on information to your supervisor then you must immediately tell the service user. You will find more information on confidentiality in Unit 1.

Interaction in health and care professionals
What you should be doing
You will develop different skills in different placements working with different people. You are unlikely to be involved in medical care, but highly likely to be asked to assist service users with daily living activities such as:

- menu planning
- assisting with food and drink
- accessing and using toilet facilities
- maintaining personal hygiene and appearance
- shopping
- cleaning and tidying
- helping service users to become comfortable
- supporting service users through communication
- reading to service users
- writing letters for service users
- assisting with simple mobility
- accompanying service users
- promoting leisure interests.

What you should not be doing
There are also very important health and safety aspects that you should observe.

You should *not* be involved in lifting and handling of service users unless you have had recognised and appropriate training from a person qualified to give such training. You should not be involved in answering any questions dealing with the details of a service user's care with family, friends or other care staff. As a general rule, you should not answer the telephone although sometimes you may be given permission to do so.

You must be aware of the need to obtain a service user's permission for any aspect of care work. A service user has the right to refuse any part of his or her care and any refusal or rejection must be reported to the supervisor.

Reflection and effective caring
You are a person with values, beliefs and interests special to you. These personal factors will have influenced your development, personality and behaviour; you must understand that it is exactly the same for your service users. You will instantly be drawn to some people and enjoy caring for them but there will be others that you don't instinctively like.

To be an effective carer, you must be able to suppress these prejudices and look in to yourself to analyse your feelings. A good carer reflects on actions, thoughts and feelings. This is called being a reflective practitioner and the purpose of this is to identify the areas in your own personal development, which need further work.

At the end of a day in placement, look back at the support you have given your service users and try to identify any difficulties, anxieties or awkward moments that you might have avoided with a different approach. You might do this by mentally running through a checklist such as the one below.

Placement venue.. Date:

Reflective practice checklist

1   How did I approach the work I carried out?
2   Was my approach positive?
3   How did the way I worked affect the service user?
4   How did the way I worked affect my colleagues?
5   How effective was my verbal and non-verbal communication?
6   Which part of today's activities did I do well?
7   What were the reasons for my good performance?
8   Which part of today's activities did I not do so well?
9   What were the reasons for the poorer performance?
10 How could I have performed better?
11 What have I learned today?
12 What would be my performance rating out of 10?   /10

Special comments relating to this placement day

_____

_____

_____

_____

_____

Assessment activity 5.9

Word-process the above checklist, leaving appropriate spaces for your responses, and save it. In your first placement, complete a daily performance analysis. Following your experience, write an account of how your performance has changed throughout the whole period of your placement, and file in your VPL together with hard copies of your completed checklists.

- How much did the checklist help you to analyse your performance?
- Do you need to modify the checklist in any way? If so, complete this in readiness for your next period of experience and include the reasons why you have made the changes.

If you repeat this assessment activity each time that you go to vocational placement, you will have excellent evidence for your VPL.

Dealing with inappropriate behaviour and abuse
Inappropriate behaviour

Inappropriate behaviour is behaviour not usually seen in the circumstances of the care setting. It is often distressing, sometimes violent and occasionally oppressive. It can also mean simply ignoring the needs of others. Inappropriate behaviour can come from service users, visitors or care-workers. In some cases you will be able to understand why the individual is acting in this manner, in other cases you will not. Understanding the reasons behind the behaviour does not change its acceptability. In most cases you will be able to refer the matter to a supervisor – you should not be working on your own. There are certain generic guidelines for dealing with inappropriate behaviour, but you must realise that each situation will be unique and developing the ability to size up the problem quickly will help.

Generic guidelines for dealing with inappropriate behaviour

1 Try to assess the size of the problem as quickly as possible and consider the approach you will use.
2 Get help if there are not enough care staff around.
3 Keep calm.
4 Think clearly.
5 Be clear in what you say.
6 Try to get the service user into a private area.
7 Repeat the request and give your reason but don't enter into an argument.
8 Use frequent eye contact but do not stare.
9 Be assertive but not aggressive.
10 Give your service user personal space.
11 Empathise with the service user.
12 Let the service user back down in a way that will not belittle or humiliate them.

Violent behaviour

Most of the generic guidelines above will be appropriate for dealing with violent people as well, but in addition you will need to know:

- how to get out of the space as quickly as possible
- how to summon help – sound an alarm, shout for help, call security or police
- not to let an attacker get between you and the door
- remove any potential weapons if it is easy to do so.

Above all, keep yourself safe, you are a student and not trained to deal with attackers. Even if there are other people such as service users in the room, as an untrained person you will be more of use bringing trained staff to their aid.

Assessment activity 5.10
Dealing with inappropriate behaviour (1)

1 Examine the above guidelines and think of a situation in your life in which you have been in the presence of an angry person and felt a bit frightened.

a) How was the situation resolved?

b) Was it satisfactorily concluded?

c) Explain how it could it have been managed in a better way.

2 Write short explanations of the meanings of the following terms:
- personal space
- aggressive
- empathise
- assertive.

3 Work through the generic guidelines point by point and suggest the purpose behind each one.

4 If you observe a demonstration of inappropriate behaviour in any of your placement experiences write a report of the circumstances and the way in which the care staff managed the incident. Comment on the management style in relation to the guidelines.

Dealing with inappropriate behaviour (2)

Earlier in this unit you learned about policies and procedures, and how to find out the appropriate steps to take in each placement when dealing with aggression and violence. Write a report comparing how different organisations respond to the different types of inappropriate behaviour.

Case Study

Mr J is a service user in the residential home where you are working for two weeks vocational placement. He likes a particular chair to sit in to watch the television in the communal living room. A new service user Mrs M came into the room straight after the evening meal, and occupied Mr J's chair. He is an ex-army man with a brusque manner and can be very sarcastic and rude. Mrs M is a timid service user, prone to bouts of weeping since her husband died recently. You anticipate the problem that might arise when Mr J enters the room.

1 How will you approach Mrs M?

2 What will you say to her?

3 Is it necessary to refer the matter to a supervisor?

Although Mr J is brusque and may distress Mrs M a great deal he is not likely to be violent.

Abuse

Sitting alongside inappropriate behaviour, there is the problem of abuse. Abuse can take many forms as you can see from Figure 5.6

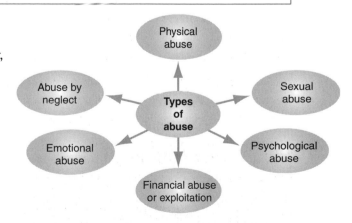

Figure 5.6 Abuse can occur in many forms

Assessment activity 5.8

Over a period of three months or one term, collect cuttings or photocopies from newspapers or magazines or refer to TV documentaries related to different forms of abuse. Obtain a copy of one placement's policy on dealing with abuse.

In a small group discuss a small selection of cases in the following ways:

- Which service user group was being abused?
- How many service users were involved?
- Who were the abusers?
- What type of care setting was involved?
- How long did the abuse continue?
- What was likely to be the short- and long-term effects on the service user?
- What signs might you have noticed if you had been working in that care setting?
- Why do you think the abuse started?
- What could you have done about it? (Your placement policy can be used here.)

You might find it helpful to repeat this exercise again using different cases before your study programme is finished to reinforce the importance of awareness of abuse.

Information

Lack of information or misinformation is probably the most likely cause of most daily difficulties arising in caring for people. Sometimes the mishap is easily overcome, many times it can mean a delay but, on other occasions, it can have disastrous or tragic consequences.

Reasons for sharing information can be:

- to safeguard a service user's care and life
- to prevent the waste of resources
- to prevent delays
- to value other people
- to communicate all the information to prevent errors and make correct decisions
- to ensure continuity of care.

Think It Over

Here are some examples of lack of information or being given the wrong information. What might be the implications of each?

1 Mrs F has two buses to catch and a long walk from her home to the first bus stop. She has her first appointment with the cardio-vascular clinic on 12 September. On arrival, she finds that the receptionist had written the date incorrectly and she should have attended on 2 September. She recalls that the receptionist was distracted by a telephone call in the middle of making the appointment.

2 The renal consultant had not received the documents relating to a case conference. He failed to attend. As a consequence, five other important, busy care-workers could not progress and their time was wasted.

3 Jo asked her friend what time the external assessment was set for on the next day. She arrived two hours late at the time she was told and missed the session. She had to wait until the following year to complete her qualification.

4 The tired house doctor omitted to prescribe an essential medicine for a service user. The service user developed life-threatening symptoms and became a medical emergency.

Assessment activity 5.9

1 Brainstorm all the different ways of passing on information to other people.

2 For each way of transmitting information say how the information could be recorded.

3 For each way of transmitting information say how the information could be stored.

4 Discuss the advantages and disadvantages of each method of recording information.

5 Discuss the advantages and disadvantages of each method of storing information.

When you have completed the activity above, you will have an excellent base for comparing the different methods of recording and storage of information in your various placements.

You can form your own opinions about the effectiveness of storage during your placement by observation and experience. For example, how easy was it to find a particular placement policy?

Some confidential information must be kept in a secure location for access only by authorised personnel. You need to find out how the information is kept secure. Could it be simply behind lock and key or is it in computerised files protected by a password that is changed regularly and known only to a few key workers?

Taking a 'worst case scenario', imagine how care-workers would feel if a service user had been diagnosed with an untreatable cancer and written case notes had been read by another service user who had disclosed the information to the victim before the care-workers had time to do so. The sick service user left a suicide note and killed herself because of the leaked information. Imagine if the 'nosy' service user had mistaken two similar names! Fantasy, you might think, but these things do happen. It is also not infrequent for an individual to overhear a conversation about a service user who is a relative or friend both inside and outside a care setting.

Make sure that you have read the organisation's policy on confidentiality and abide by its contents.

Principles of team work, work relationships, roles and responsibilities

Every care setting consists of networks and teams of people working together and it is essential that each network or team member fulfil their duties to ensure maximum efficiency in delivering service to the service user. If you have worked on a team project you will know how annoyed, frustrated and angry people can get if one team member fails to carry out their responsibility. You will also know that the whole project can be abandoned or jeopardised under such circumstances, even though other people have worked really hard. In a care setting where you are dealing with vulnerable people, it is unforgivable to jeopardise the delivery of care.

Limits of their roles and competence in vocational practice

As a student on vocational practice, you will be expected to join one or more teams of carers. You will be one of the lowest levels of people in that team, but you can still be of great value. Your role will be limited by the guidelines that you have been given by your tutor or a placement supervisor. The guidelines will differ in different placements and you should be prepared for this. At all times, you must remember that the team has the primary function of delivering the best possible care to the service user group. You will not be the most important person in the placement and there will be times when you feel in the way because the care-workers have other duties which must be carried out.

You can however, always be observant, willing, responsible and enthusiastic about the tasks you are given to do. Make notes on questions you want to ask and find suitable times to seek answers from appropriately qualified people. Taking coffee breaks with some of your team members is often more useful than arranging a break time to fit with a friend in the same establishment.

Many students feel 'task-orientated', in other words they feel guilty if they are not actually doing something rather than talking to service users. There is no need to feel this way, talking to service users in an appropriate way is valuable to both parties. This does not mean telling service users all about personal relationships or talking about yourself all the time; it means treating the service user as a real person and finding out how they feel about things and generally being a reflective practitioner.

You should always introduce yourself to a service user and explain the purpose of your presence. Never let a service user believe that you are a qualified carer, even though this might be quite flattering. If you do not know how to do something that you are asked to do, always say so politely and ask if you might observe so that you can carry out the task at a later date when you are competent. Occasionally a carer may ask you to do something that is not permitted by your guidelines, so you must explain why you cannot do it at this time.

Take the time to discover the limits of other roles and responsibilities in the team such as care assistants, porters, volunteers, etc.

Roles and relationships
Staff, service users, students, relatives and visitors

Relationships depend upon good communication between people and treating each person as an individual with unique needs, views, beliefs and choices. Where these can be seen to exist, relationships will form by right. Relatives and visitors are usually very important to service users and bring an interest in life outside the establishment. There are some exceptions to this and sometimes a service user will not wish to see a relative or visitor. The service user has that choice and the carer must communicate that information in a polite, yet assertive, way.

Relatives and friends may act as informal advocates for the service user but should not dictate the care programme to care staff or make demands or suggestions that counter the service user's wishes. Consultants and doctors have traditionally been viewed by everyone else as 'demi-gods' whose wishes must be carried out immediately, but this is slowly changing and more and more people will now challenge the medical staff as and when necessary. Nurses were traditionally seen as the 'handmaidens' of the doctors. They are now qualified professionals, often graduates, able to manage staff, plan care programmes, prescribe some medicines and act as advisers on health and illness; they are, quite rightly, held in a higher regard by service users and the general public.

Care assistants form the bulk of 'hands-on' carers and are very well regarded by service users who generally appreciate the support they give. Care assistants will also form good relationships with students on vocational placements provided they are fully informed about the purpose of the experience. Occasionally, a student might be placed with an extremely busy carer who resents the presence of the student and shows it. This can make the student feel very uncomfortable and the tendency is to complain to others about the person's attitude. Inevitably, this gets back to the carer and makes the situation worse.

Key issues

If you are experiencing difficulties with your supervising carer, you would do well to explore the following avenues to remedy the situation:

1 Stay bright and enthusiastic and demonstrate a willingness to learn.

2 Try to manoeuvre asking for jobs to do in front of other people, staff or service users, because the carer will be more pleasant in these circumstances.

3 Do not complain to people around you.

4 Carry out any task that you are given efficiently and pleasantly and let the carer know (preferably in front of others) when the job is completed.

5 Reflect on your own personality and communication skills to see if you are at fault.

6 After several days, if the situation has not improved ask the carer privately if you have caused offence in any way and would they prefer if you asked the supervisor or tutor to be re-allocated. When you have tried hard for some time, polite assertiveness may change behaviour. If this does not work, ask for re-allocation, but do not blame the carer openly; when asked for reasons explain that you need diversity of service users and experience. The supervisor will know the personality of the carer and appreciate your tactfulness.

Students are expected to maintain relationships of a professional nature with staff and service users and to be polite and courteous at all times to relatives and visitors. They will not be required to give or to receive information from or to people who visit the service user in any aspect but should refer to the supervisor in all matters.

Fontana (1990a) writes that those who have good relationships with service users in a caring field also:

- Convey a respect for them and show an ability to listen
- Put them at ease but avoid emotional over-involvement
- Clarify the help that can be given and cannot be given
- Accept justifiable criticism
- Avoid undue exercise of professional power.

Skills required to work effectively in a team

All care organisations work in teams and networks largely because care is a twenty-four-hour commitment and involves a multitude of skilled practitioners, 'hands-on' care assistants, administrative personnel, technicians, porters and security people to name only a few groups. When individuals cannot work together, the atmosphere is unpleasant for the remainder of the team, everyone begins to question the roles they perform and the whole performance suffers.

On the other hand, when people do work together within a team, there is pride in performance, everyone tries to do their very best and efficiency soars. In this situation there is a pleasant camaraderie and individuals enjoy job satisfaction even when times are difficult. Communication and co-operation, both formal and informal, between team members is essential to make everyone aware of events and able and willing to pull together. A large number of formal meetings that interfere with the actual caring role can be seen as irrelevant, whereas shared informal coffee breaks can forge team links in a very effective way.

Key issues

The team works together in an effective way when members:

- have the same professional objectives
- are able to contribute to discussion and action
- feel valued
- can be creative in their approach
- share responsibility
- suppress personal differences in the interests of team harmony
- have different skills and talents which are put to good use and complement each other.

Employees who are excluded deliberately or accidentally get extremely upset and resentful of the situation. Lack of communication is one of the most common causes of care service breakdown; sometimes it is an oversight due to forgetfulness or being called away at a crucial time, or there may be mislaid or lost information that is vital to the next course of action.

Think It Over

Think of an incident when you could not perform to the best of your ability due to lack of information or misinformation. How did you feel about the end result and about the person(s) who let you down? Have you ever failed to communicate properly to someone else? How did that turn out?

Punctuality is very important in employment and especially so when working with a team of people. A team may not be able to proceed if one member is missing and everyone's time is wasted. The late member can have no idea of the effort other people have made to arrive on time and the annoyance and frustration that can build up against them.

It is always prudent to arrive a little early for work or placement and to do this you must allow extra time for late transport, busy traffic, etc. This often means simply rising an hour earlier and preparing the items you need for work, the night before. This is particularly important if you have a social occasion the evening before work as you are more likely to wake up later. Ensure that you have a good alarm clock or someone reliable to give you an alarm call. Continually being late is one of the most damaging factors to you personally and very few people believe your excuses for being late – however inventive you are!

You have already learned that in many situations, such as dealing with unacceptable behaviour, you should refer to others. Being able to do this is also part of working within a team. Team members will have different skills, strengths and abilities and to use these to good effect other team members must be prepared to refer problems to them. This must not be viewed as getting rid of a problem on to someone else, but as providing the best service. However, this must not stifle professional, social and personal development in others; there is everything to be gained by reflecting on the expert's actions and asking questions at suitable times, thereby eventually gaining confidence and competence to perform similar tasks under the expert's supervision. As a student, you may be able to use this strategy in some simple tasks but are more likely to be able to observe the development of other workers in the care setting.

Causes of stress in the workplace and the effect on service users and staff

A large number of books have been written about the causes and management of stress in general and quite a number written solely about the stress involved in the various aspects of caring professions. Unit 7 also discusses the meaning of stress, various models of stress analysis and management. This unit asks you to look at the causes of stress in the workplace and how it affects service users and staff.

Burnout is a term used to explain how a person feels usually occurring after a long period of stress (chronic stress) when they feel stripped of motivation and enthusiasm. They are devoid of creative thinking and feel they cannot cope with anything more. Very often it can be a prelude to a complete breakdown and therefore should be taken seriously.

Care staff are continually being asked to perform more tasks and work longer hours because there is a chronic shortage of qualified care-workers. It takes several years to fully train a qualified carer and, although the government has initiated various schemes to improve recruitment, there remains an imbalance between the number of service users needing care and the number of care staff. Hospitals are particularly hard-hit by staff shortages and care staff from overseas are being encouraged to come to Britain. Large numbers of residential and nursing homes are closing because the funding for elderly vulnerable people is too low to enable the establishments to survive. Every week in local newspapers we read of specialist centres closing due to reduced or loss of essential funding.

Think It Over

It is always useful to make daily use of media reports, but do not believe everything that you read!

For one week, make a period of time to read daily and specialised media reports concerning care staff shortages, extended roles, longer working hours and stress levels.

Keep a log of everything you find and note the effects on service users and staff. Investigate stress levels, the causes and the effects in your different vocational placements. Compare your findings.

The most common *physical* symptoms of stress are:

- headache
- stomach disorders
- chest tightness
- lower back pain
- neck tensions
- chronic constipation

Other symptoms of stress can be:

- insomnia
- loss of efficiency
- loss of concentration
- irritability
- breakdown of relationships
- lack of motivation
- depression

You have learned that it is very important to have successful relationships in teams of people working together. Where there is conflict between care-workers and/or service users, there is also stress. Many people can 'switch off' when they have finished the day's work, but some people will brood over any conflict for a very long time. People can find release for their feelings by talking to others, increasing physical activity, experiencing a period of solitude or even just going into an empty room and shouting their feelings out loud.

Assessment activity 5.10

Make careful observations of an incident that involves stress in the workplace. This may be a stressful situation that needs to be managed, or a carer or service user feeling stressed and displaying unusual behaviour.

1 Record the cause of the stress if you know it.
2 Do you think that there were other underlying reasons for the behaviour?
3 How did the behaviour differ from 'normal'?
4 How was the situation resolved?
5 Could the individual have coped another way? Explain.

As with all the activities, remember confidentiality!

Equal opportunities

You will have come across several references to equal opportunities already in this book, particularly in Unit 1. You have also learned in this chapter about valuing people as individuals and respecting the beliefs and views of others.

You will need to find out about the equal opportunities policies and procedures in each vocational placement that you do and analyse how these relate to the national and legal framework. To do this you will need access to the national and legal framework. Three most important documents/organisations for you on this topic will be:

- Commission for Racial Equality: www.cre.gov.uk
- Equal Opportunities Commission: www.eoc.org.uk
- Human Rights Act 1998: www.pfc.org.uk/legal/hra98b.htm

Other useful information can be obtained from:

- Department of Social Security: www.dss.gov.uk
- Opportunity for All: www.dss.gov.uk/ha/pubs/poverty/sum/suma.htm

- Age Concern: www.age.org.uk
- British Association of Social Workers: www.basw.co.uk
- National Disability Council: www.disability-council.gov.uk
- Institute of Race Relations: www.homebeats.co.uk

You should obtain leaflets (many are free) or download the appropriate information before you go on your first placement so that you are in a position to start checking the relationship of the policies and procedures to the national and legal framework.

Some policies may discriminate positively for a particular group of people in order to 'pump-prime' against deep-rooted prejudice. You can find more information on this in Unit 1, page 15.

Key issues

You will find below a summary of the key points concerning equal opportunities:

- Prejudice involves making judgements about other people or groups of people without direct knowledge or experience of them.
- Stereotyping is closely allied to prejudice and involves believing that all members of a particular group share negative characteristics.
- Discrimination occurs when you act on prejudices and deal with some people less favourably than others.
- Most prejudices are based on things that people cannot change, such as skin colour, birthplace, appearance, gender, disability, etc.
- Ignorance, power, vulnerability, upbringing and the need to conform to a particular group lead to prejudice.
- Using reflective thinking, empathy, raised awareness, understanding, sensitivity, knowing the consequences of discrimination and a desire to treat others fairly will provide you with the tools to promote equal opportunities in yourself and others.

Assessment activity 5.16

Work as groups. Obtain a copy of the equal opportunities policy in your educational organisation or workplace and collect evidence of:

- the ways in which the establishment is meeting its obligations
- the failures to meet any obligations.

Compile the evidence on two headed flip-chart sheets and complete your findings by analysing the extent to which the policy is being met, i.e. the effectiveness of the policy.

Note: You will probably start with simple things like looking for wheelchair access and personal hygiene facilities that have been adapted for people with special needs and disabilities. However, do not forget to find out if staff members are provided with equal opportunities training and if there is a complaints procedure that people are encouraged to use if they are dissatisfied.

Effectiveness

You will need to judge the effectiveness of the policies and procedures in each vocational placement. You will be able to think of several ways to do this if you observe and listen to the events around you. When the Queen opened a new parliament session in November 2001, she quoted a passage from Burke: 'To promote evil it is only necessary for good men to do nothing.'

We could substitute injustice for 'evil' and people for 'men' and this quote would be highly relevant to equal opportunities practice. Bearing this in mind, you could focus on the presence and absence of action to promote equity.

Here are some suggestions:

- Do equal opportunities issues or rights appear regularly on the agendas of meetings?
- Are service users (and staff) advised of their rights?
- Have you seen or heard anyone supporting service users to achieve their rights?
- Have you seen or heard any discriminatory behaviour?
- Was this behaviour challenged by anyone?
- Are complaints procedures explained to service users (and staff)?
- How many complaints have been received in the last twelve months?
- Were complaints resolved satisfactorily as far as the service users were concerned?
- Have you seen any service users being assisted by an advocate?
- What is the gender mix of carers in the setting?

You can also consider practical care tasks in this way as well:

- Can individuals choose and wear their own clothes?
- Can they go to bed in their own time?
- Is there a choice of food at meal times?
- Are service users' religious beliefs catered for?
- Are people from ethnic minorities supported with their cultural differences, language, gender of carer, etc?

You will be able to use these ideas to form your own list of questions that are specific to the care setting in which you are working. When you are compiling your questions, you will also be collecting examples of practice relating to theory and evaluating the effectiveness of equal opportunities practice. It should then be possible to suggest improvements from your evaluation of your answers.

Challenging discriminatory behaviour

Discriminatory behaviour can take many forms in different care settings and with different individuals; you will need to be able to identify the behaviour and know how to challenge it – which can be difficult to do especially when the person is a good friend or someone in a superior position.

Many discriminatory remarks are hidden in humour or the individual responds with the old excuse, ' I was only joking'. Other remarks are intended to put a person down, undermine them or even be absolutely cruel. On many occasions, the discrimination occurs through sheer ignorance of knowledge about different cultures practised by ethnic minority groups of people or failing to recognise the need to provide care programmes appropriate to different cultures. Ageism, sexism, racism and discrimination against disability, sexuality and unemployment is still prevalent in today's society despite legislation. Much of this is bound up with use of inappropriate language such as:

- dolies, yobs – unemployed people
- wrinklies, oldies, old folks, dearies – elderly people (even the 'elderly' on its own can be seen as discriminatory)
- cripples, spastics – these are very unpleasant terms for people with disabilities
- Pakis, coons, wogs, Paddies, coloureds – these are unacceptable terms for people from different racial groups.

In care it is unacceptable to call service users – the renal case, the stroke in bed three, etc.

Using inappropriate language can label or stereotype, cause offence and belittle individuals, and as carers it is important to treat everyone fairly. It is also discrimination to do nothing when you hear discriminatory remarks or to say:

'It's not my problem', 'I'm not going to cause trouble', 'I will wait to see if anyone else takes it up first', or similar remarks.

You may find this rather worrying that by doing nothing, you are also part of the discrimination. For many people, discrimination is only seen as a positive action against someone and they would be shocked to be implicated by the negative aspect. Take heart from the fact that very few people have *not* been guilty of this in the past either by not wishing to cause trouble, not get involved or simply not knowing how to manage the situation. The individual who is being discriminatory will continue to do so if never challenged and the effects on those being discriminated against will continue to be damaging to their physical and mental health.

Many members of the general public continue to be unaware of their discriminatory behaviour even when they have had equal opportunity training! In many situations a person can be discriminated against from multiple directions. For example, a female Afro-Caribbean service user can be discriminated against on the grounds of age, gender, culture, race, skin colour and disability. How could you cope with that – many people have to, every day!

Case Study

Mrs S and her partner Mr B were purchasing some cut flowers in a large supermarket to take to a friend in hospital. A middle-aged male employee was wrapping the flowers chosen and handed to him by Mrs S while the two men were chatting idly. Mrs S handed over the money for the flowers and the supermarket loyalty card in her name. When the purchase was completed, the employee handed the wrapped flowers, the change and the loyalty card to Mr B. When Mrs S complained about that, both men were astonished and Mr B explained quickly that he had no intention of keeping the change. Mrs S tried to make both men see that was not the point; she felt no respect had been paid to her right to receive the items back herself. She said that if she had been a child buying flowers for her mother, she would have received change and purchase back herself. Both men thought that she was making a mountain out of a molehill, although Mr B did eventually see the point afterwards. Mrs S explained that most discrimination is so inbred that people just don't think about it.

Do you think that Mrs S was justified in her complaint?

Was this an example of sexism?

Would you have picked up on this type of discrimination or just accepted it?

What do you think might have happened if Mrs S had used a wheelchair and been accompanied by Mr B?

Do you think the incident would change the way the employee behaved next time?

You would challenge most types of discrimination by direct conversation with the individual concerned in a private room in a polite, but firm manner. If the matter is not resolved ask for support from your colleagues and supervisor. Where there is a lack of provision for people, the most appropriate method of challenge is asking for the matter to be discussed at a unit meeting and, if necessary, request training. Where there is any risk to people, then the unit manager, health and safety officer or police should be informed.

Even governments have been guilty of discrimination (an example of institutional discrimination). In the UK the age of consent for heterosexual partners was different from that of gay partners until recently. Anti-discriminatory practice is vital in providing good service that meets the needs of service users; an active approach is needed to make efforts that result in change.

Assessment activity 5.11

Think of a situation when you or someone you know was excluded from a party, meeting or activity. How did you or your friend feel? Were you angry, dispirited, devalued, belittled or offended?

Discuss the effects of discrimination if every time you went anywhere you were faced with people who discriminated against you for reason of your skin colour, gender, race, religion, culture, sexuality, age or disability.

Empowerment

In the past, professional carers such as nurses, doctors, social workers and carers generally made decisions about service users because they considered themselves to be experts on people. Nowadays, people are considered to be the experts on their own social, emotional and cognitive needs but not necessarily on their physiological care. Whereas historically the carer had the power, it is generally perceived that the service users should hold the power to control their lives as much as possible and that carers should assist the service user to make his or her own decisions whenever possible. This is known as **empowerment**.

Many service users are not able to work towards their own decisions because of their vulnerability due to illness, confusion, disability, dementia and old age. In these situations, the carer is required to reach out to the service user or their advocate using empathy and understanding and work towards an agreement, which fits in with the service user's lifestyle, culture and beliefs. A relative or family friend may be important in acting as advocate by providing details of the service user's identity that are unknown to the carer.

In addition to all the other policies and procedures that you have learned about, most care settings will have policies and procedures on empowerment to guide the caring staff on their approach. You will need to find out about the ways in which empowerment is managed in each vocational placement.

Assessment activity 5.12

Carry out this activity in pairs. Find a case study situation in which you might be frightened and confused and unable to make a straightforward decision. You can choose your own age group or gender. Some ideas are given below to guide you.

1   An older man or woman is trying to decide whether to give up their home and move into residential accommodation. The son, who they think is trying to sell the house to raise money, is pressing almost daily.

2   A fifteen-year old girl is pregnant from a 'one-night stand' with someone unknown to her at a party. Her parents are strict church-goers with a high reputation in the community. Although she would consider an abortion, she has no money of her own and the doctor is a family friend.

3   A woman in her thirties had a secret affair over a year ago with a colleague who later left the area. She has just heard from another colleague that he has been diagnosed HIV positive. She is newly pregnant by her husband with their first child and they are looking forward to the event.

Decide who will be the carer and the service user. The carer must reach out to the service user to help her reach a decision about the next step to take. The carer must not directly advise or instruct or use phrases such as 'If it was me, I would...', 'If I were you I would...' or 'I think you should...'. The service user must reach the decision of his or her choice. Remember that open questions will be more useful here.

Discuss how it felt for both parties.

Care programmes

A care programme exists to identify the most appropriate ways of achieving the objectives identified after the assessment of the service user's needs and to provide the best service possible with the available resources. Everyone who receives a service should have a care programme that fits resources to the service user and not the service user to resources. Some care programmes will be very simple whereas others will involve a number of agencies and a number of teams of different specialist carers – a so-called multi-disciplinary approach. Duplication, a waste of resources and a failure to provide some aspects of care will result if the care programme is not fully understood by all personnel involved and constantly reviewed, as the service user's needs change.

How information is gained about service users and their needs

You learned in Unit 2 the importance of effective communication skills. The carer who is assessing the service user's needs must use these to develop a working relationship with the service user to gain as much information about their problems, identity, values and beliefs as possible to plan an effective care programme. The carer must make sure that from the outset the service user is aware of the carer's role and is given as much information as possible about the nature of the service provision. Frequently, service users and/or relatives have grandiose views over the services that can be provided and the carer must clarify any misconceptions at the start.

Carers should bear in mind the influences that they personally might have on the service user during the assessment of needs. Some service users will maximise their needs while others make every effort to minimise the amount of help they require. It can be very useful to have a relative or friend, who knows the service user well, present during the assessment; the service user should be asked if there is such a person who will help them.

At regular intervals, the carer should summarise the information obtained so far and ask for confirmation. The needs assessor may also, with the service user's permission, contact other people or agencies who have been working with the service user for extra information. The service user should be absolutely clear about who will be contacted and the nature of the enquiry and the carer must be absolutely clear that permission has been granted. All care professionals are bound by confidentiality policies and by appropriate legislation and these must be adhered to. A representative from an outside agency, which has been involved with the service user, can be asked to attend the needs assessment to provide a fuller picture. The service user should be empowered by these 'helpers' and remain in control wherever possible.

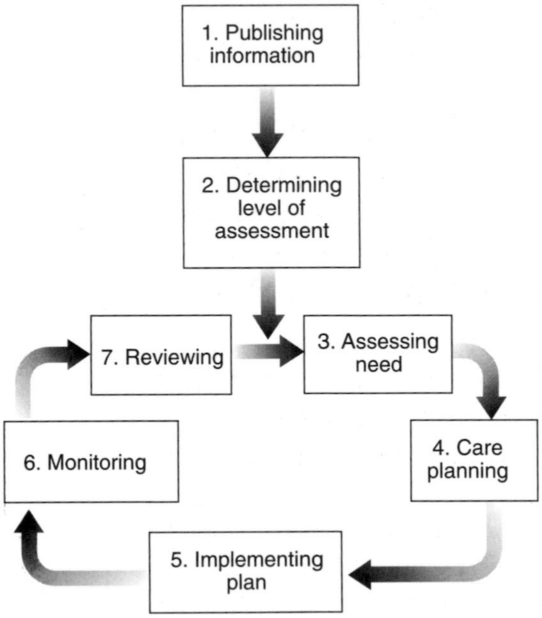

The care setting will have appropriate documentation for completion and procedures in place for the needs assessment process. You will be required to find out how the assessment process operates in your vocational placement. The assessment of needs is just one part of the care plan cycle shown in Figure 5.7.

The assessment may be a full needs assessment taking into account physical, emotional, social, intellectual and cultural needs, or it may be a partial assessment that assesses the needs to, say, cope with the tasks of daily living or to promote an improved quality of life. This will form only a part of the whole picture.

Figure 5.7 The care plan cycle

Carers need to observe the service user unobtrusively as well as ask questions. Shared activities such as cooking a meal or playing a game will often result in a useful informal dialogue. Some service users may feel more confident in expressing initial ideas if it is part of a group discussion although there will need to be a one-to-one chat later.

Own contribution to the planning for service users' needs

In this part of the unit, you are asked to take part in a care-planning meeting and make some contribution to the arrangements. You may be able to report on any observations that you have made or any events witnessed. However, you must not wait until a meeting is held to report anything; it might be important to report back to care staff immediately and this may feature in the planning meeting. When the assessment involves sharing an activity with the service user, you may be able to participate and make valuable, relevant contributions about the service user's physical abilities or state of mind for example. People with learning disabilities or communication problems might be assisted by the use of pictures or photographs to stimulate or replace discussion.

Once the assessment is over, the care plan needs to be written down and distributed in whole or in part to all key workers providing service to the service user.

How agreement is made to provide appropriate services

Once the assessor has developed a working relationship with the service user, a pre-arranged meeting is held in an appropriate setting, frequently the service user's own home. The assessor, service user and carer should be present and appropriate representatives of agencies or advocates, as the service user deems suitable to assist. At this meeting, the needs of the service users are explored; some service users will confuse 'wants' with 'needs' such as wanting a ground floor apartment to overcome difficulties with stairs whereas installation of a stair-lift will meet the need. As the needs become unravelled, the assessor will need to know those needs that concern the service user most and those that concern the carer the most.

The assessor also needs to look at motivation; in other words, which need is the service user most eager to get sorted and for which need(s) are they willing to accept intervention? It might seem strange to you that a service user can identify a need yet not require any help to address that need, but such a situation is quite common. Many people resist change or do not wish to feel they are becoming dependent on others.

The assessor will need to classify the needs into immediate needs, acute short-term needs and chronic long-term needs, and prioritise their plan. The next stage is to agree the objectives to be met in satisfying the prioritised needs; each objective must be capable of being measured and this can be quite difficult with qualitative goals such as improving social contact or emotional stability.

Any agency that is going to supply a service for the service user should receive copies of the assessment documentation and care plan. The individual who has carried out the assessment usually becomes the care manager for the service user and is responsible for the implementation of the plan and the coherence of the agencies involved, including the relatives and friends of the service user as and when necessary. The broad aim of the care plan is to promote as much independence for the service user as possible and enable them to do as much as they can for themselves. The care plan will detail the activities involved, the day and time and who will provide the service – if indeed one is required.

How care services are reviewed

As each care plan is constructed, arrangements for monitoring and reviewing the care plan should be made and recorded. There can be several reasons for monitoring care plans:

- to ensure the objectives of the care plan are being achieved
- to ensure the contributions from different agencies are satisfactorily co-ordinated
- to ensure the care services are meeting quality standards
- budget control
- to support the participants

- to make minor adjustments to the care plan
- to prepare for review.

The care manager can carry out monitoring by telephone calls, observations, visits, surveys or letters. The same person is responsible for reviewing the care plan after a specified interval of time. After a period, the care plan 'ages' and major modifications need to be made. Reviews are necessary because:

- needs require re-assessment
- objectives require change
- objectives require checking and reasons for success and/or failure noted
- costs and quality of care need to be evaluated and revised
- services may need to be revised
- any needs not met require to be assessed
- further dates for monitoring and review need to be established.

Ideally the care manager should again carry out this review. The views of the service user and carer are of paramount importance in checking progress and quality of care, but opinions of service representatives are also valuable. You will need to provide examples from your vocational placements of review situations and how evaluation is carried out in particular care settings.

Personal career goals

Many students know that they want to care for people but are unsure of the direction in which they wish to go. Other students feel that they know precisely which area of caring is preferred but feel disoriented if pulled another way. Some students, committed to a particular career choice, become aware that they may not have either the aptitude or the perseverance required and take another direction altogether, frequently returning to the caring profession later on in their lives.

This section of the unit is attempting to clarify your thoughts, aims and aspirations by careful career planning. It does not try to steer you in any particular direction and is comfortable with the notion that you may change your mind about what you wish to do once, or even several times, during your studies.

It is important to realise that:

- you should know the requirements and skills that you may require for any occupation
- you are aware of the time-scales involved in pursuing your desired job
- you understand that there are many levels of job in caring and if you do not have the requirements for a particular level, there will be other posts open to you in caring
- you should still plan your career even if you change direction
- you should understand the reasons why you are moving in a particular direction
- there are specialists who will help you with your choice(s).

As well as learning about care and care services in your vocational placements, you will also be learning and developing your own knowledge, skills and abilities about *yourself*. You will make and monitor your personal and career plans and map your existing and proposed status against career requirements.

Personal career plan

In this plan you will need to consider all your possible career goals and the intended care area(s) in which you would like to work. For example, you might choose occupational therapy as your main career goal but decide that you would be far happier working in a community care setting rather than a large hospital. You need to consider all possible options in that setting; using the same example there may be opportunities for working with children, young disabled adults, elderly people or those with a particular disability like the loss of a limb. As your experience increases, the list of possible options will grow.

Qualifications, skills and attributes required

As you identify your career goals, you will need to research the necessary requirements for those areas and match your qualifications, already gained and those you are working towards, against them. Qualifications open doors but you will need to match your skills and abilities too. It is important both to be realistic and to realise your own potential. If you do not enjoy studying for long periods at a time and have found examination success hard to come by, then it is probably not sensible to aim to be a doctor, surgeon, psychologist or pathologist for example. You could, however, consider nursing, pathology technician or community psychiatric nursing, depending on your personal views. If you do not like studying very much and prefer to learn in a more practical way then National Vocational Qualifications alongside a job in the area is likely to form your best route after your National Diploma or certificate. Which of these might be chosen could rest with whether you like to work face-to-face with people, like to work in a team or more in an office or laboratory environment. There are many different aspects to consider and research and your tutors will not expect you to make decisions at the beginning of your programme – but they will expect you to investigate and research your favoured options.

Career action plan

In a career action plan, you will detail the actions and their time-scales to achieve your career objectives. Once again you need to be realistic, particularly with time-scales, which have a habit of slipping! You will measure progress against your goals and adjust when appropriate, providing the reasons why adjustment is necessary. This will be an on-going action plan for your programme duration. For further assistance on these plans see the assessment guidelines which follow.

Assessment guidelines

It is crucially important that you record accurately the knowledge and skills that you gain in each placement and do not wait until you have almost completed your course of study. This is an essential unit, equal in depth and breadth to other essential units. However, it is a unit that cannot be completed by lecture notes, but from material and experience from your vocational placement. All your work from vocational practice will be placed in a file or portfolio called the Vocational Practice Log (VPL).

Sketchy, inadequate notes made during your period of time in the placement will cause great difficulty for you later on. If you can show that your progress, development, powers of analysis and evaluation have advanced from the first year of the course to the second, that will be exactly what your tutors are looking for. You will benefit from completing your first-year vocational placement reports in the VPL before the commencement of the second year and comparing your skills and knowledge gained from the first year with that gained towards the end of your course.

Record your findings from each placement in your VPL with dividing pages between each placement; alternatively you might prefer to divide your file into evidence collection sections, such as policies, procedures, equal opportunities practice, care programmes, etc. and have a box or code at the top indicating the placement reference.

About a week before you begin your vocational placement and with your tutor's agreement, pay an informal visit, trying to familiarise yourself with the route you have to take and the length of time you will be travelling. You will then have some idea of the length of time it will take you to reach your destination on the correct day of starting, but do remember that the starting time can make a difference. For example, if you visit one afternoon but actually need to travel between eight and nine o'clock in the morning, it could take you twice as long. You will not wish to arrive late on any morning, and certainly not the first one!

It is useful to telephone first to enquire whether you might introduce yourself when you carry out your journey practice. On this occasion, do not stay too long (carers are busy people), ask any questions that you are worried about that you know your tutor cannot answer and pick up any leaflets to read when you arrive home. Most residential and nursing homes will have publicity leaflets and many other care settings will also produce information. If you are fortunate, the supervisor will show you around and introduce you to other members of staff. If you have a placement in a large organisation this will be more difficult, but you will be able to walk around the public areas without hindrance.

Ensure that you read the information before you arrive on the correct day. Your tutor will inform you about the need for uniform, name badges and the location for the first meeting, together with any particular information that you will require. If you are working with certain service user groups, you will need to be 'police cleared'. This is nothing to be afraid of and involves completing a form, which your tutor will forward to the appropriate authorities. You can also find out if you need to sign a form of registration to indicate that you are on the premises and who to telephone if you are delayed or absent through illness. Most educational establishments will provide you with guidance notes on your student roles and responsibilities. These notes are generic and you may find that there are extra guidelines in specific placements.

Students are often anxious and fearful on their first few attendance days, worried that an emergency might happen and they will not be able to deal with it, worried that someone might shout at them, or complain loudly or that they will be ignored. It would be the same on the first day at work and everyone feels like this – the feeling will soon wear off. In an emergency, call the nearest member of staff; you are not expected to handle emergencies or crises. Do not let yourself be ignored, offer to help other members of staff in a courteous way and stay calm and reassuring if a service user becomes distressed – call a member of staff. You will not know whether this is a common occurrence and a feature of the service user's illness – most will be! Talk to someone at the placement about it in a quiet moment and you will feel much better about it.

Placement structure
Aims, policies and procedures

You will need to record the key features of the aims, policies and procedures in your workplaces and place in your file. Photocopying the policies at your own expense is acceptable but if you then place it in your VPL without reading it through carefully, it will be of little use, whereas teasing out the key features will commit the policy to memory much more effectively. It will also be much easier to compare this list with your next placement's policies than using the whole document. Plan to do this in your first few days in the placement. Find out about other policies operating in the placement and perform the same exercise.

You will find that it is much easier to remind yourself from the key features of documents when you need to consider other evidence, such as linking theory to practice, confidentiality and equal opportunities, than to work from whole policies. Do not attempt to summarise a large number of policies and procedures or you will find time passing so quickly that you will have little time left for anything else. Tackle the major topics that you will find useful for other sections of this unit, such as:

- equal opportunities, including empowerment
- bullying and harassment
- dealing with violence and aggression
- fire emergency
- lifting and handling
- confidentiality
- health and safety.

If you have difficulty in understanding the wording and terminology used in such documents make some notes identifying the problems and in a quiet, suitable moment ask a professional carer to go over these with you.

Role and responsibilities of the staff structure

There are several ways to find out about the roles and responsibilities of different levels of staff in care settings:

- You can ask members of staff, choosing a suitable time.
- You can ask them about their person and job descriptions.
- Visit the personnel section or the employment manager of the organisation.
- Use a search engine for local organisation websites under the type of care setting.
- Write a few letters to care organisations who are advertising job vacancies.
- Use the latest edition of *Career* or other career guidance references in the library.
- Look at job specifications on notice boards in care settings or job centres.
- Look at job vacancies advertised in specialist medical, nursing and social service magazines.

You will see a job description in Figure 5.8 for a position advertised on a hospital website.

Title: **D/E GRADE NURSES**

Closing Date: 31/12/03

Area: Nursing: General

Grade: D/E

Salary:

Description: FULL OR PART TIME

We require staff nurses from varying backgrounds to complement the established teams on both sites. We require nurses who prefer to work at night (although posts will be rotational and day duty will be required to meet training and development needs.) The wards accomodate medically stable patients, most of whom need nurses who are well educated in all aspects of medical nursing with expertise in social aspects of care. There is emphasis on the multi-disiplinary approach therefore applicants must have good communication skills.

D GRADE NURSING JOB DESCRIPTION JOB TITLE: Registered Nurse

GRADE: D

RESPONSIBLE TO: Ward/Unit Sister/Charge Sister

PROFESSIONAL RELATIONSHIPS: Ward/Unit multi-disciplinary team; Clinical/Directorate manager

JOB PURPOSE: The postholder will have responsibility for assessing, implementing and evaluating under supervision, the care needs of group patients.

PATIENT CARE RESPONSIBILITY: To provide safe, individualised, patient care. To participate in the maintenance and development of professional standards incorporating evidence based practice. This will be expected to include participation in the audit of clinical indicators for nursing care. Appropriate delegation, supervision and teaching to junior staff. To communicate effectively with patients, relatives and multi-disciplinary team utilising verbal and written communication methods.

DEVELOPMENT AND TRAINING: To participate in preceptorship, mentorship and clinical supervision to develop personal and professional competence. Accept responsibility for identification of personal development needs. Maintain active registration, including when appropriate attendance at formal education.

WIDER RESPOSIBILITIES: Work with UKCC Code of Conduct. Be aware of and follow Trust policies, procedures. D Grade nurses will not routinely be rostered to take charge. They may however at times be expected to take on this responsibility for personal development purposes or in the absence of a senior nurse. To act at all times as an Ambassador for the organisation. To respond positively and contribute to management of change projects, i.e. in link nurse roles or project groups. This will be expected to include initiatives such as Clinical Governance.

Figure 5.8 A job description for a nursing position
© reproduced with the permission of the Royal Liverpool and Broadgreen Hospitals NHS Trust

Service users

You will need to provide an outline description of the service users in each placement and a broad picture of the reasons behind their involvement in the setting. This will incorporate a similarly broad view of how the needs of the service users are met in the setting. You will have some idea of these areas from publicity literature of the setting but check that the overall picture is correct by discussion with staff members. This evidence can be confined to a few paragraphs; you must not ask service users systematically using direct questions relating to the problems that led to their referral and their physical, emotional, intellectual or social well-being. This might cause too much stress and would probably offend some service users. During your placement experience, you may be able to amplify your evidence further because of the relationships you make. Remember that outline statements are all that is required and you must respect confidentiality at all times.

Services and resources provided by other organisations

This will largely depend on the type of placement you are working in – a small privately owned playgroup may have very few associated organisations, whereas a community care establishment may have several associates such as diverse voluntary groups, physiotherapy and occupational therapy visits, psychology services, etc. You will need to ask staff and be vigilant in observation of visitors to the establishment to obtain this evidence.

Role and performance in each student placement

You will have a basis for this work from your tutor's and/or placement guidelines and together with the placement diary that you should keep, be able to write an accurate job description for yourself about halfway through the placement. Review your job description as your placement ends to update if necessary. It is easier to do this by keeping your word-processed work on a floppy disk. Keep one or two disks for vocational placement only. Convert your diary notes to floppy disk every few days and then complete and print out your work to put in the VPL.

You should use a tabular format that can be utilised for each placement and easily compared during each year of your programme. If you print a chart similar to the one below in landscape format you will have more space in the columns.

Name:		Placement dates:	
Title of vocational placement:			
Nature of service user group:			
Aims of placement	*Objectives of placement*	*Expected tasks*	**Comments on performance*

*The final column will assist you with evaluating your own developing skills and communication skills.

You should try to become more sophisticated in your terminology as you gain experience and become more reflective in your practice. You should be able to evaluate your work as you progress. After you have completed each sheet at the end of a placement, write a reflective report and an evaluation of performance.

As you work through your placements, you will find some of the expected tasks are similar, but some will be very different. You can however make your aims and objectives very different by challenging yourself to complete more difficult objectives. An example is suggested below for your communication skills:

Placement 1	Practise different ways of introducing yourself and find the best way for you. Practise asking open questions and some closed questions and note the service user's responses
Placement 2	Practise open questions and reflecting feeling
Placement 3	Practise opening and closing conversations with service users and summarising at the end
Placement 4	Practise total active listening
Placement 5 or as appropriate to the setting	Find and use ways to overcome barriers in communication
Placement 6	Practise prioritising any of the service user's difficulties and ways to make the service user progress towards making their own decisions. Do I offer the service user individual choice? Do I treat service users as unique individuals? How do service users react to me?

You could make charts like these for other skills and abilities so that you have a plan for developing and improving your performance with each placement and in preparation for making the links from theory to practice. In every placement you should remind yourself of the need to respect confidentiality.

Demonstrate the base knowledge and skills to be an effective practitioner

When you complete the skills and abilities planning charts as above, you will clearly be able to show the links between theory gained in lectures with the practice in the vocational area. You will also show the range of skills needed to fulfil the placement role and how to overcome barriers in communication. The ideal way is to be pro-active in your search for evidence. The last thing you want to be doing is reaching the end of your placements and trying to remember events that took place several months ago, producing second-rate poor evidence or having no evidence at all for some sections – despite having been on five or six placements. Read through the unit specifications or this unit a few times before you go into each placement and plan ahead. Remember that some placement settings will give more scope in experiencing issues like dealing with barriers to communication, so be prepared to modify your plans as you learn about each care setting.

Organisations will not expect you to deal with inappropriate behaviour in care settings, so you are required to write a report on strategy for dealing with such behaviour. You can do this at an appropriate time for you, but place it on a list of 'things to do' in your VPL to remind you. However, you are likely to witness other staff having to deal with such behaviour from service users of all ages, so be observant and watch the staff closely so that you can provide witness examples. There is a tendency when viewing incidents of this type to pay more attention to the individual causing the disturbance – after all, in many situations, this is exactly why the individual acts this way. Try to pay more attention to the professional staff and the methods for dealing with the disturbance and make notes in your break time. Keep your report on disk for modification when you have a practical incident to add.

With the permission of your supervisor, try to put aside one (or two) mornings or afternoons, perhaps during visiting time, to find out about the recording and storage of information in each placement. This does not mean you have to look at confidential files – just determine the methods used. You will also need to find out how staff share information and what the reasons are for sharing information. After your first placement when you have one set of information, try to set up a generic sheet on a computer to ask the same questions on the remaining placements with appropriate spaces for you to complete during your working time. This will not only save you time later on, but also provide you with a suitable format for comparisons at the end of placement activity.

Principles of teamwork, work relationships, roles and responsibilities

You must be able to show that you are working within the limits of your role and competence in the placement. You will have the evidence for this from:

- your job description (see above)
- the expected tasks from your chart (also above)
- a work placement report.

The latter should be available from each vocational placement; your tutor may hold these reports and you can ask for a photocopy.

You should write a report based on these documents to demonstrate the limits of your role and your vocational competence. Put this report on your 'things to do' list. You should also find the evidence to demonstrate the skills required for working effectively in a team. To recap, you are looking for evidence of punctuality, communication skills, willingness to refer and to involve others.

Two additional items for this list are reports explaining a range of roles and relationships and the causes of stress in the workplace and the effect on service users and staff. Use several pattern diagrams in your work on roles and relationships as these illustrate links between people and roles rather well.

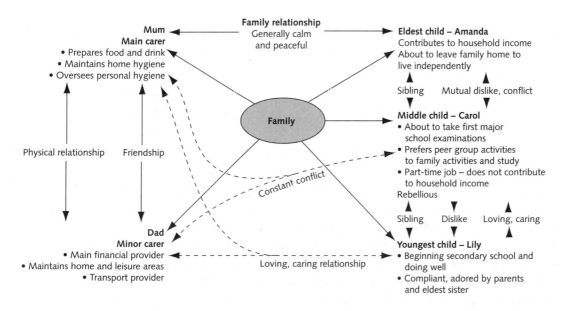

Figure 5.9 An example of family roles and relationships

You might find that one specific care setting is suitable (with permission from the supervisor) for devising your own questionnaire to research the causes and effects of stress. You should then get your questionnaire checked through by both your tutor and the supervisor if permission is granted. Use your survey as an example of primary research within your report.

Equal opportunities

You will need to write a report on the equal opportunities policy and procedure in each workplace and analyse how effective these are in the setting. You will have a sheet in your file outlining the key features of the relevant equal opportunities documents in each placement.

Examine the bullet points on page 180 of this unit and your answers to these questions should form a basis for your analysis of effectiveness. These responses will also help you to explain how staff and service users are empowered in each setting and this can be amplified by looking at (the key features of) the policies and procedures in use in the workplace.

How can staff be empowered? Here are some suggestions to explore:

- Are staff trained and developed in areas of concern to them?
- Can they contribute to the agendas of meetings?
- Are they freely able to contribute in meetings or do they feel intimidated?
- Can staff count on support from managers?
- Will managers act as advocates for staff if required?
- Are members of staff confident about their roles and responsibilities?

You can probably add more bullet points to this list in specific settings that you work in.

Finally, in this section you will need to identify examples of challenging discriminatory behaviour that you have met or read about. This should go on your 'things to do' list. As well as practical examples, stay alert for articles in the media that you can use.

Care programmes

You may prefer to leave this section until your second year and make steady progress with the other sections in the first year. You must be able to observe some care-planning meetings and have the opportunity to participate in at least one meeting. Participation will not be major and you will only be able to do this if you know the service user and have developed a working relationship with them. Make sure that you record your contribution to use as evidence. After the meeting has finished you will need to describe how information was gained about the service user and their needs and how agreement was reached to provide services. Do not leave this until later or you will find that you have forgotten some valuable points. If you feel that your memory is not as good as it might be, you could ask all participants if they would mind if you took some notes on the care-planning process. Ensure that the service user knows that you are not making notes on their difficulties and allow them to see your finished notes if required. Preferably, practise active listening and avoid taking notes. If you can observe more than one care-planning meeting then you will be very fortunate and are only required to remember the differences in the processes.

Personal career goals

This is a section that you can start even before you have been on a vocational placement! In fact, you can benefit from an early start and half-yearly monitoring, review and reasoned evaluation.

Begin by making a pattern diagram of three or four potential career goals and possible options within those areas. You will produce something like the example shown in Figure 5.10 for a student who likes working with elderly people.

This student has four career options at present. You may have more or less than this; remember that you can add or subtract career options as you progress through your course. Ideas alone are a good start, but you need to research the personal qualities and qualifications needed to realise these ambitions. The latest careers books in your libraries will provide you with the basic

Figure 5.10 Career options for working with elderly people

information, and then actually talking to carers practising those professions will provide insight. You can often do this informally at open days or evenings, so look out for these and take every opportunity to attend.

Many career guides incorporate self-tests and exercises for you to find and develop your natural aptitudes in the search for the most suitable careers (see References and further reading at the end of this unit).

The best way of providing the evidence for your research findings and your personal action plan is to set up two tables (in landscape format) on your disk that you can keep reviewing and adding to. Try reviewing and updating your sheets every four months (this can be a permanent feature of your 'things to do' list) printing out copies for your VPL after each update. Your first table might look like this, but with more entries:

Career research plan: Maisie Dolojor				
Career option	*Entry qualifications required*	*Desired personal skills and attributes*	*Date of entry and current status*	*I need to work on...*
Geriatric nursing	BTEC National Diploma Health Studies		21.12.02	
		Good health	Current health good	My fitness
		Intelligence	Reasonably intelligent	Reading more
		Ability to make relationships	Can form and sustain relationships	Client relationships
		Empathy and understanding	Learning more about this every day	Putting this into placement practice
		Ability to work in a team	Think I could	Putting this into placement practice
		Ability to work one-to-one	Think I could	Putting this into placement practice
		Excellent communication skills	Improving, less shy than I used to be	Putting this into placement practice
		Confidentiality	New to me	Putting this into placement practice
		Good management skills	Not very good, no opportunity	Putting this into placement practice
		Personal organisation	Could be better	Keeping to my time schedules and punctuality
		Time management	Not good	
		Equal opportunity practice	New to me	Putting this into placement practice
		Even-tempered	Placid	More enthusiasm
		Good personal hygiene	Yes	
		Common sense	People say so	
		Practical	Limited at present	Doing some voluntary work in vacations

Figure 5.11 Health Studies Career research plan

A new Diploma student might produce this type of table and then incorporate the items to be worked on in her placement plans to improve skills and abilities so that they can show improvement in personal development at the next chosen review date. The student would need to produce a table for each career option. This is, if you like, a macro career plan and the following table would be a micro career plan to manage personal actions.

Personal action Plan				
Date	Personal actions required	Aims	Time scale	Progress
21.12.03	Improve personal fitness by walking to college every day	To improve general health and stamina	Year one	
	Read one library book each week – seek guidance on choice from librarian	Improve literary skills and general knowledge	Term one	
	Visit Mr Kitch (elderly neighbour who lives alone) once a week	Practise improving one-to-one relationship building – voluntary work	Year one	
	Completing assignments on time with a plan of action	Improve personal organisation and time management	Course duration	

Figure 5.12 Personal action plan

A student would have more items than this and include those that he or she wished to develop from vocational practice.

End-of-unit test

1 Explain the differences between aims and objectives.
2 Distinguish between policies and procedures.
3 Name three possible barriers to communication.
4 Explain the difference between an open and a closed question.
5 What is affirmative action?
6 Provide an example of affirmative action.
7 Provide two reasons for planning a service user's care programme.
8 Why is it necessary to review care programmes regularly?
9 Name three possible causes of stress in a care setting and suggest the effects of the stress.

10 Name two pieces of legislation that are important in protecting service user information.

11 What skills are important in teamwork?

12 Explain the way in which you as a student should act when confronted by an angry non-violent service user.

13 What is the role of a student on placement when asked for information on a service user by a relative?

14 What is an advocate? Explain the circumstances when an advocate may be required.

References and further reading

Breakwell, G. (1990) *Facing Physical Violence.* Leicester: British Psychological Society

Clements, P. and Spinks, T. (1997) *The Equal Opportunities Handbook*, London: Kogan Page

Fontana, D. (1990a) *Managing Stress,* Leicester: British Psychological Society

Fontana, D. (1990b) *Social Skills at Work,* Leicester: British Psychological Society

Hopson, B. and Scally, M. (2000) *Build Your Own Rainbow*, Cirencester: Management Books

Lee, E. (1997) *Mental Healthcare*, Basingstoke: Macmillan Caring Series

Lindon, J. and Lindon, L. (1997) *Working Together for Young Children*, Basingstoke: Macmillan Caring Series

Lore, N. (1998) *The Pathfinder: How to Choose or Change Your Career for a Lifetime of Satisfaction and Success*, New York: Simon and Schuster Books

Moonie, N. (2000) *AVCE Health and Social Care*, Oxford: Heinemann

Nolan, Y. (2001) *Care S/NVQ*, Oxford: Heinemann

Parry, G. (1990) *Coping with Crises,* Leicester: British Psychological Society

Smyth, T. (1992) *Caring for Older People*, Basingstoke: Macmillan

Spink, C. (1996) *Equal Opportunities Guide*, London: Kogan Page

Thompson, N. (1996) *People Skills*, Basingstoke: Palgrave Macmillan

Thompson, N. (2001) *Anti-discriminatory Practice*, Basingstoke: Palgrave Macmillan

Trevithick, P. (2002) *Social Work Skills*, Buckingham: Open University Press

Protecting self and others

All care settings should provide a healthy, safe and secure environment. All care services should promote optimum health and well-being for service users and employees. Certainly they should do no harm!

These might seem obvious statements to make, but there are a number of potential hazards to be aware of in care settings, especially where service users are vulnerable, due to their age (whether young or old), because they are ill, or have special needs. As a care worker you must, by law, do all you can to protect your service users, members of the public, and yourself from physical, psychological and emotional injury. This is a complex challenge involving many different situations and issues.

What you need to learn

- Health, safety and security issues in care settings
- Recognising and responding to abuse
- Management of abuse care services
- Professional confidentiality

Accountability and **responsibility** are two concepts that run throughout this unit. Accountability means being able to justify your actions. In your place of work this involves keeping up to date with necessary knowledge, staying within the law, keeping to any policies and procedures that are in place and acting in a professional manner. You can be called to account to explain your actions to your employer at any time and, of course, your employer is equally accountable for his or her actions. Responsibility means working to the best of your ability at all times and carrying out your duties fully. Accountability and responsibility are not just about doing things correctly. If you are aware of someone else's wrong practice you are also duty bound to do something about it, or report it; otherwise you too can be held responsible for allowing the situation to continue unchecked.

Health, safety and security issues in care settings

In this section you will look at key health, safety and security topics in care settings (see Figure 6.1). The legislation, regulations and policies that apply to these will be described as well as the concept of risk assessment, the management of accidents and emergencies and the management of challenging behaviour.

Figure 6.1 Key health, safety and security issues in a care setting

Who is especially vulnerable to harm?

Without wishing to stereotype, certain groups of people are potentially more vulnerable to harm because of the age, stage or nature of their life experience. The table below lists some common traits to be aware of.

CHILDREN	TEENAGERS	PEOPLE WITH SPECIAL NEEDS	OLDER PEOPLE
Reliant on others for all needs	Partially reliant on others for some needs	May be reliant on others for basic needs	May be reliant on others for basic needs
May be too young to express needs or ask for help	May resent needing help, so avoid asking for it	May be unable to express needs or ask for help	May be unable or unwilling to express needs or ask for help
Body not yet developed full strength and dexterity	Less aware of limitations	May have physical or mental deficits	May have physical deficits plus wear and tear deterioration of hearing, sight, mobility
Lack of experience	Stage where authority is challenged and convention defied	May be over-trusting	May have memory loss or confusion
Less fear of danger	Less likely to consider consequences	A lack of specialised facilities for people with disabilities makes the attempt to carry out certain activities more risky	May be unaware, or in denial of physical/mental deficits

CHILDREN	TEENAGERS	PEOPLE WITH SPECIAL NEEDS	OLDER PEOPLE
Strong instinct to explore the world around them	Desire to experiment More susceptible to peer pressure		
Young children unable to read instructions	May think it 'uncool' to read instructions		May overlook instructions
Judgement for vehicle distance and speed not yet developed			Judgement for vehicle distance and speed reduced
Immature immune system	More likely to take risks and seek thrills		Less efficient immune system
More vulnerable to infection	More vulnerable to some infections	May be more vulnerable to infection	Lowered ability to heal

Policies and legislation

Legislation in the workplace is designed to protect and promote health, safety and security and prevent accidents and incidents. Legislation for England and Wales sometimes differs slightly to that of Scotland and Northern Ireland, but similar rules and principles apply across the United Kingdom and, increasingly, across Europe. You will come across different types of law that apply in your work setting:

- Common law, also called case law – has developed out of a history of legal judgments of cases. These set a precedent and guide the judgment of future legal cases.
- Civil law – concerns your private rights, where you personally take a person to court to seek justice.
- European law – is currently being integrated with British laws as a result of the European Union.
- Statute law – refers to laws passed by an Act of Parliament. The term 'statutory duty' derives from this and means you are legally obliged to do something. It is a criminal offence to ignore or defy a statute law and to do so may result in prosecution.
- Legal regulations – are developed to interpret and carry out statute law. Parliamentary committees, informed by specialist advisers, set down the regulations to apply to specific situations and circumstances in the workplace.
- National, Local and Professional Policies – are developed and written down by institutions and individual employers to demonstrate observance of statute law and legal regulations in their particular area. Policies provide guidance for employees' working practice: they spell out more specifically the 'do's' and 'don'ts' of your job.

Health, safety and security legislation relevant to a care setting

The Health and Safety at Work Act 1974 is the main law covering health, safety and security in all places of work, including care settings. The Health and Safety at Work Act enforces minimum standards and provides a framework for safe working. It sets out principles – the underlying values to our actions – that employers must interpret and apply to their work premises and working practice. A number of legal regulations come under the umbrella of the Act to address specific aspects of health, safety and security in the workplace (see the table below). You will probably find that your employer has drawn up a folder of health and safety policies, to offer specific guidelines for applying these laws and regulations in your place of work.

Statute law	Key principles
The Health and Safety at Work Act 1974	Developed to minimise the numbers of accidents to employers, employees and members of the public in the workplace or through working practice. Protection and prevention are the two main principles in this legislation.
The Management of Health and Safety at Work Act (amended 1994)	The main amendment was to introduce the concept of 'risk assessment'.
The Children Act 1989	Developed to clarify the rights of children and the duties of parents and society to protect and fulfil these rights.
The Care Standards Act 2000	Developed to regularise standards of health and welfare services available to children and adults in the community. Covers children's homes, fostering and adoption situations and care homes for older people (previously called nursing and residential homes) and for people with special needs. Imposes minimum standards – 'National Care Standards' – and checks on the suitability of people to work with children and vulnerable adults (disclosure checks). It introduced a statutory duty for employers to provide formal health and safety training as part of their induction to a job.
Legal regulations	(These come under the 'umbrella' of The Health and Safety at Work Act 1974.)
The Health and Safety (First Aid) Regulations 1981	Introduced the rule that there must be a trained first-aider for every 50 employees. In smaller places the employer must assess the need for specific first aid training. First aid equipment must be available and official records kept of first aid treatment administered.
The Manual Handling Operations Regulations 1992	Introduced to enforce safer moving and handling practices in the work place. Covers training in safe techniques and use of lifting equipment.
The Control of Substances Hazardous to Health 1994 (COSHH)	Regulates the storage and use of chemical substances that pose a danger because they are poisonous, irritant or corrosive. In a care setting this mostly refers to cleaning, disinfecting and sterilising solutions. A COSHH file detailing the hazardous chemicals in use must be kept in each workplace.

The Reporting of Injury, Disease and Dangerous Occurrences Regulations 1995 (RIDDOR)	Introduced the requirement to report notifiable diseases – those that are highly infectious – in order to identify, monitor and manage epidemics. Also introduced the requirement to report major accidents and incidents occurring in the work place.
The Fire Precautions Regulations 1999	Instituted a system of inspection of work premises by the fire brigade. Also includes regulations about training employees to respond to fire appropriately and maintain fire-fighting equipment. Anyone interfering with fire-fighting equipment, e.g. setting off fire extinguishers as a joke, can be prosecuted.

Common law	(Can be used as a defence in a court of law.)
'A duty of care'	Common law that states that all institutions, professions and employers must try to predict situations of risk in the workplace and put measures in place to prevent accident, incident and injury.
'Acting in good faith'	Common law that can protect an individual if you are shown to have tried to help another person, even though your attempt fails.

Employer and employee responsibilities

Under the Health and Safety at Work Act, both employers and employees hold certain responsibilities. Health and safety laws and regulations may seem complicated and rather theoretical – far removed from your hands on care – but they are extremely relevant to your work. If you fail to comply with them you may be disciplined by your employer or even prosecuted. The following table sets out some of the major areas of responsibility. Check whether you and your employer are sticking to the rules!

Employer responsibility	Employee responsibility
Make the workplace and working practice as safe as possible, ensuring that, at least, the minimum safety standards are enforced.	Comply with, at least, minimum health and safety standards.
Carry out and record formal risk assessment of potentially hazardous situations to employees and service users.	Take part in the on-going risk assessment process.
Provide for the adequate health and welfare of employees, including first aid provision. Have particular awareness of employees who are pregnant, post childbirth, breast-feeding, returned from sick leave or disabled.	Maintain adequate levels of personal hygiene and do not work if unwell or unfit. Bring any health issues to your employer's attention and seek medical help when needed.

Maintain, store and use equipment and materials and substances correctly.	Report to employer faulty working, wrong use or storage of equipment, materials or substances.
Provide adequate protective and safety equipment.	Use protective and safety equipment correctly.
Provide employee training in all aspects of health and safety.	Attend and participate fully in health and safety training.
Have a written health and safety statement (if there are more than five employees) and bring this to the attention of employees.	Read and take note of all written health and safety information.
Establish protocols (written statements describing the particulars about how a procedure or process should be carried out) for health and safety issues, including emergencies, specifically relevant to that workplace.	Follow health and safety protocols in your own personal working practice and do not 'cut corners'.
Provide and display written safety information and instructions.	Read and take note of all written health and safety information.
Display insurance certificate.	
Co-operate fully with health and safety officials and inspections.	Enable health and safety officials and inspections to carry out their work.

Think It Over

This activity is about responsibility for implementing health and safety legislation in the care setting. In pairs or in a group decide which of you will be 'employers' and which will be 'employees'. Discuss one or more of the following scenarios, deciding what each must do to fulfil their legal obligation:

1 A worker in a care home has come on an early shift. He complains of feeling nauseous.
2 You work at a nursery and have been asked to help plan the summer outing to a local children's farm and adventure play area.
3 You accidentally dropped the contents of a bedpan on the floor.
4 The service user you visit at home is verbally aggressive to you. You fear the service user may hit you.

Risk assessment

Risk assessment is the term used to describe a systematic examination of work situations to identify potential risks to the health, safety or security of workers, service users and the visiting public. It acknowledges that all sorts of activities in any number of environments can be potentially dangerous, but that steps can be taken – termed '**risk control measures**' – to minimise, contain or eliminate these. We carry out risk assessment in an informal way many times a day, for example, as we negotiate crossing roads or use electrical equipment. Risk assessment in the workplace is no different,

A health and safety poster

except that here the process is a legal requirement, following structured steps, and where the conclusions are formally written down. Employers are responsible for ensuring risk assessment is carried out, but all levels of employee have a responsibility to participate in the process. The risk assessment process is illustrated in Figure 6.2. Notice that it is a continuous process; there's never a point when you can say, 'That's safe – no need to look at that again!'

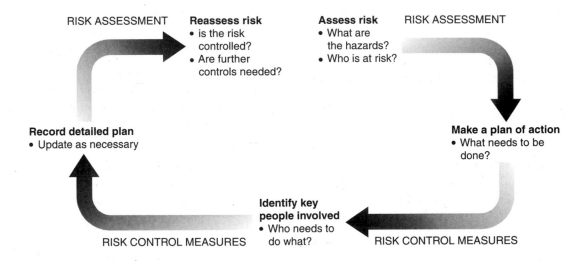

Figure 6.2 The risk assessment process

In most care settings there are numerous areas in the working environment and issues in working practice that represent health and safety hazards. Some of the key ones are described here.

Moving and handling

In a care setting these tasks may include lifting, lowering, transferring, carrying and supporting service users. You may be helping service users move up the bed, from bed to chair and from chair to toilet and bath. Always comply with risk control measures and continue to carry out further risk assessments as the service user's situation evolves. Remember that the weight of the service user is often less significant than how much they resist your moving them. Also remember that the 'mover' and the person being moved are equally at risk of injury.

There is no longer a lifting technique that is universally considered safe: all carry risks. However, important physical principles still apply to all manual handling situations, such as keeping your back straight and your knees bent and ensuring that your clothes allow freedom of movement. If you use lifting equipment, such as hoists, slip-sheets or transfer boards, make sure you receive adequate training and supervision in their use first and that equipment is in good working order.

It is crucial that you check the moving and handling policy in your place of work and keep to these guidelines. Don't be persuaded to carry out a manoeuvre that you feel unhappy or unsure about. To do so could be construed as negligence and if, as a result, a manual handling injury occurs, you could be held equally responsible. Always refer your concerns on to your immediate senior. If they are also unsure how to proceed, the matter should be taken further along the management structure.

Hazardous chemicals

In a care setting this mostly refers to cleaning, disinfecting and sterilising fluids. Hazardous can mean toxic (poisonous), corrosive (burning), or irritant and might detrimentally affect skin, eyes, breathing and liver/kidneys. They can pose a hazard to you as the care-worker if you fail to use them appropriately, also to your service users if they get hold of them and spill or swallow them, as well as to the environment if not disposed of correctly. Hazard symbols printed on the bottles and packets give you important information about the specific danger they pose, so do take notice of these (see Figure 6.3).

Figure 6.3 Safety hazard warnings – symbols are always black on a yellow background

Find out where your employer keeps the COSHH (Control of Substances Hazardous to Health) file and check the hazardous chemicals that are in use in your place of work. Follow instructions carefully, such as wearing gloves or a mask when using chemicals, and never decant solutions into other bottles. Report any wrong storage or use of these substances to your employer.

Medicines

Medicines include prescribed ones and **illicit drugs** (for example, cannabis, Ecstasy, crack cocaine and heroin) and both are potentially dangerous substances. Some prescription medicines, especially certain pain killers, and sleeping tablets, also have a 'street value' and are more liable to be abused. Correct storage, accurate administration of prescription medicines and the protection of your service users from the dangers of illicit drug use and abuse are the major health and safety concerns to do with medicines in a care setting. Most medicines are kept in a locked cupboard or trolley and are administered by trained nurses or other trained personnel.

As a care-worker you should not be asked to administer medicines and should question any such request, referring to senior management if necessary. Medicines must always be kept out of reach of children, who could mistake them for sweets with devastating consequences. Accidental overdose can occur with older people who suffer from memory problems and are unsure whether or when they have taken their medication. If you work with service users in their own homes you might need to remind them about taking medication or oversee the use of a dose box which sets out medication for a day or a week at a time.

If you work with young people you will need to be particularly aware of the possibility of teenage experimentation with illicit drugs. Signs of intoxication are a glazed look, slurred speech, elevated or depressed mood, loss of appetite or sudden binge eating, and erratic or excitable behaviour. Signs that indicate addiction include the above, but with the addition of a gradually reducing interest in personal care, appearance, motivation, concentration and interests.

Infection control

Infection control is a crucial health and safety subject in care environments, especially in a communal setting. Wherever people are gathered together there is a greater mingling of pathogens (germs). In a care setting, such as a hospital or care home, where people are there because they are frail or ill, the likelihood of pathogens being disease carrying is higher. This is compounded by the fact that these service users are also more vulnerable to disease.

There is no knowing just by looking who carries disease-causing pathogens and who does not, so the key is to treat everyone as if they are infectious, including yourself. This is called taking **universal precautions** and involves placing a protective barrier between your own and the other person's germs. The barrier might be to wear disposable surgical gloves or a mask, a protective uniform or a plastic apron. Remember that 'disposable' means just that – plastic gloves must be changed between patients or they too become an infection hazard.

If you work with young people, universal precautions are a vital part of sex education and drug awareness. The spread of sexually transmitted diseases (STDs) and HIV (Human Immune Virus) and AIDS (Acquired-Immune Deficiency Syndrome) is significantly reduced by use of condoms and by not sharing needles.

A simple but equally important element of taking universal precautions is to wash your hands between all service user contacts and contact with your own bodily secretions – most obviously after using the toilet. This significantly reduces the numbers of bacteria present, especially if you use hot water and soap, and wash every area thoroughly, drying well afterwards. When service users are self-caring it may still be necessary to make sure they wipe themselves properly after going to the toilet and help with hand washing. This is particularly so for children who may not have been managing independently for very long.

Use of antiseptic solutions helps to kill some pathogens, as well as keeping an area clean to prevent bacteria multiplying and colonising. However, overuse of antiseptics in a domestic setting (for instance, in our own homes) has led to certain bacteria becoming resistant and more difficult to kill. Disposal of human waste – urine and faeces – and other bodily fluids – blood, vomit, pus and sputum – must be carried out in a way that contains the waste safely, to prevent it from contaminating anything else and to protect workers further down the line, for example in the laundry. Most care settings follow specific procedures for dealing with each different type of waste. Examples are **clinical waste** (e.g. wipes, incontinence/sanitary pads, nappies and dressings), soiled laundry, sharp objects (e.g. broken glass), and sharp clinical waste, such as needles and syringes.

If you accidentally spill bodily fluids it must be dealt with immediately. Use gloves, dispose into clinical waste bags and follow up by disinfecting the area. In this instance, domestic staff should **not** be asked to clean up the spillage.

Key issue

Remember, never try to re-sheath a needle or separate it from the syringe: needle-stick injuries are all too common from this practice.

Food preparation and handling

This is a health and safety issue for all care-workers who help service users to prepare, cook or eat food. Bacteria quickly contaminate food if it is stored, cooked or handled incorrectly. Safety measures include maintaining high standards of personal hygiene, especially when moving between areas (for example, toilet or service user's bedside to kitchen) as well as correct management of food in terms of temperature, covering properly and cooking and re-heating thoroughly.

Thorough cooking usually kills bacteria, but raw food, such as salad, poses extra risk. For this reason, never use a knife or chopping board used for preparing raw meat or fish to also prepare a salad. If asked to save a meal for a service user make sure you re-heat it thoroughly to a high temperature and allow it to cool back down to a safe temperature for eating. All kitchens in care settings come under strict regulations and your place of work will have policies in place to guide food preparation and handling – make sure you are familiar with the rules.

Road safety

Safety on the road applies particularly to the young, the old and those who have disabilities – in other words, many of the same sorts of people who will be your service users. Children right up to the age of about 10, as well as older people, are less able to accurately judge speed and distance of moving vehicles. They may not be physically fast enough to get out of trouble in time and with older people or those with disability they might not be able to see or hear vehicles properly. If you are out with younger or older service users you may have to take responsibility for crossing roads safely. People over 70 who are still driving need to have medical clearance every year to say they are fit.

Outings

Safety during outings is important and, following some recent fatal accidents, new regulations have been drawn up. These mostly concern risk assessment and supervision. Written permission must be obtained from the service user's legal guardian (e.g. in the case of children, their parents) and they should be given clear information about the outing, its activities and the safety measures in place. Before you set off you need to think the situation through step by step. Remember that you and your service users will be away from the routines and supports that usually back you up. There will likely be both excitement and tension in the air, causing people to behave in a less predictable way. Situations can arise that you have no control over, such as changes in weather and temperature, queuing and crowding, and sudden illness or injury in your party.

Security breaches

A breach can be an external breach when someone comes uninvited into a private room, house, or institution in order to do harm. It can also be an internal breach by someone who is there on legitimate business – perhaps they work there – but who is acting in a dangerous or unlawful way. The harm might be through physical, verbal or sexual abuse, theft or vandalism.

External security breaches

In a large institution, such as a hospital, it is very difficult to keep track of who is there on legitimate business. There will be many entrances and exits and huge numbers of personnel and visitors coming and going. Security measures may include surveillance cameras, photo identity cards and uniforms for staff and a check-in procedure for visitors. In smaller homes such stringent measures are less likely, but it is still not always easy to know who should and shouldn't be there. Make sure you know the proper procedure for monitoring visitors at your place of work. If you see someone you don't recognise, the best policy is to politely ask if you can help them and then check their credentials. Bogus callers can turn up at the door claiming to offer a service, such as building work or reading a meter or even posing as a police officer. Check they are expected and accompany them if necessary.

If you work with service users in their own home you might need to remind them to never let strangers into the house, however plausible their claims, without first checking identity cards. If doubt remains, advise them to phone the company to verify the facts. Remind service users to put a chain across the door and not release this until they recognise the caller. You can remind them of this routine every time you call. Also suggest that they use only recommended tradespeople to do jobs for them.

Internal security breaches

These can be more difficult to spot. For example, thieving might just be petty and occur over a long period of time. Most places will have set procedures for checking the money and valuables of residents. Do keep to these and then you should never be wrongfully accused of theft. Always advise service users to put large sums into a bank account. Also make sure all the service user's clothes and belongings are clearly marked. If you shop for a service user, never take money directly from his or her purse. Use a book to record how money is spent, attaching receipts for proof.

Key issues

Security breaches have led to stringent security policies being put in place in many care settings. Friends and relatives of service users find the loss of an 'open door' policy excludes them from the everyday life of the facility and alienates staff.

- Think about ways around these that improve communication, without compromising safety and security.

Missing persons

People who go missing from a care setting present a worrying situation that must be dealt with urgently. The person is vulnerable to many potential dangers and separated from the usual protection and support available to them. People go missing for many different reasons. They might have deliberately run away or they could have walked out just because a door, normally closed, was open. If you work with older people who suffer from dementia and memory problems they may have become confused and wandered away. If you work with children they may have become distracted or attracted by something and wandered away. In most care settings the management of missing persons will be set out, step by step, in a policy. Here are some common steps to take:

- establish the time and place where they were last seen
- find out whether they had discussed any plans
- search the building and immediate vicinity
- check if belongings have gone
- check familiar places that the person might have headed for
- a decision will need to be made to inform the next of kin and the police.

Hopefully your missing person will be found safe and well, but it is an important element of the risk assessment process to take action to prevent the situation happening again. Service users who persistently wander create a difficult management challenge. It is never acceptable to physically restrain a person with sheets or ties, or to block them in with furniture. Try to create a safe space within which they can wander at will. Provide a range of distracting activities and include service users in helping with tasks, such as laying tables and making beds. Arrange and supervise regular and frequent trips out, even short ones to local shops, library or park.

Case Study

This describes a case that came to court in 2001. It concerns a couple in England who care for their two physically disabled daughters at home. The Health Authority there interpreted the relevant legislation by having a 'no manual lifting' policy for all employees working in care settings. This service user's house was unsuitable for the mechanical lifting aids that carers assessed were required to move the young girls around. Therefore the Health Authority refused to allow carers to assist with moving and handling tasks. Although carers helped with other care, the girls still needed to be moved a number of times a day and as a result the couple had no respite from their 24-hour care. They decided to challenge the decision and took the Health Authority to court and won. The court ruled that whilst workers must continue to avoid 'hazardous handling', the regulations cannot be interpreted with absolute, 'blanket' rules, such as 'no lifting' because this denies service users' personal freedom and right to choose.

Assessment activity 6.1

Read the previous case study carefully. Then consider the following questions.

1 Identify the main health and safety legislation – both the Act and the legal regulations – that the court would have referred to in this case.

2 What health and safety documents might the care managers also present to the court to show how they had interpreted the law to apply to care practice?

3 Describe the different responsibilities of the employer and the employee, regarding health and safety, towards these service users when their care was first taken on.

4 In note form, write your version of a care plan to meet the need of these service users to be safely moved around.

5 How would you feel about the final court ruling, firstly as the service user and secondly, as the care-worker? Include whether you feel justice has been done.

Accidents and emergencies

Accidents, emergencies and incidents do happen and cannot always be avoided, but measures, identified through risk assessment, should be taken to minimise the likelihood. Here is a list of potential hazards in the environment:

- **Kitchen** – sharp knives (cuts), cooking appliances (burns, fire, gas leaks), pot handles hanging over the edge of the cooker (could be tipped up to burn or scald), slippery floors (falls), food gone off or contaminated (food poisoning, food allergy).
- **Living room** and **bedroom** – worn or rucked carpets and rugs, obstacles such as poorly placed furniture or dropped items, trailing flexes, poor lighting (falls, broken bones, head injury), electrical goods (electric shock, fire), fires without guards (burns, fire).
- **Bathroom** – hot water (burns), wet and slippery surfaces (falls), use of electrical items near water (electric shock).
- **Stairs** – falls from a height (broken bones, head injury).

Your employer is obliged to ensure the work environment is as safe as possible, but this is sometimes less straightforward to achieve if you work in a service user's own home. Where possible, talk to your service user (or their relative or main carer) about anything you notice that is unsafe. They may not have thought about it before, so might be glad to co-operate with improvements. If not, discuss the matter further with your employer.

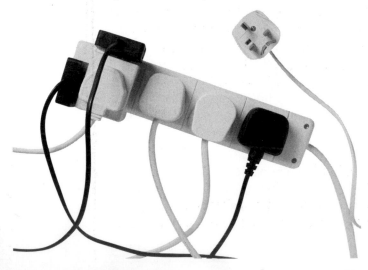

An overloaded plug socket is an accident blackspot

Case Study

Stella Mason is 85 and a resident in a care home. She is fiercely independent, enjoying a daily walk around the courtyard. She recently fell, sustained a fractured hip, resulting in transfer to hospital and surgery. Her relatives are upset and also feel angry, blaming staff for the accident. They threaten to make an official complaint stating that their mother should not have been allowed to walk if she was liable to fall. Staff maintain that Stella could have fallen anywhere, anytime, as indeed could all of us.

- What do you think – does a fall always constitute negligence on the part of staff?

- Draw out the dilemma between allowing freedom and promoting independence versus constant supervision or restraint.

- How do you assess for evidence of negligence?

Fire or gas leak

Fire or gas leaks requiring evacuation are rare events and opportunities to experience and become practised at your response to them are few and far between. Therefore, be prepared and make yourself familiar with emergency procedures. Here is a brief checklist of the responses you should make. If a number of responsible people are present, some of these responses can happen simultaneously.

Fire
- Alert people in the immediate area by shouting 'FIRE!' or activating the alarm system.
- Summon the fire service by dialling 999.
- Remove people out of immediate danger, perhaps to a nearby room, to await instructions.
- Close doors and windows to contain the fire.
- If evacuation is necessary, help people to gather at the assembly point and tell them not to return until instructed to.
- Only if it is safe to do so and you feel equal to the task should you try to tackle the fire with the safety equipment available.

Fire equipment available might be a fire blanket or fire extinguishers and some of this equipment is illustrated in Figure 6.4. There are separate extinguishers for different types of fire, for example a water extinguisher is inappropriate for an electrical fire. Take the time to read the instructions on fire equipment so that if you have to use it in an emergency you will already know what to do. Your employer must provide training on fire procedures, and local fire services are usually happy to come to your place of work and demonstrate use of equipment. Never take risks that endanger your life or the lives of others.

Gas leak
- If gas is smelled check gas appliances are switched off.
- Open doors and windows to fully ventilate the area.
- Be careful not to use matches or lighters.
- Do not use any other electronic equipment, such as light switches, telephones or buzzers as these might spark, igniting the gas and causing an explosion.

Extinguisher	Type	Colour	Uses	NOT to be used
Electrical fires	Dry powder	Blue marking	For burning liquid, electrical fires and flammable liquids	On flammable metal fires
	Carbon dioxide	Black marking	Safe on all voltages, used on on burning liquid and electrical fires and flammable liquids	On flammable metal
	Vaporising liquid	Green marking	Safe on all voltages, used on burning liquid and electrical fires and flammable liquids	On flammable metal fires
Non-electrical fires	Water	Red marking	For wood, paper, textiles, fabric and similar materials	On burning liquid, electrical or flammable metal fires
	Foam	Cream/yellow markings	On burning liquid fires	On electrical or flammable metal fires

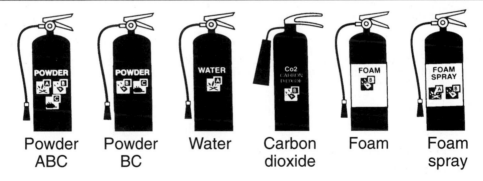

Powder ABC Powder BC Water Carbon dioxide Foam Foam spray

Figure 6.4 All extinguishers are red with a coloured zone that describes content and explains specific uses. For instance, a blue zone denotes dry powder for multi-purpose use.

- Evacuate the area and do not return until instructed to do so.
- Phone the gas emergency number – 0800 111 – from outside the building.
- Switch off the gas meter if you know where it is, but not if it is situated in the cellar.

Evacuation of a building
- Try to stay calm – don't shout or run and instruct others not to.
- Do not stop to collect belongings.
- Give clear instructions about where to assemble.
- Assist those less able to get to assembly point, using wheelchairs and taking people in their beds if necessary.
- Check everyone is out, ticking names off a list if possible.

Theory into practice

At your place of work ask two different members of staff (preferably with different roles and responsibilities) the following questions about fire safety:

- Where are the fire exits?
- Where is the assembly point to evacuate to?
- What should you do if you come across a fire?
- What should you do when you hear the fire alarm sound?
- What do you make of your colleagues' answers? Sum up your conclusions.

First aid

First aid is the urgent treatment given following sudden injury, accident or ill health. It is an excellent idea for all of us to be trained in basic first aid techniques, because, at best, they save lives! Potential first aid situations are described only briefly here and not in enough detail to enable you to respond effectively. This is because reading about first aid is absolutely no substitute for practising it with other people. If possible borrow or buy an up-to-date, comprehensive first aid manual, as well as getting signed up with a class. Remember, if you don't feel confident as a first-aider you can still be helpful in an assisting role.

First aid at work

First aid situations can occur at work, so find out what first aid policies are in place where you work. There may be a designated first-aider and emergency equipment at the ready. Be prepared and find out about equipment before, rather than at the time of an emergency. Your manager should inform you of the role you are expected to take and provide you with any necessary training.

You need to know:

- who to call for help
- actions to take or avoid before help arrives
- how to assist when help arrives
- follow up, including documentation.

Who to call for help

If the situation is clearly serious, either instruct someone to phone 999 for an ambulance, or do so yourself. Give clear information about where the accident has occurred and the key facts about the condition of casualties.

In less urgent cases, alert a senior member of staff or the first-aider. Depending on the situation, you may need to help the person to a health centre or hospital.

Actions to take or avoid before help arrives

Try to keep calm! Speed is important, but not to the detriment of clear thinking. Sometimes people going to the aid of an injured person rush in and end up getting hurt too. According to your knowledge and expertise, assess the condition of the casualty. Check whether they are conscious and the nature and severity of their injuries. Make the area safe. For example, when dealing with a road traffic accident, direct traffic and warn motorists. If inside, cordon off the area to avoid a further accident occurring and clean up any spillage or breakage. As a general rule you should not give an injured person food or drink in case it complicates their condition, especially if they may require an anaesthetic.

How to assist when help arrives
Follow the first-aider's instructions. Offer reassurance to the person hurt and to other witnesses.

Follow up, including documentation
However slight the first aid situation is, when at work the treatment you give must be recorded – usually by completing an accident or incident form. This is vital because an outcome can be more serious than it initially appears. Also in this litigious age, a person may sue for negligence and a clear record made at the time may provide a clear defence. Check the procedure at your place of work and carry it out accurately. Rather than trusting to memory, as soon after the incident as possible jot down the key facts. Make a note of the time, witness names, any equipment involved, the events as they happened and the immediate action taken.

First principles of first aid

The unconscious person
They must first be treated with the 'ABC' of first aid. This refers to three key aspects to observe for:

Airway – is there any obstruction in the mouth or throat blocking their airway?

Breathing – are they breathing?

Circulation – is there a pulse?

It is also sensible to check if the person carries a Medi-Alert bracelet or card indicating an existing medical condition.

Recovery position
The recovery position describes the position to move an unconscious person into once you have ensured they are breathing, their heart is beating and they have a pulse. The recovery position keeps the person's airway open and even if they vomit or bleed it will flow out of the mouth and not cause choking or obstruction. To achieve this position for someone lying flat on their back, follow these steps:

- Place one arm right across the chest
- Cross the same side leg over the other leg
- Roll them on to their side, facing in the same direction as the arm and leg you previously moved.

Figure 6.5 illustrates this but there is no substitute for practising with colleagues.

Figure 6.5 A person placed in the recovery position

Anaphylactic shock

This is a severe allergic reaction, sometimes to a particular food, to insect stings or to certain chemicals. Symptoms occur within minutes of contact with the substance and include redness, swelling and inflammation. The situation is quickly life threatening. A person with a known allergy may carry an 'Epi-pen' that delivers an adrenalin dose. If not, get the person immediately to a doctor.

Bleeding

Bleeding of a superficial nature can usually be stemmed by running under cold water. Severe bleeding – a haemorrhage – requires urgent attention. Apply pressure over the wound (using a clean cloth if available), or to one side of any sharp object embedded in it, and elevate the affected area. Do not be tempted to reduce pressure to take a look, because blood might well up again. If the 'dressing' soaks through, apply a clean one over the top – do not remove the old one because you'll disturb any clotting. Application of a tourniquet is a specialist skill. Attempting this without expertise could cause more harm than good and is not advised. Do remember that whether the bleeding is superficial or serious, blood is a body fluid and therefore poses a potential risk of infection to you. Take universal precautions whenever you can and wear disposable gloves.

Burns

Whether superficial or serious, burns are best treated by immersing in cold, preferably running, water for at least ten minutes. If the person has been burnt through their clothes, don't remove clothing as you may do worse damage to the skin as you take them off, but put the person under a cool shower and thoroughly saturate everything for at least ten minutes. Never apply creams, or worse, butter! A person with severe burns will lose a lot of fluid and can become dangerously dehydrated, so get them to hospital as soon as possible.

Broken bones

Broken bones are also called fractures. Children suffer 'greenstick' fractures where the bone doesn't break cleanly, but bends like a young, 'green' branch of a tree. A child may not be incapacitated by their injury, so get them checked as a precaution. It is better not to move anyone with a suspected broken bone unless they are in obvious danger, have stopped breathing, or suffered a cardiac arrest. The main first aid treatment is to prevent the break from causing further tissue damage and pain and to provide stability by supporting the joints above and below the break.

Choking

Choking is treated slightly differently depending on whether a child or an adult is in trouble. A young child needs to be bent forward – over your knee is a good, supported position. Give up to five firm slaps between the shoulder blades. Remove any obvious obstruction from the mouth, but avoid pushing it further down. For adults, the principle of treating choking is the same, but the procedure, called the 'Heimlich manoeuvre', is different. You will need training in this.

Cardiac arrest and respiratory arrest

These are usually discussed together because they frequently occur together. Respiratory arrest means a person has stopped breathing. If this is not swiftly treated the emergency continues into cardiac arrest. In cardiac arrest the heart stops beating. Artificial respiration is the process of getting air into a person's lungs by breathing for them, either by using resuscitation equipment or by blowing your own breath into their mouth. Cardiac resuscitation, or heart massage, describes the process of manually working a person's heart from the outside. If you are asked to assist in the resuscitation process, try not to panic. Remember that the person has already died, so the situation cannot get any worse and what you do may bring them back to life. Ask for resuscitation instruction at your place of work or sign up for an adult education class.

Convulsions

Convulsions (fits, seizures) – can occur at intervals in a person diagnosed with epilepsy, but also after a head injury, and as a result of drug overdose or severe alcohol intoxication. It is impossible to stop a convulsion in mid-flow so your role as a first-aider is to keep the person as safe and comfortable as possible through its course. Look up the steps you need to take in a first aid book. If you work with service users who are susceptible to fit, your employer should provide specific training.

Poisoning

Poisoning requires swift action. Where possible, identify what has been taken, how much, and at what time. In the case of deliberate overdose, check whether alcohol was taken as well. This information gives an idea of how much will have been absorbed into the bloodstream as well as other toxic effects that could be occurring. Always get expert advice.

Think It Over

Think about this yourself, or discuss it in small groups. Have you ever been injured or involved in an accident? Do you remember how it felt? Try to remember who came to your assistance and how they helped. Was it their calm manner, or authority that reassured you, or their obvious expertise? Or did they make you panic or feel insecure? Did they do the right thing at all? Use these observations to inform your approach to the next first aid situation you are involved with.

Assessment activity 6.2

This assessment activity is about emergency responses. Consider the following scenarios and identify the priority of your responses. Bear in mind the following:

- who to call for help
- actions to take or avoid before help arrives
- how to assist when help arrives
- follow up, including documentation.

1 A child in your care falls from a climbing frame and is momentarily unconscious.
2 Smoke is coming from the television in the lounge of a care home for older people.
3 You smell gas in the kitchen of a service user you visit at home.
4 You come across a patient who has apparently slipped in the toilets of the ward you work on.
5 When assessing home-care skills in a day centre, your service user spills boiling water from the kettle, scalding his arm.

Challenging behaviour

Challenging behaviour has become the acceptable term for the less politically correct labels of aggressive, violent and downright difficult behaviour! The term 'challenging behaviour' helps to remind us to deal positively with a potentially negative situation and to avoid labelling a service user as 'difficult' without looking for the reasons behind their challenging behaviour. The sorts of challenging behaviours that you might come across at work may include:

- verbal abuse – shouting, screaming, swearing
- physical abuse – biting, kicking, punching
- sexual behaviour – masturbating in public, sexual gestures, using explicit language.

In a care setting challenging behaviour, including abuse, may come from service users or their relatives and friends.

On the whole, most people are aggressive only if they feel vulnerable or attacked or their **personal space** is threatened. If someone you are dealing with displays challenging behaviour, take a step back – literally! Look at how you might be coming across to them and consider whether anything you are doing is making them feel vulnerable or attacked. Are you invading their space, ignoring them, hurting them or trying to persuade them to do something they don't want to do? Is there another, less intrusive, way of going about your task?

Aggressive challenging behaviours are more likely to occur if a person is frightened, confused or in pain. Sexual challenging behaviours often occur when a person is bored, nervous and unaware of more appropriate expression of sexual urges. In the case of a child, the behaviour could be part of a normal developmental stage of testing boundaries, learning about self-control, expressing feelings and, in teenage years, rebelling against authority. For an older person or someone with learning difficulties challenging behaviour might be a feature of their condition. Challenging behaviour from a person with mental health problems could indicate that they are responding to **delusions** or **hallucinations**. Any cultural differences must also be taken into consideration; there may be different norms about what is acceptable behaviour, plus great frustration can build up where there are difficulties understanding different languages and customs. If you work with newly arrived refugees or asylum seekers they may be traumatised, acutely fearful, extremely confused and physically, mentally and emotionally exhausted by their ordeal.

Identification and management

The identification of early signs of challenging behaviour may lead to your preventing it or reducing its impact. Be aware of the changing moods of your service users, especially in relation to things happening in their lives. Even events that you would expect to be positive, such as a trip out, a visit from a relative or a holiday can bring apprehension and increased tension. Look out for changes in body posture, tone of voice and eye contact. All of these non-verbal signs carry important information about a person's mood. Someone who is feeling angry is likely to have a tight and guarded body posture, perhaps arms folded defensively across the body. Their voice may be cold and low, revealing a forced containment of anger, or else be loud, aggressive and threatening and they may avoid eye contact or flash quick and challenging looks across at you.

Management of challenging behaviour really begins with risk assessment (see page 204). The process of risk assessment can be usefully applied both to anticipate situations that might provoke challenging behaviour as well as to assess how to handle a situation already in progress. Don't ever risk your life or the life of anyone else when dealing with a violent situation – back off, get help and try to protect those around you. Remember that however severely you are provoked you must never hit out or shout back. To do so would be unprofessional and might even be interpreted as an assault in itself. You could be officially disciplined, even lose your job, as well as ruining future references or, at worst, end up being charged in a criminal court.

De-escalation describes the process of reducing a person's rage to a point where it is possible to talk. Talking (not shouting!) is not compatible with violent behaviour – this is why the main aim of peace negotiations in a war situation is to get all sides sitting together and talking about differences rather than acting them out. Most care settings have written policies about managing challenging behaviour and it is important that you familiarise yourself with the relevant documents at your place of work. In addition you may well be offered a short, usually 'in-house' training course on **'control and restraint'** methods. This sounds rather dramatic, but most courses demonstrate safe ways of holding a person to prevent injury and contain behaviour. The diagram shows recommended ways to manage aggressive behaviour and de-escalate anger.

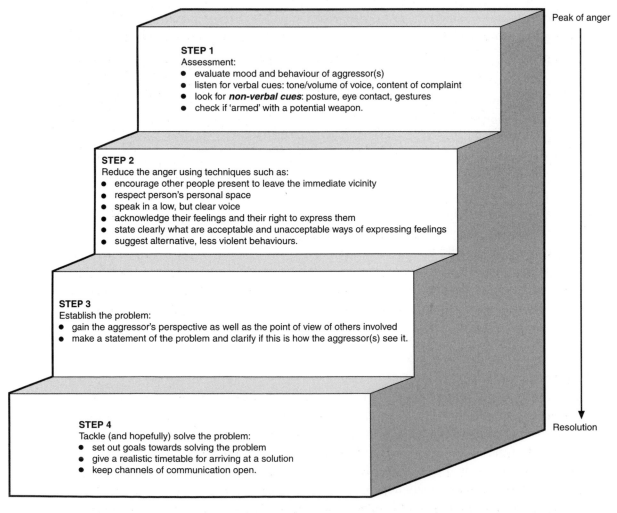

Peak of anger

STEP 1
Assessment:
- evaluate mood and behaviour of aggressor(s)
- listen for verbal cues: tone/volume of voice, content of complaint
- look for **non-verbal cues**: posture, eye contact, gestures
- check if 'armed' with a potential weapon.

STEP 2
Reduce the anger using techniques such as:
- encourage other people present to leave the immediate vicinity
- respect person's personal space
- speak in a low, but clear voice
- acknowledge their feelings and their right to express them
- state clearly what are acceptable and unacceptable ways of expressing feelings
- suggest alternative, less violent behaviours.

STEP 3
Establish the problem:
- gain the aggressor's perspective as well as the point of view of others involved
- make a statement of the problem and clarify if this is how the aggressor(s) see it.

STEP 4
Tackle (and hopefully) solve the problem:
- set out goals towards solving the problem
- give a realistic timetable for arriving at a solution
- keep channels of communication open.

Resolution

Figure 6.6 Steps for managing aggression

Assessment activity 6.3

For this activity you need to read the three short scenarios about challenging behaviour and answer the following questions.

1 You observe a colleague confronting a service user who he believes has not swallowed her medication. He attempts to open her mouth to see inside and she bites his finger and raises her arms as if to hit him.

   a) What would your immediate response be?

   b) Later, your colleague asks if you think he provoked the attack or could have prevented it. What constructive advice would you give?

2 Mr Aziz is an elderly man who is confused and partially paralysed following a stroke. He believes people, including carers, intend him harm. His manner is aggressive, he swears loudly and resists help. A multi-disciplinary team have met to discuss his care.

   a) What observations and thoughts about the reasons for his challenging behaviour can you offer to the discussion?

   b) How would you take these into account when planning Mr Aziz's care?

3 Jacob is a service user at the day centre where you work. One morning he bursts into your group in a furious temper, shouting about his benefit cheque being held up and that he has no money. When you attempt to calm him down he screams in your face that you don't understand, you're all the same and that no one cares for people who have no one. He suddenly picks up a chair and hurls it to the ground

   a) What are your priorities in responding to this situation?

   b) Write down word for word what you might say to Jacob.

   c) Give specific reasons for the words you chose.

Recognising and responding to abuse

In this section you will be looking at what abuse is, the different forms it can take and some of the people more commonly affected by it. You will explore why abuse happens and the consequences that can follow. An outline of current legislation will be given as well as clear guidelines on how to deal, in a professional manner, with suspicions and allegations of abuse.

Definitions of abuse

The subject of abuse stirs very strong feelings in people and yet many forms of abuse lie somewhere upon a continuum of what can be termed 'normal' behaviour. Who hasn't shouted, or felt so angry you could hit someone or something? We are all capable of abusive behaviour at times and have all probably been on the receiving end of some degree of abuse too. Perhaps, in part, it is this realisation and resonance that makes the subject of abuse so uncomfortable and difficult to address. Having stated that, for the majority of people, the facts and details about serious abuse are so extreme they are difficult to hear, let alone understand.

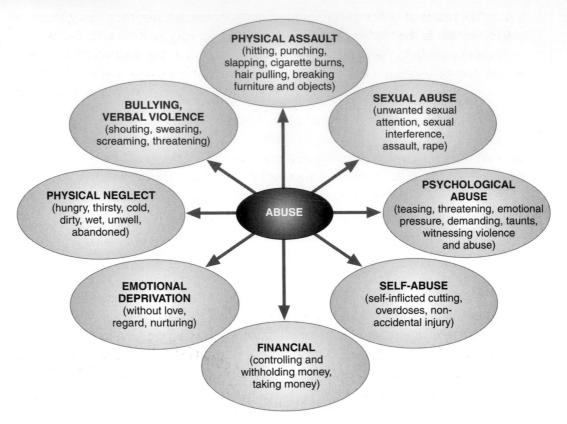

Figure 6.7 Aspects of abuse

The following are some brief definitions of types of abuse.

- **Physical abuse** is an act of violence against another (more vulnerable) person, often occurring persistently over a period of time.
- **Sexual abuse** occurs when there is unwanted and/or underage penetration or interference to a person's body for the sexual gratification of the perpetrator (person committing the offence).
- **Psychological abuse** describes a process of systematically intimidating or frightening another (more vulnerable) person, often over a period of time, in order to gain control of them.
- **Neglect** describes the failure to provide for both physical and emotional needs.
- **Financial abuse** describes the exploitation of a person's vulnerability, to steal or withhold money and make financial decisions against the person's wishes.
- **Domestic abuse** is the term given to violent behaviour occurring in the home between family members. For instance, an abusive male, perhaps the father, abuses his partner and their children witness this. This image, however, can become stereotyped and it is important to remember that domestic violence can take different forms and that women are also capable of the whole range of abusive behaviours.
- **Elder abuse** refers to any abuse of an older person perpetrated because their age has made them vulnerable to attack.
- **Self-abuse** is the term for a person who inflicts harm on their own body. Commonly this occurs through cutting with razors, glass or knives and burning with cigarettes, or through taking overdoses of medicines. Sometimes it is disguised as accidental

injury. The intent of the behaviour is not usually to commit suicide, although sometimes this is the tragic outcome. Self-abuse is not easy to deal with, but as carers we can help by focusing on the emotional pain that surely exists behind the injury. You may witness colleagues who treat such people as 'time wasters'. Do resist unhelpful labels like this because people who self-harm are no less deserving of your care.

Why and who?

Most forms of abuse are about having power and control over someone who is perceived as weaker. This is why certain groups of people are more vulnerable to being abused – children, older people, people with physical disabilities, mental health problems or learning difficulties. Abuse is also about the inappropriate expression of strong feelings. The feelings themselves might be very appropriate, but they are being inappropriately expressed when they emerge in the form of abuse.

Abuse can occur in ways that are obvious, violent and traumatic, but it is a myth to believe that all abuse *feels* abusive in the moment that it occurs. Sometimes abuse, especially sexual abuse, takes place in the context of a close and seemingly loving relationship. In the case of children, the child may not even recognise that abuse has taken place until much later in life when they are able to put a mature interpretation on childhood memories. In these cases, despite the elapsed years, the sense of betrayal can be extreme and very damaging. Even if children realise at the time that, for example, overt sexual behaviour is uncomfortable for them, it is confusing when cuddles and closeness accompany it.

The indicators of abuse

Most people who abuse will do so in secret and it is generally a well-hidden activity. A number of signs might alert you that abuse is occurring. Depression and anxiety, sleep disturbance and nightmares and poor self-esteem are commonly experienced across sufferers of all types of abuse. Other common indications include extremes of behaviour such as being withdrawn, shy and quiet or extremely noisy and demanding, especially if these traits are out of character.

The following are all indicators of types of abuse:

- Physical abuse – frequent bruises in unusual places where a person is unlikely to have fallen or reached, such as on the back, the backs of legs, ears. Also bruises in the shape of objects, such as a belt buckle. Small burn marks that could have been caused by a cigarette. Marks from string or cord around neck or wrists.
- Sexual abuse – frequent urinary tract infections and/or evidence of a sexually transmitted disease (STD). Anal and vaginal bleeding or bruising. Overt and precocious sexual behaviour and use of sexual terms, or extreme shyness and reluctance to change clothes or undress.
- Neglect – hunger and malnutrition, small stature, failure to reach usual milestones, signs of cold such as chapped skin and cold extremities, and poor social skills.
- Emotional abuse – little eye contact, inability to make decisions or choices. Little evidence of self-belief and emotionally undemonstrative.
- Self-abuse – numerous scars on arms, legs or face. May be unable to explain how injuries occurred or give outlandish explanations. Difficulty with verbalising and expressing emotions.

- Financial abuse – disappearance of bank books. Service user reports signing documents with little idea why. Sudden money worries. Insistence of a relative that they witness all conversations between carer and service user.

Theories of abuse

A number of theories exist to explain why some people are more likely to experience or perpetrate (commit) abuse. Such theories are sometimes categorised in the following way:

- Medical reasons – the abuser may suffer from a physiological condition that increases the aggressive and sexual drives, whilst also reducing the person's ability to control these impulses. The 'medical condition' of the abused person might also make them more vulnerable to abuse.
- Sociological reasons – the abuser learns from a deprived and abusive upbringing, to behave in an abusive manner, perpetuating abuse in what is termed the **'abuse cycle'** (this is discussed further later in this section).
- Psychological reasons – feelings of low self-esteem and poor self-worth result in an emotionally immature person who expresses strong feelings in an inappropriate and abusive way, or result in a person being more vulnerable to abuse.

However, whilst these categories provide some clarity, it is unhelpful and misleading to believe there are always straightforward explanations. Reasons for abuse can be very complex.

Predisposing factors to abuse

Abuse is always wrong and there can be no excuse for it, but there may be reasons why a person is more likely to resort to abusive behaviours. Most people know their abuser. It is usually a close family member or friend, or someone who is in a position of trust. Remember there is no typical abuser and you cannot spot one in a crowded street. The person could be a doctor, a teacher, a solicitor, a bank manager. It could be a man or a woman. It could be someone with a bright, cheerful, funny personality; someone you may like very much.

Some people who abuse convince themselves that the other person also finds pleasure in the activity, or that they were 'asking for it' by their provocative behaviour. These abusers might accept responsibility for their behaviour, but do not think there is anything wrong with it. Some abusers do not accept any responsibility for their behaviour and separate themselves from it completely. For example, a father who homosexually assaulted his son on a regular basis, remained aggressively homophobic in his outward behaviour, denigrating all gay men as 'poofs'. When an abuser is in denial in this way it is very difficult to challenge or confront them, especially when the person experiencing the abuse is in a less powerful position to them. Other abusers are horrified by their own behaviour and after an incident will vow that it will never happen again. However, given the same triggers that typically initiate the abusive behaviour, they feel compelled to commit the abuse again. Sometimes abuse takes place under the influence of medication, or illicit drugs or alcohol. These are never legitimate excuses for abuse, but might reduce the abusers' ability to recognise responsibility for their behaviour.

The abuse cycle

Some people who abuse, perhaps in response to their own upbringing or childhood experiences, have very unclear boundaries about what is right and wrong or acceptable or unacceptable behaviour. The phenomenon of a person who has experienced abuse going on to perpetrate abuse in later life is termed 'the abuse cycle'. However, it is wrong to assume that all those who experience abuse will go on to be abusers. Some seek therapy and recover successfully from the effects of their abuse and many are adamant that they will never inflict hurt on others, because of their experience of abuse.

Carer abuse

Cases regularly come up of people abusing the relative they care for at home. This might seem unforgivable, but consider just how hard it can be to be the full-time carer for someone you are emotionally involved with. Carers may have had to sacrifice a great deal and change their lifestyle completely in order to provide care. The stress of such physical and emotional demands, often with little acknowledgement, support, privacy or respite, can be intolerable and mental health problems among carers are common. The problems intensify if the service user has communication difficulties, confusion or displays challenging behaviour. Abuse under these circumstances is still wrong, but is perhaps easier to empathise with. It also should be mentioned that sometimes it is the carer that is abused by the person they care for. People with a mental health problem or learning difficulty may have difficulty expressing frustration and take it out on the person closest to them. These cases may need expert assessment and intervention from psychologists and other specialist therapists, so speak to your manager if you suspect that carers of your service users need support.

Figure 6.8 Why abuse happens

The consequences of abuse

The consequences of abuse can affect all aspects of a person's life. Physically the person may suffer permanent disability as a result of physical injury sustained during episodes of abuse. This might affect their potential to work or bear and raise children. Emotionally the scars can run as deep as physical wounds. Most people who experience abuse report or display signs of poor self-esteem and some suffer long-term mental health problems. They might have little belief in their worth and experience difficulty forming trusting relationships.

Key issues

Contact a voluntary organisation that offers a service to people experiencing abuse, for example, *Childline* or *Women's Aid*. You will find the addresses at the end of the book, in the telephone directory, at a public library, Citizen's Advice Bureau or on the Internet.

- Briefly describe the service offered and the ethos behind it.
- Evaluate (in brief note form) the contribution of the service, both to individuals who have experienced abuse and to our society as a whole.

Abuse and the law

The only law that specifically addresses abuse is The Children Act 1989. This requires children to be protected from abuse and gives the power to Social Services, the police and the National Society for the Prevention of Cruelty to Children (NSPCC), to remove children to a place of safety (see table below). **Child protection** is the term used to describe the process of monitoring for signs of child abuse. You may be aware of this process in action because all institutions, including schools, appoint a child protection officer whose role is to oversee and co-ordinate the recognition and reporting of abuse. A child protection register lists all children thought to be at risk and they are monitored more closely. The Children Act also requires the Secretary of State to keep a list of people who are deemed unsuitable to work with children. At present this only includes those with a criminal conviction, but a bill currently under consideration will extend this to include other evidence, particularly an employment history. This is because, under current legislation, a person can be sacked because of allegations or concerns about abusive behaviours, but walk into another job, also working with vulnerable people, without any record against them.

The law	How it protects
The Children Act 1989	Children have a legal right to be protected from abuse and must, by law, be removed to a place of safety if there is evidence of significant harm occurring. A child protection register is kept. A register of individuals deemed unsuitable to work with children is kept.
Sexual Offences Act 1976	Details illegal sexual offences, including underage sex and sex without consent, that can lead to prosecution in a criminal court.
NHS and Community Care Act 1990	This states that individuals must be provided with the means to complain about their care.
National Assistance Act 1947 (Scotland), 1948 (England and Wales)	Protects vulnerable adults, unable to provide their own care at home.
The Chronically Sick and Disabled Persons Act 1986	Protects and provides for physically disabled people.

The Mental Health Act 1983 (England and Wales), 1984 (Scotland)	Protects and provides for adults with mental health problems and those with learning disabilities.
The Care Standards Act 2000	The Secretary of State has a duty to maintain a register of individuals deemed unsuitable to work with vulnerable adults.
Health and Safety at Work Act 1974	Employers have a right to be protected from violent assault at work and risk assessment must be carried out against this possibility.
Common law	Details rights against 'assault' – grievous bodily harm (GBH) and actual bodily harm (ABH).
Civilian law	Details rights against 'trespass against the person', in the form of neglect or physical or sexual abuse.
The Public Interest Disclosure Act 1998	Protects a genuine **'whistle blower'** who exposes misconduct in an organisation (see page 230).

There is no specific law to protect adults from abuse, although government guidelines entitled 'No longer afraid' have been issued to advise about elder abuse. People with learning difficulties, physical disabilities, mental health problems or older people have certain rights and services protected under the laws itemised in the table, but none specifically address all types of abuse. However, if abuse is uncovered and evidence is sufficient to make a criminal case, the police will proceed and the matter will be tried in court. Not all cases of abuse end up in a court of law. Many are managed by working with the individual and family to improve the situation and break any abusive cycle.

Supporting and protecting someone experiencing abuse

As a care-worker you have a legal duty to report any suspicions you may have about the possibility of abuse taking place. If you fail to speak up you can be found guilty of negligence. However, do also practise caution. To make an allegation of abuse is extremely serious, with serious consequences, and the authorities are duty bound to investigate it fully. Find out what the policy for reporting abuse is in your place of work, but remember, although it is your responsibility to report your observations to your manager, it is not your responsibility to interpret or draw conclusions from them – that must be left to experts.

People who experience abuse may be very reluctant to report their situation. They may feel guilty and tainted by the behaviour itself, especially in the case of sexual abuse. They might worry about the effect of a revelation of abuse on the abuser. Everyone, such as neighbours and friends and family, would know about it. It might get reported in the media and ultimately the perpetrator might go to prison. Indeed, the abuser may have used such threats, as well as threats about violence or withdrawal of financial assistance, in order to remain undetected. The person experiencing abuse may love the person who abuses them and might be reliant on them for their care.

If a service user talks to you about abuse they are experiencing, here are some brief notes to guide your response:

- Before they tell their story explain that you are legally bound to report any evidence of abuse to your manager.
- Do not get in too deep. Explain that this is not your area of expertise and, without being directive or dismissive, suggest a more experienced colleague.
- If the person does want to continue, make sure you are able to talk in private and without interruptions.
- Make sure they understand that the matter will be treated in confidence and shared on a 'need-to-know' basis only.
- Listen attentively and let them tell their story.
- Do not express either verbally or non-verbally any doubts. Not believing a person's story can be experienced as a further abuse.
- Do not express either verbally or non-verbally any strong emotions you may feel about their story. It is not helpful for them to be burdened by your feelings as well.
- Do NOT ask ANY questions. If legal prosecution follows, any questions you ask at the time may be interpreted as 'leading questions'. The judge would then have to instruct the court to ignore all evidence associated with your questions and this could seriously undermine the case.
- Advise that any evidence (clothing, implements) be preserved and not tampered with. In the case of sexual assault, washing is not advised as DNA evidence may be affected.
- Avoid using words such as 'victim' or 'sufferer' because many people experiencing abuse report that they feel further disempowered by the negative terminology used to describe their situation.
- Be aware of your own needs and seek support and supervision from senior management.

Think It Over

This activity is about meeting the needs of a person experiencing abuse. It can be carried out individually, in pairs or in a group.

- Imagine you are in an abusive situation – it is up to you to decide your age, gender, situation and the type of abuse occurring.
- Describe how you are feeling and what you need to feel safer and better.
- Now imagine that you are a care-worker to your imagined person.
- Translate the feelings and experiences you had into needs to be met by care practice.

Assessment activity 6.4

Read through the following brief descriptions of people experiencing abuse.

1 Ellouise, who is nearly five, arrives unaccompanied to school each day, without having had breakfast and inadequately dressed for the weather.
2 Mrs Lapont informs her carer that she cannot keep the heating on during the day because of the expense. She explains that her son is very good to her and does 'all the money side of things', but that he is worried he will have to move her into a home if she can't keep the bills down and manage a little better to care for herself.
3 A newly arrived resident to a care home for dementia appears frightened when her husband comes to visit and cries out when staff leave them alone together. The husband requests a lock be fitted to allow them greater privacy.

4 A colleague often comes to work with her arms covered in plasters, saying she has accidentally burnt them or a knife slipped when cooking.

5 A student on placement in a unit for children with autism reports to you a number of incidents where a child has used explicit language about his genitals, and been overheard telling other children that 'my daddy has a very big willy'. The child has also drawn rather puzzling pictures that the student states are 'disturbing'. This coincides with the child suffering from a urinary tract infection.

For each one:

- identify the type of abuse that may be being experienced and the major signs to look for (you may suspect more than one type of abuse is occurring in some cases)
- devise a brief, bullet point plan of action for tackling each situation of abuse, bearing in mind the immediate treatment, safety and protection of the person
- identify what further facts you need to know, how you should go about finding them and who you need to hear from to establish with as much certainty as possible that abuse is occurring
- evaluate both the effectiveness and limitations of the various methods (outlined in your answers) of identifying and managing abuse.

Management of abuse in care services

This section looks at the potential for abuse to occur in the care setting, both to service users and care-workers. Guidelines are provided for recognising, recording and reporting evidence. The term 'institutionalised abuse' is explained and you will examine the forms it can take, particularly in care settings. The systems that provide protection from institutionalised abuse are explored, including staff training, staff support and the central importance of **informed consent**.

Abuse of service users and care-workers

It is a sad irony that care settings – places that are set up to provide sanctuary and support for people – can become settings for abuse to take place. Some abusers are attracted to caring professions because this gives them access to vulnerable people who are less able to resist or report abuse.

As a care-worker you too can be on the receiving end of abuse. This might come from a colleague, a service user or your manager. This is unacceptable behaviour and you cannot be expected to continue to work under such circumstances. Remember that if you make unwelcome advances, sexual or otherwise, towards another person at work, even if you only intend to tease or have fun, you can be accused of harassment or even abuse.

Case Study

Mr Barnes is the senior manager of a care home for older people. He recently interviewed Belinda Cruikshanks and appointed her as a healthcare assistant. Mr Barnes has a jovial nature and is quite physical with his staff, putting an arm round them when speaking, and making joking remarks about their personal appearance and what they might be doing in their personal life, especially when off duty. Belinda consults a local solicitor about bringing a case of sexual harassment against her employer.

- Write down two descriptions of what is taking place, one from the point of view of the employer and one from the point of view of the employee.

- What do you think each of them might say to explain or defend their position?

- What advice would you give to each?

Institutionalised abuse

Institutionalised abuse describes the situation where the culture and climate of an organisation or workplace, as well as the systems that run within it, become abusive. This can affect both the workers and the service users. Some forms of institutionalised abuse are illustrated in the Figure 6.9.

Discrimination:		Abuse:	
Sexism	☐	Sexual	☐
Racism	☐	Physical	☐
Disability	☐	Financial	☐
		Emotional	☐
Abusive systems:		**Motivating through:**	
Dictatorial	☐	Bullying and coercion	☐
Inflexible	☐	Violence	☐
Restrictive	☐	Fear or threat	☐
No choice	☐		
Informed consent not sought or obtained			☐
Unreasonable demands and expectations			☐
Unpaid overtime			☐
Individual needs not acknowledged or met			☐

Figure 6.9 The different forms of institutionalised abuse

Discrimination in the form of sexism, racism and disability, where people are treated differently or unfairly because of their race, gender or disability, are included here because people often experience these as abusive. Such discrimination can become a form of institutionalised abuse when it runs throughout the workplace, affecting many areas, such as recruitment and promotion possibilities. (See Unit 1, pages 1–10 for more information about discrimination.)

In a large organisation, such as the Health Service, the very structure that keeps clinical practice disciplined and efficient can flip over to be rigid, inflexible and unable to meet the needs and wishes of individuals. The system then becomes more important than the quality of the service offered. Have you ever worked somewhere where service users had to be up and put back to bed by a certain hour, have meals only at set times with no choice of menu, be forced to bathe against their wishes and wear communal clothing? Institutionalised abuse such as this is often due to inflexibility and a lack of thought at a management level, filtering down to dictate work priorities to the 'front-line' workers. Routines should never be more important than the individual people you care for.

Think It Over

This activity concerns situations where it is necessary to disclose unsafe or abusive practice that denies service users, carers or members of the public their rights or puts them at risk. Individually, in pairs, or as a group, consider how you would manage the following scenarios. Write down your responses in a step-by-step approach.

1 A fellow carer is filling in the weekly menu forms to order meals for all the service users. She picks the dishes randomly without asking individual residents for their preferred choices.
2 You witness a service user making a sexual pass at a new member of staff. She looks very flustered and uncomfortable, but says nothing.
3 A visitor tells you her back is aching after lifting an elderly service user, suffering from dementia, from the commode back to bed. Apparently, the service user's carer regularly requests assistance saying that they are always short-staffed and that it's the policy of the home to involve everyone in the care of service users.

Preventative measures

There are numerous preventative measures to guard against abuse. All people applying to work with children or vulnerable adults must go through a thorough recruitment system. This should include the provision of references that are checked for authenticity, as well as seeking **disclosure information** including 'criminal checks' to identify previous convictions or appearance on a **paedophile** register. Once in post, staff should be given regular training, supervision, appraisal and support. These measures keep you up-to-date with current thought and research in your area of work, and inform you about what is expected of you, particularly in terms of professional conduct. Abuse can occur when staff feel under pressure. To avoid this, extra support and recognition should be given in times of increased stress, such as staff shortage, low morale, and where staff work in isolation with service users. It is a sign of strength and not weakness to recognise when you need support at work, so do not be afraid to ask for it.

Most organisations develop policies to guide working practice. Similarly 'models of care' are adopted that reflect the philosophy, or ethos, behind the service provided and these help to reduce rigid ways of working. An example of a model is care-planning, where every area of need is identified for each service user and the care described to meet these (see pages 184–5). However, it is important to keep up-to-date with current debate, because if out-of-date models of care are held on to, and if these become more important than the actual care provided, the potential for institutionalised abuse increases again.

Preventative measures also come from outside the workplace in the form of registration and inspection. This requires organisations to maintain certain standards and to justify ways of working. The 'Patient's Charter' was set out by the government a few years ago to inform the public of the service they are entitled to and should expect. Complaints procedures also help to ensure that matters are brought to the attention of management and can (hopefully) be resolved before a more serious situation develops.

Informed consent

Informed consent is a concept designed to prevent the violation and abuse of a person's rights. It requires that a person understands what is to happen – is informed – and agrees to it – gives consent. An obvious example is before an operation, where the surgeon and anaesthetist must obtain written and signed consent before surgery takes place. Consent in a care setting is frequently more subtle though, and is given (or not!) in more informal ways. For example, when you say to a service user, 'Shall I help you to get washed?' you are seeking their consent, but it would be highly unusual to have to obtain that in writing! Rather, you wait for your service user to say, 'Yes', or to show their consent by walking along with you to the bathroom. Informed consent becomes more problematic when dealing with people who are unable to give this, due to their inability to understand the situation or communicate their wishes or feelings – a child, for example, or a person with confusion. In these cases, consent must be obtained from the person's legal guardian or representative, usually a close relative.

Case Study

Letticia Amos is a resident in a community home for adults with learning difficulties and autism. She has recently been put on new medication to help calm her during episodes of agitation. Senior staff decide to crush these tablets and mix them in with her food. Ellen Phipps, a care assistant, is asked to ensure Letticia eats all her ice-cream, feeding it to her if necessary, because her tablets have been added to it. When Letticia's father comes to visit he complains that it is ridiculous to force-feed someone food that is usually viewed as a treat, especially when Letticia is overweight anyway! Ellen realises that the father has not been informed about the medication being hidden in the food and is in a dilemma about what to do and say.

● What would you do in this situation?

● Who is being abused in this situation and how?

Reporting abuse

If you suspect or know that abuse, or dangerous or illegal working practice, is taking place you are duty bound to report it. You may need to act swiftly if you fear people are in immediate danger, but where possible take your time to think through your actions and the consequences of these. Record your evidence accurately, keeping it factual and to the point and avoiding emotive (emotionally loaded) or subjective (personal) language. Where possible, go through the usual channels of communication within the management structure. You may find that by telling the person it concerns or your immediate boss, the problem is identified and sorted out. However, if you suspect that disclosure puts you at risk or might force the problem underground, you may need to go straight to a higher authority. If you are a member of a trade union or professional body, do seek advice before you act.

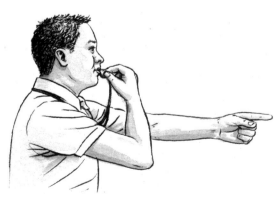

Whistle blowing

The term whistle blowing is used to describe the disclosure of misconduct within an organisation. The person who reports wrong-doing at work – whether in the form of abusive, dangerous or illegal working practice – to a higher authority, or exposes it in the media, is known as 'the whistle blower'. The Public Interest Disclosure Act, 1998 was designed to protect

Figure 6.10 Whistle blowing

whistle blowers. It came about as a result of public inquiries into scandals (for example, sexual abuse in children's homes across North Wales) and disasters (for example, the Clapham rail crash). It was discovered that individual workers had known for some time about abuse or dangerous working practice, but did nothing about it for fear of being punished by the organisation they worked for. The Act requires firm evidence and does not protect people who bear a grudge against their employers or who wish to stir up trouble.

Theory into practice

Check out any written policies on bullying and sexual harassment in your place of work. Find out whether other employees know these policies exist. Do you think they need updating? Could they be improved upon?

Assessment activity 6.5

You work in a care setting and your manager has devised an internal teaching programme, where the workers take it in turns to present a work-related topic of interest to each other. Your turn has come around and you have been asked to talk about 'the potential for abuse in care settings'. Make a detailed plan of your teaching session, set out in the following way:

1 Itemise and give brief explanations of the different ways in which abuse can occur in a care setting.
2 Describe what is meant by the term 'institutionalised abuse'.
3 Explain the strategies put in place by care services to minimise the potential for abuse taking place and for dealing with it when it does occur.
4 How might you get your audience to consider the various effects of the discovery of abuse within a care setting? Include the effect on service users, workers and the management.

Professional confidentiality

This section deals with confidentiality at work and examines the key importance of safeguarding private and personal information in a care setting. You will look at the variety of ways that confidentiality can be broken and the methods and systems in place to minimise such breaches. The legal situation will be explained, as well as specific circumstances when it is legitimate to breach confidentiality.

As a care-worker you will see and hear things about the intimate, personal, medical and psychiatric histories of your service users. This is usually necessary in order for you to give care appropriately. Professional confidentiality means keeping this information private and sharing it only with those who also need to know, in order to contribute to the service user's care. You might find it useful to think of this position as privileged and certainly one not to be threatened by gossip or indiscretion. Professional confidentiality is vital for a number of reasons:

- Trust – your relationships with your service users and colleagues are dependent on their trust in you. If you breach this you risk undermining the therapeutic effects of the relationships you have built up.
- Respect – the service user may lose faith in an organisation that has lax systems and allows breaches of confidentiality to occur.
- Safety – some information could have safety implications, such as keeping secret a person's HIV status, or the whereabouts of a family who have escaped from domestic abuse.

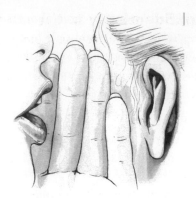

Figure 6.11 Talking about a service user's personal information is a breach of their trust

- Employment – you risk your job if you breach rules of confidentiality.
- Legal – there are a number of laws that protect the individual's right to confidentiality.

Key issues

Across the United Kingdom in schools, youth clubs, nurseries and other childcare facilities, those in charge have to seek written parental consent for photographs to be taken and published in the local paper. These might be photos of a school fete, the swimming gala or a gym display. A number of parents contact the school to exclaim over this 'ridiculous situation'. They question who would resent such good publicity for the school, the leisure centre or the gym club, denying the benefits of being included in the life of the community. The answer is stark. Local papers are regularly used by abusers as a source of information and a method for tracing the whereabouts of children protected under a Court Order. Discuss in a group the positives and negatives of this situation.

Confidentiality and the law

Confidentiality refers to the human right to have personal information kept private and for it to be shared only with those people who need to know in order to provide a necessary service. The Data Protection Act 1998 is the main piece of legislation relating to confidentiality and it covers written, spoken and electronically stored information. This states that information must be accurate, relevant and not excessive, it must be kept secure and should not be held for any longer than is necessary. Under common law, 'a duty of confidence' also provides protection. This states that any personal information given or received in confidence for one purpose will not be passed on to another person for an entirely different purpose, unless permission is given. For example, if information about a named individual has been collected for nursing or medical reasons you cannot then pass the information to a colleague doing research, or a drug company targeting treatment in this area, without first getting written consent.

Related to these laws is the Freedom of Information Bill, which is in the process of becoming an Act. This concerns your right to access information that is held by any public authority. For example, you have a right to read the medical notes written about you by your doctor (unless seeing these is judged to be potentially detrimental to your mental health).

Confidentiality in the care setting

Confidentiality affects so many aspects of the workplace. Wherever this information can be directly traced to a specific service user you must ensure it is only seen or heard by those who need to know. There are four aspects to the process of handling confidential information:

1 Receiving   3 Storing
2 Recording   4 Retrieving.

Your role as a care-worker will involve you in some or all of these aspects. You are likely to take phone calls, discuss service user care and contribute to care plans. You will liaise with colleagues and talk with service users and their relatives and friends. Off duty, you are still likely to talk about work to friends and family and at times you may need to unburden yourself about stresses at work. This is understandable – you do a tough job at the front line of public service – but the golden rule is to still maintain confidentiality. Never use names or disclose facts that are traceable to your service users or colleagues. It is your professional duty not to breach confidentiality and to report any breaches you witness. Most are accidental through carelessness or thoughtlessness, but some are malicious or for gain or profit.

Case Study

Read the following conversation overheard between two off-duty healthcare assistants.

Fay: 'I've just come off night duty – I'm dying for my bed.'

Meg: 'Talking of dying, is Bunty Harris still with us, poor soul?'

Fay: 'Yeah, but only just. It's a lot of work at night with turning her and cleaning her up and it's nearly impossible to get fluids down her. I think she's still in pain too.'

Meg: 'It'll be a blessing if she slips away soon.'

Fay: 'She'd slip away a bit sooner if they upped her diamorphine injections.'

Meg: nodding in agreement, 'Yes, perhaps they should.'

The two women go on to chat about other things.

- How would you feel if you overheard this conversation, especially if you were a relative or friend of Bunty's?
- List all the specific breaches of confidentiality.

Theory into practice

It is an interesting fact that when the law changed to allow service users to read the notes written about them, many carers recognised the need to be more sensitive and careful about the way they write notes. Notes generally have become less descriptive and more factual and less subjective (personal) and more objective (non-judgemental).

- Briefly write up, in note form, an incident or event with a service user that occurs at work this week. Describe this twice, using two different styles to report the one event: firstly use a subjective, descriptive style and secondly an objective, factual style. Remember to change the names of your service users in order to keep the information confidential!
- Compare the two reports for accuracy and authenticity.
- If your service user requested to read his or her notes, which style of report would you prefer your service user to read?

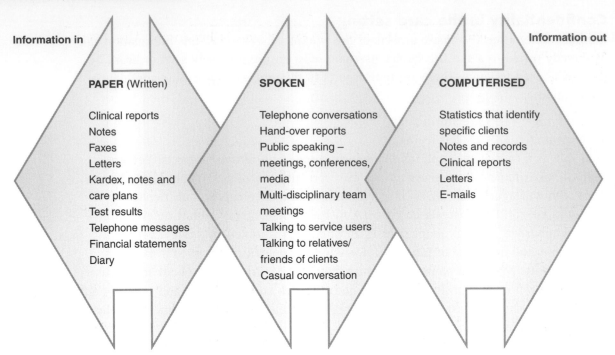

Figure 6.12 The many forms of confidential information

Keeping information safe

For paper information, the physical barriers of a locked filing cabinet or a locked room, where only designated key-carriers have access, are usually adequate. There should also be an agreed system for accepting and sending faxes, writing down phone and answerphone messages and storing papers waiting to be filed. Where paper records are shared between different care agencies or professions there should be agreed policies about access and safe-keeping.

The confidentiality of spoken information must be safeguarded. All conversations of a confidential nature, including phone conversations, must be carried out in a private place where information cannot be overheard. Over the phone, it is not always possible to confirm that a caller is who they claim to be. It is usually best to defer to a senior member of staff or explain that you are not permitted to discuss confidential matters over the phone. Sometimes you will be in the situation of asking someone else, perhaps a service user's relatives, for confidential information. Try not to put pressure on them to reveal information, and, where possible, go directly to your service user. Numerous meetings take place in care settings so be aware of items under discussion that concern confidential matters, particularly relating to individual service users. If you are unsure about what information is confidential, check with a senior member of staff.

Information stored on computers should be kept safe by using passwords and codes, as well as by limiting access.

Think It Over

This is a group role-play activity, but if you work alone look through the following scenario and consider your responses. Ideally three people are required: one to phone, one to receive the call and one to listen and observe. The 'caller', claiming to be a close family member phones to ask for information about the progress of their relative. The 'carer' does not know the caller, but must respond in a helpful and professional manner, without breaching confidentiality. The 'listener' feeds back his or her observations about the exchange.

It is helpful to swap roles and experience all perspectives. You can make brief notes about how you found this exercise.

The boundaries of confidentiality

The issue of confidentiality can include 'grey areas' where it is not easy to assess who has a right to personal information. For example, is it right to keep information about a service user's medical condition from them, because in your opinion the information will distress them unnecessarily? Also consider the situation where a service user asks you to collude with him or her by not informing a relative of certain information. These are difficult areas and there may not be one right answer. In the past many doctors and nurses kept information about terminal illness from a patient, truly believing this to be a kindness. More recently the trend has changed and most doctors and nurses would consider it the patient's right to know they are facing death. Whatever the final decision taken about confidential and sensitive information, the process of deciding should include full discussion among the key people involved. Never fall into the trap of agreeing to keep information confidential when in fact it is beyond your powers or professional duty to do so. If keeping confidentiality puts someone in danger – for example, if you are aware a person is suicidal or has committed a serious crime – it becomes your duty to breach confidentiality and report to a higher authority.

Assessment activity 6.6

This activity is divided into three sections. In each section you need to read the short scenario and answer the following questions.

1 Stewart is a new carer who has started at your place of work. As you show him around he spots a service user he knows – her family are neighbours of his. This presents a good opportunity to go through the key aspects of professional confidentiality with him.

- *a)* Briefly describe how you would explain what confidentiality means in a care setting.
- *b)* Itemise the laws relevant to confidentiality with a short-sentence explanation of each.
- *c)* Describe, giving examples, how confidentiality is protected when handling paper, spoken and electronic information.
- *d)* Give him two examples of occasions when it is considered acceptable to breach the normal rules of confidentiality.

2 Stewart seems to have taken in the facts about confidentiality, but then makes these remarks at lunch-break, 'I can't quite see what all the fuss is about. I'm not very senior so I doubt I'll get to be told anything too confidential. Even if we do let something slip, it's unlikely to be that important.'

- *a)* What can you say to Stewart to help him to recognise why confidentiality is crucial to effective care practice?
- *b)* Illustrate your point with three practical examples drawn from potential situations that could arise in a care setting.

3 As Stewart settles in you are relieved to see from his professional behaviour that he has understood the central importance of confidentiality. However, not long after he comes to you for advice about a conversation he has just had with the wife of a service user. Stewart tells you that she has shared information, strictly in confidence, about something that is against the law. Her husband has made her promise to help him to end his life. Stewart is in a dilemma and having difficulty knowing what to do.

    a) Breaching confidentiality in this situation will affect the service user, the service user's relative, the care-worker, the place of work, the profession, and possibly the wider community. Describe the impact from each of these perspectives in a way that might help Stewart to evaluate the effects of overriding adherence to confidentiality.

End-of-unit test

1 Illustrate, using two or three examples, how you demonstrate accountability and responsibility in your own working life.

2 Make a list of all the people in your life who are most vulnerable to health, safety and security risks and explain how and why.

3 Why do you think health, safety and security legislation is important? List your reasons.

4 Carry out a detailed risk assessment of any one area in your life today. Document your findings.

5 Why is it important to raise the alarm before taking action when you come across a fire? Explain the different ways in which you can raise the alarm.

6 If you were to come across a person, apparently unconscious, on the ground, what steps would you take to provide first aid? Place your responses in the order in which you would carry them out.

7 Briefly describe a situation of challenging behaviour you have experienced. How would you handle the situation now, and why?

8 List as many types of abuse as you are aware of.

9 Choose one type of abuse and list the signs and symptoms that might indicate this abuse is taking place.

10 Imagine that someone you know is experiencing racial abuse – describe how you would respond and offer your support.

11 Give three reasons why it is important to maintain confidentiality when working in a care setting.

12 What do you understand by the term 'whistle blower'?

References and further reading

Donnellan, C. (2001) *Issues Series: Sexuality*, Cambridge: Independence Press

Donnellan, C. (2000) *Issues Series: Privacy Rights*, Cambridge: Independence Press

Pre-school Learning Alliance (1991) *Accident Prevention and First Aid for use in Pre-schools*

Home Life: Code of Practice for Residential Care (1984) London: Centre for Policy on Ageing

7 Applying psychology

This unit explores the major perspectives in psychology and the ways in which they influence care practice.

The NVQ Care Value Base defines the importance of fostering the equality and diversity of people. The value system of equal opportunities requires care-workers to understand and value the diversity in the people that they work with. A phrase that is often spoken in care work is 'everybody is different', or 'no two people are the same – everyone has different needs'. But what makes people different from one another?

What you need to learn

- Major psychological perspectives
- Psychological perspectives and understanding individual behaviour
- Major perspectives and care practice

Major psychological perspectives

What are perspectives and why are they important in care work?

A perspective is a way of looking at something. There are many different ways of looking at human behaviour and trying making sense of it.

Each perspective makes different assumptions about what influences people. Each perspective can help us to understand influences on behaviour because each perspective

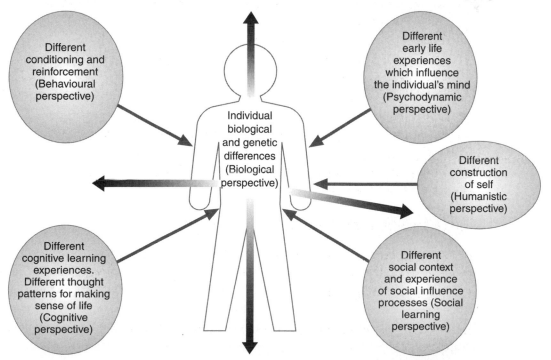

Figure 7.1 The influences that make people different from one another

may be useful in drawing our attention to important issues. The perspectives listed below are more than just theories; they are more like eye glasses, which can make the world look different, depending on which pair of glasses you put on. Different professionals may favour different theories, but no single perspective has been proved to be true or to be false. Psychological perspectives are ways of looking at life – because of this they will never be proved or disproved.

Psychodynamic theory

Sigmund Freud (1856–1939) developed a theory of the human mind that emphasised the interaction of biological drives with the social environment. Freud's theory emphasises the power of early experience to influence the adult personality.

Freud's theories are called psychodynamic theories. Freud founded a method of therapy called psychoanalysis. Psychoanalytic therapy involves exploring the impact of early experience on the mental functioning of a person.

Psychodynamic refers to the broad theoretical model for explaining mental functioning. 'Psycho' means mind or spirit and 'dynamic' means energy or the expression of energy. Freud believed that people were born with a dynamic 'life energy' or 'libido'. This initially motivates a baby to feed and grow, and later motivates sexual reproduction. Freud's theory explains that people are born with biological instincts in much the same way that animals such as dogs or cats are. Our instincts exist in the unconscious mind – we don't usually understand our unconscious. As we grow we have to learn to control our 'instincts' in order to be accepted and fit in with other people. Society is possible only if people can 'control themselves'. If everybody just did whatever they felt like, life would be short and violent; civilisation would not be possible. Because people have to learn to control their unconscious drives (or instincts), children go through stages of psychosexual development. These stages result in the development of a mature mind which contains the mechanisms that control adult personality and behaviour.

Freud's stages of psychosexual development

The Oral stage
Dynamic life energy motivates the infant to feed and activities involving lips, sucking, biting, create pleasure for the baby. Weaning represents a difficult stage which may influence the future personality of the child.

The Anal stage
Young children have to learn to control their muscles and in particular the control of the anal muscles. Toilet training represents the first time a child has to control their own body in order to meet the demands of society. The child's experiences during toilet training may influence later development.

The Phallic stage
Freud shocked Europeans a century ago by insisting that children had sexual feelings towards their parents. Freud believed that girls were sexually attracted to their father and boys were sexually attracted to their mother. These attractions are called the Electra and Oedipus complexes named after characters in ancient Greek mythology who experienced these attractions. As children develop, they have to give up the opposite sex parent as a 'love object' and learn to identify with the same sex parents. Children's experience of 'letting go' of their first love may have permanent effects on their later personality.

Latency

After the age of 5 or 6 years, most children have resolved the Electra and Oedipus complexes (Freud believed that this change was usually more definite in boys, and that in contrast girls often continue with a sexual attachment to their father). Children are not yet biologically ready to reproduce, so their sexuality is latent or waiting to express itself.

The Genital stage

With the onset of puberty adolescents become fully sexual and 'life energy', or libido, is focused on sexual activity.

Think It Over

Freud's theories are often hard to accept in a society which is 'out of touch' with nature, but have you ever watched animals such as kittens develop? Young kittens focus all their energy on getting milk from the mother cat – the life energy seems almost visible. As kittens grow into young cats they will sometimes attempt to mate with parents! Freud's theories were based on the idea that people are animals – but animals that have to adapt their behaviour to the needs of society.

Discuss with other students the possibility that we forget or even deny our inner 'animal' drives.

Freud's mental mechanisms

Freud believed that we were born with an 'id'; the 'id' is part of our unconscious mind that is hidden from conscious understanding. The 'id' is like a dynamo that generates mental energy. This energy motivates human action and behaviour.

When a young child learns to control their own body during toilet training the 'ego' develops. The 'ego' is a mental system which contains personal learning about physical and social reality. The 'ego' has the job of deciding how to channel life energy from the unconscious into behaviour which will produce satisfactory outcomes in the real world. The 'ego' is both unconscious (unknown to self) and conscious (a person can understand some of their own actions and motivation).

The 'superego' develops from the ego when the child gives up their opposite-sex parent as a 'love object'. The 'superego' contains the social and moral values of the parent that has been 'lost' as a potential partner.

The essence of psychodynamic theory is that people are controlled by inner forces, but that people do not understand and cannot explain what is happening to themselves. For example, throughout adult life a person has to find a way to release life energy that is compatible with the demands of society and with the demands of the superego. Sometimes people may feel sandwiched between the demands of their biology and social pressures. Typically today's world often creates pressure to 'achieve a good career' and maintain parental values by 'doing well'. For some people the desire to enjoy their sexuality and perhaps have children may conflict with the pressure to achieve. The way people cope with these pressures will be strongly influenced by childhood experiences, according to Freudian theory.

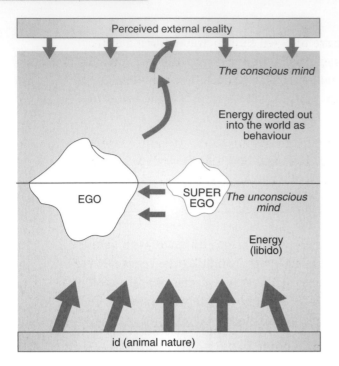

Perceived external reality

The conscious mind

Energy directed out
into the world as
behaviour

EGO

SUPER
EGO *The unconscious
mind*

Energy
(libido)

id (animal nature)

Figure 7.2 Freudian mental mechanisms

In order to understand a person's behaviour a therapist needs to be able to understand what is happening in that individual's unconscious mind. Therapists and counsellors cannot begin to understand the unconscious mind of an individual by asking direct questions. In order to understand how an early experience has influenced the unconscious mind, therapists might explore an individual's dreams. Alternatively a therapist might ask a service user to make up a story about a picture (the Thematic Apperception test) or ask them what they see in an ink blot (the Rorschach test).

These indirect conversations are a way of learning about another person's unconscious mind. Freud originally used the method of 'free association' to access the unconscious mind of his patients. This 'talking cure' involves getting the service user to relax on a couch and just explain whatever comes into their mind in response to words that the psychoanalyst says.

Erikson's development of psychodynamic theory

Erik Erikson (1902–94) based his theory on Freud's psychodynamic ideas. Erikson's first three stages of development are similar to Freud's and are developed from Freud's theory. The major difference between Freud's and Erikson's theory is that Erikson believed that people continue to develop and change throughout life. Freud only explained how early experience might influence adult life. Erikson originally stated that there were eight periods of developmental crisis that an individual would have to pass through in life. These crises were linked to an unfolding maturation process and would be common to people of all cultures because they were 'psychosexual' in origin rather than linked to aspects of lifestyle or culture.

How an individual succeeded or failed in adapting to each crisis would influence how their sense of self and personality developed. Each stage is described in terms of the positive or the negative outcomes that may happen following the developmental stage. Many people achieve an in-between outcome.

Erikson's eight life stages

1 basic trust versus mistrust
2 self-control versus shame and doubt
3 initiative versus guilt
4 competence versus inferiority
5 identity versus role confusion
6 intimacy versus isolation
7 generativity versus stagnation
8 ego-integrity versus despair

Basic trust versus mistrust
Birth to 1¹/₂ years. Infants have to learn a sense of basic trust or learn to mistrust the world. If children receive good quality care this may help them to develop personalities which include a sense of hope and safety. If not, they may develop a personality dominated by a sense of insecurity and anxiety.

Self-control versus shame and doubt
1¹/₂ to 3 years. Children have to develop a sense of self-control, or a sense of shame and doubt may predominate. They may develop a sense of willpower and control over their own bodies. If this sense of self-control does not develop, then children may feel that they cannot control events.

Initiative versus guilt
3 to 7 years. Children have to develop a sense of initiative which will provide a sense of purpose in life. A sense of guilt may otherwise dominate the individual's personality and lead to a lack of self-worth.

Competence versus inferiority
Perhaps 6 to 15 years. The individual has to develop a sense of competence, or risk the personality being dominated by feelings of inferiority and failure.

Identity versus role confusion
Perhaps 13 to 21 years. Adolescents or young adults need to develop a sense of personal identity, or risk a sense of role confusion, with a fragmented or unclear sense of self.

Intimacy versus isolation
Perhaps 18 to 30 years. Young adults have to develop a capability for intimacy, love and the ability to share and commit their feelings to others. The alternative personality outcome is isolation and an inability to make close, meaningful friendships.

Generativity versus stagnation
Perhaps 30s to 60s or 70s. Mature adults have to develop a sense of being generative, leading to concern for others and concern for the future well-being of others. The alternative is to become inward-looking and self-indulgent.

Ego-integrity versus despair
Later life. Older adults have to develop a sense of wholeness or integrity within their understanding of themselves. This might lead to a sense of meaning to life or even to what could be called 'wisdom'. The alternative is a lack of meaning in life and a sense of despair.

Both Freud's and Erikson's views of human development are based on the notion that human biology creates a 'life trajectory' where stages of crises are inevitable. Both Freud and Erikson accept that individual social experiences will interact with biology to create an individual personality. The psychodynamic view of development emphasises the importance of individual experience and the interaction of biological stages and the environment. The relationship between children and parents is seen as a key influence on the development of personality. Personal development is understood in terms of definable stages.

The idea that human development fits eight stages (or five stages) of coping with crises or change does not make intuitive sense to everyone. Whilst there may be some important ideas about emotional development in psychodynamic theory, some authors claim that these theories are too rigid to provide a full understanding of development.

Think It Over

Thinking back over your own life, did you experience times of crisis linked to issues like competence or inferiority in your own school life?

Do you think that your life will involve change through periods of crisis or more gradual and gentle change?

Freud and Erikson's theories both emphasise the role of biological and sexual development in influencing the workings of our unconscious mind. Some other psychodynamic theorists take a different view and instead emphasise the role of relationships and attachment as the primary force which influences the development of our unconscious mind.

John Bowlby, attachment, bonding and maternal deprivation

Bowlby (1953) stated, 'What occurs in the earliest months and years of life can have deep and long-lasting effects'. Bowlby studied mothers and babies in the mid 1940s, just after the end of the Second World War. Bowlby had noticed that some baby animals would make very fixed emotional bonds with their parents. For example, baby ducklings would attach themselves to, and follow, whomever they presumed to be their mother. Wild ducklings will naturally attach themselves to the mother duck. Bowlby had studied research which showed that ducklings would attach themselves to humans if humans were all that was around during a critical period when the duckling needed to bond.

Bowlby's studies of infants led him to the conclusion that human babies were similar to some types of animal, such as ducks. Bowlby believed that there was a biological need for mothers and babies to be together, and that there was a sensitive or critical period for mothers and babies to form this attachment, which is known as bonding. Bowlby (1953) stated, 'The absolute need of infants and toddlers for the continuous care of their mothers will be borne in on all who read this [book]'.

Separation

If the bond of love between a baby and its mother was broken through separation, Bowlby believed, lasting psychological damage would be done to the child. If a mother left her infant to go to work every day, or just once to go into hospital, there might be a risk of damage. Bowlby believed that children who suffered separation might grow up to be unable to love or show affection. Separated children might not care about other people. Separated children might also fail to learn properly at school, and might be more likely to turn to crime when they grew up. This theory that children who are separated from their mother would grow up to be emotionally damaged is known as a theory of maternal deprivation – being deprived of a mother's attention.

Some other researchers working outside of the psychodynamic perspective have doubted that babies are really affected so seriously by separation. Michael Rutter (1981) found evidence that suggests that it is the quality of emotional attachment between a carer and the infant that matters. Not being able to make an attachment at all may damage a child emotionally. But it is the making of a bond of love between the baby and a carer that matters, not whether temporary separations happen.

There is research that suggests that babies can and do make bonds with their fathers and with their brothers, sisters, or other carers. In one study (Schaffer and Emerson, 1964) almost a third of 18–month–old infants had made their main attachment to their fathers.

It seems that babies give their love to the person or persons who give them the best-quality affection and time.

Melanie Klein

Another psychodynamic theory which emphasises relationships has developed from the work of Melanie Klein. This theory argues that our unconscious mind is built on our early experiences of being cared for. Babies can only exist as part of a relationship with their carer. What happens in the first months of life strongly influences the way we express emotions later in life.

Figure 7.3 According to the psychodynamic perspective adult emotions are based on early experience

Alan and Ann Clarke (1976) reviewed a wide range of research. They concluded that children can recover from almost any bad psychological experience provided that later experience makes up for it. It is whole life experience and not just the first years of an infant's life that will decide whether a child grows up to care about other people, or takes to a life of crime. Although people can recover from separation and poor relationships, it is very important that infants do have a chance to make a loving relationship or bond with carers. The first part of a person's life may set the scene for what will happen next. A lack of love in early life could be a very bad start for a child's emotional development. It would be unwise just to hope that some later quality of life could make up for it.

The importance of the relationship between children and their parents, or carers, is now widely accepted. When children require hospital treatment it is now common for parents to be encouraged to stay with their children. Separation is seen as serious emotional risk for the child.

Peter Marris (1996) believes that adult emotional security and quality of life also depend on attachment. Marris argues that modern working patterns undermine the development of adult attachments and so create higher levels of stress in society. People who attend counselling for stress-related problems may be experiencing a failure to maintain appropriate attachments to others.

Assessment activity 7.1

What facilities and support does your placement setting provide to enable service users to maintain contact with their relatives? Pool your information with the information that other students can gather on their placements. Looking at your sample of agencies, write an account of the importance of attachment theory as reflected in the service provision you have researched.

At merit level you can use this analysis as a basis for an example of ways in which psychological theory assists care-workers in practice. At distinction level your analysis might be used to provide one example for evaluating the role of theory in increasing the effectiveness of therapy and interventions. To achieve this level you will need to undertake further discussion to clarify how understanding of attachment theory might improve individual carer skills and contribute to the formation of organisational policy.

Biological perspectives

Human behaviour is undoubtedly influenced by brain and body chemistry. For example, some people become touchy or irritable when their blood sugar levels are low because they have not eaten. When people have a high body temperature they may become irrational.

Genetics

The way our bodies work is influenced by genetics. Genetics contain the information and instructions needed to make living organisms. An individual person results from the interaction of their genetic pattern and their environment. It has become fashionable for journalists to talk about 'genes for' criminal behaviour, or for intelligence, or for certain illnesses. But it is extremely unlikely that complex social behaviours can be explained purely in terms of the biochemical instructions for building cell structures. As we learn more about the emerging science of genetics it is widely accepted that genetic influences interact and are intertwined with environmental influences. That is, genetics do have an influence on behaviour but not directly. Some people with certain genetic patterns may be more likely to commit crime but whether or not a crime will take place will depend on what the person has experienced and learned.

A study reported in *The Independent* on 2 August 2002 illustrates this point. An international study discovered a gene which is associated with violent behaviour in men. However, violent crime was particularly associated with a combination of having experienced abuse as a child and inheriting the gene. Professor Moffitt who led the research is quoted as saying; 'this is not really the story of a gene that has a risk for anti-social behaviour. It is a story of the interplay between a gene and the experience of maltreatment'.

Genetic differences may explain why some people become aggressive or depressed, whereas other people in similar circumstances do not. Genetics might influence how people react, but they do not directly cause behaviour.

Trait theory

Trait theorists assume that human personality is relatively stable. We are born with different tendencies to react to the world in different ways. Two famous trait theories are summarised below.

Hans Eysenck

Eysenck's (1965) theory of personality involves three central traits which describe human personality.

1. Introversion/extroversion – an individual might be either hungry for experience and excitement, in which case they will be an extrovert; or eager to avoid excitement, in which case they will be an introvert. Most people are somewhere in between these extremes.
2. Stability/instability – stability means a calm, confident and perhaps carefree approach to life. Instability means a moody, changeable and restless response to life events. Once again most people will fall somewhere in between these extremes.
3. Tough-minded/tender-minded – the tough-minded person might be careless of other people's feelings, rights or needs. Tender-minded individuals are likely to be concerned for individual feelings. Few people will demonstrate extremes of tough or tender-minded traits.

Eysenck's theory emphasised the biological basis for personality. He argued that criminal behaviour is particularly associated with high levels of extroversion and instability. Eysenck argued that people who were born with a high level of extroversion were less responsive to conditioned learning.

Raymond B. Cattell

A second famous trait theory is based on the work of Cattell (1965). Cattell argued that descriptions of human personality could be reduced to 16 basic traits. He invented a test of personality called the 16 personality factor test or 16PF test. The test results in a score and a profile on the 16 factors set out below:

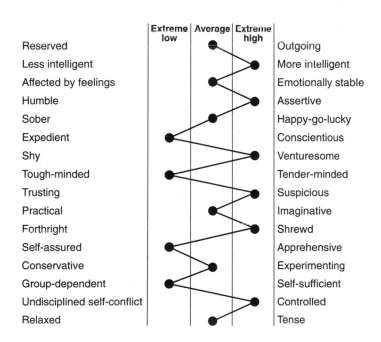

Figure 7.4 A personality profile

The assumption is that how reserved, tough-minded, or group-dependent a person is depends on their underlying biological nature.

Current ideas

Some psychologists currently work with the idea that there are five main dimensions which summarise human personality. These five basic traits are listed below:

Extroversion Being talkative, energetic	v.	Being quiet, reserved and shy
Agreeableness Being sympathetic, kind and affectionate	v.	Being cold, quarrelsome and cruel.
Conscientiousness Being organised, responsible	v.	Being careless, frivolous and irresponsible
Emotional stability Being stable, calm and contented	v.	Being anxious, unstable and 'temperamental'
Openness to experience Being creative, intellectual and open-minded	v.	Being simple, shallow and unintelligent

Figure 7.5 Five basic personality traits, Zimbardo (1992)

Humanistic perspectives

The humanistic perspective is sometimes described as a 'third force' because it is an alternative to both the psychodynamic and behaviourist viewpoints, which have traditionally been used to explain human behaviour.

The humanistic perspective can be harder to understand than the psychodynamic and behaviourist viewpoints. Behaviourism sees human behaviour as being caused by influences in the environment. The psychodynamic viewpoint emphasises the importance of early experience. Although ideas like conditioning and ego defences can be complicated, at least they fit with the common assumption that everything must have a cause. Humanistic theorists do not try to explain people's behaviour in terms of searching for causes in the environment. Behaviour is influenced by our understanding of who we are. It is the way we have come to understand our own self-concept that is important, not our early experience or conditioning.

Self-concept

Self-concept means our own knowledge of who we are. Self-concept can include the ideas shown in Figure 7.6.

Our knowledge of our own life and personality can be very complicated. A very simplified way of thinking about self-concept is to see ourselves as having a physical self, an intellectual self, an emotional self and a social self.

Each person develops their own special view of themselves. This view comes about because of the experiences which people have as they grow and develop across their

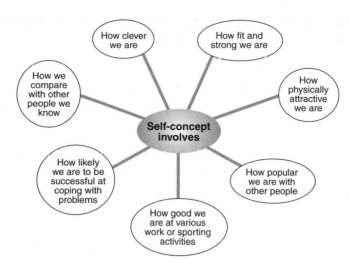

Figure 7.6 Aspects of self-concept

life-span. Self-concept may influence how we grow and develop – some examples are set out below.

- Our view of ourselves can motivate us to do things or stop us from doing things, for example, doing well at school or at sport.
- Our view of ourselves can create a feeling of social confidence or cause us to feel anxious with other people.
- Our view of ourselves can mean that we derive happiness or unhappiness from life experiences.
- Our view of ourselves can help us lead a successful and enjoyable life or it can lead us into trouble and difficulties in coping with life.

Our knowledge of ourselves changes as we go through life. The people we mix with, the experiences we have, all cause us to think differently. The way we think about ourselves may control what we attempt to do and how much confidence we have.

Carl Rogers

Carl Rogers (1902–87) created a theory of 'being', or a theory of how to live a quality life. This theory argues that each person is born with an in-built need to grow and develop to his or her full potential. This need is called the 'self-actualising tendency'. Self-actualisation means 'becoming everything one is capable of becoming'. Each person has their own individual, unique experience of life and will self-actualise in different ways. In a perfect world people would be free to grow and develop according to their own inner needs. In a perfect world everyone would be able to spend their time developing their physical, social or practical skills as they wished. People who were free to learn and grow would experience the world in a way that would enable them to live fully. They would follow their own instincts; they would be healthy, spontaneous, flexible and creative. Such people would also be able to truly experience events and sensations undistorted by the need to conform to social roles or be controlled by others.

Naturally, we do not live in a perfect world. Many people develop a self-concept which does not fit with the needs of their own inner self-actualising tendency. People deny and distort their experience of life in order to maintain a working self-concept. Many people do not lead truly happy or fulfilling lives because they live their life trying to conform to the demands and wishes of other people.

Carl Rogers identified 'conditional positive regard' as the main factor that caused people to develop an understanding of themselves that did not fit with their inner needs. Conditional positive regard means that you are only friendly towards people who meet your expectations of what is good. Conditional positive self-regard means that you only like yourself if you meet the standards that other people set for you. People like to be liked – many people adopt the values and beliefs of other people around them, not because these values and beliefs meet their real psychological needs, but because they want to be liked.

Case Study

Jodie was born with the potential for athletic abilities. Jodie's inner tendency to self-actualise includes a deep enjoyment of athletic activities such as running and body building. Jodie's parents and friends see these activities as masculine behaviour – suitable for boys but not for girls. They say things like 'you will never get a decent boyfriend if you look muscley'. Jodie's friends do not like running or going to the gym. Jodie comes to believe that she will be more popular and likeable if she drops her athletic interests. Inwardly, she feels that she should develop her abilities, but she suppresses these feelings in order to 'look good' to others. By pleasing other people and doing what they want Jodie is responding to conditional positive regard. The consequences of this are that Jodie develops a concept of herself as a non-athletic person. This concept involves a denial and distortion of her true nature, preventing her from developing in a psychologically healthy way.

In discussion with other students decide what sort of problems Jodie might experience if she gives in to the pressure to conform to other people's expectations.

Obstacles to the self-actualising tendency

Nowadays, many people live within a culture where making money is seen as the purpose of life. Activities that bring in money are good. Jobs that involve making a lot of money are praised. People may be criticised for using their time to learn music or art if this does not make money. Taking a career in care work might be criticised if the earnings are less than in other jobs. Getting conditional positive regard might depend on maximising the amount of money you can earn. Some people might follow their own inner actualising tendency; others might put the need to earn money first in order to please others and look good. Rogers would have argued that it is difficult to lead a fulfilled and happy life if you seek to look good and please others all the time.

Much of the socialisation we receive from parents and friends involves conforming to the roles which they think we should adopt. This need to conform may deny people the chance to meet their real needs. Children may learn that they will be liked only if they get the right exam grades, start the right career, find the right partner, develop the right lifestyle and so on. Many children may grow up with a sense of self that does not meet their real needs. Some children may always live with the threat of failure; their self-concept may depend on constant achievement or approval from others.

The answer to this problem is that parents, carers and teachers should supply unconditional positive regard to the children that they work with. Unconditional positive regard means that a person is accepted, loved and liked, regardless of their actions. This does not mean that actions cannot be criticised. It simply means that actions are criticised – not the person. Giving unconditional positive regard to a child means making it clear that you respect and like them even if you don't like the behaviour.

If children receive unconditional positive regard they will feel free to develop into a contented and fulfilled person. A self-actualising person does not need to pretend to be something they are not. The self-concept of a self-actualising person will fit their real experience of themselves and not be dependent on the wishes of other people.

Happiness develops from following the self-actualising tendency

Unhappiness may result from having to conform to other people's expectations of you

Abraham Maslow

Maslow (1908–70) developed a theory of self-actualisation which was similar to Rogers. Maslow's theory accepts that many people will fail to self-actualise and therefore will not live happy and fulfilled lives because their basic needs will not be met.

Maslow believed that humans have an inbuilt framework of needs. We have a range of needs which have to be met before we can truly develop to meet our full potential. If any of these needs are not met then an individual will invest their time and energy in meeting these needs rather than in progressing to the higher levels of development. These needs, called deficit needs, include:

- physiological needs – such as food, warmth, shelter, sex
- safety needs – to feel physical and emotionally free from threat
- a need to belong – a need for social inclusion and attachment to others
- self-esteem needs – a need for respect and to develop a secure sense of self/self-concept.

In an ideal world everyone would have his or her physical, safety and belonging needs met from birth. Everyone would grow up in a safe, secure, loving network of carers. The task of childhood and adolescence would be to develop a secure sense of self-esteem. Once self-esteem is established, adulthood could focus on the full development of a person's potential. Full development would include in-depth intellectual and artistic skills. In a perfect world each person would be 'free' to self-actualise. People who achieve self-actualisation might have special qualities including:

- a more accurate perception of reality
- greater acceptance of self and others
- greater self-knowledge
- greater involvement with major projects in life
- greater independence
- creativity
- spiritual and artistic abilities.

People who self-actualise achieve a high degree of satisfaction from life.

Maslow believed that only a few people have the chance to achieve self-actualisation in North American or European culture. The majority of people spend most of their life struggling with deficit needs; feeling stressed and worrying about issues such as money or about self-esteem.

Self-fulfilment needs

Self-esteem needs

Belonging and attachment needs

Security needs

Basic needs

Figure 7.7 Maslow's levels of needs

Think It Over

The Paradox of Prosperity (1999), a paper prepared for the Salvation Army by the Henley Centre, argues that although material prosperity is increasing in Western society, the chances of a fulfilling life are decreasing. By 2010 more people will experience life stress, fewer people will find satisfying relationships, fewer people will feel secure and 'safe' and fewer people will be able to meet the conditions for self-actualisation.

In discussion with other students, decide what chances you believe you may have of fulfilling your own potential.

Cognitive perspective

The cognitive perspective focuses on how we think and understand. Cognition means the process of getting knowledge by using thought and perception. The study of cognition includes the study of perception, memory and learning. Research in the fields of perception, memory and learning suggests that people build or 'construct' their own self-concept. This means that people are not simply fixed by early experience or conditioning, but that they take an active part in becoming an adult person. The study of cognition provides some evidence for the view taken by the humanistic perspective. It is possible to argue that research in the field of cognition provides scientific evidence to support the humanistic perspective.

Perception

Roth and Frisby (1986) define perception as: 'The means by which information acquired from the environment via the sense organs is transferred into experience of objects, events, sounds, tastes, etc.'

A common assumption is that what we see or hear in our mind is an exact replica of what is out there in the world. The study of perception suggests that our mind is much more complicated than this. According to Gregory (1966) when information comes to our eyes or ears we have to build (or construct) our own inner mental interpretation of what we are seeing. What we think we see always involves an act of interpretation. Humans do not experience reality directly. What we experience is our mental interpretation of what is real. An exploration of some famous visual illusions may help to explain this idea.

Look at Figure 7.8. Just looking at the vertical line in the middle of each diagram, which vertical line looks longer? Most people will see the left one as the longer; but both lines are the same length. Why is it that most people's judgement is confused by this illusion?

One explanation for the Muller-Lyer illusion is that we have learned to interpret our world using a sense of 'perspective'. The right line looks as if it is an edge which is 'towards us'; the other might look like an edge which is 'away from us.' Figure 7.9 may help to explain this idea.

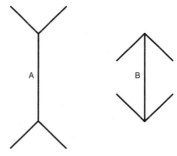

Figure 7.8 Which vertical line is the longest?

Our minds learn general principles for interpreting the world. When we see something, we then build an interpretation of it, in terms of the principles that we have learned. The illusion in Figure 7.10 provides another example of this principle.

Looking at the two horizontal lines, which line looks bigger? Most people will see line A as the bigger, but once again both lines are the same length. This illusion is known as the Ponzo illusion. Once again it can be explained that we have learned to see our world in perspective; perspective disturbs our sense of judgement in this instance. The drawing below will help to make sense of this explanation.

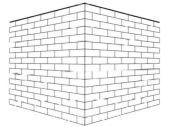

Figure 7.9 The Muller-Lyer illusion shows that human visual perception involves more than just seeing what is there

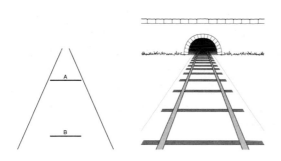

Figure 7.10 The Ponzo illusion

Figure 7.11 Young woman/old woman illusion

The world of shadows, light and colour is very complex. Making sense of something depends on an ability to organise the patterns of light that come to our eyes into something meaningful. Once we have interpreted an experience we tend to stick with that interpretation. The illusion in Figure 7.11 was invented by a cartoonist called W. E. Hill in 1915. What do you see when you look at this picture?

Once your mind has identified an interpretation of the markings on this page, you may find it hard to switch between different possible interpretations. You have developed a fixed idea of what you are looking at. This is known as 'perceptual set'. Perception involves building an interpretation of what you see.

Another example of perceptual readiness to see what we expect to see may be illustrated by the simple exercise in Figure 7.12.

TAE CAR

Figure 7.12 What do you read?

When we read, we have a perceptual set to see what we expect to see. We recognise the odd shape as an 'H' in the first word and an 'A' in the second word. We have learned to fix what we see and this may help us to read faster. Fixed interpretation of what we see may be helpful when we read, but it may contribute towards prejudice and stereotyping when applied at a social level.

People from the same culture often share the same way of seeing events, interpreting beauty and so on. People from different cultures may perceive the world differently. Zimbardo et al. (1995) write 'people from other cultures, who do not share our cultural truisms, may "see" objects or events differently. Because as we have said before, in everyday life "seeing is believing" these differences lie at the basis of misunderstanding, miscommunication and mistrust between people from different cultures'.

Memory

A tape-recorder 'remembers' exactly what was said to it. A camera 'remembers' exactly what pattern of light existed in front of the lens when the shutter was opened. Human memory does not work like these devices. Human memory is selective in that only some features of the events seem to be recorded. Human memory often appears to distort what was experienced. One theory is that memory, like perception, involves a reconstruction of what was experienced. What we remember depends on the way we have learnt to think.

Lloyd et al. (1984) suggest that only one-hundredth of the information that reaches our senses gets through to consciousness. It would appear that perhaps only one-twentieth of the information that reaches consciousness is then stored in memory. Although these statistics relate to a particular experimental situation, it may be fair to generalise that we remember only a small proportion of the events that happen each day.

There is no one, simple, explanation of how memory works. Different theorists have explored how memory might be stored, how memories might be processed and how memory for meaningful information seems to work. One of the best known models which explains how memory works is the multi-store model proposed by Atkinson and Shiffrin (1968). An outline diagram of this theory is set out in Figure 7.13.

Suppose that someone tells you their telephone number; how will your memory process this information? To begin with you will hear the information. At this stage you take the information into sensory storage. If you are not interested in the telephone number you will probably not transfer it to short-term memory. Suppose you need to use the number to make a telephone call – then you will store the knowledge 'short term' while you dial. Very often you will forget the information as soon as you have no further use for it. Short

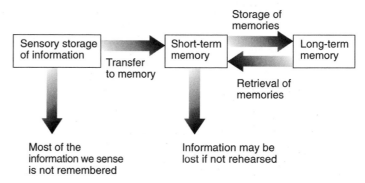

Figure 7.13 The Atkinson and Shiffrin view of memory

term means remembering something for a few seconds or minutes. We transfer information to long-term memory only when it is very important to us and we expect to have to keep recalling the information. Getting memories from short-term into long-term storage involves rehearsing the information.

An alternative way of looking at memory is not to explain it in terms of how information is stored, but in terms of how information is processed. Craik and Lockhart (1972) propose that there are different levels of processing that we can use to remember information. If the telephone number is not very significant, then we just process the information in a relatively shallow way. This means that the memory quickly becomes lost. If the telephone number was very important emotionally we might put a lot of mental effort into remembering it. The more we work on a memory and the more that memory links with important issues in our mind the more we are likely to retain that memory. If something is important to us, we will process the information more thoroughly and more meaningfully.

Schema theory

Memory works differently, depending on whether or not new information is meaningful. When you have to remember information that you do not understand – such as telephone numbers or nonsense syllables – the average person can usually remember only between five and nine 'bits' of information. This principle is often referred to as the 'magic number seven' following the research of George Miller in 1956. Memory gets overloaded with detail.

The situation is different when you are told things that link with what you already know. A schema is a mental organisation for something. If you were told a story about going shopping, you would already have a lot of knowledge about the way shops are organised; how goods are paid for; conversations with shop assistants and so on. It appears that when we hear complex information we store the information associated with schemas that already exist in our thinking. When we come to recall information, we partly recall what we were told and partly recall the associations that were made with our pre-existing knowledge. We can take in a great deal of new information linked to pre-existing schemas but our memories can become distorted in the process.

Frederick Bartlett (1932) first illustrated the role of schemas in his experiments on remembering; he used a famous story called the 'War of the ghosts' to demonstrate how memory reconstructs information based on what is already known.

When used in the UK this story is usually not remembered very well, about 80 per cent of the story is lost altogether. Besides this, the whole story becomes muddled and confused. It is very difficult for most people to remember this story because the story comes from a culture that uses schemas that most people from a European, African or Asian culture do not understand. People have to be able to connect what they hear and see to what they already know. The importance of this theory for care work is that people often don't understand the schemas that other people use.

If you work with someone with different life experiences and different schemas from your own, you may not be able to recall accurately what they have explained to you. The 'War of the ghosts' story illustrates how different patterns of cognitive organisation (schemas) can lead to misinterpretation and distorted memories when individuals work with people from different cultures and backgrounds.

Reasons for forgetting

The reasons that explain why people forget information include problems of getting information into memory (registering the information) in the first place. Very often problems with registration may be caused by not being able to link the information to an appropriate schema. This is also true of problems with storage and retrieval (recall and recognition are both forms of retrieval). Other problems include:

- Cue – dependent forgetting (we can only remember things in a similar context such as a particular room, being on land or under water).
- Motivated forgetting – Freud believed that people sometimes repressed memories that they did not want to be reminded of.
- Interference – earlier or later memory interferes with learning.

Improving memory

One of the best ways of improving memory is to develop your knowledge of an area. It may be true that the more you know about a subject, the more you can know or remember about that subject. Other ways of improving memory involve making information easier to remember. This is sometimes called the art of 'mnemonics'.

Mnemonic techniques include ideas such as:

- Imagine information to be remembered located in a familiar house or building.
- Imagine information to be remembered as being encountered on a familiar journey.
- Weave the information into a story.
- Make a rhyme or rhythm to the information e.g. One – Bun, Two – Shoe, Three – Tree.
- Link some existing memories to each new item of information.

Reminiscence therapy

When we remember we rebuild, or reconstruct, what happened in the past. Some therapists believe that we have to constantly rebuild our sense of self in order to maintain a sense of being in control of our life. We each build our own 'life story' constructed from the culturally available ideas that we come in contact with. This life story should provide us with a sense of personal value. Reminiscence therapy may be offered to older people in order to help them to maintain a sense of personal value and to adapt to changing life circumstances. Research quoted by Coleman (1994) suggests that older people, particularly, remember life events that occurred between the ages of 15 and 30. It may be that older people reconstruct their sense of self with particular reference to this period of life.

Assessment activity 7.2

Think about the last ten years of your own life; try to think of at least one happy experience that occurred in each of the last ten years. How has your memory for these happy events influenced your construction of a self-concept? Write a brief account of the way in which memory reconstructs information in order to create meaningful patterns.

At merit level you might include reminiscence therapy as an example of ways in which a knowledge of psychology can assist practical care delivery. To achieve a distinction you should undertake further discussion with others to explore how a knowledge of the reconstructive nature of memory might help counsellors and therapists to become more effective. Use your ideas to write an account of ways in which theory increases the effectiveness of professional practice.

Learning

Three different approaches to explaining what happens when we learn are set out below:

1 Behaviourists understand learning as coming about when we make associations during conditioning and reinforcement. Theorists such as Bandura argue that we learn by imitation as well as conditioning (see the section on behaviourism).
2 Experiential learning theorists argue that learning involves a process which includes thinking about and reflecting on experience.
3 Constructivists argue that learning involves us in building mental structures or schemas as we learn.

Experiential learning

In the 1940s a psychologist called Kurt Lewin argued that people could improve their learning and problem solving skills if they used a four-stage process. This process involved planning, acting, observing and reflecting. Basically the idea was that before writing an assignment it would be important to:

1 plan
2 write the assignment
3 check what you have done
4 reflect on or evaluate the quality of what you have done.

By learning to follow a process of planning and evaluation people would improve their learning skills.

David Kolb (1984) developed this theory further, emphasising the importance of using concepts and ideas as part of the process of organising learning from experience. An adapted diagram of the Kolb learning cycle is set out below:

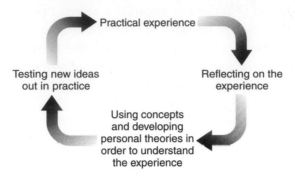

Figure 7.14 An adapted diagram of the Kolb learning cycle

Constructivist learning theory

Constructivism is a perspective which explains human development and human behaviour in terms of the way an individual builds an interpretation of the world. The way a person learns to think about and conceptualise an experience will influence how they behave and react.

Two famous theorists who developed the constructivist approach are Piaget and Vygotsky.

Jean Piaget

Piaget believed that:

- Infants, children and adults actively seek to understand the world they live in. People build mental representations, or theories, of the world in their minds because it is human nature to do so.
- Children learn through experience. Teachers can help with learning only by helping to create useful experiences. Teachers and parents do not directly cause children to learn things.
- As children grow older they develop increasingly complex ways of interpreting the world.
- Developing theories about the world involves processes called 'accommodation' (fitting new information into existing schemas), 'assimilation' (changing schemas, ideas and theories when new information is discovered), and 'equilibration' (creating a balance between theory and experience in order to make sense of the world).

A simple explanation of Piaget's theory of learning might be based on a young child's experience of animals. Perhaps a child goes to a park and sees ducks for the first time. The child has already seen pictures of animals in books and has seen other animals in real life. The child will 'take in' or assimilate the idea of 'ducks' as a new category of animal. As the child experiences more examples of ducks, the child will need to adapt their idea of what ducks can look like – this is called 'accommodation'. The child will now have a balanced theory of what ducks are, and will be able to identify them effectively.

Figure 7.15 Piaget and ducks

As they grow older the child will lose their 'equilibration' on this idea when they have to make sense of the idea that ducks are birds and not animals! Life involves constant development and changing of ideas.

In Piaget's theory, learning is a process which is constantly working to enable people to cope with or 'adapt to' their environment. Teachers should never try 'to put ideas into children'. Teachers are most successful when they create useful experiences which stimulate children to make sense, or make new sense, of their experience. Learning is about the changing of mental schemas; only the learner can change the way they think.

Children cannot learn skills before they are mature enough. Trying to teach abstract theories (such as psychodynamics) to five-year-olds would never work no matter what teaching skills a person had.

The importance of social context – Vygotsky

Lev Vygotsky (1896–1934) proposed a theory which emphasises the importance of a child's social context in influencing development. Vygotsky believed that thinking, memory and perception were strongly influenced by the culture that a child lives in. A child's understanding of the world develops from the child's interaction with other people as well as with 'the environment'.

Vygotsky's theories can be referred to as being 'social constructivist' because of his emphasis on social interaction being the major influence on the way a child builds their understanding of the world.

Vygotsky argued that:

- The culture and socialisation a child experiences will greatly influence the nature and level of skills that he or she will eventually develop.
- The quality of parental communication and teaching that a child experiences will greatly influence the skills that they develop.
- The quality of conversation, play and instruction a child receives will influence how their language and intellectual skills develop.

Vygotsky offers two important concepts to help explain how children learn; these are 'internalisation' and 'the zone of proximal development'.

Internalisation
Vygotsky believed that successful cognitive development depended on a child being able to build an internal 'understanding' of activities and skills. Internalisation might follow a process such as the example below:

A mother tries to encourage her son to complete a jigsaw puzzle. The mother explains how jigsaw puzzles work and demonstrates how to search for correct pieces and put them together. At this stage the child is socially involved with play and communication but does not understand how to do a jigsaw puzzle. The child will then attempt to find pieces of the puzzle, the mother will help him and repeat ideas to encourage him.

The child may begin to talk out loud to help him make sense of his actions. The child is beginning to learn but has not yet internalised the skill of solving jigsaw puzzles. Finally, after lots of help, guidance and encouragement the child can work on the puzzle independently. He will be excited and will say how good he is at puzzles! At this stage the child has learned how to solve the puzzle – the child has internalised the external guidance and concepts his mother provided.

If you were teaching a child to read you might ask a child to read out loud. Reading out loud helps a child to practise skills, but 'Vygotskyans' might question whether the child was internalising anything. In other words is the child really learning when they read out loud? 'Vygotskyans' might ask the child to explain the story they had read. By asking the child to explain, the teacher or parent is creating a social learning situation which requires the child to internalise ideas and concepts which they might otherwise only repeat without understanding.

The zone of proximal development

Vygotsky argued that teachers and parents should try to understand the level of thinking a child was working from, and then try to move the child on to a deeper level but always staying within what was possible for a child to understand. The zone of proximal development is the amount that a child's thinking and understanding might realistically be developed in a given subject area.

Assessment activity 7.3

- Think of one example where you have 'internalised' a concept. Think of an example where the Kolb learning cycle might explain how you've come to learn something new. Meet with a small group of others and explain your examples.
- Discuss Piaget's learning theory and the theory of internalisation in order to establish an example of each of these theories – then check your ideas with a tutor.
- Write a report which explains how a knowledge of experiential learning, Piaget's theory and the concept of internalisation can improve skills for explaining ideas.

After you have written your report, further discussion and analysis may enable you to provide a deeper level of evaluation. For a merit grade your report needs to provide evidence for analysis of ways in which theory may assist care-workers in the practical task of teaching and explaining. At distinction level your report must evidence ways in which theoretical knowledge may increase the effectiveness of interventions within a care setting.

Attribution theory

In European culture people develop their own personal theories to explain life events. People often assume that there must be a cause for everything. If you fail any exam there must be a reason. You might attribute your failure to not having worked hard enough – in other words it was your fault. Or you might attribute your failure to external conditions, perhaps the room was too hot, or you were not guided to revise the right things – in other words other people are to blame.

Attribution theory explores how people attribute causes. Some people tend to explain life events in terms of internal causes. Success at a job interview would be explained in terms of 'I am very clever' or 'I am very good at interviews'. Other people tend to explain life events in terms of external causes; 'I got the job because they liked me' or 'I was very lucky'. The way we learn to attribute causes will be influenced by the social context that we grow up in. Nevertheless, attribution theory is an aspect of cognitive functioning.

Think It Over

The different psychological perspectives attribute causes of behaviour in different ways. The psychodynamic and cognitive perspectives attribute behaviour to the internal workings of the mind. The behaviourist and social learning perspectives attribute behaviour to environmental influences. The biological perspective attributes causes to biology. The humanistic perspective is unique in that it argues against attribution. Within the humanistic perspective cause is irrelevant – carers need to understand the service user and not interpret the service user's views in terms of their own judgement or attributions. The humanistic perspective is non-judgemental. Discuss with others why the humanistic perspective is not interested in causes.

The behavioural perspective – behaviourism

Behaviourists believe that learning is the main force that influences our actions and reactions. People are seen as being immensely adaptable – they adapt to the environment and life experiences that they encounter.

Russian physiologist Ivan Pavlov (1849–1936) and American psychologists Edward Thorndike (1874–1949), John Watson (1878–1958) and Burrhus F. Skinner (1904–90) all worked to develop theories of learning. These theorists believed that the environment controlled behaviour. The way people developed skills and abilities was entirely due to the learning experiences which they encountered.

Edward Thorndike studied the way that animals learn. He noticed that animals would often learn by trial and error. For example, a hungry cat would experiment with ways of escaping from a cage in order to receive a reward of food. When the cat discovered actions that helped it to escape, it would remember those actions. Thorndike believed that any action that produced a good effect would become stamped into the mind of the animal. In 1898 Thorndike wrote an article in which he explained the 'law of effect'. The 'law of effect' means that actions are governed by their consequences. Animals and humans will learn to repeat actions which produce good effects and to avoid repeating actions which have bad outcomes. This theory provided a foundation for the development of behaviourism.

Radical behaviourist theorists believed that theories of conditioning and reinforcement could explain all human behaviour.

Conditioning

In 1906, Pavlov published his work on conditioned learning in dogs. Pavlov had intended to study digestion in dogs, but his work ran into difficulties because his animals anticipated that their food was due to arrive. Pavlov became interested in how the dogs learned to anticipate food.

Pavlov was able to demonstrate that dogs would salivate (or dribble) whenever they heard a noise, such as a bell being rang, if the noise always came just before the food arrived. The dogs had learned to associate the sound of the bell with the presentation of food. It was as if the bell replaced the food – the dogs' mouths began to water to the sound of the bell. He called this learning by association 'conditioning'.

'Conditioned learning' isn't really such a big discovery. Oscar Wilde (a famous author of the time) is reported to have said, 'Doesn't every intelligent dog owner know that?' In the first half of the last century many people believed that learning by association (conditioning) represented the discovery of the basic mechanism whereby learning took place. It was easy to assume that all learning, and perhaps all intellectual and emotional development, were due to learning by association.

Many people develop conditioned avoidance of certain foods. If you eat something and feel bad afterwards, you may become conditioned to avoid that food for the rest of your life.

Case Study

Jessica, a 3-year-old, was given some jelly to eat whilst she was in a nursery. That day she was not feeling very well. Jessica had never eaten jelly before, and she was sick soon after eating the jelly.

Because Jessica is not used to jelly she will learn to associate eating jelly with being sick. What kind of learning is this called? Is it likely that Jessica will soon forget the experience and enjoy eating jelly next time it is offered?

Conditioning is not always about unpleasant experiences. Very enjoyable experiences may cause conditioned associations of pleasure. A simple example might be having a really enjoyable meal at a restaurant. You might associate enjoyment with the restaurant and seek to repeat the experience as often as possible. Some problems people develop, such as a constant need to go shopping, may involve conditioned associations of pleasure with the activity of shopping. The person gets pleasure but also some very large bills!

Case Study

John Watson undertook a range of research which showed how conditioning works in both animals and children. He demonstrated how both rats and birds developed fixed patterns of behaviour due to conditioning. He also demonstrated that he could create a conditioned fear in a young child. The child, known as Albert, was conditioned to become afraid of a pet white rat. When Albert was shown the rat Watson would bang a steel bar with a hammer in order to create a loud unpleasant noise. The unpleasant noise became associated with the rat and Albert became afraid whenever the rat was presented. Albert also became afraid of things that looked like the white rat, such as a fur coat, a rabbit and a false beard. Watson was able to demonstrate the power of conditioned learning at a time in history when researchers did not work with the ethical principles that would be applied nowadays! It is not known whether Albert remained afraid of animals during his later life or not!

Watson is also important because he founded the idea of behaviourism in 1913, arguing that only the study of behaviour was truly scientific.

Skinner's theories of conditioning

Skinner argued that learning is caused by the consequences of our actions. This means that people learn to associate actions with the pleasure or discomfort that follows from action. For example, if a child puts some yoghurt in their mouth and it tastes nice, they will associate the yoghurt with pleasure. In future they will repeat the action of eating yoghurt. On the other hand if the yoghurt does not taste good they may avoid it in future. This principle is similar to Thorndike's 'law of effect' – behaviour is controlled by past results associated with actions.

The terminology of conditioned learning

Classical conditioning (Pavlovian conditioning) – learning to make association between different events.

Operant conditioning (Skinnerian conditioning) – learning to repeat actions which have a reinforcing or strengthening outcome. In other words, people learn to repeat actions which have previously felt good or are associated with 'feeling better'.

Reinforcement

Skinner believed that learning could be explained using the idea of reinforcement. Reinforcement means to make something stronger. For example, reinforced concrete is stronger than ordinary concrete, when a military base is reinforced, it becomes stronger. A reinforcer is anything that makes a behaviour stronger.

Case Study

Amita is an infant who is eating while sitting in a highchair. Amita accidentally drops the spoon she is eating with. Amita reacts with surprise that the spoon has gone. Her mother picks the spoon up and gives it back to Amita, smiling and making eye contact as she does so. This makes Amita feel good. Amita's mother goes back to her own dinner and stops looking at Amita. By accident Amita drops the spoon again. Once again mother gives Amita attention and the spoon is returned. Once again Amita feels good. Half a minute later Amita drops the spoon on purpose – dropping the spoon has become reinforced. The consequences or outcomes of dropping the spoon feel nice – it is followed by attention.

Think It Over

Without understanding reinforcement parents might say that the child is being naughty, or that she is playing a game. Stressed parents could even take the food away – to stop her being naughty!

- Amita's another is teaching her to drop the spoon although she doesn't mean to teach her to behave like this. What is the kind of learning experience that Amita is having called?
- Discuss with other students whether it is ever right to use a word like 'naughty' to describe the behaviour of a young child. In groups, discuss whether or not you believe that children's bad behaviour might be caused by learning experiences.

Skinner would have argued that 'naughtiness' was an adult misunderstanding. What is happening is that Amita's behaviour of dropping the spoon is being 'reinforced' by her mother. Reinforcement is happening because Amita is getting a 'nice feeling' each time she drops the spoon and her mother gives it back.

Behaviour	Outcome	Consequences
Drop the spoon	Smiles, attention	Reinforced behaviour
	Return of the spoon	The spoon is continually dropped.

It is important to remember that life experiences cause conditioning. Most conditioning happens without anyone planning or intending it. Reinforcement and punishment frequently take place in educational and social care settings. They happen whether or not anyone intended reinforcement or punishment to happen.

Positive and negative reinforcement

Reinforcement always involves things getting better for the individual who receives it. Both positive and negative reinforcement make behaviour stronger. The term *positive reinforcement* is used to identify pleasurable outcomes for the individual who is reinforced. The term *negative reinforcement* is used to identify a situation where something which is unpleasant ceases. For example, a child at school may be bored during their lesson. Poking the child next to them with a pencil may relieve the boredom. The child may receive negative reinforcement that makes them feel better, as a result of their disruptive behaviour. The reinforcement is 'negative' because an unpleasant state of boredom has ended. Negative reinforcement is an important distinction, which is very useful when explaining problems like phobias and anxiety states.

The opposite of reinforcement is punishment; punishment has the result of blocking behaviour whilst reinforcement always strengthens it.

Imitation learning

Albert Bandura (born 1925) argues that conditioning only partly explains what is happening when people learn. He argues that people also learn from what they see and hear and that people often imitate or copy others without external reinforcement or conditioned association taking place.

Bandura was able to demonstrate that children will copy the things that they see adults do in a famous experiment done in 1963. Children who saw adults behaving aggressively toward a 'bobo doll' were much more likely to get aggressive toward the doll when they had a chance to play with it than were children who saw more usual behaviour. This experiment confirmed that we are not just influenced by reinforcement, we are also influenced by what we see in the media and what happens to other people. Bandura argues that people will model themselves on other people who appear to be being rewarded or 'reinforced'. People copy or model themselves on people they associate as being like themselves, but who seem successful.

Think It Over

If people imitate what they see others rewarded for, how might the following life experiences influence a person?

- Seeing an elder brother or sister praised for school achievement.
- Seeing a friend being praised and looked up to because of violent behaviour.

- Seeing a neighbour do well from trading shares on the Internet.
- Seeing a person gain respect and being 'looked-up to' because they deal in drugs.
- Seeing a person being praised and thanked for caring for a relative.

Social learning theories

Behaviourist theories and imitation learning theory explain human experience and behaviour in terms of environmental influences. If you want to know what causes someone to be aggressive or to take drugs then it is important to look at the social influences which teach an individual how to behave.

Social role

Actors have to learn the parts they play in films and plays. These parts are called roles. Actors are expected to conform to the expectations the audience will have of their part. Everyday life may also involve acting a part; other people have expectations as to how we should behave. When we conform to the expectations of others we may be performing a social role.

Think It Over

What expectations do other people have of you as a student? Whose expectations influence you? The 'role set' of people that influence you probably includes other students, teachers, parents and family. How far do the expectations of these people cause you to behave the way you do?

Social categorisation and social identity

In order to play effective social roles people have to have a sense of who they are. Erikson (1963) argued that the development of a sense of identity was an essential life task. A sense of individual identity is necessary in order to be able to work and socialise with others. People with an inadequate sense of self are more likely to lead isolated and withdrawn lives.

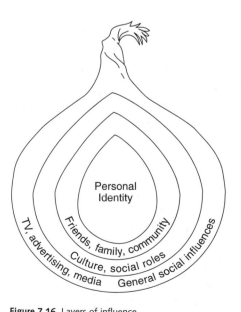

Identity is learned through the process of socialisation and subsequent life experience. A range of social factors influences learning during socialisation. These factors may be portrayed as layers of influence which affect the development of identity.

Primary groups are small groups where you know each group member personally – such as your family. Secondary groups are large networks of people where you will not know everyone who belongs to the group – such as members of your gender or racial groups.

Figure 7.16 Layers of influence

Theory into practice

Write down 10 responses to the question 'I am?'

You might tend to write things like caring, considerate, clever and so on. These might describe your personal identity. On the other hand you may have described aspects of your social group membership such as woman, black, Muslim.

People categorise themselves in terms of the groups that they identify with. Gender, religion, race, class, age group and social roles such as mother or sister signify groups that we may identify with. If we belong to a particular age group, for example, we may categorise ourselves as being like other people who are the same age as us. People who are older may be seen as 'not like me'. It is possible to divide the world up into people 'who are like me' and people 'who are not like me'. An 'in-group' is a group that you identify with – people 'who are like me'. An 'out-group' means people who are different.

Tajfel (1981) argued that individuals develop social identities based on groups that they identify with. In some situations, personal identity will give way to social identity. For example, a thoughtful and caring individual may also be a football club supporter. When they join in with other supporters they may become abusive to supporters of other teams. Social identity takes over from the individual's 'personality' and behaviour conforms to the expectations of the group.

Social identity theory argues that much of human behaviour is caused by an individual conforming to the expectations of the social groups that they identify with. It argues that it is wrong to try to explain everything in terms of individual personality.

Hedy Brown (1996) explains that individual judgement can be seriously affected by group membership. People's views can become more extreme or 'polarised' when they mix with other members of an in-group. Brown's research suggests that people trust ideas that come from people they see as being similar to themselves.

Social impact theory

Social impact theory suggests that a lot of our actions are influenced, or even caused, by the people who surround us. Put simply, humans often behave like sheep and simply copy what others are doing. A lot of our actions are performed in order to conform to the expectation of others. People are great conformists. If you need an explanation for why people tell racist jokes or commit acts of vandalism do not look inside their heads. Instead, we might be better off looking at the social context that surrounds the person. For example, a person might vandalise a bus shelter because they are copying their friends. They may not be able to give a logical explanation for their actions.

Social impact theory developed from the work of Bibb Latane and John Darley who investigated 'bystander apathy' in the late 1960s. Their research discovered that when people are alone they will often come to the assistance of another person who has collapsed. When people are part of a group and that group generally ignores the person in need, then individuals will follow the lead of the group and not provide assistance to a person who has fallen down. The theory says that most people are not directed by inner moral values, but that they take their cue from what other people are doing. It is all right to do things if everybody else is doing it. We respond to the 'social impact' of the people that surround us. We go with the crowd and seek to fit in with the social norms of others.

265

Assessment activity 7.4

Whilst on placement you should keep logbook records of interactions that take place. Use your notes to look for examples of the influence of socialisation, social group membership, prejudice, labelling and stereotyping. Share your examples with other students and discuss how these issues can influence care settings. Write a report which describes an example of how care settings may be influenced by:

- socialisation
- group influences
- prejudice, labelling and stereotyping.

To achieve a merit grade you will need to write a report which identifies some of the influences on the attitudes of care-workers that you have met. During your placement you might interview care staff in order to learn more about their perception of the influences on their attitudes, beliefs and values. Your discussions with staff might provide a basis for this report. At distinction level you will need to critically evaluate the degree to which social influences affect service delivery. In order for your report to achieve this criteria, it may be useful to debate how far social group membership, socialisation and prejudice influence the quality of interaction and the support given by care-workers.

Key issues

An overview of the theories

Perspective	Famous key theorists	Key features	Possible catch-phrases
Psychodynamic	Freud, Erikson, Bowlby	Early experience has a major impact on the development of our conscious and unconscious mind. Adult personality and behaviour are governed by the unconscious as well as the conscious mind. Bowlby stressed the importance of attachment as the key feature of early experience.	The human mind is like an angel (the conscious mind) riding a wild beast (the unconscious mind). The first few years of life are critical.
Biological	Eysenck, Cattell	Genetics influence the biology of our nervous system. This influences our personality traits.	We are born with our personalities. You can't change your nature.
Humanistic	Rogers, Maslow	Neither the environment nor our early experience control our personality and behaviour. People	The purpose of life is to develop your potential.

Perspective	Famous key theorists	Key features	Possible catch-phrases
		have an in-built tendency to develop their potential – this is called self-actualisation. Problems with conditional regard (Rogers) or unmet deficit needs (Maslow) prevent people from fulfilling their potential. An individual's view of themselves (self-concept) will control the development of their personality and behaviour.	Understanding, respect and value represent the key ways to help others.
Cognitive	Piaget, Vygotsky, counsellors such as Ellis	This approach explores the processes involved in human thinking including perception, memory and learning. The constructivist perspective explains how people build their own internal systems of thinking. The way people learn to think influences how they act.	We are not controlled by the things that have happened to us – but we may be enslaved by our interpretation of events.
Behaviourist	Pavlov, Watson, Thorndike, Skinner	Human behaviour and personality are learned through classical conditioning and reinforcement. Bandura emphasised that people also learn through imitating the behaviour of others.	People are just complex machines. Behaviour can always be measured and controlled.
Social learning	Tajfel, Latane	Human personality and behaviour are influenced by the social expectations of others. People conform to group expectations or norms. An individual's sense of self is strongly influenced by group values.	If you want to understand a person's behaviour then look at the company they keep. We are all other people!

Psychological perspectives and understanding individual behaviour

Working in care involves working with vulnerable people. Children may be vulnerable because they have not yet learned to understand themselves and the world they live in. Adults with learning difficulty may be vulnerable because they do not have a high level of cognitive skills and abilities. Older people may experience ill-health, loss of abilities, loss of social support and a fear of death among other problems.

When people are vulnerable they may often experience threat. Threatened people may react with challenging behaviours including verbal or physical abuse, violence and threatening behaviour. Self-harm may result from a reaction to stress, or from the depression which might result from feeling threatened.

Think It Over

Imagine working with an older man in care. One morning you go to help this person to get ready for breakfast and he becomes angry and verbally abusive. There is no obvious reason for the aggression. How would the different perspectives try to explain aggressive behaviour? Figure 7.17 sets out some starting points.

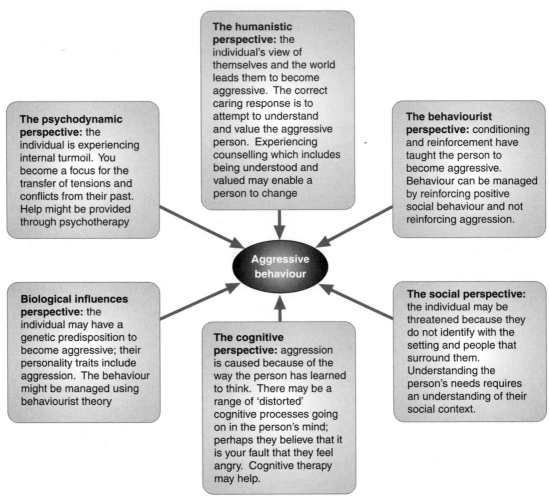

The humanistic perspective: the individual's view of themselves and the world leads them to become aggressive. The correct caring response is to attempt to understand and value the aggressive person. Experiencing counselling which includes being understood and valued may enable a person to change

The psychodynamic perspective: the individual is experiencing internal turmoil. You become a focus for the transfer of tensions and conflicts from their past. Help might be provided through psychotherapy

The behaviourist perspective: conditioning and reinforcement have taught the person to become aggressive. Behaviour can be managed by reinforcing positive social behaviour and not reinforcing aggression.

Biological influences perspective: the individual may have a genetic predisposition to become aggressive; their personality traits include aggression. The behaviour might be managed using behaviourist theory

The cognitive perspective: aggression is caused because of the way the person has learned to think. There may be a range of 'distorted' cognitive processes going on in the person's mind; perhaps they believe that it is your fault that they feel angry. Cognitive therapy may help.

The social perspective: the individual may be threatened because they do not identify with the setting and people that surround them. Understanding the person's needs requires an understanding of their social context.

Aggressive behaviour

Figure 7.17 Analysing anger using the different perspectives

An evaluation of the different perspectives

Coping with challenging behaviours involves the use of skilled communication techniques. Before a care-worker can use skilled communication techniques they have to be able to control their own emotions. It is usually very difficult to control emotions unless you can understand what is happening. Perspectives are useful because they:

- can help to explain what is happening
- can help care-workers to understand and manage their own emotions
- can suggest possible ideas for working with distressed or vulnerable service users.

The biological perspective

It is important to remember the biology of stress when trying to understand people who are aggressive. If an individual believes that they are threatened their stress response will be activated. The stress response prepares the body to fight or run away. The stress response is a powerful automatic reaction. The adrenal glands stimulate adrenalin secretion which increases blood sugar levels, blood pressure and heart rate. A whole range of other biological changes occur in the body, as set out in Figure 7.18. Initially a person's senses may become sharper and the individual may be more alert. If the feeling of threat continues over a long period the individual may become 'burned out', experiencing fatigue, exhaustion and potentially withdrawal and depression.

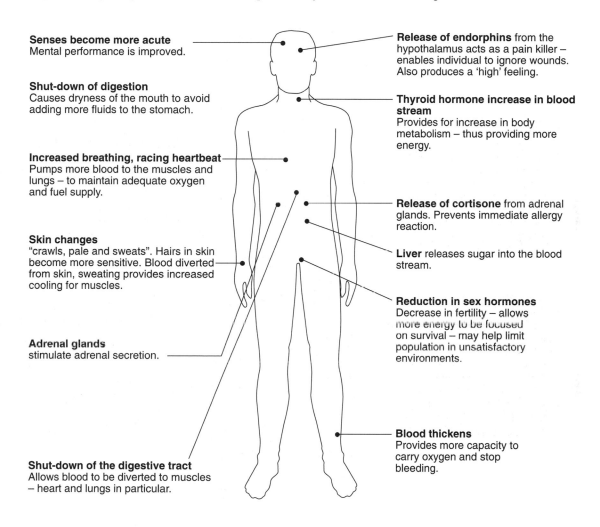

Senses become more acute
Mental performance is improved.

Shut-down of digestion
Causes dryness of the mouth to avoid adding more fluids to the stomach.

Increased breathing, racing heartbeat
Pumps more blood to the muscles and lungs – to maintain adequate oxygen and fuel supply.

Skin changes
"crawls, pale and sweats". Hairs in skin become more sensitive. Blood diverted from skin, sweating provides increased cooling for muscles.

Adrenal glands
stimulate adrenal secretion.

Shut-down of the digestive tract
Allows blood to be diverted to muscles – heart and lungs in particular.

Release of endorphins from the hypothalamus acts as a pain killer – enables individual to ignore wounds. Also produces a 'high' feeling.

Thyroid hormone increase in blood stream
Provides for increase in body metabolism – thus providing more energy.

Release of cortisone from adrenal glands. Prevents immediate allergy reaction.

Liver releases sugar into the blood stream.

Reduction in sex hormones
Decrease in fertility – allows more energy to be focused on survival – may help limit population in unsatisfactory environments.

Blood thickens
Provides more capacity to carry oxygen and stop bleeding.

Figure 7.18 Physiological reactions to stress

Whilst the stress response is operational, it will influence the individual's behaviour. As the body is prepared for fighting, stressed individuals are more likely to respond to frustration with acts of verbal or physical aggression. If care-workers have to work with stressed service users it will be important to remember that service users may not be able to consciously control their stress response. Only the removal of 'the threat' might lead to the stress response being switched off. It is not always possible for care staff to remove the threats that a service user might feel. It is possible however to learn 'calming skills,' which might help to reduce the intensity of the stress response.

The behaviourist perspective

This perspective offers some straightforward ideas on understanding and managing aggressive behaviour. Carers need to learn advanced communication skills but these skills might be coupled with the concept of reinforcement. Aggression will become stronger if it leads to 'a good outcome'. So if an individual is ignored, leading to them becoming aggressive, which in turn leads to their needs not being met, then the aggressive behaviour will become stronger. When care staff seek to manage aggression using behaviourist theory they will seek to reinforce calm or co-operative behaviour. Perhaps a care-worker will say: 'I am sorry that you are upset, would you be willing to sit down and talk to me?' If the aggressive resident does sit down, the care-worker might attempt to reinforce co-operation with thanks and non-verbal messages of gratitude. The care-worker would try not to reinforce angry and aggressive behaviour. This might involve not showing an emotional reaction such as anger or fear in response to the service user's behaviour. Instead, the care-worker might aim to remain assertive and respond with statements such as, 'I am sorry you feel that way, but please can we continue to talk?'

The care-worker would be employing the concept of reinforcement in order to help them manage the situation. If the service user experiences a good outcome when they engage in co-operative behaviour, co-operative behaviour may become stronger and aggressive behaviour may become less frequent.

The humanistic perspective

Mostly the different perspectives emphasise different important aspects of human experience. The perspectives don't necessarily disagree. Humanistic theorists do often disagree with behaviourists, however. The idea of a managing another person's behaviour is contrary to the ideal of respecting and understanding another person's sense of self. A carer working within the humanistic perspective would not think 'how do I control this person's behaviour?' Instead they would attempt to build a deep understanding of the service user which would enable the service user to discuss their feelings and needs. Within this safe, non-judgemental and supportive relationship, issues such as verbal abuse could be confronted in a caring way, which would meet the self-esteem needs of both carers and service users.

The cognitive perspective

Cognitive theorists would be interested in the thought processes that the aggressive individual was using. Perhaps the aggressive person attributes their feelings to the worker. They might think, 'If I feel angry – it can only be because someone has made me feel this way, somebody must be treating me badly'. From this thought, the next step may be to decide ' Yes it's my carer that makes me feel bad – they must be punished'. Many people allow their emotions and feelings to control what they think. Aggression and violence result directly from feelings of frustration or unhappiness. The individual may use 'distorted' cognitive processes to justify and guide their behaviour. Cognitive therapists might attempt to work with the individual's thought system. (See the section on counselling on page 275.)

The psychodynamic perspective

According to this view, we are all driven by unconscious struggles and issues which may go back to our early childhood. Early power struggles between the aggressive person and their father may still linger in their unconscious mind. The carer's actions may be associated with tensions from the individual's past. It could be that the aggressive individual transfers the emotion they once felt towards their father to the carer.

The psychodynamic perspective would argue that aggressive behaviour cannot always be explained logically. A great deal of human experience and action is bound up with unconscious motivations. It is a mistake to assume that human behaviour is, or should be, logical.

A detailed explanation for this person's aggression could be found only during a process of psychoanalytic therapy. Psychoanalytic therapy would involve an attempt to explore the unconscious motivations, which have come to exist within the individual's mind.

The social perspective

This perspective might alert us to the critically important issues associated with the social identity of the aggressive individual. Gender, race and class (amongst other group membership variables) can have a major impact on how individuals understand themselves and their world. Social role or in-group/out-group conflict could be an issue to consider when seeking an explanation for events.

Addiction

Drugs which influence mental processes and emotions are called psychoactive drugs. Drugs such as cocaine and heroin create physiological and psychological dependence in the individuals who use them. Addiction occurs when a person requires the drug in order to function and will suffer painful withdrawal symptoms if drug use is discontinued. The perspectives may help us to understand addiction by focusing on different issues.

Biological perspective
The biological perspective is central to understanding the reasons for drug abuse. Psychoactive drugs interact with brain chemistry, influencing the way nerve cells communicate. Drugs such as cocaine and 'crack' cocaine increase the activity of neurotransmitters in the brain, resulting in feelings of euphoria, well-being and alertness. The intense feelings of pleasure can easily create psychological dependence on the drug, whilst prolonged use also results in physiological dependence when brain chemistry has adapted to the presence of the drug.

Whilst the biological perspective explains the chemistry behind addiction, only a small percentage of people in the UK are dependent on or addicted to drugs such as heroin and cocaine. It might be unwise to attempt to understand drug abuse simply in terms of brain chemistry. An obvious issue is that some people are regularly exposed to the availability of drugs and others are not. Social explanations may be equally central to understanding why some people become 'addicts', whilst the majority of people do not. Being part of an 'in-group' which promotes drug use might greatly contribute to a process of becoming dependent on drugs. Adopting a social identity as a drug user might also contribute to dependence.

Behaviourist perspective
The behaviourist perspective would emphasise the powerful nature of reinforcement. Drugs create pleasure – pleasure reinforces or strengthens the behaviour that is associated with the pleasure.

Humanistic and cognitive perspectives
The humanistic and cognitive perspective would explore why some individuals think it

is appropriate to experiment with drugs whilst others might seek to avoid the risks associated with addiction.

The psychodynamic perspective might usefully remind us that people do not always function in a purely rational way. Freud believed that as well as life energy (or libido), the unconscious mind also contained a self-destructive death wish, which he called the thanatos drive. According to Freud, self-destruction is a necessary part of the human condition. Not everyone 'chooses life' – as the film *Trainspotting* pointed out.

Case Study

When Callum was a young boy his mother and father had constant arguments. Callum often felt ignored and rejected. Callum's father left his mother when he was 8 years old. Callum has not seen his father since. Callum lives with his mother on a housing estate that has a high incidence of crime. Drugs are easily obtainable in the neighbourhood. Callum says that there are no good job opportunities, but his friends are all impressed by the wealth and power that the local drug dealers appear to have. Callum refuses to talk to his stepfather and feels that he does not belong in the flat that his mother and stepfather share. Like many people on the estate, Callum has experimented with cocaine and heroin. Callum gets a great deal of pleasure from taking cocaine, which he describes as making him feel alive.

Callum becomes dependent on cocaine.

In discussion with others decide the extent to which Callum's behaviour can be understood in terms of each of the theories below:

- positive and negative reinforcement
- unconscious conflicts
- the biochemical effects of cocaine
- the social context, norms and values of the neighbourhood
- cognitive learning experiences
- a distorted sense of self.

Phobic behaviour

A phobia is an irrational fear. For example, it would be perfectly rational to be afraid and nervous if you believed there was a deadly poisonous spider in the room. Common household spiders in the UK are not poisonous and not known to be harmful to humans. Even so, many people in the UK react as if they face a life-threatening experience when they encounter a spider. Some people are afraid of heights, some are afraid of crossing water. Some individuals are afraid of moths or butterflies. Agoraphobia is a fear reaction which can prevent people from leaving their own home. Claustrophobia is a fear of enclosed spaces. The perspectives might explain these fears as in Figure 7.19.

Behaviourism and negative reinforcement

The behaviourist explanation would explain that spiders behave in unusual ways – they walk on eight legs! Our attention is bound to be drawn to them. If we react with surprise when we encounter a spider it may create a very mild sense of tension. If we respond to that tension by withdrawing, or even perhaps by killing the spider, we may

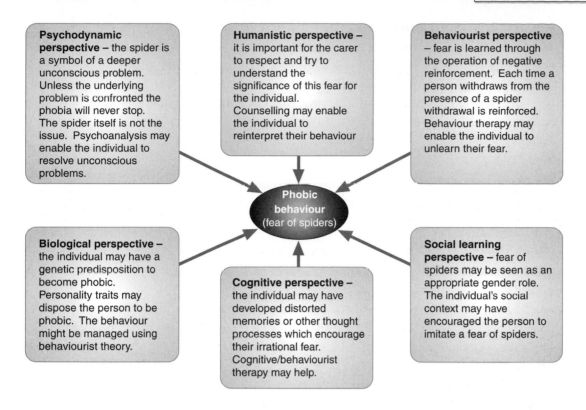

Figure 7.19 Phobic behaviour and psychological perspectives

experience a mild release of tension. That mild release of tension will create negative reinforcement. We feel better once we have got rid of the spider. If we keep withdrawing from encounters with spiders we will negatively reinforce ourselves until withdrawal becomes a learned reaction. At this point we will no longer be able to control our behaviour. Our conditioned reactions will force us to withdraw.

Figure 7.20 Different perspectives will explain obsessive behaviour in different ways

Obsessive and compulsive behaviour

Many people have routines that they feel compelled to repeat. Some people may need to check their door locks repeatedly before going out or going to bed. Some people have an obsessive routine which involves checking that electrical or gas appliances are switched off. Some individuals develop an obsessive concern with food hygiene or hand washing. Service users sometimes invent routines such as tapping the ground with their foot 10 times. This routine is then repeated, perhaps to the annoyance of other people who are nearby.

Why do people develop obsessive behaviours? Figure 7.20 on the previous page may summarise the standpoint of the major perspectives.

Assessment activity 7.5

Work with a group of about six others. Collect details of socially challenging behaviours either from discussion with others in placement settings, or from the newspapers or TV. Take it in turns to describe an example of an anti-social or challenging behaviour. Each member of the group should then take it in turns to explain the behaviour using one of the perspectives.

Use this work to write a report which describes the main concepts involved in each of the major psychological perspectives. At merit level your written report should include a discussion of the value and limitations of each perspective for explaining issues such as aggression, phobias, prejudice and drug abuse. To achieve a distinction you may need to undertake additional discussion work in order to analyse the assumptions, strengths and weaknesses involved in each perspective. At distinction level your report must provide an in-depth critical evaluation of the perspectives.

Attitudes, prejudice and stereotyping

Historically the word 'attitude' was used to describe the physical posture of a body or statue. Nowadays the word to has come to mean 'mental posture of mind'. Attitudes can be expressed in the way we think (cognition), the way we react emotionally (affective response), and the way we behave. Just knowing how somebody thinks is not enough to be able to predict their behaviour. There are documented examples of people with discriminatory mental attitudes who do not to behave in discriminatory ways; equally there are many examples of people who profess anti-discriminatory attitudes who perform discriminatory acts.

The term 'prejudice' implies a negative pre-judgement and the power to do harm to others. A stereotype is a simplified and fixed thought pattern used to classify the world.

Some people display prejudiced attitudes whilst others do not. How would the perspectives explain prejudice?

A psychologist called Adorno (1950), working within the psychodynamic perspective, explained that people who had experienced an authoritarian upbringing would be more likely to express harsh prejudiced views as an adult.

Eysenck (1965) proposed a trait of a 'tough-mindedness' versus 'tender-mindedness' to account for people who held harsh prejudiced views. Traits are generally assumed to be predominantly caused by an individual's biology.

Tajfel (1978) proposed the theory of social identity, which can be used alongside other theories of social group membership to explain prejudice as a psychological reaction aimed at maintaining social identity. In-group/out-group conflict might also explain prejudiced behaviour from the standpoint of the social perspective.

The process of self-categorisation explained by Tajfel involves thinking processes; the cognitive perspective might help us understand these processes in greater depth.

The behaviourist perspective might argue that some individuals experience tension and frustration in their lives. Blaming others and being prejudiced might help to relieve tension and frustration. Anything that makes you feel better will be reinforced and you will repeat the actions.

Major perspectives and care practice

Counselling and psychotherapy

The word 'counsel' was originally used to mean giving advice. A king would have counsellors to advise them on issues like taxation and military strategy. Nowadays the term counselling is used to describe a form of therapy which is based on an in-depth understanding of at least one of the psychological perspectives, together with highly advanced interpersonal communication skills.

Counselling is different from:

- Giving advice – advice means giving other people helpful information
- Guidance – guidance involves helping other people to make decisions such as decisions about managing debts or about child-care.
- Supportive skills – carers often provide social support to lonely or distressed individuals.

Advice, guidance and supportive behaviour do require carers to develop skilled communication techniques, but counselling requires a greater depth of therapeutic knowledge and understanding of communication. Some counsellors base their approach on a single psychological perspective whilst others combine perspectives when they work with service users. Combining perspectives is called an eclectic approach.

Psychodynamic counselling

When a service user discusses their concerns with a psychodynamic counsellor, the counsellor will be aware that what is said comes only from the service user's conscious mind. Most problems that people experience will involve difficulties at an unconscious level. The psychodynamic counsellor has to find ways to access the service user's unconscious motivations and needs, which go beyond the surface level of the service user's conversation.

Within each person's unconscious mind the id and the superego are in conflict. Our unconscious minds are full of tensions. Individuals develop mental defence mechanisms to prevent their unconscious tensions from controlling their conscious life. For example, people can deny or repress memories that are unpleasant. Bad experiences in early life may be deliberately forgotten and locked away in a person's unconscious mind. A service user may tell their counsellor that they had a happy childhood – although in reality they may have experienced abuse. The memory of abuse is repressed in a person's unconscious mind and no longer available to the conscious mind because of mental defences. Psychodynamic counsellors believe that what a service user says is only part of the story that they need to find out.

The aim of psychodynamic counselling is to enable service users to become more able to control their emotional life and free individuals from being controlled by the forces of their unconscious mind. The ego needs to be able to control the id. Service users can achieve insight into their own mental conflicts through the skilled interpretation offered by a therapist.

McLeod (1998) lists the following characteristics of psychodynamic methods:

- *Free association* – free association is where the service user says whatever comes into their head. Unconscious issues may slip out during this process.
- *Discussion of dreams and fantasies* – dreams and other products of a person's imagination may provide the counsellor with an insight into the workings of the service user's unconscious mind.
- *Identifying defence* – the counsellor will seek to identify the defences that the service user uses in order to cope with their emotional situation.
- *Use of the counselling relationship* – McLeod notes that psychodynamic counsellors 'tend to behave towards their service users in a slightly reserved, detached, neutral or formal manner. The reason for this is that the counsellor is attempting to present himself or herself as a blank screen on which the service user may project his or her fantasies or deeply held assumptions about close relationships'. Psychodynamic counsellors expect service users to transfer their assumptions about relationships into the counselling relationship. So, for example, a person who was used to being dominated might behave submissively towards their counsellor. Transference is a key concept to explore within psychodynamic work.
- *Interpretation* – the counsellor will seek to interpret the meaning of the service user's statements and behaviour. Interpretation is a difficult skill which takes extensive training and practice to develop.
- *Projective techniques* – counsellors will sometimes use artwork or images to prompt communication. Children might be observed while they play to assist the counsellor in interpreting fears or worries.

Humanistic and person-centred counselling

Carl Rogers founded the person-centred approach to counselling. Person-centred counselling is one of the best-known humanistic approaches. This approach rejects the assumption that we are influenced by our unconscious mind. Instead, the basic assumption is that everyone is born with a self-actualising tendency. This means that everyone has the potential to grow and develop as a happy, fully functioning, creative person. In practice social pressures often distort this fully functioning sense of self. People often lose their sense of joy in living and instead spent their lives worrying about how successful they are, or what other people think of them.

The point of counselling is to help people to reassess their sense of self and develop a deep understanding of their own self-worth. Once people are in touch with their own actualising tendency they will be able to resolve their own problems without relying on help or advice from others.

Carl Rogers originally proposed 'six necessary and sufficient conditions of therapeutic personality change'. These six conditions define how person-centred counselling works. The six conditions are set out and briefly described below.

1 *Two persons are in psychological contact* – this means that they can listen to and understand each other.
2 *The service user is in a state of incongruence, being vulnerable and anxious* – this means that the service user's sense of self is distorted – probably by the need to live up to other people's expectations. A distorted sense of self creates vulnerability and anxiousness.
3 *The therapist is congruent or integrated in the relationship* – this means that the counsellor or therapist is in touch with their own actualising tendency and is able to value and respect both themselves and the service user.
4 *The therapist experiences unconditional positive regard for the service user* – this means that they experience a deep respect for the service user.
5 *The therapist experiences an empathetic understanding of the service user's internal frame of reference, and endeavours to communicate this to the service user* – this means that the counsellor develops a deep understanding of the ways in which the service user thinks about and experiences their life.
6 *The communication to the service user of the therapist's empathetic understanding and unconditional positive regard is to a minimal extent achieved* – this means that the service user believes that their counsellor has understood and respected them.

If a counsellor can achieve these criteria then that is all that is needed to help a person to re-evaluate their life. When an empathetic relationship takes place, the service user will be able to explore and re-evaluate their sense of self. The counsellor does not analyse or try to interpret the problems that the service user expresses. Genuineness, respect and understanding within a relationship can empower people to solve their own problems.

Cognitive-behavioural counselling

Cognitive therapy takes the view that human unhappiness and problems are often caused by the way we think about and understand our lives. Cognitive therapy aims to help people to re-examine and change the way they think. Cognitive-behavioural approaches combine an emphasis on thinking processes with a focus on creating changes in behaviour. This approach is quite different from the person-centred approach because the counsellor does interpret what the service user says and does aim to change the service user's behaviour. Cognitive-behavioural counsellors do not use the concept of an unconscious mind.

An early cognitive-behavioural therapist called Albert Ellis argued that counselling should challenge the 'crooked thinking' and 'irrational beliefs' that service users develop. The job of the counsellor is to help service users to understand how their thinking has 'gone off the rails'. Ellis listed ten irrational beliefs which prevent service users from adopting a positive, problem-solving attitude to life. These belief systems can lead individuals into distress and self-pity. The ten beliefs quoted from McLeod (1998) are listed below:

1 I must do well at all times.
2 I am a bad or worthless person when I act in a weak or stupid manner.
3 I must be approved or accepted by people I find important.

4   I am a bad, unlovable person if I get rejected.

5   People must treat me fairly and give me what I need.

6   People who act immorally are undeserving, rotten people. People must live up to my expectations or it is terrible.

7   My life must have few major hassles or troubles. I can't stand really bad things or difficult people. It is awful or horrible when important things don't turn out the way I want them to.

8   I can't stand it when life is really unfair.

9   I need to be loved by someone who matters to me a lot.

10   I need an immediate gratification and always feel awful when I don't get it.

A person might come to counselling saying things like: 'I can't go on, I failed my last test, I've got no future', or: 'I want to die, my boyfriend rejected me so I guess I'll never be loved'. A cognitive-behavioural counsellor would attempt to challenge these statements and bring out the irrational thinking into the open. They might say something like: 'I'm sorry you failed or were rejected. You must feel bad, but can you explain how you get from "I've had an unpleasant experience" to "I can't go on"? What has one failure got to do with your reason for living?'

The therapist would try to separate the emotion of distress from the thought processes which help to maintain this distress.

Therapeutic interventions – bereavement counselling

Young children develop an attachment to their carers – the loving relationship referred to as bonding. Adults usually transfer this attachment behaviour to a sexual partner. When this attachment is broken, a person is likely to be unable to accept the degree of change which has been imposed on them. Quite often bereaved individuals experience an urge to search for the dead person. The need to search is due to the grieving person's emotional inability to cope with the separation. During this stage of grief bereaved individuals might be described as using the defence of denial – they are denying the reality of the loss, at least on an emotional level.

Later on, bereaved people may experience strong feelings, such as guilt, anger or despair. Experience of these emotions may help an individual to develop a degree of detachment from the dead person.

Eventually a grieving individual will usually reorganise his or her understanding of self, together with their expectations and habits. At this stage the person has to rebuild their life to takes account of the change that has occurred.

Most grieving individuals find support from friends and family, and this support enables them to make appropriate mental adjustments. Some people will seek professional or voluntary counselling to help them to adapt. Bereavement counselling will aim to help a person to fully express and experience the pain of their loss and to slowly work to build new ways of coping with life.

Counsellors working within the psychodynamic perspective may interpret their role as partly to help the person maintain appropriate and effective ego defences. Denial, anger and guilt may represent defensive behaviour that assists a person to get through their day-to-day life whilst experiencing the emotional turmoil which follows the loss of an attachment to another.

Counsellors working within the cognitive perspective might interpret their role as assisting an individual to build new understandings or in other words to change their thought processes. Much of the support that the counsellor might provide would be similar to the support provided by a psychodynamic counsellor. Cognitive approaches would ignore the notion of ego and unconscious mind. Humanistic counsellors would aim to value and understand the service user, so as to enable the service user to develop their own solution to grief.

All bereavement counsellors would aim to listen to and support the grieving person. The interpretation of the grieving process might vary between the different perspectives.

Assessment activity 7.6

How do the three main approaches of cognitive-behavioural, psychodynamic and humanistic counselling interpret the idea of self? Choose a case study, such as a person who seeks counselling after the break-up of a relationship. In a group, discuss and write a report on how the three main approaches might interpret the impact of bereavement on the individual's sense of self.

At merit level your report can be used to evidence ways in which psychological theory can assist care-workers in practice. At distinction level your report could include a debate on the nature of self. This debate could help to evidence a critical evaluation of some perspectives. The debate could also explain how theoretical knowledge might increase the effectiveness of therapy.

Group and family therapy

The social perspective takes the view that individual behaviour can be properly understood only if we understand the social circumstances that surround a person. Family therapy goes further in that it applies 'systems theory' to the interpretation of individual behaviour. Family therapy sees a family as a system; it is not possible to understand why a particular family member behaves the way that they do unless the dynamics of the entire family are understood. Families and other groups build their own private belief systems; is only by understanding these private systems that we can help individuals.

For example, perhaps a child will develop an eating problem. A family therapist would want to know what the significance of this problem might be within the child's family. Perhaps the mother and father are close to splitting up their relationship, but because of the child's problem they stay together, focusing their attention on the child's needs. If the child was to be well perhaps the parents would stop putting aside their differences and perhaps the relationship would break up. As long as the child has a problem, the child can keep mother and father together.

The child is unlikely to have thought this strategy through on a conscious level, but the family system has created the environment where the child needs to remain ill. The family therapy approach would argue that the more traditional perspectives often misinterpret individual motivation. A great deal of human behaviour can be understood only in terms of group or family dynamics.

Stress management

One way of working with people who are stressed is to teach them relaxation skills. One technique is to learn to progressively relax different groups of body muscles. This technique was developed as long ago as 1929 by a Dr Jacobson. The service user learns the feeling associated with physical relaxation as compared to being tense. When the individual recognises that they are becoming tense, they can inhibit tension by switching on a relaxation response. As well as practical skills, stress management often involves a wide range of cognitive therapy. Psychologists or counsellors may help individuals to explore their own coping strategies and support systems.

Desensitisation

Phobias and fears can become unlearned using a systematic behavioural therapy. Firstly the fear will be investigated. Perhaps, for example, a person is afraid of spiders. The therapist will seek to map out what is the most feared situation – perhaps a spider walking over the service user's head. The therapist may try to find out what sort of thing causes mild anxiety – perhaps seeing a photo of a spider. The therapist will also need to know of some more situations which create tension on a range between mild to extreme tension.

Desensitisation to a fear of spiders might start off with the service user holding a photo of a spider and then using their learned relaxation skills in order to stay calm. Staying calm will weaken the conditioned learning between the spider and the anxiety reaction. The service user would then be asked to gradually encounter increasingly stressful situations, using their relaxation skills to inhibit tension on each occasion. Eventually the conditioned fear would become unlearned once the individual could stay calm while a spider walked on their arm.

Cognitive approaches are often combined with behavioural techniques. An individual may be asked to go through all the 'unlearning steps' involved in relaxing in the presence of spiders – using their imagination. In other words to imagine holding a photograph of the spider, to imagine a spider on their face. Imagining not being afraid may help with later practical training to unlearn a fear.

Techniques such as desensitisation work on both a cognitive and a physiological level. Relaxation aims to switch off the stress response.

Case Study

Claire has been receiving support from a counsellor for work-related stress. She has been advised to try and balance her life with more leisure activities and guided in ways in which she might re-think the significance of being successful at work. Claire has also been taught 'emergency relaxation skills'. Emergency relaxation involves being taught to use breathing exercises to create a relaxed feeling and switch off the stress response. Claire can now recognise when she is becoming tense, she can make herself relaxed just by thinking the word 'relax' and starting her breathing exercises.

Assessment activity 7.7

Details of the physiology of stress are set out on page 269. Use these details as a basis for small-group discussion to explore how a stress management programme, which uses relaxation skills, might affect the physiological processes involved in the stress response. Write a report which explains how stress management may affect physiological processes.

At merit level, your report might provide evidence of ways in which psychological theory can assist care-workers in practical situations. At distinction level, a detailed discussion of cognitive – behavioural approaches might evidence ways in which theoretical knowledge can increase the effectiveness of therapy.

Behaviour management

Case Study

Jack attends a college programme for people with learning difficulty. He is 19 years old. Nearly every day he will sit or lie down in the main entrance to the college. He cannot explain why he does this, but his behaviour creates a lot of difficulty for other users of the college.

Behaviourist learning theory offers an approach to managing challenging behaviour. First it is necessary to define exactly what the challenging behaviour involves. Judgemental terms such as 'badly behaved', 'awkward' or 'difficult' are not helpful in understanding or managing behaviour. Behaviourist psychologists would set out to observe and monitor exactly what takes place. Jack's behaviour would be recorded in detail. Psychologists would want to know how often Jack sat in the doorway, what times of day he did this, how long he stayed there and exactly what he did in the doorway. By measuring and defining Jack's behaviour psychologists could establish a 'baseline' for the behaviour. A baseline means a measurement of the behaviour pattern.

Once a challenging behaviour is defined, it is possible to try to monitor what happens before the behaviour occurs and what the consequences of the behaviour might be. Herbert (1981) explains a strategy for understanding behaviour referred to as the ABC method. 'A' stands for antecedents – what happened before the behaviour; 'B' stands for behaviour – the defined behaviour; and 'C' stands for consequences – what happens after the behaviour.

By carefully monitoring antecedents, behaviour and consequences it may be possible to identify the operation of reinforcement. For example, Jack might spend some time sitting alone, perhaps becoming bored and frustrated. After periods of isolation Jack goes and sits in the doorway. The consequence of this behaviour is that Jack becomes the centre of attention. Jack may be receiving reinforcement for the behaviour of sitting in the doorway. Or put another way, people are unintentionally teaching Jack to sit in the doorway.

Behaviour management always involves reinforcing an alternative behaviour. It would be inefficient and ethically wrong to try to change Jack's behaviour by punishing him. It would be impractical to ignore him – health and safety legislation would forbid an organisation to ignore a person causing a hazard.

A management strategy might involve a support worker monitoring Jack to prevent periods of isolation. The support worker might offer reinforcement for behaviour such as asking questions. If Jack feels bored, he might substitute asking questions for lying in the doorway if he learns that asking questions produces pleasurable consequences. If

Jack does lie in the doorway it would be important to try to persuade him to move with a minimum of attention. Hopefully Jack will learn that the consequences of 'asking questions' are more pleasurable than the consequences of lying in the doorway.

Using reinforcement as part of a management strategy is unlikely to be straightforward. Jack may respond differently to different people. If a support worker can establish a relationship and understand Jack, then Jack may find that person's attention much more reinforcing than the attention of someone that he does not like. In practice, the cognitive and humanistic perspectives are usually important in helping workers to implement effective management strategies. It will be important to try to understand Jack's feelings and to build a supportive relationship with him. Jack's involvement in learning a new skill may be critical in order to establish effective reinforcement.

Interventions aimed at reducing crime

Harrower (2000) notes that 'according to the 2000 British Crime Survey, the average chance of becoming a victim of violence in 1999 was 4.2%. Why is there such a risk of crime and what can be done to reduce re-offending behaviour? Figure 7.21 summarises the interpretations that different psychological perspectives might offer in relation to this problem.

The role of custodial and community sentencing

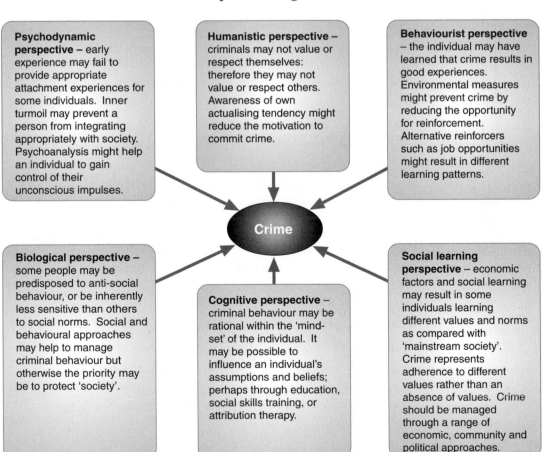

Psychodynamic perspective – early experience may fail to provide appropriate attachment experiences for some individuals. Inner turmoil may prevent a person from integrating appropriately with society. Psychoanalysis might help an individual to gain control of their unconscious impulses.

Humanistic perspective – criminals may not value or respect themselves: therefore they may not value or respect others. Awareness of own actualising tendency might reduce the motivation to commit crime.

Behaviourist perspective – the individual may have learned that crime results in good experiences. Environmental measures might prevent crime by reducing the opportunity for reinforcement. Alternative reinforcers such as job opportunities might result in different learning patterns.

Biological perspective – some people may be predisposed to anti-social behaviour, or be inherently less sensitive than others to social norms. Social and behavioural approaches may help to manage criminal behaviour but otherwise the priority may be to protect 'society'.

Cognitive perspective – criminal behaviour may be rational within the 'mind-set' of the individual. It may be possible to influence an individual's assumptions and beliefs; perhaps through education, social skills training, or attribution therapy.

Social learning perspective – economic factors and social learning may result in some individuals learning different values and norms as compared with 'mainstream society'. Crime represents adherence to different values rather than an absence of values. Crime should be managed through a range of economic, community and political approaches.

Crime

Figure 7.21 Crime prevention and psychological perspectives

There are three major ways of interpreting the purpose of sentencing:

1 *Retribution and deterrence* – the idea of retribution is that victims and their relatives may feel better if they are compensated by the suffering of the perpetrator of the crime. Punishment provides retribution and may also deter others from committing crime.

2 *Rehabilitation* – the idea of rehabilitation is that prison or community service may provide an opportunity for therapeutic change. Individuals may learn alternatives to criminal behaviour. Sentencing may result in reduced re-offending due to therapy rather than deterrence.

3 *Management* – the idea of management is that serious offenders should be isolated from the rest of the community. Society is protected from offenders once their liberty is restricted. Prison is not necessarily intended for rehabilitation, deterrence, or retribution. The idea is simply to make society safer by removing dangerous people.

None of the major perspectives in psychology argue that punishment in itself will result in therapeutic change. Radical behaviourists, such as B. F. Skinner, taught that punishment was inefficient as a way of controlling behaviour. Whilst punishment can block a behaviour it does not guide a person into learning new alternative behaviours. Only positive reinforcement is likely to result in therapeutic change. The punishment, which follows from sentencing, is most likely to be associated with being caught by the police – not with the original crime!

Attempts to use punishment as a therapeutic approach have been tried. Aversion therapy attempts to condition an individual to associate discomfort with a specific action. For example, a person with a serious alcohol problem can be given a drug which causes them to become sick soon after they take alcohol into their body. The punishment of becoming sick becomes conditioned with drinking alcohol. This therapy may assist some individuals who genuinely wish to stop drinking. The conditioning can be easily unlearned once an individual has left the therapeutic programme. Aversion therapies are unlikely to provide an effective approach to reduce crime.

Interventions aimed at reducing offending

Brewer (2000) reviews the following interventions:

- *Token economies* – tokens are given as reinforcers for desired behaviour within a closed institutional setting. The idea is to use positive reinforcement to teach new habits to offenders.
- *Social skills training* – individuals are taught new social skills to improve their relationships and employment opportunities.
- *Cognitive-behavioural approaches* – these training programmes aimed to improve sensitivity towards others and improve the ability to control emotion.
- *Anger control programmes* – a specific cognitive-behavioural approach aimed at increasing self-control.
- *Psychodynamic therapy* – aimed at achieving personality change.

In general it would appear that these interventions do influence individuals, but there is insufficient evidence of a major reduction in re-offending behaviour following release. A famous study by Martinson (1974) – quoted in Brewer (2000) – concluded that 'nothing works' when it comes to using therapeutic approaches to change criminal behaviour. Brewer (2000) summarises more recent evidence which suggests that behavioural, cognitive-behavioural and community programmes are effective in some

283

settings. A modern conclusion might be that some rehabilitative therapies work – some of the time.

One important way of preventing criminal behaviour centres on reducing the opportunity for crime and improving local environments. A famous example of environmental management of crime stems from a 1982 journal article called 'Broken Windows'. The idea was to crack down on (or reduce tolerance of) minor crimes and anti-social behaviour. In this way the local environment would improve, there would be fewer 'broken windows' and the police would be in control of the streets. This approach was introduced in 1992 in New York and is often attributed with achieving a major reduction in serious crime in that city.

Assessment activity 7.8

Choose a specific example of crime and, working with a small group of others, discuss possible ways of reducing the incidence of this crime. How might punishment and reinforcement influence offending behaviour? Write a report which evaluates the role of punishment and reinforcement within the justice system.

For a merit grade your evaluation may contribute to your explanation of the major psychological perspectives. Your report might also contribute to the critical evaluation of the major perspectives required at distinction level.

End-of-unit test

1   Describe two major features of the psychodynamic perspective which differentiate it from other psychological interpretations of behaviour.
2   Describe two major features of the humanistic perspective which differentiate it from other psychological interpretations of behaviour.
3   Describe two major features of the cognitive perspective which differentiate it from other psychological interpretations of behaviour.
4   Describe two major features of the behaviourist perspective which differentiate it from other psychological interpretations of behaviour.
5   Describe two major features of the social learning perspective which differentiate it from other psychological interpretations of behaviour.
6   In what ways might an individual's genetic inheritance influence their social behaviour?
7   If a counsellor or therapist stated that they used an 'eclectic approach' what would this mean?
8   A service user is regularly aggressive and verbally abusive to the care staff who work with him. Describe three different explanations for general aggressive behaviour and relate these explanations to the appropriate perspective.
9   A service user has a strong fear of spiders. Describe three different explanations for how this fear may have come about and relate these explanations to the appropriate perspective.
10 Relate the following explanations of substance abuse to the appropriate perspective:
    • Positive and negative reinforcement
    • Unconscious conflicts

- the biochemical effects of drugs
- the social context, norms and values of the neighbourhood
- cognitive learning experiences
- a distorted sense of self.

11 Some individuals are prejudiced towards people who are different from themselves. How might the following the theoretical perspectives start to explain the origins of prejudice?
- psychodynamic theory
- trait theory
- behaviourist learning theory
- social theories of learning.

12 Explain the central aim of the following types of counselling:
- psychodynamic counselling
- humanistic counselling
- cognitive-behavioural counselling.

13 Describe the main difference between individual and family therapy.

14 Within the theory of behaviour management, what is the ABC approach to understanding behaviour?

15 Why is positive reinforcement more useful than punishment for modifying behaviour?

References and further reading

Atkinson, R. C. & Shiffrin, R. M. (1968) 'Human memory: A proposed system and its control processes'. In Spence K. W. and Spence J. T. (eds) *The Psychology of Learning and Motivation*, Vol. 2. London: Academic Press

Bartlett, F. C. (1932) *Remembering*. Cambridge: Cambridge University Press

Bowlby, J. (1953) *Child Care and the Growth of Love*, Harmondsworth: Penguin

Brewer, K. (2000) *Psychology and Crime*, Oxford: Heinemann

Castells, M. (1997) *The Rise of the Network Society*, Oxford: Blackwell

Cattell, R. B. (1965) *The Scientific Study of Personality*, Harmondsworth: Penguin

Clark, A. M. & Clark, A. D. B. (eds) (1976) *Early Experience: Myth and Evidence*, Somerset: Open Books

Craik, F. I. M. & Lockart R. (1972) 'Levels of processing', *Journal of Verbal Learning and Verbal Behaviour*, 11, 671–684

Dollard, J., Doob, L. W., Miller, N. E., Mowrer, O. H., and Sears, R. R. (1939) *Frustration and Aggression*, New Haven, CT: Yale University Press

Erikson, E. (1963) *Childhood and Society*, New York: Norton

Harrower, J. (2001) *Psychology in Practice – Crime*, London: Hodder & Stoughton

Herbert, M. (1981) *Behavioural Treatment of Problem Children*, London: Academic Press

Lloyd, P., Mayes, A., Mansstead, A. S. R., Mendell, P. R. & Wagner, H. L. (1984) *Introduction to psychology – an integrated approach*, London: Fontana.

Marris, P. (1996) *The Politics of Uncertainty*, London: Routledge

Moxon, D. (2000) *Memory*, Oxford: Heinemann

Rutter, M. (1981) (2nd edn), *Maternal Deprivation Reassessed*, Harmondsworth: Penguin

Schaffer, H. R. and Emerson, P. E. (1964) 'The development of social attainments in infancy', *Monographs of Social Research in Child Development*, 29 (94)

Zimbardo, P. G. et al. (1992) *Psychology and Life*, London: HarperCollins

Zimbardo, P. G. et al. (1995) *Psychology: A European Text*, London: HarperCollins

This unit is part of the core of your qualification and is internally assessed by your tutors from the portfolio of evidence that you will compile as a *result of your work experience*. You also will need to produce a Vocational Practice Log from your work experiences for Unit 5, which is equivalent to the value of two units. You will realise that vocational placement recording, analysis and interpretation are vitally important in this qualification as it occupies three-eighths of the unit core.

Your tutors will have determined the pattern of unit progression that you will take so you may already be familiar with Unit 5; if not, you are advised to read the first two sections of Unit 5 to get a feel for this unit as well.

What you need to learn

To achieve this unit you must learn about the following:

- Reflect purposefully on your own vocational practice
- Identify and evaluate sources of information about care
- How to apply concepts, theories and research to care practice.

Unit 8 is particularly focused on developing both your personal skills and those you will need to be an effective carer. You will explore your personal qualities and strengths and your weaknesses and shortcomings because you will need to build up the former and overcome the latter. Much of this will occur naturally with constantly reflection on your attitude, behaviour and actions in education, leisure, home and work time. As a consequence, you will be able to plan your learning more effectively both on this programme and in work, whether this is vocational placement or professional.

Exploring and evaluating information sources will help you with all the unit work in the programme and enable you to keep up to date during your career.

The final part of the unit helps you to understand and carry out research into care practice; you might think that after this programme has been completed you would not be involved in research again. However, when you are a professional carer there is always the possibility that you might be engaged in research in one capacity or another. You might be part of a working party designated to explore a system or practice or you might be involved in reviewing a particular change that has taken place and need more information. You are also extremely likely to engage in project or research work in the next step in your career progression, so employing the right skills at the beginning can save you many wasted hours later on. Another benefit of developing research skills early in your education is the confidence that you will acquire, letting you approach project or research work with enthusiasm.

Reflect purposefully upon your vocational practice

To reflect, in this context means to think back about something; add the word 'purposefully' and it changes the sentence into thinking back in order to do something about it. You are looking back at the things you have done in your caring to effect a change where or when this is necessary. An individual who never changes as a result of learning will not be effective in their practice. As a carer, you will desire to be as effective as you can. Many good, professional carers keep a type of diary, especially for this purpose, known as a reflection log. During a busy day it is easy to forget even important issues, and spending a few minutes recording and reflecting is extremely valuable, and sometimes vital, to the professional carer.

Assessment activity 8.1

Keep a reflective log of your communication skills in school or college activities for one week by spending a few minutes at the close of each day thinking about:

- what you said
- the way in which you said it
- the body language that you displayed
- unexpected negative responses and behaviour
- pleasure and/or praise given to others.

At the end of the week answer the following questions:

1 What were the circumstances when you felt that you had communicated well?
2 How was this dialogue received?
3 What were the circumstances when you felt that you had communicated less well?
4 How would you improve the dialogue referred to in question 3?
5 Did you aggravate or irritate anyone (this week) because of either the way you spoke or the words used?
6 Was this intended? If so, why?
7 Did you ever consider the other person(s) feelings or views during your conversations?
8 Have you verbally abused anyone or been offensive (in the widest possible sense) this week? Why?
9 How can you avoid behaviour like this in the future?

You will have thought more deeply about your communication skills to friends, family and peers. There are many more questions that you could ask yourself. Write down two more searching questions and answer them.

Next write down three particular points for you to address in your general communication and keep to them without conditions. For example: 'I will say something nice to a person at least once during a conversation'.

During this activity, you will have begun to reflect on your communication skills, a vitally important area, but not the only one. You might reflect on the ways in which you respond to other people who ask you to carry out boring or unpleasant tasks, or how do you respond to people who are continually giving advice or interfering in a task that you are doing. How do you respond to Mr M who asks you for a urine bottle urgently, when you are helping another service user to dress? How do you behave when a frail service user asks if you will help her to the bathroom just as you are going off duty?

Literally, there will be hundreds of opportunities to reflect on your practice in the course of a week, but remember the words are – 'reflect purposefully' in order to make positive changes in the future.

Reflective practice is closely associated with Donald Schon who wrote a book called *The Reflective Practitioner* in 1983, and followed this with other works. Since that time, many practitioners have taken up the challenge and found the process so rewarding that it has become a major thrust in training programmes dealing with people, and care training programmes in particular.

Why has this become such an important issue? Working with people is often complex and there can be a multitude of influences on problems, so there is no standard way to approach such complexities. You cannot always expect to get perfect answers from the experts. There are theories and guidelines to inform care practice but often practice informs theory as well. We must use reflection to see how the theories that we have learned will work more effectively and again we must use the practical experience that we gain, with reflection, to further inform the theory. This will seem very difficult at first because you are not used to analysing tasks and emotions, but practice makes perfect – you will soon develop a set of skills which will provide you with job satisfaction and high quality caring experience. Observing skilled practitioners at work will enhance your skills and do not be afraid to ask questions at an appropriate time if you do not understand the reason for doing something a certain way. To be a successful reflective practitioner, you need to understand yourself as well. It might be that a service user did not respond in the way that you expected because of your approach. The next section will help you to understand the 'inner you' much better.

Personal attributes, shortcomings and prejudices relevant to care practice

An attribute is a quality or characteristic; just as you are not usually given to criticising yourself, so you are not used to praising your good qualities. Recent television programmes concerned with groups of people living together in isolation, whether it is on an island, in the jungle or simply in a house, have produced many instances of participants describing how they got to know themselves better during the experiences. Some of the participants have been in their fifties and sixties so, clearly, they have not been trained to look at their inner self in the way that you are going to do.

At school and college you will probably have had to write about yourself many times and you described your age, physical appearance, position in the family, etc. This time it is different, you will need to recall your feelings about different things, what makes you feel good, bad, mad or sad. If you have difficulty beginning such a personal account, try asking your family, friends, peers and tutors to list your good points and the 'not-so-good' or shortcomings in an honest way. If you explain that you will not be upset or angry with them, you are far more likely to reach a true picture of yourself. An alternative way is to ask them to complete an anonymous questionnaire giving you a rating for a quality. Here is one example of a question you might ask.

'On a rating of one to ten, where ten is excellent and one is very poor, how would you rate my ability to empathise with people?'

Make sure that you are clear what the question is asking and if necessary clarify in simpler words such as:

'How would you rate my ability to put myself in someone else's place in order to understand their feelings?'

Assessment activity 8.2

1 Design a short questionnaire of at least twenty questions to present for completion to a group of people who are well known to you to find out more about your attitude, behaviour towards others, temperament and other attributes. Alternatively, or as well, repeat the above but concentrate on shortcomings. If you are really brave and earnestly wish to receive good feedback, include people who you think are not well disposed towards you. Write an account of your findings and say whether you were surprised or not.

2 Using the long list of adjectives and nouns below, make a photocopy to work on and highlight all the words which you believe apply to you. Use a dictionary to find unfamiliar words.

loyal	placid	volatile	punctual	angry
moody	sulky	calm	sarcastic	cynical
pleasant	keen	enthusiastic	egotistical	humble
clown	serious	silly	even-tempered	moaner
quiet	reserved	articulate	chatterbox	organised
apologetic	patronising	conscientious	biased	helpful
co-operative	hesitant	compliant	uncooperative	proud
weak	average	stern	envious	leader
follower	reliable	loner	perseverer	neat
clean	sensible	teaser	compassionate	sensitive
callous	cruel	practical	excitable	alert
aware	imaginative	creative	problem-solver	joker
worker	blamer	cheat	friendly	cheerful
plodder	dedicated	happy-go-lucky	supportive	forgetful
sympathiser	truthful	liar	considerate	timid

Sort the words that you have identified as applicable to you into attributes and shortcomings.

3 Using the material from questions 1 and 2, write an account of how these will influence your care practice.

A few words of warning, you are using self-criticism in a constructive way to help improve your practice. Do not be downcast at the shortcomings; most people never attempt an exercise like this and we all have our downside. When you are aware of these, you will make efforts to minimise them – most people never do! Do not forget to praise yourself for your strengths – you can build these up further, now you have identified them.

Assumptions are made when you take things for granted. Assumptions are usually based on arrogance and are definitely based on prejudices.

Case Study

Most of a class group are going to the school disco – the last few days are exciting as everyone discusses what to wear and who they hope will attend. At the actual dance, everyone is surprised to see Emily there because she uses a wheelchair and had only recently joined the school. No one thought to include her in the conversations because they all assumed that she would not be going. During the evening, Emily talked to a few people and appeared to be enjoying herself. Matthew, a caring young man, asked Emily if she would like to dance and those people around her looked embarrassed and stared at their feet. Emily whooped with delight and said she had been waiting all evening for someone to ask her, and wheeled herself onto the floor. Emily and Matthew danced the rest of the evening together and had a really good time.

The following day, a few of Emily's peers apologised to her but the rest excused themselves by saying they had assumed she could not dance. A few said that they thought she should not have come because it was embarrassing to them.

Discuss this story in small groups in terms of assumptions, prejudices, arrogance and discrimination. Place yourselves in Emily's shoes and discuss the effects of the behaviour of the class on her. How would you have felt if Emily was Chandra and male, and he had asked you to dance? Why?

We all have prejudices, often they lie hidden and denied. We can only combat our prejudices by exposing them and reflecting on them. You need to develop clear ideas about how you view people who are different, and to ask yourself whether you can justify your opinions in a fair way.

Prejudice

While prejudice can be positive and helpful, it is negative prejudice that is the most damaging and this is our concern. In an ideal world where there is no negative prejudice, there should be no requirement for positive prejudice. However, that world is light-years away and positive prejudice is often required to combat deep-rooted, continuous, and often hidden, negative prejudice.

Prejudice arises mainly from our upbringing because we have heard unfair views and even perhaps unacceptable comments and behaviour from peers, friends, family and colleagues about certain groups of people over and over again. This is almost like 'brain-washing' and much of it lies hidden in our sub-conscious mind. You may hold different views and have been ridiculed for them and have learned to suppress such opinions 'for a quiet life'. This is known as conforming.

The major forms of prejudice are against:

- people from different races and cultures
- people who practise different religions
- disabled people
- elderly people or young people
- gay and lesbian people
- gender differences
- homeless, poor and deprived people.

These are often called minority groups and are said to suffer from 'marginalisation'. This means being pushed to the edge of society, but if you added all these groups together they would become the major part of society because there are a lot of people in these groups.

Stereotyping

When you have little or no knowledge about a person or group of people, you tend to make them fit into certain patterns or characteristics. Sometimes this is based on some knowledge of another person in a similar group and you lump all your ideas together about that group. Elderly people might be afraid of young teenage males, particularly if they are from a different ethnic group and travel around in 'gangs'. Teenage girls become suspicious of older, friendly males, especially if a high-profile rape or murder case has happened recently. Clearly, there are individuals who will commit criminal acts against people in vulnerable groups and others, and common sense dictates some patterns of behaviour to ensure safety. The point being made here is that we must be prepared to treat people as individuals and not fit them into a mould dictated by our thoughts on certain groups, called stereotyping. There is a close link between prejudice and stereotyping. The key to unravel stereotyping is to combat our ignorance and find out more about the differences between people so that we do not imagine things to fill the gaps. Conformity and ignorance cause prejudice and stereotyping.

Figure 8.1. What stereotyping might you apply to the people shown? Why might you have reached these conclusions?

In the past few years, the number of legal and illegal immigrants into this country has multiplied and public concern has reached high levels, fuelled by media coverage on housing, benefits, the rise in street crime and so on. Adult, white, British men and women tend to be the most vocal opponents of immigration policy because they feel that people from ethnic minority groups will eventually swamp them. They feel vulnerable, even though they form the powerful majority. Here are some statements that are made frequently when members of this powerful group meet each other:

'I would send them all back to where they came from immediately.'
'Why should our tax money be spent on people we don't want here?'
'Is this what we fought for in two World Wars?'
'They breed like rabbits and we will soon be overrun.'
'You cannot get a job/benefits unless you are black, one-legged and gay.'
'The value of our houses drops like a stone when they move into the area.'
'They don't mix with us or even speak our language.'

Think It Over

How often have you heard similar statements by people you know? How often have you nodded or kept silent? We are just as guilty of prejudice as if we have said those things.

Imagine that you or a member of your family was brave enough to speak out for someone who has been unfairly treated, beaten or thrown into jail and this was a country with a military junta in charge, or there was no free speech or democratic process. Your life would then be in danger and everyday you would expect the secret police to come for you and all those whom you loved. Would you not try to get out to another country that upheld human rights? Many of our immigrant people in the UK have been forced to flee from their home country. They have come here to seek asylum from persecution or the threat of death in their own country.

Do any of the people who make the sort of statements referred to above attempt to empathise with these asylum seekers? Usually not, because they are wealthy and powerful compared to immigrant people. The same people are not heard complaining when a rich Swiss banker or Hollywood film star relocates to Britain. Can you imagine what it must be like to come to another country like Britain with a different language, food, customs, education, culture, housing, monetary system, legal system, transport network and so on? It must be terrifying but at least, they are not in living in constant fear for their lives.

Assessment activity 8.3

In groups of three or four, invite a person from another culture or race to talk to you about themselves, their family life and their culture. Try to invite someone (or their parent) who came to this country as a migrant.

Once you get to know about another culture it ceases to become a threat as you become more and more interested in their lives.

The constructive use of work experiences for learning purposes

You have already learned that it is vitally important to keep records from your work experience, both for this unit and Unit 5. Both units are part of the core of your qualification and you cannot get this information from textbooks. You will also collect information such as policies, procedures and guidelines on various topics from your placements. Get into the habit of filing these correctly at the end of each day; make a plan for reading through or, even better, making notes of key points and retain these carefully. When you keep work on floppy disks, label these and keep back-up disks in case of damage or loss. If you are unfortunate to lose work then it cannot be credited to you; it is your responsibility to guard your work carefully.

Sometimes, a friend or peer may ask you for information or notes from a placement that they have also attended, often due to their negligence, disorganisation or lack of diligence. This can put you in a very difficult position, you may not wish to offend but feel obliged to help. Many times, good students have lent not-so-diligent students work that they have produced over a long period of time. Many times, this work has not been handed back due to the person suddenly leaving, carelessness or envy. It is wise not to lend your work to others, and to remember that both of you are guilty if copied work is discovered by tutors or moderators. You are not doing the 'borrower' any favours, because they are cheating the system and are not themselves learning through their own experience. How did that person analyse their shortcomings honestly – did it include copying other people's work? Almost certainly not!

Reflection log

On page 287 of this unit, you learned about keeping a reflection log. It would be helpful to go over this again. Every hour you spend making notes that will be useful and recording information will save you hours later on when you come to present your information for assessment. Take another look at Unit 5, pages 168–9, and see how much time you will save by working through your own charts. Keep the formats on disks so that you can print off a blank chart to take into placement with you. Use spare minutes usefully to start and/or complete paperwork. You will often get tips from care staff on points that you probably would not have thought of by yourself. However, a word of warning, do not worry about paperwork if there are care tasks to do and this includes giving service users comfort or company if they are in need.

Reflective practice

You have already learned about reflective practice, so reviewing the principles will be useful at this stage.

- It is important to recognise the influences in your own development because these may direct the way that you think.
- Identification of these influences helps us in questioning the ways in which we work and our relationships to colleagues and service users.
- Analysing personal strengths and shortcomings helps us to build on the former and overcome the latter.
- Be constructive not destructive with self-criticism.
- Reflect on your performance at regular, short intervals.
- Keeping a reflective diary is a sign of good professional practice.
- Use reflection to improve performance.

Listening skills

Part of reflective practice and good care work is using the right listening skills. You might think that you always listen to people, but the type of listening in care work is not just hearing what has been said, but active listening to everything going on during the conversation. This might include:

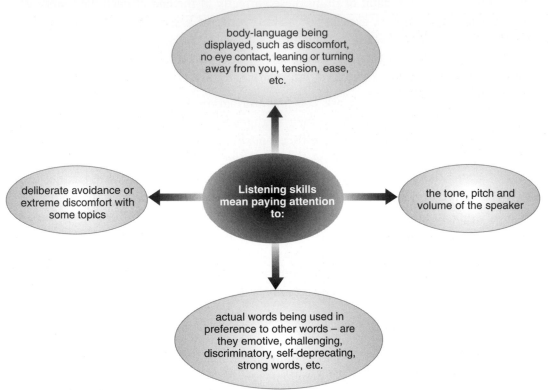

Figure 8.2 Reflective listening

Good communicators check the meaning of a service user's words by paraphrasing at regular intervals. This means repeating the sense of the conversation in your own words. If you repeated the service user's words parrot fashion, the service user might think that you were poking fun at them. At the end of each part of the conversation check not only the sense of the words, but also how you think the service user feels about it. For example, a middle-aged man with a younger wife might be telling you the story behind his wife leaving him with three young children and taking up with a younger man. You might respond with, 'You must feel angry/devastated/depressed/lost because your wife has left you and you have three children to care for', and he replies that he is delighted that she has gone! This was not what you expected and if you had not tried to reflect his feelings, you could have carried on for a long time getting it all wrong.

Towards the end of a conversation, it is wise to summarise what has been said, particularly if you or the service user have some follow-up tasks to do. It is useful to start with a phrase such as:

- 'Just to make sure that I have got everything right...'
- 'Can I just check this through with you?'

Body language

You should think about your own body position and posture when you are listening to someone and the acronym SOLER is a reminder to check these points quickly.

S – sit squarely on to your speaker (not sideways or half turned away).

O – have an open posture (not arms and legs crossed or folded).

L – lean slightly towards the service user.

E – display frequent eye contact, but not staring.

R – relax.

Assessment activity 8.4

Work in small groups of three people. Choose a role from service user, carer or observer, rotating so that each person practises each role. The carer must use active listening skills with the service user in a small scenario. After the carer and the service user both report on how the conversation went for them, the observer provides feedback on the carer's listening skills. A few scenarios are suggested below but the group is encouraged to imagine and own their own scenario.

The service user describes:

- how they do not want to live any longer following the recent death of a spouse
- failure to give up an addiction
- the effects of discrimination at work
- inability to manage at home unsupported
- the effect of a disability on a relationship.

J. Miller (1996) writes about points for good communication:

- Good communication does not just happen. It needs to be thought about and optimised for each individual service user.
- All forms of communication are important: verbal, non-verbal and symbolic, and it is the combination of messages which people give and receive which need interpretation and thought.
- Listening is at least as important as talking.
- Enhancing the ability of the service user to communicate is a way of empowering the service user and increasing choice.
- Hierarchies often present barriers to open and equal communication.
- Care-workers who work with people who rely predominantly on sign language work best when they know that language and the different meanings which service users attach to signs.
- Self-knowledge and awareness of our own communication patterns enhance the ability to communicate with others.
- Setting an example of good communication encourages others to do the same.
- Working with people from different cultures and/or with a different language to the worker may be a challenge but should never be seen as a barrier.
- Time for communication is vital. Care-workers may not be able to set aside large parts of the working day just for communication but they can show an openness to communication and should try never to be too busy to listen. If everything a service user wishes to say cannot be said at the time, a particular time for communication should be set aside later.

There is a lot to think about here for our own practice.

Conflict

Occasionally in care work you might be called upon to manage conflict between a service user and a carer or between two service users. The (incorrect) assumption being made here is that you will not see two carers in conflict! If this situation arises, keep well out of the conflict, do not take sides and remain pleasant to both parties; it will be up to the parties concerned or managers to deal with the situation. Carers should know how to avoid conflict and it is not part of your role to gossip.

Unit 6, pages 217–18, dealt with managing aggression and violence. Although it is not part of a student's role, you may find yourself in the presence of such inappropriate behaviour. You should review this section.

Non-violent conflict should also be left to professionals to deal with. But engaging the angry person in dialogue may help to calm the situation as most people desire their points of view to be understood. Good listening skills are very important here, and in a student role that is all you can do. You cannot make promises for future action and it is essential that the service user be allowed to calm down in a quiet place and given respect and dignity. The professional carers will resolve the situation in the best way. This often involves exploring the options to move forward and negotiating with the service user as to the most appropriate option to achieve success. Negotiating is a highly complex skill, particularly with people who feel they have been treated unfairly and should be practised only by those who have had training.

Assessment activity 8.5

Using scenarios of your own or those suggested in Assessment activity 8.4, and working in the same group of three roles, try producing options for the best way forward and negotiating with the service user on a preferred option. Let the service user show moderate anger or hostility towards the carer. Debrief afterwards how the dialogue felt to the participants and let the observer comment on the interaction. Change roles until each person has been in the negotiating role.

Note: this activity is to increase awareness and does not constitute specialist training.

Teamwork

It is clear from the issues raised in this section, that it is unlikely that each carer will possess all the skills necessary to perform each and every task to its optimum conclusion. Carers work in teams to maximise each person's different skills and ensure that the care the team gives is the most effective. Some people will be better at calming people down, others better at negotiating and others at being firm and assertive when necessary. This is not to say that, after careful observation and appropriate training, carers should not attempt to acquire further skills and improve others. This must happen otherwise personal and professional development would be stifled and job satisfaction lowered. However, a number of people working in the same area with the same group of service users do not constitute a team. A team is a group of people working together to achieve common goals and sharing the same philosophy regarding the aims and objectives of the organisation, agency, unit or residence. The team will inevitably have a leader who will be responsible for the team achieving the common goals. A good leader will:

- value the team and show this
- respect the views and opinions of the team members
- concentrate on the team working together to achieve its goals
- be accessible to all members of the team
- implement decisions taken by the team
- hold regular, meaningful team meetings
- encourage all team members to participate in team meetings
- build on strengths of team workers and encourage individuality
- minimise shortcomings of team members by appropriate development
- institute evaluation of changes made in the working practices of the team.

Teamwork requires planning, organisation, good communication, flexibility, adaptation, sound working relationships, negotiation and partnership.

Team meetings in care settings should also involve representation from service users, just as in your school or college student representatives should be invited to major committee meetings.

Thoughtful verbal and non-verbal communication is important between team members as well as excellent written records to ensure continuity. Partnership encompasses willingness to share information and ideas with others, including service users. An open-minded approach is required, with the ability to work with all members of the team. It does not involve feeling threatened and being possessive about certain aspects of your work.

Think It Over

Cast your mind back to a time when you were part of a team, perhaps you were carrying out project work, preparing a presentation or playing a sport. Did the team function well together or did some people under- or over-perform? Try to analyse the way the team and its leader functioned using the qualities described above.

Consider whether our party politicians work as a team to govern the country.

Make appropriate use of feedback from service users, work supervisors and course tutors

Have you always made effective use of feedback? Have you grumbled or complained about a mark or grade that you received for a piece of work? Did you reread the work carefully and take on board the comments that were made? Did you try to improve your coursework in the light of the comments you received? If you did not, then it is unlikely that your next piece of work improved significantly.

We all need feedback from the people we talk to, the work we present, the actions that we carry out. We look for praise and the best type of feedback is that which praises the strengths of what we do before commenting on the weaknesses.

Think It Over

Remember how you felt when you received some work back with a grade but no comments at all. Even if the grade was a good one, did you still feel disappointed at the lack of specific feedback? When a poor grade is received with no comments at all, it is natural to feel a little aggrieved about it. Sometimes students are even heard to wonder if the work was read!

Positive or negative feedback is helpful in caring because both the giver and the receiver learn more about themselves. Using feedback as a tool for monitoring one's own performance can be very effective.

Sometimes people do not want feedback because they feel threatened and defensive about the interaction, even if it went well. Some people are so used to negative feedback that they even have difficulty responding to positive feedback. They assume the giver is not telling the truth; this often happens when people have been deeply hurt in the past and have a 'victim' culture. None of us will know how we come across to other people if we do not ask. Our perceptions of ourselves can be vastly different to others' views about us. Some carers can be very sensitive to service user's feelings, but because they have difficulty showing warmth and smiling the service user thinks that they are 'miserable' and uncaring. These carers would be astounded at the views of the service users.

Think It Over

In the USA it is common practice for strangers to call out to you 'Have a nice day' or similar pleasant comments. In the UK, sadly, one is suspicious of total strangers calling out pleasantries and as a result it takes a few days in the USA to acclimatise. We tend to think that someone new offering flattering comments is after some payback of some kind.

It is vital therefore when giving or receiving feedback to consider the personality and experiences of the other person and modify the comments in an appropriate way. Giving feedback of a constructive nature in a care setting can be a difficult thing to do.

G. Egan (1990), described three purposes of feedback and these are summarised below:

- *confirmatory* – when feedback lets service users know that they are progressing towards their goals
- *corrective* – when feedback lets service users know that they have strayed from the goals set and the information helps them to get back on course
- *motivating* – when feedback includes ideas for improving performance and suggests the consequences of doing well and doing not so well.

When feedback is not given freely, there is not usually any reason why you should not ask for feedback, but do not ask in a way that indicates that you require praise or you will not necessarily get a truthful answer. It is better to ask open questions that allow the person choice in their reply, using phrases such as:

'How do you feel about...?'

'What was the best thing I did for you and what was the worst thing...?'

'Could you tell me how you found my...?'

'What would you say were my strengths and weaknesses in...?'

Being assertive in vocalising the need for feedback can be very rewarding for both parties if they are open-minded about constructive feedback. A tutor or carer may find that they have not explained a topic as well as they might and effect a change in the future.

Absorbing feedback

It is not uncommon for a student who is struggling academically to feel that feedback from a tutor or course tutor is personal and that they are not liked or favoured as much as other students who receive more favourable comments. This is nearly always not so; a tutor is anxious for you to do well. They are not choosing you for a friend, they have a job to do and this is to support you to gain your chosen qualification or award. Their feedback has one major aim: to improve your performance.

It is common for students to look at the grade given for work and possibly read the final comment. The work is then filed away with a vague intention of reading through again at a later date. This rarely happens and so mistakes are repeated over and over again. Set aside perhaps half an hour each evening to review work and absorb the comments and feedback. If necessary, jot a few notes down to remind you of the key critical points and have this with you when you prepare the next assignment. When you are unsure of the key points, take a few minutes at a suitable time to ask the tutor. Some tutors will be happy to look at a plan of your intended work well beforehand to identify any irrelevancies and point you in the right direction. But remember that tutors do not like students to appear the day before the deadline and say that they do not understand the assignment. Time management is always important.

Support

You will need to know where to find support in vocational practice and school or college. It is difficult to say specifically as all organisations are different. Your first port of call should always be your course tutor. This is the person who is managing your programme of learning and they will not be too happy if you have asked for support from all and sundry and they are unaware of your problems or needs.

In vocational practice it may not be possible to get hold of your tutor if the matter is urgent as he or she is usually visiting your peers or teaching. In this case, if the matter concerns placement then your immediate supervisor is the person to talk to, but do not forget to inform your tutor of the situation as soon as you can. It may be possible to telephone school or college and leave a message that you would appreciate a visit as soon as possible.

Figure 8.3 People who can support you

Do not forget your peers or (with caution) service users. The last group has to be with caution as nearly all your service users will have problems of their own and you will not wish to add to them. Many service users having long-term care are, however, extremely knowledgeable. When collecting information from non-professional people be sure to check the validity and reliability of the information.

Identify and evaluate sources of information about care

When you begin your programme of study, you will most likely have little or no specific information about caring for others. You may have practised in a caring way before commencing studies but even so you will have minimal underlying theory. During your studies you will have to find a great deal of information to back up and improve your practice. You will use libraries extensively but not exclusively, learn from lectures and visiting speakers, leaflets, brochures and periodicals. Alternative sources are newspapers, radio, television and the Internet, but above all, you will learn from *people* both in school or college and in the workplace.

Assessment activity 8.6

Choose an activity you have carried out either on your own or with a group of your peers and make a pattern diagram of all the sources of information that you explored. Alternatively, start to compile the list when you commence your next substantial piece of work.

Keep your answers to the following questions on a floppy disk or in a notebook kept just for this purpose.

- Do you think that you used enough different sources?
- Which sources proved the most useful?
- Why were these sources so good?
- Which sources proved to be of little value to you?
- Why were they of little value?
- Did you notice and record any useful information for future reference in the source material?

Evaluation

Always evaluate (describe the strengths and weaknesses) your sources of information and record your findings. Try to do this every time you carry out work, it could save you a great deal of time in the future. There is a tendency to choose sources at random when we have work to do and discard them if they are too simple or difficult or irrelevant – and we go through this time-wasting exercise every time! Making a source disk or notebook will facilitate information searching. You could use a specified place for recording the meaning of difficult or technical words. It is annoying to come across a word or phrase that you have investigated before and still not remember the explanation.

Identify and evaluate library resources

Nowadays, good study programmes have a library induction built into the programme at an early date. If you have not been on an induction, ask your tutor if it can be arranged for your group. Libraries contain much more than hardback and paperback books – most will keep several good daily newspapers and a multitude of weekly, monthly or quarterly magazines or periodicals. In an educational library, many magazines are quite specialised and related to specific programmes of study. There would be little point in spending precious library resources on magazines to do with civil engineering if this was not included as a study programme in the establishment. New magazines appear and others decline but the librarian is not clairvoyant and does not have unlimited resources. It is necessary therefore to vocalise your needs and get others to support you (particularly your course tutor) if a change is desired.

Most libraries have a bank of computers for members to use and some have special software that may relate to your course. The librarian often has first claim on past test and examination papers and copies of course syllabuses. Nearly all libraries have strong career advice sections alongside current prospectuses from major institutions of higher education (HE). This is often the location of information on application forms to HE, and booking appointments with careers advisers, counsellors and other general personnel with broad student pastoral care roles. The library staff will certainly know how to find this information and will be pleased to assist you. Committee reports, annual reports and relevant papers and documents from departments in local and national government will be filed in the reference section along with dictionaries, thesauruses, valuable and extensive reference tomes, telephone directories, street guides, rules and regulations of authoritative bodies and a plethora of other material. Educational establishments and public libraries keep fiction, travel, biographical and autobiographical books and many of the latter will also lend out musical CDs, videos and even paintings to hang on your walls.

Finding your material – library classification systems

Fiction books are usually stored in alphabetical order in groups such as crime, thrillers, romance and so on. Textbooks are found under topics like Health, Biology, Physics, and Chemistry according to the particular classification system used by the library. The most common in UK libraries is the Dewey Decimal system. Each subject has a unique number. This means that all books on a given subject are found together on the shelves. There are ten major subject areas each divided into ten related smaller subject areas. In the Dewey system there are one thousand subject areas called classes. Books at this level will cover one subject only, such as Sociology, but will cover all aspects of that subject in a basic way. Most of your core textbooks will be found here. Examples of the classification sheets are seen in Figure 8.4.

Dewey Classification System

000 Generalities
010 Bibliographies and catalogs
020 Library and information sciences
030 General encyclopedic work
040 Unassigned
050 General serials and their indexes
060 General organizations and museology
070 News media, journalism, publishing
080 General collections
090 Manuscripts and rare books

100 Philosophy and psychology
110 Metaphysics
120 Epistemology, causation, mankind
130 Paranormal phenomena
140 Specific philosophical schools

300	**Social sciences**	470	Italian languages, i.e. Latin
	310 General statistics	500	**Natural sciences and mathematics**
	320 Political science		510 Mathematics
	330 Economics		520 Astronomy and allied sciences
	340 Law		530 Physics
	350 Public administration		540 Chemistry and allied sciences
	360 Social services; associations		550 Earth sciences
	370 Education		560 Paleontology, paleozoology
	380 Commerce, communications, transport		570 Life sciences
	390 Customs, etiquette, folklore		580 Botanical sciences
400	**Language**		590 Zoological sciences
	410 Linguistics	600	**Technology (applied sciences)**
	420 English and Old English		610 Medical sciences
	430 Germanic languages, i.e. German		620 Engineering and allied sciences
	440 Romance languages, i.e. French		630 Agriculture
	450 Italian, Romanian, Rhaeto-Romanic languages		640 Home economics
	460 Spanish and Portuguese languages		650 Management and auxiliary services
			660 Chemical engineering

Figure 8.4 Some classifications of the Dewey Decimal system
© OCLC Online Computer Library Center Inc.

Another classification system used in university libraries is the Library of Congress system (LC). Reading LC numbers is quite a skill and involves call numbers that can begin with one, two or three letters.

The first letter represents one of the 21 major divisions of the system, for example 'Q' is science. The second letter represents a sub-division so 'QE' is Geology and all books in the 'QE's are about Geology. A third letter may denote a particular area such as Europe. After the letters there are numbers. The first set of numbers defines the subject of a book. The next group of numbers, called 'cutter numbers' is a coded representation of the author of the book or the organisation's name or title.

A typical book number might look like this:

QE534.2. B64

Your tutor will identify relevant books and periodicals, which will be useful for your studies. If this does not happen then ask for a list. Obtaining a copy of the unit specifications will also direct you to helpful publications and as you are reading this book, you will find suggestions for further reading at the end of each chapter.

The Internet

The Internet is the world's largest computer network; a network is a collection of computers linked together for two-way (or more) communication. Really, the Internet is a network of networks allowing any computer to tap in.

There are masses of books giving you advice on using the Internet and you are highly recommended to use one or two as this chapter can only provide principles and guidelines. If you are a recent school-leaver you will probably be very familiar with the

Internet already, but if you are a mature student this may be a new experience for you. Computers connected to the Internet show an icon on the menu; click this and you will access the Internet. The Internet can be used for e-mail (electronic mail) that is devastating postal businesses, chatting to people in chat rooms (take care here), games, news, weather, buying and selling, but, above all, information retrieval from the world wide web (www). You need a browser to explore the web and the most common ones are Microsoft Internet Explorer and Netscape Navigator. As well as surfing worldwide, you can explore local and regional areas too, which might prove very useful to you especially if you reside in a rural community.

Searching

To retrieve information from the Internet, you will need to use a search engine, a programme devoted to searching for information. Some programmes are indexes and others are directories. A directory is a listing that is divided into named categories rather like a table of contents in a book. An index is a list of keywords collected from a lot of websites, that is updated regularly and containing many more entries than directories.

Some major search engines are:

Yahoo!
Altavista
Ask Jeeves
Google
Web Crawler
Infoseek
Excite
Lycos

Figure 8.5 A search engine

A word of warning – you can waste hours and hours of time searching the Internet for material and find some items more quickly from a book.

Using key words for your search helps to refine the number of websites that you will be referred to. It is not uncommon to be directed towards ten thousand web pages – impossible to look at. Using a question mark at the end can help with some engines like Ask Jeeves.

Marking useful sites

You will find some pages that you will want to visit over and over again because they are really useful in your work. You can mark these pages and compile a list by clicking on 'Favourites' with Microsoft Explorer and 'Bookmarks' on Netscape Navigator.

Some browsers take a long time to search for specific pages and this can be frustrating if you have not much time. Broadband, now available in some parts of the UK, can speed this up tremendously. You can also save images from the web by right clicking your mouse and choosing save image/picture and choosing a file for storage. Nearly all the web is copyrighted, however, so you might need permission from the author to use it. Like most files, you can also print pages from the web by clicking the 'print' button. It is a good idea to check how many pages are in the document before you do this. It is common for directories and indexes to change and you can update by accessing http://net.gurus.com/search/

Libraries, commercial businesses, colleges and schools offer short courses on various aspects of information technology so if you are not confident using a computer it may suit you to enrol on such a course.

Training opportunities

Whether you are at school or college or have moved on to more professional training, you should take any opportunity to undertake further training. People who never move on in their thinking, never move on in life. Whenever you apply for a post, interviewers will always want to know about the further training opportunities you have undertaken and there is usually a place on an application form for adding these. People will not regard you in a good light if this space is blank and you have nothing to say here. This is because you may not be actively developing yourself, your knowledge, value base and your skills to improve your performance at work. Training courses are expensive and only a few are held, at long intervals apart; when budgets are tight, training usually suffers so make the most of the opportunities as soon as you can.

As well as the benefits already mentioned, there is also the opportunity to:

- take a step back and be more objective about work problems
- discuss new concepts, processes and procedures
- share complex issues with other colleagues
- see how other colleagues tackle issues
- work through set issues with colleagues and teachers
- learn about new initiatives to be implemented in the future
- make new friends and have the opportunity to socialise in a different way.

Many training courses are off-site and even residential to enable members to focus on the agenda without being called away to everyday matters. You might be fortunate to be able to take some small courses leading to qualifications within your programme. Many educational establishments offer this addition. You might be able to take First Aid or Food Hygiene awards that will help you gain casual employment to assist you  with the financial aspects of your studies. There is usually the opportunity to take information technology awards at different levels of expertise.

Take every chance to increase the learning that you do both at work and on placement. Attend all appropriate staff development sessions even if it means not participating and being an observer. Go to fire-drill practices and fire lectures, listen to lifting and manual handling instructions, attend talks on the prevention of cross-infection – there is a lot you can do if you demonstrate enthusiasm.

Making progress

At some point, you will need to determine your next career move; will you be moving on to university to take professional qualifications or will you commence employment and progress through the vocational qualification route? There are advantages and disadvantages with either course of action and you should consider these very carefully.

Assessment activity 8.7

Invite a career adviser to speak to your peer group about the relative merits of professional and vocational qualifications. After asking clarifying questions, compile a list of advantages and disadvantages for both routes of access for you, personally. Compare your findings and discuss your conclusions with a small peer group.

Managing your time

Study skills seem a boring subject but if you have not got the skills for studying you are far less likely to be successful. 'I managed at school', you say, but study skills for life are a bit different. In this qualification and those still to come, you are expected to apply your knowledge more, develop concepts and analyse facts. Previously, at GCSE standard, you were spoon-fed your knowledge. You carried out a lot of the work at school supplemented by homework. Now you are expected to carry out your reading, investigating and coursework in your own time, taking into effect vocational placement, lectures/classes, leisure time, socialising. If you have a casual job as well, life can become very difficult! General problems faced by all students include:

- finding time
- using time effectively
- defining the tasks
- exploring resources
- completing the task before the deadline
- evaluating your work
- absorbing the feedback.

This might sound fine, but remember that you are collecting evidence for other units at the same time, particularly Unit 5 from your vocational placements, and you will not be working on one assignment at a time. You may have four or five in various stages in any given period.

Start with making yourself a *realistic* timetable indicating the periods that you will spend in study. Allow yourself some time for socialising, but realise that you cannot commit yourself to an advanced programme of study and still go clubbing three or four nights each week. Explain carefully to your friends that you must study for designated periods in the week. When there is some event that you really want to go to then you must give up something else to pay back the time or not go at all.

How much time will you need? This is difficult to estimate because different people work at different speeds and if there is a lot of background reading and note-taking to do in preparation for particular assignments, this takes longer. Start with making about twenty hours available in the week and adjust as you feel it is necessary. Having some free periods in the educational week can help to reduce the amount of spare time that you will need but *only if you use them properly*. When you prefer to spend your free periods chatting to friends in the coffee bar, then you cannot take these off your overall commitment. To use this time effectively you will have to get organised by having the right materials with you to do the work. The best way forward is to use a 'rough' book or a large diary in which to record all the items that it is essential to remember. Date each page and repeat the tasks that did not get completed from the previous day. By splitting the tasks up you will soon be able to work on several assignments at once and know how much time that you will need. A typical page might look like Figure 8.6.

November 6th

1 Try to find the Equal Opps Handbook in library.

2 Read through Ass.2 in Communication & Supp before handing in.

3 Make a pattern diagram of idea for research project.

4 Read through returned assignment and note the comments from Applying Sociology .

5 Plan the structure of my job description in Voc. Prac in nursery.

6 Write tasks for day after tomorrow and the weekend.

Figure 8.6 Use a rough book to keep track of your tasks

This student is well ahead of himself because of his careful planning and should be able to complete assignments with time to spare. He is sharing his time between different units and therefore feels less strain due to the built-in variety.

You could design a table with your computer and print enough copies for say, two weeks at a time. You will not need to have too many rows as you are limited by the time available. The chart could look something like Figure 8.7.

Date:	Things to do today	Tick if done
1		
2		
3		
4		
5		
6		

Figure 8.7 A tasks list can be useful

Some members of your peer group might mock you because of your organisation, but it will not be long before they are asking to borrow something.

Looking for references early pays dividends in another way. Other students, set the same assignment, will be searching for the same books a few days before the completion date and there are never enough copies to go round.

Tools for the task

This might seem like a lot of work spent in organisation and you are frantic to complete your next assignment. If you do not get organised early on, this is how it will always be; panic, panic, panic. This is not a good feeling and if you fall ill or have to take time off for any other reason, you will never catch up. Doing your research early in small chunks means that you can do some work away from classes. You can always use some holiday time to get organised. Developing your own organisational skills like this will pay off when you move on to your next qualification. Keeping your files in order from the first day will also help tremendously. You will have different classes every day and if you keep a file for classes only, together with your rough book and/or diary, you will not need to carry several files each day. Place in this file your task list and any work to do if you have free time.

Take ten minutes in the evening to remove the day's pages and file appropriately. It is worth investing in a small wallet designed to carry your floppy disks, they are not expensive and the disks will be kept clean and safe. As well as keeping your paper files in order, start from the beginning to label your disks, electronic folders and files in an orderly fashion. Disks are relatively inexpensive now and having one for each unit will be beneficial.

Do make sure that you also carry a supply of writing materials. Nothing annoys teachers more than students who come to classes without the tools for taking notes.
A pocket dictionary is a useful addition to your daily bag as you will need to check on the meanings or spellings of some words. Basic English grammar and numeracy (see Assessment activity 8.8) are also important skills and you can be referred to appropriate library texts by your tutor if you require these.

Structuring your work

Ensure that the work you produce is structured and relevant, using clear sub-headings if necessary. When you hand-write work, do make sure it is readable. Tutors find work that is hard to read frustrating and it can get put at the bottom of the pile. Either put the given task at the top of the first page or, preferably, a clear title or make sure that the issues are presented clearly.

It is permissible to use quotes from sourced books and therefore give credit to the author; if you do not then you are committing plagiarism. Be in no doubt, your tutor will recognise when you are lifting whole sections from texts or if you are copying the work of a peer. In the latter case, both pieces of work are marked down and if you were the person who compiled the work then you will be very upset. You will not learn new ideas or correct terms, develop your own style or read fluently when you create a 'patchwork' essay from many books. Write in your own words, using sourced quotes, if you need to, and have a beginning, middle and end. Place different views, ideas, issues, etc. in separate paragraphs. When you are asked to present an argument, compare and contrast, and analyse and do not forget to give opposing views. When the tutor requires a conclusion, make sure that there is one at the end.

Note-taking

The way in which you take notes from a text depends on whether you own the book or not. When the text is yours to keep, you will save time by highlighting or underlining the important sections. You cannot do this with borrowed books so you must take notes on paper or card. You will need to pick out the key points rather than copy the whole text. Write the author, date and title against the note so that if you need to refer back to it, you know immediately which book to use. You will also require this detail for a bibliography at the end of the work.

Notes written in lines are called linear notes, but you can also write patterned or diagrammatic notes. You can make your own code for certain links such as an arrowhead pointing towards an effect or an intermittent line meaning a cause; coloured lines could mean also links to something else and so on.

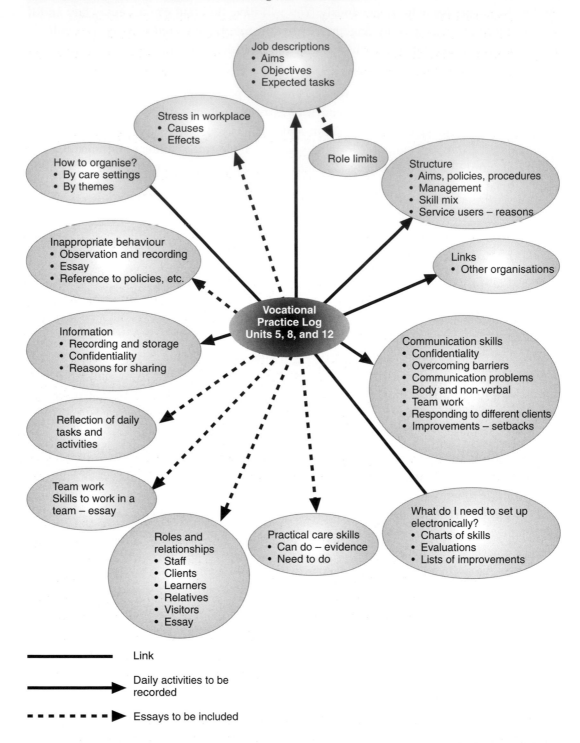

Figure 8.8 Example of a patterned diagram

Taking notes is a complex active skill and you need to be constantly asking yourself questions such as:

- 'What do I need to remember from this?'
- 'What is the main theme?'

- 'Will these notes be useful or can I get the same information from my textbook?'
- 'Have I understood the principles behind this?'

Some people find that when they read a text they cannot remember it afterwards. Taking notes on what you are reading can help the information to 'stick'. Very few people remember material on a first reading so you will need to read important passages or the notes several times. The more times that you read a passage through the more will stick.

How the media and current affairs contribute to effective care practice

Most newspapers demonstrate preference for certain political parties and their reporting inevitably displays bias. You must bear this in mind when you use newspapers in your work.

Assessment activity 8.8

Spend about an hour in the library reading the same news item in *The Times*, *The Independent* and the *Daily Mirror*. Analyse the way in which the particular article is presented. Choose an article which has some relevance to your programme on, say, the NHS or an aspect of social services.

1 Can you see the political affiliations in the way that the article has been written?
2 Are there differences in the style of language?
3 What does this tell you about the reader group that the paper is targeting?
4 Have the papers included emotive words or case studies to grab the reader's imagination?
5 Does the layout of the page influence your perception of the news?
6 Explain why you preferred one report rather than the others.

Reading reports like this can be very helpful in raising issues or starting campaigns to make changes and keeping up-to-date with new initiatives. Many news items appearing first in the press as leaks can be deliberate and stem from someone in government circles. For instance, if you read in a press release a suggestion that income tax was going to rise 5 per cent in the next budget to pay for schools and hospitals, you would be horrified, assuming that you will be paying income tax now or in the near future. On budget day, if the rise was only 2 per cent you would be highly relieved. This is known as 'spin' or public relations. The government of the day gets the rise of 2 per cent practically unopposed and comes out looking good. Newspapers can be manipulated to achieve the aims of officialdom.

Another point to remember is that many people get large sums of money for selling their stories to newspapers. Do not believe everything you read – newspapers are interested only in stories that sell; reporting that everything in the country is working well is not news. There may be 200,000 hip operations successfully carried out in a year, but the newspapers report only the few that were not successful. Use newspapers, preferably broadsheets rather than tabloids, but be aware of commercial and political bias, money-making and negative (often sensational) reporting.

Other media

Television and radio broadcasts are also extremely useful, but have some drawbacks. Unless you have your own television in a quiet room it is difficult to concentrate on what is being said and what images are being shown. Taking notes is particularly difficult, as you have to take your mind off the sound and the images to write. The results often feel unsatisfactory because you have missed other chunks. Due to the high cost of making televised programmes, a lot of material is squeezed into either half an hour or an hour. If you have already covered the theory in class, the television becomes really useful because imagery is so much more powerful than the written word; getting the theory from the programme is very much more complicated. Animation, graphics and using fibre-optic cameras can enable us to see objects and understand concepts in a way that is impossible from writing.

Television controls us in that we have to be present at the appropriate time and have a set that can receive the right channels. The written word is much more controlled by us; we can pick up a book when we want to. However, we cannot get current up-to-the-minute material from books or even magazines. The former are out of date before they are printed, and even the latter may be written three to six months ago. With both television and radio, you have to be aware that you are still getting someone else's version of events and this may have a bias too.

Radio is seen to be a friendlier medium, available from a cheaper, more portable set than television. As there are no visual images to focus on, we can be doing other daily tasks or taking notes if we wish. Radio consists of people talking or listening to music. Radio can feel more accessible as many programmes dealing with current affairs have 'phone-in' type programmes and listeners can give their views or tell their experiences. This can be valuable feedback in a way the other media fail to do effectively. There are 'phone-in' programmes on television, but somehow they lack the vibrancy of radio. Although the radio has become less popular than TV, many hundreds of thousands of people still listen to the radio, particularly at home and when travelling around in vehicles. You can hear broadcasts on care practice and the reactions of concerned people immediately.

Government publications

Green Papers are government publications that bring forth discussion on a matter; Green Papers precede White Papers. White Papers are a set of proposals published by central government or one of its departments. When you wish to know future changes for the NHS or the social services, you will examine the relevant White Paper.

Documents like these are published in part and/or in full on a website offered by the Department of Health of Her Majesty's Government. You can find this website for official papers at http://www.doh.gov.uk/publications/wgpaper.html. You can also find useful statistics for services like community care on this site.

An easier way of keeping your practice current is to examine press reports of the keynote speeches given by leading politicians, eminent judges and departmental heads like chief constables. Look for the date after the speech or paper is made public. Actual dates of the specific content are usually speculative articles written by relevant journalists. Press reports present the gist of the content in a manner that can be understood by the general public readership so the language and style have been modified. Government publications are often lengthy and difficult to analyse, whereas journalists will do the job for you and often add useful additional background material.

White and Green Papers	Date
Reform of the Mental Health Act: Proposals for consultation	1983
Our Healthier Nation	February 1998
Valuing People: A new strategy for learning Disability for the 21St Century	
Adoption – A new approach	December 2000
Reforming the Mental Health Act	December 2000
Saving Lives: Our healthier nation	
Smoking Kills – A White Paper on Tobacco	1998
Modernising Social Services — Promoting independence, improving protection and raising standards	December 1998
The Food Standards Agency: A force for change	January 1998
The New NHS	December 1997

Figure 8.9 Some Green and White Papers

Assessment activity 8.9

Access the Department of Health website and click on statistics for home care services. Find the table that shows the 'Service intensity percentage of total households receiving home care, 2001'.

Write one page of linear notes to explain the statistics in the table. Ask a tutor to check your explanation. If you can interpret a table like this, your numeracy skills are good.

Notice how many lines of writing it takes to explain one table. Tables and charts are excellent ways of presenting complex figures.

How to apply concepts, theories and research to care practice

Concepts are ways of thinking that enable us to understand and make sense of the world about us. They help us to recognise situations and guess what will happen next. We use words to express concepts, labelling them and grouping them together. Theories involve the use of concepts; they are systems of ideas, which interpret and explain things.

Theories are also couched in words and labelled, often using the name of the person who first developed the theory. Concepts and theory then inform practice, but practice also informs and changes theory. This can occur only when people apply theories and concepts to their work and consider their impact carefully.

P. Trevithick (2002) said:

> 'As practitioners we need to work in a learning culture where curiosity, enquiry and exploration are encouraged and where opportunity, encouragement, time and resources to update our knowledge are seen as priorities. This would, hopefully, encourage many more practitioners to write and to engage in research and this, in time, may provide the link that is needed in the theory-practice divide.'

This leads us on to the next section concerning the purposes of research and the benefits to be obtained from it.

The skills of critical thinking

Earlier in the chapter, you were strongly encouraged to work towards becoming a reflective practitioner, reviewing and reconsidering your actions, tasks, behaviour and communication on a daily basis, with a purpose of improving your performance as a care-worker. Pause a moment – what about the *way* in which you think? This is influenced by your own experiences, upbringing, teachers, etc. and may itself be flawed. We also have to consider the way we think about our thinking to avoid bias, inaccuracies and discrimination. The art of doing this is called critical thinking and it is used in many professions, including health and social care.

You are only just getting used to reflective practice and already you are being introduced to the skills of critical thinking. It seems like hard work but if we look at the qualities of a critical thinker according to one writer you will see that it is not too complex.

S. Ferrett (1997) considered that a critical thinker:

- asks pertinent questions
- assesses statements and arguments
- is able to admit to a lack of understanding or information
- has a sense of curiosity
- is interested in finding new solutions
- is able to clearly define a set of criteria for analysing ideas
- is willing to examine beliefs, assumptions and opinions and weigh them against fact
- listens carefully to others and is able to give feedback
- sees that critical thinking is a life-long process of self-assessment
- suspends judgement until all facts have been gathered and considered
- looks for evidence to support assumption and beliefs
- is able to adjust opinions when new facts are found
- looks for proof
- examines problems closely
- is able to reject incorrect and irrelevant data.

Trying to sum up all these points, a critical thinker can be thought of as a 'doubting Thomas' who enquires into all manner of practices and shuns instincts, assumptions and beliefs for accurate relevant facts using set criteria.

Carrying out research which focuses on the unique and better qualities of each individual human being is said to be research that has used the humanistic approach. It is derived from humanistic psychology, first described by the psychologists Adler and Maslow, who developed the theory of the hierarchy of human needs (see Unit 7).

As a student of a care programme, you need to consider the effects of simply asking people questions because the very nature of this invades someone's privacy. Should you carry out research on any aspect of the care of service users, this may affect their compliance, emotions, attitudes and behaviour to name only a few. Considering these means that you have ethical issues to take into account in your research. You should discuss the ethical issues you have identified at a very early stage of your research because you may not obtain permission to carry on. Ignoring ethical issues will not solve your problems, as you are far more likely to be stopped if you have not cleared the project through your supervisors. You cannot prevent people from mentioning your work to others and you certainly cannot ask them to refrain from doing so. Try to imagine how you would feel as a service user being part of your student research.

Whatever the subject of your research, however much data you collect and however wonderful your presentation of results, you will not convince an audience or reader of any points by having a one-sided weak argument. For conclusions to be drawn with validity and reliability you must have a balanced argument or debate. The points you make must be logical and argued on both sides. When you are becoming a critical thinker this will start to happen naturally as a process of the logical thought and questions and answers you devise and seek.

Assessment activity 8.11

These days on television (and radio) there are many advertisements for credit control through financial organisations. Listen to one or two of these and follow the one-sided arguments for placing all your debts under one banner with these agencies. Why are they not presenting the viewing or listening public with a balanced argument? What facts would you need to find out? Why are you not likely to get out of financial trouble in the long term?

On completion of a project, research paper or simply an essay, you should be able to judge the worth and value of what you have done. This means using your evaluative skills. Traditionally, younger students find this hard to do. Most students conclude with expressing satisfaction with their achievement and perhaps mentioning the area(s) they found difficult. You will find below some questions, of a necessarily general nature, to help you to develop evaluative skills. You will need to customise the questions in the light of the subject matter.

- Did the work match the targets I set out to achieve?
- Why am I satisfied or not satisfied with the work?
- How well or not did I manage the time resource?
- Did I use adequate resources?
- Have I used any other people's opinions to check the quality of my work?
- How much of the work is original (to me)?
- How and why would I change my methodology if I needed to repeat this work?

- Did I take shortcuts or abandon parts resulting in inferior work? If yes, state the reason.
- Is the work compatible with the value base of health and social care?

Assessment activity 8.11

Take two pieces of recent work, graded or ungraded, and use the questions above to evaluate your performance. Modify the questions as appropriate and add any others you feel are necessary to provide an honest evaluation. Ask your tutor for feedback on your evaluative skills only.

The concepts of action research

You will be familiar with the use of the word research, but probably have not come across the term action research, although you have most likely carried it out at school quite often. Action research is a quicker way of saying 'let's study what is happening in our establishment and make it better'. Put in a more refined way, action research is the process by which practitioners try to study their problems scientifically in order to guide, modify and evaluate their decisions and actions. It is usually carried out in three steps:

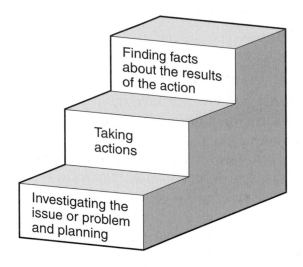

Finding facts about the results of the action

Taking actions

Investigating the issue or problem and planning

Figure 8.10 Action research

When you come to plan your project in the workplace you should ask your supervisors about changes that might have taken place recently. Find out about the changes, plan your project, and fact-find about the results of the change. It might be that there is a project sitting waiting for you to tackle. If the change has been carried out in more than one area, it would be helpful to include one or some of these as well. Collecting data from more than one source will provide baseline information (where everyone has started from), guide immediate action (the systems implemented may not be exactly the same) and you and others will be better able to assess their progress over time.

To provide you with the relevant information, ask yourself the following questions *before* you begin to collect data:

- Why am I collecting this data?
- How is this data related to the issue/problem?
- What will the data tell me about the problem?
- What precisely am I going to collect data on?
- Where am I going to collect the data?
- What is the size of sample that will suffice?
- How long will I collect the data for?
- Will this time-scale be adequate?
- When will I collect the data?
- How often will I collect the data (daily, twice-weekly, weekly, monthly)?
- Who will collect the data?
- How will the data collected be analysed?
- Who will I share the data with?
- What ethical issues must I consider?
- Will I use the humanistic approach or not?
- Whose permission will I need?
- Where will the data be stored?
- Who will have access to the stored data?
- What resources will I need?
- Are these resources available to me?
- How will the results of this project affect my care practice?
- How will the results of this project affect general care practice?

This is a very long list of questions, but if answered honestly and positively, you will be well on the way with your action research project and will have met the criteria for a pass as well. Collecting the data will be relatively easy once you have found the answers to these questions.

Use tables, pie-charts and graphs to display your results graphically, as these are more easily and quickly understood than a lot of written material.

Having no set project from the workplace, you will have to use an innovation concept. This means trying to think of something appropriate to the workplace and your own development. Make a pattern diagram of all the ideas that you have and discuss them with your supervisor and course tutor. You will find that you will be prioritising your work in the workplace, school and college in carrying out your project. This means deciding the order in which you would do things. Although it is tempting to sacrifice everything else for the project that you are anxious to complete, your work with service users should be your first priority. After this, you can list your tasks in order. Your task list, referred to earlier, will help you to prioritise your work tasks.

The purpose of your vocational placement is to acquire the knowledge, skills and understanding appropriate to the caring profession. Although you will spend a large part of your time in formal education, you are also learning on the job.

At the conclusion of each vocational placement, take an evening to reflect and evaluate the experience that you have acquired using the three categories of knowledge, skills and understanding. Having done this, you will be able to plan your strategy for learning on the next placement.

End-of-unit test

As this unit is concerned with development rather than factual knowledge, the unit test has been modified to probe your personal and professional development.

1 Explain three ways in which you have demonstrated that you are becoming a reflective practitioner.
2 Describe three ways that you have recently promoted anti-discriminatory practice into your everyday or working life.
3 Describe how you have organised the way in which you collect evidence for this unit or Unit 5.
4 Explain how you have identified your strengths and weaknesses.
5 Describe three ways in which you have handled potentially confrontational incidents.
6 Explain how you have made constructive use of feedback.
7 Provide three examples of changes you have made in the way you communicate with service users.
8 Relating the theory you have learned to the practice, describe the performance of a team in which you have been a member.
9 Describe the way in which you used information resources to complete a piece of work.
10 Describe any learning opportunities that you have taken advantage of during your programme that were not included in the official course of study.

References and further reading

Belson, W. A. (1981) *The design and understanding of survey questionnaires,* Aldershot: Gower

Egan, G. (1990) *The Skilled Helper: A Systematic Approach To Effective Helping,* Pacific Grove, CA: Brooks/Cole

Fontana, D. (1992) *Social Skills at Work,* Leicester: British Psychological Society

Miller, J. (1996) *Social Care Practice,* London: Hodder & Stoughton Educational

Nolan, Y. (2001) *Care S/NVQ 3,* Oxford: Heinemann

Oppenheim, A. N. (1985) *Questionnaire design and attitude measurement,* Aldershot: Gower

Owen, D. and Davis, M. (1991) *Help with your project,* London: Edward Arnold

The Good Study Guide (2002) Buckingham: Open University Press

Thompson, N. (1996) *People Skills: A Guide to Effective Practice in the Human Services,* Basingstoke: Palgrave

Trevithick, P. (2002) *Social Work Skills: a practice handbook,* Buckingham: Open University Press

Unit 9 Care services

This chapter aims to put into context the role that the state plays in providing welfare services in the UK. We will consider historical perspectives on welfare and care services and how they have evolved to influence contemporary thinking about, and enactment of, social policy. You will need to evaluate the current structure of social care provision, based on an analysis of legislation, political ideology, public opinion and changing social needs, including demographic issues.

What you need to learn

- The concept of welfare
- The structure, function and development of social care organisations in the UK
- Contemporary social care service issues

The concept of welfare

The idea of 'welfare'

Figure 9.1 Who should welfare be for – the worst-off or everyone in need?

'Welfare' is not a new or even a recent idea. Current ideas about welfare have developed over time. The way we understand and use the term today can be traced back to ideas about human needs, 'rights' and the responsibilities of the individual and the state. In particular, present-day ideas about welfare are closely related to beliefs about the role that **central government** should play in meeting the daily living needs of the most vulnerable people in society. We'll refer to the historical debate over what are the government's welfare responsibilities when we consider the different perspectives on welfare provision later in the chapter. However, before we look at this, we should first clarify the meaning(s) of 'welfare'.

What is welfare?

'Welfare' is sometimes used as a synonym for 'well-being'. For example, care-workers may express a concern about an individual's 'welfare' or say that they are acting to protect a service user's 'welfare'. In this sense the term is associated with a person's social, emotional or psychological 'health'. The term 'social welfare' is also used in a similar way to refer to, or express a concern for, the 'health', needs or interests of a particular social group or society more generally. For example, 'the social welfare needs of asylum seekers' has been a concern for organisations who work with and support asylum seekers who are fleeing persecution in their home country.

'Welfare' is also used to refer to the *forms of help* that are provided for vulnerable people. In this sense 'welfare services' in the UK include such things as social housing, social security benefit payments, general education and the provision of advice, counselling and support services. The concept of welfare, as it is understood and used in the UK, therefore includes individual human (non-medical) needs and the services and forms of support that are provided to help people who are unable to meet their own needs independently.

Think It Over

What kinds of care services qualify as social welfare services? Identify services that are designed to meet the social welfare needs of children, disabled adults and older people. Remember to avoid listing *health* services.

A history of social welfare provision in the UK

Modern social welfare provision in the UK has its roots in the eighteenth and nineteenth centuries. The beginning of organised social welfare provision is linked to the changes in British society over the course of the eighteenth and nineteenth centuries. This period saw massive social changes and upheaval in British society that resulted in difficult social conditions, new kinds of social relationships and the emergence of new political institutions.

The industrial revolution and urbanisation

At the beginning of the eighteenth century Britain was mainly an agricultural country with a rural population. However, during this and the following century there was a massive growth in population and a shift in the location of most people from rural to urban areas. **Industrialisation** was a key factor stimulating the movement of people from rural to urban areas. Industrialisation involved a change from traditional agricultural and craft methods of work to methods that were mechanised and factory-based. Instead of working for themselves and their families in a traditional way, people were now increasingly working in the new factory-based system. The availability of work in factories attracted people to the areas where they were located, so large population densities grew up there. Many metropolitan area and larger cities that now exist in the UK can trace their origins back to an industrial past and the process of urbanisation that occurred in the eighteenth and nineteenth centuries.

Manchester was a mill/factory town

The rapid growth of urban areas, and the changing social and work relationships that accompanied this, had major effects on living conditions and quality of life during the industrial revolution. Historical evidence shows that the effects of large-scale industrialisation and urbanisation included:

- housing shortages and squalor
- sanitation problems
- poor standards of public health
- high unemployment
- widespread poverty.

Governments during the eighteenth and nineteenth centuries were not very involved in social issues or in providing care or welfare services for vulnerable groups in the population. In fact, law and order and the economy were really the only issues that members of the aristocracy (a powerful social elite who made up governments during this period) were concerned with. Gradually this situation changed as expectations about who should govern the country and about political rights for ordinary men (but not women!) began to change. Governments became more involved in responding to major social problems, particularly poverty, as people demanded more from them. Dealing with social problems eventually came to be seen as part of the government's task in managing the country as a whole.

The emergence of welfare provision

Industrialisation, urbanisation and an increasingly democratic political system are considered to be key factors that provided the conditions for the emergence of welfare provision in the UK. The first major area of state involvement in social welfare was in response to the problem of poverty.

Poverty has been a problem affecting sections of the British population for centuries. It was a serious, and worsening, problem in the eighteenth and nineteenth centuries. Industrialisation, and the changing nature of worker-employer relationships in particular, had a significant effect on poverty levels. In the new industrial system people became employees rather than self-employed farmers and crafts-people. However, factory production required fewer workers than agricultural and craft-based production because new machines performed tasks faster and more efficiently than people had done previously. Additionally, because of the large numbers of workers looking for employment in urban areas, factory owners were able to keep wages levels low. When trade slumped, factory owners could also lay their workers off at short notice to cut their own costs. Poverty was the result because, without jobs, people had no other sources of income or support. At this point, there were no social security benefits, no redundancy pay and no social care services that people today are able to call on. The result for some was abject poverty, starvation, sickness and even early death.

Responding to poverty

The identification of poverty as a social problem and the responses to it in the eighteenth and nineteenth centuries provide examples of the two different ways of thinking about 'welfare' that we identified earlier. On the one hand, a person's welfare was seen as threatened or damaged by the experience of poverty. At the same time, the help provided for them included some of the first examples of organised welfare services for vulnerable people in the UK.

Social welfare provision for people in poverty was first dealt with through the **Poor Laws** of 1598 and 1601. These laws required that people in each local parish should pay a 'poor rate' tax that would be distributed to poor people. People who were in need of welfare support were classified as either 'able-bodied poor' and sent to work in the local workhouse or were given money called 'outdoor relief' or a place in an almshouse (an early hospital) because they were too old or sick to work. This system changed at the end of the eighteenth century when it was overwhelmed by the growth in the numbers of people in poverty. The result was a harsher **workhouse system** and a change in attitude to both poverty and the welfare services being offered by the state.

One of the key questions that people began to ask about poverty at the end of eighteenth century was 'are people poor through no fault of their own or is poverty their own fault?' This kind of question, seeking a cause and trying to attribute responsibility, still influences the response of governments and individuals to welfare provision in the twenty-first century.

Think It Over

Do you think that some people are more deserving of state help than other people? Reflect on your personal beliefs and discuss your ideas with a class colleague. Both of you should be able to justify the viewpoints that you have on this issue.

In the late eighteenth and early nineteenth centuries it was increasingly felt that people should be encouraged to meet their own welfare needs and should be discouraged from using or relying on the state or other people to do so. As a result, the workhouse system was increasingly seen as a last resort because it was so awful and came to contain only orphans, the old and sick and people who really had no other choice. People who had welfare needs began to develop and turn to other sources of welfare provision and support.

From the mid-nineteenth century onwards, the main alternatives to the state workhouse system were **mutual aid** and voluntary 'charity' schemes. Mutual aid schemes were popular in the late nineteenth century. They are the origins of trades unions and friendly societies. They enabled workers to pool resources into small-scale local savings funds that they could draw on in times of hardship. As these schemes grew they developed into housing and worker co-operatives that could provide welfare services which enabled members to avoid the workhouse in times of hardship. **Philanthropists** were rich, middle-class Victorians who were keen to use their wealth to help (and morally reform) those in poverty. Philanthropists often saw voluntary welfare provision as being an expression of their religious beliefs. Quaker families, such as the Tukes, Cadburys and Rowntrees for example, were important providers of social welfare from the nineteenth century onwards. Many present-day voluntary organisations can trace their origins back to nineteenth-century philanthropists.

Changing approaches to welfare

The belief that poverty was a person's own fault or could easily be avoided by hard work was being challenged by the end of the nineteenth century. A shift in social attitudes away from individualist, 'survival of the fittest' notions to 'collective' beliefs about the rights of all people to a basic standard of living in reasonable social conditions played a part in this.

The first 30 years of the twentieth century saw a series of 'welfarist' governments elected to power. Liberal and then Labour Party governments gradually extended the role of the state as a provider of health and social care in response to a growing interest and concern about welfare issues. Many of the new welfare services were introduced as a result of governments passing legislation (see Figure 9.2 for example). The effect of this was to establish a political platform and a public appetite for what was to be a watershed in the history of welfare provision in the UK.

The Education (Provision of Meals) Act (1906) introduced free school meals for poor children

The National Insurance Act (1911) introduced unemployment benefit for workers

The Education Act (1918) raised the school-leaving age to 14

The Subsidised Housing Act (1919) provided for local authority council housing

Figure 9.2 Legislation introducing social welfare provision

Welfare provision since 1945

William Beveridge

In 1941, Sir William Beveridge, an academic and government adviser, was asked by Prime Minister Winston Churchill to lead a committee of civil servants investigating the welfare schemes of the time. The result of their work was a set of ideas and principles that radically changed health and social welfare provision in the UK from a minimum state intervention model to one that came to be described as a '**welfare state**' model.

The Beveridge Report

The final report produced by the committee led by Sir William Beveridge was called *Social Insurance and Allied Services* (1942). It is now widely known, and will be referred to, as the *Beveridge Report*. In it the committee identified what they believed were the main social welfare problems facing the UK and set out suggestions for reforming the welfare system in a way that tackled these problems. The *Beveridge Report* identified five 'giant evils' that were affecting the welfare of the population and the development of the nation. These were:

- want (poverty)
- disease (ill health)
- ignorance (lack of education)
- squalor (poor housing)
- idleness (unemployment).

The Beveridge plan proposed a social security system that would provide universal welfare benefits for British people. The aim of establishing a system of social security was to abolish the social problem of 'want', or poverty. This meant that a minimum level of income would be available, without means-testing, to everyone as a (universal) right.

Many other ideas were also proposed to tackle the other 'giant evils'. The most notable of these was the proposed development of a National Health Service. This would be founded on the basis of three main principles:

- services would be available to all on the basis of real, clinical need rather than on the basis of ability to pay
- services would therefore be free at the point of delivery
- services would be comprehensive, covering all people in all parts of the country.

When the report came out in 1942, the UK's health system was fragmented and unco-ordinated. Services were provided through private, voluntary and local authority (council) organisations and individual practitioners and were inadequate to meet the health care needs of the population.

The 'welfare state'

The term 'welfare state' is used to refer to both the idea of state (government) responsibility for providing welfare services and also to the institutions or organisations through which these services are delivered. A variety of social legislation passed in the 1940s led to the emergence of a welfare state era of health and social care intervention in the UK that lasted until the late 1970s.

Key issues

Legislation extending welfare provision into the 'welfare state' era included:

The Family Allowance Act (1945) – introduced cash benefits for all children under 16 years old, except the first.

The National Health Service Act (1946) – introduced a nationalised system of health care provision that was free, universal and comprehensive.

The National Insurance Act (1946) – introduced an insurance scheme that was intended to fund a variety of cash benefits (unemployment, sickness, maternity and widow's benefit included) to those who contributed.

The National Assistance Act (1948) – introduced benefits provision for people not covered by the National Insurance Act (1946) because they couldn't contribute from their wages. This legislation provided money and accommodation, particularly for people 'in urgent need'.

Health and social care services that were funded and run by the state expanded a great deal between 1947, when the NHS was officially 'born', and the early 1970s. The NHS was very popular in its early years. The number and range of health care services available to people expanded significantly, new hospital and community facilities were built to cope with the increased work load and large numbers of people were trained and employed to provide care on behalf of the NHS.

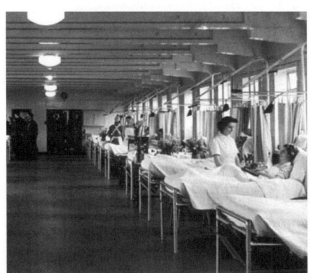
The new NHS in 1947

It gradually became clear that the NHS was not, as originally thought, going to reduce demand for health care services by making the British population healthier. By the 1970s, the size of the service was also resulting in significant funding and organisational problems. In particular, the national system contained service duplication and there was a lack of co-ordination between various parts of the NHS at local and national levels. The response was a reorganisation of the structure of health and welfare services (see Figure 9.3).

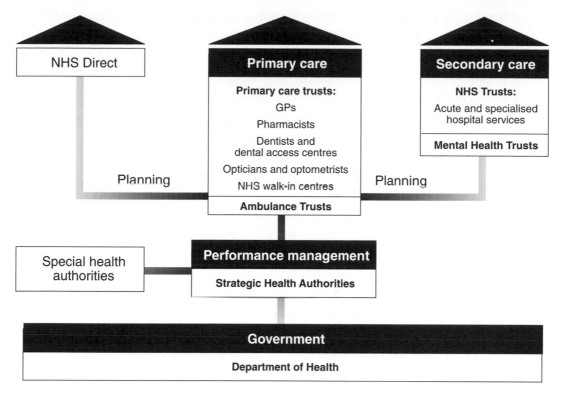

Figure 9.3 The reorganised structure of the NHS

One of the main effects of the reorganisation was to separate responsibility for provision of health and social care services. Social care and other forms of welfare, such as housing and education, became the responsibility of local authorities (councils). Local government did have some responsibility for primary health care before this reorganisation. This was now given to the new Area Health Authorities and Family Practitioner Committees.

The development of a social care system

The British social care system is not just the result of a 'welfare state' reorganisation in the early 1970s. The present-day system has its roots in the nineteenth century, with the voluntary sector playing a significant early role in social care provision. Voluntary 'social work' developed because of poor social conditions and poverty in the late eighteenth and nineteenth centuries caused by industrialisation and urbanisation. State-funded and-run social work services gradually emerged during the first half of the twentieth century and were expanded significantly as a result of the 'welfare state' developments that occurred after 1948. Local authorities took on responsibility for social care and welfare-related work with children and families, people with disabilities, older people and people with mental health problems in particular. All of these service user groups were viewed as having welfare needs that made them vulnerable.

Despite the expansion of the welfare state, the social care and welfare system developed without the equivalent of a National Health Service. Local authorities were responsible for social care, social work and some other forms of welfare provision (housing and education, for example) in their geographical areas. However, there was no central body or overall plan governing or guiding social care and welfare provision. The result was a complicated and poorly integrated system that had lots of overlap and co-ordination problems. Local authorities also developed different kinds of organisational structures,

323

making it harder for them to work with each other and for other agencies to relate to them.

In 1968, the Seebohm Committee investigated the provision of social care and proposed that all local authorities should merge their social care provision into a 'social services department'. The Local Authority Social Services Act (1970) brought these new departments into existence and integrated personal social care and social work provision in the way we recognise today.

Key issue

How are your local social care and social work services currently being developed to meet local care service needs? Carry out some research into the immediate and future plans that are proposed by your local authority.

Restructuring the welfare services

Between 1948 and the late 1970s, there was general agreement between the main political parties in the UK that the 'welfare state' was a good thing that should be supported and maintained by governments. This political consensus first began to break down in the late 1960s when economic problems began to affect the UK. These problems caused people to ask questions about government's ability to pay for the welfare state. The services being offered by the welfare state were funded through income tax. Because the welfare state was now so large and costly, full employment of the population was required to produce the amount of income tax required to fund the welfare system. Increasingly, the economic problems of the 1970s and the growing levels of unemployment meant that high levels of government welfare spending could not be sustained. As a result the political consensus on welfare gradually broke down. New ideas began to emerge about the role of the state and people's rights to health and welfare provision.

The Conservative Party, led by Margaret Thatcher, challenged the consensus view that the government should fund universally available and free welfare services. When they were elected to government in 1979, the Thatcher-led Conservative Party set about rethinking the role of the state in the provision of health and welfare services.

Challenging the 'welfare state'

One of the aims of the Conservative governments of the 1980s and early 1990s was to reduce the direct involvement of the state in the funding and provision of welfare services. The aim was to shift some of the responsibility onto private and voluntary sector providers as well as placing greater responsibility on the individual and their family for meeting personal welfare needs. The Conservative governments of this period felt that the state had gone too far in providing welfare and had, in fact, trapped some sections of the population in 'welfare dependency'.

Welfare provision during the 1980s was 'reformed' through a reduction in the range of services available, the introduction of means-testing and eligibility criteria and by increasing the use of voluntary and private sector organisations as providers of specialist forms of social and health care.

Health

Despite this, the NHS was not privatised, though some services, including cleaning and catering, were 'contracted out' to private providers. Charges for prescriptions and other services were also extended during this period.

Important 'reforms' in the organisation and provision of healthcare during this period included the introduction of an **internal market** in which new National Health Service Trusts had to compete against each other for contracts to provide care. The purchaser-provider 'internal market' system was intended to improve efficiency and raise standards in the NHS.

Housing

The Conservative governments of the 1980s and early 1990s also made attempts to significantly reform the provision of housing in the United Kingdom. In an attempt to create a 'property-owning democracy', the Thatcher-led governments introduced a scheme where council-house tenants could buy their homes, thereby taking them out of public ownership. At the same time, local authorities who had traditionally provided 'council' housing were restricted from building more homes and were

Typical council housing of the 1980s

required to work in partnership with private and voluntary sector housing providers. These Conservative governments fundamentally altered housing welfare provision.

Education

Education, a key area of welfare state provision and expansion since 1948, was also the focus of government reform in the 1980s and 1990s. The aim was to reduce the degree of state control and increase the amount of 'choice' available to parents and their children. In effect, the Education Reform Act (1988) allowed schools to 'opt out' of local authority control and take on 'grant-maintained' status. This was made more controversial as it saw an increase in the use of selection criteria by grant-maintained schools. This went against the principles of a comprehensive system that was accessible to all. At the same time, the funding restrictions imposed on higher and further education providers and the introduction of repayable student loans in place of grants, heralded the end of an expanding, free, state-run education service.

Thatcher's Conservative governments redefined the approach to health and welfare provision by the state. Consensus on the 'welfare state' was over but welfare services were still required and a lot of the organisational structures and services that first emerged in the 'welfare state' era were still around. The aim of the New Labour governments, first elected in 1997, has been to 'modernise' the organisational structures and practices of the state welfare system in order to create a welfare system that is efficient, cost-effective and targeted at those most in need.

New Labour's approach to social welfare provision

New Labour's approach to welfare funding and provision has been to accommodate and reform the changes made by the previous Conservative governments. Many 'Old Labour' supporters were hoping for a return to a large-scale 'welfare state' system in which the government took responsibility for funding and providing universal, free welfare services. However, since New Labour were elected to power they have adopted an approach to welfare that built on some of the Conservative reforms and rejected others. For example, rather than returning to universal and free welfare services the New Labour approach has been to target those most in need of welfare services, such as housing and social security. This was also a Conservative government strategy. New Labour have introduced eligibility criteria to control demand and limit access to these services. The purpose of state 'welfare' under New Labour has been to provide opportunities for 'social inclusion' to the most vulnerable rather than to return to universal provision. Targeted welfare means making welfare recipients responsible to do their best to help themselves. If they do not, then the welfare services are withdrawn.

Tony Blair has led New Labour since 1997

Think It Over

When do you think a person is at risk of being 'socially excluded'? Identify the kinds of personal or social situations that you believe lead to social exclusion.

The New Labour approach to social welfare provision has removed the competitive 'internal market' element from the state system and has halted attempts to privatise aspects of the state welfare sector. However, New Labour's approach also involves an acceptance that private and voluntary organisations, as well as families, do have an important part to play in the delivery of welfare services. The current approach of New Labour is that the state does not have to be the main provider of welfare services, but that it should take responsibility for funding and regulating public welfare provision. This is a significant change from the ideas underpinning the early welfare state. Nevertheless, the legacy of the welfare state still influences New Labour's policy-making and service provision in this area. Like all previous governments, New Labour has to meet the welfare needs of the British population in ways that are affordable, effective and politically acceptable.

Perspectives on welfare provision

Social care and welfare services are generally provided as a way of responding to social problems such as poverty, unemployment and housing shortages. However, it is also important for us to identify and consider the kinds of thinking that underlies any decision to provide welfare services. As well as being created for practical purposes, the form, extent and focus of social care and welfare services reflect the political beliefs and programmes of the government and local authorities who commission and allocate funding for services. These packages of ideas are known as **ideologies.**

Ideas about welfare needs and rights

Historically, the ways that governments have thought about the concept of 'social welfare' (and the kinds of services they believe ought to be provided), have tended to be closely linked to broader political ideas. However, increasingly in the twenty-first-century UK, the close link between political parties and welfare ideologies is weakening and new ideologies reflecting the priorities of women, minority ethnic groups and welfare service users are being developed. Before we consider these, it is important to outline what is known as the **political spectrum** and the welfare ideologies that fit into this.

The political spectrum

Political ideas have been described in terms of a left–right spectrum of positions for over a century. Figure 9.4 below illustrates the beliefs that exist within the spectrum and locates the position of the main political parties on it.

You will be able to work out from the diagram that whilst some members of the Conservative Party may have quite right-wing views, other may have more centrist views like those of Liberal Democrats and some Labour Party members. The spectrum provides a guide to the types of political position that are taken by parties and politicians in the UK, but doesn't say what these positions involve in relation to social care and welfare provision. The three mainstream approaches to social care and welfare

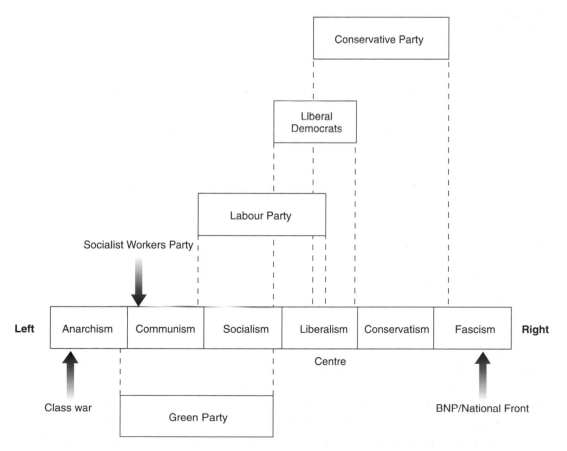

Figure 9.4 The political spectrum

provision that we need to consider are the collectivist, democratic socialist and 'New Right' perspectives.

The collectivist approach

This approach to social policy and welfare is associated with Marxist and radical socialist political ideas. People who hold these views generally oppose the capitalist economic system because they see it as the main cause of social inequality and problems. The collectivist approach to social welfare is one in which central government takes responsibility for funding and delivering social welfare and care services for all members of the population. In particular, the aim of this approach is to create a social environment in which all members of society can thrive and develop. In practice, this means that a large amount of welfare funding has to be obtained through taxation and spent on comprehensive, universally available public services. The collectivist approach aims to achieve equality (and therefore remove social inequality) in society. The political party most closely associated with the collectivist approach to social care and welfare was the old Labour Party (pre-Blair). However, despite having some sympathy for the idea of universal welfare and state responsibility for funding and development of a 'welfare state', the old Labour Party never implemented the more radical aspects of this approach and New Labour has moved even further away from it.

The democratic socialist perspective

This approach to social care and welfare provision involves significant central government involvement in, and control of, service funding and provision but not as much as the collectivist approach. The democratic socialist approach involves the government developing a welfare system that protects vulnerable members of society and prevents the worst effects of social and economic inequality, such as abject poverty and homelessness. The democratic socialist approach involves a belief that the better-off and more able members of society have a duty or responsibility to support those who are 'in need'. This tends to result in social care and welfare services that are selectively targeted at those people who meet needs assessment and eligibility criteria. Democratic socialist ideas were very influential when the 'welfare state' was created and to varying degrees have influenced central government and care professional's thinking about service development and provision ever since.

The New Right perspective

The New Right approach to social care and welfare presented a powerful challenge to democratic socialist ideas from the mid-1970s onwards. The New Right approach focuses on individual freedom and liberty and includes the belief that governments should 'interfere' as little as possible in people's lives and personal problems. The New Right approach to social care and welfare provision tends to make distinctions between 'deserving' people who require services through no fault of their own and 'undeserving' people who are seen as lazy, irresponsible and the cause of their own problems. Politicians and social policy-makers who hold New Right beliefs tend to argue that a state welfare system creates a dependency culture in which these 'undeserving' people rely on the state for help instead of helping themselves. As a result governments influenced by New Right ideas limit the amount of state social care and welfare provision, impose stricter eligibility criteria to limit access to these services and encourage people to take more responsibility for their own welfare and that of their families. The New Right approach encourages voluntary and private sector organisations to offer cost-effective, high-quality social care and welfare services for 'customers' as an alternative to state welfare. The Conservative governments of the 1980s and early 1990s, and increasingly the New Labour governments, developed a policy approach that reflected many of these ideas and encouraged people to purchase services (such as health insurance) privately.

Feminist perspectives

Feminism is a relatively new and important approach to social welfare development and social care service provision. Feminist approaches primarily focus on issues and express ideas from the perspective of women. There are a variety of different types of feminism rather than a single ideology or approach. Feminists are often critical of social care and welfare provision on the grounds that 'traditional' welfare services are based on male assumptions about gender roles in which women are seen as 'natural' carers and men are seen as 'breadwinners'. Feminists support women-centred services and a welfare system that addresses child care and family issues in a flexible and unbiased way.

Influences on welfare provision and service development

A number of factors have influenced the development of state welfare services since governments first began taking some responsibility for welfare provision in the eighteenth century. Particularly important amongst these factors have been the impact of poverty, social exclusion and demographic issues.

The impact of poverty

We said earlier that poverty in the eighteenth and nineteenth centuries was a key factor that influenced governments to begin providing basic welfare services for vulnerable people through the Poor Law system. Initially, cash benefits for unemployed adults were provided only as a last resort and able-bodied people were expected to work, in very harsh workhouse conditions, for the small amounts of money they received. Despite these attempts to provide a 'safety net' system, many people living during the Victorian era experienced severe poverty. Whilst mutual aid and voluntary charity schemes developed to supplement this very basic system, it was not until the middle of the twentieth century that a more concerted effort was made to deal with widespread poverty in British society.

The development of a state system that sought to tackle 'want' (poverty) was one of the most important welfare developments in the twentieth century. The response at the time, and which remains a significant part of welfare provision, was the development of a social security system of welfare benefits. In this sense 'poverty' was seen as the inability to meet basic and material needs because of a lack of money.

Key issues

A number of pieces of legislation were passed with the aim of tackling poverty:

The **National Insurance Act (1946)** created an integrated universal system of social insurance. The goal was to cover all major personal risks (such as sickness and unemployment) and pay out benefits that would support people when they had no income from paid work.

The **National Assistance Act (1948)** established a means-tested allowance for unemployed people who were unable to contribute to the national insurance scheme because their income was too low.

It was hoped that poverty would be removed by this system of state welfare. However, despite these hopes poverty continues to affect sections of the British population. As a result it continues to be a factor influencing the provision of, and reasons for, welfare services. Welfare benefits are now available to individuals who meet eligibility criteria. These targeted cash benefits are increasingly offered as part of a 'welfare package' that also includes education and job training opportunities that are designed to get people back to work.

It is likely that the state will continue to be involved in providing social security benefits and other welfare services to tackle poverty for as long as politicians recognise it as an important social issue that individuals cannot resolve simply through their own personal efforts.

Social exclusion

The term social exclusion is sometimes used as a synonym for poverty. However, whilst poverty may be a part of social exclusion, there is more involved. The New Labour government identified social exclusion as a major problem affecting sections of the British population in 1997. In response they set up a Social Exclusion Unit to develop policy and services that would tackle and reduce this problem. The Social Exclusion Unit defined the phenomenon in the following way:

Social exclusion is a shorthand term for what can happen when people or areas suffer from a combination of linked problems such as unemployment, poor skills, low incomes, poor housing, high crime environments, bad health, poverty and family breakdown.
Source: Social Exclusion Unit, 1999

The New Labour government has said that it intends to tackle the problems of social exclusion in a 'joined up' way rather than trying to deal with the linked problems individually. This will involve reforming the organisations that deliver welfare services so that they can tackle the various problems, and meet the multiple needs of socially excluded people, in a co-ordinated way. Since different governments tend to slowly rather than radically change welfare service provision, it is likely that this 'joined up' way of thinking about social exclusion will remain an influence on welfare policy for the immediate future.

Demographic issues

Demography is the study of population characteristics and trends. Social welfare policy and the provision of welfare services have been heavily influenced by patterns of population change since industrialisation and urbanisation of the eighteenth and nineteenth centuries. At this point in history social problems, including poverty, overcrowding and high unemployment, occurred as a result of a growth in the population during a period of economic change. Inevitably these demographic changes led to the emergence of new welfare needs and pressure for service provision.

Similarly, a range of demographic factors were taken into account by politicians and social service planners when the 'welfare state' was being developed in the middle of the twentieth century. For example, initially welfare services were designed for a country damaged by war. Those with welfare needs included a large population of men returning from fighting the war and, shortly after this, the large number of young children born in the post-war baby boom.

Politicians and service planners do not just look at the numbers of people in the population when considering how demography may affect welfare needs. They also consider, often by making assumptions, how lifestyle patterns are likely to affect future welfare needs. For example, at the time when the 'welfare state' was being planned, it was assumed that men would go out to work, whilst women would stay at home to raise families. It was also assumed that full employment could be achieved and that the majority of men in the population would be able to contribute taxes to pay for the welfare state. When unemployment rose and lifestyle patterns changed, demographic factors had to be reconsidered in order to adjust services to meet changing welfare needs. Since the 1950s, lifestyle patterns, the age structure and the ethnic composition of the British population have all changed considerably. As a result, welfare service planners have had to adjust their predictions about the need for welfare services in the future.

Think It Over

What kinds of welfare problems do you think are likely to occur over the next thirty years? Think about likely changes in the size, composition and lifestyle of the population when making your predictions.

A wide range of demographic factors, including migration, longevity, the incidence of disease and illness, as well as the age and sex structure of the population, are now taken into account by governments and service planners when predicting future welfare needs and service requirements.

Assessment activity 9.1

Social exclusion has been identified as a major social problem and the focus of government welfare programmes. In this activity you are asked to explore and define the nature of this problem and to analyse how central government is tackling it.

1 Define what social exclusion involves. You should clearly explain the causes and impact of social exclusion on individuals and communities that experience it.
2 How has central government attempted to tackle the problem of social exclusion? Analyse and explain the major pieces of legislation and policy initiatives that have been developed to improve social exclusion.

The structure, function and development of social care organisations in the UK

The modern social care system is composed of **statutory** (state or government), **voluntary** or not-for-profit, and **private** sector organisations. Additionally, a large proportion of social care services are provided by the families and friends of people who need forms of support and help that are classified as 'social care'. These people are sometimes referred to as informal carers, though more typically they are simply called **carers** in social care settings. This is known as a '**mixed economy**' care system because it is based on different types of service provider. In the next section, we will explore the structure and function of the modern social care system, looking particularly at the roles that central government and carers play and also outlining the general organisation and structure of the system.

The role of central government

The term central government is used to describe both the people and the level of government responsible for making decisions that affect social care policy, funding and service organisation throughout the UK. The key policy-making groups in central government are government politicians.

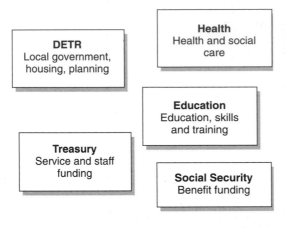

Figure 9.5 Government departments which have welfare functions

The government of the UK is formed by the political party that wins the most seats in a general election. Some members of the winning political party are appointed to ministerial posts by the Prime Minister, and are given the title Secretary of State. The Secretary of State for Health, who leads the Department of Health, has the lead role in developing policy ideas about personal social care services as well as about health care. Other members of the government have welfare-related policy roles that focus on housing and homelessness, employment and training, and disability support, for example. Policy on welfare benefits is the responsibility of the Secretary of State for Social Security.

Government politicians are supported and assisted in making social care policy by a range of advisers and civil servants. The government politician's role is to develop the broad policy ideas about what kinds of social care and welfare services ought be provided. They do this by translating the ideological principles that their party believes in, such as 'equality' for example, into practical approaches to social care – for example, by making services accessible to everyone. The government's advisers and the permanent, non-political civil servants who work in the **Social Services Inspectorate** within the Department of Health develop plans for putting government social care policy into action. As well as identifying how much money, or funding, the plans will cost, the Inspectorate identifies how statutory social care and welfare services should be organised, offers guidance to Local Authorities on service delivery and inspects the performance of local authority social services departments.

Why does central government create social welfare policies?

The need for social care and welfare services was described in a policy document titled *Modernising Social Services* by the New Labour government in the following way:

Social services are for all of us. At any one time up to one and a half million people in England rely on their help. And all of us are likely at some point in our lives to need to turn to social services for support, whether on our own behalf or for a family member. Often this will be at a time of personal and family crisis – the onset of mental illness, the birth of a disabled child, a family break-up, a death which leaves someone without a carer they had come to rely on.

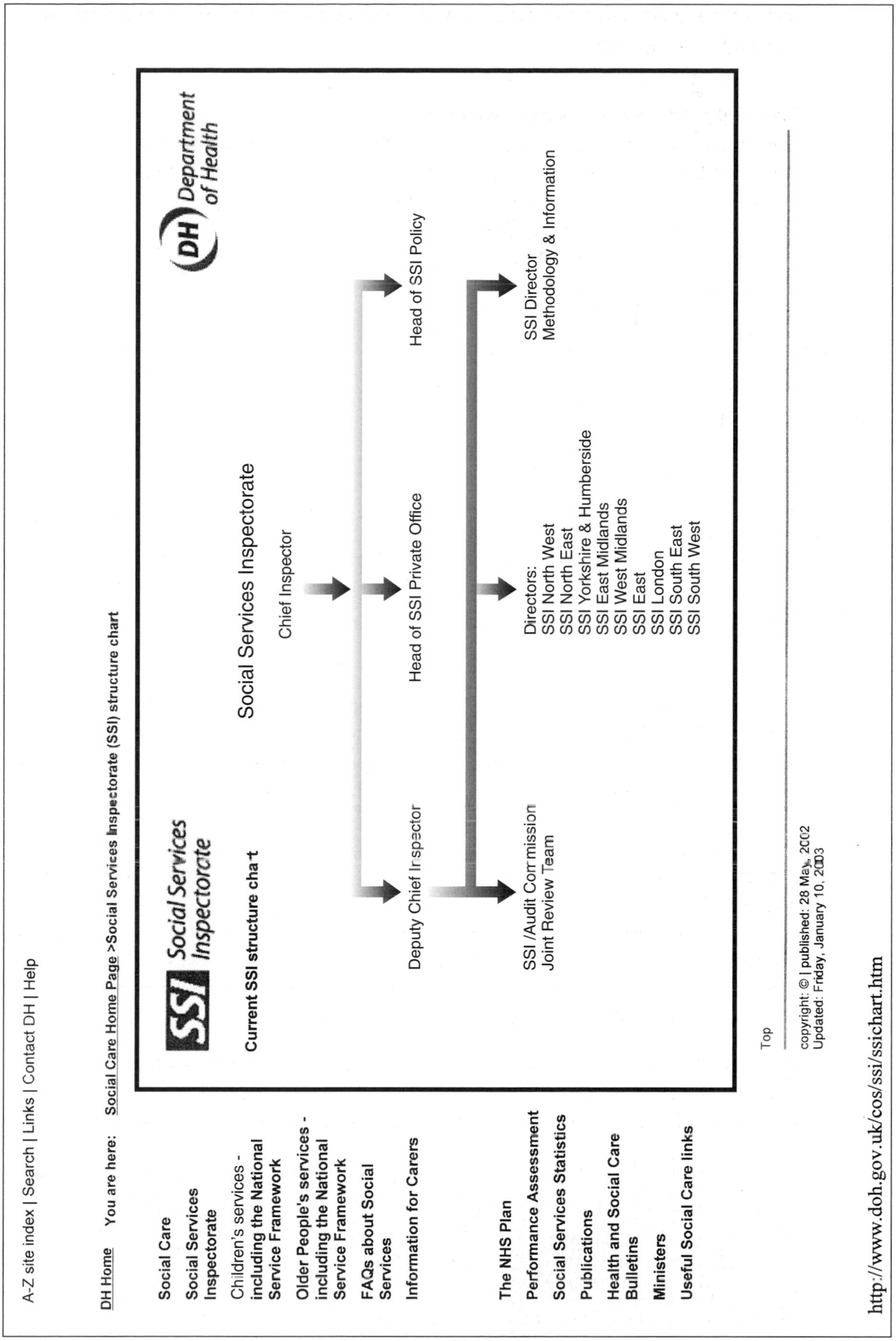

A-Z site index | Search | Links | Contact DH | Help

DH Home   You are here: Social Care Home Page >Social Services Inspectorate (SSI) structure chart

SSI *Social Services Inspectorate*

(DH) *Department of Health*

Current SSI structure chart

Social Services Inspectorate

Chief Inspector

Head of SSI Private Office → Head of SSI Policy

Deputy Chief Inspector

SSI /Audit Commission
Joint Review Team

SSI Director
Methodology & Information

Directors:
SSI North West
SSI North East
SSI Yorkshire & Humberside
SSI East Midlands
SSI West Midlands
SSI East
SSI London
SSI South East
SSI South West

Social Care

Social Services
Inspectorate

Children's services -
including the National
Service Framework

Older People's services -
including the National
Service Framework

FAQs about Social
Services

Information for Carers

The NHS Plan

Performance Assessment

Social Services Statistics

Publications

Health and Social Care
Bulletins

Ministers

Useful Social Care links

Top

copyright: © | published: 28 May, 2002
Updated: Friday, January 10, 2003

http://www.doh.gov.uk/cos/ssi/ssichart.htm

Figure 9.6 The Social Services Inspectorate
Source. Department of Health website. © Crown copyright

We all depend on good social services to be there at such times of crisis, to help in making the right decisions and working out what needs to be done. And more widely, we all benefit if social services are providing good, effective services to those who need them. Any decent society must make provision for those who need support and are unable to look after themselves. Breakdowns in services for young offenders, homeless people, or people with mental health problems can have damaging consequences for other people as well as the individuals themselves. Factors such as demographic changes, and changes in the patterns of family life, are likely to mean that the need for social services will increase in the coming years. With recent advances in health care, more people, including those with profound disabilities, are able to live longer, and they rely on effective social services to achieve more fulfilling lives.

Social services, therefore, do not just support a small number of 'social casualties'; they are an important part of the fabric of a caring society.

Key issue

What role should private sector organisations play in the provision of social welfare services? Research the arguments that are put forward in favour of this and assess them against the claim that central government has a fundamental, moral responsibility to provide care for vulnerable people in society.

The structure and organisation of welfare

The current social care and welfare system in the United Kingdom has its origins in the nineteenth century. The system that we now have has evolved out of a Victorian system based on friendly societies, trades unions and self-help. Before the creation of the 'welfare state' in 1948 central government played only a small part in funding and delivering social care and welfare services. From this point onwards the statutory (government) social care system began to grow. The voluntary (not-for-profit) sector continued to operate and develop alongside the growing statutory social care sector throughout the second half of the twentieth century. Informal, family-based, social care and support was also a significant part of social care and general provision throughout this period (and remains so).

A 'mixed economy' of social care

The Wolfenden Committee on Voluntary Services first described the social care system in the UK as a 'mixed economy' of care in their 1978 report. This term refers to the fact that social care and welfare service providers (organisations, individual practitioners and carers) are funded, and provide access to services, in different ways.

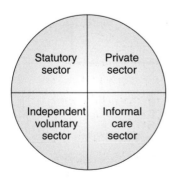

The mixed economy of care consists of four different but related sectors of care provision

Statutory sector social care and welfare organisations are largely funded by central government. The funding comes from the Treasury who collect it by imposing income tax on UK employees. As a result, a significant proportion of statutory social care services are free or are charged for on a means-tested basis. This means that service users pay some or all of a charge levied for the services they require

Figure 9.7 The mixed economy of welfare

depending on their income ('means') and ability to afford it. The structure of the national system of statutory social care provision is outlined in Figure 9.8 opposite.

As you will see, there is a distinction in the structure between the national policy-making and funding part of the structure which is provided by central government and the organisation and delivery of social care services locally by local authority social service departments. These came into being after the **Local Authority Social Services Act 1970** was passed to create an organisation that would deliver statutory social care and social work services within defined local areas. The role of local authority social services departments is discussed in more detail below.

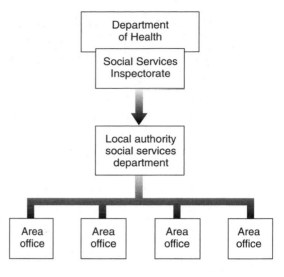

Figure 9.8 Statutory social care

Voluntary sector social care and welfare organisations obtain their funding from a variety of sources. The source that they are most often associated with is charitable giving or fund raising. This occurs when people or businesses donate money in order to support the cause, issue or service user group that the voluntary organisation works with. Increasingly, voluntary sector social care organisations receive money from government, private organisations (such as insurance companies) and fee paying individuals to provide social care or welfare services that are no longer available from state providers. This source of funding increased significantly in the 1990s when the 'internal market' policy of the Conservative governments required local authorities (as 'purchasers') to make 'contracts' with private and voluntary sector care 'provider' organisations.

The private social care and welfare sector consists of care businesses and private practitioners. These care 'providers' obtain their funding by charging fees for their services or, as we have just seen, through making contracts with government, other businesses or individuals. Supported housing and residential care for older people, people with learning disabilities and people with physical disabilities are areas of social care that are delivered largely by the private sector.

The role of local authorities

A local authority is a local government organisation that administers and provides various public services for a defined area. Local authorities are responsible for everything from managing and maintaining local roads to collecting the community charge and providing local library services. However, the area of their work that we are most interested in relates to their significant social care and welfare responsibilities. Local authorities are responsible for housing homeless people, protecting vulnerable children who are 'at risk' of abuse or neglect and for providing a statutory social work service. Most local authorities spend over 20 per cent of their annual budget on the services offered by their social services departments.

The current social care and welfare roles of local authorities, first came into existence in 1971. The Seebohm Committee (1968) proposed that a single 'social services department' should be created. This would involve merging the specialist children's, mental health and welfare departments that previously existed into a more generic personal social services department. The Local Authority Social Services Act 1970 created these social services departments and led to local authorities taking on a general social care responsibility whilst handing responsibility for primary health care back to the NHS.

Local authorities have historically had a broad range of social care and welfare responsibilities. These have included the provision of public sector (council) housing, responsibility for primary and secondary education and responsibility for the broad range of services to meet the non-medical, personal care and support needs of vulnerable people. The present social care and welfare role of local authorities is described in more detail below. However, it is important firstly to identify the relatively recent changes that have occurred in the social care and welfare role of local authorities in order to understand the current situation.

The changing role of local authorities

Local authorities are largely controlled by, and are required to respond to, the policy approach adopted by central government. During the 1990s the Conservative governments, and the New Labour governments that succeeded them, developed policies that significantly altered the social care role and structure of local authorities. The key policy change was the introduction of an 'internal market' in social care based on new purchaser–provider relationships. Local authority social services departments were effectively divided into 'purchaser' and 'provider' sections, and were required to 'purchase' a significant proportion of social care and welfare services from the private and voluntary sector 'provider' organisations. This is in contrast to the situation in the 1970s and up to the mid-1980s when local authorities were the main providers of social care services.

Figure 9.9 The purchaser/provider relationship

The NHS and Community Care Act 1990 introduced the 'internal market' changes that altered the role and structure of local authorities. As a result of the 1990 Act, local authority social services departments became the lead organisation for the provision of social care in a particular location. Instead of being the provider of the social care services that people required, their role changed to being the assessor of social needs and the purchaser of 'care packages' (largely from the private and voluntary sectors) for service users who met needs assessment and eligibility criteria. Whilst there was a significant shift in the social care provider role of local authorities during the 1990s, they still retain responsibility for social care service provision in areas that are seen as social (and political) priorities and which, typically, are sensitive.

Personal social care services for adults

Services for people over 18 who need help with essential everyday tasks are often referred to as 'community care'. People may need help for many different reasons. It may be, for example, because they are old and frail, or they have a disabling illness, or perhaps they are losing their sight or hearing or becoming less mobile than they were.

It may be because they were born with a disability, or are having problems as a result of an accident. It may be because they are suffering from a mental illness that makes it difficult to cope with everyday living. They may need help just for a short while, so that they can regain their independence, or they may need help for the rest of their lives. Local authority social services departments will assess a person's need for help in this area but do not usually provide the services required themselves. They will provide information and advice about the services that are available and an assessment of the help people might need.

Local authorities assess more people who have social care needs than they are able to arrange services for. They purchase, or in some cases directly provide, services only for people who have the greatest need. This usually means that the person has to be 'at risk' if they are not helped. Eligibility criteria are used to work this out.

Social care services for children

Local authorities have a long history of providing services to help and protect children. The Children Act 1989 is the key piece of legislation affecting the provision of services for children. Local authority social services departments generally provide day care and child protection services to meet their responsibilities under the Children Act 1989. As part of their responsibilities, social services departments must provide services that prevent children from becoming the victims of abuse or neglect. This includes compiling and maintaining an 'at risk' register. Local authority social care services are usually designed to help children remain with their families as far as possible and to offer assistance to families in difficulties or under pressure. Among the social care services typically provided by local authorities for children are:

Local authorities provide limited care for children under school age

- social work services; to offer advice and organise assistance
- child protection services
- residential care for children unable to live with their families
- a fostering service
- an adoption service
- family support services for children in need, including children with disabilities
- family centres.

Local authority social services departments also have a legal responsibility to assess and register private and voluntary child-care services. People who wish to work as childminders providing day care for children under 8 years for more than two hours a day must be registered with a local authority social services department.

Social care services for older people

Local authorities tend to offer a range of social care services for vulnerable older people. Usually, a local authority will employ social workers in a care management role to carry out needs assessments and purchase care packages for older people who need considerable help. Local authorities aim to provide social care services that enable service users to be as independent as possible and to remain living in their own homes.

To achieve this, social service departments provide services for the carers of older people, as well as for older people themselves. Where older people need more care than can be offered at home, a social service department will conduct a needs assessment and may purchase residential care for older people who require this. Older people who have limited savings can be assisted with the costs involved in moving into residential or nursing home care. Among the social care services typically provided by local authorities for older people are:

- advice and information services
- assessment by a care manager to identify individual needs and ways of meeting those needs
- assessments by specialist workers such as occupational therapists and sensory impairment workers
- assessment of carers' needs
- domiciliary care to support older people with personal and social care needs in their own homes
- community meals services
- day care in the form of day centres, lunch clubs, local day care groups, day care within a residential or nursing home setting
- laundry services
- respite care away from home, or within the home
- special equipment and adaptations to help maintain independent living
- special equipment for older people who are blind, partially sighted or are deaf or hard of hearing.

Many of these services are means-tested and may require a financial contribution from the service user. Local authorities tend to develop their own eligibility and means-testing rules.

Services for disabled people

Local authority social service departments provide a range of specialist personal care and support services for people with physical, sensory and learning disabilities. An individual assessment of needs is usually carried out by a care manager and other specialist care staff, such as occupational therapists, in partnership with the disabled person and their carers. The aim, again, is to identify ways in which the person can be helped and supported to live as independently as possible. The disabilities team in a social services department will typically provide a joint health and social care assessment service with NHS colleagues, care management, occupational therapy assessment, advice and daily living equipment, carer advice and support, including respite care services.

Services for mental health

Mental health provision is a major area of work for local authority social services departments. Specialist mental health teams tend to work in partnership with other agencies that provide mental health services, such as NHS Trusts, voluntary sector, user support and self-help organisations. Social services departments have a statutory responsibility to provide Mental Health Act assessment services and also provide a range of support and after-care services for people who use hospital or community-based mental health services. Frequently this involves working with housing agencies and health services as well as assessing the social needs of people of working age who have serious and enduring mental health problems. Where a person with mental health problems also has a carer, social services departments offer an assessment of need to the carer. Local authority mental health social workers aim to work in partnership with service users, encouraging their independence whilst finding the least intrusive way to offer help and provide effective support.

Carers

Carers (or 'informal carers') are those adults, children or young people who look after someone who is elderly, disabled or unwell in some way, providing them with a substantial amount of care on a regular basis. In the UK, the majority of people in receipt of care are cared for by an informal carer. The 1990 General Household Survey suggested that there were about 6.8 million carers in the UK.

> *It is estimated that Oxfordshire has 67,000 adult carers. It is difficult to provide an exact number as many do not perceive themselves as carers as such, but rather as family, friend or neighbour. It is also difficult to estimate the number of young carers. National statistics suggest the figure could be as high as 3% of children and young people. If this is the case there could be 2,000–3,000 young carers in Oxfordshire. Social Services is working with the county's three carers' centres, the Carers' Forum and the NHS to contact carers, in order to offer help and support.*
>
> Source: Oxfordshire County Council Social Services Department website

Services for carers

Most carers are not professionally trained and, in some cases, receive little support from professional care-workers or care organisations. However, local authority social services departments do have some legal responsibilities to provide carers with services.

The Carers (Recognition and Services) Act 1995 gave carers the right to an assessment of their own needs when the social care needs of the person they cared for were being assessed. This was a significant step forward as it acknowledged the burden of caring that fell onto many relatives and made support for informal carers a priority. However, despite providing a right to have their needs assessed, the Act did not

Care for older people includes day respite and residential care

provide carers with any subsequent rights to receive services themselves even if the assessment indicated that they needed them. Many social services departments see carers as being 'part of the solution' to an individual's care needs and assume that carers will offer considerable amounts of care informally when care packages are being planned. As a result of the 1995 Act, carers' needs must also be taken into account when these care packages are being planned. One of the strategies adopted by social services is to offer carers the use of **respite services**. This can involve the cared-for person going into a residential home on a planned, short-term basis to allow the carer to take a break. Alternatively, attendance at a day centre or 'sitting schemes', where someone replaces the carer temporarily in their own home, can be offered to give the carer breaks from caring during the day. The aim of these strategies is to relieve the caring burden from the carer at least temporarily so that they can undertake shopping or other essential tasks or enjoy some social and recreation time.

The most recent legislative development in this area is the **Carers and Disabled Children Act 2000**. The Act came into force in April 2001. It gives social workers the right to assess the needs of carers of adults even where the cared-for person refuses an assessment of their own particular needs or has rejected community care services for themselves. The Act also allows local authorities to provide certain support services direct to carers who have a parental responsibility for a disabled child. Local authorities have the power under this Act to make direct payments to carers who wish to purchase services to meet their own assessed needs and those of the disabled child and family.

In their work with carers, local authority social services departments generally aim to:

- work in partnership with people caring for those who need care and support
- reduce, as far as possible, the stresses and strains on carers and their families caused by caring for a person who is disabled, unwell or infirm
- offer sensitive and confidential services that take into account the needs and wishes of both carers and the people they provide care for
- provide services to relieve carers of the caring responsibility for some of the time.

Theory into practice

Further information on both the Carers and Disabled Children Act 2000 and government policy towards carers can be found on a website set up for the purpose of informing carers and the general public about carer issues. The website can be found at www.carers.gov.uk. Further information can also be obtained from carer support organisations in your local area or from national organisations such as the Carers National Association (www.carers.uk.demon.co.uk), Crossroads caring for carers (www.crossroads.org.uk) and the Princess Royal Trust for Carers (www.carers.org).

Assessment activity 9.2

Organised social care and welfare provision is a relatively recent development in the UK. In this activity, you are asked to outline the history of this area of care provision and to identify and evaluate the legislative and service development milestones that have led to the evolution of the current social care system.

1 Describe the government's role in creating social policy. You should analyse, using examples, how political perspectives influence the focus and outcomes of government social policy-making and welfare service provision.
2 Describe the major pieces of welfare legislation and the historical development of welfare in the UK since 1945. You should also critically evaluate the impact of the welfare state system on current care service provision.
3 Outline the current structure of social care provision by the state, voluntary and independent sectors.

Contemporary social care service issues

Social care services are provided, and develop, within a society that has social, political and economic dimensions and which is constantly changing. In modern society, there is an expectation that central government has a responsibility to identify the key social problems that are faced by the population. In particular, social policies, and the services that put them into practice, are expected to play a part in promoting positive, purposeful social change for vulnerable and marginalised groups in society whilst also providing immediate, practical help to support those most in need.

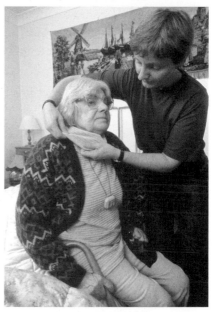

Central government policies currently prioritise a number of issues that will shape the structure, delivery methods and focus of social care services in the UK over the next decade. These include issues relating to provision of care in the community, the changing nature of the relationship between care professionals and service users and the goal of targeting social care services to meet the needs of those people who are most likely to benefit but are hardest to reach.

Care in the home can be delivered by a variety of providers

Care in the community

Community care (or care in the community) is a shorthand term that describes the mixture of help, support and care that allows people to go on living in their own home rather than having to move into residential care. In a wider sense, community care is an extension of the help that people in a local community – families, friends and neighbours – have traditionally given to those who need it. Care in the community has been a major policy goal for social service providers since it first appeared on the political agenda in the 1950s. Community care has its origins in the investigations into problems associated with mental hospitals during this period. The result of these inquiries was a proposal to develop a new community-based approach to the provision of long-term care that reduced dependency and avoided taking service users out of society. Community care has, to one degree or another, remained an important issue ever since.

Community care developed significantly from the mid-1970s onwards with the closure of many residential institutions and the re-provision of services in community settings. During the 1980s the pace of welfare reform increased and community care developed further. The 1990s saw another significant shift towards greater provision of care in the community as a result of the NHS **and Community Care Act 1990**. This formally required local authority social services departments to move away from providing institutional, residential care, and to adopt the role of enabling service users to access appropriate support services in their local communities.

The current aim of the community care policy is to provide help, support and care for older people, people with learning, physical and sensory disabilities, and, more controversially, people with mental health problems in their own homes. Today, community care is delivered by professional organisations as well as by informal carers. Local authority social services departments, NHS Trusts, voluntary organisations and privately run agencies are all involved in the delivery of community-based social care services.

The form that community care takes varies considerably throughout the country and according to service users' particular needs. Different people have differing needs. Some people cannot continue living at home without continuous specialist professional help, whereas other people find that some relatively minor additional help from professional services can enable them to continue living independently despite their disability, health problem or other difficulty. Local authority social services departments play an important part in helping people get the community care services they need. To facilitate this they can provide information and advice as well as needs assessments.

Community care has had a significant impact on the lives of social care service users, their carers and social services professionals since it was brought into practice. It has also had an impact on the attitudes of members of the general public towards the individuals and organisations they see living and working in their communities. Many social care service users have benefited from the shift to care in the community. Adults with learning disabilities, and some people with long-term mental health problems, have probably benefited most. People in these groups are now able to live less restricted, more normal lives than would have been the case if they had moved into long-term institutional care. However, community care services for frail older people and some people with mental health problems have been criticised for failing to provide enough help and support to meet the complex needs of these service users. As a result, the perceptions of some members of the general public, who have read or heard about the relatively rare incidents of neglect and harm that have occurred, is that community care involves poor-quality, uncoordinated and under-funded care service provision. The likelihood is that care in the community will remain the key strategy for the delivery of social care services for the foreseeable future. The professional and political issues associated with it will require policy-makers and social care practitioners to continue searching for the most effective ways of delivering services and developing relationships with service users in community contexts.

Assessment activity 9.3

Community care has aroused controversy since the policy was first introduced as a way of delivering forms of health and social welfare provision in the 1970s. In this activity you are asked to define what community care involves and to assess the implications and effectiveness of this approach to welfare provision.

1 Using examples, define what community care involves.
2 Outline the implications, both positive and negative, of delivering social care and welfare services using a community care approach. You should consider the implications of this from the perspective of service users, their families and service providers.
3 Evaluate the effectiveness of the community care policy as a method of delivering care for people who have a need for continuing care services. Again, you should consider both the positive effects and the negative outcomes that have occurred.

The emergence of care 'consumers'

There has been a significant shift in the nature of the relationship between care professionals and service users over the last fifteen years. The power and 'expert' status of professionals has gradually been challenged whilst the entitlements and 'consumer' rights of care service users have been asserted and strengthened in a variety of ways. Central government initiatives such as the Patient's Charter and legislation such as the Children Act 1989, the NHS and Community Care Act 1990 and the Carers and Disabled Children Act 2000, have fixed the principle of service user involvement and consultation in law. Additionally, care professionals and provider organisations have developed codes of practice, value bases and charters to restate and focus their care relationships. These acknowledge that the care system has moved away from a situation where professionals have the greatest power, to one in which they work collaboratively to establish partnerships with service users.

Social care service providers are now required to be more democratic and open to service users taking control of decision-making about their own care provision. In effect, service users have used initiatives such as advocacy services, self-help groups and the support provided by new legal rights to shift their role from that of passive recipients of care 'given' to them by expert, paternalistic professionals, to being active, involved and powerful 'consumers' of care services. Social care service providers, in the shape of organisations and individual practitioners, now need to find ways of acknowledging and working with the new 'consumer' orientation of many social care service users. Increasingly this involves providing service users with a budget (direct payments) to purchase care that meets their personal needs. Additionally, care organisations must ensure that appropriate advocacy and complaint systems are in place to enable service users to express their views and wishes in respect of service provision. The requirement to find ways of empowering social care service users within and through care relationships, and of respecting their developing 'consumer' orientation are issues that all professional practitioners and care organisations now need to focus on.

Theory into practice

Charters of rights, service user agreements and professional codes of practice have all had a significant impact on the relationship that care providers have with service users. Obtain information from local care organisations to identify your rights as a 'consumer' of their services.

The issue of marginalisation

Social care services have always been developed to meet the needs of the most vulnerable members of society. However, there is considerable evidence that some social groups fall through the 'safety net' provided by statutory services and become gradually less 'visible', more marginalised and harder for care organisations to reach. These groups include homeless people, the long-term unemployed, disabled people, members of many minority ethnic groups and people with enduring mental health problems. However, this is not a definitive list. Members of some of these social groups do receive social care services, whilst other people become 'lost' to the current care systems. Social policy initiatives have been developed by central government to address the problem of marginalisation. The current term given to the issue is 'social exclusion'. The characteristic that most 'socially excluded' people share is that they are poor. This has various consequences that lead to increased personal vulnerability and a need for social care services and support.

A key challenge facing social care service providers, particularly local authorities who provide statutory services, is finding ways of identifying 'marginalised' people in need of social care services. Targeting services so that they are accessible and are actually taken up by 'socially excluded' individuals is also an issue for care organisations who have tended to be unresponsive to non-traditional needs and unwilling to adapt to the requirements of marginalised groups. In essence, social care organisations and professional practitioners face the challenge of building new partnerships and finding new ways of working in order to address the needs of socially excluded communities.

Think It Over

Why do you think that some people become 'lost' to local social care services? Try to identify reasons why some socially excluded people may not wish to receive help and why others may not be able to obtain it despite wanting to.

The issue of abuse

Abuse against children and vulnerable adults can take the form of physical, emotional and sexual abuse and neglect. Local authority social services departments have a statutory responsibility to establish services that protect children and vulnerable adults from abuse and neglect. During the 1980s and 1990s a number of inquiries were held into widely reported cases of abuse within care establishments. Cases of individuals being abused within families are still a regular feature of newspaper and television reports. Given the increasing awareness of all forms of abuse, social care providers have to continually address the issue of how to develop systems for identifying and responding to incidents of abuse as well as finding ways of protecting those most at risk of experiencing abuse. All local authority social services departments have child protection teams and prioritise this area of work. Increasingly, new care standards for residential care for children, vulnerable adults and older people, include guidelines on prevention of abuse and require care providers to develop systems for reporting and responding to abuse allegations. The development of legislation and policy guidelines, the changing attitudes of the general public and the police and a more proactive approach to prevention have all made abuse a priority issue for social care professionals and provider organisations. There is no reason why the issue will assume a lower significance in the future.

Key issues

Protecting vulnerable adults from abuse

A policy document titled *No Secrets* was issued in 2000. It provides guidance on developing and implementing multi-agency policies and procedures to protect vulnerable adults from abuse. The aim of *No Secrets* is to ensure that key local agencies, particularly, but not only, health, social services and the police, are able to work together to protect vulnerable adults from abuse both at home and within residential settings.

Assessment activity 9.4

This assessment activity requires you to investigate aspects of the work of a local social care organisation. Ideally, this will be a local authority social services department or a voluntary organisation that provides social care services.

1 Describe and explain how a social care organisation tackles the problem and effects of social inequality and the abuse of vulnerable people within the local community.

2 Identify and evaluate the effectiveness of the strategies that are used by your chosen social care provider for challenging abuse and inequality.

3 Make reasoned recommendations to improve access to the services offered by your chosen social care provider organisation.

The issue of funding and privatisation of welfare services

The funding of social care and welfare services has always been a politically sensitive issue for central government. The government's social policy commitments require it to raise a large amount of money each year. Traditionally, this is achieved by imposing taxes on income.

Taxation

Income taxes tend to be unpopular with the general public. At the same time as not wanting to pay taxes, people tend to want high-quality, easily accessible, and ideally free, social care and welfare services. The challenge for governments is to ensure that the services people require are provided within the funding available. How can this be achieved?

Funding initiatives

The days of central governments paying for a fully funded welfare state through taxation appear to be over. At the beginning of the twenty-first century, central governments increasingly look to the private and voluntary sectors for new sources of welfare funding. Strategies such as the Private Finance Initiative (PFI) and Public-Private partnerships (PPP) have been introduced to increase the amount of private money being put into social welfare provision. This is likely to continue given the reluctance of political parties to increase taxation. It suggests that the private and voluntary sectors will have an important role to play in the future provision of welfare services.

Privatisation of social care provision

During the 1980s, 'privatisation' of care services became a major political issue. The Conservative governments of the time were very keen to reduce public spending on

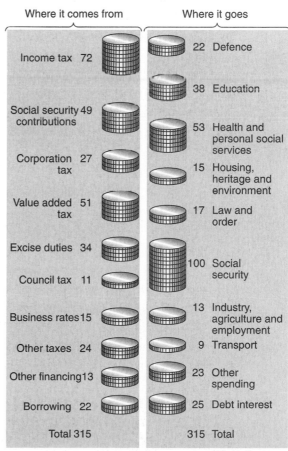

Where it comes from	
Income tax	72
Social security contributions	49
Corporation tax	27
Value added tax	51
Excise duties	34
Council tax	11
Business rates	15
Other taxes	24
Other financing	13
Borrowing	22
Total	315

Where it goes	
22	Defence
38	Education
53	Health and personal social services
15	Housing, heritage and environment
17	Law and order
100	Social security
13	Industry, agriculture and employment
9	Transport
23	Other spending
25	Debt interest
315	Total

Figure 9.10 UK Tax spending 1997–8

social care. They did so by increasing the private provision of some forms of care. In particular, provision of residential care for older people, people with learning disabilities and people with physical disabilities was largely taken over by private and voluntary sector providers.

Despite the apparent separation between public and private social care, a significant proportion of 'private' care is actually funded by the public sector. This includes long-term care for service user groups such as the elderly, those with learning disabilities and people with chronic mental illness. These are areas where voluntary or profit-making organisations have won contracts from the state to specialise in providing these services, and are able to compete on price and quality with the state sector.

Privatisation is an ideological as well as an economic issue. People who believe in a 'free market' tend to believe that the state provides low-quality services and has no incentive to prevent people requesting unnecessary services or to reduce dependency on state welfare. The issue of 'privatisation' of welfare remains a contentious one because of the conflicting political issues involved.

Assessment activity 9.5

Finding sufficient funding to meet the demand for social care and welfare services is a difficult and ongoing struggle for both governments and provider organisations. In this activity you are asked to explain how limited resources are prioritised in the social care system and to explore the concept of resource rationing.

1 Explain how financial and other non-monetary resources are prioritised and allocated in social care service provision generally.

2 Describe and explain why some service users groups and areas of social welfare practice (e.g child protection) receive priority when care organisations allocate financial budgets.

3 Explain what the term 'resource rationing' means and outline both the arguments for and against the rationing of social care and welfare provision.

End-of-unit Test

1 Identify three different kinds of social welfare provisions that are available in the UK.

2 In what ways are welfare services different from health care services? Describe the main distinctions between the two as you understand them.

3 Describe the impact of nineteenth century urbanisation and industrialism on the need for welfare services in the UK.

4 Identify the five 'giant evils' referred to in the Beveridge Report of 1942.

5 Describe the main effects that the Beveridge Report had on the provision of welfare services in Britain during the 1950s and 1960s.

6 Explain why the Conservative government of the 1980s objected to the growth of a 'welfare state' in the UK.

7 Describe the main ways in which the Conservative government of the 1980s sought to change Britain's welfare system.

8 Explain the term *ideology*, referring to two contrasting examples of political ideologies in your answer.

9 Identify two statutes that were passed with the aim of tackling poverty in the UK.

10 Explain the term *social exclusion* and identify three reasons why it occurs.

11 Describe the role that central government plays in the development and provision of welfare services in the UK

12 Using examples, explain the term 'mixed economy of care'.

13 Summarise the role that local authorities play in the provision of social care services.

14 Define the term 'informal carer' and describe the contribution that such people make to the provision of social care and welfare services.

15 Identify the main reasons why community care remains a controversial way of delivering social care and welfare services in the UK.

References and further reading

Braye, S. and Preston-Shoot, M. (1995) *Empowering Practice in Social Care,* Milton Keynes: Open University Press

Care Homes for Older People: National Minimum Standards, London: Stationery Office, 2002

Gottesman, M. *Residential Care: An International Reader,* London: Whiting & Birch ltd

Home life: A Code of Practice for Residential Care, London: Centre for Policy on Ageing, 1984

Nolan, Y. (2001) *S/NVQ Level 3: Care,* Oxford: Heinemann

This chapter covers a broad range of issues which relate to the promotion of health. It looks at the various perspectives on health, including the biomedical model and the social model, comparing these with your own understanding of health and other lay viewpoints. It explores the factors which underpin good health before moving on to consider differing types of health promotion activity including primary, secondary and tertiary prevention.

You will learn about the differing and complementary approaches to health promotion and the people and organisations who play a part in promoting health, before considering the ethical issues which face them. You will also consider the constraints on health promoters – whether financial, political or simply lack of knowledge.

You will explore the opportunities for health promotion around specific topics and target audiences and how the current national policy is supporting those types of initiative. You will consider the role of major organisations like the NHS and the role of the private sector and mass media in promoting health.

Finally you will consider more practical aspects of being a health campaigner or educator such as what targets you might focus your work around, how to select the appropriate leaflets and posters and how to plan, implement and evaluate an effective health promotion campaign.

What you need to learn
- Concepts of health and health promotion
- Ethical issues involved in health promotion
- Contemporary key themes
- Health promotion campaigns

Concepts of health and health promotion

Think It Over
What do you think about when you hear the phrase 'health promotion'?

Write down words, phrases, pictures it makes you think about.

Now try to write a couple of sentences, which will be your starting definition for health promotion. Keep this to hand, you will come back to it throughout this first section.

Models of health
Lay models of health
The term 'lay' refers to a non-professional viewpoint, that is, the models of health held by the public at large (as in the table below) as opposed to professionally or

scientifically phrased perspectives. To the public the term *healthy* is usually associated with not being ill, that is, a negative perspective which is best summarised as 'not knowing what you had till you lost it'. More positive perspectives might talk about building up your strength, being on good form or having resistance to infections; these areaspects of physical health which emphasise the need for strength and robustness for everyday life.

The body as a machine	Has strong links to the medical model of health, in that it sees illness as a matter of biological fact and scientific medicine as the natural type of treatment for any illness.
Inequality of access	As above, this perspective is rooted in a reliance on modern medicine to cure illness but is less accepting because of awareness that there are great inequalities of access to treatment.
The health promotion account	This model emphasises the importance of a healthy lifestyle and personal responsibility, e.g. if you are overweight, it is simply a matter of your own choice of diet and lack of exercise which has led to this.
God's power	Health is viewed as part of spirituality, i.e. a feature of righteous living and spiritual wholeness. This might be seen as abstinence from alcohol consumption because it is an impure substance which is unholy but also can lead to immoral activity.
Body under siege	The person exists in a sea of challenges to their health, be they communicable diseases such as colds and flu or stress at work, etc.
Cultural critique of medicine	Science and the medical model on which healthcare is based can oppress certain groups (that is, they can take away their rights to self-determination). The way health care manages pregnancy could be used as an example of oppressive practice against women, or the treatment of minority ethnic groups.
Robust individualism	Best summarised as 'It's my life and I will do with it what I choose'.
Will power	Suggests that we all have a moral responsibility to remain healthy. This relies on strong will power to manage our health e.g. to eat the right things, take regular exercise and drink moderately.

Therefore, people's notion of what being healthy means varies widely and is shaped by their experiences, knowledge, values and expectations as well as what others expect them to do.

Theory into practice

What does being healthy mean to you?

In Column 1, tick any statements which seem to you to be important aspects of your health.

In Column 2, tick the six statements which are to you the most important aspects of being healthy.

In Column 3, rank these six in order of importance – put '1' by the most important, '2' by the next most important and so on down to '6'.

For me, being healthy involves:	Column 1	Column 2	Column 3
1 Enjoying being with my family and friends	_____	_____	_____
2 Living to be a ripe old age	_____	_____	_____
3 Feeling happy most of the time	_____	_____	_____
4 Being able to run when I need to (e.g. for a bus) without getting out of breath	_____	_____	_____
5 Having a job	_____	_____	_____
6 Being able to get down to making decisions	_____	_____	_____
7 Hardly ever taking tablets or medicines	_____	_____	_____
8 Being the ideal weight for my height	_____	_____	_____
9 Taking part in lots of sport	_____	_____	_____
10 Feeling at peace with myself	_____	_____	_____
11 Never smoking	_____	_____	_____
12 Having clear skin, bright eyes and shiny hair	_____	_____	_____
13 Never suffering from anything more serious than a mild cold, flu or stomach upset	_____	_____	_____
14 Not getting things confused or out of proportion – assessing situations realistically	_____	_____	_____
15 Being able to adapt easily to changes in my life such as moving house, changing jobs or getting married	_____	_____	_____
16 Feeling glad to be alive	_____	_____	_____
17 Drinking moderate amounts of alcohol or none at all	_____	_____	_____
18 Enjoying my work without much stress or strain	_____	_____	_____
19 Having all the parts of my body in good working order	_____	_____	_____
20 Generally getting on well with other people	_____	_____	_____
21 Eating the 'right' foods	_____	_____	_____
22 Enjoying some form of relaxation/recreation	_____	_____	_____
23 Hardly ever going to the doctor	_____	_____	_____

Biomedical model

Probably the most widely known model of health is that which first developed in the early part of the nineteenth century and has come to dominate all others in the western world, i.e. the biomedical model. Its history lies in the developing understanding of how the various parts of the body might work together to ensure good health. This scientific view of health and body functioning is summarised by Jones (1994) as shown below:

The medical model of health

- Health is predominantly viewed as the absence of disease.
- Health services are geared towards the treating of the sick.
- A high value is placed on specialist medical services.
- Doctors and other qualified experts diagnose and sanction treatment.
- Main purpose of health services is curative – to get people back to work.
- Disease and illness is explained by biological science.
- It is based in the understanding of how diseases arise, emphasising risk factors.
- A high value is placed on scientific research methodology.
- Quantitative scientific evidence is generally given higher value than lay or qualitative evidence

Social model of health

Although the biomedical model has contributed greatly to increase in life expectancy it is public health measures, based on the social model of health, which have contributed most to the decline in mortality during the twentieth century.

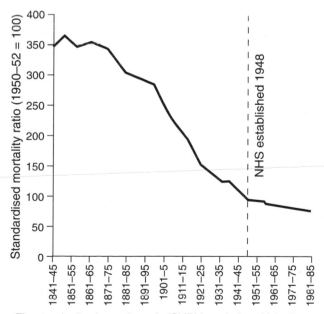

The standardised mortality ratio (SMR) is an index which allows for differences in age structure. Values above 100 indicate higher mortality than in 1950–52 and values below 100 indicate lower mortality.   (Source: OPCS)

Figure 10.1 Declining mortality rates during the twentieth century

Living conditions and environment can affect health

A social model of health emphasises that to improve health it is necessary to address the origins of ill-health. That means addressing social conditions which make ill-health more prevalent in some groups than others. Its underlying philosophy is that the health differences between individuals and social groups is the result of a complex mixture of behavioural, structural, material and cultural factors which together affect health. The social model has strong links to the lay models of health because it recognises that people often have firmly held views about their own health, which are sometimes at odds with those of professionals. For example, the need to address damp conditions in housing and its link to childhood asthma might be prioritised by people living in those conditions, as opposed to the need to tackle parental smoking as prioritised by health services.

Think It Over

- How has the environment in which we lived changed in the last 100 years to improve health?
- What types of social and environmental issues would you include as key factors influencing health expectation today?
- What three things would you suggest as changes which would greatly improve the health of your local population?

A holistic concept of health

One of the most widely known definitions of health is the 1948 World Health Organization (WHO) definition: 'A state of complete physical, mental and social well being'. However this illustrates the difficulty in attempting to define health when you consider two alternative definitions shown below and the range of broad dimensions to health:

- Physical health – concerned with body mechanics.
- Mental health – the ability to think clearly and coherently, strongly allied to emotional health.
- Emotional health – the ability to recognise emotions and express them appropriately. The ability to cope with potentially damaging aspects of emotional health, e.g. stress, depression, anxiety and tension.
- Social health – the ability to make and maintain relationships with others.
- Spiritual health – can be about personal creeds, principled behaviour, achieving peace of mind or religious beliefs and practices.
- Societal health – wider societal impact on our own individual health, e.g. the impact of racism on people from a minority ethnic culture; the impact on women of living in a patriarchal society; the impact of living under political oppression.

It is important to recognise that these are not alternative models of health but all different dimensions of health; together they build a holistic concept of health which embraces all the various aspect discussed previously

Key issue

Some definitions of health:

A satisfactory adjustment of the individual to the environment.
Royal College of General Practitioners, 1972

By health I mean the power to live a full adult, living, breathing life in close contact with what I love. I want to be all I am capable of becoming.
Katherine Mansfield

The extent to which an individual or group is able on the one hand, to realise aspirations and satisfy needs and on the other hand, to change or cope with the environment. Health is therefore seen as a resource for everyday life, not the objective of living: it is a positive concept emphasising social and personal resources as well as physical capabilities.
World Health Organization, 1984

Assessment activity 10.1

Consider the information given to you in Figure 10.1 and the bullet list above. Also think about the changing environmental impact on health over the last hundred years. What limitations does this suggest for the medical model of health? How does the social model offer a more favourable perspective?

Factors affecting health

Margaret Whitehead mapped the influences on health, shown in Figure 10.2, reflecting the range of influences which a social model of will recognise:

Figure 10.2 The Dahlgren/Whitehead model showing the underpinning influences of health inequalities

If we base our investigation of health promotion on this model of health, then it is necessary to consider the wide range of influences on health. These factors would include social class, gender, race, unemployment, age, disability and lifestyle.

Disability

Disability is the consequence of an impairment or other individual difference. The disability a person experiences is determined by the way in which other people respond to that difference. It can have serious social consequences, which in turn can harm that person's health. In the past, being left-handed was considered a disability and left-handed people were banned from certain jobs. Today we are more accepting of that difference, but this does not apply for all such differences; for example, people with a disability are three times more likely to be unemployed, with all the attendant health impacts described below.

Social class

Social class has long been used as the method of measuring and monitoring health inequalities. Since the Black Report of 1980, it has been clearly identified and acknowledged that those from the lowest social groupings experience the poorest health in society.

I	Social class grouping	Example
II	Professional	Doctors, engineers
III	Managerial/technical	Managers, teachers
IIIN	Non-manual skilled	Clerks, cashiers
IIIM	Non-manual unskilled	Carpenters, van drivers
IV	Partly skilled	Warehouse workers, security guards
V	Unskilled	Labourers

Traditionally social groups within society have been broken down into the six groups shown above, however, it has been accepted more recently that these groupings are no longer representative of the population. Therefore for the 2001 census the National Statistics Office reclassified the population into eight layers as shown below.

The National Statistics Socio-economic Classification

1   Higher managerial and professional occupations
    1.1 **Large employers and higher managerial occupations**
         e.g. chief executives of major organisations
    1.2 **Higher professional occupations**
         doctors, lawyers

2   **Lower managerial and professional occupations**
    middle management in bigger organisations, departmental managers,
    e.g. physiotherapy or customer services, teachers, etc.

3   **Intermediate occupations**
    clerks and bank workers, etc.

4   **Small employers and own account workers**
    painter and decorator or small manufacturing company owner, etc.

5   **Lower supervisory and technical occupations**
    builders, joiners, etc.

6   **Semi-routine occupations**
    unskilled labouring jobs

7   **Routine occupations,**
    assembly line workers, etc.

8   Never worked and long-term unemployed

However we choose to classify the different social strata, most recent research suggests that it is the countries with the smallest income *differences* rather than the highest average income, which have the best health status. Where income difference is large, such as in this country, the following inequalities can be seen:

- Children in the lowest social class are five times more likely to die from an accident than those in the top social class.
- Someone in social class 5 is three times more likely to experience a stroke than someone in class 1.
- Infant mortality rates are highest amongst the lowest social groups.

Age

As one might expect, as people get older they are more likely to experience a wide range of illnesses. The health inequalities recorded above remain in the older generations but are often compounded by the loss of income that comes with retirement. This significantly increases the proportion of the population who are living on benefits as compared to other age groups in the population. Another factor is the longer lifespan of women, which means that because women make up a higher proportion of the older population there are often higher rates of illnesses specifically associated with women.

Gender

Men and women have widely differing patterns of ill-health. In the main this can be best summarised by saying that men suffer a higher rate of early mortality (deaths) whilst women experience higher rates of morbidity (illness). There are many specific examples which illustrate these points, and they are linked to physiological, psychological and other aspects of gender characteristics influenced by the differing roles that the two genders are expected to adopt by society. Typically men are less likely to access routine screening and other forms of health service, whilst women who are viewed as the carer in the family are more able to do so and therefore may be identifying potential health problems earlier. The result of these differences may be seen as:

- under the age of 65, men are 3.5 times more likely to die of coronary heart disease
- suicide is twice as common in men as in women
- women experience more accidents in the home or garden whilst men experience more accidents in the workplace or sports activities.

Race

Black and minority ethnic groups have higher risks of mortality from a range of diseases such as diabetes, liver cancer, tuberculosis, stroke and heart disease. Infant mortality and mental illness have also been highlighted as problems amongst **Afro-Caribbean** men. However, establishing the cause of these variations has proved difficult. Medical interventions have tended to concentrate on cultural practices but this does not acknowledge the compounding factors of poverty and low employment levels in these groups. However, racism must play a part in the experiences of minority ethnic communities in contact with health services and as a causative factor in leading to a higher than average experience of poverty and unemployment in these groups.

Attitudes

Revisit the lay definitions of health on page 349. It is possible to see how people's differing attitudes to health will influence their behaviour. A person who believes in the robust individualism model might well choose to smoke and take regular exercise, because these are both satisfying and that individual believes in their right to choose. This however would be a difficult position for someone who subscribes to the health promotion account or the will power model, both of which emphasise personal responsibility to maintain health. In this situation that person's decision would appear to be contradictory. Therefore our own attitudes to health are essential to the behaviours we adopt.

Lifestyle

It is a common assumption that lifestyle choices are simply a product of our attitudes to health; as a consequence, people routinely make judgements about the behaviours of others. 'That woman shouldn't be smoking when she is pregnant' or 'that person who is overweight should go on a diet or take more exercise' might be typical examples of what is termed 'victim blaming', in other words our lifestyle is a choice we all make. But there is now considerable evidence that choice is quite limited in many cases. For example, the vast majority of people who smoke are first recruited at a very young age before they are mature enough to make an 'adult choice'. The complex nature of the environment and its impact on health choices is also important. For example, choosing healthy nutritious food is as much a feature of availability in the shop and access to the shops which provide it, as it is of personal choice. Therefore it is unfair to make simple assumptions about people's health behaviours.

Unemployment

For a small minority unemployment actually leads to an improvement in health, but for the vast majority being unemployed leads to significantly poorer health. The unemployed have higher levels of depression, suicide and self-harm and a significantly increased risk of morbidity and mortality from any cause. Unemployed men at both census dates in 1971 and 1981 had mortality rates twice that of the rest of other men in that age range and those men who were unemployed at one census date had a mortality rate of 27 per cent above the national level.

Assessment activity 10.2

Look at the Dahlgren/Whitehead grid for mapping health inequalities on page 353. Using the examples below, try to plot the issues which might affect the health of the two case studies given below.

First consider all the factors which impact on your own health, starting at the centre with the issues that you can least influence and working outwards to think about issues like the work environment, local neighbourhood, etc. before going on to think about more national issues like our long working hours, high car dependency, etc. Then you can begin to explore the case studies of people who might figure in socially excluded groups.

- a teenage single parent excluded from school, living alone in a council flat, with little or no support from her parents or

- a gay man, living with his partner, who is 'out' to close friends but not to work colleagues.

Components of health promotion

Prevention is a term generally used to refer to action taken to prevent ill-health before it starts. However it is more accurately used to refer to a broader range of actions covering three levels:

Primary prevention

This is an attempt to eliminate the possibility of getting a disease, e.g. the childhood immunisation programme would be an example of a health protection activity under this heading. Other examples here would include smoking education as part of personal and social health education (PSHE) in schools or leaflets and posters for use in promoting healthy eating.

Secondary prevention

This addresses those people identified as being in the early stages of a disease, usually through early detection of symptoms. Action here focuses on addressing the underlying causes in order to alleviate any further symptoms. An example here might be action to address raised blood pressure taken by a doctor who identified those symptoms as part of a routine check up for a patient. This might be drug therapy but equally could be a referral to a physical activity scheme for promoting regular exercise run as a collaboration with the local leisure services departments (usually referred to as an **exercise on prescription scheme**). This sort of scheme might also be used for people who are overweight and people with mild depression, so a range of secondary prevention issues are addressed through one scheme.

Tertiary prevention

This refers to the control and reduction (as far as possible) of an already established disease. This is not easily distinguishable from medical care but it is possible to consider issues such as increasing the capacity of the individual to manage their condition and their own health. This might refer to supporting and enabling people with a history of heart attacks to regain their confidence to live a more fulfilling life as far as possible. It could also apply to some one suffering from Parkinson's disease being supported in learning about and managing their condition as independently as possible.

Approaches to health promotion

The term health promotion covers a wide range of different activities, all of which have a part to play in promoting health. None of these differing approaches is essentially the right way, they are simply different aspects which complement each other. The balance between them is very much a choice based on personal perspective, influenced by our own life experience, personal standpoints and values, as illustrated in the wide range of differing lay perspectives on health. Ewles and Simnett characterise these differing approaches into five broad headings which are summarised in Figure 10.3:

Approach	Aim	Example – smoking
Medical	Freedom from medically defined disease and disability.	*Aim* – freedom from lung disease, heart disease and other smoking-related disorders. *Activity* – encourage people to seek early detection and treatment of smoking-related disorders.
Behaviour change	Individual behaviour conducive to freedom from disease.	*Aim* – behaviour changes from smoking to not smoking. *Activity* – persuasive education to prevent people starting and persuade smokers to stop.
Educational	Individuals with knowledge and understanding enabling well-informed decisions to be made and acted upon.	*Aim* – clients will have understanding of the effects of smoking on health, resulting in a decision whether or not to smoke, which they then act on. *Activity* – giving information to service users about the effects of smoking. Helping them to learn how to stop smoking if they want to.
Service user-centred	Working with clients on the service users' own terms.	Anti-smoking issue is considered only if service users identify it as a concern. Service users identify what, if anything, they want to know and do about it.
Societal change	Physical and social environment which enables choice of healthier lifestyle.	*Aim* – make smoking socially unacceptable, so it is easier not to smoke than to smoke. *Activity* – no smoking policy in all public places. Cigarette sales less accessible, especially to children, promotion of non-smoking as social norm. Banning tobacco advertising and sports' sponsorship.

Figure 10.3 Five approaches to health promotion

Assessment activity 10.3

Evaluate the following examples of health education approaches to smoking. Try to identify what model of health promotion it is based on and the level of health promotion it illustrates:

- a community support worker discussing an action plan for stopping smoking with a service user

- a teacher showing a group of children a set of diseased lungs in a jar
- a youth worker working with a group of young people to develop their decision making skills
- a community worker working with a group of single parents on an estate who have expressed a desire to stop smoking, to create their own support group
- a doctor prescribing nicotine replacement therapy for a smoker who has been told they have to give up by their consultant
- a national television campaign to encourage smokers to quit smoking with 'Quitline', which offers support on how to quit
- a person working with a quit smoking group for people who have suffered a heart attack.

Health promoters and their role

If you review the Dahlgren/Whitehead model of the determinants of health on page 353, it is possible to see how the promotion of health is multi-layered. It starts with the individual and their health and lifestyle choices, and moves on through local issues and organisations to broader influences at both national and international level.

International

Organisations operating at this level would include a range of charities such as Christian Aid, Oxfam, and Save the Children; as well as pressure groups such as Greenpeace and key statutory organisations like the United Nations, European Commission, World Health Organization (WHO) and UNICEF. The WHO in particular has been instrumental in shaping and influencing health policy across many nations through its 'Health For All by the Year 2000' programme. This has been crucial to a move away from medically dominated models of health promotion to a broader based approach, encompassing social and environmental influences.

National

The greatest potential for improving the health of the population lies at the national level with government. Simply put, the single most effective action at any level to address the level of health inequality is to raise benefit levels. As the first health strategy 'The Health of the Nation' identified, to raise health status required a cross-government commitment from all departments. This is again recognised in the subsequent documents like the Aicheson Report on tackling health inequalities and 'Our Healthier Nation', both of which identify key roles for a range of government departments including:

- Department of Health
- Department of Social Security
- Department for Education and Skills
- Home Office
- Department of Environment, Food and Rural Affairs.

Think It Over

Investigate the role these departments can play in promoting health. You can do this by visiting the website for the government health strategy 'Our Healthier Nation':

www.ohn.gov.uk/govwide/govwide

From here you will find links to the roles individual departments can play in the health strategy.

What examples can you find for:

- the Home Office
- Trade and Industry
- Education and Skills?

You can find examples of key targets and activities for national government contribution to improving health on pages 361–2 where it deals with the NHS plan, Health Improvement Programmes and the contribution of national policies across government.

However, the government is not the only national organisation which contributes to the promotion of health. There are many other national level organisations which have a part to play in promoting better health. Some examples are shown in Figure 10.4 below.

Organisation type	Examples
Voluntary organisations – these organisations produce educational materials such as those on sexual health issues from the FPA or safety from RoSPA. They have become acknowledged as being authoritative on their subject and may be the sole supplier of literature in that field. Also campaign on specific issues, e.g. MIND campaigning for improved mental health services.	Family Planning Association (FPA) Royal Society for the Prevention of Accidents (RoSPA) National Childbirth Trust (NCT) National Association of Mental Health (MIND)
Professional organisations – set professional standards and codes of conduct, can strike off professionals who are proved to have breached them and therefore stop them practising. Nurses cannot be employed without a current registration with the UKCC, therefore it is an effective mechanism for managing the quality of their profession.	British Medical Association (BMA) United Kingdom Central Council for Nursing, Midwifery and Health Visitors (UKCC) Institution of Environmental Health Officers (IEHO)
Trade unions - advocate and negotiate for their members on issues such as pay and working conditions. They can also co-ordinate activity to campaign for changes to these, e.g. through strike action or 'working to rule'. For example the teaching unions have had several periods when they have	Public sector workers (UNISON) Teachers (NUT, AMMA, NASUWT) Miners (NUM)

either withdrawn support for out-of-hours activities or resorted to strike action in response to government activity which affected their working conditions.

Commercial and industrial organisations – see page 375 for more detailed discussion, but there are roles for large private agencies here, e.g. in delivering an efficient and effective rail network which can reduce road traffic and hence pollution levels.

National Rivers Authority (NRA)

Railtrack

Figure 10.4 National agencies which can contribute to health promotion

Local

Whilst national government policy will remain the most effective tool for enabling health to be promoted, it is at the local level that national policy is translated into practice. This relies on a range of local agencies working together effectively on health issues with a common purpose. Examples of local partner agencies and their potential roles are set out in Figure 10.5.

Agency	Role
Primary Care Trust	Have three key responsibilities: • improve the health of their local population • develop local primary health care services • commission other local health services in line with local health needs.
Local Authority	• The provision of good quality affordable housing. • Tackling crime and issues of community safety through careful planning and design of estates. • The provision of leisure activities for all age groups. • The provision of safe areas for children to play. • Providing affordable nursery and crèche facilities to support working parents. • Tackling poverty through welfare rights advice and benefits take-up campaigns. • Tackling environmental issues of refuse, noise and dog-fouling. • Attracting inward investment into an area. • Provision of sound, high-quality education.
Police	Increasingly the police are active partners in many local initiatives, either through direct interventions such as those around drugs issues, or working through partnerships such as Community Safety, where the issues of crime and disorder can be addressed across organisational boundaries, e.g. working with the youth and community service to address youth-related problems. This might mean co-ordinating the activities of these two services to address adult perceptions of neighbourhood nuisance involving young people.

Council for Voluntary Services	An umbrella organisation for a wide variety of local voluntary sector organisations. The organisations they represent will vary from one area to another but usually have a high proportion of support groups for people with specific illnesses or disabilities. They offer a gateway for statutory organisations to communicate with many voluntary sector groups and carers.

Figure 10.5 Local partners

Informal networks

Finally we must acknowledge the part that informal networks of families, friends and neighbours play in influencing our health decisions, beliefs and environments. It is now widely acknowledged that the vast majority of medical consultations are from lay members of the community. This is the consultation we have with other family members about how best to deal with our cold or flu, or the old lady on the landing above, who knows a great deal about homeopathic remedies for backache. Lay knowledge is increasingly seen as an essential tool for screening out minor illness and ailments from the healthcare system.

Ethical issues involved in health promotion

If you consider the wide variety of lay perspectives on health and the various models of health promotion, it is easy to see how confusing it can be to try and define what is ethical and what is not in terms of health promotion activity.

Ethical decision-making in health promotion

The danger with health promotion activity is that health promoters may become fixed on the goal of improved medical or physical health to the detriment of other aspects of holistic health. It is all too easy for professionals to adopt a judgemental approach, deciding what is best for the individual to the exclusion of that person's right to autonomy. It is important to remember that empowering people is an integral part of effective and ethical health promotion work. To enable health promoters to make ethical judgements about the work they undertake, the following questions should be considered:

- Will they be able to choose freely for themselves?
- Will I be respecting their decision, whether or not I approve of it?
- Will I be non-discriminatory – respecting all people equally?
- Will I be serving the more basic needs before addressing other wants?
- Will I be doing good and preventing harm?
- Will I be telling the truth?
- Will I be minimising harm in the long term?
- Will I be able to honour promises and agreements I make?

These points are as equally applicable to a one-to-one service user/professional scenario, or to a planner considering alterations to local roads in a housing estate. The most challenging question is who to consult. It is impossible to consult a 'community' because no one person or group can accurately reflect the views of the entire community. So, in this case the planner would have to consider a range of approaches including postal surveys, consulting key people who work in the area, key people from the local community and any local community groups. Taken together these views might give a more accurate assessment of the situation.

If working ethically is challenging for this planner, imagine how difficult it can be for people working one-to-one with service users who are possibly vulnerable or viewed as being 'at risk'. Here they must strike a balance between protecting their vulnerable service user and yet trying to respect that person's autonomy and right to make their own health choices. In some cases this may be relatively simple to address, e.g. a care-worker may engage a service user in discussion about the benefits of stopping smoking and if the service user expresses a preference to continue to smoke then they can respect that choice and have ethically addressed the smoking issue with their service user. But some situations are less easy to assess. Consider these two examples:

- A social worker supporting a young woman who has been abused within the home environment and smokes, possibly as a result of the trauma she has experienced. Is the social worker promoting the service user's health if they challenge their smoking in some way?
- A learning disability support worker who learns that one of their service users is having a sexual relationship with another service user in their sheltered accommodation. Should the worker intervene and express concern?

In both cases the ethical principles still apply but the right thing to do is not as easily identified. In some cases it may require the care-worker to intervene for the greater good of the service user, e.g. in the second example, it would be up to the care-worker to assess whether the service user was competent to choose to have a sexual relationship or whether they were being coerced by their partner.

Any organisation with caring responsibilities will have clear policies which deal with confidentiality, and when and how it is appropriate to breach the service user's confidentiality in their own interests. Staff require clear procedures backed up with supervision and training to enable them to operate ethically, protecting the service user but providing for their self autonomy as well.

Case Study

Lucy is 14 and currently living with her parents. She had previously been thrown out of the house briefly when they found out she had been using cannabis. Your concerns as her social worker are that Lucy is quite immature and easily influenced by others, which in the past has led to her being in trouble with the police and has often caused conflict within the family, sometimes leading to outbursts of violent behaviour from her father. Lucy has just told you that she is having sex with her current boyfriend, who is 15, and has asked you for advice about contraception methods and how to obtain them.

- What advice would you give Lucy about her relationship with her boyfriend?
- What advice would you give her about contraception and how would you help her access it?
- Under what circumstances (if at all) would you tell her parents?
- If you tell them, what position does that put you in and how will it affect your relationship with Lucy?
- How would you explain to Lucy your decision to tell her parents?

Constraints on health promoters
Financial

Whilst much local health promotion activity may be viewed as being relatively cheap in relation to the illness it seeks to prevent, it is also hard to measure the precise outcome of the work. Therefore the investment of two or three hours time by a practice nurse to help someone quit smoking is considerably less expensive than the cost of extensive treatment for lung cancer. However it is impossible to state categorically that the nurse's time led to that individual quitting. Many other factors might have influenced the outcome; it is not an *attributable* outcome.

Health promotion historically has had to compete against clinical treatments for funding where it is easier to attribute the outcome to the investment (the person receives their treatment and gets better), and in many cases the issues are significantly more emotive to deal with.

Assessment activity 10.4

Promoting physical activity is probably one of the best health promotion investments there is. If a person becomes more active it has great potential benefit on their physical, mental and social health.

Now imagine that you are trying to convince your local primary care trust to invest in a 'Chairobics' scheme for older people cared for in local care homes. The scheme will train care-workers to run gentle exercise sessions with their service users to maintain strength, stamina and suppleness. However, there are also competing bids for additional emergency crisis beds in those homes to deal with pressures caused by influenza outbreaks, etc.

- Start by finding out how being active can improve your health. This is the information you would need to enable you to market this approach.
- What model of health is it likely that the decision-makers will be working to?
- How will this present problems for you in selling your proposal against the emergency beds?
- What problems might you have in identifying future success of your scheme compared to the success of the emergency beds?

Political

As one government leaves office and another arrives, wholesale change may alter the landscape of health promoting activity. For example, the concentration on individual responsibility in the Conservative government's *Health of the Nation* White Paper is in stark contrast to the Labour government's 'Our Healthier Nation' health strategy of 1997. This emphasised that health improvement relies on a contract where both individual and government play their part in the process, the individual taking responsibility for maintaining their own health and

Prime minister Tony Blair making an acceptance speech

government providing a supportive environment, e.g. through job creation or environmental action.

Think It Over

- Name three things which might influence health which might be changed as a result of a change in government.
- When politicians talk about health they are usually focusing on one aspect. What aspect is this and what model of health does it reflect?
- Why do you think politicians continue to talk about health in this simplistic way instead of in a broader holistic fashion ?

The Black Report (1980) illustrated the widening health gap between rich and poor in the country. However, it was suppressed by the Conservative government, and the word 'inequalities' was largely replaced by the less emotive term 'variations' because of their sensitivity to that word. Government action in other areas led to compounding inequalities, e.g. the introduction of Clause 28 forbade schools from 'promoting homosexuality' creating a climate where schools felt unable to address issues of sexuality. The Conservative government of the time ensured that the initial HIV awareness campaign of the 1980s avoided any reference to risk-taking behaviours, which were deemed too sensitive for the public and ran with a theme of 'AIDS – don't die of ignorance'. This left many people asking – what is this ignorance, and how do you catch it?

Knowledge

As the knowledge base for health promotion develops, health messages change, leading to confusion within the general population. Good examples here are the change in physical activity recommendations for promoting heart health. This has changed from 30 minutes of vigorous activity three times a week, to building 30 minutes of moderate activity five times a week. It is not unusual when asking people what they understand the current message to be, to receive either of these recommendations or a mixture of the two. This can place considerable demands on health promoters to remain up to date and can leave them in the same state of confusion as the rest of the population.

Acquiring new evidence to create health promotion campaigns can be difficult. Health promotion is often excluded from scientific research networks because its approach runs counter to the prevailing scientifically based research culture. Health promotion outcomes are less easy to measure. Health promotion research is often carried out in naturalised settings and frequently generates qualitative data, which is not valued as highly as quantitative findings.

Service user groups

Every service user group brings with it their own ethical considerations, be it an individual or a whole population approach:

Smoking cessation advice for a service user

Working with lifestyle change is fraught with ethical concerns. Two of the most important issues here would be the service user's right to self-determination and the need to remain non-judgemental. For example, the role of a social worker in discussing smoking with a pregnant woman, where the social worker has considerable knowledge about the potential damage to the unborn child and the possibility of further health damage if the mother continues to smoke after the birth. However, to be an ethical health promoter they must respect the service user's right to choose whether to continue smoking and not allow the service user's decision to continue smoking (if that is the case) to change the relationship.

Should a care-worker tell this mother not to smoke or drink?

Think It Over

A social worker has gone to visit a woman who is pregnant. She is a smoker and has not given up smoking for her pregnancy.

- What three pieces of information might a social worker most want to convey to the mother in the picture above?
- What things will they have to be mindful of when having this discussion?
- Are there any specific issues which might present problems for them in doing this in the mother's own home?
- Why is it appropriate for them to have this discussion with the mother?

Helping people with learning disabilities with community living

People with learning difficulties usually have difficulties understanding, learning and remembering new things, and in applying that learning to new situations. Because of these difficulties, the person may have difficulties with a range of social tasks, for example communication, self-care or awareness of health and safety. If we consider the health promoting principle of supporting autonomy and empowering people, it is possible to see the challenge this presents for supporting community living for people with learning difficulties. The approach most favoured when supporting people with their community living is termed 'person centred'.

Being 'person centred' or using a 'person-centred approach' means ensuring that everything is based upon what is important to that person, from their own perspective. It requires a fundamental shift of thinking from a 'power over' relationship to a 'power with' relationship. The five key features of people-centred planning are illustrated in Figure 10.6 on page 367.

Children learning about healthy eating

With the government's recent initiative to ensure every child of primary school age is offered a piece of fruit each day, the issue of healthy eating is at the forefront of school health promotion work. However there are many other attendant issues for consideration when addressing healthy eating in a personal social and health education lesson:

- Does the school have a nutrition policy to manage all aspects of nutrition on its premises?
- Does the school have a tuck shop or vending machines, and if so are healthy choices available through them?

Family members and friends are full partners – person-centred planning puts people in context of their family and communities. The contribution that friends and families can make are recognised and valued and gives a forum for creatively negotiating conflicts about what is safe, possible or desirable to improve a person's life.

Reflects a person's capacities, what is important to a person – (now and for the future) and specifies the support they require to make a valued contribution to their community. Services are delivered in the context of the life a person chooses and not about slotting people into 'gaps'.

The person is at the centre – person-centred planning is rooted in the principles of rights, independence and choice. It requires careful listening to the person and results in informed choice about how a person wants to live and what supports best suit the individual.

Builds a shared commitment to action that recognises a person's rights – it is an ongoing process of working together to make changes that the person and those close to them agree will improve a person's quality of life.

Leads to continual listening, learning and action and helps the person get what they want out of life – learning from planning can not only inform individuals but can affect service delivery as a whole and inform and inspire others to achieve greater things.

Figure 10.6 The five key features of person-centred planning

- If it generates essential income, what would be the likely impact of closing it to restrict sales of sweets and sugary drinks?
- Does the school canteen offer a range of options with interesting healthy options as part of that menu?
- When discussing healthy eating with children are parents involved at all?
- Does the school have a policy on snacks which children can bring to school? Some schools ban crisps, chocolate and sugary drinks.

A key issue to introducing any policy is ownership. It is relatively easy to write or copy a policy from someone else, but the people who it affects do not 'own' it, that is they have no sense of it applying to them. Therefore, policy development of the type identified above often takes time to allow these people to be consulted and involved as much as possible along the way. This would allow a school time to identify to parents not only why they had decided to adopt a nutrition policy but also time to identify what the likely implications are for them as a parent of a child in that school. This reduces the likelihood of someone breaking the policy when it is introduced because everyone understands why and how it will operate.

Screening

Screening was defined by the American Commission on Chronic Illness in 1957 as:

...the presumptive identification of unrecognised disease or defect by the application of tests, examinations and other procedures which can be applied rapidly. Screening tests sort out apparently well persons who may have a disease from those who do not.

Screening a well population is a contentious issue, with many attendant problems; for example, are we right to be medicalising a well population in this way? For health promoters there is considerable responsibility to consider what is an ethical position for discussion of screening programmes, such as those for:

- breast screening
- cervical screening
- HIV screening of pregnant women.

These screening programmes raise many questions, not least of which is the service user's right to choose. In some cases, such as HIV screening of pregnant women, this is done without the women's consent as a part of a wider population screening programme to monitor HIV patterns. In the case of breast screening, women below the age of 50 are not deemed to be at risk and are excluded from the programme.

Screening for some conditions remains an imprecise science. Recent media coverage of cervical cancer screening problems emphasises the difficulty of ensuring that all the people who take cervical smears are adequately trained and that the laboratory screening process itself has limitations and will inevitably miss some positive smears. The international debate for breast cancer is just as contentious with a debate raging about the effectiveness of the screening programme. Some Scandinavian countries consider it to have little or no impact on survival rates for breast cancer.

Think It Over

One of the most contentious screening programmes is that for breast cancer. There is conflicting evidence as to the effectiveness of the programme. If you were a nurse and someone asked you whether they should attend for breast screening, what would you tell them if you had the following background information available to you?

Background information for breast screening

- Every year your chances of dying from breast cancer are 1 in 2400, after screening they may be about 1 in 2900 (Rodgers, 1990).
- Breast cancer screening offers the possibility of less radical treatment for breast cancer (Austoker, 1990).
- Treatment of breast cancer may include lumpectomy, mastectomy, radiotherapy, chemotherapy, hormone treatment.
- The woman's breast will need to be compressed to 4.5 cm (Forrest, 1990).
- 14,000 women will need to be screened to save one life (Rodgers, 1990).
- 142,000 women will be recalled with some false-positives and some over-diagnosis (Rodgers, 1990).
- For every seven women found to have breast cancer, six will not live any longer as a result of early diagnosis (Rodgers, 1990).
- Some breast cancers will be missed at mammography (Rodgers, 1990; Skrabanek, 1989; Woods, 1991).
- Some cancers will develop in the three-year interval (Forrest, 1990).
- The cost of saving one life from screening is £80,000 (Rees, 1986).
- *Individual* benefit cannot be guaranteed (Skrabanek, 1989).

Contemporary key themes

The recent emphasis on improving health in national policy has meant a need for local health promoters to ensure that their work addresses these targets and themes. As we have already seen, health promotion activity can struggle to identify funding unless it shapes its work along these major policy themes.

NHS policy linked to key targets

The Health of the Nation was this country's first-ever health strategy (as opposed to health services). It was published in 1992 with a stated aim of ensuring that 'action is taken whether through the NHS or otherwise, to improve and protect health'. It initiated action at three levels:

- the Department of Health was given the lead role
- it commented on the contribution the state and the individuals could make to improving the nation's health
- it set a range of national health targets.

'Saving Lives – Our Healthier Nation'

This was the follow-up health strategy released by the Labour government as it came to power in 1997. *Our Healthier Nation* proposed to tackle the root causes of ill-health – including air pollution, unemployment, low wages, crime and disorder and poor housing. It focused on prevention of the main killers: cancer, coronary heart disease and stroke, accidents and mental illness and included a wide range of service providers including local councils, the NHS, and local voluntary bodies and businesses.

Main targets from *Our Healthier Nation* are:	
Cancer	To reduce the death rate in under-75s by at least 20%.
Coronary heart disease and stroke	To reduce the death rate in under-75s by at least 40%.
Accidents	To reduce the death rate by at least 20% and serious injury by at least 10%.
Mental illness	To reduce the death rate from suicide and undetermined injury by at least 20%.

The NHS plan (2000)

The NHS plan was the Labour government's policy paper, which outlined their intentions in modernising the NHS. It aimed to tackle the health inequalities that divide the UK and set national targets for tackling health inequalities with the relevant supporting investment such as:

- A £500 million expansion of the 'Sure Start' projects.
- A new Children's Fund worth £450 million over three years for supporting services for children in the 5-13 age bracket which will improve educational achievement, reduce crime and improve attendance at schools, etc.
- A more effective welfare foods programme with increased support for breast-feeding.
- A 15 per cent cut in teenage conception.

- The number of smokers to be cut by at least 15 million by 2010.
- Every child in nursery and aged 4-6 in infant school to be entitled to a free piece of fruit each school day.

In 2001 the government added targets for addressing the inequalities in health which had been further documented in the Aicheson Report of 1998. These targets were:

- Starting with children under one year, by 2010 to reduce by at least 10 per cent the gap in mortality between manual groups and the population as a whole.
- Starting with health authorities, by 2010 to reduce by at least 10 per cent the gap between the fifth of areas with the lowest life expectancy at birth and the population as a whole.

Measuring progress

Measures of progress developed to help monitor progress towards the targets of *Our Healthier Nation* also contributed to the Performance Assessment Framework for the NHS. These indicators look across a wide range of service areas and allow comparison between health authority areas and in some instances between NHS trusts. They cover six key areas:

- Health improvement – to reflect the overarching aims of improving the general health of the population and reducing health inequalities, which are influenced by many factors, reaching well beyond the NHS.
- Fair access – to health services.
- Effective delivery of appropriate healthcare.
- **Efficiency.**
- Patient/carer experience.
- Health outcomes of NHS care.

Case Study

The aim of Sure Start is:

To work with parents-to-be, parents and children to promote the physical, intellectual and social development of babies and young children – particularly those who are disadvantaged – so that they can flourish at home and when they get to school, and thereby break the cycle of disadvantage for the current generation of young children.

Sure Start is a cornerstone of the Government's drive to tackle child poverty and social exclusion. By 2004, there will be at least 500 Sure Start local programmes. They will be concentrated in neighbourhoods where a high proportion of children are living in poverty and where Sure Start can help them by pioneering new ways of working to improve services. To date, 128 have started work and another 66 programmes are working on their plans. Local programmes will work with parents and parents-to-be to improve children's life chances through better access to:

- family support
- advice on nurturing
- health services
- early learning.

The design and content of local Sure Start programmes will vary according to local needs. But all programmes are expected to include a number of core services including:

- outreach and home visiting
- support for families and parents
- support for good-quality play, learning and childcare experiences for children
- primary and community healthcare, including advice about family health and child health and development
- support for children and parents with special needs, including help getting access to specialised services.

Carry out some research by reading a national newspaper (a broadsheet is preferable) for a week, and collecting any stories that relate to child poverty. In a group discuss why it is important to break the cycle of disadvantage and poverty at a very early stage in a child's life, and write a report evaluating the roles and responsibilities of health promoters in preventing children suffering from inequality as a result of the financial position of their family.

Health Improvement Programmes

Introduced as part of the changes set out in the 1997 White Paper *The New NHS – Modern Dependable* the Health Improvement Programme (HImP) was described as being 'an *effective vehicle for making major and sustained impact on health problems ... focusing action on people who are socially excluded'.* All HImPs should include information about how national targets are being addressed, local health targets, action plans for delivering these targets, identify local health partnerships and this information should be made accessible to all. The key feature of the HImP, or its successor the Modernisation Plan, is that they describe the local actions; they identify what the targets are and what needs to be done to address them locally, including how the necessary finance will be made available to do that.

Health promotion topics

With such a broad agenda to cover it is hard to decide what areas of activity should be prioritised within health promoting activity. The five topics selected here represent key national health concerns which relate to the targets set out in *Our Healthier Nation.*

Diet

The proportion of both men and women who are overweight or obese has steadily increased since 1980. This is a major risk factor for a variety of illnesses but coronary heart disease (CHD) in particular. Poor diet, that is one containing too much fat and salt and not enough fruit and vegetables, is directly related to:

- diabetes
- raised blood pressure
- raised cholesterol levels
- weight gain.

All of the above are major factors in circulatory disorders such as CHD and stroke. Diet is also thought to account for about a quarter of all deaths due to cancer in this country, particularly colorectal and stomach cancer. The current trends show that the proportion of fat in our diets, which contributes to many of these problems, has remained the same since the early 1980s and shows little indication of reducing. In 1996 61 per cent of men and 52 per cent of women were clinically obese, with an increase in obesity amongst quite young children. This may relate to evidence found by the Department of Health (reported in 1989) that the main sources of dietary energy for children were bread, chips, milk, biscuits, meat products, cakes and puddings, whilst some vitamin intake levels were below the minimum daily recommendation.

Exercise

Surveying the activity levels of the general population is a relatively recent phenomenon. Until the Allied Dunbar Fitness survey (in 1995), this country had no accurate picture of the current levels of physical fitness within the adult population. The results of that and other subsequent surveys have not been encouraging, the message clearly being that we are an increasingly sedentary population. This may be caused by increased reliance on the car, children being transported by car due to safety issues, less tolerance of children playing in the street, an increase in less active occupations, a wider range of other recreational activities such as Playstations, PC games and multi-channel TV.

Whatever the causes, the results are indisputable – we are less active as a nation, and this will contribute to a range of health problems, not just CHD but also a range of other illnesses, including depression, osteoporosis, high blood pressure and diabetes.

Sexually transmitted disease

The government first set targets for improving the sexual health of the population in *The Health of the Nation*, where it focused on a reduction in rates of gonorrhoea and a reduction in the rate of conceptions amongst the under-16s by 50 per cent by 2000.

By the time of *Our Healthier Nation,* some of these priorities had changed, although tackling teenage pregnancy remained an issue with the UK having the highest rate of live births to teenage girls of anywhere in Europe. Therefore a target of reducing by half the rate of teenage conceptions by 2010 was retained, but with a fresh focus on teenage pregnancy as a social exclusion issue.

The government also recognised a worrying reversal in HIV trends, with increasing levels of new infections, particularly amongst the heterosexual population. In 1996 nearly 3000 new cases were recorded, emphasising concerns about complacency amongst young people in particular, where evidence showed a reduction in safe sexual practice and an increase in risky sexual behaviour, for instance when holidaying abroad.

Clearly, lack of safe sexual practice also brings with it a risk of contracting other forms of sexually transmitted disease, and at this time there has been a steady rise in rates of both gonorrhoea and chlamydia. Between 1995 and 1997 there was a 53 per cent rise in rates of gonorrhoea and a 47 per cent rise in rates of chlamydia amongst the 16-19-year age group. These are both areas of considerable concern, with chlamydia particularly being the single most preventable cause of infertility in women.

Smoking

The link between smoking and ill-health is now well documented. 'Smoking is the single most important modifiable risk factor for CHD in young and old.' (*Our Healthier Nation* section 6.5) A lifetime non-smoker is 60 per cent less likely to have CHD and 30 per cent less likely to have a stroke than a smoker. Smoking mirrors other patterns of ill-health in that the highest levels are in the lowest social groups. Although the proportion of young people who smoke is similar across all social groups, by their mid 30s, 50 per cent of young people from higher social classes have stopped as opposed to only 25 per cent from the lowest income groups. The result is that about one-third of the smokers in the population are concentrated in only the lowest 10 per cent of earners in the country.

Skin care

The major cause of ill-health associated with skin care is malignant melanoma or skin cancer. Skin cancer is distributed in the reverse pattern to other forms of cancer both regionally and by social class. It is most common in the south-west and east and in social classes 1 and 2. The incidence of malignant melanoma amongst men in class 1 is nearly five times that for men in class 5 and this is repeated for women where the difference is approximately twice that of class 5 for class 1.

Social class	Men	Women
I	150	(97)*
II	108	111
IIINM	115	95
IIIM	57	67
IV	67	58
V	(34)*	(51)*

National average rate shown as 100

*Figures in brackets are those based on very small numbers

Figure 10.7 Incidence of Skin Cancer by Social Class 1984

The major cause of malignant melanoma (skin cancer) is exposure to the sun, which explains both the regional and social variations. In the northern areas of the country the number of days where lengthy exposure to the sun is likely is far fewer than in the south. The variations by social class are most usually explained by the use of tanning facilities and holidaying abroad, which those with greater disposable income can afford.

Sunscreen is an effective protector against sun exposure

Since the advent of the cheap package holiday this gap has narrowed as more and more people have greater access to holidays in hotter countries with stronger sunlight levels. Countries such as Australia have led the way in addressing this problem, with campaigns such as 'Slip, Slop, Slap', which have been adopted in many other areas world-wide.

Theory into practice

The current sun safety messages are:

Seek the shade – especially at midday

Hats on – use a wide-brimmed hat

Apply sunscreen of at least SPF 15

Don't burn – it won't improve your tan

Exercise care – always protect the very young

- How often do you see people following this advice?
- Why might people choose not to follow this advice?
- What wider principle does this illustrate?

Agencies involved

Delivering the health improvement agenda is clearly a multi-layered approach, as suggested in previous sections, with many partners at every level. Here we consider some key partners in the process.

Government

Government action to effect improvements in health take place across all departments as we have already seen in the first health strategy *The Health of The Nation*. This is illustrated by the work of the Department for Education and Employment (DfEE), which has been instrumental in leading the development of the National Healthy School Standard and reducing the levels of unemployment through initiatives such as the modern apprenticeship and the 'New Deal'. The Department of Social Security has been responsible for raising the levels of benefits and targeting them at those most in need, particularly families with young children as recommended by the Aicheson Report. This theme has been further supported by the introduction of the Sure Start and Sure Start Plus programmes for supporting families in most need.

On a wider front the Department of Health has targeted additional resources to those areas identified as being at most need through the creation of Health Action Zones for large-scale health projects across a wide range of sectors, including education and housing. The Home Office has also played its part in addressing the issue of fear of crime through the introduction of Community Safety Strategies, which are local community plans to address crime issues through partnerships led by the local authorities.

NHS

The primary function of the NHS is to treat sick people. Although health promotion activity could and should be a feature of many health service roles, in practice this aspect of health activity is the poor relation of the primary goal of treating the sick. Recent government reorganisation of the NHS has emphasised its health improvement role, specifying that Health Authorities have the lead role in developing HImPs and giving Primary Care Trusts a primary function of 'to improve the health of their local population'.

There are several key roles within the NHS with very active parts to play in promoting health. Examples of these include:

- *Public health doctors* – have a key role in assessing the patterns of ill health locally and identifying what types of health care provision and health-promoting activities are required to improve health locally
- *Health visitors* – have a public health role in local communities, working at a neighbourhood level to identify local health need and support community activity to address those needs
- *Specialist health promotion services* – a small, specialised service which supports the development of the health-promoting role of others, and the development of new services and policies which can promote health locally.

Private sector

In the private sector the commercial pressures mean that if an organisation does not generate an income, it will quickly go out of business. However as the public become more health conscious, the private sector responds to serve that need. Therefore, it is not unexpected to see the changes in the leisure industry, for example, where there is:

- an increasing number of leisure facilities
- a refocusing on promoting active lifestyle rather than body-building or elitist exercise
- a whole new market for sportswear and advice, such as personal trainers.

This move within the marketplace has been joined by developments in other areas such as private practitioners in health fields such as alternative therapies, chiropractors, nutritionists, counsellors, etc. Increasingly, organisations buy in specific consultants for stress audits and advice on managing stress within organisations. In the home this response to a health-conscious population is probably best illustrated by the extent to which local supermarkets have responded to public concerns about **Genetically Modified foods,** in the case of at least one retailer proclaiming that none of its products contain GM foodstuffs. A similar picture has developed for organically grown foods, where this niche market has gradually grown to occupy a significant proportion of the local produce on offer, the public clearly being prepared to pay the additional costs associated with those products.

Mass media

The mass media clearly has a major part to play in the health education of the public at large. It serves this purpose in three ways:

Advertising
Publicity is paid for in the form of specific adverts carried on television, radio or in the printed media. This is most usually national campaigning due to the high cost. Campaigns include those to raise awareness of benefit entitlements, publicity for the national smoking quitline, HIV and safe sex awareness campaigns and the television 'stop smoking' adverts featuring John Cleese run at major quit periods, such as New Year or in the run up to National No Smoking Day.

Free media coverage
Health promotion also often benefits from free media coverage of major campaign launches such as those for teenage pregnancy and National No Smoking Day. However, this type of media coverage also brings many attendant problems. The biggest problem is the lack of control over the final content of any article a health promoter may contribute to. Health is a very political issue and therefore news items about health issues present reporters with many opportunities to present a story in a particular light

North West tops the table as lung cancer link highlights smoking

Free help at hand to kick cigs habit

Cigarettes? They just make me sick!

Figure 10.8 National No Smoking Day headlines in the press

as a means of creating a more 'interesting' story. For example, the issue of tackling teenage pregnancy provides many opportunities for the media to reinforce the stereotypical view of feckless young mothers who get pregnant to obtain council housing accommodation. The evidence simply does not support that view but it is perpetuated as it is deemed more newsworthy.

Internet
With the rapid rise in use of online services, people will increasingly be able to access information directly through the use of the Internet. Whilst greatly improving access to this will remove much of the control and screening which other forms of media provide, it is increasingly easy for people to set up their own websites and enable others to access information which is not regulated in any way.

Theory into practice

What examples of health information/campaigning can you find in the printed media? Collect any examples in your own newspaper and magazines from a seven-day period. This exercise will be more effective if you work with others to maximise the number of different papers and magazines you can cover.

What examples did you find which were:

- paid for advertising?
- unpaid coverage of new information?
- news coverage of new services/health-related projects?

What are the messages being conveyed in these pieces?
Did you find any examples of the same information presented differently in various papers and magazines?
What problems do you think this might present for the health promoter seeking media coverage?

Health promotion campaigns

Health policy linked to health promotion

As you have already seen, the key targets set by the government are those from *Our Healthier Nation*. If you look back to these targets it is possible to see how the government has translated its headline targets into local/national health policy. This has primarily been through the implementation of National Service Frameworks (NSFs) which have been introduced in three of the four target areas. Each service framework introduces a national blueprint of how that health target is to be addressed, for example if you look at the coronary heart disease NSF below, you will find both the main standard areas and the detail of standards 1 and 2. These deal with the prevention aspects of the strategy.

The coronary heart disease NSF covers all aspects of CHD from primary prevention, right through to tertiary care for people with existing heart conditions. The aim of this approach is to ensure that every district in the country has similar levels of service provision and a co-ordinated approach to preventing heart disease. Each standard has specific targets which must be achieved within a given timescale.

The coronary heart disease NSF

Standard 1 – the NHS and partner agencies should develop, implement and monitor policies that reduce the prevalence of coronary risk factors in the population, and reduce inequalities in risks of developing heart disease.

Standard 2 – the NHS and partner agencies should contribute to a reduction in the prevalence of smoking in the local population.

The remaining standards deal with aspects of treatment for people with existing heart conditions, detailing service standards to be achieved which contribute to aspects of secondary and tertiary prevention:

Standards 3 & 4 – preventing CHD in high-risk patients.

Standards 5, 6 & 7 – heart attack and other acute coronary syndromes.

Standard 8 – stable angina.

Standards 9 & 10 – re-vascularisation.

Standard 11 - heart failure.

Standard 12 - cardiac rehabilitation.

Specific examples of initiatives which have resulted from this approach would include:

Smoking
New smoking cessation support services are to be established in every district in the country. This is allied to major campaigns programmed at strategic times in the year, such as New Year and National No Smoking Day to encourage people to give up smoking and use available services.

Healthy eating
Every child in the country will be offered a piece of fruit in a similar scheme to the free school milk approach to encourage them to adopt healthier diets. This approach adopts a medical model which focuses on the disease people experience or are prevented from experiencing.

The Older People's NSF
Perhaps more interesting is the Older People's NSF which adopts a different approach by focusing on a population group. Here the emphasis is more holistic, recognising the issues which are relevant to that group, e.g. age-related discrimination as well as treatment services.

Standard 1 – rooting out age discrimination
NHS services will be provided, regardless of age, on the basis of clinical need alone. Social care services will not use age in their eligibility criteria or policies, to restrict access to available services.

Standard 2 – person-centred care
NHS and social care services treat older people as individuals and enable them to make choices about their own care. This is achieved through the single assessment process, integrated commissioning arrangements and integrated provision of services, including community equipment and continence services.

Standard 3 – intermediate care
Older people will have access to a new range of intermediate care services at home or in designated care settings to promote their independence by providing enhanced services from the NHS and councils to prevent unnecessary hospital admission and effective rehabilitation services to enable early discharge from hospital and to prevent premature or unnecessary admission to long-term residential care.

Standard 4 – general hospital care
Older people's care in hospital is delivered through appropriate specialist care and by hospital staff who have the right set of skills to meet their needs.

Standard 5 – stroke
The NHS will take action to prevent strokes, working in partnership with other agencies where appropriate.

People who are thought to have had a stroke have access to diagnostic services, are treated appropriately by a specialist stroke service, and subsequently, with their carers, participate in a multidisciplinary programme of secondary prevention and rehabilitation.

Standard 6 - falls
The NHS, working in partnership with councils, takes action to prevent falls and reduce resultant fractures or other injuries in their populations of older people.

Older people who have fallen receive effective treatment and rehabilitation and, with their carers, receive advice on prevention through a specialised falls service.

Standard 7 – mental health in older people
Older people who have mental health problems have access to integrated mental health services, provided by the NHS and councils to ensure effective diagnosis, treatment and support, for them and for their carers.

Standard 8 – promoting an active healthy life in older age
The health and well-being of older people is promoted through a co-ordinated programme of action led by the NHS with support from councils.

You can find information on all the NSFs at the Department of Health website: www.doh.gov.uk.

Methods and materials

Interaction

It is hard to quantify the extent to which individual face-to-face interaction can contribute to health campaigning. However, it is clear that the general public hold certain groups, such as doctors, nurses, teachers and environmental health officers, in high regard within society and therefore respect the information they obtain from them. This creates considerable potential for promoting key health messages simply through the day-to-day routine of work. This might mean a doctor suggesting to someone that they consider giving up smoking when they attend for a health check, or a district nurse suggesting that moderate activity is still possible and potentially beneficial for an older service user whilst visiting them at home.

Leaflets

Leaflets are the backbone of health education activity. They can serve a wide variety of purposes such as informing people about local services, providing information about specific health conditions, giving advice about specific health promotion issues or engaging people in thought about broader health considerations. In many cases leaflets are designed to support specific health campaigns, such as those for immunisation and National No Smoking Day. A leaflet is a relatively simple tool, but it is important to consider a range of questions when designing or using a leaflet

- Who is this leaflet for? A drugs leaflet appropriate for secondary school children will not be appropriate for primary schools.
- Who produced the leaflet? Will they have an interest in the information? If it is a commercial company, such as a drug company, will this mean they have been selective in their reporting of the information?
- How long ago was it first produced? Is the information still relevant or accurate? For example, information on drug-related harm changes very rapidly.
- Is the language level used appropriate to the target audience? Is it too adult, does it include abbreviations or technical terms?
- Is it well designed, i.e. will it grab the attention of the reader from amongst the other leaflets and posters? Will it connect specifically with the target audience?
- Are the key messages clearly identified or are there too many other distractions?
- For the particular leaflet and target audience, where is the best place to display it?

Theory into practice

As we have already seen, the HIV and AIDS awareness materials of the late 1980s were roundly criticised for the lack of clear information and message. Imagine you are a health promotion worker who has been commissioned to devise a leaflet to raise awareness of HIV risk amongst older people. The reason for this request is a recognition that there are a large number of older people who are leaving failed marriages, without having the benefit of good health education on HIV risk which many young people now get in school. These people require some specifically targeted information which will meet the above criteria to help them manage their risk as they embark on life as a single person again.

You might want to start by:

- collecting some existing sex education literature for comparison
- ensuring you have the correct information to hand for your leaflets content
- identifying relevant local services to include in this leaflet.

Posters

Posters provide an excellent tool for first catching the attention of the target audience and supporting the key broad messages you might then develop in more detail within a leaflet. Hubbey (1993) divided the factors which draw attention to a poster into two groups – physical and motivational characteristics. Clearly a poster needs to be eye-catching and big enough to attract attention. It will need to be in colour, or if in black and white it will need to use this for dramatic effect. Wording should be minimal and very bold. Posters need to be targeted carefully at places where the target audience will see them and routinely changed after a short period.

Physical characteristics	Motivational characteristics
Size – the whole of the poster as well as parts within it like key lettering.	Novelty – unusual features or surprising objects.
Intensity – bold headings.	Interest – items of interest to the target audience.
Colour – use of primary colours such reds, greens and orange.	Deeper motivations – e.g. fashion and sex.
Pictures – using photographs and drawings.	Entertainment or humour.

Plan, prepare and conduct a campaign

Dignan and Carr (1992) describe effective planning as 'requiring anticipation of what will be needed along the way towards reaching a goal. This statement implies that the goal is defined...'. Therefore, to plan effectively requires a clear understanding of what you are trying to achieve and therefore that a health promoter define clear aims and objectives before commencing any form of action. Planning should provide you with the answer to three questions:

- What am I trying to achieve?
- What am I going to do?
- How will I know whether I have succeeded?

Objectives

It is important to start by differentiating between an aim and an objective:

- Aim – a broad goal.
- Objective – a specific goal to be achieved.

Any one aim may have several supplementary objectives within it, whilst objectives are usually defined as being SMART:

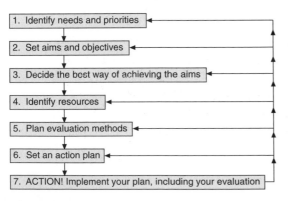

1. Identify needs and priorities
2. Set aims and objectives
3. Decide the best way of achieving the aims
4. Identify resources
5. Plan evaluation methods
6. Set an action plan
7. ACTION! Implement your plan, including your evaluation

Figure 10.9 Planning model of Ewles and Simnet

Specific – are defined in terms which is clear and not too vague.

Measurable – when the work is finished we can see whether the objective has been achieved or not.

Achievable – the target is realistic, i.e. within our power to change.

Relevant – is focused on addressing the issue within our broad aim.

Timed – we have agreed a timescale by which we expect to have delivered this objective.

Objectives which are not SMART are not aids to effective planning and may be aims which require breaking down further into specific objectives. Without this level of detail an objective becomes unmeasurable and therefore evaluation of the work is undermined.

Identification of target audience

Identifying your target audience for a campaign starts with the question, 'what is the health need which I should be addressing?' The need for a campaign will usually come from one of four sources:

Normative need – defined by an expert or professional according to their own standards, where something falls short of this standard then a need is identified, e.g. percentage of people who are overweight or obese.

Felt need – needs which people feel, i.e. things we want. For example people might want their food to be free of genetically modified products.

Expressed need – a felt need which is voiced. For example, the felt need to have genetically modified free food becomes an issue of public debate with pressure groups focusing public debate on the issue.

Comparative need – arises from comparisons between similar groups of people, where one group is in receipt of health promotion activity and the other is not. Examples here might be one school a having well-thought-out and planned PSHE curriculum and another not.

Theory into practice

If you were to undertake a piece of health promotion activity locally, how would you start to identify local needs which would frame the aims and objectives of your work? Think about:

- Where could you go?
- Who could you ask?
- What information might be available for you to use?
- How would you decide whether this information is a reliable basis for your decision-making ?
- What type of need from the four categories above do most health education campaigns like those for smoking, healthy eating and exercise focus on?
- What problems can you foresee for your work if it focused solely on this type of need?

As a health promoter the first action in undertaking any campaign is to identify the source of the need we are considering and this will identify whom we are targeting.

Liaison with other agencies

Health promotion is rarely effective when the activity is focused within one organisation. As we saw at the beginning of this chapter the causes of ill-health are so broad that it requires a wide-ranging response across agencies to influence health for the good. This is reflected in current government thinking through statutory duties to work in partnership on planning mechanisms such as the local community plan, HImP, community safety strategy and so on.

Effective partnership working is based on having:

- clear objectives
- a shared vision
- an understanding of where the partnership fits with other pressures/priorities
- an open approach to learning from the partnership
- partners with a strong ownership of the partnership
- the capacity to change mainstream service provision
- the right people with the appropriate level of authority to make this happen
- clear reporting and monitoring systems
- clear communication channels, within and across organisations
- the ability to pool budgets and release existing resources
- a commitment to evaluating their progress and the outcome of their work.

[Summarised from *Kings Fund* findings Autumn 2000]

Construct research tool

It is likely that as part of the work a health promoter will need to conduct some form of research, perhaps to identify the need as suggested earlier or to assess whether they have achieved the objectives as part of the evaluation process. When carrying out any research it is important to consider the following steps:

1. Define the purpose of your research.
2. Review the existing literature – has your research already been carried out somewhere else?
3. Plan the study methodology for the investigation.
4. Test the methodology by carrying out a small-scale pilot.
5. Review the findings of your pilot and review your methodology in the light of these findings.
6. Carry out the research.
7. Analyse the information.
8. Draw your conclusions based on your findings.
9. Compile a report of your findings for the target audience identified in step one.

As part of the research you might choose to use various types of research tools, a short summary of some basic tools is set out below.

Link to national campaigns

Inevitably a high proportion of campaigning activity is linked to national campaigns. This is for two primary reasons.

Most national campaigns are better resourced through the provision of leaflets, posters, supportive media coverage, possibly access to small-scale funding and national advice on operationalising your work locally. In the past this role was taken on by the Health Education Authority who both produced the materials and supported the role of local practitioners in activities for major campaigns such as National No Smoking Day and Drink-wise Day. However, the HEA has now been replaced by the HDA, which has a very different role, and the production of key campaigning materials has passed to the Department of Health. However, it is important to recognise that most government departments produce what might be considered campaigning material for health promotion. Examples might include:

- road safety pamphlets and cycling information from the Department of Transport
- energy conservation and recycling information from the Department of the Environment
- information for parents on helping your child to read from the Department for Education and Employment
- advice on benefits from the Department for Social Security.

Most national campaigns support key national strategies and therefore offer opportunities for local agencies to identify how they are supporting government programmes locally. For example, all local health services will be expected to address the issues of smoking and therefore National No Smoking Day presents a high-profile opportunity to link in with a national campaign and report that action in the performance monitoring activity for the services involved.

Assessment guidelines

Assessment for this unit depends upon your evaluation of a national campaign (local campaigns are not appropriate for this assessment exercise). Good examples of campaigns which you should be able to find information on include:

- National No Smoking Day
- Teenage Pregnancy Campaign
- Meningitis vaccination campaign
- Flu vaccination campaign.

In each case you will be able to find existing information which will help you:

- identify the level of need for that campaign both nationally and locally
- identify the types of activities which are undertaken locally to support the national campaign
- review and assess the level of impact the campaign has on the public awareness of the issue
- assess and evaluate the success of the campaign in achieving its goals.

This is an opportunity to review an existing campaign against key assessment criteria which will determine your pass level. To achieve an E grade pass at this level you must:

- accurately explain the model of health used in the campaign
- clearly define the components and approaches in the campaign
- explain in detail the ethical issues involved in the health promotion campaign

- describe major factors affecting the health of individuals and the roles and responsibilities of health promoters at all levels
- outline the campaigns links to key themes and priorities for health promotion
- fully describe the target audience methods and materials used for the campaign
- provide a justified conclusion on the effectiveness of the campaign.

For a Merit grade you must also:
- show the links between the approaches used by promoters and relevant models of health
- clearly explain ways in which major factors affect the health of individuals
- provide a detailed explanation of the reasons for key themes and priorities in health promotion
- analyse the positive and negative factors contributing to the effectiveness of the campaign.

For a Distinction grade you must also:
- evaluate the roles and responsibilities of health promoters
- analyse the links between major factors which influence health and the key themes and priorities for health promotion
- make detailed and supported recommendations for the next stage of the campaign

Usually, national campaigns are commissioned with an evaluation element built in, therefore that information is open to scrutiny. Your starting point for obtaining this background information could be your local health promotion service, and nationally the Health Development Agency (HDA).

End-of-unit test

1 Describe the key features of each of the following lay accounts of health:
- The body as a machine.
- The health promotion account.
- God's power.
- Body under siege.
- Robust individualism.
- Will power.

2 Give five key features of the medical model of health.

3 Complete the following table to identify the relevant aspects of health or their key features.

Aspect	Description
	concerned with body mechanics
Mental health	
Emotional health	
	the ability to make and maintain relationships with others
Spiritual health	

4 Identify whether the following statements are true or false.
- The disability a person experiences is determined by the way in which other people respond to their difference.
- Since the Black Report of 1980, it has been clearly identified and acknowledged that those from the lowest social groupings experience the best health in society.
- Because women make up a higher proportion of the older population, there are often lower rates of illnesses specifically associated with women.
- Suicide is twice as common in women as in men and women experience more accidents in the home or garden whilst men experience more accidents in the workplace or sports activities.
- Black and minority ethnic groups have higher risks of mortality from a range of diseases such as diabetes, liver cancer, tuberculosis, stroke and heart disease.
- Men unemployed at both census dates in 1971 and 1981 had mortality rates twice that of the rest of other men in that age range and those men who were unemployed at one census date had an excess mortality of 27 per cent.

5 Explain what each of the following means and give a suitable example.
- Primary prevention.
- Secondary prevention.
- Tertiary prevention.

6 Give three examples of international agencies, and state their role in promoting health. Give a suitable example of work each might undertake.

7 Place the following organisations into the relevant category in the table

IEHO   MIND   UNISON   BMA   NCT   NRA   UKCC
NUM   Railtrack   NUT   FPA   RoSPA

National Agencies which can contribute to health promotion	Examples
Voluntary organisations	
Professional organisations	
Trade unions	
Commercial and industrial organisations	

8 List five issues which a health promoter would need to consider for ethical decision-making in a piece of health promotion work.

9 Describe three features of screening programmes which contribute to them remaining a contentious issue.

10 What were the four headline targets for improving health in *Our Healthier Nation?*

11 Describe the role and main features of the Health Improvement Programme (HImP).

12 Identify which of the following statements are true or false:

12.1. The proportion of both men and women who are overweight or obese has steadily declined since 1980.

12.2. The current trends show that the proportion of fat in our diets has remained the same since the early 1980s.

12.3. In 1996 61 per cent of men and 52 per cent of women were clinically obese.

12.4. The current recommendation for physical activity levels which promote heart health is to be vigorously active for at least 30 minutes three times per week.

12.5. Between 1995 and 1997 there was a 53 per cent rise in rates of gonorrhoea and a 47 per cent rise in rates of chlamydia amongst the 55–60-year age group.

12.6. A lifetime non-smoker, is 60 per cent less likely to have CHD and 30 per cent less likely to have a stroke than a smoker.

References and further reading

Certificate in Health Education Open Learning Resources, 1995. London: The Health Education Authority

Ewles, L. & Simnett, I. (1999) *Promoting Health – A Practical Guide,* Oxford: Baillière Tindall

HM Government (1999) *Saving Lives – Our Healthier Nation,* HMSO: The Stationary Office

HM Government (1992) *The Health Of the Nation,* HMSO: The Stationary Office

HM Government (1997) *The New NHS – Modern Dependable,* HMSO: The Stationary Office

Jones, L. (1994) *Social Control of Health and Health Work,* Basingstoke: Macmillan

Jones, L. & Sidell, M. (1997) *Promoting Health – Knowledge and Practice,* Buckingham: Open University Press

Jones, L. & Sidell, M. (1997) *The Challenge of Promoting Health – Exploration and Action,* Buckingham: Open University Press

Moonie, N. (2000) *Advanced Health and Social Care,* Oxford: Heinemann

Naidoo, J. & Wills, J. (1996) *Health Promotion – Foundations for Practice,* Oxford: Baillière Tindall

Sir Donald Aicheson, (1998) *The Independent Inquiry into Inequalities in Health,* HMSO: The Stationery Office

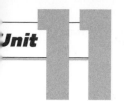

Practical caring skills

The unit is both complementary and supplementary to units 5 and 8, which focus on the skills, knowledge and understanding required in order to benefit from vocational placement and working in a care setting. The particular focus of this unit is the theoretical knowledge and practical skills required to accomplish the desired holistic care of the individual service user.

The student will gain competence in practical caring skills, learn how to deal with sensitive issues and understand how issues concerning resources affect care-workers and service user's choices. They will learn how the theories of care have evolved to reach the standards of care for modern society and how up-to-date thinking and knowledge impact on current practice.

The final part of the unit relates to working with others, including managers, and understanding the mechanisms for personal and professional progress.

What you need to learn

- Describe the knowledge required in a care setting
- Key caring skills
- Requirements of an effective training programme

Describe the knowledge required in a care setting

The title of this section is ambitious, given that there are a large number of diverse professional carers and thousands of books have been written, and will continue to be written, on essential knowledge required for the multitude of professions involved within care settings. One unit cannot hope to cover all these, but you will see that there are many common threads in today's care professions.

Current theories of care

You may find this section complex and confusing on first reading. There are many difficult technical terms for types of theories and paradigms (explained below) as there is no single theory of care. You may need to re-read the section and carry out further reading. As this forms a considerable chunk of the unit assessment, you will need to understand the basic terminology before you can begin to collect information for your evidence.

Psychology and sociology form part of the fundamental platform on which the various theories of care stand. However, it is the application of these disciplines to 'problem people' and the problems people have that forms the puzzle. Furthermore, many experts have developed theories on which these disciplines grew and some were diametrically opposed to each other or in conflict in whole or in part. Making sense of the theories that currently underpin care is not easy, with care itself having many branches. As time, good practice and sound research provides more in the way of knowledge, skills and understanding some theories fall by the way while others grow in strength.

In order to cope with the world around us, human beings try to impose order by seeking patterns, looking for regularity and explanations. This is how theories are built; models are constructed to place some order on the chaos.

Theories no longer fitting the facts are discarded and new theories put forward to better explain and manage events. A successful theory should describe and explain, so that prediction and control are brought about.

Theories in social work

In the 1920s and 1930s, social workers had only **psychoanalytical theory** to help them out, based on the ideas of Sigmund **Freud**. Freud believed that the present mood and behaviour of an individual was due to early childhood experiences and only by releasing those experiences under analysis could the individual be helped. Post-1930, some workers including Otto Rank, realised that a helping relationship with a service user was more likely to achieve success and becomes an experience in itself. They were looking at the present and not the past. This was called the '**Functionalist school**'.

Figure 11.1 Conflict often existed between different theorists

The 1960s saw a huge proliferation of theories that could be applied to social work and there were so many, that in the 1970s an inventory had to be made to make sense of it all.

Social functioning

Rationalisation followed, with an attempt to bring some unity to social work practice and this was called '**social functioning**'. This provided social work with not only its terms of reference but also broad perspectives. However, as it turned out, social functioning was also short-lived, as unifying social work theory proved impossible. In the 1970s, the works of Whittaker (1974), Leonard (1975) and Burrell and Morgan (1979) tried to explain theoretical ideas by using **paradigms**. A paradigm in social science indicates a large concept in which a particular way of making sense of society, including all those theories, beliefs, values and methods, are placed. Burrell and Morgan (1979) produced four paradigms in a framework which demonstrated vertical and horizontal relationships (see Figure 11.2).

David Howe (1987) provides more easily identified names without detracting from this work. The functionalists become 'the fixers' who are the experts, can diagnose problems and using expertise and knowledge devise 'treatment' to fix the problems. Put simply, parents in a discordant partnership might be advised to seek counselling to solve the problems of a problem child. The **interpretivists** become the 'seekers after meaning' who

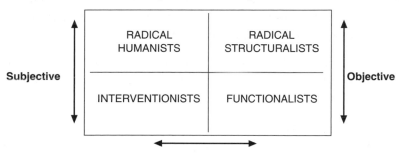

Raisers of consciousness
believe that the nature of society is largely to blame
for clients' problems rather than the individual.
Major theme is to change society such that the
consciousness of the client is raised to a level, at
which they can resolve own problems.

Revolutionaries
wish to change the materialist, capitalist,
powerful society to one that empowers
working class and those disadvantaged
by age, gender, culture and economics.

Seekers after meaning
strive to see the problems of a client from their point
of view. The relationship between the social worker
and the client is pivotal to understanding the problem
and, together, reaching conclusions for resolution.

Fixers
diagnose the problem of a client and
using their knowledge, skills and
understanding organise treatment so
fixing the problem.

Figure 11.2 Theories applied in social work

strive to understand things from the other person's point of view. The relationship
between service user and social worker is of paramount importance and appropriate
questioning, with warmth, sincerity and empathy, will draw out the details around the
problem. They will consider the question of direction of progress together. This is a
service user-centred humanistic approach.

The **radical humanists** are called 'the raisers of consciousness' who believe that the
nature of society and the way in which, for example, the members of the working class
are treated as objects rather than human individuals is largely the cause of the problems
of the individual. The approach is still centred on the service user, i.e. subjective, but
indicating that society is at fault, not the individual. Out of this paradigm, we find the
beginnings of women's studies and feminism. Women have been valued only because of
their performances as wives and mothers, doing things for others. Single-parent
mothers, widows on low incomes and prostitutes can all be seen to have problems, not
within themselves, but in coping with the world in which we live.

A major theme in this paradigm is to change the society in which we live, so social
workers will press for refuges for battered wives, unmarried pregnant girls, greater
benefits for those on low income and so on. The aim is to raise their level of
consciousness to a situation where they can resolve their problems.

Subjective and objective approaches
Radical humanists and interpretivists both apply subjective approaches.

Radical structuralists are renamed 'the revolutionaries'. They believe that the interest of
society in material wealth and power is paramount and the working-class members are
merely pawns in the game. The way forward is to change the capitalist society and the
powerful structures which trap poorer people. One member of a political party, when
speaking of unemployment, maintained that the non-working man should get on his
bike and find work.

This is a minor example of the power of the state; shuffling people around to eke out a living – possibly having to leave wife and children at home and stay in lodgings. Probation officers and child abuse specialists have long recognised that the majority of cases that they deal with come from poor homes where there is inequality and deprivation. Fixers and revolutionaries are objective in their approach.

Linking theory to practice

Should you ask a social care-worker which paradigm they favour in their work, most will look perplexed, many will say they use common sense and some theory, in fact isn't common sense and practical skill rooted in theory? They will use a combination of these paradigms to suit occasions although functionalism is common. Theories need to be linked to practice or they become abstractions, and this is one of current dilemmas of social work. Linking theory to practice sounds straightforward, but such links are in their infancy in social work and currently many articles appear in the professional media to attempt to address the situation. For if practice is not linked to theory how can we begin to predict and control, let alone describe and explain? Practice must also inform theory, and practice is not a fixed body of knowledge, but dynamic and changing.

Currently, there is still a gap between theory and practice in social work, but it narrows as professionals strive to tease out the key issues. Howe (1987) says at the end of his book:

> *Those who wish to explore the heavens, first must build telescopes and map the stars. We have been mapping social work theories. We have been finding out where they are. We have looked at what they do; and we have seen where they lead us. Good practice requires social workers to know where they are and where they are going. Quite simply, there is nothing better than a clearly held theory to give the worker a good idea of place and a strong sense of direction.*

Theories in nursing

Before the 1950s, it was difficult to argue that nursing was a profession; professions must have a discrete body of knowledge to call on. The public and other caring

professions saw nursing mainly as being 'handmaidens' to doctors. The last 50 years have seen a tremendous build-up of knowledge, skills and understanding that can be identified with nursing and used as the focus of practice, although some still maintain that this expertise does not justify professional status. In the USA, nursing became an all-graduate profession, shifting learning into institutes of higher education. This is occurring in the UK now and those exiting with a Diploma in Higher Education are encouraged to extend their knowledge to graduate status.

To be considered as a profession, we need **nursing theory** to underpin the specific body of knowledge that is required. To recap, a theory is an explanation of a collection of concepts that describe, explain, predict and control phenomena.

Theories need to be applicable to practice or they become an abstraction. Such links are constantly being explored through research and greater understanding. Practice also informs theory, resulting in a changing body of knowledge and more research projects are aiming towards a closure of the **theory–practice gap**.

Theories

Pearson *et al* (1996) has divided nursing theories, which can be diffuse and complex, into:

1 **Personal theories** – based on developing a personal explanation of events. These can be based on assumptions and prejudices but can also lead on to more developed theories.
2 **Local theories** – theories held by a group of people, in a particular setting and time, to explain events. These also can be based on assumptions and prejudices, but can be a source of new ideas for research.
3 **Grand theories** – theories that explain particular events in a field of study, very often developed as a result of observation of outcomes. Models of care (see below) fit into this category as well as many recommendations for managing pressure sores, leg ulcers, etc.
4 **Epistemological theories** – theory of knowledge from the world about us and from other disciplines such as sociology, physiology and psychology that have a broad influence and can be used within nursing theory.
5 **Metatheory** – definitions of theory and explanations of origin.

Nursing paradigms

Once again, we meet paradigms where groups of related theories are collected together in an organised way. Nursing has three master paradigms:

1. **Positivist paradigm** – a theoretical idea becomes a hypothesis that can be tested, measured and verified. Results will be repeatable and so predictions and control are possible for well-defined concepts. Many controlled trials are carried out in nursing using the methods developed by physiologists and statisticians. Deduction occurs with the goals of prediction and control.
2. **Interpretative paradigm** – theory is seen to be embedded in practice by listening, observation and study of people, rather than by experimentation to prove hypotheses. This is more concerned with the experience of ill-health than cause and effect of disease. Goals are description and understanding.
3. **Critical paradigm** – creates theory from practice to assist in changing to a more desired state, possibly to understand the self more. Relates theory to practice in a meaningful way.

Each paradigm has much to offer nurses and nursing practice although many individuals will prefer one approach to another.

Abstract models of care

Further underpinning this drive towards professional status was the generation of abstract models of nursing care: 'A model of nursing care is a collection of knowledge, ideas and values about nursing, which determines the way nurses and individuals work with patients and service users' Wright (1990).

In other words, organisation becomes integral to the way nurses both think and practise. Any nurse or team of nurses can create an informal model of care for their use, but this can pose problems when team-nursing with other individuals, and there is a tendency to expect everyone else to share views and beliefs. Many models were created in the USA and UK experts modified some of these for use here. The most common model is that devised by Roper in Scotland, based on the **activities of daily living**, known as Roper's or the ADL model. In fact, the ADL model does not apply the holistic approach referred to in the next section, but rather partitions the mind and body into activities (sometimes called a '**reductionist** approach'). This has generated some criticism from some experts but it is still the most widely used model in the UK. Different philosophies are employed in other models of care.

'Activities of daily living' used in Roper's model of care

maintaining a safe environment	personal cleansing and dressing
communicating	controlling body temperature
breathing	working and playing
eating and drinking	mobilising
eliminating	sleeping
expressing sexuality	dying.

Key issue

Some other models of care include:

Orem	Minshull
Peplau	Logan and Tierney
Roy	Neuman

Try to find out something about each of them.

Holistic approach

The **holistic approach** is fundamental to many current theories of care; you can think of it as a 'wholistic' approach as the word is a more modern variation of the Greek word *holos* meaning whole. This approach treats the whole person as a union of body and mind. In other words, it is not sufficient to treat the symptoms of a condition alone; one must consider the influence of other parts of the body and the mind as well. It can be thought of as rather like a cake – the butter, sugar, flour, eggs and milk all have distinct properties and appearances of their own, but when mixed

Figure 11.3 The whole is more than the sum of the parts

together and baked to produce a cake, we have something entirely different with a unique taste and appearance.

There are many examples where body and mind work as one. For example, a form of the skin disease psoriasis erupts with extra stress. Stress alone produces a multitude of physical symptoms and is a major factor in heart disease and so on. Caring for a service user in a physical way only will not be sufficient, as people will not be helped to solve problems and an extended period of suffering and cost will follow. Consider the examples above: expensive treatment will not solve the problems if the underlying cause is stress.

Thus the mind and body (some will add the spirit as well) must be treated as one – this is the basis of the holistic approach.

EU regulations

The European Union (EU) was created in 1993 and replaced the European Economic Community (EEC) in existence since 1973. The European Communities Act (1972) stated that rights created out of the European Community treaties should have effect in UK law.

The UK population and government have to abide by the EU **regulations**, directives and decisions. Regulations are binding in a court of law in the UK. Directives are also binding but the member state has power over the application of the directive, although this does not apply to the NHS, which is bound by directives. **COSHH (1988)** is such a directive and has been operative for a number of years now. When UK law and European law are at odds with one another, the European law is supreme.

British people are also signed up to the **European Convention on Human Rights (1953)** and bound to the **Human Rights Act (1998)** so can bring actions to the European Commission of Human Rights if they feel they have been treated unjustly in the matter of human rights.

Other legislation that forms part of some or all care

- Access to Health Records Act (1990)
- Access to Medical Reports Act (1988)
- Children and Young Persons Act (1933)
- Children Act (1989)
- Chronically Sick and Disabled Person's Act (1970)
- Disability Discrimination Act (1995)

Assessment activity 11.1

1 Write a description (in your own words) of the main theories on which care practice is based.

2 Using examples from the past and the present day, show how these theories have influenced the practice and skills of carers.

3 Write a critical evaluation of the theories of care practice.

Key caring skills

Basic anatomy
Structure and functions of blood

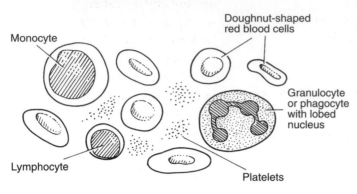

Monocyte

Doughnut-shaped
red blood cells

Granulocyte
or phagocyte
with lobed
nucleus

Lymphocyte

Platelets

Figure 11.4 Different blood cells

Blood consists of straw-coloured plasma in which several types of cells are carried (see Figure 11.4). Plasma is mainly water in which various substances are dissolved, such as gases like oxygen and carbon dioxide, nutrients like glucose and amino acids, salts, enzymes and hormones. There is also a combination of important proteins collectively known as plasma proteins: these have roles in blood clotting, transport, defence and osmosis.

The most numerous cells in the plasma are red blood cell (erythrocytes) which are bi-concave in shape, very small and packed with iron-containing haemoglobin that is responsible for combining with oxygen from the lungs. In the mature state, these cells have lost their nuclei (and consequently their power to divide) in order to have a larger surface area and carry more haemoglobin. They have a limited life of approximately 120 days.

White cells (leucocytes) are larger cells, which are less numerous and have various roles in defending the body against infection. There are several types, but the most numerous are the granulocytes, phagocytes and polymorphs that are capable of engulfing foreign material such as bacteria and carbon particles. Granulocytes carry lobed nuclei and granules scattered throughout the cell material. Large monocytes are also effective at engulfing foreign material (phagocytosis) and both granulocytes and monocytes are able to leave the circulation and travel through tissue.

Lymphocytes are smaller cells containing round nuclei and clear cytoplasm. They assist in the production of antibodies which form part of the plasma proteins. Thrombocytes or platelets are not full cells but products of the fragmentation of much larger cells. They play a vital role in blood clotting.

The functions of blood can be listed as follows:

- main system of transport throughout the body – oxygen, carbon dioxide, nutrients such as amino acids and glucose, antibodies, urea, etc.
- defence against disease – clotting, action of leucocytes
- temperature regulation – distribution of heat from warmer places such as the liver and muscles to cooler places such as limbs to maintain an even temperature
- aids in reproduction by stiffening the penis during insemination of the female.

Lymphatic system
The lymphatic system also forms part of the cardiovascular system. The lymphatic system begins as closed-ended lymphatic capillaries which lie in the spaces between cells (see Figure 11.5). They unite to form larger and larger vessels passing upwards eventually to join the great veins in the neck. At several points in this lymphatic circulation, the lymph passes through small nodules known as lymph nodes, which are

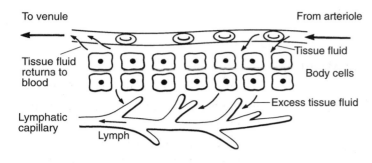

Figure 11.5 The relationship between blood capillaries, cell and lymphatic capillaries

scattered about the body in groups. Lymph nodes contain lymphocytes and macrophages which destroy any microbes which have entered the lymphatic vessels from the tissue spaces. They do this by initiating the antigen-antibody response (sometimes called the immune response) and by macrophages carrying out phagocytosis, which destroys the microbes.

The cardiovascular system

The heart is a muscular pump which forces blood around a system of blood vessels, namely arteries, veins and capillaries. Blood carries dissolved oxygen to the body cells and at the same time removes carbon dioxide and water. However, blood also distributes heat, hormones, nutrients and enzymes around the body as well as transporting urea between the liver and the kidneys for excretion with many other products.

The adult heart is the size of a clenched fist, located in the thoracic cavity in between the lungs, protected by the rib cage (see Figure 11.6). It is surrounded by a tough pericardium that contains a thin film of fluid to reduce friction. The heart is a double pump, each side consisting of an upper chamber (the atrium) and a lower chamber (the ventricle). The right-sided pump contains deoxygenated blood and is totally separate from the left side that contains oxygenated blood. Each chamber has a major blood vessel entering

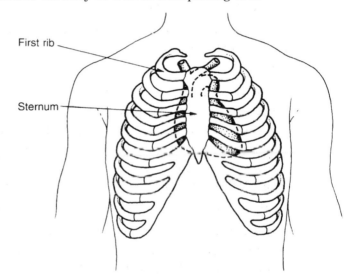

Figure 11.6 The thoracic cavity and heart

or leaving the heart. The veins pour blood into the atria and the ventricles bear arteries that carry blood away from the heart.

It is helpful to remember that atria have veins, ventricles have arteries: A and V in each case – never two As or two Vs.

The right pump receives blood from the body tissues, having offloaded its oxygen, and pumps the blood to the lungs for re-oxygenation. The left pump receives blood from the lungs, fully loaded with oxygen, and distributes it to the body tissue. You will notice the blood travels twice through the heart in one circuit around the body. This is known as a double circulation. Figure 11.7 illustrates this, but notice how the right and left halves have been artificially separated.

One circulation is to and from the lungs and is known as pulmonary circulation. Whenever you see or hear the word pulmonary you will know that it is referring to the

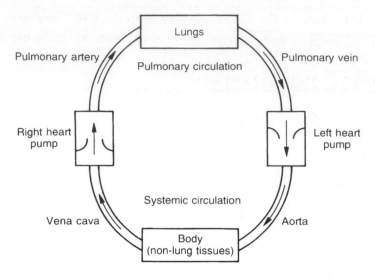

Figure 11.7 Double circulation: blood flows through the heart twice in one circuit

lungs; so the artery taking blood from the right ventricle is the pulmonary artery and the vein returning blood from the lungs to the left side of the heart is the pulmonary vein(s) – in fact there are four of these. The other circulation is called the systemic circulation because it carries blood to and from the body systems, except the lungs of course!

The main artery of the body is the aorta which leaves the left ventricle, and the main vein returning blood to the right atrium is the vena cava. There are two divisions of this vein, the superior and inferior venae cavae returning blood from the head/neck and the remainder of the trunk respectively.

The semilunar valves are located where the main arteries leave the ventricles. All these valves have the same purpose – to ensure that blood flows only one way through the heart.

You will also notice the septum dividing the right and left sides of the heart, valve tendons and papillary muscles in the ventricles. The papillary muscles contract and pull on the valve tendons a tiny fraction of a second before the main ventricular muscle contracts, so that the contraction does not force the tricuspid and bicuspid valves inside out. The valves make noises when they close, but not when they are open (rather like clapping your hands) and these noises are the heart sounds doctors listen for with a stethoscope.

Theory into practice

Ask to borrow a stethoscope and listen to either your own or a partner's heart sounds. They make sounds rather like lubb, dup, lubb, dup.

By counting each pair of lubb, dups for the duration of one minute, you would have a very accurate measurement of heart rate.

Think It Over

Study the labelled diagram of the heart (Figure 11.8) and find all the major blood vessels you have studied.

You will need to examine the diagram of the heart again to see four valves labelled. Two of these, the tricuspid and bicuspid, are located at the junctions of the atrium and ventricle on each side.

You can remember these because the TRIcuspid valve is on the RighT side (a rearrangement of the letters) so that the other side, the left must be the bicuspid valve.

The *myocardium* is the name for the heart muscle.
The *endocardium* is the name of the smooth endothelial lining of the cavities.

Superior vena cava

Semilunar
valve or
pulmonary valve

Arch of aorta

Pulmonary artery

Endocardium

Myocardium

Left atrium

Right atrium

Bicuspid valve

Tricuspid valve

Semilunar
valve or aortic
valve

Right ventricle

Left ventricle

Inferior vena cava

Septum

Branch of coronary
artery

The *chordae tendineae* and *papillary muscles* tie the edges of the
valves to the ventricular wall and stops the blood from
flowing backwards.

Figure 11.8 A section through the heart

Heart murmurs are extra sounds heard between the normal heart sounds. Some are significant and indicate problems, while others carry no significance. They are usually the result of disturbed blood flow.

Blood vessels

These tubes, together with the heart, make up the circulatory system (see Figure 11.10). The main types of blood vessel are shown in Figure 11.9.

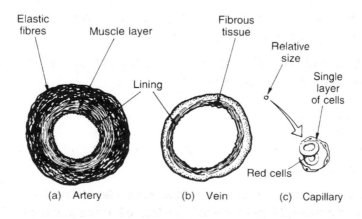

Elastic
fibres

Muscle layer

Fibrous
tissue

Relative
size

Single
layer
of cells

Lining

Red cells

(a) Artery

(b) Vein

(c) Capillary

Figure 11.9 Blood vessels, transverse sections

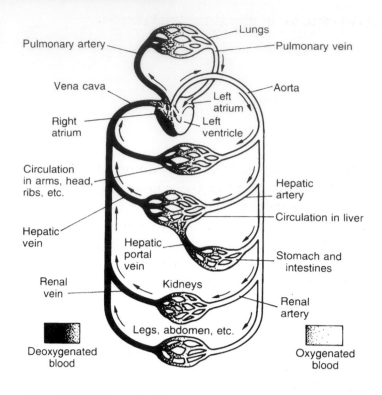

Figure 11.10 The human circulatory system

They are:

- arteries
- veins
- capillaries.

Each type has functional and anatomical differences.

Cardiac output

Each ventricle has a capacity of approximately 70 ml of blood. This is called the stroke volume as it is the quantity expelled at each beat of the heart. With moderate exercise and stressful circumstances the stroke volume can increase to 110 ml or as high as 140 ml in strenuous activity! Heart rates at rest vary a great deal, but in untrained people it is usually between 60 and 80 beats per minute. Cardiac output is the volume of blood expelled in one minute so is the result of heart rate multiplied by stroke volume.

Functions of the cardiovascular system can be listed as follows:

- circulate blood around the body
- assist with absorption, transport and distribution of digested food materials
- assist with the elimination of waste products of metabolism
- create blood pressure that is vital to distribute body fluids
- transport dissolved gases to their appropriate destinations to maintain respiration
- transport blood cells and antibodies important in the defence of the body to appropriate locations
- regulate the temperature of the body
- transport hormones to their target organs
- regulate the flow of blood to appropriate organs when required, such as exercise or in critical situations.

Breathing and respiration

There are two definitions crucial to your understanding of the respiratory system. These definitions are as follows:

- Respiration – this is the release of energy from the breakdown of food molecules.
- Energy – best described as a stored ability to do work.

The respiratory system comprises the anatomical structures and the physiological processes that take the vital oxygen into the body and transport it to the body cells where aerobic respiration can be carried out and, at the same time, eliminate its waste products. Respiration and energy release can take place only inside body cells.

The study of the process of respiration is facilitated by the subdivision into four distinct parts:

- breathing
- transport in the blood
- gaseous exchange
- cell respiration.

Breathing

The chest or thorax is an airtight box containing the lungs and their tubes, the bronchi (see Figure 11.11). There are two lungs (right and left), each with its own bronchus, which unite to form the windpipe or trachea. The trachea joins the back of the throat or pharynx, which connects with both mouth and nose, which are of course open to external air. All these tubes are lined with mucus-secreting ciliated cells and have either C-shaped rings or small plates of cartilage in their walls to prevent collapse. Mucus is a sticky, white, jelly-like material which lubricates and traps dust particles that can enter by external passages.

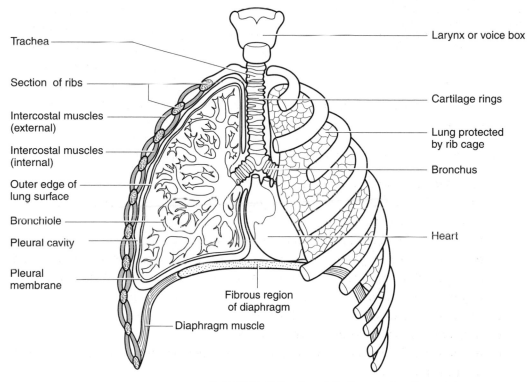

Figure 11.11 Section through the thorax to show the respiratory organs

The lungs themselves have a thin, outer covering of a membrane called the pleura and are located behind the chest wall which is also internally lined with pleura. Between the two layers of pleura is a thin film of moisture, which exerts surface tension, so allowing the two layers to slide up and down but not allowing them to pull apart easily. This means that when the chest walls move, the lungs are usually pulled with them.

Forming the wall of the chest, outside the pleura, is the bony rib cage with two sets of oblique muscles joining them together – these are known as the intercostal muscles (*inter* means between; *costal* means ribs). A sheet of muscle called the diaphragm forms the floor of the chest. The diaphragm is dome-shaped, with the highest part in the centre

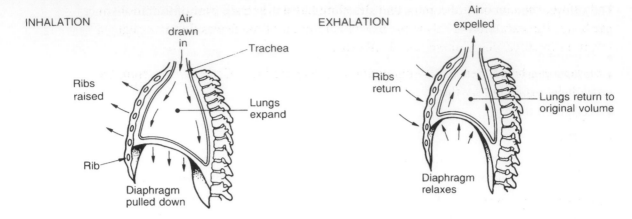

Figure 11.12 Changes during inhalation and exhalation

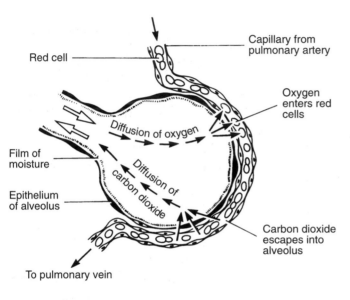

Figure 11.13 Gaseous exchange in an alveolus

and the edges firmly attached to the lowest ribs. The chest is an airtight cavity with the trachea being the only way for air to enter.

Gaseous exchange

Inside the lungs, smaller and smaller branches of the bronchi, called bronchioles, open into thousands of air sacs, each containing a cluster of alveoli. Each air sac with its alveoli and bronchiole looks rather like a bunch of grapes on a stem.

The wall of each alveolus is only one cell thick and surrounded on its outside by tiny blood vessels called capillaries – these, too, have walls only one cell thick. The air in each alveolus is separated from the blood in the capillary by very thin walls, only two flat cells thick. A film of moisture in which the respiratory gases dissolve lines each alveolus. The walls of the alveoli contain elastic fibres capable of expansion and recoil. The process by which gases exchange across these walls is called **diffusion** (see Figure 11.13).

Excretion

As you take in the raw materials to sustain life and living processes, so waste products are produced as a result of the chemical reactions that make up the metabolism. Waste products can be gases, such as carbon dioxide, water, salts and nitrogenous materials. Carbon dioxide and some water can be removed by exhaling air from the lungs, but the main route out of the body for most of the water, salts and nitrogenous materials is in the urine produced by the kidneys and voided from the bladder and urethra.

You may think that faeces or stools eliminated from the rectum or back passage are also waste material. In fact, most of this material has mainly passed through the centre of the body (from the mouth to the anus) and therefore has not become part of the 'flesh' of the body. The exception to this is the brown coloration of the faeces that is a pigment left from the breakdown of old red blood cells.

Excretion can be defined as the elimination of waste products of metabolism from the body. It is carried out by the:

- lungs
- liver
- kidneys
- skin.

The renal system

The renal system consists of the two kidneys and the tubes leading from them to the bladder called the ureters, the bladder and the urethra (see Figure 11.14). the only difference between males and females is that the urethra in the males is longer and also serves as part of the reproductive system as it is used to convey semen (spermatozoa and gland secretions) during copulation. Short renal arteries leave the aorta to enter each kidney and renal veins carry the blood from the kidneys to the inferior vena cava. The kidneys are dark red in colour because they receive one quarter of the cardiac output.

The kidneys

Each kidney holds approximately one million microscopic units called nephrons that are responsible for producing urine. Urine travels to the bladder down the ureters and is voided at regular intervals from the bladder via the urethra.

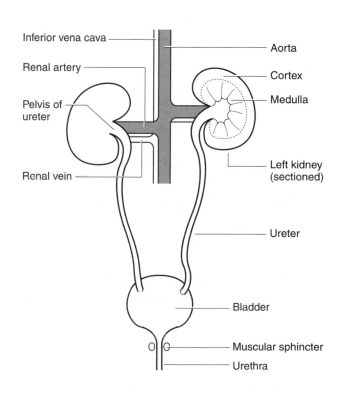

Figure 11.14 The renal system

The kidneys of some people fail to work effectively (renal failure) and they must either have regular dialysis to remove the waste products by a kidney machine or have a kidney transplant.

The alimentary canal

Ingestion is the act of food being taken into the mouth, chewed and rolled into a small ball suitable for swallowing (a bolus). The bolus passes quickly down the oesophagus into the stomach. Strong muscles in the wall of the stomach churn the food into a loose paste called chyme.

Chyme leaves the stomach to enter the small intestine. Two very important organs pour juices onto the chyme in the first part of the small intestine to help further breakdown.

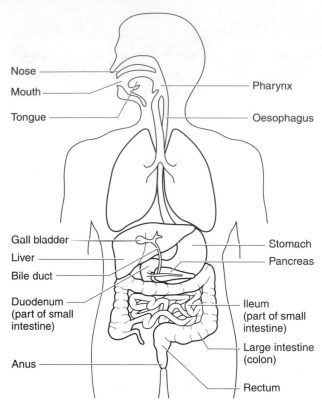

Figure 11.15 The alimentary canal

- the liver pours bile on the chyme.
- the pancreas pours an enzyme-rich juice onto food that continues the breakdown of all three major food components (protein, starch and fat).

The large intestine returns water into the blood by reabsorption. By the time the food residue has reached the last part of the large intestine, known as the rectum, a semi-solid motion has been formed. Faeces contain cellulose, dead bacteria, and scraped-off gut lining cells. It is coloured brown by the bile pigments formed from the breakdown of dead blood cells.

Movement

Bones cannot move by themselves: they need muscles to pull them into a different position. Muscles always pull, never push. This means that there must be at least two muscles to effect a movement; one muscle pulls to displace the bone and the other pulls to return it to its former position.

One of the best examples of bone and muscle working together can be seen in the flexing and extending of the forearm. Flexing means decreasing the angle between two bones and extending is the reverse action.

Sexual reproduction

Male gametes are spermatozoa produced in large numbers by the male testis and delivered in glandular fluids into the female body by tubes or ducts that emerge through an erect penis capable of insertion into the female vagina (see Figure 11.17).

Female gametes or ova are usually released singly every four weeks by the ovary. The ovum enters the oviduct and travels slowly towards the uterus or womb. It may or may not become fertilised during this journey, depending on whether sexual intercourse or insemination occurs at the right time.

When fertilisation has taken place, the resulting cell – known as a zygote – undergoes many cell divisions to

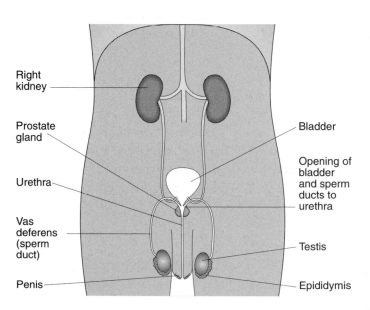

Figure 11.16 The male reproductive system

form the embryo, its coverings and umbilical cord through which it receives nourishment during the pre-birth stages. After about eleven days, when the tiny embryo has reached the uterus, it begins to embed itself in the thick wall of the uterus, where it undergoes further growth and development for about 40 weeks. This period is known as gestation and, at the end, uterine muscle contractions expel the foetus (the name given to an embryo after two months) from the mother's body through the vagina.

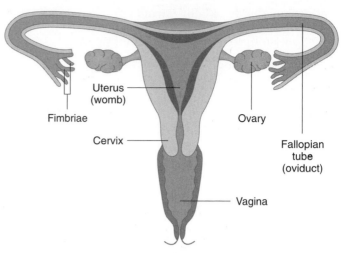

Figure 11.17 The female reproductive system

The nervous system

To conserve energy, the body systems need to work together in harmony to produce maximum efficiency. This efficiency should not be impaired even when external and internal changes take place. The role of the nervous system is to control and co-ordinate the different body systems and to respond appropriately to changes in the environment.

The central nervous system (CNS) is composed of the brain and spinal cord; the cranial (from the brain) and spinal nerves from the peripheral nervous system that connects the CNS with all parts of the body. Within the CNS are hundreds of thousand of nerve cells or neurones with long processes wrapped in connective tissues that from the nerves. Neurone are excitable cells (similar to muscle cells) which respond to stimuli by creating tiny electrical impulses that can cause muscles to contract or glands to secrete.

Stimuli received by the sense organs scattered around the body initiate impulses which travel along sensory nerves to the CNS, or impulses can be generated by the workings of mind and intelligence.

Control of internal organs and processes such as heart and breathing rates, peristalsis (gut movements), balance and sexual intercourse are carried out by the autonomic system of nerves connected to the brain and spinal cord.

The endocrine system

Some glands in the body pass their secretions directly into the bloodstream and not down tubes or ducts. These glands are called endocrine glands and the active materials in their secretions are hormones. Hormones cause a change in a target organ that may be close at hand or some distance away. Some hormonal secretions affect only one place in the body, but others have an affect on the entire body. The major hormones and their actions are shown in the table overleaf.

Endocrine glands and their hormones control and co-ordinate the behaviour of other cells and in this regard they have a similar role to the nervous system. Their action is much slower than the nervous system because hormones travel to their target organs via the bloodstream.

Further details of anatomical and physiological processes can be found in the companion to this book, *BTEC Health Studies*.

Endocrine gland	Major hormones	Summary of the actions of the hormones
Hypothalamus – also part of the brain	Releasing and inhibitory factors that control other endocrine glands	Stimulation and inhibition of many glands, particularly the pituitary gland
Pituitary gland – anterior part	Growth hormone	Skeletal, muscular and soft-tissue growth
	Adrenocorticotrophic hormone (ACTH), also known as corticotropin	Stimulation of the hormone cortisol from the adrenal cortex
	Follicle stimulating hormone (FSH), also known as follitropin	Stimulates the production of gametes form the gonads
	Luteinising hormone or lutropin	Causes ovulation and the formation of the corpus luteum in females. Causes testosterone to be secreted from the testis in males
	Prolactin	Stimulates breast-milk formation after childbirth
	Thyroid stimulating hormone or thyrotropin	Stimulates the thyroid gland to produce thyroxine
Pituitary gland – posterior part	Antidiuretic hormone, also known as vasopressin	Causes water reabsorption in the second renal tubules and collecting ducts
	Oxytocin	Causes rhythmic contractions of uterine muscle in childbirth
Thyroid gland	Thyroxine	Regulates growth and development and controls the basic metabolic rate
Parathyroid glands	Parathyrin	Controls calcium in blood and body tissues
Adrenal glands – the medulla	Adrenaline and noradrenaline	Stimulates the fright, fight and flight response to stress. Involved in the regulation of blood sugar
Adrenal glands – the cortex	Cortisol	Involved in regulating blood sugar and repair of body organs damaged in degenerative diseases
Pancreas (islets of Langerhans)	Insulin and Glucagon	Regulation of blood sugars
Ovaries	Oestrogen and progesterone	Growth and development of primary and secondary sexual organs and female secondary sexual characteristics
Testes	Testosterone	Growth and development of primary and secondary sexual organs and male secondary sexual characteristics

Safe disposal of clinical waste

Pathogens are disease-causing micro-organisms and must be considered to contaminate all **clinical waste**. Safe **disposal** of all clinical waste such as dressings, bandages, and removed sutures (stitches) must be carried out to prevent infection. The Department of Health and Social Security has issued guidance on the methods of disposal and the colour coding of containers used for waste and most establishments have a policy for waste disposal.

- Yellow bags (sealed after use) are for clinical waste disposed of by incineration.
- Sharps boxes (often yellow, but well labelled) are for syringe needles, scalpels and other sharp instruments and are also incinerated.
- Yellow bins are for human tissue, also incinerated.
- Black plastic bags are for domestic waste, plastic drinking cups, discarded cardboard boxes, dead flowers, etc.
- Bed linen removed from a service user's bed should be bagged immediately on removal and treated according to the policy of the establishment.
- You are unlikely to be inside an isolation unit, but here policies dictate double-bagging to reduce the risk of spreading infection further.

Theory into practice

Write a short description of the way in which the items listed below are disposed of in your care setting

- a dressing which has been used to cover a wound
- dirty bed linen removed from a service user with incontinence
- a contaminated needle from a syringe used to deliver a local anaesthetic.

Moving and handling service users

First and foremost, you should not be involved in moving and handling service users or using equipment designed to assist in moving and handling without thorough training by a qualified instructor. Large organisations, such as hospitals, will have an appointed moving and handling co-ordinator, who will also update employees each year on the principles and practice of moving and handling operations. This is so important that it is covered by several pieces of legislation and regulations.

Health and Safety at Work Act (1974)

Employers must:

- ensure that employees are not exposed to foreseeable risks of injury
- develop a no-manual-handling policy in practice
- provide information, instruction, training and supervision necessary to ensure health and safety
- maintain a working environment that is safe and without risks to health and adequate as regards facilities and arrangements for welfare at work.

Employees must take reasonable care of their own health and safety and that of other people who may be affected by their actions.

The Manual Handling Operations Regulations (HSE, 1992)

- All equipment should be available with full instruction in its use.
- All staff must be trained in the use of equipment they are expected to employ.
- Equipment must be in good working order.
- Equipment designed for shared use should have guidelines for disinfection.

Equipment must be:

- compatible with the surroundings, other equipment and mechanical aids
- designed to reduce or avoid manual handling
- easy to use, move, adjust and maintain.

Risk assessments, including working with others to move a service user manually in exceptional circumstances, are complex and you should decline politely if you are asked and are untrained.

Dietary requirements

Most of us believe that we are eating a healthy (balanced) diet, but we hear much more about the risks to health nowadays than ever before. Experts agree that the UK population was healthier during World War II when food rationing existed and people consumed much less sugar, fat and protein.

Food chemicals making up the bulk of our food are called **macronutrients**. These provide energy, materials for growth and repair and cell structure and function.

Carbohydrates

About 60 per cent of our daily intake should be carbohydrates such as starch and sugars; when these are broken down by digestive enzymes large quantities of energy are released, fulfilling half of our energy requirements. Complex carbohydrates such as porridge, bread, rice, cereals, pasta and chapattis are better for us because they take longer to digest, are filling and provide slow-release energy. Convenience foods (which also can contain high fat levels), sweets, biscuits, chocolate, crisps and snack foods release their energy swiftly, creating peaks of energy that fade away rapidly leaving a feeling of hunger again. This last list is also believed to increase the incidence of certain conditions such as tooth decay, atherosclerosis (narrowing of the arteries from fatty plaques), obesity and mature-onset diabetes. Many processed foods contain 'hidden' sugar so you should check the labels on the packaging – even baked beans contain sugar.

Protein

Body cells can be considered as tiny bags of protein, so to achieve growth in children or to repair and replace body cells in children and adults every individual requires a supply of protein in their diet. Proteins are made of chains of **amino acids**; both these materials contain nitrogen so are often referred to as nitrogen-containing compounds. When there is a large turnover of tissue protein in the body as a result of the disease process, or when excessive quantities of protein are consumed, the amino acids are degraded in the liver to form urea (also a nitrogen-containing compound). Urea travels into the bloodstream to the kidneys for elimination in urine. High-protein diets produce extra work for the liver and kidneys and some experts believe that kidney stones and osteoporosis are a possible result.

Rich sources of protein are meat, fish, eggs, nuts, peas, beans, lentils, soya and tofu, while bread, milk and cereals contain less but still significant quantities. Vegetarians can get all their protein requirements from plant sources providing that they eat a wide variety of plant foods. Often recommended is a diet containing peas, beans or lentils with bread, rice or cereals.

Theory into practice

Imagine that you are helping to choose a main meal and pudding (for three days) from a wide-ranging menu for a service user who is:

1 a vegetarian adult
2 a non-vegetarian adult.

The meals must be different each day and supply at least half their daily dietary requirements.

Think It Over

Why do pregnant women and breast-feeding mothers require more protein in their diet than the average female?

Why do post-operative service users require more protein and Vitamin C?

Fats

Fats or lipids are the last of the macronutrients and are found in dairy products, nuts, meat, oily fish, cereals and even some fruits. In addition fat is added to food during cooking and processing. A totally fat-free diet is pretty uninteresting and bland, so individuals soon get tired of it.

Fat is a concentrated source of energy releasing twice as much (35kJ per gram) as either carbohydrate or protein (17kJ per gram). Note that protein is used for energy only when consumed in excessive quantities, as its main role is growth and repair.

Everyone needs some fat in their diet to build cell membranes, form steroid hormones, insulate the skin against heat loss, dissolve the fat-soluble vitamins and protect some organs. However, most people in Western societies consume too much fat and this can lead to obesity, heart disease and many other related conditions.

Energy

Energy requirements vary according to gender, age, race and degree of physical activity and so typical figures in tables of energy requirements may not suit each service user. The energy requirements for a healthy adult should be sufficient to maintain a steady body weight. You will know what happens when too much food energy is consumed – body weight increases, mostly as fat. When too little is consumed, the body tissues will begin to break down and body weight is reduced.

Alcohol also breaks down in the body to provide energy but it provides no other useful materials such as vitamins, minerals or NSP (non-starch polysaccharides), so it is not recommended to supply energy requirements with alcohol.

NSP

Also supplying bulk to the meal but not supplying energy is NSP or non-starch polysaccharides. This used to be known as roughage, fibre, cellulose or sometimes bran but these terms are being withdrawn, to be replaced by NSP.

There is no NSP in animal and dairy products; it is to be found in plant foods such as fruit, vegetables, peas, beans, lentils and cereals. The recommended intake is 12g per day from a selection of five fruit or vegetable portions consumed daily. NSP prevents bowel disorders and stimulates peristalsis.

Fluids

Adults should have a fluid intake of 1.5-2.0 dm3 each day, preferably much of this to be water that does not supply energy needs. Tea, coffee, carbonated drinks and fruit juices may, if taken in excess, present other problems.

Vitamins and minerals

Micronutrients in our food, which do not supply energy needs, are needed in only small amounts and are necessary to the efficient functioning of the human body. Micronutrients are the vitamins and minerals found in our food.

Name	Rich sources	Functions	Additional comments
FAT-SOLUBLE VITAMINS			
A	Carrots and leafy green vegetables	Maintain healthy epithelial (lining) tissues	Stored in the liver and released when required.
	Liver and fish liver oils	Maintain a healthy immune system	High intake is associated with foetal defects so pregnant women advised to avoid liver, liver products and pâté
	Butter and most margarine	Promote twilight vision	
	Eggs	Promote growth and bone development in children	
D	Butter and most margarine, some milk and eggs	Assists in the absorption of calcium, so is important for healthy, hard bones and teeth.	Most people gain adequate supplies from the action of sunlight on the skin
	Oily fish, added to breakfast cereals	Deficiency leads to rickets in children and osteomalacia in adults	
E	Eggs, cereals, plant oils	Helps to safeguard cell membranes and lipids from damage	Known anti-oxidant
	Nuts and dark leafy vegetables		

Name	Rich sources	Functions	Additional comments
K	Liver, green vegetables, margarine and plant oils	Assists in clotting of blood Plays a part in energy release Bacteria living naturally in the gut produce forerunner of Vit. K	People on long-term antibiotics may need extra supplies
WATER-SOLUBLE VITAMINS			
C	Green vegetables and potatoes Citrus fruits, strawberries and black/redcurrants	Maintains connective tissue Helps wounds to heal Deficiency results in fatal condition of scurvy. Lack of C leads to more infections and delayed healing	Smokers need more than non-smokers. Anti-oxidant
B1 Thiamine	Meat, cereals, green vegetables	Helps in energy release from fat and carbohydrate	
B2 Riboflavin	Meat, cereals, eggs, liver and yoghurt	Assists in energy release	
B3 Niacin	As for B2	As for B2	
B6 Pyridox-amine	Liver, cereals, beans, meat and fish	Maintains efficient nervous and endocrine systems Assists with the metabolism of proteins	Bacteria living in the gut manufacture some B6
B12	Meat, fish, eggs, offal (particularly liver) and yeast extract	Required for efficient manufacture of red blood cells and the healthy function of the nervous system. Deficiency gives rise to pernicious anaemia and is not uncommon in vegans, vegetarians and people who have gastric surgery.	Also known as the intrinsic factor from the stomach lining In past times, people with pernicious anaemia had to eat raw liver to obtain this vitamin
Folic acid	Offal, green vegetables, and cereals	Required for efficient blood cell production	Prevents spina bifida during pregnancy

Figure 11.18 Table showing the functions and sources of vitamins

In older textbooks, you may find that the average quantities of food chemicals are known as RDAs (Recommended Daily Allowances) but these were replaced over ten years ago by the term Dietary Reference Values or DRVs. You can find up-to-date DRVs in a Department of Health publication listed in further reading.

Trace amounts of naturally occurring inorganic substances known as minerals are required in a healthy diet. The most important are:

- Calcium – most important for bones and teeth development (see also Vitamin D) this mineral also has a role in blood clotting, and nerve and muscle physiology. Found in dairy products including yoghurt, leafy green vegetables and canned fish.
- Iron – essential for the transport of oxygen by red blood cells. Iron deficiency leads to iron-deficiency anaemia. Iron is found in meat, cereal products, potatoes and green leafy vegetables. Vegetarians are again more likely to become anaemic, together with children and adults with food fads.
- Iodine – necessary for the manufacture of thyroxine hormone that controls the rate of metabolism in the body and is important in the growth of children. It is found in seafood, and dairy products, but in the UK table salt also has added iodide.

Theory into practice

Most establishments supply a variety of breakfast cereals to choose from. Examine the nutrition labels on at least four packets of cereal and discuss the availability of the micro-nutrients listed from a breakfast meal for an adult service user. You may take into account the milk usually added to the cereal.

Safe food handling

Study leading to one of the Food Hygiene certificates within your study programme will be most beneficial to you, although you will learn about basic food hygiene in the following paragraphs.

Food poisoning outbreaks are not uncommon in the home and in care settings. When an outbreak occurs in a care setting, vulnerable service users may be very ill or die (most often new babies and older people), staff absences will increase, public confidence is eroded and establishments may have to close temporarily. All this is also very costly, eroding the budget for other uses. As a consequence therefore, improved education in food handling and stricter controls have been imposed.

The main pieces of legislation and support are:

- Food Safety Act 1990 – major piece of legislation relevant to food, manufacture and materials in contact with food.
- Food Standards Agency (1998) – enforces food safety procedures and policies to protect public interests because of fears over food safety.

Other legislation includes:

- Food Act (1984)
- EC Food Safety Legislation
- Food and Drugs Act (1955, 1984).

The different types of bacterial food poisoning are:

- *Campylobacter* (the most common)
- *Salmonella*
- *Listeria*
- *Escherichia coli* (*E. coli*)
- *Clostridium staphylococcal.*

As well as bacterial food poisoning, which is by far the most common, food may also be contaminated by chemicals, viruses, fungi, human products such as hair and finger nail-clippings, machine parts and glass. Food poisoning is usually characterised by vomiting, diarrhoea and pain, although some other types such as botulism may cause more serious symptoms that are often fatal. Many bacteria cause illness through the poisons or toxins that they produce and these cause food to be rushed through the bowel, hence the diarrhoea and pain.

Food that is thoroughly cooked and served immediately is unlikely to cause bacterial food poisoning. This is of course almost impossible in large institutions like hospitals and large restaurants or cafeterias. Food cooked a long time before serving is responsible for many outbreaks, particularly if not kept hot (above 63°C). Food kept at room temperature is also potentially dangerous as the bacteria double their numbers every twenty minutes. Inadequate thawing of food, especially poultry and meat, may mean that the interior of the food never reaches a sufficiently high temperature to kill any bacteria. Large turkeys at Christmas can be particularly dangerous as the insides of the carcasses are usually contaminated with Salmonella. Re-heating previously cooked food is not safe as it rarely reaches the temperature of the original cooking, as the dish might be spoiled by this.

Incorrect refrigerator temperatures (should be below 5°C) and cooling food for too long before refrigeration are potential sources of trouble. Low temperatures only inhibit bacterial growth; bacteria are not killed, and so continually opening a refrigerator door or putting in warm food will raise the temperature above a safe level.

Raw food should always be considered contaminated whereas thoroughly (just) cooked food can be thought of as safe. Cross-contamination can occur if knives or other utensils are used on raw food and then cooked food. It can also happen if raw food is allowed to drip or come into contact with cooked food in a refrigerator. Cross-contamination can also occur through chopping boards, especially wooden ones, and dishcloths; the latter should not remain bunched up and wet after using, but spread out and allowed to dry.

Personal hygiene

Personal hygiene of the food handlers is of paramount importance. They should thoroughly wash their hands after touching any part of their (or anyone else's) body, including the hair. Avoid smoking as touching of the lips occurs and ash is unpleasant around food. Any illness, particularly of the bowel, stomach, skin, nose and throat, should be reported so that other duty maybe assigned; any skin wounds or abrasions should be covered with a highly coloured waterproof dressing. It is particularly important to wash hands thoroughly after using the toilet as food poisoning bacteria lurk in everyone's intestines.

Food should be kept clean and covered, and utensils and equipment clean. Any spills should be wiped up thoroughly and the area left clean. 'Clean as you go' is the key phrase in kitchen hygiene. Pets, flies and insects should not be allowed in a kitchen area as they carry contamination. Kitchen waste should be wrapped and placed in covered bins.

Failure to observe the guidelines can result in prosecution under the Food Safety Act referred to earlier.

Personal hygiene requirements
Washing and bathing

Different people have different views on how often they wish to wash or bathe and generally it is considered to be their choice. The carer might wish to encourage (or more rarely, discourage) washing or bathing by careful reasoned explanations (see the box below), but cannot enforce the action. Having obtained the service user's agreement and co-operation, you can plan and prepare for the activity.

Does the service user:

- prefer a bath or a shower?
  The choice in a setting may be limited or the service user may find that one of these choices is unsuitable due to physical disabilities. Hindu and Muslim culture advocates the use of running water for bathing.

- need constant assistance or only with particular aspects such as removing some clothing?
  It is also prudent to check with your supervisor as the service user may have an unrealistic view of their abilities and the bathroom can be a major hazard area.

- need regular supervision?
  Some service users prefer to manage themselves while others will need checking every few minutes.

- prefer a carer of the same sex when bathing?
  Service users from some cultures (such as Muslim and Hindu) will receive care only from an individual of the same sex and others may prefer it.

- wish his or hair to be washed or otherwise managed?
  It is the custom in some cultures, such as Sikhism, not to cut hair.

Think It Over

What would your responsibilities and those of your employer be when assisting a service user with their personal hygiene requirements?

All service users should have their privacy respected by door or curtain closure and the number of carers should be restricted to those who are strictly necessary. When the service user is adamant about not having a shower or bath, regular washing should still be encouraged. Service users might need to be gently reminded that a visit to the toilet or the use of a bedpan or bottle is a good idea before bathing.

Many service users will need a considerable time to complete their cleansing routines and this also needs to be taken into account, as they should not be rushed. Hurrying causes the feeling of well-being to diminish and can lead to more errors resulting in accidents. Ensure that all the equipment necessary for the individual to bath or shower is close to hand and that the water is at the preferred, safe temperature. Baths are available with extra or integral seats, hand-rails, handles, walk-in doors, non-slip mats and hoists for lifting people in and out. There is also a wide variety of seats and hand-rails suitable for use in showers. Buzzers, to enable a service user in difficulties to call a carer, should be at hand.

A service user should be encouraged to wash (and dry) all the areas that they can manage themselves, so be aware that they will need to be able to reach all those areas. Assistance can be offered where it is necessary. Clean up the wash room after the service user has finished and been accompanied back to the living area.

When a service user is confined to bed, bowls of warm water can be provided with closed curtains for privacy and assistance where necessary. Bed baths need two carers. As each part of the body is washed, rinsed and dried make sure that the remainder is covered up with a towel to prevent chilling. Use two or three facecloths (one for face, one for body and one for the genitals) and change the water regularly. When the service user is rolled over for access to the back of the body, change the sheets if required.

Always be observant when a service user is washing, or being assisted to wash, for skin changes such as pigmentation, moles, eczema, dermatitis, swellings, scratches, bruises, etc. and bring these to a supervisor's attention.

Clean-shaven male service users can feel uncomfortable if stubble is allowed to grow unchecked. Many service users will be able to shave themselves if the equipment and toiletries are provided close at hand together with hot water. Protect the service user's chest with a dry towel and wear suitable protective clothing including gloves if you are carrying out the task for him. Here again there will be many personal preferences for a carer to explore if it becomes necessary to give assistance or to perform the task for the service user. Remember to rinse and dry the facial area after shaving and before after-shave.

As with bathing, establish agreement and co-operation and plan the task with the service user. Ask for feedback as you are proceeding with the activity.

Think It Over

After a service user has shaved (by himself or by a carer) what will you do with:

- wet towels
- blood-stained towels
- used razor blades?

Theory into practice

You are likely to be very nervous the first time you have to shave someone else and this will be particularly so if you are female and have never shaved even your own face. Ask your tutor for help getting practice; he or she may be able to provide a few model heads from a training salon or failing that you might try using a smooth football or inflated balloon. You could cover the 'facial area' with a strip of fine velvet or flannelette to give a textured feel to the surface. When you have had some practice like this, try to persuade a close male member of your family or a friend to let you try to shave them. Do not forget to ask for feedback from them and prepare for the task as if it is a real service user. You can also try shaving someone else's legs to get the feel of working on a service user. Confidence will be gained with competence.

Intimate hygiene

When you are looking after young and middle-age female service users, you may have to assist with menstrual hygiene. The principles are the same for any intimate personal hygiene requirements, so you should be able to plan your procedure as before.

Think It Over

- Female students – in pairs or groups of three, consider all the issues involved in caring for a new female service user who is about to menstruate.
- Male students – in pairs, consider how you would manage a situation when a female service user is anxious and reserved and you suspect that she is embarrassed about impending menstruation. When you have done this to the satisfaction of your tutor or female colleagues, then sit in and listen or contribute to the other discussions.

When you are old enough to care for other people, you are also deemed old enough to be able to discuss the real issues in care, including a topic such as this. Giggling and embarrassment have no place in learning to care, so handle the topic with responsibility; being able to discuss issues sensibly with colleagues will soon dispel any initial discomfort that you might feel.

Mouth and teeth

Most service users will be able to cleanse their own teeth and mouth, but again some may need some assistance. You will have vast amounts of experience for this so communicate with the service user and offer to do the parts that they cannot manage in a gentle fashion. Rather like the need for clean skin, bacteria and food particles will build up if the mouth is not cleaned, leading to gum and tooth disease.

Theory into practice

Bring in your dental care materials, disposable gloves, a bowl, paper towels and a bottle of water and try to clean a partner's teeth. Change over when you have finished. Feedback on the process to your partner and discuss the most difficult parts.

Discuss how it felt for both of you.

Toilet needs

Going to the toilet is another potentially embarrassing topic and needs to be discussed with sensitivity. Not getting to the toilet in time is even more embarrassing for the service user than asking for assistance. Discuss toilet needs with your service user in a private, dignified way. Actually getting to the toilet is the first problem if the service user has a difficulty with mobility; alternatives are to use a commode, bedpan, or bottle for males. Many service users can access toilet facilities by using a wheeled chair because they can manage on their own for a short time but cannot walk far. Toilets should have call buzzers easy to reach. The service user should be allowed privacy once the toilet is reached and assistance with clothing (if necessary) has been given. Toilets can be adapted with supporting rails and raised seats for those service users who have difficulty getting on to the lavatory. Hand-washing facilities should be close to the toilet area and assistance with cleaning may be required. As you may be dealing with body fluids, disposable gloves should be worn.

For more details about managing personal hygiene requirements, particularly for service users who are very ill, consult a more specialised text in caring such as *Care NVQ Level 2* in the further reading list.

Use of aids and adaptations to support self-management

You are learning how to work with service users to identify their needs and the various ways in which you can support them to meet those identified needs.

Providing support to service users must be done in a safe way that enables them to maintain their self-respect and dignity, as well as promoting independence and free choice. Everyone needs physical care at some time in their lives; as helpless babies we could not have survived without physical help from a parent or carer. Physical assistance may be temporary, such as a service user with a fractured leg requiring a Zimmer frame or crutches, or it may be permanent, such as a service user with a progressive degenerative condition such as Parkinson's or Alzheimer's disease. Never assume that an elderly service user requires physical assistance; some people are fiercely independent and feel offended if offered help. It is also wise not to assume that an elderly service user in residential accommodation needs physical help, as there are many reasons why an individual may not live independently. In fact, it is better to assume that each service user is capable of managing their own daily living activities and alter what you do to suit each person. Sensitive communication will soon ascertain whether assistance is required.

Daily living activities might include:

- shopping
- preparing and eating food and drink
- washing, dressing and undressing
- using the lavatory
- housework
- gardening
- reading, writing, calculating, hobbies
- answering telephones or doorbells
- moving about or going to see friends.

Most of us take these activities for granted, but for some service users they can be very difficult and almost impossible without some physical help. Every day more and more aids and adaptations become available and there are even large shops where you can explore all manner of physical aids. General ideas are all that can be incorporated into part of a chapter like this, so you will find it beneficial to visit a care centre where aids are on display or obtain catalogues from suppliers.

Be pro-active and explore the wide range of physical aids and adaptations for yourself. Find out whether there is a centre for supplying assistive devices within easy travelling distance of your home or college and arrange for a group from your class to visit. Such a centre may be a commercial outlet or part of the NHS or Social Services. Ask at the branches of nationwide chemists for a catalogue of physical aids for disabled people, if not immediately available they may be able to arrange for one to be sent to you.

Explore the numerous online catalogues on the Internet; many websites are based in the USA but use the search engine to find the Disabled Living Foundation in the UK. This is an excellent site for providing lists of suppliers of equipment, short resumés and prices. Many county council and city websites have sections on services for the disabled and these can be supplemented by voluntary organisation websites such as the National Multiple Sclerosis Society.

Here are a few websites to get you started:

- www.abledata.com
- www.maxiaids.com
- www.nationalmssociety.org
- www.freedomlivingdevices.com

Dressing

We use clothing for privacy, well-being, warmth and protection as well as to express our identity and personality. A service user should be given the choice of his or her clothing, although you may provide helpful suggestions. 'You always look so nice in that cosy warm dress' is more likely to gain acceptance than 'You can't wear that, it is much too cold'. When clothes are too thin for the climate, they can be layered with other garments in a fashionable way. When clothes are too warm for the climate, they feel uncomfortable and the service user will soon want to change. If the service user is elderly, the thinning of the skin and inactivity may mean that he or she experiences the weather in a different way from busy carers, so the service user may know exactly what is right for them. If you are laying out the clothing for the day, respect the service user's choice and take into account religious and cultural influences and the difficulties of fastenings. You will find some ideas to help service users retain independence when dressing in the box below.

Aids and adaptations to help with dressing and undressing

- button hooks, one-hand button rotation devices to help with fastening buttons.
- touch and close tape ('velcro') can replace buttons
- stocking aids
- replace stockings with tracksuit bottoms and socks for warmth and comfort
- touch and close fastenings on shoes
- specially fitted shoes
- elastic laces convert lace shoes into slip-on shoes
- long shoe horns and special shoe removers reduce bending down
- large zip pullers
- hooked stick for pulling clothes over the shoulders.

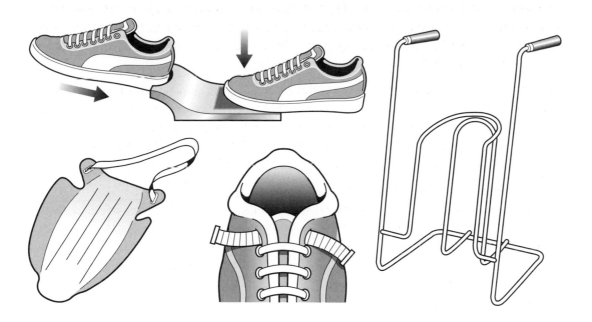

Figure 11.19 *Adaptations for dressing*

When helping a service user with one good limb and one stiff or less flexible limb, remember the rule:

- when dressing, stiff limb first
- but undressing, stiff limb last.

Washing and bathing

You have already learned much about washing and bathing in the previous section; take the opportunity to re-read this part before continuing.

Powered bath-lifts, costing several hundred pounds, allow the seated service user to be lowered into the bath safely. Somewhat less expensive are turning bath seats that allow the service user to sit outside the bath and turn swinging the legs over the bath side. Relatively inexpensive are bath seats, which hang over the sides of the bath. Some baths may incorporate a seat into the design and others can recline after the service user has

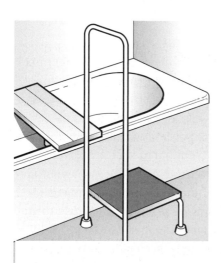
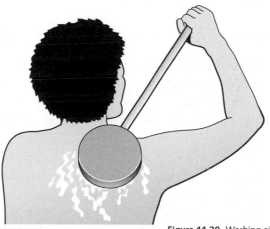

Figure 11.20 *Washing aids*

entered. Some baths, often advertised on TV, are taller with doors that open to allow the service user to walk in and sit down. There are a wide variety of inexpensive inflatable pillows and cushions for using in the bath. Babies can be bathed in a baby bath inside the adult bath.

Showers can have plastic seats with a hole in the centre to allow cleaning and water drainage.

Grab-rails and handles are essential around bathing areas and hand basins, so that the service user can hold on if required. Non-slip bath mats can be placed inside and outside the bath areas because soap and water can make these areas slippery. Soap on a rope is useful in showers as it can be hung from the shower and does not slip to the floor. There are many types of containers that can be attached to shower equipment to hold sponges, shampoo and other washing essentials.

Taps which are hard to turn can have adaptations fixed on to them and arthritic hands will find these a lot easier to use. Bath and sink plugs are available with extra long and thicker pulling attachments.

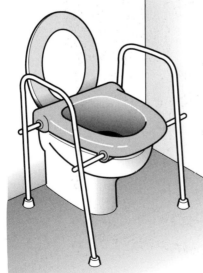

Using the lavatory

Young children can have access to an adult toilet by an easily cleaned step and an inner seat that slots into the adult seat. They may require help in cleaning after a motion has been passed and moist wipes are now available, some specially for children. All children should learn to wash and dry their hands thoroughly after using the toilet, and girl children taught to wipe their genitals from front to back, as this helps to prevent bacteria from the anal region invading the urethra and causing cystitis. Toilets in residential and nursing homes should be well signed with plenty of appropriately placed hand-rails. Guard-rails around toilets assist and protect wheelchair users and raised seats are available for those who find standard toilet seats too low. Places to put walking sticks are useful as they tend to fall to the floor.

Cooking and feeding

All manner of kitchen tools come with longer and wider handles covered with non-slip rubber for a better grip. Cutlery can be altered in the same way as well as coming with angled fork tines, blades and bowls. There are specially designed 'holding' tools for managing equipment such as graters. It is almost impossible to grate some cheese if you have only one functional hand. Tipping equipment for kettles and saucepans help service users use them more easily and safely. Kitchens can be specially designed or adapted for wheelchair users to be at a lower level.

Figure 11.21 Toilet aids

Figure 11.22 Kitchen equipment

Mobility aids

Inaction leads to less action; in other words, although it can be hard to watch a service user struggling to accomplish something and not take over, you are helping that service user to keep mobile and remain independent. If you imagine a big wheelchair looming over the service user every time that you do something for them, it becomes easier to cope with not intervening. Mobility aids are provided to enable the service user to keep their independence as much as possible and to restrict other people's aid as much as possible.

The simplest, oldest and most familiar walking aid is the walking stick. Change has happened here too, many come in folded designs for service users who may need the stick only at certain times. Some have large handles so that the weight can be spread

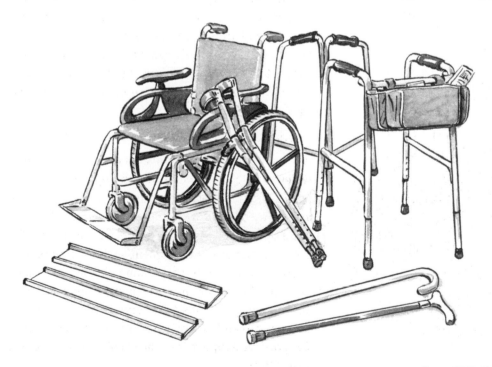

Figure 11.23 Mobility aids

over a larger area. Walking frames provide more support than sticks, also come in folded designs and with wheels for pushing. Trays and bags can be fitted to frames for carrying items around. There are some frames with attached seats for a rest while moving. Ordinary walkers can be awkward to manoeuvre around corners and there are three- and four-wheeled walkers with brakes that are much more flexible.

For service users with very little mobility there is the familiar wheelchair with large rear and small front wheels, brakes and foot rests. Apart from the usual type that needs someone to push it, there are self-propelling wheelchairs and others are powered by batteries. Folded designs are available to fit into the boot of a car and some cars are fitted with mini-hoists that lift the folded chair into the boot. Portable ramps are available to enable a wheelchair user to climb to a higher level when there is no disabled access. Some wheelchairs cost many hundreds of pounds and the ultimate accessory in mobility is, of course, a specially adapted car costing many thousands of pounds.

Sitting

Perching stools are high chairs with or without backs and an angled seat. They are usually used in kitchens and bathrooms when a service user needs to sit for a while, perhaps to iron or peel potatoes, but can get up again quickly and easily.

Elderly and disabled service users may spend quite some time in their chairs so that a chair with correct support is necessary and these can be designed with high or low seats to suit the individual. Chairs with tipping seats enable the user to stand again easily. Chairs with arms and cushioned seats are best for sitting at a dining table. Cushions are used to support weak or paralysed arms.

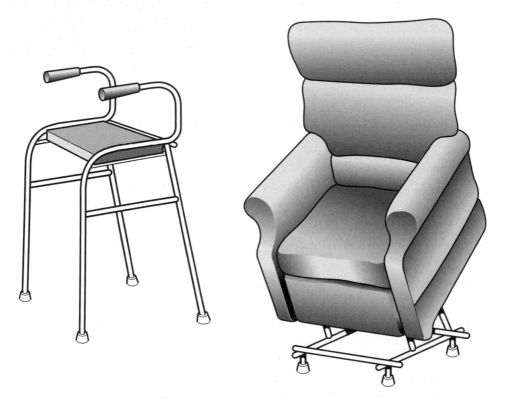

Figure 11.24 Perching stools and tilting chairs

Sleeping

Beds that are higher than standard are favoured for more elderly service users with firm but not hard mattresses. Bed-rails are used for confused service users who may wander in the night and supports that can be tucked under the side of the mattress are good for preventing bedclothes from weighing too heavily on damaged legs. /\-shaped pillows and bed-rests enable service users with heart and breathing difficulties to half lie in bed.

Providing that they are used in accordance with the manufacturer's instructions, both ripple and water mattresses are excellent for the prevention of pressure sores for people confined to bed for long periods.

Senses

Vision

Many service users will use spectacles to help their vision and prescriptions should be kept up-to-date as eyesight changes over time. Books in large print and Braille enable service users with impaired vision to enjoy reading. Talking books are valuable to people with little or no vision and many service users lead normal working lives with the help of a guide dog.

Magnifying glasses or plastic sheets allow a service user to participate in hobbies such as knitting, sewing or doing jigsaws and there are even large lettered and numbered playing cards for games (and special holders to put them in).

Pads of paper and thick, black, felt markers are handy to have around to communicate to people who have impaired sight and are also deaf.

Which cabinet minister of the UK leads a full working life with the help of a guide dog?

Hearing

The most common aid for receiving sound is the hearing aid and most people will be familiar with the standard designs of these. Hearing aids need good maintenance and frequently a service user will switch them off and forget about it. You will need to check the functioning of hearing aids regularly.

Headphones can be useful, especially for listening to music and TV. Induction loops are in use in many public buildings and these enable people using hearing aids to pick up electronic signals without background noises. Churches, cinemas, theatres and public halls are generally fitted with induction loops. Doorbells with flashing lights and specially adapted telephones are also available to hearing impaired service users.

Planning and implementing activities for individuals and groups

We explore the world and society about us through a range of different interests and activities. Very few people have no interests at all, and these are generally people with whom it is difficult to both start and continue conversations. Even if two people have totally different interests, there are still common threads in both – how much time the interest takes, how much it costs and so on. We have different interests at different stages of our lives. Some people may drift in and out of an interest over many years while other people are intensely interested for life, learning all the time. Activities and interests promote an individual's health and well-being, making them a whole rounded type of person with a view of 'self'.

You will have learned about meeting the needs of people and have probably come across the acronym PIES.

Physical needs – many activities will stimulate physical activity, such as ballroom and line dancing, but even completing a jigsaw will promote fine motor skills,

Intellectual needs (or mental activity) – sitting in a chair, bed or wheelchair and conversing with a group of visitors, staff or other service users will stimulate mental activity. More intense pursuits might be completing puzzles and crosswords, playing games that involve strategies, following a knitting pattern or other instructions and debating the daily news items.

Emotional needs – playing games with others, discussing the life events of family and friends, watching some films, reading, reminiscing, taking part in religious practices and being part of the festive events will all have strong emotional attachments as well as meeting other needs.

Social needs – most of the leisure pursuits already mentioned will have social connotations as well. Perhaps you can think of others, particularly involving visits or outings.

There are some important points to bear in mind when planning activities:

- Never force people to do activities; use encouragement and persuasion.
- Respect people's decisions.
- Never say that it will be good for them; this is likely to produce resentment and is judgemental on your part.
- Do not stereotype individuals and assume that they will, or will not, be interested in the said activity.
- Plan for some people to make last-minute decisions to attend or withdraw; if tickets have to be bought then you should explain that there is a deadline date for decisions to be made.
- Where the activity involves payments, keep excellent financial records and try not to accept payment at a time when you are involved in other tasks and unable to document the receipt. Try to give simple, dated, named receipts for payment.
- Consider each individual's needs for the activity.
- Ensure that health and safety issues have been covered and are in line with the policy of the organisation or group.
- Allow plenty of time, especially if travelling is involved.
- Give everyone involved the same information and repeat the guidance as many times as necessary with the particular service user group.
- Notify and leave a record with an appointed person of the details of the activity including the names (and addresses and telephone numbers if necessary) and make sure that this person will be available during the time of the activity (particularly if travel is involved).
- Notify relatives and guardians as necessary. Obtain written permission for a minor if a visit is planned.

- Carry a fully-charged mobile phone if travelling and take copies of all relevant documentation (including insurance documents if required) with you.
- Make lists of the items you need to take with you and prepare this well in advance.
- Have more helpers than necessary in case someone is unavailable on the day. Ensure that the helpers know the details and the tasks that they will be expected to carry out.
- Plan the activity well beforehand.

The list above seems long and daunting and may be unnecessary for simple in-house activities, such as setting up some tables for playing whist or 'Beetle', but most of these guidelines will be essential if organising a coach to take a group of service users to a pantomime for example.

Try to make travelling time interesting by researching the route and giving information about the places you are travelling through. You could ask people if they know the area better than you and can tell others about it. When involved with a group of children or people with learning difficulties on an outing, make sure that they have some written details to give to an adult if they get lost and some form of common group symbol, like a brightly coloured rosette, for easy recognition.

Assessment activity 11.2

Describe, in your own words, the practical skills required by care-workers with examples from your own practice.

Requirements of an effective training programme

The need for formal training

You will have been in formal education for most of your childhood and adolescence. Education is seen as having wide goals, and aims to demonstrate many ways of thinking and doing to encourage the development of choice and self-determination. Training on the other hand can be seen as having narrow goals from planned episodes of learning, leading to a demonstration that there is a right way to do things. Choice is strictly limited and not encouraged. Training exists largely in the skills area but not exclusively so (Rogers 1986.).

In order to train individuals in the right way of doing things, there must be clear instructions or specifications such as those found in NVQ programmes.

Informal training may be somewhat haphazard, often disparagingly referred to as 'learning alongside Nelly' and ticking off the items on a checklist. Such training may be excellent and some may be abysmal; largely this depends on the competence of 'Nelly' and her ability to communicate in a satisfactory way to a trainee. Caring has evolved into a sophisticated profession using electronic aids, complex equipment and service user-centred planning. Informal training, although still playing a minor part, has been downgraded to give way to formal training that means all trainees have a foundation level from which they can progress.

Formal training – methods, duration, internal and external
Nursing qualifications

Many changes have occurred in nurse training over the last twenty years and there is considerable movement towards an all-graduate profession. Current training courses are three-year, full-time programmes, leading to either a Diploma in Higher Education (Dip.H.E.) or a degree (B.Sc., B.A., or B.N.). Dip.H.E. students are encouraged to top up the diploma to degree status. Nowadays, programmes tend to be equally split between academic theory and clinical practice. Placements can vary from an Accident and Emergency department in a busy local hospital to assisting in a small rural health clinic. The first half of a programme is the Common Foundation Programme taken by all trainees before selecting the branch programme for the remainder. Most Schools of Nursing offer more than one branch, but sometimes do not offer all options. See Figure 11.25 for the structure of some nursing programmes.

Although some hospitals still offer nurse training, they are now linked to institutions of higher education and financial support can be by non-means-tested bursaries. When you complete your BTEC National Diploma, you will have the entry qualifications to most professional qualifications.

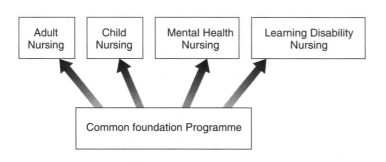

Figure 11.25 Nursing programme structures

Professions allied to medicine

- University physiotherapy – programmes are mainly three-year courses combining a mixture of clinical practice and academic study. Some courses integrate theory modules with clinical practice modules throughout the course, whereas others end-load the programme with practice. Physiotherapy courses are very popular and require at least Grade Bs at A- level standard and some require sciences. You would need to contact the institution to see if this qualification is acceptable with or without a science A-level.
- Occupational therapy – courses are structured in similar ways to physiotherapy and involve three years full-time study.
- Social work – courses are mainly three-year full-time courses and some include the CCETSW Diploma in Social work. Programmes may cover optional pathways such as working with children and families or adult services.

Many degrees in social work can be taken with other major subjects such as social policy, gender studies and counselling. There may be age restrictions and a requirement for previous experience for entry to many programmes.

For other external university courses, consult careers guides, *The Good University Guide*, *Which Degree 2002/3* or individual university prospectuses.

Learning and training while you are in work is possible in various ways via the NVQ system of qualifications. The basic level is NVQ 2, and this is available in a variety of vocational areas including Care. You will need an assessor, who in turn has both your work and her assessments verified by an internal and external assessor. You will be awarded the qualification when your practical training is judged competent and you have presented a portfolio of evidence against the standard specifications. NVQ Level 3 can be used as entry to professional nurse training and other occupations. Management skills can be assessed in similar ways at levels 4 and 5.

Specialist programmes can be run internally and externally by part-time or full-time attendance at institutions of higher education.

Management qualifications and specialised programmes are taken as part of an individual's personal and professional development. You will find more references to these in Unit 8.

Key caring skills

There are some skills in caring that you will learn about over and over again because they are pivotal to giving good quality service; this section contains information about these key caring skills.

Principles of good practice – key working

When a team of multi-disciplinary workers is caring for a service user, it is essential that there should be a team leader to co-ordinate all the actions (and ideas) of the team. This ensures that everyone knows their particular role and those of other team members. This person is the main worker to get in touch with for issues concerning service user care. The team leader is called the key worker and this way of working is known as key working.

Think It Over

What will be the advantages and disadvantages of key working?

Effective communication skills

You have already come across several chapters concerning communication skills and this will be an excellent place at which to review this work. A few points worth remembering are worth repeating here in the form of bullet points:

- You may have built up a good relationship with a service user who then feels more comfortable talking to you than with a counsellor. However, you are likely not to have been trained as a counsellor and using some counselling skills such as active listening and reflective feelings does not mean that you are a counsellor. Ensure that you and the service user recognise the basis on which you are talking.
- Do not be too hasty to interrupt a service user telling you of a problem; often, during the conversation, a service user may make more sense of the problem and reach either a solution or a range of options for themslves.
- It may be useful to explore with the service user the worst and the best scenario relevant to the problem. This often shows the service user that the worst is not that bad after all.
- It is often valuable to focus on one problem at a time so asking the service user what troubles them the most is a good starting point.
- Recognise your own limits and do not be afraid to refer the service user to a more experienced practitioner.

- Recognise when enough is enough and the service user clearly does not wish to pursue the topic further on that occasion. Service users may need more time to come to terms with telling their problems to another person.
- Do not be in any hurry to give advice, rather let the service user make their own mind up about things. Giving advice is a difficult thing to do and if the course of action resulting from the advice fails, you are likely to be blamed for it.
- Remember that you should be an active listener and as a consequence, you should not be talking as much as the service user. Verbal prompts are often all that is necessary during the major part of a service user's story.
- Do not be judgemental about any aspects of a service user's problem and keep your emotions in check.

Safety

Make sure that you are fully aware of the organisation's health and safety policy, Health and Safety at Work Act, COSHH, RIDDOR, Food Safety Act and the Manual Handling and Lifting Regulations and that you abide by the regulations. Do not be afraid to ask your superior if you are in any doubt about any aspect relating to your work in the care setting. Make sure that you understand the principles behind cross-infection and the methods employed to eliminate cross-infection. Attend fire lectures and take part in fire drill.

Confidentiality

Think It Over

Imagine that you are being cared for temporarily and every time that you see two carers talking quietly together, you are sure that they are discussing you personally. Your stay would become very uncomfortable and distressing and your health and well-being might become seriously impaired through stress. You would not feel able to discuss any problems with your carers and would surely not feel that they deserved your co-operation and trust.

This is what can happen to service users who feel that personal information, even if it is relevant to their care, is being given to all and sundry, including visitors, other service users and relatives. Keeping personal information to only people who need to know and even then, with the service user's permission, is the basis of confidentiality.

Each organisation will have a confidentiality policy that must be strictly adhered to. Make sure that you read and understand this policy and how it applies to you both inside and outside the workplace. Never use the name of a service user if you are telling people how your day has been and be careful even then. It is ridiculously easy to pinpoint a service user when you know the unit in which someone works. Many people may demand information from a carer and in some cases very angrily. If you are a student, reply politely that you cannot divulge information and refer the person(s) on to a more senior professional. Personal information applies to written documents also, so you may have to check the identity of a person to whom you are authorised to pass on information.

Theory into practice

Try to think of three specific imaginary events that could mean you have to break confidentiality with a service user. Ask some qualified staff whether they have had to breach confidentiality about an event or conversation.

Record notes about these in your Vocational Practice Log (VPL, see Unit 5) or reflective diary and describe how you might feel if you had been the carer involved. Remember not to use names of either the carer or the service user.

You will also find other references to maintaining confidentiality in this book.

Clear procedures

During learning or training, it is essential that clear procedures be provided so that the novice is comfortable and confident with the task ahead. However, the student should always understand that the service user is an individual and may have his or her own needs. Caring for others is a dynamic, adaptable, person-centred vocation, assisted by clear procedures but not hidebound by them.

You will find a clear procedure for taking a service user's oral temperature described below:

Equipment required – tray, appropriate thermometer, watch with a second hand, alcohol-impregnated swabs, tissues, receptacle for disposable items.

Procedure:

1 wash hands
2 gain agreement and co-operation
3 ensure that the service user has not partaken of anything hot, had a hot bath or exercised recently
4 assist service user to a comfortable position if necessary
5 prepare the thermometer according to the manufacturer's instructions
6 place the thermometer in one of the pockets between the base of the tongue and the floor of the mouth
7 ask the service user to close lips around the thermometer but not to bite it
8 leave for the appropriate length of time
9 remove the thermometer when the maximum temperature has been reached
10 read the temperature recorded by the thermometer
11 leave the service user comfortable
12 dispose of equipment safely
13 record the temperature in the service user's documents, compare with previous temperatures and report any changes or abnormal findings.

Internal and external factors

There are many factors that promote and hinder good practice; some factors will exist inside the organisation and some will impinge on the organisation from outside influences. You can only learn about a few examples in this chapter, but you must be aware and alert for the factors influencing good practice in each care setting.

Figure 11.26 Recording an oral temperature

Frequently individuals may feel that they are in a 'no win' situation because they have had awareness of certain principles of good practice raised in their training or learning experience (and may even be asked to provide evidence for qualification or registration), yet the supervisor (or mentor) perhaps trained later, and is not at all enthusiastic, or even refuses to pursue that way of thinking. The opposite could also happen – the supervisor, after consultation with the staff, has changed the method of working and is in fact researching new ground that is at odds with your learning.

> ### Think It Over
> Look at the procedure outlined on page 427 and try to provide reasons for the different steps 1 to 13.

Human resource problems

A shortage of carers during an influenza epidemic or at holiday time might make an already overloaded care team less inclined to have long discussions with service users and problems may go unnoticed. A busy care team might collect the care documents from the bedside or trolley for updating and not consult the service user at all about the care plan. The care team knows the theory of person-centred care but does not put it into practice. Despite all the initiatives and emphasis on information giving, many service users will still complain that they have been told very little detail about their care.

Figure 11.27 Chronic bed shortages in some care settings cause problems

Attempting to meet government targets places the care staff in some difficult dilemmas. Newspapers reported recently that a male service user in hospital returned from a visit to the toilet to find that his bed had been occupied in his absence. His protests merely produced a response that his bed had been reallocated. After spending a few hours in the corridor, he discharged himself and went home. This was not service user-centred, good information giving or best practice!

Physical resource problems

As well as human resource problems, there are physical

resource problems that influence good practice. Newspapers sensationalise the number of needy service users who have to wait on trolleys in corridors until beds become vacant. Frequently service users are sent home at inconvenient hours because their beds are needed urgently by service users in greater need.

Surgery is cancelled at short notice due to the shortage of beds, the availability of operating theatres or more urgent cases. Newspapers report that some service users have had their operations cancelled many times.

Assessment activity 11.3

1 Explain how the values and principles that you have learned about will provide the foundation for your own and others' good practice.
2 Justify the strength of influences on and the relative importance of values and practice.
3 Describe and discuss the role of the key worker and his or her contribution to the values and principles in care practice, the service users and other care-workers.

Dealing with sensitive issues
Death

Caring for a dying person can be challenging; most people will feel some sense of inadequacy and even fear. It can be difficult to know what to say to the service user and to the relatives. Many people shy away from communication at such times and this can be interpreted as insensitivity. Although it is important to keep self-control, you will not be letting the side down if you display emotion. Relatives will think that you cared for and supported the service user. You will often feel pain for the distressed relatives and also feel some guilt that you, and your team, were not able to prevent the death.

There is no written statement that tells you what to say when a person dies, and if you say nothing at all, you may regret at a later date not having said something. When difficult questions are asked of you, it is all right to say that you don't know. Do not try to be vague and non-committal in your answers as the relatives will think that you are hiding something from them. care-workers in general, and doctors in particular, do not always realise that every word uttered by them is analysed and dissected for a hidden meaning when the relatives are at home. Hearing the words, 'as well as can be expected' can be particularly fraught. What do they expect? Surely this means that there is a life-threatening illness present? And so on....

There is also a fear of what more senior people will think of what you have said. For instance: 'Am I allowed to say anything?', 'Do my thoughts mirror those of my superiors?', 'Will I get into trouble over what I say?', 'Is anything I say likely to lead to litigation?'

As a result of all this turmoil passing through their mind, a carer often ends up saying very little, trying to be reassuring or referring the questions to someone else. Do not be hurt if service users or relatives choose to talk to someone else, particularly if you are young and/or inexperienced, but you can ask if there is anything they would like to talk about. Neither tell people 'not to be silly' nor 'not to worry'; this rarely helps as quite clearly they are worrying about it.

Remember that your physical presence can be reassuring, especially if you use a comforting touch as well. Everyone can feel frightened and alone at such times. You will experience different expressions of emotion from the participants, and should remain calm and supportive. Any requests to see the deceased are usually agreed to and it is recommended that the face and, perhaps, a hand are left uncovered so that the relatives can see and touch their loved one.

Think It Over

In a group try to describe all the emotions that you would feel when someone close to you has just died. Role-play how you might respond, if you were a carer, to those emotions. Discuss the responses in your group and say whether they might have been appropriate or not. Try to analyse your feelings about dying and death through discussion.

Cultural and religious needs

Caring for a service user either from a different culture or who practises a different religion can involve meeting different needs other than the standard PIES. Some teachers add another S into PIES for spiritual needs. In the last section, you learned how to be sensitive in the presence of death.

Many denominations of Christians believe that if you accept the teachings of Jesus Christ and worship God, you will go to heaven, a place of happiness, when you die. The body is laid in a coffin and either buried or cremated after a Christian service in a church or chapel. Roman Catholics have similar rites, although it is more frequent for a priest to visit the bedside of a dying person to pray for them and give comfort.

Hindus believe in reincarnation, and the idea that if you lived a good life this time then you will have an even better life next time and vice versa. Hindus are cremated. This is done outside in India, but must be in a crematorium here in the UK. The body of the deceased is washed and scented paste rubbed into the skin. Presents, to Shiva, are often included in the cremation and prayers are said over the body.

Muslim law prevents a loud display of grief over the deceased and passages from the Koran are said over the body. The body is washed three times by people of the same sex as the deceased, before being covered with fragrant plants and spices. Wrapped in three sheets of white cloth (used on a visit to Mecca, if the pilgrimage has been taken) the body is buried facing the throne of Allah in Mecca. There are no expensive headstones on Muslim graves. Once again, the spiritual destination depends on the balance of good deeds against sins in life. Muslims believe that heaven is a paradise where beautiful maidens will attend them, so death for them is not so threatening.

Orthodox Jews permit no organ transplantation or post-mortem and the body must be ritually purified.

Food and culture
Menu planning also needs careful thought because apart from individual likes and dislikes, different cultures have different practices such as:

- Hindus are often strictly vegetarian.
- Jews do not eat any products of the pig, never eat meat (which must be drained of blood) and dairy foods together, and eat only specially prepared food known as kosher food.

- Muslims also do not eat pig products, meat that has not been drained of blood and do not drink alcohol.

Theory into practice

Invite some visitors from different cultures for about a half an hour visit and find out what their practices are with regard to:

- requirements for prayer
- food
- dress
- personal hygiene
- childbirth
- dying and death.

You will also discover that customs differ in interpersonal relations between different people. Japanese women tend to fix their eyes on the base of the neck when they are speaking, some black sub-cultures maintain eye contact when speaking but avert their eyes when listening, this is the opposite to most Western speakers.

Medication

On first consideration you may think that this is not an issue for particular sensitivity but, perhaps you are thinking of taking a painkiller for a headache or something similar. Service users may be seriously ill, physically frail, elderly or very young and may have learning disabilities, so taking medicines may be quite difficult for them. Many service users have been taking medication of one type or another for a great many years and have become weary and apathetic. It is well known that service users who are on haemodialysis (blood cleansing) for many years while waiting for kidney transplants become intensely weary of spending three to four hours on a kidney machine three times each week, and long-term multi-medication can have the same effect.

Although you should not be involved in the actual distribution or giving of medicines, you could be asked to assist a service user with taking a medicine. You should always wash your hands and check that the medicine is for the right service user. Tact and gentle persuasion may be required from you. Some medicines may taste unpleasant or cause unpleasant side effects such as indigestion and the service user may be reluctant to take it. An outright refusal should be reported to your supervisor straight away. The service user might try to delay taking the medicine but you should be wary of this, as some service users will then dispose of the medicine. It is better to re-present the medicine in five or ten minutes. Injections can be a particular difficulty with some service user group members and it is wise not to say it will not hurt; rather, suggest some pleasant activity afterwards. Try to make medicine-taking part of a child's play rather than interrupt the activity. Stress the benefits to be obtained from taking the medication and refer any questions to the supervisor. Try to learn about the medication that your service users have regularly.

Financial matters

People can be very touchy and secretive about their finances or equally they can be quite happy-go-lucky and somewhat careless with money. If you are collecting or making payments for a service user who cannot do this for themselves, you must protect both of you in a straightforward common sense way. Keep the service user's money and bills safe in a closed bag or wallet and obtain dated receipts or stamped counterfoils for everything. If you can, obtain photocopies of the records to keep in the service user's file in case of loss. You may shop for the service user, so keep the money and goods safe and all till receipts and totals recorded as before.

Having outline knowledge of available benefits can be useful in assisting or information giving to service users on low incomes. Some service users refuse to apply for extra benefits through pride or shame. You can point out the advantages of claiming extra benefits but must abide by a service user's personal decision. You can get more information on appropriate benefits from the new One Stop Shops, Social Services, Benefit Agencies or Citizens' Advice Bureaux.

Some service users cannot complete forms by themselves, become confused at long forms or never get around to it. One Stop Shops will provide someone to help complete the form or will ask the questions over the telephone and send the form for signature. It is also possible to have a home visit from a benefit manager to assist. Most extra benefits have to be applied for regularly, often annually, and failure to complete the forms may result in loss of benefit.

Occasionally you may be asked to perform a task that is against your personal beliefs or even illegal. Even though you are providing a service for the service user it is acceptable to say that the task is unacceptable to you. For example, you might be a practising Methodist and do not believe in gambling so cannot place a bet for a service user. Some matters of dubious nature might have to be referred on to your supervisor.

Personal care issues

You have learned about many aspects of this topic on pages 412–5 and are advised to review this section. Most of us, at some times of our lives, are very sensitive about our bodies and their cleansing.

British culture, and other cultures as well, have influenced many of us to perform personal care in private rooms such as the bathroom and the bedroom. With the size of families falling, there is usually enough space to accomplish private personal care if that is desired. To be accompanied when washing, toiletting and doing other intimate activities may seem bad enough to many people, even when indisposed, but for the carers to use loud voices or leave curtains and doors open is acutely embarrassing to most. Where curtains are the only private barriers both voices and toilet noises are embarrassing and inhibiting for service user and listeners.

Curtains are sometimes inevitable, but every effort should be made to use a carry chair or commode when the service user is able. Stand outside the closed curtains and ask if the service user has finished or is 'decent' before entering. Ask visitors to give the service user a few moments of privacy should personal care be required when they are present. Do not assume that the visitor's presence is acceptable to the service user, many couples have not seen each other naked for a very long time and some not at all. The service user will soon say if he or she does not mind the visitor being present or requires their help.

Respect of needs, feelings and wishes of service user, relatives and friends

Reference has been made to the wishes and feelings of service users in Unit 8. Care is service user-centred and if the service user does not wish to see either friends or relatives, then this desire should be politely made clear. Although it might be awkward for the carer, as the visitor may have travelled some distance only to be declined, practically it is even more difficult, particularly in a hospital setting. At visiting times, the doors are open and visitors sweep in looking for their target individual – they are at the bedside or in the dayroom so quickly, that the service user has little time to act. This is so especially if the service user does not expect the visitors. Sometimes many visitors turn up at once and this can be extremely tiring for the service user. Although many establishments have rules stipulating the maximum number of visitors, the rules are rarely enforced unless the service user is seriously ill. Not only can this be exhausting for the service user, it can be tiring for other service users nearby.

Relatives particularly, and some friends, can make demands 'on behalf of the service user'. This can be tricky to handle as in their presence the service user becomes compliant swept along by their dominance. Unless the service user has expressly wished for, needs and agrees to an appointed advocate, any demands are best left until the visitors have left and a quiet word with the service user will then clarify the situation. Sometimes the views of friends and relatives can be useful in clarifying or explaining the nature of any problem (valuable where communication difficulties exist) but this should only occur with the service user's permission.

When the service user is adamant that a certain course of action, such as treatment, medication, etc. does not take place, there must be no enforcement or bullying to change that decision.

Resource issues

If you read newspapers often, watch news and documentary programmes on TV and/or read specialist care magazines, you will have become aware of constant reference to issues about resources, or more often lack of resources. Bear in mind that media publicity is nearly always focusing on the negative aspects of care, as these are seen as worth reporting. Mrs J having had a successful planned hysterectomy in the local hospital is not going to get the journalists that excited, but 82-year-old Mr P, waiting on a trolley for 48 hours after a stroke, certainly might! You are likely to obtain a biased view of resource issues from media perusal so, try to restore the balance by asking pertinent questions (see Unit 8 pages 286–316), being observant and reflective about the resources in your own organisation and those of other care-workers.

Effects on the service

Resource management can be possible only if sufficient adequate incoming data is supplied to the resource manager. The manager must know how much the care of each service user costs the service, how many service users need the service and for how long. Coupled with those questions that need answering is the crucial query regarding the effectiveness of the resources on which the money was spent. Care staff then, have to supply data on resource usage and cost, but also on the effectiveness of the care received. Perhaps you should first reflect on the definition of effectiveness and its companion word – efficiency, also used a great deal in the world of resource management.

> *Definition of effectiveness*:
>
> Effectiveness is concerned about the quality or benefit derived from the outcomes of care rather than the routine inputs.

> *Definition of efficiency:*
>
> Efficiency is concerned with improving performance or output for the same input.

Care staff are therefore *accountable* for their actions and need to show effectiveness and efficiency in their caring skills. To accomplish this, relevant data identified by management must be gathered in addition to their caring duties. As we live and work in the electronic age, much of this is gathered via computers and networks, but this means that care staff must be able to operate computers accurately and confidently.

Prioritising

Prioritising is a task that consultants and NHS managers have to take on. Regrettably, with an ever-increasing demand for investigations and treatment as well as long-term care, the caring services can no longer care for everyone across the nation at all times. There are waiting lists for heart by-pass operations, joint replacements, organ transplants and a multitude of other treatments and someone has to decide the order of the things to do. This is called prioritising and it is not an easy task. Is it better to carry out one expensive heart by-pass operation or three hip replacements? The former might save the individual's life for a further five or ten years, but the latter might enable three more people to lead a normal life because they have regained mobility and become pain-free. To prioritise in a non-partisan way with common sense and clear judgement, statistics must be collated and analysed to determine the most effective ways of spending NHS resources.

Service user choice

During care planning, where a range of options are offered to the service user, they have the choice of resources and may not wish to partake of any of them for various reasons. The service user is the primary decision-maker and providing that the care team provides clear explanations with advantages and disadvantages of the course of action, it is still their decision.

Multi-disciplinary care planning

The multi-disciplinary care team will prepare the care plan and co-ordinate the resources that are to be provided with the service user's agreement. Care plans are reviewed at regular intervals to update the plan and check that the action taken is efficient and effective. Resources may be changed, added or removed when the review has taken place. You can read more about care planning in Unit 5, pages 156–197.

Assessed risk-taking

The risks associated with hazards in employment must be assessed by your employer under the Management of Health and Safety at Work Regulations (1992). This includes the use of any chemical substances, moving and handling service users or loads, dealing with aggression and violence, travelling over wet floors, managing electrical equipment, handling soiled linen and a huge variety of other work tasks.

A hazard is a potential danger, but the risk of the hazard causing harm to someone may be low or extremely high. This is the reason for assessing and recording the level of risk. Take a hypothetical example: a vinyl floor tile has a slightly protruding corner but it is located behind a radiator fixed to the wall – the hazard exists and could in theory cause an individual to fall or trip. However, due to the location nobody's feet can get near the hazard so the risk is very low, practically zero.

Had the tile been placed in the centre of a busy corridor, the risk would have been extremely high and remedial measures would have to be taken as soon as possible. In the meantime, the tile should be cordoned off and an appropriate warning notice arranged or the tile could be removed pending replacement. The remedial action is known as a 'risk control measure' and it is taken to reduce the risk. Risk control measures are an obligation for the employer, who usually transfers the responsibility to a suitably qualified person.

It is the responsibility of the employee to report any hazards that become apparent and to take reasonable steps to ensure his or her safety and that of others. Accidents and injuries must be reported so that the health and safety officer can investigate the incident in the light of re-occurrence, i.e. a risk analysis.

Theory into practice

1 Think about three hazards and remedial control measures that you encounter either in school or college or in a care setting. Try to find out who carried out the risk assessment and the findings.
2 Invite a health and safety officer to your group to talk about risk assessment and risk control measures.
3 Investigate how risk assessments for moving and handling service users is carried out in one care setting.

Requirements of an effective training/induction programme

To 'induct' someone is to install a person, literally, into a seat or place. Consequently you may like to consider an induction programme as introducing you into a position. A large number of organisations plan induction programmes for new employees, although you may have started work already. This is because to carry out a programme effectively you may have to wait until sufficient new employees have entered the organisation. Where an organisation takes in a number of people at a specific time there will be no need to wait.

Selection of personnel
Who to involve and criteria to be considered

Largely this depends on the type of programme that is being arranged so it is difficult to be very specific. When the programme is an induction course for a programme of study such as NVQ in Care, the person in charge of the staff development unit would welcome the new entrants and explain the purpose and nature of the qualification. A programme of events for the day will follow this, if this has not been sent out previously and speakers will be introduced. Usually, the new group members are asked to introduce themselves and say a few words about where they work and why they want to do the programme. Frequently a flip-chart is used to record the group members' feelings about what they want from the programme.

A tutor would distribute paperwork relevant to the programme and explain the order in which it would be tackled. The tutor would advise on useful reference texts and possibly books and files to buy.

A mentor or support person might explain their role of facilitating access to resources. A librarian might arrange an induction to library resources and explain the systems behind the library classification and borrowing books. An assessor would describe his or her role and an internal verifier explain how verification takes place. The tutor would need a second session to explain how a portfolio is developed and the importance of clear cross-referencing. Successful students may participate by explaining how they found the programme useful and the benefits that can be gained. They may also bring along their completed portfolios so that beginners may actually see the products of the course.

When the members are new to the location, domestic arrangements will have to be explained such as toilet and fire exit locations, times of coffee and lunch breaks, etc.

On the next occasion, or quite early in the session, important legislation such as the Health and Safety at Work Act and COSHH will be explained and so the work begins.

Other training and induction courses will have different content relevant to the type of work involved although there will be many common features.

A renal ward in a large teaching hospital has the following induction course for nurses and care assistants.

- Local ward induction – t*his will involve a tour and explanation of the different bays and storage rooms.*
- Introduction to staff
- Clinical profiling – *an explanation of the work of the ward and the problems that service users face.*
- Ward work package – *how the work is organised on the ward.*
- Arrange study days for:

  a. Mandatory induction – *involving safety, confidentiality, etc.*
  b. Lifting and handling.
  c. Cardio-pulmonary resuscitation.
  d. High-dependency workshop – *many service users are seriously ill and may need intensive care.*
  e. Supervisory.
  f. Venepuncture.
  g. Intravenous study day.
  h. Vascular access package.
  i. Cannulation.

Think It Over

Explore the terminology of your study programme.

Do you know the meanings of f. – i.? If not, try to find out for yourself.

Skills audit analysis

Group or individual skills can be measured and recorded in a process called a skills audit. An audit is essentially another word for account, so a skills audit is an account of the skills of an individual or group of individuals. Skills audits are carried out to find out either the staff development required or to change the structure of an organisation. The first stage is to find out the skills required to perform a job role, followed by an analysis of the skills each carer has and this is followed by an analysis of results to determine the staff development required. In some cases, if there are carers surplus to requirements in another area of the organisation, staff changes will be implemented.

The end result of a skills audit can form the basis of a training needs analysis that drops into a staff development plan. The organisation will improve by developing the employees in the most appropriate ways to improve the quality of the service. Having a skills audit on record will also facilitate the selection of employees for internal progression.

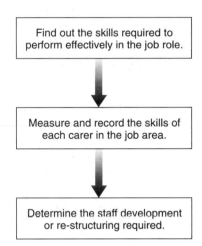

Figure 11.28 Steps in a skills audit

Think It Over

Imagine that you are a care assistant in a large organisation and have successfully completed your NVQ level 3 in fairly rapid time. You have completed an updated skills audit for the unit where you work.

How will the skills audit help with:

- identifying the areas for improvement within the organisation
- reducing the staff development budget
- selection of internal candidates for progression
- improving the quality of the service
- improving the matching of people to jobs?

Staff appraisal/supervision/mentor

Staff appraisal (also known as performance appraisal/evaluation) is a non-threatening way of creating dialogue between either a peer and a colleague or a manager and an employee. The purpose of the appraisal is to formally evaluate an individual's performance and to feedback to the employee so that adjustments to performance can be made. Initially, when appraisal is introduced, employees fear that it is a 'stick that the organisation will use to beat them with' or to enforce redundancy, demotion or unemployment. As a result, appraisal awareness sessions will have to be held as part of staff development for all employees. In addition, appraisers will have to be trained to use the appraisal system correctly.

Both parties must have a written, formal appointment to meet in a quiet room where they cannot be overheard or seen by others. The process is confidential to the participants, although a copy may be lodged with the human resources (personnel) unit (HRU) in a secure place.

In an appraisal system, there are set criteria that have to be discussed, such as services to service users, working relationships, communication, problem-solving, managing change, etc. After discussion, agreed statements or bullet points will be added in an information or response column. 'Maintains confidentiality as appropriate' and 'uses listening skills' might be two sub-sections to the communication criteria. The appraisee will explain how they feel that their performance matches up in these regards. Staff appraisal forms are quite detailed and the participants may have to meet several times before the process is finished and both parties agree to sign the document.

Falling naturally out of the appraisal process should come agreed targets and goals for the future and requests for staff development. The latter is forwarded to the HRU, who will inform the appraisee of any suitable opportunities for staff development.

At agreed intervals, and in line with the staff appraisal policy of the organisation, the appraisal process will be reviewed and progress on goals and staff development noted. Further targets will be agreed. The usual interval between appraisals is one year. Disciplinary and grievance procedures are not part of the appraisal system and the employee should be supported for improvement in performance.

You will find information on supervision and mentoring in Unit 8, pages 286–316.

Staff development plan

Methods of selection and implementation

As mentioned earlier, one of the purposes of staff appraisal and a skills audit analysis is to determine those individuals who desire to undergo further staff development. Staff development can be extremely expensive and individuals who drop out of courses due to a lack of commitment, personal problems or an inability to study or work at the enhanced level are both wasting precious budget and denying the opportunity to someone else. Even with a highly intelligent, committed member of staff the opportunity might arise at an inappropriate time due to young children, divorce proceedings or caring for a sick or dying relative.

Of course, these types of life-changing events can arise, and do, after a programme has been started, so continuous support by the staff development unit (SDU) is important during selection and implementation. A care team, supervisor, manager or mentor might put forward a name for staff development, but the SDU must ensure that the right person has been selected at the right time and with the desire to participate. Flattering as it may be, to be selected in this way, it is of paramount importance that the individual is given information about the rigours of the staff development. Many individuals will assume that staff development equates with increased salary and this may not be the case. A frank, open discussion on life after development must take place because if the motive is purely financial, at some, usually difficult, stage the individual or their family members will pose the question 'is it worth it?'

Theory into practice

When you become involved with team-working in your vocational placement make enquiries about the frequency of staff development for the team and the nature of the development.

While you are waiting for this opportunity ask your course tutor and your head of department (or suitable alternative) similar questions about team staff development. The responses to both these enquiries will help you to get a feel for team development.

Staff meetings – informal/formal

Formal staff meetings need not occur regularly, but when they do should be purposeful. An agenda should be circulated to all staff, together with the time and venue several days before the due date. Staff off-duty can then decide whether to attend, although in most cases they will not be paid for attendance.

An indication of the length of the meeting is useful for those with other commitments so that arrangements can be made. Minutes should be recorded for those unable to attend. The agenda should be compatible with the time allocation and the chairperson should limit speakers appropriately and encourage views from others that have not yet spoken.

Informal staff meetings take place much more frequently, but tend to involve only those present at the time. They are useful for airing problems and discussing tactics, but it is important that the views of others not present should be taken before decisions are made. Informal meetings can lead to formal decision-making meetings where all are invited. Participation in formal and informal meetings contributes to both personal and staff development.

Training can take place in informal meetings as well as more organised staff development. Both types of staff meeting may highlight a request for a training opportunity from the staff. This might lead to an SDU involvement and has implications for both internal and external resource implications currently unplanned for in the SDU budget.

Assessment activity 11.4

Use examples from working in care settings to illustrate your answers.

1 Define the term 'training need'.

2 Explain the training needs and development that might be required for the following people:
- a school-leaver with some GCSE qualifications employed as a care assistant
- a recently qualified staff nurse who has joined a high-dependency unit
- a newly appointed supervisor (with adult nursing qualifications) in a residential home for elderly mentally ill people.

3 Describe the benefits of training and development to:
- each individual
- the organisation.

Working in teams

You will find information that is useful to you on working in teams and leadership qualities in Unit 8, pages 286–316.

Multi-disciplinary teams

A multi-disciplinary team is a group of health or social care-workers contributing to an individual service user's care. There may be a wide variety of professional people in the team working together to improve the health and well-being of the service user. Each person may hold a different view of the way in which the improvement is to be managed, according to the particular discipline of their profession, but it is essential that each person has a picture of the role others will play. Every discipline will have its own knowledge, skills and understanding underpinning the practice although there will be many common or overlapping branches.

Most teams will have a leader who will organise and meld the work of others. Traditionally, this used to be the doctor or the social worker, but this is now changing as it has been recognised that to meet the needs of individual service users this may not always be suitable. Nowadays, a nurse or physiotherapist may lead a team for a certain period of time and as the service user's needs change so the make-up of the team and the leader may change. It is essential that conflict does not arise between members of such a team and each person can only justify their membership of the team if they are providing a unique service for the service user. Conflict should not arise if each person is fully aware of their aims and what they believe in. Many caring professions work from **models of care** and it is beneficial for teams to understand these different models.

Case Study

A 75-year-old man from the residential unit in which you are working is going in to hospital tomorrow to have a prostatectomy (an operation to relieve pressure around the urethra leading from the bladder). Previously he had acute retention of urine and had to be catheterised for relief. He is likely to be hospitalised for one week before returning to his home where you work.

1 Who are the care professionals that are likely to be involved in his care team? Give a brief description of their main aims.

2 Compare and discuss the results with another group member and modify your list as appropriate.

3 Discuss who would be best to act as the multi-disciplinary team leader and whether this would change as he improves.

Two years later, the same service user presented with similar problems, but this time, an investigation and examination revealed the existence of a non-treatable prostate cancer. He was placed in the care of a palliative care team.

4 What is palliative care and who are likely to be the professional carers who might work in a palliative care team?

5 Compare this team with the team involved in prostatectomy care.

Individual development needs

Service users in different settings with different needs will require the services of different teams of people. Professional carers are likely to be members of different teams at any one time serving the needs of several different service users and being part of their individual department team as well. You can see how important it is for carers to work well in teams.

As well as the development of the individual carer, it is equally important for teams to undergo development. This might be about the process of teams working together such as building trust, avoiding conflict, appreciating each other's roles and so on. On the other hand, it could be researching new issues or ways to move forward, always with the service user's health and well-being as the primary consideration. The leader of the team together with the staff development officer are usually the key personnel to co-ordinate staff development.

Think It Over

When you have been a member of a team, what type of development did you have to further the progress of the team? How did this relate to team-working as a process or increasing knowledge, skills and understanding of the aims and beliefs of the team?

Consider the role of a team manager for a sport you are interested in. The players have different backgrounds, clubs, styles, etc., and only come together occasionally in preparation for a game. How would you as team manager begin to knit the team together?

Assessment guidelines

Much of the assessment for this unit is in the form of written accounts that require you to tease out your learning and apply it to current care practice. You will need to have experienced two or three care settings and collected relevant information from them before attempting to complete assessments. You may well experience a theory–practice gap for yourself and thus, be able to comment meaningfully in your work.

Student activities 11.9A, 11.10A, 11.18 will form part of your assessment evidence and to conclude this, you will need to complete the task below.

Assessment activity 11.5

1 Find and describe examples from your practice of caring that show how your knowledge, skills and understanding mirrors that of current practice and thinking.
2 Describe, with examples, the impact made by current thinking and knowledge on care practice.
3 Explain ways to evaluate the benefits to a care organisation and a carer of keeping up to date in knowledge and thinking.

End-of-unit test

1 Explain what is meant by:
- a concept
- a theory
- a paradigm.

2 Describe briefly the range of options available to assist a service user with mobility.

3 You are intending to invite a group of children from a local school to sing carols to the service users of a residential home. Explain the planning that will be required.

4 Describe the meaning behind 'assessed risk taking'.

5 What is the purpose of staff appraisal?

6 Explain six ways of ensuring food is safe.

7 Why should assisting a service user to take medication need to be treated with sensitivity?

8 Explain the different purposes of the nursing process and a model of care.

9 Find three examples from your care setting where care practice has been updated to be in line with current thinking.

10 Explain the difference between a subjective and an objective approach in care theory.

11 Which laws and regulations underpin moving and handling service users?

References and further reading

Adams, R., Dominelli, L., Payne, M. (2002) *Social Work –Themes, Issues and Critical Debates,* Basingstoke: Palgrave

Department of Health (1991) *Dietary Reference Values for Food Energy and Nutrients for the United Kingdom,* London: HMSO

Department of Health (1998) *Saving Lives: Our Healthier Nation,* London: HMSO

Hogston, R. et al. (2002) *Foundations of Clinical Practice,* Basingstoke: Palgrave

Howe, D. (1992) *An Introduction to Social Work Theory,* Aldershot: Ashgate

Jamieson, E., McCall, J. and Whyte L. (2002) *Clinical Nursing Practices,* Edinburgh: Churchill Livingstone

Jolley, M. and Brykczynska G. (1992) *Nursing Care – the challenge to change,* London: Edward Arnold

Leonard, P. (1975) *Explanation and Education in Social Work,* British Journal of Social Work, Vol. 5 No 3.

McHale, J. and Tingle, J. (2001) *Law and Nursing,* Oxford: Butterworth Heinemann

Nolan, Y. (1998) *Care: NVQ Level 2,* Oxford: Heinemann

Nolan, Y. (1998) *Care: NVQ Level 3* Oxford: Heinemann

Pearson, A., Vaughan, B. and Fitzgerald, M. (1996), *Nursing Models for Practice,* Oxford: Butterworth Heinemann

Stretch, B. (ed) (2002*) BTEC National Health Studies,* Oxford: Heinemann

Wright, S. (1990) *My Patient – My Nurse,* London: Scutari Press

12 Lifespan development

This unit looks at the different life stages during human growth and development. It deals with the different major life events, life chances, diversity and equality issues that affect people's development, including psychological theories of development.

What you need to learn

- Life stages
- Psychological theories of lifespan development
- The influence of life events

Life stages

It is traditional to see life as involving certain definite periods of development. Terms like infant, child, adolescent and adult have been used for centuries to classify the age-related status of individuals. During the last century it was common to assume that there was a universal pattern to both physical and social development. During infancy, childhood and adolescence, a person would grow physically and learn the knowledge and skills they needed for work. Adulthood was a time when people would work and/or bring up their own family. Old age was when people would retire. Children would be grown up by the time their parents reached old age.

Developmental tasks – Havighurst and Castells

An American theorist called Havighurst described the developmental tasks of the different life stages (Havighurst, 1972). Some examples of these stages are listed below:

Infancy and early childhood
- learning to walk
- learning to take solid foods
- learning to talk
- learning bowel and bladder control
- learning sex differences and sexual modesty.

Middle childhood
- learning physical skills necessary for ordinary games
- learning to get along with peers
- learning an appropriate masculine or feminine role
- developing basic skills in reading, writing and calculating
- developing concepts necessary for everyday living
- developing conscience, morality and a scale of values.

Adolescence
- achieving new and more mature relations with peers of both sexes
- achieving a masculine or feminine role

- accepting one's physique and using the body effectively
- achieving emotional independence of parents and other adults
- preparing for marriage and family life
- preparing for an economic career.

Early adulthood
- selecting a mate
- learning to live with a marriage partner
- starting a family
- rearing children
- managing a home
- getting started in an occupation.

Middle age
- assisting teenage children to become responsible and happy adults
- reaching and maintaining satisfactory performance in one's occupational career
- relating to one's spouse as a person
- accepting and adjusting to the physiological changes of middle age
- adjusting to ageing parents.

Later maturity
- adjusting to decreasing physical strength
- adjusting to retirement and reduced income
- adjusting to the death of one's spouse
- establishing satisfactory physical living arrangements.

Castells

Manuel Castells (1996) argues that life has changed so much that the notion of adolescent, adult and later life transitions is no longer relevant for many people:

> *Now, organisational, technological and cultural developments characteristic of the new, emerging society are decisively and undermining this orderly life cycle without replacing it with an alternative sequence. I propose the hypothesis that the network society (the world today) is characterised by the breaking down of rhythmicity, either biological or social, associated with the notion of a life cycle.*

Biological, social and economic influences on development are changing because:

- Science is now prolonging life and health for many people – retirement need not be seen as necessary at a set age
- Reproduction no longer has to start in early adulthood. It is now possible for women to give birth in their 50s.
- People's life plans no longer need to focus on taking a set job role for life.
- Retirement can be optional and even a temporary condition that can take place at any age.
- Gender family and reproductive roles are no longer perceived as fixed. One in five women will not have children in their life. A substantial number of people may not marry. Two in every five marriages end in divorce.

We now live in a rapidly changing world where many people can choose their own style of living and plan families, careers and social roles with less and less reference to age. Even so, there are some generalisations about biological, social and emotional development which can be made at the beginning of a new century. These generalised patterns of development may help care-workers to understand the needs of people who become service users in the next decade or so.

Physical growth and development

Infancy (0–2 years)

Every individual has a unique pattern of growth and development. This is because there are so many factors influencing our progress. It would be logical to say that each one of us begins from the moment a sperm nucleus from the father joins with the nucleus from the mother's ovum, but the exact time of this process, known as *fertilisation*, is usually unknown. To obtain a more recognisable starting date, doctors will ask a pregnant woman for the starting date of her last menstrual period and add on two weeks. The period when the ovum is available for fertilising by the sperm is halfway between menstruations.

There is, however, a great deal of controversy over when an embryo becomes a human being. This has largely arisen from discussions about abortion. In Britain, the Abortion Act (1967) allowed termination of pregnancy up to the 28th week of gestation; but after lengthy debates in Parliament, the limit was reduced to the 24th week. The debate continues, however, as babies can now survive if born at 24 weeks, owing to the great advances made in modern techniques. Many groups think that the limit should be reduced even further. Some pressure groups (such as Life) and many individuals consider that all abortion is wrong and human life is sacred from the moment of fertilisation.

The fertilised ovum, now known as a *zygote*, is one of the larger cells in humans and is just visible to the naked eye. Imagine the smallest dot you can make with a very sharp pencil and this is about the right size. After a short rest period it begins to divide, first into two cells, then four, eight and so on. Quickly the tiny structure becomes a ball of smaller cells – a *morula*. These cells begin to become organised into different areas. Some will be destined to form the new human being, but for a while the majority of the cells are preparing to become its coverings and developing placenta. It is important that these parts are ready to secure the food supply for the developing being as soon as the structure enters the womb, or uterus, of the mother. All the time so far has been spent in travelling down the Fallopian tube leading from the ovary into the uterus. At about a week old, the tiny structure, a hollow ball of cells known as a *blastocyst*, arrives in the uterus. The next few days are vital to the embryo. It must bury itself in the *endometrium*, the thickened lining of the mother's uterus and secure a food supply before the mother's next menstruation is due. If this does not happen, the blastocyst will be swept out of the mother's body with the products of menstruation and will die. Once embedded in this way, a process called *implantation*, the tiny embryo releases a hormone into the mother's blood which prevents the next menstruation.

Never again will growth be so rapid. By the third week after fertilisation (week 5 of the pregnancy calculation), the embryo has grown to be 0.5 cm long and has started to develop a brain, eyes, ears and limbs. Some individuals might class the development of the brain as being significant in the date of becoming a human being. There is even a tiny heart pumping blood to the newly formed placenta to obtain nutrients and oxygen from the mother's blood.

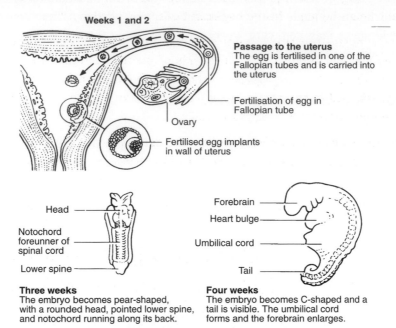

Weeks 1 and 2

Passage to the uterus
The egg is fertilised in one of the Fallopian tubes and is carried into the uterus

Fertilisation of egg in Fallopian tube

Ovary

Fertilised egg implants in wall of uterus

Head

Notochord foreunner of spinal cord

Lower spine

Forebrain

Heart bulge

Umbilical cord

Tail

Three weeks
The embryo becomes pear-shaped, with a rounded head, pointed lower spine, and notochord running along its back.

Four weeks
The embryo becomes C-shaped and a tail is visible. The umbilical cord forms and the forebrain enlarges.

Internal organs at five weeks
All the internal organs have begun to form by the fifth week. During this critical stage of development, the embryo is vulnerable to harmful substances consumed by the mother (such as alcohol and drugs), which may cause defects.

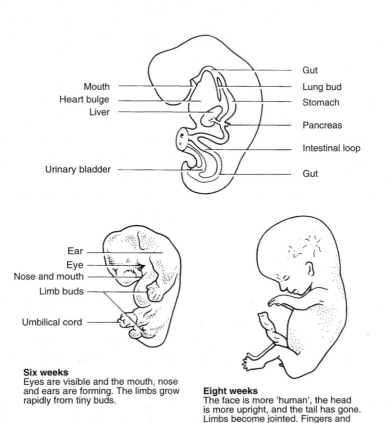

Mouth
Heart bulge
Liver

Urinary bladder

Gut
Lung bud
Stomach

Pancreas

Intestinal loop

Gut

Ear
Eye
Nose and mouth
Limb buds

Umbilical cord

Six weeks
Eyes are visible and the mouth, nose and ears are forming. The limbs grow rapidly from tiny buds.

Eight weeks
The face is more 'human', the head is more upright, and the tail has gone. Limbs become jointed. Fingers and toes appear.

Figure 12.1 Embryo development

The embryo continues to grow and develop at a fantastic rate until at week 8 all major organs have formed and there is a human-looking face with eyes, ears, nose and mouth. Limbs have formed fingers and toes, and the body length has increased to 3 cm (Figure 12.1). The name changes again – from now until birth it is called a *foetus*.

Growth and development of internal organs continues and the next main stage is at 20 weeks. The mother will begin to feel movements of the foetus, weak at first but getting stronger as the pregnancy progresses. The midwife can hear the heart beats through a trumpet-shaped instrument called a *foetal stethoscope*. The heart beats are very fast and difficult to count without experience.

The foetus is clearly male or female because the external sex organs have developed and the total length is now around 24 cm. The weight of the foetus is close to 0.5 kg already.

As you can see from the table, at 9 months (40 weeks) the foetus is ready to be born. It is about 50 cm long and weighs around 3.5 kg.

Time in months of pregnancy	Length in centimetres	Weight in kilograms
1	0.35	Almost none
2	3.5	0.05
3	8.5	0.1
4	15	0.2
5	23	0.4
6	30	0.75
7	38	1.5
8	45	2.0
9	51	3.5

A newborn infant, often called a *neonate*, is a helpless individual and needs the care and protection of parents or others to survive. The nervous system which co-ordinates many bodily functions is immature and needs time to develop. The digestive system is unable to take food that is not in an easily digestible form such as milk. Other body systems, such as the circulatory and respiratory systems, have undergone major changes as a result of birth – the change to air breathing and physical separation from the mother. A few weeks later, the baby's temperature regulating system is able to function properly and fat is deposited beneath the skin as an insulating layer.

Key principles of development

The term 'growth' is used to describe a change in the quality of some variable. For example, a child might become taller as they get older. We would say that they had grown taller. The word 'growth' does not explain what has happened – only that height has increased. If we assumed that the child's genetic programme is primarily responsible for an increase in height, then we might use the term 'maturation' to explain what we believed was happening.

The term 'development' describes changes which might be complex and qualititative as well as quantitative. The word 'development' is used to describe most intellectual, social and emotional change, where complex factors interact to create different patterns of change in different individuals.

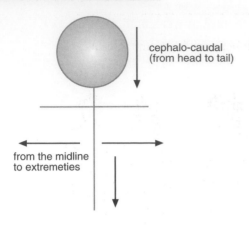

cephalo-caudal
(from head to tail)

from the midline
to extremeties

Figure 12.2 The sequence of development

Although development is a continuous process, it is not an even one affecting all parts of the body equally. However, development always follows the same sequence. The upper part of the body, particularly the head and brain, progresses extremely rapidly, while the lower part of the body, particularly the lower limbs, follows more slowly. This type of development is said to be **cephalo-caudal** and it means 'from head to tail'. Arms and legs, called 'the extremities', develop later than the heart, brain and other organs in the mid-line of the body. So as well as being cephalo-caudal, development is also from the midline to the extremities. The reason for this is not hard to find: most vital organs are controlled by the brain and protected by the trunk. As the baby is dependent on the mother for nourishment, limbs are not essential to early survival.

Think It Over
Look back at the diagrams showing early development and you will notice the unusual overall shape of the infant's body and the strange proportions of the different parts compared to the whole. For example, measure the length of the whole 8-week-old foetus and then measure the length of the head only. You will find that the head is approximately 50 per cent of the total length, whereas the arms and legs are quite small and weak.

Early childhood (2–8 years)
During childhood, different parts of the body grow at different rates.

The nervous system, sense organs and head grow very rapidly from birth to 6 years. A 6-year-old's head is 90 per cent of the adult size, and he or she can wear a parent's hat! The reproductive organs remain small and underdeveloped until the onset of puberty (between 11 and 16 years), and then they grow rapidly to reach adult size. General body growth is more steady, reaching adult size at around 18–20 years, but with three 'growth spurts' at 1, 5–7 years, and puberty.

When the skeleton first forms it is made of a flexible material called *cartilage*. This is slowly replaced by bone which is visible on x-rays. Each bone passes through the same sequence of changes of shape as it reaches maturity in a healthy adult. Bone age is, therefore, a useful measure of physical development. Height and weight standards are often associated with age, but are less useful because of the enormous differences which can occur in different individuals.

Puberty and adolescence (9–18 years)
Both boys and girls enter puberty between the ages of 10 and 15 years; this is when the secondary sexual characteristics develop and the sexual organs mature so that reproduction becomes possible. Puberty is the physical change which accompanies the emotional changes of adolescence and is caused by the hypothalamus – part of the brain influencing the pituitary endocrine gland to secrete hormones known as gonadotrophins.

Think It Over

Look at Figure 12.3. Write notes on the changes you can see between birth and 8 years.

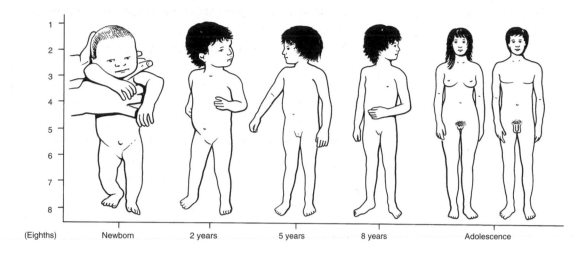

(Eighths)   Newborn   2 years   5 years   8 years   Adolescence

Figure 12.3 Growth profiles from birth to adolescence

In girls the gonadotrophin stimulates the ovaries to produce the hormone oestrogen and, in boys, the testes produce testosterone. Experts are still not sure why the hypothalamus seems to be important. Pubertal changes have occurred earlier in western countries with improved nutrition. It is also well recognised that, in the condition of anorexia nervosa, reproductive processes fail when an individual's body weight drops significantly.

Puberty is accompanied by a growth spurt in height, and weight increases are due to muscle building in boys and fat accumulation in girls.

Around the age of 10 to 11, but sometimes starting earlier, the breasts of girls start to swell, and pubic hair begins to grow. This is followed around one to two years later by the first menstruation, called the menarche. One hundred years ago the menarche occurred at an average age of 14.8 years; in 1988 it had reduced to 12.5 and a current research project indicates that it is now closer to 10 and 11, with breast budding and pubic hair appearance around 8 and 9. Early menstruation is often scanty, irregular and of brief duration; puberty is said to be complete when full, regular expected menstruation

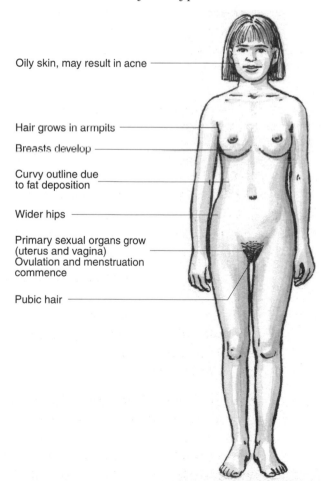

Oily skin, may result in acne

Hair grows in armpits

Breasts develop

Curvy outline due to fat deposition

Wider hips

Primary sexual organs grow (uterus and vagina) Ovulation and menstruation commence

Pubic hair

Figure 12.4 Female body changes at puberty

449

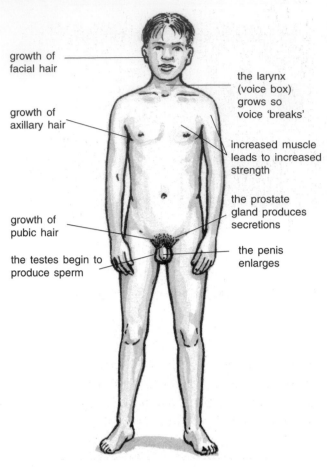

growth of facial hair

the larynx (voice box) grows so voice 'breaks'

growth of axillary hair

increased muscle leads to increased strength

the prostate gland produces secretions

growth of pubic hair

the testes begin to produce sperm

the penis enlarges

Figure 12.5 Male body changes at puberty

occurs. During this time, the pelvic bones widen, underarm (axillary) hair appears and fat is deposited around the body to produce a curvaceous figure with full breasts (see Figure 12.4).

The whole process takes three to four years to complete and very little growth in height occurs after puberty. Oestrogen is the hormone largely responsible for the physical changes but a second hormone produced during the second half of each menstrual cycle, i.e. progesterone, promotes glandular development of breasts and uterine linings.

Puberty in boys lags behind that of the girls by about two years, so at some time girls can be both taller and heavier than boys; boys eventually overtake girls in height and weight by the end of puberty (see Figure 12.5). The table below identifies male and female secondary sexual characteristics.

Male	Female
1 Enlargement of testes and penis	Enlargement of breasts and nipples
2 Pubic, facial, underarm hair growth	Pubic and underarm hair growth
3 Increased muscle and bone size leads to increased strength	Increased fat deposited under skin leads to increased curvy shape
4 Voice deepens (breaks)	Onset of menstruation.

Influences on growth
Inherited characteristics

Height and build are thought to be controlled by a number of genes as well as environmental influences. An individual's height, for example, may depend on the proportions of 'tall' and 'short' genes that they have inherited from their parents. Tall parents may have more 'tall' genes than shorter parents and are thus likely, but by no means definitely, to pass on more 'tall' genes to their children. Average height parents are more likely to pass on fairly equal mixtures of 'tall' and 'short' genes. However, during certain types of cell division that precede the production of ova and sperm, there are random exchanges of genes. It is quite possible for a child of average parents to have a larger 'allocation' of 'tall' or 'short' genes than any brothers or sisters and so to be unusually tall or short.

Environmental factors

Children who live in deprived or disadvantaged circumstances may have their growth and development affected by poor home situations, such as inner city high-rise flats with no recreational areas and damp infested interiors. Parents who smoke cigarettes tend to have smaller than average children who do less well at school. Alcoholism in families affects the health and welfare of children, as do any other circumstances that cause anxiety in the home environment. Living close to nuclear establishments has recently been shown to affect children's health, particularly in the incidence of serious diseases such as cancer.

Figure 12.6 Pollution can seriously affect children's health

Nutrition and diet

Malnourishment will affect growth directly, and this could be the influence of too little food or food of the wrong type. A child whose main meals consist of chips or similar foods with inadequate protein, fruit and vegetable content, may appear well-nourished, but lacks essential foods to promote healthy growth and development.

Think It Over

How far do you think genetic influences affect the height and build of people and how far are issues such as diet and lifestyle involved in influencing shape and size?

Physical development

Adulthood and middle age (19–65)

After puberty, there is little further growth in height but muscle building often continues with increased work and leisure pursuits. Some weight gain is often experienced slowly from the mid-twenties onwards, usually as a result of less strenuous activity and more sedentary work patterns. This is by no means universal and depends very much on the influences dictated by lifestyle.

Between the ages of 45–55, females experience a decline in fertility, eventually resulting in a complete cessation. This is called the 'menopause'. Menstrual periods become irregular, sometimes scanty and sometimes heavy, and may be accompanied by night sweats and feelings of bloatedness as well as mental and emotional changes such as anxiety, tiredness, confusion and periods of weepiness.

Males can experience physical changes in the same way, although of course not the menstrual changes. These form the basis of the so-called 'male menopause' ascribed to a decline in the levels of testosterone. At least 20 per cent of men are thought to experience changes due to low testosterone levels as they get older. The figure may even be as high as 50 per cent.

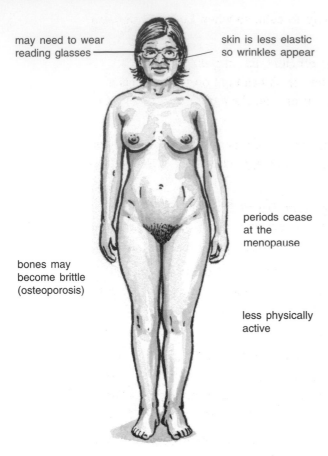

may need to wear reading glasses

skin is less elastic so wrinkles appear

bones may become brittle (osteoporosis)

periods cease at the menopause

less physically active

Figure 12.7 Some physical changes become obvious as people get older

Men are still able to father children well into their 70s and 80s – assuming the absence of disease and that they were fertile in the first place.

As people get older, they begin to show some wrinkles, greying hair, 'middle age spread', less elastic skin, less muscle firmness and a reduced inclination to be strenuously active. The eyesight begins to change. The focal point for accurate work such as reading gets farther and farther away and reading glasses usually become necessary. One in two people over the age of 60 will experience serious hearing loss.

Loss of hair may affect both sexes in the middle years of life, but it is much more common in men. Hair loss in men occurs first from the temples, then the crown of the head, with a gradual widening of the bald area to the sides of the head.

Older people are usually less active than younger people, but often still continue to take in the same amount of food. This usually results in a gradual thickening of the trunk, arms and legs, often called 'middle age spread'. Many people regard this as an inevitable stage in getting older, but generally it is a result of not matching food (and therefore energy) intake with energy output.

Later adulthood (65+)

Physical and mental changes occur as time passes. Not many people live to be over a hundred years old – the average lifespan is around 85 years of age in the West.

Sexual activity may decline only a little or a lot, very often depending on the usual life pattern of the individual. Elastic tissue, present in many organs, degenerates with age and this is most readily seen in wrinkled skin. Blood capillaries are more fragile so bruising occurs from relatively small injuries.

The number of nerve cells in the central nervous system steadily decreases from quite a young age and they are irreplaceable. This loss, unnoticed at first, begins to show as one gets older. It results in poorer memory, difficulty in learning new skills quickly and slower reaction times. Senses are less acute, particularly taste, smell and hearing.

The progressive loss of hearing which can come with age is known as *presbyacusis* – sounds are less clear and high tones less audible. It occurs with the degeneration of the sensory hair cells of the cochlea (in the inner ear) and of nerve cells.

The focusing power of the eye weakens with age, beginning at around 45. Often after the age of 65 there is little focusing power left – *presbyopia*.

As the body ages it gradually loses its sensitivity to cold, so when body temperature drops an old person may not feel the cold.

Heart, breathing and circulation all become less efficient, causing difficulty with climbing stairs and hills, and with strenuous exercise. A healthy young adult has a blood pressure around 110/75 mm of mercury, but around the age of 60 years this is 130/90 or higher.

Muscle thins and weakens, while joints become less mobile and total height shrinks. Wound healing and resistance to infection decline with age. Functions of organs like the kidneys and the liver slowly decline.

However, there are positive aspects to growing older. Despite the decline of physical systems, a combination of tolerance, wisdom and experience built up over the years enables older people to avoid the mistakes made by younger, inexperienced people.

Healthy older people may have greater emotional control and a more developed understanding of their self-concept than younger people. Socially, older people may have more time to appreciate other people and their environment.

Developmental abnormality and delay

Developmental abnormality is a general term that may simply be a variation from normal in the structure or physiology of a cell, tissue or organ. Alternatively the term may refer to a physical malformation or deformity, such as a curvature of the spine, or a mental or behavioural problem, such as aggressive attitudes towards other children.

Developmental delay happens when a baby or youngster has not shown new abilities within a 'normal' time range and is displaying a type of behaviour not usually seen at a particular age. The term is generally restricted to children under 5 years. Remember that when the words 'normal' time range are used, there may be an incredibly long time range considered as normal such as in walking ability or bladder control.

Causes of developmental delay may not be known, but some of the major known causes are:

- brain damage (before, during and after birth, or during infancy)
- poor interaction with carer(s) usually parents
- severe disease of organs or organ systems of the body
- serious visual disability
- serious hearing disability
- low intellectual ability
- poor nutrition or starvation.

Developmental progress is checked as a matter of routine if the child is taken regularly to baby and well-child clinics and problems may be highlighted by the health professionals who carry out the checks. More commonly, parent carers are the first to notice that their child is not acquiring new skills at the same rate as other children of the same age and contact their health visitor or family doctor. A full assessment is carried out consisting of:

1 full developmental assessment
2 thorough physical examination
3 visual testing
4 hearing tests.

The child may then be referred to an appropriate specialist for advice and/or therapy. Professionals will try to estimate the severity of the developmental delay and its probable cause. Appropriate treatment or therapy will be advised so that the child can be assisted to achieve his or her maximum potential.

A premature baby (born before 37 weeks of the pregnancy) will develop the new skills and abilities somewhat later than a baby born at full-term. For example, a baby born four weeks early will be approximately four weeks late in learning to smile. The premature child has usually caught up with other children of the same age group by his or her first birthday.

Biological and social consequences

Biological consequences of a developmental disturbance can depend on the specific nature of the delay, For instance, a child with cerebral palsy, which affects all aspects of motor (muscular) control, will have difficulty in controlling head movements and make slow movements. Some affected children have stiff, contracted muscles, others floppy (hypotonic) muscles and some writhing movements. There is enormous variation in the degree of disability and intelligence among those with cerebral palsy. This disorder may cause feeding difficulties, sitting up and walking disabilities, problems with speech or lack of bladder control and the possibility of serious renal infections. The variation is immense, but it is also important not to stereotype children with cerebral palsy; many affected children are able to lead independent, normal lives with a near-normal life expectancy.

Other developmental disorders resulting in physical disability include:

- toxoplasmosis
- rubella
- effects of drugs known as teratogens such as thalidomide
- irradiation
- spina bifida.

Theory into practice

Research the conditions listed above and write short notes on the biological and social consequences that might occur.

Social consequences usually arise from the perceptions of other people or society in general to the person with a disability.

Think It Over

In small groups of three or four, discuss the effects of these perceptions on the person with the disability. Write the effects you have suggested on a flip chart sheet and discuss in class. Afterwards, make your own notes on the key consequences.

Has this activity changed any of your attitudes or behaviour to someone with a disability? Discuss this.

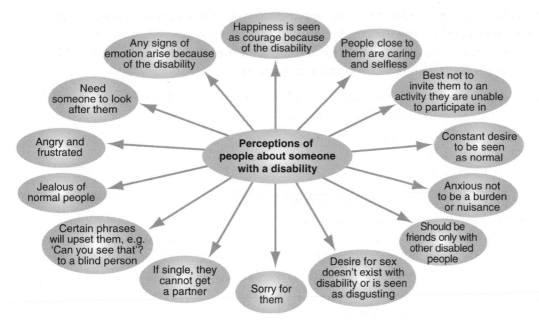

Figure 12.8 Some of the perceptions of society towards disabled people

Impact of disability

The impact of disability within the family unit can be enormous. Some families withdraw into themselves to protect themselves from pity and curiosity. This could result in social isolation. Other families become expert on the disability and seek as much help from services as they can, thus widening their social horizons, knowledge and skills. Caring for a disabled person can change relationships within a family. Often non-disabled brothers or sisters feel that they do not get enough attention. Attention-seeking behaviour patterns may emerge. Partners may also feel neglected and relationships can break up as a result of increased tensions and frustration.

The carer's own quality of life can diminish as time and effort is given to the child; this can lead to resentment, bitterness, anger and frequently depression due to feeling increasingly trapped. In many situations there may be emotional feelings of guilt or self-blame. In addition to all this, there is often a lack of financial resources or suitable, willing helpers to offer support.

Models of disability

A model is a framework of theory around which people can work. There are two major models of disability that you need to be aware of: the medical model and the social model.

The medical model

The medical model is based on the medical causes of disability, in other words if you have a hearing impairment it may be due to the dysfunction of the cochlea in the inner ear. The Disability Discrimination Act (1995) is based on the medical model because the causes of disability are attributed only to medical causes.

The medical model has been criticised for its:

- narrowness
- implication that the individual is flawed, faulty and second class

- leading to 'disability' being used to describe the lack of opportunities for disabled people who cannot carry out 'normal' activities because of impairment(s)
- ignorance of the large number of social factors which may also influence 'day-to-day' activities
- use of value judgements that other means of speech, mobility, communication, etc. are abnormal
- implication that the legitimate requests for adjustments to buildings, walkways for example are to accommodate the abnormal.

Key issue

Disability Discrimination Act (1995)

The Disability Discrimination Act states that a person has a disability if he or she has a physical or mental impairment which has a substantial and long-term effect on his or her ability to carry out normal day-to-day activities if it affects one or more of the following:

- mobility
- physical co-ordination
- ability to lift, carry or move everyday objects
- eyesight (unless corrected by spectacles)
- perception of the risk of danger

- manual dexterity
- continence
- speech
- hearing
- memory – ability to concentrate, learn or understand.

The social model

The social model of disability, developed in the early 1970s, stated that disablement was the result of any behaviour or barriers that prevented people with impairments choosing to take part in the life of society. It does not imply that impairments and physiological differences do not happen, but says that aspects of life can be changed so that disablement does not occur. In the example above, hearing impairment is only a barrier to day-to-day living because a British Sign Language interpreter is not provided. This model does not attach value judgements on 'normality' but describes disablement as a consequence of social organisation – which could be changed!

The discrimination produced by the social organisation produces disablement.

Assessment activity 12.1

If you have a placement working with children, or with people with learning difficulty, then interview a member of staff about the usefulness of the concept of normal and delayed development within that setting. Alternatively you may be able to arrange to meet with someone who works with children or with people with a learning difficulty in order to gain their views.

Write a report which explains the concepts of normal and delayed development. To achieve a merit grade your report must explain how life events may be associated with the labels of 'normal' and 'abnormal' development. To achieve a distinction grade your report must critically analyse the assumptions built in to the concepts of normal and abnormal development. At distinction level you should debate alternative ways of conceptualising the development of people with a range of disabilities using a range of sources to support your ideas.

Lifespan social, emotional and cultural change

The life story of an individual person will involve the interaction of their genetic structure with the social context and events that make up a person's environment. Human development can also be influenced by the interactive nature of human behaviour and thought. People are not simply moulded into shape by circumstances – people can make choices and interact with their environment in ways in which will influence how they adapt to their environment.

This section provides an overview of life stages and describes some of the social, cultural and emotional issues which people have to adapt to.

Infancy

On average, infants will follow a moving person with their eyes during the first month of life. They will also show an interest in face-like shapes. By two months an infant may start to smile at human faces and may indicate that they can recognise their mother. By three months an infant may make sounds and smile when an adult talks. At five months, infants can distinguish between familiar and unfamiliar people. By six months an infant may smile at a mirror image.

It is as if babies come into the world prepared to make relationships and learn about others. Infants try to attract attention, they will smile and make noises to attract adults. It may be the case that infants have an in-built need to make a relationship that will tie or bond them with their carer. The development of a social and emotional bond of love between a carer and infant is one of the key developmental issues during infancy.

Early childhood

A child's attachment to parents and carers is just as strong as in infancy, but children no longer need to cling to carers. As children grow older they start to make relationships with other children and learn to become more independent. Young children still depend very much on their carers to look after them however and they need safe, secure, emotional ties with their family.

Close emotional bonds provide the foundation for exploring relationships with others. Attachments within a family setting provide a child with opportunities to learn from others. As a child grows he or she will copy what other adults and children do. Children learn attitudes and beliefs by watching the behaviour of parents, brothers, sisters and other relatives toward them. Parents and families create a setting or context in which children learn expected social behaviour. This process of learning social rules is called socialisation.

Socialisation

Socialisation means to become social – children learn to fit in with and be part of a social group. When children grow up within a family group, they will usually learn a wide range of ideas about how to behave.

Families and similar social groups develop attitudes about what is 'normal' or right to do. Sociologists call these beliefs 'norms'. Each family will have norms that cover how people should behave.

By 2 years, children usually understand that they are male or female. During the socialisation process, children learn how to act in masculine or feminine ways. Boys may copy the behaviour of other male members of the family, and girls may copy the behaviour of other female members. Sociologists call this learning a gender (male or female) role. Learning a role means learning to act as a male or female person.

During childhood, children learn ideas about what is right or wrong. They learn the customs of their culture and family, they learn to play gender and adult roles, and they learn what is expected of them and what they should expect from others. Socialisation teaches children ways of thinking, and these ways of thinking may stay with a person for life.

Primary socialisation
Not everything that a child learns during primary socialisation within the family group is learned by copying adults. Children also spend time watching TV, listening to radio and playing computer games. Children will be influenced by the things they see and hear over the media as well as their experiences within the home.

Cultural influences
Children are influenced by the family and friendship groups that they grow up with. But every family and friendship group is different. Families and small social groups are influenced by the culture that surrounds them. The culture that surrounds a child will be influenced by assumptions and expectations associated with:

- ethnicity (or racial identity)
- religion
- social class
- lifestyle
- geographical location.

The culture which surrounds a family or small group will create different assumptions within that group. These assumptions are referred to as norms or expectations as to what sort of behaviour is appropriate. Different family habits about meal times for example, will be strongly influenced by the lifestyle of that family. Ethnicity, religion and social class will strongly influence a family's lifestyle and therefore what the child comes to believe is 'normal'. Small groups of teenagers will also form expectations of what behaviours are 'normal'.

Culture will create a major influence on individuals throughout their lifespan. Different people have different beliefs about what is morally right and wrong, about norms of politeness and about what people should aim for in life. All these differences will be influenced by the ethnicity, religion, social class and lifestyles that an individual identifies with.

Friendships
Young children enjoy playing with others and will often see children that they play with as being their friends. Three- and 4-year-olds will often show a need or even a preference for being with parents rather than with friends. This is sometimes called 'safe base behaviour' where the child seeks affection and reassurance from parents.
By 7 years most children will express a preference for playing with others rather than needing the security of being in close contact with carers.

Friendships become increasingly important as children develop independence. Older children will see friendships as based on trust. Friends are special people who are trusted – not just people who are available to play with.

As children grow older they become increasingly independent. Friendship groups become increasingly important and can exert a major influence on behaviour. For a few individuals the norms and beliefs of friends may conflict with the values and norms learned during primary socialisation.

Secondary socialisation

As children grow older they go to school and learn to read and use computers. The range of influences on them grows larger. Even though children make friends and learn new ideas at school, however, the main group experience for most children will still be with their family and kinship group. Children's needs for love and affection and the need to belong to a group will usually be met by the family. If a child is rejected or neglected by the family, he or she will be at risk of developing a low sense of self-worth and poor self-esteem.

During adolescence the importance of the family group begins to change. Between 11 and 15 years adolescents become very involved with their own group of friends. Most adolescents have a group of friends who influence what they think and believe, usually people of the same age. This is the second influential group to which people belong, and it creates a second type of socialisation, that sociologists call secondary socialisation.

Think It Over

Try to remember when you were 14 or 15 years old. Can you recall what you and others in your class at school thought about the following topics? What sort of beliefs and values did your parents have at that time? Which beliefs are closest to your beliefs now?

1 It is important to get a good job.
2 It is bad and dangerous to use drugs.
3 It is important to go out and have a good time.
4 Wearing the right clothes to look good is a priority.
5 Saving money is a priority.

Socialisation does not finish with secondary socialisation. People continue to change and learn to fit in with new groups when they go out to work and when they start their own families.

Primary socialisation = First socialisation within a family or care group.

Secondary socialisation = Later socialisation with friends and peer groups.

Change and transition during adolescence

Adolescence can involve major pressures to change and adapt as people go through rapid social and physical development. Sources of pressure may include:

- The need to make new friendships when transferring schools.
- Coping with change within a family group. (Nearly one in four children may expect divorce or the loss of a parent within their family before the age of 16. One in eight children will live with one or more step-parents.)
- Coping with academic pressures to succeed and achieve good school results.
- Developing friendship networks and making relationships with 'best friends'.

- Balancing the beliefs and demands of family and the beliefs and values of friendship groups.
- Understanding sexuality and making sexual relationships.
- Coping with the transition from school to work – some adolescents and young adults experience a loss of self-esteem during this transfer.

Towards late adolescence people will begin to think about, plan or take on job responsibilities. Adolescence is a time when many people actively seek new experiences in order to explore the world and develop skills and knowledge needed for later life. Fifty years ago, the change from adolescent exploration to taking on adult responsibility was often quite obvious. Starting work or marriage could mean the start of a settled adult lifestyle. Nowadays, many people continue to explore social relationships and are constantly learning new skills and knowledge for most of their adult life. For many people the transition from adolescent social lifestyles to 'adult social lifestyles' is no longer clearly marked in Western culture.

Early adulthood – 18–45

In the UK the right to vote begins at 18, and 18 years of age is usually taken as defining the social category of adulthood. Early adulthood is often a time when people continue to develop their network of personal friends. Most young adults establish sexual relationships and partnerships. Marriage and parenthood are important social life events which are often associated with early adulthood.

Think It Over

Look at Figure 12.8, which describes the number of sexual partnerships that people claim to have had in the previous year. The pattern seems to suggest that as people become older there is an increasing tendency to have just one partner. Is this to do with age, or is it to do with culture, or is it both?

Number of sexual partners in the previous year: by gender and age (1998)

England		Percentages				
	16–19	20–24	25–34	35–44	45–54	All aged 16–54
Males						
None	48	14	7	8	11	13
One	24	49	78	80	82	71
Two or more	28	38	16	13	8	16
All males	100	100	100	100	100	100
Females						
None	30	17	9	10	13	13
One	37	53	81	86	85	76
Two or more	33	30	10	4	2	11
All females	100	100	100	100	100	100

Figure 12.9 Table showing sexual partnerships

As in all periods of life, early adulthood involves the need to adapt to social and emotional pressures. The demands of family and careers are a source of growing pressure for many young adults.

Balancing work and relationships is not the only change or transition which young adults need to adapt to. Adult life can contain a range of transitions and changes that create a need for social and emotional adaptation.

Holmes and Rahe (1967) produced a catalogue of life events which people frequently have to adapt to. Barrie Hopson (1986) states that this general index was found to be consistent across European countries and with the cultures of Japan, Hawaii, Central America and Peru. Naturally, the amount of work needed to readjust to a life event differs for each individual. Each person has particular vulnerabilities, strengths and weaknesses. The Holmes-Rahe scale is no more than a general overview originally researched in the USA in the 1960s.

Life event	Value	Life event	Value
Death of partner	100	Son or daughter leaving home	29
Divorce	73	Trouble with in-laws	29
Marital separation	65	Outstanding personal achievement	28
Going to prison	63	Partner begins or stops work	26
Death of a close family member	63	Begin or end school	26
Personal injury or illness	53	Change in living conditions	25
Marriage	50	Revision of personal habits	24
Being dismissed at work	47	Trouble with boss	23
Marital reconciliation	45	Change in work hours or conditions	20
Retirement	45	Change in residence	20
Change in health of family member	44	Change in schools	20
Pregnancy	40	Change in recreation	19
Sexual difficulties	39	Change in religious activities	19
Gaining a new family member	39	Change in social activities	18
Business or work adjustment	39	Mortgage or loan less than one year's net salary	17
Change in financial state	38		
Death of a close friend	37	Change in sleeping habits	16
Change to different line of work	36	Change in number of family get-togethers	15
Change in number of arguments with partner	35	Change in eating habits	15
Mortgage larger than one year's net salary	31	Holiday	13
		Major festival, e.g. Christmas	12
Foreclosure of mortgage or loan	30	Minor violations of the law	11
Change in responsibilities at work	29		

Figure 12.10 The Holmes-Rahe life-event scale
Source: Reprinted from the *Journal of Psychosomatic Research*, Vol. 11, Holmes, T and Rahe, R., Social Readjustment Rating Scale pg 214, with permission from Elsevier Science

The value scale suggests that on average the death of a partner involves ten times the change, and perhaps the threat, that being caught for speeding does. Changing to a new school is half as stressful (on average) as a new sibling being added to the family.

The Homes-Rahe scale may be a useful list of changes and transitions that might happen to adults. But it is important to remember that few people are 'average'. In your own personal life you may rate some issues as far more or less stressful than the scale suggests.

Middle adulthood – 46–64

Early adulthood is particularly associated with starting a career, making relationships and partnerships, and for many people starting a family. 'Middle adulthood' from 46 to 64 years of age is likely to be more associated with maintaining work roles, relationships and meeting family commitments. Early adulthood may focus on developing a lifstyle which has to be developed and maintained as life progresses. The issues identified by Homes and Rahe (1967) are relevant across the whole of the adult lifespan.

One of the distinctions between middle and early adulthood is the increasing significance of having to support parents as well as children. Some 'middle age' adults find that time pressures actually increase as they become older and that it can be very difficult to balance the demands of financing their chosen lifestyle, meeting commitments to own children, commitments to parents, commitments to a partner and/or friends, and commitments to the local community.

Key issue

The Henley Centre report 'The Paradox of Prosperity' (1999) reports:

- 82 per cent of the UK population (aged 15 and over) claim to suffer from stress.
- Almost a quarter of the UK population claim to have suffered a stress-related illness in the previous year (1999 research).
- Workplace absenteeism, largely attributed to stress, cost UK businesses £10.2 billion in 1998.

Later adulthood – 65+

The age at which men can access the state pension in the UK is 65. After 2010 this will also become the age at which women can access the state pension (it is still 60 years of age at present). 65 is therefore seen as a possible age to use as a social definition of being 'elderly'.

Most 65-year-olds do not see themselves as old, however, and some writers distinguish between the 'young-old' (65 to 80) and the later years (80-plus). Many 80-year-olds will still reject the term old however!

As with all periods of life there are immense variations in how life is experienced. A person's social class, wealth, health, gender and ethnicity (race) may have far more significance on the type of life they lead than their age as such. Key age-related issues include:

- Retirement – the great majority of people over 65 do not undertake paid employment in order to maintain their lifestyle.
- Free time – the majority of people over 65 no longer have to care for children, although some may act as carers for relatives or friends. For those who are free of work and care pressures, retirement can represent a time of self-development when they can indulge interests in hobbies, travel, socialising, and learning for its own sake. For some others, retirement and loss of a care role creates a feeling of uselessness and loneliness.

- The risk of disability – as life progresses, physical impairments may influence mobility, hearing, vision, memory and general performance of daily living activities.
- A person's enjoyment of later adulthood may be influenced by the level of financial resources they have; their perceived health, including what people believe they can do; and their network of support from community, family and friends.

Successful ageing

What counts as successful ageing may vary from one culture to another. One hundred years ago, just reaching the age of 70 might have been seen as a wonderful achievement in its own right. The roles open to older people may vary depending on their family and community context. Elders have been traditionally respected in many Asian and Caribbean communities. For some people cultural and family tradition will provide a secure sense of achievement and purpose in later life. An older person, who is fortunate enough to belong to a culture or family which provides a secure a role in later life, may simply perceive growing older as a positive and natural development. The idea of successful or unsuccessful ageing may be difficult to understand.

Successful ageing implies being able to lead a happy and fulfilled life

For many people in Europe, adapting to later life presents a range of social, economic, mental and physical challenges. Successful ageing implies the ability to lead a happy and fulfilled life given a range of threats and uncertainties which may face many older people.

Expectations

Successful ageing involves the ability to avoid, minimise, or adapt to loss, change and threat. An individual's ability to avoid unwelcome changes, or to adapt to change will depend on the economic, social and emotional resources which they have developed during their life.

For many people successful ageing will be influenced by the lifestyles, relationships and habits that they have established earlier in life. The type of work that a person undertook in adulthood will influence the savings and pension arrangements that the person will have. The friendship and family networks that the person established during their adult life may continue to support them during later life. A person's expectations and perceptions of ageing will be influenced by their experiences from childhood onwards. An individual's self-concept in later life will be strongly influenced by adult life experiences.

Preparation

In terms of preparation for later life, the following principles may have general relevance for many people.

1   **Physical exercise** – a lifestyle that involves moderate physical exercise may help to prevent cardiovascular disease and preserve flexibility and balance. Cardiovascular disease might contribute to towards a loss of intellectual performance as well as a range of mobility and other health problems. Moderate physical exercise may help to prolong life as well as to maintain physical and mental abilities.

2 **Maintaining social networks** – maintaining a healthy sense of self-esteem and self-concept may be easier if an individual has a satisfying social life. Friends, family and community links can provide physical and emotional support during the later life.

3 **Avoidance of stress and poverty** – some people argue that money does not create happiness. Whether or not this is true there is evidence that low income is associated with poor health (Blaxter 1990, the Aicheson Report 1998). A lack of financial resources is likely to provide a cause of stress for many people. People who are dependent on state benefits may also tend to have less choice with respect to their housing and the environment in which they live. Adequate financial resources may help to enable people to feel in control of their lives. Financial planning represents an area of preparation which may contribute to successful ageing, even if only to avoid the stress of poverty.

4 **Developing a positive view of self and ageing** – successful ageing and happiness have a lot to do with expectations and the way in which an individual makes sense of life. Where individuals have deeply held religious, philosophical, or cultural views which supply a sense of purpose, they may find it easy to maintain a sense of self-esteem. Where an individual sees themselves as being socially useless or isolated, it may be harder to maintain self-esteem. If they think of themselves as facing a process of decay and decline they may feel depressed. If they can perceive the whole of their life as important and meaningful they may be able to adapt to physical changes in a positive way.

Think It Over

At what stage of life would you plan to ensure that your relationships, health, wealth and self-concept would help you to age successfully?

You might find this a difficult question – perhaps because so few people do plan for later life. Many people feel that they cannot control their life and that establishing resources for later life is a matter of luck rather than judgement! How far does socialisation influence a person's belief that they can be in control of their own life?

The final stage of life

For many people the final stage of life will involve a major process of emotional adjustment. The cultural norms and social support networks which surround an individual will have a major influence on how they adjust to dying.

Some people will fear death and refuse to think about it. Other people may have strong religious or personal beliefs which protect them from stress. Some older people may feel ready to let go of life as they experience physical decline. Some prepare for their own death by thinking through and reflecting on the purpose of their lives and the things that they have achieved.

Some people who face death may want to see family, friends and relatives and perceive the act of dying as being socially important. Some may need social support to help them cope with the process, others may prefer to die alone. Each individual may have their own personal social and emotional needs at this stage of life.

Assessment activity 12.2

Work with a small group of colleagues in order to compile a list of the biological influences and a list of the social influences that have affected you so far in your lives. Thinking about older people that you know, such as parents and grandparents, imagine how social and biological influences will affect you until you are in your 80s.

Use your discussions to produce a report which describes the roles of social and biological development throughout the lifespan. To achieve a merit grade your report must use a range of sources and must discuss social and biological perspectives of human development. To achieve a distinction grade your report must provide a critical evaluation of the relative importance of biological and social perspectives. At this level your report will also discuss ways in which biological and social influences interact to influence lifespan development.

Death as the final stage of growth

Being ready to die, not angry, afraid or depressed, might represent the final achievement that a person makes during their life. Self-concept develops across our lifespan and the sense of self that we invent is never really finished until we die. Our lives will have influenced others and have left a mark on history. The world might not be exactly the same if you had never existed.

Many of the world's great religions believe that the self that we have created (or soul) is in some way 'kept on record', and that this self will be recreated in heaven or some type of afterlife. Acceptance of death may involve making sense of finishing a life, but a sense of self-esteem will be important during the process of dying, just as in every other stage of adult life.

Infancy	Emotional attachment and bonding.
Childhood	Adapting to social roles and norms. Learning social skills. Making friends.
Puberty	Adapting to own sexuality. Developing new friendships. Adapting to norms of peers. Developing social skills.
Early adulthood	Adapting to demands of work and finance, relationships/ family.
Middle adulthood	Adapting to change in roles. Coping with unwanted change.
Late adulthood	Adapting to reduced stamina and possibly to disability.
The final stage of life	Making sense of one's own life and accepting death.

Figure 12.11 Adaptation to life events

Influences on development – an overview
Intellectual and cognitive development

Cognitive development covers the development of knowledge, perception and thinking. Over the past 40 years the study of cognitive development has been dominated by the work of Jean Piaget (1896–1980) and his colleagues. The study of 'object permanence' and 'conservation' refer to aspects of Piaget's theory of development. Piaget originally developed his theories of cognitive development by observing and questioning young children. When his own children, Jacqueline, Laurent and Lucienne were born, Piaget was able to illustrate his theory by observing their actions.

Piaget's theory of cognitive development specifies that children progress through four stages:

1 the sensorimotor stage – learning to use senses and muscles (birth–$1^{1}/_{2}$ or 2 years)
2 the pre-operations stage, or pre-logical stage (2–7 years)
3 the concrete operations stage, or limited logic stage (7–11 years)
4 the formal operations stage – formal logic/adult reasoning (from 11 years).

Piaget believed that the four stages were caused by an in-built pattern of development that all humans went through. This idea and the linking of the stages to age-groups are now disputed. There is some agreement that Piaget's theory may describe some of the processes by which thinking skills develop.

Infant sees object

Infant watches carer hide object

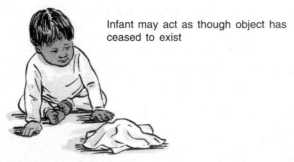

Infant may act as though object has ceased to exist

Figure 12.12 The sensorimotor stage

1 Sensorimotor stage

Throughout life we have to learn to adapt to the circumstances and puzzles that we come across. This process starts soon after birth.

To begin with, a baby will rely on in-built behaviours for sucking, crawling and watching. But babies are active learners. Being able to suck is biologically necessary so that the baby can get milk from its mother's breast. The baby will adapt this behaviour to explore the wider range of objects by sucking toys, fingers, clothes, and so on. If the baby is bottle-fed, he or she will be able to transfer this sucking response to the teat on the end of the feeding bottle. Learning to respond to a new situation, using previous knowledge, is called *assimilation*. The baby can assimilate the bottle into his or her knowledge of feeding. Later, when the infant has to learn to drink from a cup, he or she will have to learn a whole new set of skills that will change the knowledge of feeding. This idea of changed internal knowledge is called *accommodation*. People learn to cope with life using a mixture, or balance, of assimilation and accommodation as their internal knowledge changes. (See Figure 12.12.)

Spatial awareness

Young infants do not have adult eyesight. Their brains and nervous systems are still developing and their eyes are smaller in proportion to their bodies. They are effectively short-sighted, able to see close detail better than more distant objects. Piaget's observations convinced him that infants were unable to make sense of what they saw. If a 6-month-old child was reaching for a rattle and the rattle was covered with a cloth, then the child would act as if the object had now ceased to exist. It was as if the object had been absorbed into the cloth!

Think It Over

The world for the infant might be a very strange place. If we close our eyes we will be able to use our memory for spaces, 'our spatial awareness', to walk around a room with our eyes shut. According to Piaget, young infants have no memory of visual objects when they close their eyes. If they can't see an object, it no longer exists.

Piaget believed that young infants would have great difficulty making sense of objects and that they were unable to use mental images of objects in order to remember them.

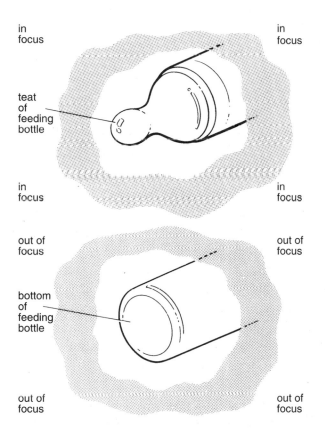

Infants will also have great difficulty in making sense of objects. If a feeding bottle is presented the wrong way round, the young infant will be unlikely to make sense of it. The infant may not see a bottle as we would – they will see an unusual shape.

As adults, we have a vast visual or spatial memory for objects – but something of the sensorimotor experience might be imagined by looking at illusions.

Toward the end of the sensorimotor period, children would begin to internalise picture memories in their minds. Piaget noticed this in his daughter, Jacqueline, at 14 months of age. Jacqueline had seen an 18-month-old child stamping his feet and having a temper tantrum. The next day, Jacqueline imitated this behaviour. Jacqueline must have been able to picture the behaviour in her mind in order to copy it later.

Figure 12.13 An infant will not recognise a feeding bottle if it is offered the wrong way round

At the end of the sensorimotor period, children are regarded as being able to remember images and to make sense of objects that they see.

Think It Over

Look at the picture opposite. What do you see? Can you see a picture of both an old and a young woman? If not, it may be because you are not familiar with the visual patterns involved. Try to get a friend or colleague to help you see both images.

Piaget guessed that the young infant may be unfamiliar with almost everything that surrounds him or her. An infant would be unable to interpret what objects like feeding bottles were, or even to know that their own body ended and that there was an outside world.

Object permanence

The sensorimotor period ends when the child can understand that objects have a permanent existence. The child knows that objects still exist even if he or she is not looking at them (see Figure 12.14).

Figure 12.14 Understanding the concept of object permanence (around 18 months)

2 Pre-operational stage

Pre-operational means pre-logical. During this stage Piaget believed that children could not operate in a logical or rational way. Between 2 and 4 years of age, children were pre-conceptual – they could use words and communicate with adults, but they might not really understand what they were saying. For example, a 2-year-old might use the word 'cat' to mean any animal that he or she sees, and might not really have the same idea of cat that an adult has. By 5 years of age a child might name objects correctly, but still not understand the logic behind things that he or she says. Pre-operational children don't always understand how *meaning* works in language.

Egocentricity

The pre-operational child is not only pre-logical, but according to Piaget, the child is also unable to imagine other people's perceptions. In a now famous experiment, Piaget showed 4–6-year-old children a model of three mountains. Piaget moved a little doll around the model and asked the children to guess what the little doll could see. Piaget gave the children photographs which showed different views of the mountain. The children had to pick out the photograph that would show what the doll saw. Children were also invited to try using boxes to show the outline of the mountains that the doll could see.

The young children couldn't cope with this problem. They chose pictures which showed what *they* could see of the model mountains. Piaget concluded that children could not understand other people's perspectives. Children were centred on their own way of seeing things – they were *egocentric*. Egocentric means believing that everyone will see or feel the same as you do. To understand that other people can see things from a different view, a child would need to de-centre his or her thoughts. Piaget believed that pre-operational children could not think flexibly enough to imagine the experiences of other people.

Observations of play might suggest that Piaget's view of egocentric thought is correct. Young children might speak with other children when they play, but they do not always seem to listen to others or watch others for their reactions. Piaget believed that emotional and social development were strongly influenced by cognition. The child's ability to reason and use concepts would lead the development of social skills and emotional development. Children might learn to de-centre and understand others' viewpoints when they could use concepts and make mental operations that would free them from being dominated by the way things look. This freedom from egocentricity and the ability to think logically comes with the development of concrete operations.

3 Concrete operations stage

Children in the concrete operations stage can think logically provided the issues are 'down to earth' or concrete. Children can solve logical puzzles provided they can see examples of the problem that they are working with. The concrete stage implies an ability to think things through and 'reverse ideas'. Very young children have problems with verbal puzzles like, 'If Kelly is Mark's sister, who is Kelly's brother?' At the concrete stage, children can work out the logic of the relationship – Mark must be Kelly's brother if she is his sister. They can explore relationships in their minds. In terms of spatial ability, 7- to 11-year-old children are likely to be able to imagine objects as they would look from various directions. Drawing ability suggests that mental images are much more complex and complete.

Children of 8–11 years may tend to concentrate on collecting facts about topics that interest them. But their real understanding may still be limited compared to older children and adolescents.

4 Formal operations stage

When children and adolescents develop formal logical operations they have the ability to use their imagination to go beyond the limitations of everyday reality. Formal operations enable an adolescent or adult to see new possibilities in everything. Piaget stressed the ability of children to use formal deductive logic and scientific method in their thought. With formal logic, an adult can develop hypotheses about the puzzles that life sets. The adult with formal operations can reason as to why a car won't start. Adults can check their hypotheses out. Perhaps the car won't start because there is an electrical fault. Perhaps the fuel isn't getting into the engine. Is the air getting in as it's supposed to? Each hypothesis can be tested in turn until the problem is solved.

Hypothetical constructs and abstract thinking

The adolescent or adult with abstract concepts and formal logic is free of the 'here and now'. They can predict the future and live in a world of possibilities.

... but adolescents see themselves differently

Although Piaget originally emphasised logic; the ability to 'invent the future' may be the real issue of interest for many adolescents. For example, an 8-year-old will understand how mirrors work and even understand that people can dress differently, change the way they look, and so on. The 8-year-old is likely to accept that the way they look is just 'how it is', and is very unlikely to start planning for a change of future image. With hypothetical constructs an adolescent can plan to change his or her appearance and future.

Many adolescents will have theories or concepts about the way people in their social group should look. In order to make relationships, it will be important to present themselves in the right way, to be seen as being attractive. Adolescents and adults may spend time planning their image. Body-building, diets, new clothes, new jewellery, new hairstyles might be chosen to create the desired appearance. People build or construct an idea of the person they want to be. Because they have the mental power to think through various possibilities, they are able to re-design the way they look.

Was Piaget's view of cognitive development the whole story?

Over the past 25 years a range of research has built up which suggests that human development is not as straightforward as Piaget's theory of stages suggest.

Object permanence

Berryman *et al.* (1991) quote research by Bower (1982), which suggests that 8-month-old infants have begun to understand that objects have a permanent existence. Bower monitored the heart beat of infants who were watching an object. A screen was then moved across so that the infant couldn't see the object for a short while. When the screen was removed, sometimes the object was still there and sometimes it had gone. Infants appeared to be more surprised when the object had disappeared. This should not happen if 8-month-old infants have no notion of object permanence.

Bower suggests that infants can begin to understand that their mothers are permanent from the age of five months. Infants begin to understand that their mothers move and exist separately from other events. Berryman *et al.* (1991) state: 'It seems that Piaget may well have underestimated the perceptual capabilities of the infant, and that some sensorimotor developments take place at an earlier age than he suggested'.

Conservation

The reason why children got 'logical' tasks wrong may not be that they are completely illogical or egocentric. Part of the reason why children got the tasks wrong may be that they did not fully understand the instructions they were given. Another reason may be that Piaget was right and that young children do centre on perception. They judge things by the way they look. Even so, this may not mean that they have no understanding of conservation.

Bruner (1974) quotes a study by Nair which used the water and jars problem. This time the experiment used language and ideas that would be familiar to the child. The adult experimenter started with the two full, clear plastic tanks and got children to agree that there was the same water in each.

The adult then floated a small plastic duck on one tank of water, explaining that this was now the duck's water.

Children could now cope with the change. Many children would now say that the two amounts of water were the same because the duck kept his water.

Children may be able to make logical judgements if the problems are made simple and put in language that they can understand. Bruner believed that in the original jars problem, young children may have centred their attention on the way the jars looked. Young children might have understood that water stayed the same, but they became confused because their picture (or iconic) memory suggested that height should make volume bigger.

Egocentricity

Piaget believed that young children were unable to de-centre their perception from the way things looked, to be able to understand logical relationships. Pre-operational children were supposed to be egocentric to the point where they could not imagine that anyone could see or experience things differently from themselves. Paul Harris (1989) reports that children as young as 3 years of age do understand others' perspectives and do try to comfort others even though they are not themselves distressed. Nicky Hayes and Sue Orrell (1993) quote research from Barke (1975) who found that 4-year-old children could choose a view that a *Sesame Street* character could see – and from different positions. Hayes also quotes research from Hughes (1975) who found that young children were able to hide a doll from another doll using partitions. The children could imagine who would see things at different angles.

Piaget's belief that pre-operational children are completely egocentric may not be safe. Modern research does not confirm his original findings.

The influence of inherited and environmental factors on cognitive development

Piaget believed that cognitive development was due to an *interaction* between environmental learning and genetic influences. He understood that genetic influences and environmental influences combined to create a new system, on which development depended.

The system which enables a person to learn and understand involves the regulation of knowledge through *assimilation* and *accommodation*. For example, consider the experience of learning to swim. Learning to float to begin with is not easy – you have to get the feeling of how it works. Once you've got the idea, then it's easy. This learning comes in a kind of automatic way. You may not be able to remember how you did it. Piaget thought that learning to float was 'regulated' by an automatic correcting and 'fine tuning' action. He called this *autonomous regulation* – you gradually get the 'feel' of how to do something.

If you are going to swim, you will have to experiment with arm and body movements. At first you may get it wrong and take in mouthfuls of water. Eventually you may get

Figure 12.15 The ability to use concepts can help in the improvement of skills

the actions right. You learn by activity or by what Piaget called *active regulation* – trial and error type of learning.

A lot of skills, such as listening or non-verbal communication, are learned by active trial and error and fine-tuning of our behaviour. We do not learn them by thinking about them but through practice.

If you want to be a really good swimmer and enter swimming competitions, you will probably need *conscious regulation* of your learning. This is where you do work out and conceptualise what you are doing. You will need to work out a training routine, you will need the right diet, you may need to improve the way you turn your body and use arms and legs to swim. To get it right you may need to get your mind involved. The same applies to learning to listen, to communicate with people in social care, or to reassure people who are upset. Basic skills might be developed naturally or unconsciously, but advanced skills require the ability to analyse or to evaluate what you are doing using concepts.

Piaget believed that people often started to learn from practical action. Skills could be dramatically improved by learning to use concepts to analyse action, and then autonomous, active and conscious regulation systems could be used together. With the ability to use concepts, mature learners can imagine a situation or skill that they want to improve. Imagination may even help competitive swimmers to improve their skills.

It may be that children do learn skills by learning practised actions and only later being able to conceptualise them. Some adults may be able to learn by using concepts before they try practical activities.

Think It Over

Think of a skill that you have. Did you learn it through practical work? Could you improve it by analysing and evaluating it?

Intellectual development during adulthood and later life

Many adults will need to continue to develop their mental skills. Adults who work in professional jobs may develop special mental skills where they control and monitor their own thought processes. This ability is sometimes called *metacognition*. Many adults will specialise in particular styles or areas of mental reasoning.

Zimbardo (1992) suggests that adulthood may involve learning to cope with continual uncertainties, inconsistencies and contradictions. Logic alone may not be sufficient to cope with life. Skilled judgement and flexible thinking are needed. Some psychologists have gone on to call this adult stage of advanced thinking a *post-formal stage* – adding a fifth stage to Piaget's theory. As people grow older, happiness may depend on thinking skills that many cultures have referred to as wisdom.

Each person will develop unique physical and personality features. No one person is exactly the same as another due to the immense complexity of interaction between factors which influence development. One way of looking at influences on development is to identify three different types of influence.

1 The development of each person will be influenced by their **genetic inheritance.**
2 Each person will be influenced by the **environment** in which they develop. Environmental influences include nutrition, housing, cultural context and economic circumstances.
3 The developing **self-concept** of each person will cause that individual to interact with their environment in unique and unpredictable ways.

Human development involves the interaction of all three types of influence. People are not simply determined or fixed either by their genetics, or by social influences or even by their own ideas and wishes!

The interaction of genetics and environment

Genes control the sequence of human development, so many abilities like walking and talking seem to 'unfold' from within a growing child. This unfolding process is often called maturation. Maturation is not simply a matter of genetics however. The environment a person grows up in will influence how development unfolds.

For example a foetus may grow according to a genetic pattern, but growth will also be influenced by the diet and habits of the mother. Alcohol may damage the foetus's nervous system at certain stages of development. If a mother smokes it can harm her unborn baby. Diet during pregnancy may also influence the lifespan health of the child.

Environmental explanations

Environmental influences can be understood as working at different levels. Children are immediately affected by the behaviour of people in their family. But the people in a family are influenced by wider issues such as culture and economics. One way of looking at influences is set out in the diagram on page 475.

Self-concept

The way a person makes sense of the world they live in will have a central influence on their behaviour and on what happens to them during their life. A great deal of individual happiness and misery may be caused by an individual's interpretation of life. For example, if you believe that you are 'no one' unless you are wealthy you may become suicidal if you fail to 'strike it rich'. On the other hand if you believe that friendships are more important than money, you could be happy despite a failure to become rich.

Promoting good health across the lifespan

Health campaigns have different time spans and cover diverse target areas. Many are focused on issues raised in the government publication *Our Healthier Nation*, for example accident prevention, cancer, coronary heart disease and strokes and mental health. A more recently publicised campaign is 'Five-a-day', referring to the need to consume more fruit and vegetables (at least five pieces each day) in our diets. To encourage children to eat more fruit, a National School Fruit Scheme will be introduced in 2004 when children in nursery education and 4- to 6-year-olds in infant schools will be given a free piece of fruit every day. To find out about current national health campaigns like this either contact your local health promotion unit (HPU) or log on to:

- www.open.gov.uk - and select 'h' for health in the index
- www.doh.gov.uk - this website will provide you with the address, telephone number and e-mail address of your local HPU as well.

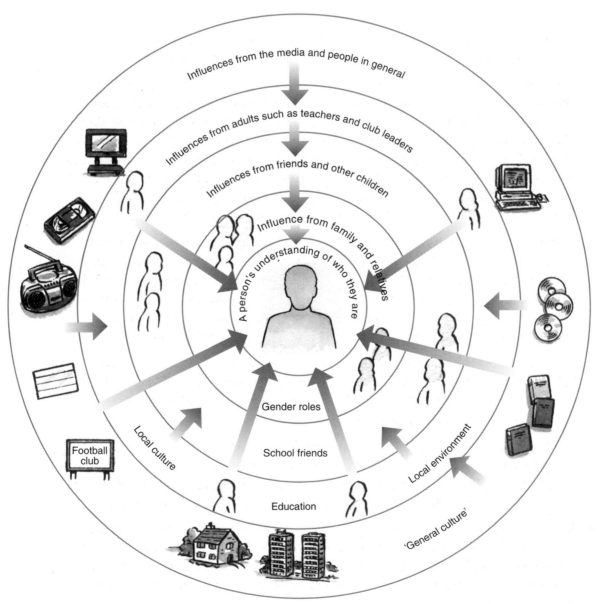

Figure 12.16 Circles of social influence

Psychological theories of lifespan development

Please see Unit 7 for coverage of psychological perspectives. The developmental theories of Piaget are explained on pages 466–492 of this chapter. Kohlberg's theories are explained below.

The work of Lawrence Kohlberg

Piaget provided a theory of intellectual development, But Kohlberg developed these ideas further with specific reference to the way people develop their sense of ethical and moral reasoning.

Children's beliefs about what is right and wrong are strongly influenced by the beliefs of the people they live with and mix with. The way children talk about what is right and wrong is influenced by their level of intellectual development. Kohlberg (1976) published his ideas about how children and adults might progress through six different stages of moral thinking. These stages are outlined below:

1 *Punishment and obedience* – things are wrong if you get told off or punished for doing them. You should do what you are told because adults have power.

2 *Individualism and fairness* – you should do things that make you feel good or get praised, and avoid things that get punished. It is important to be fair to everyone. For example, 'If I help you, you have to help me!', 'If I get pushed in a queue, then I have the right to push other people!'. There is a simple belief that everyone should be treated in exactly the same way. For example, if everyone gets the same food, this must be fair. Children at this stage will find it hard to work out that 'the same food' is not fair because it will discriminate against some people and not others. If everyone is given meat, this will be good for some people, but not for vegetarians!

3 *Relationships* – as children grow older, relationships with others become important and children begin to think about the way they are seen by others. At this stage, children start to think about 'good' behaviour as behaviour that pleases others. Being good is about meeting other people's expectations of you. Ideas of loyalty, trust and respect come into children's thoughts and feelings. For example, a child might think 'I can trust my friend to keep a secret because they are a "good person"'.

4 *Law and order* – adolescents and adults start to think in terms of a 'whole society'. Rules and laws are seen as important as they enable people to get on with each other. Being good is not only about relationships with friends and family, but also about relationships with people in general.

5 *Rights and principles* – some adolescents and adults develop an understanding of what is right or wrong in terms of social principles and values. Laws are valid and must be obeyed because of social consequences or the principles of justice which should govern society. Laws can be changed depending on the needs of society.

6 *Ethical philosophy* – adults who reach this stage will believe in a system of ethical reasoning. The individual will follow a system of values and principles which can be used to justify and guide action. Laws and regulations are judged in relation to the individual's own system of reasoning, and individuals take personal responsibility for their own actions.

These levels of moral judgement are strongly influenced by the level of cognitive development and education that an individual has received. The first two stages rely on pre-logical or pre-operational thinking. Stages 3 and 4 are associated with concrete logical thinking. Stages 5 and 6 require formal logical thought. Many adults do not ever develop clear systems of reasoning about moral and ethical issues. Research quoted by Cohen (1981) suggests that the majority of adults may not generally use formal (or operational) thinking in their daily lives. The majority of adults probably do not develop to stages 5 and 6 as outlined in Kohlberg's theory.

Think It Over

When people you know discuss equal opportunities what sort of debate takes place? Do people concentrate on what can happen to you if you break the rules or on things being the same for everyone? Such a debate might suggest that moral thinking is at levels 1 or 2. Do people discuss equal opportunities in terms of relationships or the need for a just society? This might put the debate at Kohlberg's levels 3 or 4. If people discuss the relativity of value systems or the ethical context of equal opportunities then this would be a discussion at levels 5 or 6.

In real life much adult debate might focus on levels 2 to 4.

Case Study

Stephen is now 20 years old. Stephen appeared to enjoy a healthy and happy childhood but he never did very well at junior school. When Stephen was 12 years old his mother and father got divorced and his mother remarried. Stephen did not get on well with his new stepfather. Stephen stayed at school until he was 18 but never did very well in his exams. He went to work for a DIY store as his first job but found that he could not get on with the other staff. Stephen left his job because of arguments with his employers.

An overview of psychological theories of lifespan development

How the different psychological theories would explain issues in Stephen's life

Behaviourist theories – conditioning (Pavlov and Skinner)
Perhaps Stephen did not get sufficient reinforcement to motivate him to be successful in school work?   Perhaps Stephen's environment conditioned him to avoid certain activities or learn to give up on some tasks?

Learning theories – imitation (Bandura)
Perhaps Stephen did not grow up in a culture where success in academic work was rewarded? Perhaps Stephen copied role models who were not successful in academic work?

Psychodynamic theories
Freud and Erikson's theory would explain Stephen's actions in terms of unconscious struggles in the mind. Perhaps his inability to get on with others is linked to his relationship with his mother and rivalry with his stepfather? Perhaps Stephen's

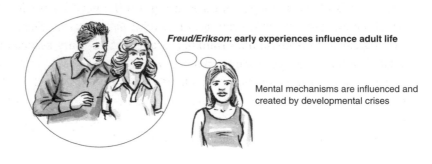

Freud/Erikson: early experiences influence adult life

Mental mechanisms are influenced and created by developmental crises

Piaget: children progress through stages of cognitive development

Child matures in stages
Adults may facilitate or help but children build their own systems of thinking

I can work it out

Skinner and Bandura: children are conditioned to learn from their experiences

Reinforcement or punishment

That's good!

I like this. I'll keep doing it

Learning by imitation: Bandura

I can copy that

Rogers' theory

Unconditional regard

The child is free to develop — Inner experience guides development

Conditional regard

We won't like you unless...

The child develops a sense of self based on what others would like him or her to be like

Figure 12.17 The major psychological theorists

emotional development and achievement at school has been disturbed because of tensions between his parents. Erikson's theory would emphasise the struggle Stephen might have to develop a working identity or sense of self. Parental conflict and poor relationships with others might prevent Stephen from developing an effective identity. Perhaps this will interfere with his ability to relate to others, love and work?

Bowlby might have questioned whether Stephen had developed a secure attachment to his mother during the first years of his life. It could be that the divorce triggered deep unconscious problems to do with an unsatisfactory level of security and attachment. Stephen's problems with work might be a symptom of deeper emotional problems which date back to early childhood.

Humanistic theories – Rogers and Maslow

Rogers might have been concerned that Stephen has not grown up in an environment which has encouraged him to build a positive sense of himself that fits with his potential. Perhaps Stephen has experienced contradictory pressures to please different people in different ways. Perhaps Stephen has been unable to develop a satisfactory, positive self-concept that fits his needs.

Maslow might have emphasised the deficit needs which are probably unmet in this case study. Steven's need for emotional safety and for love and belonging may not have been met – perhaps since the age of 12 when his mother and father got divorced. Maslow might have also questioned whether Stephen had had a chance to meet his self-esteem needs. Without a sense of self-esteem, emotional safety and belonging Stephen might find it hard to cope with life.

Cognitive theories – Piaget

Perhaps Stephen did not have the right kind of experiences to help him develop an effective understanding of his world? Perhaps Stephen's intellectual and emotional development was restricted because of the difficulties at home?

Biological perspective

Theories which emphasise genetic explanations would probably explain poor academic performance and poor social skills in terms of a lack of aptitude or genetic potential for these activities.

There may be some truth and value to be taken from all of these theories.

Assessment activity 12.3

Write a report which describes the major psychological theories of lifespan development. One way of starting this report might be to undertake an interview with an older person in order to gain an understanding of the major issues and events in their life. You should keep the person's name and personal details anonymous, but you could use your outline material as the basis for a report which explains the major psychological theories of lifespan development. Can you interpret the person's life in terms of the life stages described by Freud and Erikson? How might attachment theory have been relevant to the person's life history? How might reinforcement have influenced their learning? How might the development of self-concept have taken place? You could present your conclusions to a group of colleagues.

To achieve a merit grade your report will need to compare the different theories and include an analysis of the commonalities and differences between the major psychological perspectives. To achieve a distinction grade your analysis must provide a critical evaluation of the usefulness of the different psychological theories in influencing understanding of human development.

You need to provide a written description of the relationship of lifespan development perspectives to care practice. In order to evidence this criteria you might use your report on psychological theories of lifespan development to include a discussion of the usefulness of perspectives. For example, you might discuss the value of attachment theory when working with children, the usefulness of reinforcement theory when working with people with challenging behaviours and the usefulness of self-actualisation theory in trying to understand what motivates individual people.

To contribute towards a merit grade your work should include a discussion of the value of these concepts in helping carers to work effectively with service users. At distinction level, your work must evidence a critical analysis of these theories and their value for guiding care practice.

The influence of life events

Life events

Buddhism teaches that apart from birth and death the only certainty in life is that there will be change. Each individual will experience change differently. Changes such as moving house, losing a job, or divorcing a partner may be immensely stressful for some people. Yet other people may be able to cope with these changes with ease. Going to school, getting a job, leaving home, marriage, parenthood, retirement, grief and ageing are all common events that involve change. Many individuals will not experience all of these life events.

Change

Some life events result in a permanent change to an individual's self-concept. Life events that change self-concept often involve:

- a sense of *loss* for the way things used to be
- a feeling of *uncertainty* about what the future will be like
- a need to *spend time* and/or money and/or emotional energy sorting things out
- a need to *learn* new things.

Common life events that can change an individual's understanding of themselves

Starting school

Some people are taught at home because of travelling problems or personal needs. Most people go to school and many people will remember their first day.

Starting school can involve a sense of loss. This might be the first morning your mother and family have left you to cope with lots of other people on your own. You might cry because you miss them.

Starting school usually gives children a sense of not knowing what to expect from all the strange new people they meet. Starting school involves spending time and energy learning lots of new things – how to find your way in the building, how to get on with other people, what you have to do and so on.

Some children miss their family; some are frightened by other children and teachers. Some children get confused about what to do and find school hard to cope with. Starting school can be a negative experience.

Some children feel safe even though their parents or carers are not with them. Some children feel that it is exciting to meet new people rather than being afraid. Some might find school interesting and may be proud that they are 'grown up' enough to start school activities. Starting school can be a positive experience, involving increasing independence – it all depends on how each child is helped to cope with the change.

The birth of a sibling

Gaining a new brother or sister may change a child's relationship with their parents. Children's reactions to the new member of the family can be very varied and reactions differ depending on how old the child is and how large the family is. Very often children have mixed emotions. Children may feel pleased that they have a new brother or sister, but they may also feel jealous that their new sibling gets the attention that they would like for themselves. Some positive and negative feelings associated with gaining a new brother or sister are listed below:

Positive	Negative
The child feels important because they can care for the new infant	The child may feel rejected because parents spend more time with the infant
The child is pleased because there are more people to play with	The child may think of themselves as having been replaced in their parents' affections
The child feels increased self-esteem because they are the older child	The child may feel that their attachment to their parents is threatened
The child makes a new attachment with the brother or sister	The child may feel that they are in competition with the new brother or sister

Leaving home

Moving out from the family home can be a major life event. Sometimes leaving happens gradually. A person might go away to study or work but return home at weekends or at the end of term. Sometimes people may leave home to marry and the major life event is getting married. Some people leave home after a dispute with parents – some 'run away' rather than leave. Other people do not leave their family home during their early adult life.

For some, leaving home is a great change. Some people will miss their family and feel a loss of company. They may feel uncertain about their future and how to cope with a new house or flat. People who leave home will need to spend a lot of time and energy sorting their new home out. There is much to learn about paying bills, buying food and doing your own housework. Many find that the change is a positive experience. However, people who feel that they have been forced to leave, perhaps to find work, or because of arguments, might see the change as a negative life event. For many people, 'having your own place' is the final thing you need to be an independent adult.

Marriage

In Britain, marriage is the legal union of one man to one woman. Gay and lesbian couples are currently excluded from being legally registered as married although gay and lesbian marriages can be formally acknowledged and certificated in London. Some other cultures permit a husband to have more than one wife or a wife to have more than one husband. The legal definition of marriage in Britain at the moment still restricts marriage to one man and one woman.

Many heterosexual couples live together without marrying – some go on to marry after living together for some years, but about half of all couples who live together do not go on to marry the partner they have lived with. Current trends suggest that perhaps about one in five people will never be married during their lives.

Marriage involves a commitment to live with a partner permanently. It ties financial resources and networks of family relationships together. Marriage is a big change in life. It can involve moving house and leaving your family. This may cause a sense of loss. Many people feel some anxiety about getting married; are they marrying the right person, will they both get on together, what will living together for ever be like? A marriage and coping with married life involves a lot of time, money and energy. Living with a partner involves a lot of learning about their needs and their ways.

For some people marriage is among the most positive changes that can happen in life. Others regard it as involving a loss of freedom or even as a relationship where one person dominates or exploits another.

Think It Over

How positively or negatively do you and your friends see marriage? What rating would you give it on a five-point scale?

Divorce

At present roughly one in three marriages is likely to end in divorce. Half a century ago many people stayed married despite being unhappy with their partner. In the past it was often difficult to get a divorce and there were likely to be serious problems over money and finding somewhere to live following divorce – particularly for women.

Divorce is much more common nowadays, and many people who divorce go on to re-marry. Each year over a third of marriages are likely to be re-marriages. Nearly a quarter of children in Britain may expect their parents to divorce before they are 16 years old. Although many people experience divorce negatively, it may often be better than living in a stressful relationship. Sometimes people develop a new and more positive self-concept following divorce. Agencies such as Relate provide counselling services to help people to understand the emotions involved in partnerships. Counselling may help some people to decide whether it is best to divorce or not.

Childbirth and parenthood

Becoming a parent involves a major change in life. Many parents experience their relationship with their child as an intense, new, emotional experience. There may be strong feelings of love and a desire to protect the child. Becoming a parent also involves losses. Parents can lose sleep because the baby wakes them up. They may find that they cannot go out very easily – parents can lose touch with friends and social life. Parents can lose money because either they have to pay for child-care or give up full-time work to care for their child. They can lose career opportunities if they stay out of full-time work to bring up a family. These losses can sometimes place a relationship or marriage under stress. Sometimes a parent can even become jealous of the time and attention that a child receives from the other parent.

Becoming a parent can involve some anxiety about the new role of being a parent; 'will the baby be all right?', 'is the baby well?', 'is the baby safe?', 'am I being a good mother/father?'. New parents usually seek advice from family, friends, doctors and health visitors. Parenthood involves a lot of pressure on time, money and energy. A new infant will need clothes and toys, nappies, cot, high-chair, food, car-seat and so on. They need lots of attention. Carers will need time and emotional energy to care for the child. Parents often need advice on caring skills – there is often new learning to be a good parent and always lots to learn about the child as a new relationship develops.

Case Study

Zeph and Steve had been married for three years before deciding to start a family. When Zeph realised she was pregnant she was very excited. Steve and Zeph both planned for the baby. They bought some things like a cot, clothes and toys before the baby was born. Steve and Zeph also decorated 'the baby's room' in the house. Zeph took maternity leave from her job to have the baby, but later decided that she would take a 'career break' to look after the child. Steve was happy with this but it did mean that they had less money to live on.

As the baby grew older Steve and Zeph said how much they loved her, but they often felt tired. Steve had to do overtime to pay all the household bills and felt tired when he got home. Zeph felt he should take turns looking after the baby. Neither of them went out very often and although they never argued before the baby was born, they did occasionally get annoyed with each other.

Both Zeph and Steve said that becoming parents was the most exciting and best thing that had ever happened to them.

Think It Over
Parenthood involves a great mixture of problems and joy for many people – do the problems outweigh the joy among the people you know, or does the joy outweigh the problems?

Retirement

Many people born in the 1940s, 1950s or 1960s grew up expecting to work for an employer until they were 60 or 65. Often, people expected to stay with the same employer for the last fifteen or 20 years of their working life.

The nature of work and employment are rapidly changing. Many older people will work as self-employed or temporary workers in the future. Retirement may become very flexible with some people effectively retiring in their 40s and others continuing to take on work in their late 60s and 70s. Retirement can represent a major change for people who have worked in a demanding full-time job and then suddenly stop working.

A sudden break from full-time work might cause a feeling of loss. Work roles influence self-concept. A person's self-concept and self-esteem can change following retirement. A person may lose their routine and perhaps their work friends when they retire. Some people may not be prepared for the leisure time they have, and may not be sure what to do each day. Some people say that retirement makes them feel useless – they are retired because they are no use to anyone. People who have to live on the state pension alone may experience a loss of income. Some older people live below the poverty line.

On the positive side, people with private pensions and savings often have the time and money to travel and thoroughly enjoy themselves. Some people see retirement as a time of self-fulfilment, a time when they harvest the rewards of a lifetime's work. Retirement can lead to greater freedom and the opportunity to spend more time with family, relatives and friends.

Bereavement

People can lose their partners at any stage of life. As couples grow older the chances that one person will die increase. Bereavement means losing someone you loved. Bereavement causes a major change in people's lives. There is a very strong sense of loss – you might lose the main person that you talked to, the main person who helped you; you lose your sexual partner, a person who you shared life with and a person who made you feel good. Living without a partner can involve great uncertainty. Your partner may have helped with sorting out household bills or with shopping or housework – now you have to do it all yourself. Bereavement can mean you have to learn to live a new life as a single person again. Coping on your own can take a lot of time and energy.

People who try to cope with a major loss often experience a feeling of not being able to believe that their partner is really dead. Later, people may become very sad and depressed as they miss the person in their life. People may feel strong emotions of anger or guilt as they struggle to cope with loss. Finally, people have to learn to live what might feel like a new life as a single person again. Few people describe bereavement as a positive life event, but the final outcome need not be sadness or grief. Over time people can change and can take a positive outlook on life again.

The case study illustrates the emotions and changes that an individual might go through during bereavement:

Case Study

Jack had been married for 22 years when his partner unexpectedly died of a heart attack. They had been very close. When Jack was first told about the death he showed little reaction. Friends had to persuade Jack not to go into work the next day. Jack had said that it would give him something to do, take his mind off things. Later, at the funeral, Jack said that he felt frozen inside and that he did not want to eat. It was some weeks later that Jack said he felt better because he could talk to his partner, sitting in a chair late at night. Jack admitted that he never saw his partner, he just felt a presence.

As time went on, Jack said that he felt he could have done more to prevent the heart attack; if only he had noticed some signs, if only they hadn't smoked. Jack felt angry with their local doctor. His partner had seen the doctor only two months before. Surely, if the doctor was any good, they should have noticed something! On occasions, Jack just became very angry and bitter about how badly everything had gone; perhaps he was to blame?

Months later, Jack explained that he had sorted his life out a bit. Whereas his partner had used to organise things, he had now learned to cope alone. He explained that he spent time with a close friend, 'a shoulder to cry on' as he put it.

After a year and a half, Jack still misses his partner but he now says that the experience has made him stronger: 'It's as if I understand more about life now. I feel – if I could cope with this loss – well, there isn't much I can't cope with'. Jack has now become involved with the local voluntary support group for people who are bereaved. He says that helping others has helped him: 'It has given me new meaning and purpose in life. I think everything in life has a purpose – things are meant to happen to you. I had a good life before and now I've got a new life to lead.' Jack says that, 'life feels OK now'.

Jack has come through the experience in a positive way even though he will always wish that his partner had never died. Bereavement can lead people to start what might feel like 'a new life'. Bereavement need not be understood as totally negative.

Trauma and abuse

The word 'trauma' means a wounding experience. Abuse may often result in wounding experiences. Abuse can include criminal acts of violence or acts of neglect. Some forms of abuse are listed below:

- Physical abuse – this includes hitting, wounding or any act which causes physical pain or distress.
- Sexual abuse – this includes the sexual exploitation or humiliation of others
- Emotional abuse – this includes bullying, blaming, and damaging or threatening others' self-esteem.
- Financial abuse – this includes taking other people's property or money.
- Neglect – this includes failing to provide food, medical care, affection or attention.

Abuse and trauma can cause lasting damage to a person's sense of self-esteem. Experiences of abuse in childhood may result in the individual failing to develop a sense of self-confidence and self-worth. Some victims of abuse may be more at risk of becoming withdrawn and depressed as their life progresses.

Other victims of abuse may become perpetrators of abuse when they achieve a position of power. For example, a person who has been put down and bullied may repeat this behaviour with his or her own children. Some victims of abuse may become self-destructive, others may fail to make loving relationships or to be able to sustain employment.

In general, experiences of abuse and trauma during childhood may have a negative impact on the individual's mental health and well-being in later life.

Assessment activity 12.4

Produce a report which uses examples to indicate the effects of major life events on development. One idea for evidencing this is to use a case study – perhaps the previous case study you might have used to explore theories of lifespan development – in order to identify the effects of major life events. As well as identifying the influence of psychological factors you might identify how major life events influence the well-being of the individual you interviewed.

Your work might contribute to a merit grade by providing additional evidence to explain social perspectives of development. At distinction level your work might tackle a critical analysis of developmental theories and their value for care practice.

The impact of social marginalisation

The term 'social marginalisation' means to put people at the edge of the community – excluded from the opportunities which other people enjoy. The government uses the term 'social exclusion' to refer to the same problem. Whichever term is used, it refers to the fact that some people are born into an environment that offers less chance of leading a healthy and fulfilled life than for other people. Some people are disadvantaged in terms of their opportunity for social and economic development.

Social exclusion

The government set up the Social Exclusion Unit in December 1997 to explore ways of improving opportunity and reducing social exclusion. This group produced a report in 1999 called *Opportunity for All – Tackling Poverty and Social Exclusion*. In this report the government states:

Our aim is to end the injustice which holds people back and prevents them from making the most of themselves. That means making sure that all children, whatever their background and wherever they live, get a first-class education, giving them the tools they will need to succeed in the adult world. And it means making sure that children can live and play in clean, safe environments, and that the community in which they live is thriving and supportive. Put simply, our goal is to end child poverty in 20 years.

Source: *Opportunity for All – Tackling Poverty and Social Exclusion* (Page 1)

The government says its goal is 'that everyone should have the opportunity to achieve their potential. But too many people are denied that opportunity. It is wrong and economically inefficient to waste the talents of even one single person.'

The *Opportunity for All* paper also states that:

- The number of people living in households with low incomes has more than doubled since the late 1970s.
- One in three children live in households that receive below half the national average income.
- Nearly one in five working-age households has no one in work.
- The poorest communities have much more unemployment, poor housing, vandalism and crime than richer areas.

The report goes on to say that the problems which prevent people from making the most of their lives are as follows:

- *Lack of opportunities to work* – work is the most important route out of low income. However, the consequences of being unemployed are more far-reaching than simple lack of money. Unemployment can contribute to ill-health and can deny future employment opportunities.
- *Lack of opportunities to acquire education and skills* – adults who are without basic skills are substantially more likely to spend long periods out of work.
- *Childhood deprivation* – this is linked with problems of low income, poor health, poor housing and unsafe environments.
- *Disrupted families* – the evidence shows that children in one-parent families are particularly likely to suffer the effects of persistently low household incomes. Stresses within families can lead to exclusion and, in extreme cases, to homelessness.
- *Barriers to older people living active, fulfilling and healthy lives* – too many older people have low incomes, a lack of independence and poor health. Lack of access to good-quality services is a key barrier to social inclusion.
- *Inequalities in health* – health can be affected by low income and a range of socio-economic factors, such as access to good-quality health services and shops selling good-quality food at affordable prices.
- *Poor housing* – this directly diminishes people's quality of life and leads to a range of physical and mental problems. It can also cause difficulties for children trying to do their homework.
- *Poor neighbourhoods* – the most deprived areas suffer from a combination of poor housing, high rates of crime, unemployment, poor health and family disruption.
- *Fear of crime* – crime and fear of crime can effectively exclude people within their own communities, especially older people.
- *Disadvantaged groups* – some people experience disadvantage or discrimination, for example, on the grounds of age, ethnicity, gender or disability. This makes them particularly vulnerable to social exclusion.

The Social Exclusion Unit paper *Opportunity for All* (1999) explains that some communities are 'trapped outside mainstream society'.

The problems deprived communities face include:

- unemployment
- lack of educational opportunities
- high crime
- poor health
- poor services.

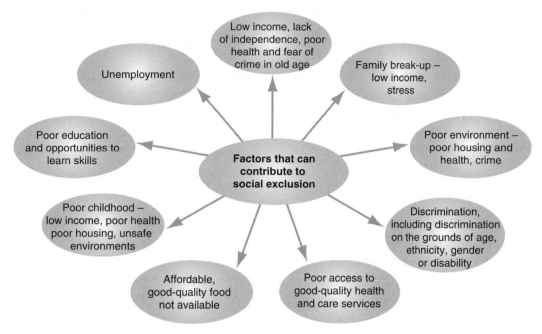

Figure 12.17 Factors which can contribute to social exclusion

Growing up and living in the most deprived neighbourhoods may greatly restrict an individual's chance of developing their full intellectual, social or emotional potential. The problems of poor facilities and crime may stop employers from starting businesses. Poor facilities and crime may help to cause unemployment. This in turn may contribute to poor facilities because people have little money to spend. Growing up in a neighbourhood with widespread unemployment, crime and poor facilities may do little to motivate children to achieve a good education. If people do not achieve a good standard of education they may find it harder to get jobs. The problems 'feed off' each other, creating housing estates and areas which are stressful to live in. Neighbourhoods may have a major impact on a person's life chances of growing up to lead a fulfilled life.

How problems are concentrated in poor communities

Unemployment

The *Opportunity for All* paper notes that 'unemployment rates are twice as high in the 44 most deprived local authority districts compared with the rest of England.' Inner cities often have 'extreme concentrations of joblessness, perhaps because inner city residents do not have the education and skills needed for the jobs that are available.' The report also notes that race discrimination is likely to be a factor in creating unemployment in many communities.

Crime

The *Opportunity for All* paper notes that 40 per cent of all crime may happen in just 10 per cent of areas in England. 'The most deprived local authority districts in England experience poor housing, vandalism and dereliction two or three times higher than the rest of England.'

Poor services

The *Opportunity for All* paper notes that 'Of 20 unpopular local authority estates in England surveyed in 1994, none had a supermarket or a range of shops, and no more than five had a post office, a GP/clinic, a launderette or a chemist.' Poor communities tend to have:

- a poor range of shops
- above average cost for food and essentials (one study found that food in small shops can cost 60% more than in supermarkets)
- poor public transport
- poor access to information technology and even telephones
- poor access to financial services.

Source: adapted from *Opportunity for All – Tackling Poverty and Social Exclusion*

The disadvantages found in some housing estates and communities mean that life is both more stressful and shorter than for people in wealthier areas. The *Opportunity for All* paper quotes a study which suggests that mortality (death) rates are 30 per cent higher in the most deprived local authority districts in England as compared with the rest of the country.

Education

Education levels in the poorest communities are lower than for the country generally. The government regards the improvement of primary and secondary school achievements as a major priority, in order to equip people with the skills needed to achieve jobs and careers.

The Acheson Report (1998) notes that schools in deprived neighbourhoods are likely to suffer more problems than schools in more affluent areas:

Schools in disadvantaged areas are likely to be restricted in space and have the environment degraded by litter, graffiti, and acts of vandalism.

This contributes to more stressful working conditions for staff and pupils. Children coming to school hungry or stressed as a result of their social and economic environment will be unable to take full advantage of learning opportunities. Stress, depression and social exclusion may reduce parents' capacity to participate in their children's education. (page 38–39.)

Social class is a major factor which influences access to higher education. In 1998–99, 31 per cent of people under the age of 21 were undertaking a higher education course at university or college. But 72 per cent of young people from the professional classes were taking a higher education course compared with only 13 per cent of children from an unskilled background. (Source: *Social Trends* 2000). *Social Trends* notes:

Young people (aged 21 and under) from the partly skilled and unskilled socio-economic groups are particularly under-represented in higher education in Great Britain. The participation rate for the unskilled group more than doubled, from 6% in 1991/92 to 13% in 1998/99. However, their participation rate is still only a fraction of that for the children of professional families. This, in part, reflects lower achievements at A-level and equivalent for these groups. (Source: *Social Trends* 2000).

It is likely that the combined effects of poor resources, low expectations and the need to earn money often influence young people from low income families to give education a low priority.

The government is now introducing new initiatives such as 'Connexions' and Educational Maintenance Allowances to encourage young people from low-income families to achieve A-levels and access to higher education. In the past there were strong environmental influences which tended to exclude people from a working-class background from the higher levels of educational achievement.

Cultural influences

The term 'culture' is used to identify different patterns of beliefs, customs, expectations and patterns of behaviour, which exist in different social groups. Different ethnic groups may have different values or norms defining the expectations for members of that community. An individual's culture is also influenced by religion and by social class or lifestyle factors.

An individual's family and the local area, or community, where they grow up may also influence the norms and expectations that a person develops.

People develop different beliefs, values, habits and assumptions because of the social experiences they have during their life. Culture can influence how people understand themselves, because different cultures create different ideas about what is normal or right to do. These ideas maybe referred to as norms. Some norms which influence what we think of as right or wrong to do are listed below:

Different norms about food
Different religions forbid different foods. Muslim and Jewish people do not eat pork. Most Hindus and Buddhists do not eat any meat.

Different ethnic traditions surround the way food is eaten. White Europeans will eat cold food such as bread with their fingers but not hot food. Asian customs allow certain hot foods to be eaten with the fingers. Many white British people will not eat snails, frog legs, snake, insects, dog or cat. Snails and frog are eaten by other Europeans and some other cultures do not restrict what can be eaten.

Different norms about education
Children born into middle-class families are likely to be taught that they must do well at school and have a good career. Children in other families may not be socialised in the same way. Asian and South East Asian cultures often stress the importance of educational achievement.

Different norms about behaviour
Some families and communities may emphasise norms about keeping appointments, never being late, and being organised for work. Other families may emphasise relationships and being honest with your friends. Different communities have different views on issues like drug-taking. Some families see using drugs as a very serious crime, others do not think this way.

Different norms about sex, marriage and gender roles
Different religions and different families and communities have different beliefs about marriage. Many religions teach that sexual behaviour is only acceptable within marriage. Some communities have beliefs that women who become pregnant outside of marriage bring shame on their family. Other families and communities believe that sexual behaviour is entirely a matter for individual free choice.

A person's sense of self, and what they think of as being important, will be influenced by the norms of other people around them. What a person expects to eat, how much they value education, their attitude to drugs and sex, will all be influenced by culture. Culture will also influence how a person understands him or herself. For example, whether a person thinks they are good or not will be influenced by culture. Self-esteem (how much a person values themselves) will be influenced by cultural expectations. The development of a sense of self, or identity, is a critical task that must be achieved if an individual is to lead a successful life – according to Erik Erikson (1902–94). Some more detailed theory on the development of self-concept can be found earlier in this unit.

Think It Over

Thinking about your own life, can you identify some of the norms and expectations that you have learned? How far has your own self-concept been influenced by belief systems in the local community that you belong to?

Alternative models for the provision of care – cultural differences in health

There is evidence of major differences in the general health of different ethnic community groups. The Department of Health published a health survey for England in 1999. This survey recorded self reported bad or very bad health by age and ethnic identity.

The government's Social Exclusion Unit states that people from minority ethnic communities are at a disproportionate risk of social exclusion. The Social Exclusion Unit's publication *A National Strategy for Neighbourhood Renewal* published in 2000 states:

there is a significant lack of information about minority ethnic groups in society, and about the impact of policies and programmes on them. But the available data demonstrates that, while there is much variation within and between different ethnic groups, overall, people from minority ethnic communities are more likely than others to live in deprived areas and in unpopular and overcrowded housing.

(pages 1-2 of summary to the report).

The Social Exclusion Unit's report emphasises the links between deprivation and membership of various ethnic minority communities. People from ethnic minorities make up 6.5 per cent of the population of Britain but 56 per cent of these people live in the 44 most deprived local authorities in Britain. Section 2.36 of the report states that 'infant mortality is a hundred per cent higher for children of African-Caribbean and Pakistani mothers, compared to white mothers'. Section 2.37 of the report states that 'some ethnic groups are also at much greater risk of suffering specific conditions or diseases than white people. For example, Pakistani and Bangladeshi people are more than five times more likely to be diagnosed with diabetes than white people, and African Asian, Indian and African-Caribbean people three times more likely. Pakistani and Bangladeshi people are also more likely to suffer coronary heart disease than other groups (50 per cent more than whites). African-Caribbean women have higher rates of diagnosed hypertension than others (80 per cent more than whites).'

Theory into practice

Go to http://www.cabinet-office.gov.uk, or look for 'Social Exclusion Unit' on the Internet. See if you can get the most recent information on the health needs of ethnic minority communities.

Specialist services to meet the needs of minority communities

The government's National Strategy for Neighbourhood Renewal concludes that much of the variation in the quality of health between ethnic minorities and the general population is due to differences in economic prosperity. Measures designed to improve employment opportunities may therefore improve the quality of health for ethnic minority groups.

In addition to policies aimed at improving the economic status of disadvantaged groups, the national strategy document includes the following strategies for meeting the needs of minority ccommunities.

- The Department of Health's race equality agenda requires health authorities, primary care groups and primary care trusts to 'give due regard to identifying and meeting local population health service needs, including those of minority ethnic groups' (section 7.4). Monitoring and target and target setting mechanisms must be used to ensure that inequalities in the health of ethnic minority Communities are addressed.
- 'Mental health services are required to plan and implement their activities in partnership with local communities in order to ensure that they meet the needs of minority ethnic communities and performance measures have been defined that include monitoring the experience of services by minority ethnic groups' (section 7.5).
- The government will develop action plans for improving services for older people from ethnic communities in partnership with local minority ethnic led voluntary organisations.
- The government will 'produce training material for social care staff to work with ethnic minority older people and those with mental health problems' and fund projects to improve service delivery and share good practice (section 7.6).
- The government will gather additional information on teenage pregnancy and produce good practice guidance for local co-ordinators of services relevant to teenage pregnancy in order to meet the needs of local ethnic communities (section 7.7)
- Work closely with the black African voluntary sector to increase awareness of HIV and AIDS.
- 'Make explicit the need for coronary heart disease services... to be accessible to everyone taking account of race, culture and religion' (section 7.8).

Assessment activity 11.5

Working with a small group of others, use the Internet to gather as much information as possible on social exclusion. Share your information to help you to produce a report which clearly explains the ways in which social and cultural influences can cause people's lives to develop in different ways. This report might explain how social exclusion restricts the opportunities open to individuals. The report should explain the sources of discrimination and disadvantage that may exist for some members of ethnic minority groups.

Your report might contribute to the evidence required for a merit grade by providing evidence of using a range of sources to explore social perspectives. Your report might also contribute to the evaluation of the relative importance of social perspectives required for a distinction grade.

Biological and environmental factors

What are genetics?

Steve Jones (1993) explains that genetics is a language, 'a set of inherited instructions passed from generation to generation'. Jones argues that genes are like the words in a language. The way genes are arranged can be seen as the rules for language – a grammar. Genetics also has a literature, 'the thousands of instructions needed to make a human being'.

Genes contain the information or 'the instructions' needed to make living organisms. At a molecular level this information is held in DNA (deoxyribonucleic acid). Each cell nucleus in a living person contains this genetic material.

Every individual person is a unique creation made from the inseparable and intertwined influences of genetic instructions and experience. To be alive, you will have had to have a code (genetics) to guide the construction of your body. That body could not have been built if there were no materials and no environment to build it in. Some individuals may have a genetic design or potential to grow tall, but they will not achieve this potential if they do not have enough protein in their diet as a child. The environmental and genetic influences interact. An individual, a phenotype, is the result of an interactive process, not just an example of an underlying genotype or genetic pattern.

Some very powerful genetic influences

We have known for many years that particular conditions result from genetic influences. Genes are carried on chromosomes. Usually a person has 23 pairs of chromosomes in each cell nucleus. These pairs are made up of one set of chromosomes from the mother and one set from the father. It is possible for a person to be born with three 'number 21' chromosomes, instead of two. Where this happens, the three-chromosome pattern causes 'Down's syndrome.' A person with Down's syndrome may have a learning disability and may have a physical appearance which includes a rounded face and shorter height. The extra genetic material on the additional chromosome clearly has a strong influence on the individual's development.

Richards (1993) identifies Huntingdon's disease and hereditary ovarian and breast cancer as two areas of disease which are linked to a *dominant genetic pattern*. This means that it only requires one parent to have the genetic pattern for children to inherit the illness. Other inherited diseases like beta-thalassaemia and cystic fibrosis may only be passed on if both parents carry the genetic pattern responsible for these illnesses (a *recessive pattern*). Increasing knowledge has enabled tests to be designed to show whether a person is carrying one of these genetic patterns. These patterns could lead their children to develop an illness later in life. Counselling can be offered to people who are found to carry the genes for these illnesses, to enable carriers to plan their lives and avoid passing the genes on to children.

Genetic influences and environmental factors

Dominant genes and chromosome abnormalities may have dramatic influences on individuals. Most genetic influences are likely to be more complex.

A rare disease which is caused when two carriers produce a baby is phenylketonuria or PKU. People with PKU cannot process phenylalanine, a substance found in most diets. So in the past, babies with PKU became poisoned. They did not develop intellectually and were likely to die from their genetic defect. Nothing can be done to change the genetic make-up of people with PKU. But nowadays most babies have no problem with the illness. At birth, they are tested for PKU and a special diet can be given if the test is positive. The special diet means that the genetic inability to process phenylalanine has no effect. So people with PKU grow up to be healthy and intelligent. PKU is caused by genetics, but is made harmless by the right environment.

Think It Over

Are genetic or environmental influences most important when thinking about PKU? The answer may be that it is a mistake to try to separate genetic and environmental influences. In some senses, PKU is 100 per cent genetic and 100 per cent environmental.

Findings at the Patterson Institute for Cancer Research in Manchester (1995) suggest that about one person in ten inherits a general susceptibility to cancer.

Some genetic diseases only happen if a person also catches a virus to trigger the disease response. Some cancers are genetic but come into operation because of diet. Some genes may cause cancer if triggered by chemicals or radioactive substances.

One of the reasons for studying the human genetic code is to find answers to the puzzles of genetically inherited disease. There may be ways in which environmental influences, drugs, vitamins and so on, can influence the effects of our genetic code. The environment may often be able to 'un-cause' the consequences of our original genetic plans.

Figure 12.19 Are genetic or environmental influences at work here?

How the environment can modify genetic influences

If genetics and environment are inseparable when understanding disease, then what of studies of personality and ability? Plomin (1989) reviews research on the heritability of

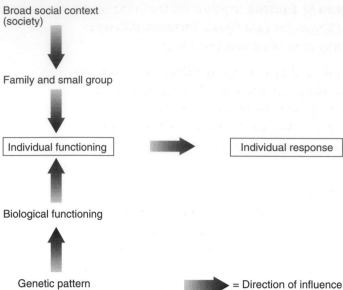

Broad social context (society)

Family and small group

Individual functioning → Individual response

Biological functioning

Genetic pattern → = Direction of influence

Figure 12.20 Different levels of explanation for behaviour

personality and intellectual factors. Personality traits and intelligence test results provide measures which can be studied in relation to potential inheritance. This area is highly controversial, but Plomin claims evidence that traits like extroversion and ability are influenced by genetic inheritance. Plomin also finds evidence that genetic influences are inseparably linked to environmental influences. It is not simply that intelligence or personality is passed from parents to children.

Think It Over

Imagine a man in his forties. He goes to his doctor with complaints of being short of breath, sometimes feeling dizzy, and being generally unfit and unwell. The doctor discovers high blood pressure. If the doctor knew a little more about the person he or she could diagnose the situation as follows:

'Well as I see it, you are an unemployed member of social class 5 (lower class). Your social habits involve excessive drinking, smoking, lack of exercise, and a poor high-fat, high-sugar diet. Your life situation provides you with little chance of changing your ways. Your family won't really support you to change your lifestyle – you are poor. Frankly you have little chance of recovery – expect to die!'

Or alternatively the doctor could have said:

'Well, tests of your genetic pattern suggest that you are at risk of developing heart disease. Some people are lucky, but I'm afraid you've inherited a tendency to heart disease – nothing I can do about that, it was all fixed before you were born – expect to die!'

Hopefully there are no doctors who would behave as in these two examples. The advice actually given would be more like:

'You have a history of heart disease in your family and it seems that you are not doing the right things to help yourself. I can't help you with money, jobs or family, but there are some things that we could do – would you take up an exercise programme if you had someone to help you? Would you follow a diet? Would you give up smoking? Can you find a sense of purpose that would make these things possible? You aren't guaranteed to live a long life if you can do these things – but at least you can try!'

The first two reactions are deterministic. The make-believe doctor is interpreting the social or the genetic pressures on an individual as fixing (or determining) what will happen. Social influences do affect people – statistics provide evidence of this. Genetic influences do affect people. But what happens to a person depends on the interplay of these factors. They also depend on the reaction of the individual. There are different levels of explanation that can be used for any area of human behaviour.

Society, belief systems, wealth, and social roles, all have a strong influence on the way families and friendship groups behave. Individuals are socialised to behave in terms of the norms and values that they learn in these groups. Genetics also influence our biological nature. Aspects of ability, temperament and susceptibility to disease will also influence how we react. The influences of biology and social groups have been interacting in us since our birth.

The interaction of nature and nurture

The debate about inherited and environmental influences is sometimes referred to as the *Nature* (inherited influences) *versus Nurture* (environmental influences) debate. This is a poetic way of putting the issues that may go back to Shakespeare. Shakespeare created the character Caliban in his play *The Tempest*. Caliban is described as a person 'upon whose nature nurture could never stick'. This means that he was fixed by inheritance. The nature/nurture debate was going on long before genes or chromosomes were discovered.

Can criminal behaviour be influenced by genes? Professor Patrick Bateson, writing in *The Independent* (18 February 1995) commented on articles claiming that biological make-up might hold the key to criminal behaviour, or that unemployment might be the cause. He said, 'The sad thing was the determinism that accompanied the media coverage of the claims. It was obvious that, in certain quarters, the dreadful old nature–nurture debate was rampant once again'. Later, he states, 'By degrees, both sides in the nature–nurture dispute have come to appreciate that behavioural development cannot be treated as though it were wholly under the control of the genes or wholly influenced by the environment.'

Figure 12.21 The nature–nurture debate will continue to run and run

It is possible to look at issues like temperament, language learning and the in-built reactions of babies and say that these are all genetic, and so, therefore, a certain proportion of language or personality is genetic. Bateson argues that this is wrong. To explain why, Bateson uses the example of baking a cake. A cake is more than the ingredients that go into it. A cake is the result of a process. When a cake is mixed and later baked, the butter, sugar, eggs, flour, milk and raisins all alter. The taste of the cake and the texture of the cake is different from the taste of the cake mixture. Bateson argues that human development is a process. The contribution of environment and the contribution of genetics is impossible to separate:

'You would not expect to recognise each ingredient and each action involved in cooking as a separate component in the finished cake... The development of individuals is an interplay between them and their environment. Individuals choose and change the conditions to which they are exposed; then they are themselves changed by those conditions to which they are exposed.'

The question as to how much human development is due to environment and how much is due to genetics could be answered by saying that it's a bit of both. But even this answer is wrong. The influence of both nature and nurture is an influence on a process. Development is a process. Jones (1993) states:

'An attribute such as intelligence is often seen as a cake which can be sliced into so much "gene" and so much "environment". In fact the two are so closely blended that trying to separate them is more like trying to unbake the cake. Failure to understand this simple biological fact leads to confusion and worse.' (Page 227.)

Human beings are infinitely more complex than mixing and baking a cake. The cake stays baked – it becomes a finished product. Humans are never finished. Human learning and change continue until an individual dies. Although the cake metaphor is limited, it does provide a way of understanding why it is unwise to separate the influences of nature and nurture.

A conclusion would appear to be that nature and nurture cannot be usefully abstracted from the process of development, but that nature and nurture form a process of interaction which progresses across the lifespan of any organism. Environment may completely override genetic influences, as in PKU, or genetic influences may sometimes have powerful effects, depending on the environment with which they interact.

A European perspective

Britain has been a member state of the European Community (EC) since 1967. The twelve members of the European Community were Great Britain, Belgium, Denmark, France, Germany, Greece, Ireland, Italy, Luxembourg, the Netherlands, Portugal, and Spain. In 1991 these Governments signed the treaty on European Union. The EU or European Union has comprised 15 member states since 1994 when Austria, Finland and Sweden joined. It is possible that further countries main join this Union and that the EU may continue to expand.

Munday (1996) provides an analysis of social support within Europe. Munday quotes Abrahamson's 1992 models of welfare within Europe. According to this analysis, there are four distinct approaches towards social care within the different states that make up the European Union. These four approaches or models are described below as:

The Latin welfare model
The Latin welfare model is exemplified by Greece, and associated with provision in Spain, Portugal and Italy. Here people rely heavily on their own family, communities, the Church and charities for social care and economic support.

The institutional or corporatist model
The institutional or corporatist model is particularly associated with Germany and Austria. Here workers access independent welfare organisations through insurance and other arrangements associated with their employment. People who are not permanently employed may be at a disadvantage compared to people who work full-time for large corporations.

The residual welfare state model

The residual welfare state model is particularly associated with the UK. Here the state still continues to co-ordinate and provide some services, but the state is withdrawing from this role and encouraging people to rely increasingly on family, voluntary and commercial sector provision of social care services.

The social democratic welfare model

The social democratic welfare model is exemplified by countries such as Sweden and Denmark. Here the state takes responsibility for providing social care and welfare support. Private sector and voluntary sector provision is limited.

There are considerable variations on the level and nature of provision within the European Union. There are also variations in the level of provision within member states. For example, services in Spain vary from one region to another. Different patterns of welfare provision are partly due to the historical and economic circumstances of the different member states. The wealthier member states have historically been able to fund a larger scale of state provided welfare provision. Political tradition has also influenced models of provision. State intervention to support individuals and families has been a tradition in France and Denmark.

Assessment activity 12.6

The European Commission for Employment and Social Affairs provides extensive information on social policy within Europe. The Mutual Information System on Social Protection in the EU member states and the European Economic Area provides comparative tables on social protection in the member states. This information can be accessed from http://europa.eu.int/comm/employment.

Working in a group, you might each like to select one issue such as maternity benefits, family benefits or healthcare and analyse the different levels of provision provided across the different member states of the EU.

End-of-unit test

Read the case study below and answer the questions that follow.

Case Study – Matthew

Matthew has always lived on a crowded housing estate on the fringe of the capital with his mother and stepfather. He was very distressed when his parents divorced ten years ago, but has come to accept his new family. Matthew is now 17, working for important examinations that will influence his future. He has spent considerable time with his career adviser but is still confused about his plans on leaving school.

School life has not been easy for Matthew; as an only child he found it difficult to make friends with other children and had trouble learning to read. He was well behind the reading ability of his peers by the age of 10.

Matthew enjoyed physical games at school but his chronic asthma restricted his ability. This also led to being bullied for a while and he began to dislike school.

Case Study – Matthew

At secondary school, Matthew worked hard and began to find schoolwork more interesting and easier to do resulting in some highly pleasing GCSE grades and a place in the sixth form.

1 Describe the major changes in personal relationships that might have occurred as Matthew passed through infancy, early childhood, childhood and adolescence.

2 The psychodynamic perspective stresses the importance of early experience in influencing personality. Explain some key stages that this perspective might have predicted for Matthew.

3 Matthew developed chronic asthma but others living in the same locality did not. Suggest some reasons for this.

4 Matthew lagged behind his peers in his reading ability. Suggest four explanations, which might account for differences in learning performance as children develop.

5 If the housing estate where Matthew lived also had high unemployment and crime levels, suggest how these environmental influences might have affected Matthew's education and career perspectives.

6 Matthew enjoys being at school now and finds learning much easier; explain how this change might have occurred, linking your ideas with 'skills development'.

7 Place the following motor skills into gross and fine categories:
   a stands without support
   b builds a tower of six or more cubes
   c catches a ball
   d runs up and down stairs one foot at a time
   e uses a pincer grasp to pick up fine objects
   f holds a rattle without dropping it
   g rolls from front to back

8 Describe the symptoms that could be alleviated in a middle-aged female by hormone replacement therapy

9 List four secondary sexual characteristics that feature in a male passing through puberty.

10 The psychodynamic theorist Eric Erikson believed that late adulthood involved a particular life crisis. Give the main points of the eighth crisis which older people may expect to experience within this theoretical perspective,

References and further reading

Aicheson, D. (1998) *Independent Inquiry into Inequalities in Health,* London: HMSO

Bee, H. (2001) *Lifespan Development,* Needham Heights, MA: Allyn and Bacon

Berkman, L. F. and Syme, S. L. (1979) 'Social networks, lost resistance and mortality', *American Journal of Epidemiology,* 109, Oxford: Oxford University Press

Berryman, J. *et al.* (1991) *Developmental Psychology and You,* London: BPS Books and Routledge

Black, D. *et al.* (1980) 'The Black Report' in Townsend, P. *et al.* (1988) *Inequalities in Health,* Harmondsworth: Penguin

Blaxter, M. (1990) *Health and Lifestyles,* London: Routledge

Bowlby, J. (1953) *Child Care and the Growth of Love,* Harmondsworth: Penguin

Bowlby, J. (1969) *Attachment and Loss,* Vol. 1, London: Hogarth Press

Broiler, J. (1974) *Beyond the Information Given,* London: George Allen & Unwin

Castells, M. (1996) *The Rise of the Network Society,* Oxford: Blackwell

Clarke, A. M. and Clarke, A. D. B. (eds) (1976) *Early Experience: Myth and Evidence,* Somerset. Open Books

Cohen, D. (1981) *Piaget: Critique and Reassessment,* London: Croom Helm

Denny, N. W. (1982) 'Ageing and cognitive changes', in B. Wolmail (ed.) *Handbook of Developmental Psychology,* Harrow: Longman Higher Education

Erikson, E. (1963) *Childhood and Society,* New York: Norton

Gross, R. (1992) (2nd edn) *Psychology,* Sevenoaks: Hodder and Stoughton

Harris, P. (1989) *Children and Emotion,* Oxford: Basil Blackwell

Hayes, N. and Orrell, S. (1993) (2nd edn) *Psychology: an Introduction,* Harlow: Longman

Hayes, N. (1995) *Psychology in Perspective,* Basingstoke: Macmillan

Henley Centre (1999) *The paradox of prosperity,* Henley Salvation Army

Holmes, T. H. and Rahe, R. H. (1967) 'The social readjustment rating scale', *Journal of Psychosomatic Research* 11, 213-18

Hopson, B. (1986) 'Transition: Understanding and managing personal change' in Herbert, M. (ed.) (1986) *Psychology for Social Workers,* London: British Psychological Society and Macmillan

Jones, S. (1993) *The Language of the Genes,* London: Flamingo/HarperCollins

Klinnert, M. (1984) 'The regulation of infant behaviour by maternal facial expression', *Infant Behaviour and Development* 7, 447-65

Kohlberg, L. (1976) 'Moral stages and moralization: The cognitive-developmental approach' in Lickona, T. (ed.) *Moral Development and Behaviour,* New York: Holt

McGarrigle, J. and Donaldson, M. (1975) 'Conservation accidents', *Cognition* 3, 341-50

Meggitt, C. (1997) *Special Needs,* Sevenoaks: Hodder and Stoughton

Moonie, N. (ed.) (2000) *Advanced Health and Social Care,* Oxford: Heinemann

Plomin, R. (1989) 'Environment and genes', *American Psychologist* 44 (2) 105-11

Rose, S., Lewontin, R. C. and Kamin, L. J. (1984) *Not in our genes,* Harmondsworth: - Penguin

Schaffer, H. R. and Emerson, P. E. (1964) 'The development of social attainments in infancy', *Monographs of Social Research in Child Development* 29 (94)

Schaie, K. W. (ed.) (1983) *Longitudinal Studies of Adult Psychological Development,* New York: Guilford Press

Segall, M. H. *et al.* (1990) *Human Behaviour in Global Perspective,* Needham Heights: Allyn and Bacon

Social Exclusion Unit (1999) *Opportunity for All,* London: HMSO

Social Trends, Vol. 30 (2000), London: HMSO

Wason, P. (1974) *Psychology of Reasoning: Structure and Content,* Cambridge, MA: Harvard University Press

Zimbardo, P. G. *et al.* (1992) *Psychology and Life,* London: HarperCollins

Glossary

Abuse cycle	Term to describe the learned behaviour of abuse, causing its perpetuation down from one generation in a family to the next, so the abused child becomes the abusing adult. Please note that abuse does not inevitably lead to an abuse cycle.
Accommodation	A process which happens when existing knowledge is changed to fit with new learning.
Adolescence	Usually understood as the period between 13 and 18 years when full adult responsibility is not required but when people are more independent than children.
Advocacy	Arguing a case for another. In law an advocate argues a legal case for a service user. In care work an advocate tries to understand and argue from a service user's perspective. Advocates should be independent of care providers.
Advocate	A person who stands in for a service user by understanding the service user's perspective and arguing a case in their place.
Aggression	A strong emotion which focuses on achieving one's own desires at the expense of others.
Analysis	Refers to the process of making sense of research data. Researchers can use a wide variety of methods of data analysis. Their choice depends on the nature of the data and the purpose of their research.
Assertiveness	The skill of negotiating for your own needs whilst respecting the needs of others. Avoiding the tendency to 'fight or to run'. Clearly explaining your own case.
Assimilation	Changing our understanding of an issue in the light of new knowledge.
Attachment	The emotional process that results in a loving relationship between people. John Bowlby emphasised the importance of attachment during the early years of a child's development.
Attitude	A mental pattern or posture which can influence thinking, emotions or behaviour.
Attribution theory	The way individuals interpret, explain or assign causes to events that happen.
Attribution therapy	A form of cognitive therapy that seeks to influence the way in which a person explains events, e.g. helping a person to understand that negative emotions are not always caused by the unjust behaviour of others.
Auditory	Sensory information taken in through the ears (hearing).
Bereavement and loss	A process of transition or coping with change following a loss.
Body language	The language of non-verbal communication; messages we send with the body.
Body movements	The speed and type of people's movements sends messages to others. Movements of the hands, eyes, head and body may communicate emotions such as anger and happiness.
Bonding	Making an emotional attachment to a person. Babies usually make an attachment to carers during the first year of life.

Boundaries	A boundary is a line that you may go up to but must not cross. Boundaries define the limits of a carer's role.
Buffering	Partners, friends and family may help to protect a person from the full stress of life changes and conflicts. This protection is called buffering.
Care management	This involves assessing and identifying the needs of individual service users in order to develop and purchase care packages that will meet the individual service user's needs.
Care plan cycle	A continuous system for assessing, organising and reviewing the management of an individual's care.
Central government	Refers to the departments of state, such as the Department of Health and the Department of Social Security, that are responsible for the planning and funding of social care and welfare services.
Challenging behaviours	Overtly aggressive or sexual behaviours that are difficult to manage because they are socially unacceptable.
Child protection	A legal process in place wherever children are cared for, involving screening procedures and recording and reporting evidence of potential harm against individual children.
Clinical waste	Anything to be disposed of that is contaminated with body fluids.
Cognition	A term which covers the mental processes involved in understanding and knowing.
Communication cycle	The process of building an understanding of what another person is communicating.
Communication difficulties	Blocks or barriers which prevent communication. Examples might include blocks which prevent people from receiving a message, or making sense of a message or understanding a message.
Concrete operations	The third stage of intellectual development In Piaget's theory. At this stage, individuals can solve logical problems, provided they can see or sense the objects with which they are working. At this stage, children cannot cope with abstract problems.
Conditional positive regard	This is a form of social control identified by Carl Rogers who worked within the humanistic perspective.
Conditioned learning	Learning by association. Classical conditioning was described by Pavlov. Operant conditioning where a behaviour is strengthened by reinforcement was described by Skinner. Conditioned learning forms an important part of the behaviourist perspective.
Confidentiality	A care value and part of the NVQ value base. Information about service users must be kept secure and private.
Conservation	The ability to understand the logical principles involved in the way number, volume, mass and objects work.
Constructivist learning theory	The theory that each person builds their own system of thinking in order to be able to understand and cope with life. Constructivist learning theory belongs within the cognitive perspective of psychology.
Control and restraint	The process of managing aggressive behaviour safely, by means of physical manoeuvres and tactics.

Counselling	A form of therapy which is based on an in-depth understanding of at least one psychological perspective, together with advanced interpersonal communication skills.
Culture	The collection of values, norms, customs and behaviours that make a group distinct from other groups. Differences in culture can lead to verbal and non-verbal messages being interpreted in different ways.
Data	Items of information obtained by the researcher. These can be numerical (quantitative date) or non-numerical (qualitative data).
Data Protection Acts 1984, 1998	Provide people with legal rights with respect to the confidentiality of information.
De-escalation (of aggression or violence)	This is the process of reducing the level of a person's anger, calming them to a more appropriate expression of feelings.
Deficit needs	These are the physiological needs, safety needs, belonging needs and self-esteem needs that represent the four deficit needs described in Maslow's hierarchy of need.
Delusion	A fixed false belief that is not shaken by logic or evidence to the contrary.
Demographic trend	Change in the structure (composition), location or other feature of a defined population of people.
Desensitisation	A technique based on the theory of conditioned learning, which aims to help people to unlearn an association between the emotion of fear and some situation or object.
Developmental delay	The term used when a baby or young child has not shown new abilities within a 'normal' time range.
Deviance	is used by sociologists to refer to behaviour that is defined as, or claimed by some to be, contrary to the dominant norms of a society or social group.
Directive	A direction from the European Union that must be complied with but the implementation can be varied according to the practice of the member countries.
Disability	The loss of ability. Ability is socially constructed; i.e. it depends on the perceptions of individuals, which in turn are influenced by social beliefs.
Disclosure process (standard or enhanced)	Screening process undertaken by employers to check whether a prospective employee has a criminal record or is on a paedophile register.
Discrimination	The different, usually unfair treatment of a person because of an aspect of their person, such as gender, race or religion.
DRV (dietary reference value)	Indicates the levels of nutrients that should be present in diets.
Eclectic	An approach which draws on a range of perspectives or theories. An eclectic approach to counselling would involve combining ideas from different perspectives and authors.
Ego	A term used in psychodynamic theory to describe the decision-making component of the mind. Ego has some similarity with the notion of 'self' used in other perspectives.
Egocentricity	An inability to understand that other people's perceptions or feelings can be different from your own.

Elder abuse	Abuse directed at older people, commonly by their carer.
Embryo	The first eight weeks of human development in the womb.
Emotional intelligence	The ability to manage and use one's own emotions to achieve personal goals. The ability to stay calm in stressful circumstances may be influenced by emotional intelligence.
Emotional support	Listening and conversational work which supports other people's individuality and self-esteem.
Empirical	A term that is used to refer to evidence or data-based research. For example, *empirical research* involves the collection of data whereas *theoretical research* involves the development of new theories or ideas.
Empowerment	Giving power to others. Enabling other people to make their own decisions and to control their own lives.
Epistemiological theory	A theory incorporating knowledge frequently culled from more than one academic discipline.
Equal opportunities	Ensuring that all people have equal rights in law and society and in the accessibility of services to promote full potential of individuals.
Ethics	The moral principles or guidelines for behaviour that researchers are expected to follow. Confidentiality is an example of an ethical principle that researchers generally follow.
Ethos	The philosophy and beliefs that influence and shape actions.
European Union	The union of 15 European countries in 2002 which is likely to expand to include more countries in future.
Excretion	The elimination of waste products of metabolism.
Experiential learning	Learning from experiences. The 'Kolb Learning Cycle' is an example of one theory which explains how experience might provide a focus for the development of understanding.
Extended family	A type of family structure in which a nuclear family live in the same household or in close association with other related kin such as grandparents, aunts and uncles, for example.
Eye contact	Eye contact provides an important source of non-verbal communication.
Facial expression	The face is an important area which sends non-verbal messages.
False consciousness	Term used by Marxist sociologists to refer to a way of thinking about life and social conditions that is the product of a ruling ideology rather than the individual's own experience of social oppression.
Feedback	Getting information from others which is 'fed to you' to help you learn adjust and develop your skills.
Fertilisation	The point in time when a sperm nucleus from the father joins with an egg nucleus from the mother.
Foetus	The named given to the developing life within the mother's womb from week 8 to week 40 (birth).
Formal operations	The fourth stage in Piaget's theory of intellectual development. People with formal logical operations have the ability to solve abstract problems.
Functionalism	Establishing successful, helpful relationships with service users so that the positive experience positively benefits both parties.

Funnelling	A system for organising questions so that closed or focused questions are always 'lead up to' using general open questions to prepare the respondent.
Gaze	Allowing the eyes to meet with other people's eyes and exchange information. Gaze is an important part of non-verbal communication.
Gender	Term used by sociologists to describe the social and cultural attributes that are expected of men and women in a society.
Genetic code	A set of instructions passed on from one generation to another for building a living organism.
Gestures	Non-verbal messages sent using the arms, hands and fingers.
Grand theories	Theories that are based on observation and study in a particular field as means to explaining events.
Hallucinations	False impression, commonly something seen or heard, that is believed to be real.
Holism	Treating the service user as a whole person rather than just dealing with one particular problem in isolation.
Holmes-Rahe scale	A scale of life events which may put pressure on individuals to make a social readjustment.
Hypothalamus	Part of the brain that has functions including controlling many of the pituitary gland hormone secretions.
Hypothesis	A suggested but unproven explanation of something. Hypotheses are predictions of what will or won't happen. Researchers who propose hypotheses in their research usually conduct experiments to test their predictions.
Id	A term used in psychodynamic theory to describe the 'powerhouse' of drive energy that motivates the behaviour. Instinctive drives develop from the Id.
Identity	The understanding of self which an individual needs to develop in order to cope with life in modern society.
Ideology	A 'package' of ideas or beliefs that influences a person's thinking and decision-making.
Illicit drugs	The unlawful use of prescription medicines or street drugs.
Imitation learning	Learning to imitate or copy the behaviour of others.
Income	Money that an individual or household gets from work, investments or other sources.
Independence	Freedom from dependence on others. The right to choose and control one's own lifestyle. Adolescence is seen as a time of growing independence in Western culture.
Individuality	The sense of self that people develop from their own life experience. Individuality is influenced by culture, religion, gender, age, ethnicity and social class.
Induction	An introductory programme for work or study.
Industrialisation	The period from the mid-eighteenth century until the end of the nineteenth century when Britain saw a change in production methods from a craft and agricultural economy to a factory-based, industrialised economy.
Informed consent	Gaining agreement from the individual or their next-of-kin prior to any treatment, procedure or aspect of care, where the

person is made aware of all the necessary information in order to make a decision.

In-group   A social group which an individual identifies with. A group that an individual is 'in with'.

Institutionalised abuse   Where the workplace or working practice allows behaviour that causes harm to occur unchecked. This can affect both the workers and the service users.

Internal market   This was developed in the mid-1980s and early 1990s in care to improve efficiency and increase competition between care providers and care purchasers.

Internalisation   Internalised learning is deeply understood learning which is likely to be remembered for a long time and which an individual can use to solve problems. The importance of internalisation was stressed by Vygotsky.

Interpersonal interaction   Interpersonal interaction includes every type of communication between people.

Interpreting   Interpreting involves communicating meaning from one language to another.

Interpretivism   Looking at problems empathetically i.e. from the service user's perspective.

Labelling   Identifying people as members of a particular group where people are expected to conform to stereotyped assumptions about that group.

Learned helplessness   The process of learning to give up and withdraw when a person comes to learn that they cannot control important life events.

Levels of need   Abraham Maslow proposed a theory of different levels of need. Communication skills have a part-play in meeting the needs of others.

Listening skills   The ability to build an understanding of another person's views. These skills may include reflective listening, questioning skills, the ability to interpret non-verbal behaviour, show respect for others and use the communication cycle effectively.

Literature review   This is conducted in the early stages of a research project. It involves searching and reviewing possible sources of background information on the topic area in which the research will be carried out.

Local authority   An administrative body that has responsibility for the local government of a specific geographical area.

Local theories   Theories developed by a group of people, working in a particular setting at a defined time, to explain events.

Macronutrients   Large molecular food components releasing energy on breakdown and forming the major bulk of the diet.

Means testing   Involves assessing a person's income and wealth against a set of criteria to determine whether they are eligible for a specific service or benefit. A mixed economy of care involves provision of care services by statutory or government, private and voluntary organisations as well as by informal, unpaid carers.

Medical model   A way of explaining disability in terms of physical impairments as opposed to the barriers created by social assumptions.

Menarche   The onset of menstruation.

Menopause	The end of a woman's fertility.
Metabolism	The sum total of the chemical reactions taking place in body tissues.
Metatheory	A definition of a theory that also explains its origins.
Micronutrients	The parts of a diet that do not release energy on breakdown and are required in minute amounts.
Mnemonics	Techniques which help people to remember information.
Model	A framework incorporating theories in an orderly way in order to progress.
Motor development	How muscles co-ordinate and pull together to enable more and more complicated movements to occur.
Multi-disciplinary	A collection of specialists from different disciplines working together for a purpose.
Muscle tension	Tension within the muscles of the face, neck, or arms may send messages about our emotional state.
Naturalistic approach	Researchers who wish to investigate and understand the feelings, beliefs and way of life of specific groups of people.
Negative reinforcement	An outcome which strengthens or reinforces behaviour. Negative reinforcement means that a bad situation improves or gets better and this improvement strengthens the behaviour associated with it.
Non-verbal communication	Our eyes, faces and bodies send messages to others. Our tone of voice also sends messages which are separate from the verbal content of a conversation.
Non-verbal cues	Information expressed without speaking; for example, through body posture, gestures or facial expression.
Norms	Social rules that define what is expected of an individual in a given social situation or patterns of behaviour.
NSP (non-starch polysaccharide)	The new name for fibre or roughage.
Nuclear family	A family structure that consists of two parents and their children.
NVQs (national vocational qualifications)	A system of gaining qualifications at the same time as carrying out the daily activities relevant to a specific vocation.
Object permanence	The understanding that objects exist whether they can be seen or not.
Oestrogen	Hormone produced by the ovary (and placenta) that is mainly responsible for secondary sexual characteristics in a female.
Operant conditioning	Conditioning caused by reinforcing outcomes which cause a behaviour to become strengthened.
Orientation	The way people face or look when communicating is part of their non-verbal communication.
Out-group	A social group which is the opposite of an 'in-group'. A group which an individual is not a member of, and the individual may feel hostile towards.
Pace of communication	The speed of a person's communication may be part of their non-verbal message.
Paedophile	A person who finds sexual gratification with children.
Paradigm	A large concept involving theories, beliefs, values and methods to make sense of an aspect of society.

Patriarchy	A form of society in which men hold power and use this to dominate the lives and restrict the opportunities of women.
Peer group	A group of people who share common characteristics or circumstances, and feel themselves to be like one another.
Perception	Our experience of the world as filtered through our sense organs.
Personal care	The legally accepted term to describe intimate assistance with bodily functions, such as toileting, bathing, dressing and feeding for people unable to carry out these functions independently.
Personal space	The space between people when they communicate. It is the psychological concept of an area around the body that is only breached with consent, or by a person you are intimate with. Also called body space.
Personal theories	A theory developed by a person to explain events.
Philanthropist	A wealthy person who voluntarily donates their money or other resources to welfare services for the benefit of others.
Phobia	An irrational or unreasonable fear which influences an individual's behaviour.
Pituitary gland	A small endocrine gland that lies under the hypothalamus; it secretes many hormones including those that stimulate the primary sexual organs.
Population	The specific, clearly defined group of people on whom a research investigation is based.
Posture	The way a person positions his or her body. Posture is part of an individual's non-verbal communication.
Poverty	The lack of sufficient income in order to meet needs and improve material circumstances.
Prejudice	A pre-judgement or fixed idea which may result in harm to others.
Pre-operational	The second stage of Piaget's theory of intellectual development. A pre-logical period when children cannot reason logically.
Presbyopia	Long sight that develops from the mid-forties onwards in many people.
Primary research	An investigation in which the researcher collects their own data.
Primary socialisation	The first socialisation that takes place during early childhood.
Primitive reflexes	Reflexes which are present in the newborn, but disappear after a few months to be replaced by learned responses.
Probes	These are short questions used to follow up an answer that a person has given in an interview. Probes are used to try to find out more information.
Prompts	These are statements or words that are offered to another person in an interview, in order to prompt them to continue speaking.
Proximity	The distance between people when they speak, may combine with other non-verbal messages to convey messages such as affection, anger or fear. (See Personal Space).
Psycho-analytical theory	An analysis of unconscious mental processes and some mental disorders by allowing and encouraging an individual to recall childhood experiences, dreams, etc.
Psychodynamic	A psychological perspective which interprets human behaviour in terms of a theory of the dynamics of the mind.

Puberty	Period of physical and sexual development during adolescence.
Qualitative research	Based on the collection of non-numerical data. Researchers who carry out this type of research typically talk to and observe people or situations and collect a wide variety of data. They tend not to count or measure things.
Quantitative research	In contrast to qualitative research, this is based on the measurement and analysis of numerical data. Researchers who carry out this type of research often conduct experiments or carry out surveys. They produce statistics to summarise and explain their findings.
Questioning	An important skill which can be used to keep a conversation going. Questions can be closed i.e. allowing only one answer, or open – inviting a range of answers.
Radical humanism	A way of thinking that helps service users with problems by believing that the difficulty lies with the way society treats the individuals.
Radical structuralism	A way of thinking that tries to change wealthy and powerful influences on the working class, believing that these authorities are responsible for service user problems.
Reconstructed family	One in which two previously separate nuclear families combine to form a new family structure.
Recovery position	A position that keeps a person's airway open even when unconscious.
Reflection	Reviewing and analysing your thoughts and actions for the purposes of improvement.
Reflective listening	This involves a reflecting another person's ideas back to them. Reflective listening is a way of building an understanding of another person.
Reflective practitioner	Practising reflection as a regular part of your daily care activity.
Regulation (E.U.)	A rule from the E.U. that must be complied with.
Reminiscence therapy	A form of therapy where an individual uses the memory of their past to strengthen their current self-concept and self-esteem.
Research process	A systematic approach to conducting a research investigation.
Research proposal	A provisional plan that sets out the intended research project and describes the approach that the researcher would like to take.
Research question	A clear, focused question that the researcher intends to seek an answer to by conducting a research investigation.
Risk assessment	A systematic process of anticipating possible risks and injuries.
Risk control measures	Preventive actions taken to minimise assessed risks.
Ruling ideology	A term that is used by Marxist sociologists to refer to the dominant set of ideas that are developed and applied by those in power in a society.
Sample	A proportion, or part, of the overall research population. Researchers usually try to select a sample that is representative of the larger population.
Sampling	Term given to a variety of methods for selecting individuals or groups of people from the population for the research sample.
Schema	An organised pattern of thought.
Self-abuse	Abuse directed at oneself.

Self-actualisation	An important need identified by Maslow which explains that individuals need to fulfil their potential. Most people spend their life focused on deficit needs and do not achieve self-actualisation.
Self-actualising tendency	A natural tendency to develop and grow identified by Carl Rogers. According to Rogers everyone is capable of responding to their inner self-actualising tendency.
Self-concept	The understanding of self. A set of concepts which describe what we are like.
Self-esteem	How well, or how badly, a person feels about himself or herself.
Sensorimotor	The first stage in Piaget's theory of intellectual development. Infants learn to co-ordinate their muscle or motor movements in this stage.
Sincerity	Being real and honest in what we say and do when we are being supportive to others.
Skills audit	Assessment of the skills or attributes, relevant to employment of an individual, department or unit.
Social class	The hierarchical division of a society into groups based on wealth, income and occupation.
Social control	A concept used by sociologists to describe processes that are developed and applied within society to ensure conformity to the dominant norms and values that exist.
Social exclusion	Being excluded from opportunity – people with fewer life chances to become economically prosperous than the majority of people.
Social mobility	Movement up and down the social class hierarchy.
Social role	A set of expectations which guide an individual's behaviour in specific circumstances.
Social skills training	Training to use verbal and non-verbal behaviour to achieve the desired effect on others in social situations.
Socialisation	The process of learning the norms, values, culture and roles of a society.
Sociological perspective	Way of viewing and understanding the structures and processes that exist within society.
Spatial awareness	The ability to make sense and respond appropriately to objects in space.
Statistics	Numerical 'facts' that summarise the quantitative data that a researcher has collected and analysed.
Statutory sector	Part of the welfare system that is funded and run by government (central and local) bodies.
Stereotyping	A fixed set of ideas and assumptions which can be used to classify others.
Stress response	The physiological processes which result from a mental perception of threat.
Submissiveness	Feeling that others needs are more important than your own – giving in to others.
Supportive skills	Warmth, understanding and sincerity can be used together to create a safe supportive emotional context.
Testosterone	Hormone produced from the male testis that is responsible for the secondary sexual characteristics in a male.

Theory	An explanation of concepts that describes, explains, predicts and controls phenomena.
Trait	A stable quality within an individual's personality which may influence their behaviour.
Transcribing	Process of writing down, usually word for word, the recorded comments or interviews that a researcher has obtained from research participants.
Transition	Periods of major change in life such as starting work, having children, or retiring from paid employment.
Translating	This involves changing recorded material from one language to another.
Trauma	A wounding experience, the word can be used to describe physical or emotional damage.
Unconscious mind	Within psychodynamic theory the unconscious mind contains drives and memories that influence our behaviour. An individual is not conscious of these influences on their behaviour.
Understanding	An essential part of being supportive is to build an understanding of another person's individuality.
Universal precautions	Preventive measures taken to avoid potential contamination from body fluids.
Urbanisation	Forms of social change that resulted in the growth of densely populated towns and cities during the industrial revolution of the eighteenth and nineteenth centuries.
Value base	A system of values which guides behaviour.
Variable	A factor that can change.
Verbal communication	Spoken messages which use words.
Warmth	The ability to listen to others in a non-judgemental and supportive way.
Wealth	The value of the property and other investments and savings owned by a person. Wealth includes the value of houses, pensions, savings and other personal possessions.
Welfare	The provision of non-medical services and different forms of personal and emotional support for vulnerable people who are unable to meet their own social or personal needs.
Welfare state	A term used to describe the growth in statutory services, including the NHS, welfare benefits system and local authority services that emerged after the Beveridge Report (1942).
Whistle blowing	Disclosing the facts about misconduct in an organisation to a higher authority or the media.
Workhouse system	An early form of basic support and provision for people who fell into severe poverty and were unable to meet their own basic needs for food and shelter.
Zone of proximal development	The limits of development which apply to a particular area of understanding within any individual. The concept of a zone of proximal development might focus teachers on the way they should seek to explain an idea.

Useful addresses

Health and Safety Executive
HSE Infoline
Caerphilly Business Park
Caerphilly
CF83 3GO
Tel: 08701 545500
www.hse.gov.uk

Child Accident Prevention Trust (CAPT)
18-20 Farringdon Lane
London
EC1R 3HA
Tel: 0171 608 3828
www.capt.org.uk

Royal Society for the Prevention of
Accidents
Head Office
Edgbaston Park
353, Bristol Road
Edgbaston, Birmingham
B5 7ST
Tel: 0121 248 2000
help@rospa.co.uk

St. John Ambulance National
Headquarters
27, St John's Lane,
London
EC1M 4BU
Tel: 08700 10 49 50
www.sja.org.uk

Childline 0800 1111
www.childline.org.uk

Women's Aid
Everton House
47, Old Cabra Road
Dublin 7
Tel: 0117963 3542
www.womensaid.ie

Domestic Violence Data Source
PO Box 21O
Brighton
BN1 3RP
www.domesticviolencedata.org

Data Protection Act & Freedom of
Information Act
Information Commissioner
Wycliffe House
Water Lane
Wilmslow
Cheshire
SK9 5AF
Tel: 01625 545 745
data@dataprotection.gov.uk

Websites

Commission for Racial Equality website: www.cre.gov.uk

Data Protection Commissioner's website: www.dataprotection.gov.uk

Disability Rights Commission website: www.disability.gov.uk

www.doh.gov.uk - Main Department of Health website.

Equal Opportunities Commission website: www.eoc.org.uk

www.givingupsmoking.co.uk - The NHS quit smoking website.

www.healthpromis.hda-online.org.uk - The national health promotion database for England, links to publications, surveys, reports, books, research, etc.

www.mindbodysoul.gov.uk - Provides accurate and up-to-date health information for young people.

www.nhs.uk/nationalplan - The NHS national plan website, targets and progress to date.

www.ohn.gov.uk - Gateway for the *Our Healthier Nation* website.

www.quick.org.uk - Quality information checklist for young people to assess the quality of information they find on the Internet.

www.wiredforhealth.gov.uk - Wired for health provides teachers with access to relevant and appropriate health information.

Index